Also by Lupe DiDonno and Phyllis Sperling

HOW TO DESIGN & BUILD YOUR OWN HOUSE

HOW TO REDESIGN & RENOVATE YOUR HOUSE OR APARTMENT

HOW TO REDESIGN
& RENOVATE
YOUR HOUSE
OR APARTMENT

BY PHYLLIS SPERLING
AND LUPE DIDONNO

ALFRED A. KNOPF   NEW YORK   1991

THIS IS A BORZOI BOOK
PUBLISHED BY ALFRED A. KNOPF, INC.

Library of Congress Cataloging-in-Publication Data

Sperling, Phyllis.
  How to redesign & renovate your house or apartment / by Phyllis Sperling and Lupe DiDonno. — 1st ed.
    p. cm.
  Includes bibliographical references and index.
  ISBN 0-679-72803-1 (pbk.)
  1. Dwellings—Remodeling.   2. Apartments—Remodeling.
I. DiDonno, Lupe.   II. Title.   III. Title: How to redesign and renovate your house or apartment.
TH4816.S64   1991
643'.7—dc20   90-52950 CIP

Manufactured in the United States of America

We dedicate this book to:

the memory of Dr. Louis Aronowitz,
   and to
Ruth Aronowitz
parents of Phyllis Sperling

   and to

Encarna Herrera
   and
Jose Exposito,
parents of Lupe DiDonno

ACKNOWLEDGMENTS

We would like to thank the following people for their help and advice in the writing of this book:

Kate Altman, interior decorator
Angelo Caputo, contractor
Jake Cohen, cabinetmaker/jeweler
Ronald V. DiDonno, architect
Tore Hansen, structural engineer
Clem Labine, publisher
Samuel Lomask, mechanical engineer
Augustin Maldonado, architect
Jonathan Poore, architectural designer
Patricia Poore, publisher
George Rehl, architect
Herman Sands, architect
Arthur Spaet, mechanical engineer
Michael Trencher, architect

We gratefully acknowledge our editor, Jane Garrett, for her help, encouragement, and patience.

CONTENTS

Contents
x

HOW TO REDESIGN & RENOVATE YOUR HOUSE OR APARTMENT

INTRODUCTION:
WHY RENOVATE?

At the start of a renovation project you are full of anticipation and good ideas. At the end of the long process you are rewarded with your vision realized, your residence transformed. In between are months of planning (hours poring over catalogues and trekking through showrooms) and construction (dust and disruption), as well as possible delays, cost overruns, and frustration. House-and-home magazines are filled with titillating "before and after" stories, whereas books are written about the pitfalls of the process. You may ask, "Why bother?" The answer is: It is most definitely worth the effort.

You probably have at least one reason for wanting to renovate your house or apartment.

For most people the pressing need is for more usable living space. A new baby needs a bedroom, a flourishing home-based business needs office space, stereo-blaring adolescents need a recreation room. New domestic technology has created space problems in addition to making our lives easier. Where do we put the microwave, food processor, computer and printer, CD player, or Nautilus machine? Many homes are large enough but poorly organized or laid out, with a lot of wasted space that could be turned into living space or desperately needed storage. In an apartment or row house, with finite available square footage, a radical reevaluation of the layout may provide solutions. In a freestanding house there are more options: alter the floor plan, convert an attic, or construct an addition.

Renovation can also be a way to personalize your environment. There is something very reassuring about living in a place that was designed especially for you. There is a place to display your ceramics collection, and a large window perfectly frames the view you love. You finally have the French doors to the balcony that you have fantasized about and a large bedroom with a skylight over the bed. The bathroom has a shelf for your radio, room for all your cosmetics, and a soaking tub.

There are strong aesthetic reasons to renovate. Your house may be dull and characterless, with small, dreary rooms and long, narrow hallways. The kitchen and bathrooms are inefficient or unattractive. Much can be done to add character to a house that was originally poorly designed. On the other side of the coin, many people undertake the arduous chore of reconstruction in order to preserve the historic character of their period homes. A good many formally gracious old houses and apartments have been unsympathetically "modernized." Restoration-minded renovators study the architectural style of the house, examine documented prototypes, and attempt to reconstruct the house as it was originally built.

Finally, there are the practical reasons for renovating: to upgrade or repair a deteriorated building, to make a house more energy-conserving or maintenance-free, and to increase the real estate value of the property.

THE SCOPE OF THE RENOVATION PROJECT

Not every renovation is disruptive, expensive, or time-consuming. A minor renovation project may entail removing nonstructural partitions, replacing windows and doors, substituting new cabinets for old, and adding closets and cupboards. Moderate-sized projects would include adding a greenhouse or installing a new bathroom or kitchen.

Adding one or more rooms to a house would be considered a major renovation. The term "gut renovation" refers to the process of entirely removing the interior fixings of a house, rearranging the interior spaces, and replacing kitchen, baths, and mechanical systems. Remodeling a barn or burned-out masonry shell would require an equal amount of work.

Any renovation project, regardless of its rationale or scope, requires an enormous amount of forethought. This book outlines the sequence of steps between planning and completion and discusses available options at every juncture. With it in hand you should be able to monitor your renovation with confidence.

PART ONE: SCHEMATIC DESIGN

1

SOME IMPORTANT DECISIONS

Renovating your home can be challenging, stimulating, and, ultimately, very satisfying. The end product, a place that reflects your idea of "home" and your sense of style, should provide years of comfortable use. On the other hand, there is no denying that renovation can be a complicated, time-consuming, and difficult task. This book has been designed to assist you with your renovation project. We guide you through the various phases (from the initial planning to the installation of the door hardware) so that you develop an understanding of how the process works. The information contained in the following chapters should be very useful whether you are contemplating an extensive renovation or some minor changes, and whether you are working with a professional team (designer and contractor) or are planning to do as much of the work yourself as you can.

There are several options available when it comes to how much of the renovation you will attempt to do yourself. (See Chapter 26 for a further breakdown.) After reading this book you may decide to design the project on your own (depending on its scope and the law) but leave the construction to a general contractor. Or you may decide to hire an architect, engineer, or interior designer to provide design and construction drawings, but you plan to administer the construction by purchasing most of the materials yourself and hiring subcontractors to do all of the labor. Yet another option is to take on many of the tasks that your design and construction skills (and the law) permit and hire others to do the rest. If you elect any of the above options you will

need to consult additional resources (books and videotapes) written exclusively for each phase of the technical planning and construction. They will offer a wealth of detailed information that is beyond the scope of a single book. A fourth option is to hire both professional designer and general contractor.

Whichever option you choose, this book attempts to demystify the renovation process so that you can become an involved member of the design-build team. We often recommend that even the handiest man or woman would be better off hiring a professional to undertake some of the more skilled or risky operations. Even in these instances, we include design and construction information so that you can monitor the work of the hired professional.

There are a number of reasons why doing it all yourself is not feasible, if not outright impossible. Realistically, most of us don't have the time or the talent to tackle all aspects of the work. Legally, there are many areas of the design and construction process that are restricted to professionals. In terms of the planning and design phases, most municipalities require that plans for the renovation be filed with them and approved before construction can begin. More often than not, the building department will not take applications from an owner but will require that plans be filed by a licensed architect or engineer. In terms of the construction phase of the work, there are many areas of the project that by law you will not be allowed to touch. For example, most municipalities will not permit anyone other than a licensed electrician to wire the electrical panel box. Other communities require that a licensed electrician install all of the wiring. Not to be overlooked is that some of these tasks are outright dangerous and should be undertaken only by someone who has studied or apprenticed in the trade for years.

If you are planning a renovation, either large or small in scope, we suggest you read this book from cover to cover before proceeding further. When you have finished you will be in a better position to decide which parts of the renovation you want to tackle by yourself and which aspects should be handled by a professional.

The rest of this chapter deals with what is in store for you if you do decide to hire a professional designer and/or a general contractor, and provides a general overview of the various phases of the project.

WHY HIRE A DESIGN PROFESSIONAL?*

You may be considering doing all of the planning by yourself for the following reasons: (1) for the challenge and satisfaction of the work, (2) in order to save money, (3) because you feel that the job is too small to warrant the attention of a designer, (4) because you are not sure what kind of designer to hire or what services to expect from a design professional.

All of these reasons are to some extent valid. The design process *is* very stimulating and you *may* save money by not hiring a designer. On the other hand, if you are not an experienced designer and you do all of the design work yourself, you may not turn out a very successful design. Furthermore, if you decide to do all of the planning by yourself, and you don't know what you are doing, it may end up costing you more money instead of less. You may have to rip out and rebuild whole parts of the project because you did not allocate enough space for an item, or you were not aware of a legal requirement. It may be worth your while to extend your budget and hire a professional. As for the third reason, if you think your project is too small to warrant the attention of a designer, reconsider. Some very small projects, such as the redesign of a staircase or bathroom, may benefit by having technical and artistic input.

Before making a decision, you should be aware of the range of services a design professional can provide. First, he or she will offer assistance in organizing the project. Second, a design professional will explore a number of alternative solutions to a programmatic or aesthetic problem. Third, he or she will develop a set of construction drawings and will help you find a reliable contractor with a competitive price. Fourth, the designer will be your agent when it comes to dealing with the contractor and all other authorities.

In almost all cases, you contract separately for design and construction services. You hire a designer, and when the design work is complete, you hire a contractor. The design professional, like your lawyer, is your representative. The designer works for you, helps you find the best and most reasonably priced contractor, and protects your interests when dealing with suppliers and contractors. A very different approach is taken by design-build firms that design and build the project for one fixed price. The advantage of this system is that you have an estimate of the total project cost somewhat earlier in the game. The disadvantage is that if you don't like the quality of construction, you can't rely on the designer to fight for you, since he is working with the contractor as a team.

WHO IS THE APPROPRIATE PROFESSIONAL FOR THE JOB?

If you decide to hire a design professional, you may have trouble deciding which professional to hire—engineer, architect, architectural designer, interior designer, or interior decorator?* This question is complex and the answer will depend on the nature and scope of your project. Although their services often overlap, each of these professionals has a particular range of expertise.

Because they offer a wide spectrum of services, it is somewhat difficult to articulate the differences between the design professionals. A project

---

*Architect, engineer, interior designer, or interior decorator

*You may not have a choice in the selection of a design professional. If your renovation project entails changes in the roofline, an alteration of the structure, a change in the room count, or the relocation of plumbing fixtures, etc., the law may insist that you hire an architect or engineer whether you want to or not. Many municipalities require that plans for these renovations be filed with the building department, and only licensed architects and engineers (and in some states, with limitations, interior designers) are permitted to file. The law ensures that any item of design that may affect your health and welfare, such as a building's electrical wiring or structural framing plan, is designed by someone whose expertise is certified.

that is purely technical in nature (either structural, mechanical, or electrical) will be suited to an engineer. For example, if you are renovating a house for the primary purpose of rewiring, an electrical engineer would be the professional to take charge of the project. Engineers are technical planners but have no training in visual design. Almost all engineering schools have four-year, post-high-school programs. In most states a graduate engineer must work for at least two years before sitting for the licensing exams in his or her engineering specialty.

Projects that involve both technical planning and aesthetics (such as the redesign of most of the house, the relocation or radical alteration of kitchen and bathrooms, or the addition of one or more rooms) are best suited to an architect who specializes in renovation or residential design. An architect is trained to organize a building functionally, spatially, and technically, giving equal weight to its interior spaces, exterior form, and structural/mechanical systems. An architect designs the renovation in its entirety, integrating input from consulting engineers, and prepares plans and details showing floor, wall, and roof construction, door and window details, mechanical systems, door hardware, and plumbing fixtures. Architectural services often go beyond the overall design and planning to include the design of built-in furniture, the selection of paint and upholstery colors, carpeting, and other furnishings. In most large towns and cities you must use an architect or engineer for any job that requires filing.

An architect is a professional who is registered (which is the same as licensed) by the state in which he or she practices after having passed the registration examinations. For the most part,* to qualify for the exams a candidate must have graduated from an accredited architectural school (five years as an undergraduate leading to a B.Arch. degree, or three years as a graduate student leading to an M.Arch. degree). In addition, a candidate must have worked under the supervision of a registered architect for at least three years before qualifying to take the exams.

A graduate of an architectural school who does not have a license is called an architectural designer, but he is not permitted by law to call himself an architect or to practice architecture.

Interior designers are professionals trained in interior-space planning and design, historical context, interior materials and finishes, cabinetry and furniture details, color and pattern, and (de-

pending on the school he or she attended) some level of education in lighting and mechanical equipment. Many interior design firms have access to ancillary professionals to cover the technical areas of the projects. An architect, mechanical engineer, or lighting designer may be part of the design team.

The education of an interior designer is not as standardized or as regulated by the state as that of an architect or engineer. Most interior design programs are either two or four years long. Most states do not have a licensing procedure for interior designers.

A decorator helps you coordinate finishes and furnishings reflecting your specific requirements and taste. He or she organizes all the elements (color, texture, and pattern of wall and floor coverings, window treatment, accessories, lighting fixtures, furniture, and fabrics) and presents appropriate possibilities for you to choose from. The decorator may place the orders and arrange for fabrication of custom items, oversee the delivery and installation of all these items, and take care of all of the related bookkeeping. Decorators recommend painters, wallpaperers, cabinetmakers, and other tradespeople and may coordinate their work.

Selecting a design professional need not be an either/or proposition. Many people planning a renovation hire both an architect and an interior designer (or decorator) and have them collaborate. This sometimes works, and sometimes leads to problems. We have found it advantageous to clearly outline the distinct responsibilities of each professional at the very outset of the project. This tends to avoid unnecessary argument later on.

HOW DO I RETAIN A DESIGNER?

Once you have decided which of the design professionals is best suited to work with you on your renovation project, you are left with the task of selecting a specific designer or firm. There are a number of things to look for when you hire a designer or architect: quality of design work, similar renovation experience, references, personality compatibility, license to practice, and fee structure. Unless you have a special relationship with a particular designer, you may want to interview three or more professionals.

In finding candidates to interview, the best source is references from your friends, especially from people whose projects have been completed.

*There are some variations from state to state.

They will have had direct experience with the designer during both the design and construction phases, and if they are still saying good things about him or her, you can count on the recommendation. If you are new in town, you may have to resort to the phone book, or to a recommendation by a contractor. If these are your sources, you must be especially careful in investigating the reputation of the recommended professional before signing on.

Call the design professional and make an appointment. Generally, if you visit the firm's office for the initial interview, you will not be charged. If you ask the professional to come to your house or apartment to give you "ideas," you may be expected to pay for the consultation. If you want to consult with a great many designers to see who has the most innovative ideas, expect to pay for the privilege. Generally, an interview is not the best time to pick the designer's brain. Some design professionals will give you some wonderful ideas on the spot that may prove impossible to execute for legal, structural, or other reasons. There are other, more reliable ways to determine the creativity of the designer.

Ask the design professional to show you a portfolio of work already completed. This portfolio may be in the form of a loose-leaf binder of 8" × 10" glossy photos of projects or may be in the form of slides projected on a screen. Ask specifically to see renovation projects similar to the one you are contemplating. Don't worry too much if the designer has not done a project exactly like the one you have in mind. Designers should be somewhat flexible and their portfolios should reflect the various functional and stylistic requirements of their former clients.

You can learn a great deal from the portfolio. If you are contemplating renovating your brownstone to restore most of its original Victorian charm, you might think twice about a designer whose work is strictly slick marble and mirrors. There are some designers who have one vision, and one vision alone, and tend to impose that one style on their clients. On the other hand, a single-style designer might be your best choice if you happen to like his particular style. For example, in your search for a designer to renovate your brownstone you may find a professional with extensive brownstone experience and a flair for Victorian design. If you love each and every one of his or her projects, hire that designer (after checking references, of course) to renovate your brownstone.

That doesn't mean necessarily that a contemporary designer or one who has never worked on a brownstone is incapable of doing an excellent restoration of your house. When you look at the portfolio, note the versatility of the designer. If all of the projects have the same look, and that is definitely not the look you want, you may wish to interview more designers. If the portfolio has a diversity of projects, each one reflecting a somewhat different personality (demonstrating the designer's ability to integrate the sensibilities and tastes of the owner), it is a good indication of the designer's willingness to develop your vision for your brownstone.

If you are looking for a knock-your-socks-off design, search the portfolio for innovative and creative ideas, such as new uses for ordinary materials, unusual use of space, and the like.

It is not enough to judge the quality of a design professional's work from photographs. Photographs tend to blur sloppy detail work, so that it is not noticeable. Ask to see one or two of the projects. You will be concerned about the designer's ability to monitor the contractor. If the construction work on most of the designer's projects is poor, it may not speak well for the designer's ability to create good construction details or to monitor the contractor.* There are many designers who have brilliant vision but are unable to execute that vision in drawings and details that can be read by a contractor.

In addition, ask for a list of references. Ask for the telephone numbers of the owners of projects that are similar to yours. Call at least three of the references and ask about their experiences with the designer:

· Was the professional sensitive to your needs and requests?
· Did he or she execute the project to your satisfaction?
· Were services provided in accordance with your agreement?
· Would you use the designer again?
· How did the designer interact with the contractor?
· Did you feel you were well represented?

When speaking to the references, keep in mind that almost no renovation jobs progress 100 per-

---

*Very often a poorly executed job is the fault of the contractor. Although it is part of the designer's responsibility to make himself familiar with the work of the bidding contractors, very often a client insists on hiring a contractor whom the designer does not recommend. It is sometimes the case that the low bidder's price is so tempting, the owner believes himself able to forgive a multitude of construction sins. There is very little justification for hiring a bad or sloppy contractor. It has been our experience that the client who claims to be "not fussy" when he accepts the lowest bidder is the one who makes the most noise when the job does not come out right.

cent smoothly. Most jobs take longer to build than expected and often cost somewhat more than what was anticipated. This is especially true for renovations, since many problems cannot be anticipated because they are hidden in the walls.

One of the most important, and often overlooked, qualities of a design professional is his or her personality. It is essential that you feel comfortable with the professional you are working with. After all, this is a collaboration, and you must feel that you will be an equal partner. We have heard many stories of clients who were totally intimidated by the designers they hired. The initial interviews and conferences are like a courtship. If you are uncomfortable with the designer at the beginning, your relationship with him will probably get worse, not better.

During the interview with the design professional, be sure to ask for his credentials and check whether he is licensed or affiliated with a professional organization. Also, request a review of how the work will be organized and determine how often you will be consulted before the design is finalized. Inquire about his fee structure, frequency of billing, and the designer-owner contract he prefers to use. Ask about the contractors he usually recommends for these kinds of projects and if he thinks it will be difficult to attract a very experienced contractor. (Your job may be too small for a specific contractor.) If you want to use a specific contractor, ask the designer if he or she is amenable to the idea.

Last but not least, you should discuss the scope of the work, what you expect to be done, and your budget. Perhaps your budget is unrealistic for the amount of work desired. Don't expect the designer to be able to give you a price for the remodeling of an as yet undesigned kitchen or bathroom. The range of renovation costs for these items is so broad that no one will be able to give you a price until all of the items are designed and specified. (Even after the design and working drawings are complete the designer will not be able to provide you with much more than a guestimate of the cost. Remember, the designer is not the builder, and only the builder can provide a price.) You may speak to five designers about your projected job and your budget. If four out of five of them tell you that your budget cannot possibly cover your projected renovation, don't hire the designer who says that your budget is sufficient.

We suggest that when you get a copy of the contract you have your lawyer review it before you sign it. Most architects use the American Institute of Architects (AIA) form, which is regarded as standard. Some professionals use a letter of intent for very small projects. Discuss all of the above with your attorney before proceeding.

HOW MUCH WILL THE DESIGN WORK COST?

As a general rule, it is hard to say which type of design service (architect, interior designer, or interior decorator) is the most expensive and which is least costly. The various design professionals use different fee structures. A design professional may use one of a number of systems to determine how he will charge.

The most common fee structure, used by architects and many interior design firms, is based on a percentage of construction cost derived from competitive bidding on a project. For a small residential project this percentage can range between 12 percent (considered very low) and 20 percent, with an average of about 16 percent. This fee covers full services:* design schematics, sketches and models (if called for), consulting engineering fees, working drawings and specifications, administration of the bid, the writing of the contract, and administration of the construction. Not covered by this percentage are the cost of a survey, building department filing fees, the cost of a building permit, and printing, mailing, and photographic costs. Before signing a contract with the designer you will agree to a billing and payment structure. For example, an architect generally charges about 5 percent of the estimated fee when he or she is retained. The client is billed monthly or periodically on percentage increments: 10 percent more when the schematic planning is completed, 20 percent more for preliminary design, 40 percent more for the contract documents (working drawings and specifications), 5 percent more to conduct and review the bid, and the final 20 percent for administration of construction. The retainer is credited at the end of construction. All of this is based on a percentage of the estimated construction cost. If the job turns out to cost more or less than the original estimate, the amount paid to the designer is adjusted accordingly. Also, if the client makes radical changes or alters the scope of the work after the majority of the drawings have been completed, or asks the designer to provide drawings for built-in furniture, the de-

*Each designer's contract is different. It is important to read your contract thoroughly and not depend on the very general outline of services and fees that we include in this chapter.

signer may be entitled to additional compensation.

Another common method of billing used by design professionals is based on an hourly rate. This fee structure charges the client by the hour at one price for experienced, licensed personnel and another, lower price for drafting personnel. You are billed monthly in proportion to how much effort was expended on your behalf by the firm. Very often there is an upset cost, based on a percentage of the actual cost of the project, so that the fee does not go through the roof. The upset fee is generally a bit higher than the ordinary percent of estimated cost would have been, had that method been chosen. Many design professionals prefer the hourly rate to the percent-of-estimated-cost method for small domestic projects. To put it bluntly, some clients absorb huge amounts of time in deliberating the alternatives available, selecting finishes, or changing their minds after the drawings are done. This, of course, is the prerogative of the client. The designer, however, likes to know he is being paid for all the time consumed by changes and deliberations. The client who knows what he wants, makes decisions easily, and tends to stick to them can profit handsomely from this method.

Some interior decorators and designers have an entirely different method of billing. You buy the wallpaper, carpet, or sofa from the decorator at the gross (retail) price, and the decorator buys the item from the showroom at the discounted wholesale (net) price. The markup at the showrooms varies from 20 to 50 percent. If you pay $10,000 for a carpet (whose net price is $6,000), $4,000 may be retained by the designer as his fee for services rendered. Although these percentages seem high, these fees are often justified by the enormous amount of time it takes some people to select furniture and finishes. If the decorator spends four days shopping for $400 worth of powder-room wallpaper, even a 50 percent profit is low.

Some decorators split the markup with their clients. They purchase the $10,000 rug for $6,000, charge the client $8,000 for the item, and keep $2,000 as commission. (The tax due on the rug, which is additional, is paid to the decorator, who passes it on to the state. Sales tax is a percentage of the retail price, which in this case is $8,000.)

Another variation on the percentage theme is the designer who bills by the hour and charges an additional amount, about 10 percent of the wholesale price, for any showroom item purchased. In the case of the carpet, you pay the designer by the hour for the shopping time and you pay about $6,600 for the item ordered. In this case, the advantage goes to the client who can make quick decisions.

Another compensation structure is the fixed fee, agreed on in advance by both client and designer. The contract signed to seal this agreement should carefully outline all of the services expected by the client for the fixed fee.

WHAT SERVICES CAN I EXPECT FROM A DESIGN PROFESSIONAL?

The Design Phase

Once you have outlined the general scope of the work, established a budget, and signed a contract, the design professional should begin to take accurate dimensions and photographs of the areas under consideration for renovation, research the files of the building department or historical preservation societies for existing plans and photographs, and sit down with his clients and prepare a detailed program of requirements. It is sometimes helpful to provide your designer with a "wish list" of items that you would like included. Make sure the designer knows which items you definitely need to include and which are pure fantasy. In addition, the designer should be made aware of the number of people living in your household, their ages, and their special needs.

Simultaneously, the design professional should be investigating the legality of this renovation. If you are planning an extension, the building and zoning codes must be examined to determine the boundaries and criteria for the extension. If you are planning to make exterior changes to a building located in a historic-landmarked area, the appropriate preservation authorities must be consulted. If the house is in a rural area, wetland and floodplain maps must be checked. In addition, fire, environmental, and building codes must be strictly followed when redesigning both the interior and the exterior of the building. The design professional should be familiar with the rules. It is best to find out in advance if the authorities will allow you to go ahead with what you are planning. Unfortunately, you will not get a final go-ahead until you have officially filed the drawings. We have found, however, that advance research and informal visits to the various authorities tend to minimize potentially expensive disappointments in the end.

With a drawing of your existing house or apartment in one hand, a list of your requirements in the other, and the building code open on the desk, the design professional can begin to examine the options. There may be more than one way to redesign the layout. The designer should present you with the various options at your next meeting. It may take a number of sessions to finalize the design direction. After a direction is chosen, appliances and plumbing fixtures should be selected since these influence the size and shape of the rooms they are in.

The final stages of the design process are often frenetic and time-consuming for the client since many small decisions must be made, often entailing visits to supply houses and showrooms. The material and color for all the floor finishes must be selected, as well as the faucets and towel bars for the bathroom, the counter and backsplash for the kitchen, and all the lighting fixtures. All of these items must be checked to see if the colors work well together and the items are available within the time frame, and to make sure that the items selected are appropriate. Of course, there are the inevitable blunders. A classic example involves the renovator who ordered an antique brass faucet for his bathroom lavatory. The fitting took months to obtain because it was out of stock. When it arrived, the renovator realized that the antique brass looked out of place with all of the chrome fittings in the room. This was a moot point, however, since he had inadvertently ordered a set with handles spaced 4″ apart that could not be installed into the holes on the lavatory, which were spaced 8″ apart.

Every construction project has a thousand little details that must be coordinated and it seems inevitable that some mistakes will be made (by you, the designer, the contractor, or the supplier). On a well-run job, however, these errors are kept to a minimum and are corrected without acrimony and long delays.

It is a good idea, if possible, to have all of the finishes and fixtures selected before the drawings are sent out for bid. If every item has been specified on the drawings, the contractor is able to give you a fixed price that covers the complete renovation. If you have not chosen the faucet sets (which can cost from $60 to $600 per set) or the kitchen flooring ($200 for vinyl sheeting, $2,000 for granite tiles), it will be hard for you, the designer, or the contractor to establish a fixed price for the total project.

If you have not selected all of the fittings and fixtures before the job goes to bid, you may ask the contractor to provide you with an allowance for each item. For example, if you have not selected the door hardware, the contractor may provide you with a $100 allowance per door. If the hardware you finally select costs more than the allowance, you will have to pay the contractor the difference. If it costs less, he owes you a credit.

Another option is to specify that the contractor will provide the installation of the fittings, fixtures, or hardware as part of the bid price, but you will supply these items.

The final set of drawings produced by the designer are the Contract Documents. These documents consist of the Working Drawings, written Specifications, the General Conditions, and the actual contract. The Working Drawings consist of the plans, elevations, and details of the construction. Dimensions and notes should be included, such as the size of the bathroom, the location of the light switch, and the model number of the toilet. The Specifications are a book of notes that outlines the expected quality of the work. The wood type and the finish for the cabinetry are specified, as are the door hinges and pulls. The contractor is instructed to use specific materials and methods in the installation of the ceramic tiles, and even the composition of the grout is specified. The General Conditions cover general notes, common to all jobs. One important condition is that the contractor must visit the job before he submits a bid. A bidder must take into account the conditions on the job: Is there electricity? Are the roads wide enough for his equipment? Will the family be living in the apartment while the renovation is in progress? The contract is either written by the designer or provided by the contractor. This is a legal document that binds owner and contractor (the designer is not a part of this agreement), committing the contractor to deliver the renovation at a fixed price and within a time frame, and the owner to pay. There are other contract options, but this fixed-price document is the most commonly used.

If you expect to use the services of a general contractor, the Contract Documents (now called the Bid Package) are sent out to a number of contractors (recommended by the designer or by people you trust), who will do a breakdown cost analysis to determine the price of the job. After each contractor has submitted his bid, you and the designer have to decide who will be awarded the contract. You are not bound to select the lowest bidder. If the prices are not too far apart, you will be better off selecting the contractor with the best reputation for quality work or for delivering the job on time for the price agreed upon. If you have a contractor that you know and love, you need not send the job out for general bid at all. The price can be negotiated. This is an informal process. The contractor gives you a preliminary price. This price should be checked with your designer, who has experience with similar projects, to see if it falls in line with the general market. If the price is fair but above your budget, sit down with the designer and contractor and see which items can be cut or which materials substituted. Most design professionals, however, feel that you will get the best price from a contractor who knows the job is being competitively bid.

Generally, the drawings required for filing are not as extensive as those required for a bid. Since most building departments do not require such specific details as finishing materials and hardware, the plans of the project can be filed before they are a complete bid package. Hopefully, you will have the plans approved when your contractor is ready to begin construction.

The Construction Phase

A general contractor (G.C.) schedules the job, hires the subcontractors, purchases the materials, and orders the fittings and fixtures. If the construction company that successfully bids your job is large enough (unlikely on a small, domestic renovation), all of the electricians, plumbers, tile installers, and plasterers work directly for the G.C. Most likely, the G.C. that you hire is a carpenter who works on the job alongside his or her workers (or a manager who heads his own carpentry crew) and subcontracts the electrical, plumbing, fine cabinetry, or tile installation to companies that specialize in these trades.

The contract between owner and contractor will specify the work (usually the drawings, specifications, and general conditions in the bid package) and a schedule for payment. Most contracts require that at least 10 percent of the contract price be paid in advance of construction, and 10 percent retainage be withheld until all of the work is complete. In between, the schedule outlines the percentage to be paid after rough partitions are installed, the wiring completed, the plumbing finished, etc. Periodically, the contractor submits payment requests to the design professional for review and approval. If a request is in order, it is approved and transmitted to the owner for payment.

It is the G.C.'s responsibility to schedule the plumber, electrician, or plasterer when that trade is needed on the job, and to call for scheduled inspections by the building department as required by law. On the average, general contractors charge between 15 and 30 percent above labor and material costs as their overhead and profit for managing the job. You may be tempted to eliminate these management costs and oversee the project yourself. Think twice before considering this option, especially if you have had no previous construction experience. In the first place, you will have to learn the sequence of activities on a construction project so that you will know when to call in the various trades. Second, many of these subcontractors are working on other projects and may not come on the day you need them. A G.C. can hold a carrot of future work over their heads as an inducement; you don't have that leverage. Third, a contractor has established a network of sources and suppliers, whereas you will have to start from scratch. Fourth, some municipalities will allow only insured contractors to pick up the building permit. The insurance premiums (providing you can get workman's compensation and liability insurance) may exceed the cost of hiring a general contractor. In spite of these drawbacks, we have known some astute people who have undertaken the management of their renovations and have actually enjoyed the process.

An alternative to hiring a G.C. is to hire a construction manager at a weekly salary or on a time-and-materials basis. A construction manager performs all of the G.C. functions, but you handle all of the payments to the subcontractors. A contractor who works on time and materials charges you by the hour for his managerial functions and submits bills to you for all materials purchased and all subcontractors hired.

One of our clients divided the functions of a G.C. between himself and an experienced builder. He paid the contractor a weekly salary to manage the day-to-day, on-site aspects of construction while he managed the financial end. The builder prepared a detailed list of every item and every trade that would be needed for the job. The client arranged for the purchase of all the materials and supplies and negotiated prices with all of the subcontractors. The builder, himself an experienced carpenter, was on the job site at all times, receiving deliveries, calling in the subcontractors when required, and making sure that everyone was working. They were both very satisfied with the arrangement, and, frankly, so were we.

Some people are under the impression that the designer will manage the construction. This is not the case. The contractor is legally responsible for constructing what has been detailed in the plans. If there is a discrepancy, he must point it out to the designer. The designer's responsibility extends to periodic site visits to ascertain if the contractor is building the project the way it was designed and specified. The designer must be available to answer the contractor's questions, correct discrepancies, solve unforeseen problems, and comment on the quality of the work. In addition, the contractor submits requests for payment periodically as the work progresses. The designer approves these requests on the basis of satisfactory completion of the work and in conformance with the schedule of payments outlined in the contract. The approved request is paid by the owner. The chain of command is from you to the designer to the contractor, and vice versa. If you want to make a change while the job is in progress, you should speak to the designer and not directly to the contractor. The designer negotiates a price with the contractor and, with your

approval, issues a Change Order. The designer is not responsible if the contractor takes shortcuts that are not easily seen on inspection, or if the project comes in late, or if you approve a change (without consulting the designer) that turns out to be illegal.

When the project nears completion, the designer issues a Punch List, outlining what still must be completed before final payment is made. The contractor calls for final inspection by the building department (if required) and all bills are settled. A certificate from the Board of Fire Underwriters is given to the owner, if one is needed. If required by the municipality, a new or revised or amended Certificate of Occupancy is applied for and issued. When the contractor completes all of the items on the punch list and all bills are paid, the project is considered complete.

2

ASSESSING YOUR NEEDS

There are two approaches to the redesign of any apartment or house. One is to start with a list of your functional needs and to begin master-planning the house around these priorities. The second approach is to study the style and proportions of the house and to make the preservation of these qualities the major design determinant. This chapter approaches the redesign strictly from a functional point of view, whereas Chapter 3 focuses solely on the style and character of the building.

Whichever approach you choose, be sure that the other determinant is not neglected. A functional approach need not result in ruining the style of the existing building. Rooms can be reorganized without destroying their original character or detailing. Additions can be constructed that are sympathetic to the existing façade. Conversely, even if your first priority is the preservation or reconstruction of a period house, there is no need to sacrifice space, privacy, and indoor plumbing. Unless you are restoring a historic monument to period conditions, much can be done to integrate functional bathrooms, compatible electrical fixtures, and modern kitchen equipment into a gracious period piece.

The first step a design professional takes in any renovation is an assessment of a client's needs and an evaluation of the existing building. An analysis of needs focuses on the spatial, organizational, and life-style requirements of the people who will occupy the house or apartment. An evaluation of the existing premises is made in terms of its physical condition, aesthetic potential, histori-

cal context, and the size and distribution of its interior spaces. By following the steps outlined below, a relative stranger (the designer) becomes acquainted with the individuals living in the house or apartment and the potentialities of the space that is to be renovated. Although you may be very familiar with both your needs and the potential of your existing residential space, we suggest you follow these steps as well. You may find that we cover some points that you may have otherwise missed. In addition, we hope to teach you the first rule of architectural design: compromise.

THINKING ABOUT YOUR REQUIREMENTS

Some people about to renovate are quite sure of their needs: more closets, a new bedroom, an overhauled kitchen. Many renovators, however, are less sure of their exact requirements short of knowing that they need more space and they want the place to look "better." We include this chapter for readers who wish to follow the redesign process from the beginning. We feel that a careful analysis of your household's needs (especially in comparison with your existing space) may be of value and ultimately may save you money. For example, one of our clients saw the need to build an additional four rooms onto his existing house. He claimed that he needed a gym,

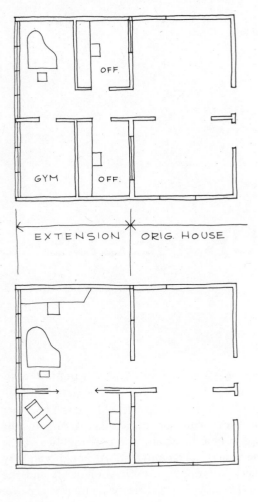

ILL. 1

a home office, and a practice room to contain his piano and recording equipment. His wife, a writer, needed her own office. The four rooms were to be small and cramped since the site adjacent to the house was small. Two of the rooms would face the blank wall of a neighbor's garage. After questioning the client on how he was going to use those three rooms, we reminded him that he could occupy only one of them at a time. We suggested that instead of his three tiny rooms he might be happier with a single large room which would contain gym equipment on one side and the piano and recording equipment on the other. The word processor would be built into a cabinet that could be opened to the room or closed off from it. The room would be pleasant and airy with a view to the backyard and perhaps a skylight or greenhouse extension. As an added bonus, his wife's office would be more generously proportioned than was originally anticipated (Ill. 1).

If your budget and existing space are tight you will have to seriously differentiate between what are real needs and what are "wish list" items. An audiovisual screening room, a private gym, and a lap pool may be fine if you are renovating a château. On the other hand, if you are redesigning a five-room apartment for your family of four, the private-gym fantasy may have to be abandoned and the exercise equipment incorporated into another space.

The design analysis that follows focuses on (1) functional needs—that which allows us to carry out our household activities efficiently—and (2) aesthetic imperatives—that which pleases the eye and enlivens us. Careful and thoughtful planning and a good eye for proportion will satisfy these two design categories.

The third ingredient, that which makes a house or apartment into a home, is less tangible than the first two. It is the elusive "something" that satisfies our psychological need to feel comfortable and secure. It generates the good feeling we get when we return home from a particularly hard day at work and close the front door behind us. No matter how many times we cross that familiar threshold, the feeling that we are in the embrace of our own private world should be there; in fact, it should grow more intense with time. We sleep best in our own bed, in a room with our imprint, surrounded by the pictures we have chosen to hang on the walls.

We feel that the more time, effort, and hard thinking you invest personally in designing your environment, the happier you will be in it. This does not mean necessarily that you should make all design decisions on your own. What we suggest is that you think about the atmosphere you wish to create. A home's environment should mirror the life style of its inhabitants, their tastes and sense of style.

FUNCTIONAL CONCERNS

An analysis of the way you live should be the starting point of the design process.

Private Spaces

Most households consist of individuals who sometimes need to be together and sometimes want to be alone. We need to be alone in order to nap, think, study, or have a private telephone conversation. All people, children included, need to withdraw on occasion to put together the events of the day or to ponder a decision. The place a person chooses for this private contemplation is a room or area that is felt to be one's own. The bedroom is the most likely candidate. Most people seem to have a particular attachment for the place where they sleep. Perhaps we shed our inhibitions when we take off our clothes. The bedroom need not be the only bastion of privacy in the house. The kitchen, when the rest of the family has deserted it, is another choice; so is the bathroom. Each member should feel that there is at least one spot in which he or she may be alone and undisturbed.

The private areas of the house are the bedrooms, studies, or home offices which are to be used by one or two members but not by everyone. Private spaces can be large or small, bright or dark, open or closed. Some people consider the bedroom to be their sanctuary to be used to take morning coffee, read the paper, or make early morning calls. Often they retire to their bedrooms as soon as they finish dinner, toss off their clothes, don their pajamas, and watch TV or read in bed. Others might use the bedroom minimally. They would prefer to spend most of the time they are awake in the living room. It makes sense that these two kinds of bedrooms be designed differently. The former requires a small sitting area as well as room for the bed and TV; the second bedroom could be very basic.

Traditionally, individual bedrooms are the only private spaces in a house. Adult privacy is provided by the master bedroom, which is larger in area and has direct access to a private bathroom. The secondary bedrooms become the children's spaces and are generally smaller, sharing a common bathroom. Although this arrangement has proven efficient for many families, it is not necessarily the model for every family. A household with visiting children, frequent guests, kids away at college, whose foremost concern is flexibility, may be happiest with a large area that can be easily partitioned into any number of smaller spaces. This space can be divided in accordance with changing needs (Ill. 2).

Another family may find that it is essential to separate adult private and communal areas from the children's bedrooms and playroom. The adult area might be a single space that accommodates sleeping, relaxing, working, and grooming in a group of areas. The children may prefer to play and work together but do not wish to share bedrooms. Their private space could be a large com-

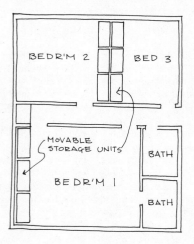

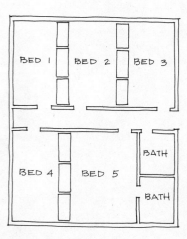

ILL. 2

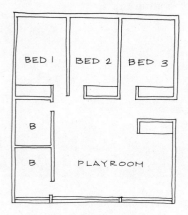

ILL. 3

Thus far we have used the terms "room" and "space" almost interchangeably. A "room" is usually defined by physical boundaries such as walls and partitions, doors, floors, and ceilings. A "space" is an area in which a specific activity is likely to take place. For example, an area near the kitchen can be set aside for dining. It need not be a room surrounded by walls. It could be a corner of the living room or kitchen, a balcony overlooking the family room, or the center of a greenhouse. Any number of locations are possible as long as the original criterion of being close to the kitchen is maintained.

Spaces are defined by visual rather than physical boundaries. These boundaries are provided by light, texture, color, materials, furniture, changes in floor level or ceiling height, and so on. A space can be partially enclosed by low walls or it may be totally free of them. The ceiling above it can be raised or lowered. It can be dramatically lit with a skylight. A free-standing fireplace or a "floating" bookshelf can partially enclose it. All of these elements manipulated in various ways set this space apart from any other space in the house, giving it a different use or setting a different mood. (See Chapter 9.)

A house should be thought of as a relationship of spaces, not a collection of rooms. Achieving the proper space interaction to satisfy your needs is what constitutes a successfully designed house or apartment. The spaces can relate to each other directly or indirectly and sometimes they might overlap. For example, the need for privacy and sound control will determine the distance between the bedrooms and the noise-producing areas of the house. Functional criteria will place the kitchen in close proximity to the eating spaces. A need for supervision may lead to the placement of the children's play area close to the kitchen or as an alcove adjacent to the family room.

Space can be defined by visual rather than physical boundaries. In this house, one space is separated from another by a change in level, ceiling height, or plane. Architects, DiDonno Associates

munal playroom-workroom with small sleeping rooms and bathroom facilities closely related (Ill. 3).

Other private areas are a painting or music studio, home office, woodworking shop, sewing or hobby room, personal gym, sauna, and steam room.

Joint Activities

Most of the activities of the household are communal. The family usually dines together at least once a day and most of us prefer to watch the ball game with company rather than watch it on separate sets in separate rooms. The shared spaces—the living room, dining room, kitchen, and playroom—are the places in which to share ideas and experiences. These spaces should have a warm and comfortable feeling, conducive to such exchange. For some people a room filled with pictures and treasures collected on vacations creates such a feeling. People who love the outdoors are likely to feel happiest in a room that embraces the outside.

Special demands are often made on the joint-activity areas of our homes. Many households differentiate between formal and informal areas. Some houses have formal parlorlike living rooms for company and more informal family rooms for TV viewing. Many houses and apartments have parallel spaces for eating: one formal for company and holiday meals, the other in or near the kitchen for daily dining. Others do not feel the need for so rigid a space hierarchy. They choose to use the same space for all kinds of purposes, both formal and informal. Each household has its own ideas on how to make best use of its space; it is the quality of space and not the quantity that is vital to good design.

Special attention should be focused on the design of these joint-activity areas. What kinds of activities actually take place in the communal areas of the house? What kinds of experiences do you hope to have in these spaces? What kind of "feeling" should the rooms have?

The shared areas of the house are where people gather to talk and argue, watch TV or look at the fire, read out loud or to themselves, prepare food, eat, gossip, listen to music, entertain friends. The activities to be housed in these areas will be as varied as the age groups within the family. The communal areas are also used for entertaining friends in large or small groups, with varying degrees of formality, and for sweet-sixteen and slumber parties and community-group meetings. Play areas accommodate activities that may at times be unharmonious, such as a quiet game of chess and a noisy computer game. Work areas might be used by someone preparing a term paper

on the word processor while another family member is consulting with his boss on the telephone. Dining areas may be required to accommodate Boy Scouts eating pizza, a formal dinner party for six, the baby's high chair and solo breakfasts, but, hopefully, not all at the same time.

Once you have established the activities or combination of activities that are to take place in these areas, you should try to envision the environment or "feeling" you wish to create in the space. You may prefer to interact with family and guests alike on a small, intimate scale. A large space of ballroom proportions would be useless and feel uncomfortable. Perhaps a series of small spaces would be more appropriate.

A family might feel the need for a large entertainment space for the adults, a big playroom to be used exclusively for the kids, and a range of smaller spaces for study, piano lessons, private tutoring, and word processing. If the construction budget and the space available are unlimited, all these spaces can be accommodated. Unfortu-

This room, which embraces the outdoors, was designed to maximize views to the meadows and mountains beyond. Renovation architects, Sands and Sperling; photographer, Phyllis Sperling

Assessing
Your Needs
19

nately, most people will find that they must work with finite space and a limited budget and will have to make compromises.

Service Areas

The service areas are the kitchen and bathrooms, garage, laundry, and storage areas. The kitchen is best located adjacent to both the inside and outdoor dining areas. It should be accessible from either the front or back door so that you won't have to haul groceries across forty feet of wall-to-wall carpeting to get to the refrigerator. The kitchen can be at the hub of the house, open to the living and dining areas, or in a separate room. (More about kitchens in Chapter 7.)

The most critical question asked about bathrooms is how many are required. Many families have managed with one bathroom for years and it may be all that your household requires. As a general rule, we recommend two complete bathrooms for three to four people and two bathrooms and a powder room (which has a lavatory and toilet but no tub or shower) or three bathrooms for five or more in the family. These need not be luxurious and may have either a tub, stall shower, or tub-shower combination. The bathroom may or may not have a window, but most municipal ordinances require all bathrooms to be either mechanically (using a fan and a duct to the outside) or naturally (through a window) ventilated.

It is most practical to locate the full bathrooms on a hallway adjacent to the bedrooms. If planned correctly, the bedrooms, hallway, and bathrooms should be somewhat isolated from the communal spaces of the house so that a bather need not walk through the living room in bathrobe and slippers. Many designers provide a separate bathroom for the master bedroom. Some more luxurious houses are provided with a bathroom off each bedroom. The powder room should be located near the living areas but not directly off the living room or dining room. It is best located off a hallway or the entry foyer. If you have a two-story house it is a good idea to have a full bath on each floor. (More about bathrooms in Chapter 8.)

At one time closets and storage areas were created out of the leftover space between rooms and at the ends of halls. Built-in closets were considered so unimportant that many beautiful and gracious homes were constructed with virtually no clothing closets. Today closets and storage space are at least as important as bathrooms and bedrooms. Most of us find that we need a lot of area in which to hang our clothing and store such paraphernalia as cross-country, downhill, and water skis.

Clothing closets are ideally located in or very near the bedrooms of the people they serve. Extra closet space can be located in any part of the house. These closets can be used to store the winter wardrobe in summer and the summer clothing in winter. This system necessitates a twice-yearly switching of the closets' contents. General storage can be located just about anywhere. In tight quarters space to store suitcases and other seldom used items is often found above closets in hung ceilings (designed to take the load of the items being stored) and under platforms (Ill. 4). See p. 22 and Chapter 13 for more storage ideas.

HOW MUCH SPACE DO YOU ACTUALLY NEED?

Although we feel that the quality of a space is more valuable than its quantity, we recognize that the size and shape of a room are important factors in how it works, looks, and feels. It is difficult to quantify the aspects of good design in regard to size and proportion; the best we can do is offer some suggestions as to how you can develop a sensitivity to size and compile a list of standard room dimensions.

As a starting point in learning about size and proportion, we suggest you measure rooms that feel "right" to you (whether in your own house or a friend's). You can "pace off" a room by stepping toe to heel across the room (most men's shoes are about a foot long or you can adjust

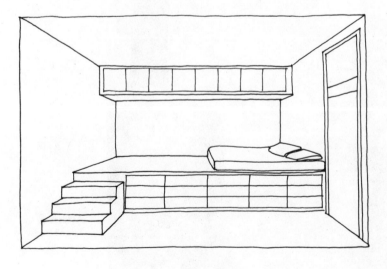

ILL. 4

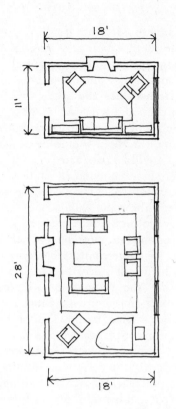
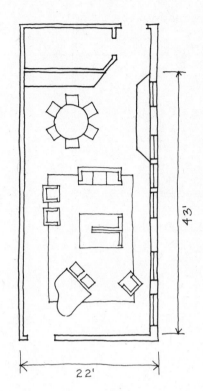

ILL.5

accordingly). At some point in the design process you should measure your own furniture and existing rooms and draw them to scale (Chapter 4, Inset II) to get some idea of the size of your house or apartment and to have some means of comparing the size of the existing rooms with the ones you are planning. It takes a while to get a good idea of how big (or small) rooms should be.

Proportion refers to the relationship of length, width, and height. A nicely proportioned room is either square or rectangular but not overly long and narrow. The ancient Greeks believed that the ideal proportion conformed to the golden rectangle of 1:1.43, and felt that a room's length should never exceed twice its width. We agree that 1:1½ is a good guide to room proportion. Rooms 20' × 28' or 14' × 20' are considered well-proportioned.

The height of a room is critical as well. A large room (20' × 28') with a very low ceiling (8') may feel more like a finished basement than a ballroom. The same room with a ceiling height of 22' will actually look small and somewhat institutional. A ceiling height of 12' to 14' would be most appropriate. Any small room with a disproportionately high ceiling will look smaller than an equivalent room with a lower ceiling. For exam-

ple, a 14' × 14' bedroom with a 14' ceiling height would look like a smaller room than the same room with a 9' ceiling. To apply the Greek proportion to room height, we use the width of the room to determine the ideal ceiling height, which would be 0.7 as great as the width. For example, if the room is 20' × 28', the "ideal" ceiling height would be 0.7 of 20', or 14'. The ideal height for the 14' × 14' bedroom is about 9'. These Greek ideals are not actually adhered to by contemporary designers, but we include them as guidelines.

Many families find that one living space is ample for sitting, reading, playing, and entertaining friends. Other families require multiple rooms for these functions. The living room can be as small as 200 square feet (11' × 18') or as large as 500 square feet (18' × 28'). The former space will feel intimate but is large enough to accommodate a small party. The latter space is amply sized to accommodate large parties. Anything over 600 square feet is baronial in size but may seem overscaled for a simple tête-à-tête. A space this large will require multiple seating arrangements to make it work as a living room. The above dimensions apply to the family room and the playroom (Ill. 5).

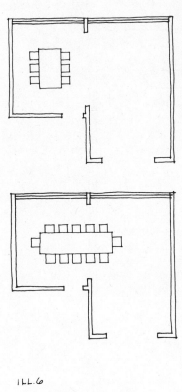

ILL. 6

Dining rooms are often sized to fit the furniture they will house. A large room that accommodates both living and dining requires less overall space for the dining functions than if they were contained in a separate room. In the case of a large dinner party with an expanded table the dining area can "spill over" into the living space (Ill. 6).

Bedrooms can be any size. A single twin bed is 39" wide and 75" or 80" long. The smallest bedroom could include a bed and a dresser and pivot space (make sure you adhere to code requirements) (Ill. 7). Keep in mind, when designing children's bedrooms, that most children over the age of ten have sleep-over dates. The bedroom should be large enough for a foldout cot or trundle bed. (If this doesn't work, be prepared to offer the guest room or family room to your kid for these mini–slumber parties.) A queen-sized bed is 60" wide by 80" or 84" long and dictates the minimal size of a bedroom for two people at about 10' × 11' or 9' × 12'. (These dimensions do not include closets.) More space is required for bureaus, lounge chairs, desk space, or exercise machinery.

If you have a lot of kids and are tight on space, you may consider combining the bedrooms in some novel way. Two children's rooms can be reconstructed as three rooms. A large bedroom

can be divided into two tiny private sleep-study areas with a joint play space. A high ceiling may allow for a more elaborate arrangement which partially piles one room onto another (Ill. 8).

Home office and study sizes depend on their function and what you want to put into them. If you build in desk space on both long walls of a room, the room should be at least 8' wide. This room will be adequate for only one person since there is not enough circulation space around the chairs for two or more. If two people are to use the space, the room should be 9' or 10' wide.

A clothing closet must be at least 2' deep to accommodate clothing on hangers. A depth of 2'-3" is more comfortable. Any depth over 2'-6" is inefficient since the increased depth will not permit the hanging of additional clothing. A walk-in closet with hanging on opposite walls can be 5'-6" wide, but a width of 6' or 6'-6" is more comfortable. These closets can be any length. A less effective closet (but useful in awkward spaces) is one with two rods, one directly behind the other, which hangs clothing two rows deep. This closet is useful primarily for storing out-of-season wardrobes or other seldom used items since you have to remove most of the clothing on the front row to get to the clothes in the back. Linen closets can be as shallow as 18" deep but should not exceed a depth of 24" (Ill. 9).

Kitchen and bathroom sizes and proportions are detailed in Chapters 7 and 8.

Outdoor space comes in all sizes and shapes depending on where you live. If you are one of the few city dwellers with a penthouse, balcony, or backyard, consider yourself lucky. Good design will maximize this space so that it is attractive and useful. If you have a choice in relocating the outdoor living and dining areas, consider

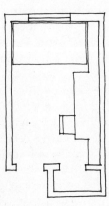

ILL. 7

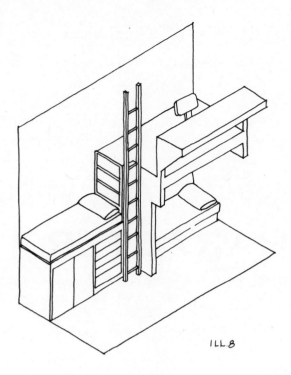

ILL.8

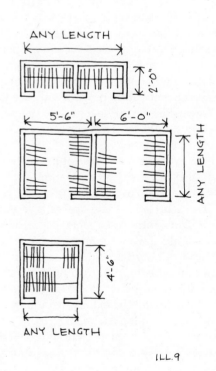

ANY LENGTH

2'-0"

5'-6"   6'-0"

ANY LENGTH

4'-6"

ANY LENGTH

ILL.9

SOME PLANNING CONSIDERATIONS

The organization of the living space is very much dictated by the size and nature of the household. A family with small children has different needs than a household of adults or one of adults and adolescents. A single person or an adult couple living without resident children can exercise a great deal of design flexibility in planning a renovation. Such houses can have showers in the living room, balconies over the living room as bedrooms, or totally partition-free interiors. Of course, this arrangement can work with a family with children as well. It is our experience, however, that a completely open space does not work for most families with children. The noise factor is enormous and the lack of audio privacy ensures that there is no place to retreat for an intimate encounter, parental argument, or private telephone conversation.

A house designed for a family with young children should include play space and room to accommodate the kids' toys and paraphernalia: bikes, baby swings, strollers, games, dollhouses. Large children's bedrooms can serve as play areas, but they are likely to be too far away from the central areas of the house for parental supervision. A playroom off the kitchen is a good idea for a household with young children. The playroom can double as a guest room or a study if it is provided with doors that can be closed for privacy. The problem with designing a house around babies and young children is that children grow up very fast. A family that designs a house around the needs of a two-year-old will find that the child is three years old, going on four, before the construction is completed.

We have found it hard to convince the parents of young children that very soon their progeny will be demanding separate bedrooms and private space. Parents who open the playroom to the kitchen so that they can supervise their children find it hard to believe that in a short four or five years they may actually prefer to have the kids (now teens) play with their friends in some remote part of the house. If you have small children, try to have the foresight to incorporate the needs of adolescents in the scheme of things.

As a final consideration, if possible, try to provide space for guests. This room can be a "flexible" room, sometimes study, sometimes guest room, sometimes playroom.

these spaces as you would the interior spaces when you plan the redesign of the floor plan. Any outdoor space will be more useful if it is located adjacent to the communal areas and has good access to the kitchen.

3
STYLE AND CHARACTER

We have all dreamed of the kind of house we want, its spaces, its style, and its character. The reality of the marketplace, however, often presents us with houses and apartments that are not quite what we had in mind. We may have been looking for a new home but buy a turn-of-the-century building instead because of location, financing, availability, or simply chance. In the process of renovating these buildings to suit our specific needs or to upgrade them, we should work with their style and character.

"Style" and "character" are often used interchangeably although they have very different meanings. Style refers to those elements in a house that place it in a particular time period. An old house would generally represent a style of its time. A new house, on the other hand, may attempt to revive a style of the past or represent a current style. The character of a house relates to those elements in it that give it a distinctive quality. Many houses have a great deal of character without belonging to any particular style.

STYLE

The changing nature of styles is clearly apparent in most houses. We are all relatively familiar with styles such as Colonial and Federal. There are few people who are fortunate enough to own original homes of these periods. Most of us fall into a much broader category of hybrid housing styles. Even houses in historic-landmark neighborhoods are seldom pure examples of a given style. There are many Victorian homes with Colonial Revival detailing and Cape Cods with Georgian doorways. Presently, it is not uncommon for builders and developers to arrive at an efficient house plan and then envelop its façade with a period "look." The result is often a contemporary open-plan house wrapped in Colonial trimmings. If you are among those whose house is of a particular style or styles, the renovation process will take yet another dimension. The style (or predominant style) of a house should be seriously considered when planning a renovation.

Each style has its own sense of proportions and scale. It also has distinctive detailing (or lack of it). When we think of a Victorian house, the imagery is one of tall, ornate spaces. We envision intricate plans with unusual-shaped rooms. The exterior would have asymmetrical massing with turrets and oriel windows. In contrast, a traditional farmhouse brings to mind low-ceilinged rooms with wide-plank floors and small windows. The plan and the exterior would be simple with spartan detailing and a large front porch.

From the 1600's to the present numerous styles have evolved throughout the United States, each with its own set of proportions, scale, and detailing. In many instances the style originated from basic functional needs, as is the case with Colonial houses. The great majority of American housing styles up until the 1900's, however, evolved from an attempt to re-create styles which were fashionable in Europe at the time. After the turn of the century American housing styles started to develop in their own right with the emergence of the Craftsman movement and Prairie houses. The modern movement had an impact internationally and houses quite consciously shed their traditional trappings. Even today, however, eclectic housing styles are very much alive and well, and within the architectural profession a revival of historicism in buildings seems to be a very popular design approach. The Glossary of Major Housing Styles at the end of this volume attempts to describe some of the most popular ones. Be advised that there are numerous books that cover this subject in much greater detail.

CHARACTER

The character of a house or apartment is one of its most important assets. Defining what we mean by character is relatively tricky. Driving through some of the older neighborhoods we often come across houses with lots of "character." When we look at these buildings we see strong rooflines, projecting porches, and interesting window treatments. Their walls are sometimes covered with brick, intricate patterns of wood siding, or a combination of materials. They may display architectural features such as bay windows or greenhouses. The way in which a house is sited also contributes to its character. A rural house may sit nicely at the top of a hill or hugging a rock formation while an urban house may fit unobtrusively within the street fabric. Character is also influenced by landscaping. A house surrounded by dense vegetation is quite different in character from one which is landscaped with a formal garden. The exterior character of a house is related to its massing, materials, siting, and landscaping.

When we walk inside a house or an apartment, we find that the sizes and heights of the rooms help to define its character. The character of a loft apartment in a warehouse is quite different from that of an apartment in an old luxury building. The loft would most likely have one large open space surrounded by enormous windows. The old luxury apartment will probably have many varied-sized rooms serving specific functions. A house with small rooms may feel cozy and intimate. Large rooms and high ceilings give an aura of grandeur. Symmetry or lack of it also has an impact on character. Symmetrical rooms tend to be more formal than those which are not. The quality of light within a house also relates to its character. Skylights and large window areas enable the house to embrace the outside. Conversely, small windows sparingly located could give a sense of protection. Character also relates to finishing materials. Floors become a prominent feature when covered with decorative wood parquet or with interesting tile patterns. A room displaying walls of rough brickwork is totally different from one with the slick covering of mirrors. The detailing of a house such as the woodwork around the windows and stairs is also integral to its character. A house may have special architectural features such as marble mantels or window seats. The size and proportions of rooms, their layout, the quality of light, materials, and detailing all play a role in giving a house its character.

EVALUATING YOUR HOUSE FOR STYLE AND CHARACTER

A most important question you need to ask yourself at the beginning of your renovation project is whether or not you are pleased with the way your home looks. Examine the house from the outside. Walk through all those spaces and rooms you

---

INSET I/THE DIFFERENCE BETWEEN RENOVATION, RESTORATION, AND REMODELING

Most buildings are renovated or remodeled; few are restored. Remodeling a building involves cosmetic work. Walls are painted, cabinetry may be upgraded, and the bathroom fixtures may be changed. Technically speaking, remodeling does not involve structural or mechanical work. In a renovation a building is made sound and ready for use. Structural and mechanical systems are generally upgraded. Attention may or may not be given to the architectural integrity of the building. In restoring a building, not only is it made sound but its appearance is brought back to what it had been at some previous time (usually when it was originally built). This approach is taken with buildings of historical importance.

Old buildings with no claim to fame are often "adaptively" restored. Adaptive restoration takes into account the overall architecture of the building while also incorporating elements not always in keeping with the original design. For example, a house may feature an exquisitely restored dining room which is serviced by a contemporary kitchen.

know so well. Carefully evaluating those elements of your house that you want to retain and those that you do not is a key issue in the process of renovation.

General Issues

· Is the house or apartment representative of a particular style or styles? Is it your basic, comfortable builder's classic? Can it be classified at all?
· Is there anything about your home that gives it a special character?
· Is there a particular architectural feature that is very important to the overall design of the house? Is it a feature that you love? Can the renovation expand and build on this feature? Would you rather forget it ever existed?

The Interior

· Is the house made up of a series of rooms that are very formal? Would you like to retain the formal character? Would you rather make it more casual?
· Do the rooms have a particular spatial hierarchy? For example, some rooms are definitely suited for entertaining whereas others are geared for relaxing.
· What are the proportions of the rooms? Are they large or small, tall or low? Do you like the proportions? Do you hate them?

This old warehouse loft was converted for contemporary residential use. The round form in the center (which hides the powder room) divides the kitchen from the living room. Renovation architects, DiDonno Associates

· Does the house have any detailing? Which aspects of the detailing do you like the best? Which ones can you do without? If the house lacks detailing, would you like to incorporate some in your renovation plans?
· What are the predominant materials used for the interior finishes? Do you like them? Are you ready for a change?
· Are there any particular architectural features that display a high level of workmanship? Can they be saved and incorporated into the renovation plan?

The Exterior

· Do you like the proportions of the house? Do they need improvement?
· How do you feel about the size of the windows and doors? Are they too big, too small, or just right?
· Are the windows and doors of particular architectural interest?
· Are these windows and door openings providing you with the quality of light you are comfortable with? Do you need more light?
· Are the windows located so they take full advantage of the views?
· Is there detailing on the exterior?
· What are the predominant building materials used on the outside of the house? Do these materials give the building a rich texture? Is the house lacking in texture?

CHOOSING A DESIGN DIRECTION

There are several design approaches that can be taken when planning a renovation (Inset I). The first and perhaps the easiest is to work toward re-creating the style of your house or apartment. A second, not uncommon approach is for the renovation to contrast the existing style and character of the building. Yet another one is to give character to a nondescript house.

Option 1: Re-creating the Existing Style and Character of Your House

If you decide to take this direction, the first thing that needs to be done is to clearly identify the style of your house. A trip to the library to familiarize yourself with the various books on the subject would be most helpful. There exists a wealth of books that can guide you through the various styles. The local historical society (if you are lucky enough to have one) can be an excellent

After numerous renovations, this 1840's townhouse had lost most of its original layout and detail. Through research of similar period buildings and careful study of the surviving decorative elements, the building was restored to its original plan and style. Restoration architects, DiDonno Associates

source of pictorial information. These societies usually keep good photographs of neighborhoods and houses similar to yours. In addition to the style, try to find out the date when the house was built and by whom. The more you can find out about your building or buildings of that period, the easier your job will become.

The next step is to find out which are the key elements within that particular style. Each style has its own proportions and details. For example, Victorian buildings have traditionally had very tall ceilings. Should your house be of this style, any renovation effort would need to maintain the ceiling heights. Dropping the ceiling in the parlor from 12' to 8' will substantially change the house. When you look at proportions in a style, you should look at the windows and doors, ceiling heights, and the sizes of rooms. Whenever you are

replacing or adding any of these elements, keep them within the same proportions.

A close look at the detailing is also valuable. Federal homes are elegant in their simplicity of detailing. At first glance, they look relatively crisp and unadorned. A closer look, however, reveals a wealth of fine, consistent detailing. Any renovation effort which attempts to stay within an original style should display the same degree of detailing as the original building. Detailing features to look for are the window and door moldings, floor patterns, wainscoting, fireplaces, stairs, transoms, railings, hardware, ceiling moldings, etc. Should these architectural features be deteriorated, it is usually easier to try to repair them if at all possible than to replace them. When you have no choice but to replace, try to keep it in character by matching the material you are replacing in scale, color, texture, and design.

Finally, a renovation effort attempting to remain within a style should keep to the original layout of the building. Let's take a house or apartment with a formal plan. Rooms are ample and clearly defined as living room, dining room, and separate kitchen. Opening up the kitchen and making a gigantic kitchen–dining room space will detract from the architectural integrity of the building. The room you have just created may be lovely, but certainly not in keeping with the style of the house. You may do better by redesigning the kitchen to make it more efficient within the given space constraints.

Option 2: Contrasting the Existing Style of Your House

In architectural and interior design magazines, we often find photographs of homes and apartments showing contrasting styles. This eclectic approach has become relatively popular, particularly with owners of older homes who, although respectful of the style and character of the building, choose to give their renovation effort a different, often contemporary solution.

To successfully contrast the existing style and character of a house or apartment is not an easy design problem. More often than not, the homes you see published have been designed by architects or other design professionals. This approach requires a careful evaluation of those elements in the building which give it its uniqueness. It also entails learning how to keep some of these elements while adding others that will enhance the original. In short, it requires a sophisticated design sense.

One way to start is to survey the entire house or apartment with a critical eye to its proportions, layout, and detailing. You need to decide which rooms or areas in the house have proportions that

This country house, originally lacking both style and character, was given a new identity by relocating the entrance, adding a storage room, and resurfacing with hori-

you like and which ones can benefit from a change. For example, your house may have small rooms with low ceilings that you find both comfortable and cozy. These are pleasant spaces which you would like to maintain. None of these rooms, however, are of sufficient scale or space to accommodate your requirements for a family room. Perhaps the best solution is to add an extension to the house which could have a tall ceiling, a double-story space, or maybe even a greenhouse. Keeping the building intact while at the same time introducing a space unlike any other in the house can offer a welcome change.

A close look at the layout and hierarchy of spaces is also important. The owner of a loft apartment with large, two-story-high open spaces may like the exuberant feeling of the overall space but prefer to dine in a more intimate and formal environment. Carving a separate area out of the existing living-dining room can satisfy his criteria. It could be a small cube of space with a

low ceiling that floats within the larger space of the apartment. This new room could be designed symmetrically and have a formal approach.

Materials and detailing also offer opportunities for contrast. A home rich in detail may benefit by having new elements such as stair railings and built-in furniture of simple design. The beauty of the original work may be enhanced by the spartan quality of the new additions. Conversely, the introduction of ornate architectural elements in an otherwise stark environment could provide the interest that had been previously lacking.

Option 3: Giving Character to a Nondescript House

We are familiar with homes that meet all our functional requirements. They have the right room count, enough bathrooms, and a kitchen of the appropriate size. Yet the house leaves us cold;

zontal siding. See Chapter 26, illustrations 1 and 2, for the working drawings of this alteration. Renovation architects, Sands and Sperling; photographer, Herman Sands

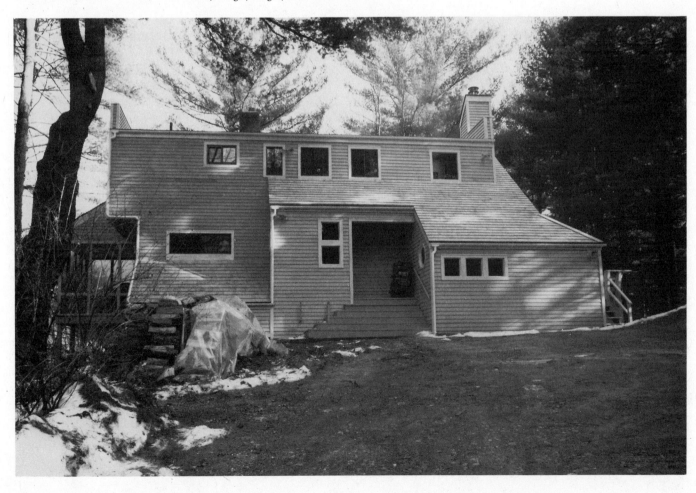

there is nothing interesting about it. The house sorely needs something to make it special.

As in the previous design approaches, attention needs to be paid to the proportions and layout. One of the problems the house may have is that there is too much "sameness." Every room is of approximately the same size and height. Windows and doors are all the same. A solution may lie in combining two rooms into a larger space. You may have to modify the structure of the roof to do this. If you can't afford to lose any rooms, perhaps you can open up one of the exterior walls into a window wall. Another solution can involve raising the ceiling height by taking down the existing ceiling and opening up the room to the attic space. You may give the house variety by playing with the proportions of the rooms and their openings.

The house may have sameness of texture. There is little detailing and no variety of materials. Adding trim to the windows and doors or replacing the stair railing with a new and interesting one would most certainly help. Introduce new materials of contrasting colors and textures. The kitchen floor could have the rough texture of quarry tile or smooth-surfaced tile with an interesting pattern. The living room may have the richness of wood parquet floors, the slick covering of marble, or a carpet of an unusual color.

Special features such as fireplaces, greenhouses, and skylights always give character to an otherwise dull space. Rooms with lovely fireplaces have traditionally been favorites. There is a special appeal to rooms with a greenhouse. It could be that they offer the feeling of being outside within the comfort of our home. Skylights, as many and as large as possible, have transformed the space of even the most banal of cottages.

4

GETTING READY
TO DESIGN

MEASURING YOUR HOUSE OR APARTMENT

Now is the time to measure and draw your existing space. If you are planning a relatively major renovation, you should take detailed measurements of the existing premises and draw an accurate, scaled set of floor plans. These floor plans are important for three reasons. First, you will need them as a basis for any structural or mechanical drawings. Second, you may need to file your drawings with the local building department and get its approval before beginning construction (Inset I). Third, and most important in the design process, floor plans are very useful in understanding the way the space actually works and/or is put together. You are able to see relationships in a floor plan that are not immediately visible when you live in or walk through a space. A floor plan

lets you see how the various rooms, closets, and hallways fit together, very much like pieces in a jigsaw puzzle. The plan allows you to envision the living space as a whole rather than as a series of independent rooms and benefits the design process immeasurably.

For example, you may be living in an apartment with a traffic flow that necessitates your walking through the living room to get to the bedroom. Since you use the living room as an office and sometimes as a guest room, you may want to be able to close it off from the rest of the apartment. Your immediate solution to the problem is to construct a corridor on one side of the living room. This, unfortunately, narrows the living room considerably but is the only solution that immediately presents itself. On drawing the floor plan, however, you note that the hall closet and the bedroom closet back up to each other. By remov-

INSET I/FILING PLANS WITH THE BUILDING DEPARTMENT

It is very difficult to provide guidelines on what sort of renovation needs to be filed with the building department and what is considered "cosmetic." It is our advice that you check with the building department before you do anything, even if you think it is minor. Certainly an addition to the house, the conversion of a porch or garage to a habitable room, the construction of a deck or cov-

ered porch, and the raising of the roof to provide another level must be filed in most municipalities. Painting, replacement of kitchen cabinets, the installation of new windows, and the repair of existing mechanical and electrical equipment usually do not have to be filed. We suggest you consult your local building department or talk to an architect or an engineer if you intend to do any of

the following: demolish or construct partitions, invade the structure of the building in any way, move the kitchen and/or bathrooms, change the number of rooms in the apartment or house, replace the water supply, sewage disposal, or electrical system. Many municipalities require that renovation plans be filed by a licensed architect or engineer.

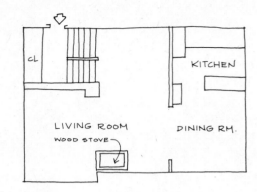

ILL. 2

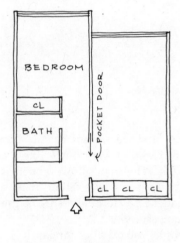

ILL. 1

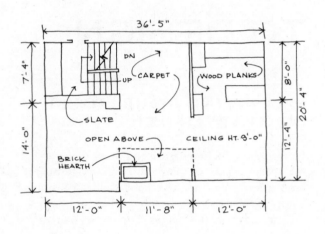

ILL. 3

ing the partition between them you create a corridor from the hall to the bedroom. This eliminates the need for a hallway through the living room. New closets can be built to make up for the ones lost (Ill. 1).

Although it is possible for one person to measure a building, it is much more efficient to have two people (or, ideally, three people). If three people are available, one draws the diagrams and records the measurements, the second holds one end of the tape, and the third holds the working end of the tape and calls out the dimensions.

To make a set of floor plans you must first measure the interior of the house or apartment and then draw it to scale. Before measuring the premises take a pad and pencil and walk through the place drawing a rough schematic of the rooms and corridors and their interrelationships. The schematic should show door openings but need

not show windows or any other details (Ill. 2). This schematic will be helpful when laying out the final plan. Next, with a rigid, retractable tape (if you are working by yourself you will need a tape about 30′ long) take the overall dimensions (length and width) of each room and all corridors and closets. Measure the distance between floor and ceiling and note if any part of the ceiling is lower than another. Note the material on the floor and walls (Ill. 3).

The next step is to make an enlarged, freehand drawing of each room in turn (including kitchen, baths, entry foyer, and closets). These schematics should show doors and arches, windows and window trim, any indentations or niches in the space, closets and closet doors, radiators, pipes (both vertical and horizontal), the location of electrical outlets and lighting fixtures (Ill. 4). Before taking detailed measurements it is a good idea to recheck

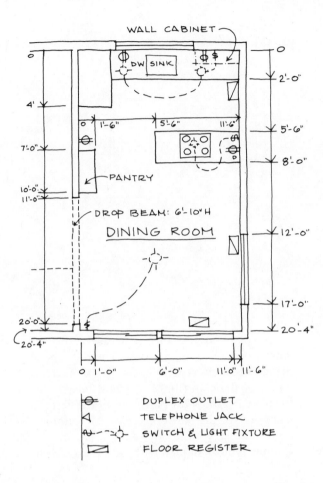

WALL CABINET

DW SINK

4'

7'-0"

PANTRY

DROP BEAM: 6'-10" H

DINING ROOM

0

2'-0"

5'-6"

8'-0"

12'-0"

17'-0"

20'-4"

10'-0"
11'-0"

20'-0"

20'-4"

0 1'-0"   6'-0"   11'-0" 11'-6"

1'-6"   5'-6"   11'-6"

⊖ DUPLEX OUTLET
◁ TELEPHONE JACK
$ SWITCH & LIGHT FIXTURE
▭ FLOOR REGISTER

ILL. 4

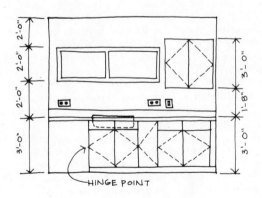

2'-0" 2'-0"

2'-0"

3'-0"

3'-0"

3'-0"

1'-8"

HINGE POINT

ILL. 5

overall dimensions. Double-checking your work is always useful and particularly so if you will be drafting in a place remote from the one you are measuring. It is very upsetting to have to return to retake a critical measurement when your long lines of dimensions do not add up.

Begin at one corner of the room and measure along the wall from the corner to a window opening. Record the dimensions. Next, keeping the zero end of the tape near the corner, measure and record the distance to the other side of the window opening. Continue measuring the length of the wall, always leaving the zero end of the tape at the corner (Ill. 4). (When you get to the end of the wall, check to make sure that this dimension is the same as your overall for the room.) Go back and measure the depth of the window and any projections along the way. When the first wall is finished, attack the adjacent wall repeating the steps above. Continue measuring around the room, from corner to corner, and include the closet-door openings and all indentations, niches, and column projections. When this step is completed, go back and measure the widths of the window trim and the door molding. Measure and note the depth of the window, the height to the windowsill, and the distance from the sill to the top of the window opening. Measure the width, height, and depth of the door itself and note on your sketch the direction of the door swing. For a complete reference set, measure the height of the baseboards and note any trim on the walls and ceilings. Some rooms may have beam drops, places in the ceiling where the structure shows. Note the beam drops on your drawings and approximate their dimensions (Ill. 4). Draw an elevation if you need one (Ill. 5).

Before leaving the room, measure and note the height, width, and depth of the radiator or baseboard. Note any pipes or valves that are visible in the space. Look for and note any electrical panel boxes, gas meters, air conditioners, or duct openings. In addition, locate each of the electrical outlets on the drawing. Draw the approximate location of the overhead lighting fixture and locate all wall switches. Turn on all of the switches to determine which outlets and fixtures each controls. Draw a broken line between switch and fixture (Ill. 4).

Draw and measure each room in turn. For the bathrooms, note all the items enumerated above. In addition, measure the lavatory cabinet and the toilet. If possible, note the exact location of the toilet on the floor. If you are partially renovating the bathroom, note the distance between the hot and cold valves of the lavatory and of the tub set.

Measure the tub (width, length, and height) and note the location of the drain and the faucets. Note the size of the tiles and whether this material covers all or only part of the walls.

In the kitchen, note the width of the cabinets and locate the sink and the gas outlet.

DRAWING TO SCALE

Before laying out your floor plan, determine the scale you will use and the paper size required (Inset II). If the whole house or apartment measures 40' × 100', you will need a piece of paper larger than 10" × 25" if you are using the ¼" scale. If you choose the ½" scale, the paper will have to be larger than 20" × 50" to fit the entire plan on one sheet. Generally, architects use a scale of ¼" = 1'-0" for the floor plan and the ½" scale for separate, detailed plans of the kitchen and bathrooms.

Begin with your sketch of the overall dimensions of the house or apartment. First, block out the major dimensions of the whole plan before detailing any single room. (All too often an inexperienced drafter starts at one end of the paper and draws room after room in great detail only to find that he has run out of paper and can't fit the

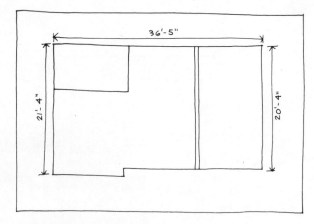

BUILDING LENGTH: ± 37'-0"
SCALE TO BE ¼" = 1'-0"
37 ÷ 4 = ABOUT 9"
PAPER TO BE MORE THAN 12" LONG

ILL. 6

whole plan on the sheet.) Measure the entire length of the floor plan (in scale) on the paper and make sure it is centered. Do the same for the width of the plan (Ill. 6). Begin at one corner of the plan and draw the partitions of the first room. Allow 6" for the partitions and walls around the room, and draw the adjacent rooms and halls. Complete the floor plan with light lines and check

---

INSET II / DRAWING TO SCALE

In order to make a hard-line drawing of what you have measured, you will need the following drafting equipment:

· Drawing board about 24" × 30" with a resilient surface such as chipboard (resembling shirt cardboard)
· T square long enough to cover the length of the board
· Architect's scale (one that has ¼" and ½" scales)
· Pencil and eraser
· Triangle (at least 12" long, either 45° or 30°-60°)
· Drafting or masking tape
· Roll of tracing paper

This is a minimum list and the items can be purchased at most good art supply stores. Don't buy expensive varieties of the equipment listed unless you intend to make drafting your career. Other drafting equipment that might be useful: an erasing shield, drafting brush, bathroom fixture template, mechanical drafting pencil and the corresponding pencil sharpener.

The architect's scale divides the inch into ¹⁄₁₆'s. Look at the end of the scale and note the markings: 16, ¼, ³⁄₁₆, and at the opposite end: ½, ⅛, etc. Look at the line of numbers to the left of the ¼ marking: 0, 2, 4, 6, and so on. The ¼" scale divides the inch into four parts. Architects use this scale to represent feet, letting ¼" represent 1'. The measurement from the 0 to the 4 is actually 1" but using the scale ¼" = 1'-0" it represents 4' (below). To use the ¼" scale to represent 27'-6", draw a line from the 0 to midway between the 26" and the 28" mark. Next measure back from the 0 and count six fine lines, which represents 6". The line (which is actually 6⅞" long) is 27'-6" at the ¼" scale.

The T square is used to draw a series of parallel horizontal lines. The cross end of the T square slides up and down the left (or right) side of the drawing board. The T square is held in place by the left hand while the right hand draws the horizontal line. The triangle is used to draw a series of parallel vertical lines. The short side of the triangle rests on the top edge of the T square and slides along it. Hold the assembly in place with your left hand while using the vertical edge of the triangle to guide your line. If this is uncomfortable, invert the triangle.

To begin a drafting project, cut a sheet of paper from the roll and place it on the table. Make sure the lower edge of the paper lines up with the bottom edge of the T square before taping the four corners to the drawing board.

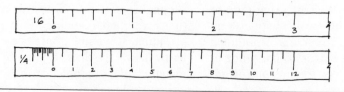

In general, zoning laws regulate building location, type, size, and setbacks.

Ordinances prohibit the construction of a factory in a residential neighborhood (or a residence in an industrial zone). Some businesses will not be permitted in a strictly residential zone. Many municipalities allow only dentists and doctors to conduct business on a residential street. Even if you are allowed to practice your trade adjacent to your home you may be required to provide on-site parking for your clients' automobiles.

Zoning laws often prohibit the renovation of a single-family residence into a two-family house if the district is restricted to one-family usage. (The conversion of a multifamily building into a single-family residence would be permitted.)

Most districts have ordinances that cover building height, overall size, and setbacks from the property lines. Many areas limit the height of the building to two or two and a half stories or a specific number of feet. In some communities houses larger than a specified size cannot be constructed unless the property is oversized. Zoning ordinances often limit the percentage of lot coverage. As an example, you may not be permitted to construct an addition to your existing house if the new construction falls outside of the 40' front, 30' rear, or 15' side property setback lines or if the total building (original house plus addition) covers more than 25 percent of the lot.

---

all dimensions to see if they conform. If there are any discrepancies, make sure you transferred the dimensions correctly from the sketch to this drawing. If that is not the problem, you might have made an error in taking the original dimensions. If there are large blocks of empty space between the partitions that you can't account for (and you did not make any errors), it is likely that there are pipes or flues hidden in these chases.

If the overall plan is correct, go back to your detailed room sketches and fill in the door and the window widths and any indentations or articulations in the space. Go on to the next room and complete the drawing. Note all critical dimensions, especially in areas you plan to change. When you complete all of the rooms, go back and add light fixtures, switches, electrical outlets, pipes, radiators, fireplaces, and other architectural details (Ill. 7). The symbols for these items can be found in Illustration 4.

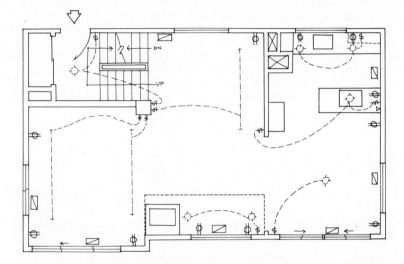

ILL. 7

RESTRICTIONS IMPOSED BY THE MUNICIPALITY

Before investing a great deal of time in fruitless labor, you should be cognizant that a number of outside factors may restrict your design freedom (see Chapter 26 for more information). If you are considering changing the usage of the building to anything other than a one-family house or if you are considering constructing an addition to the building, you may be affected by the zoning laws (Inset III). In addition, most municipalities (but not all) have adopted building codes and guidelines that may restrict your design options still further. The codes are designed to protect you from structural collapses, undue fire risk, and poisonous building materials. In almost every case the restrictions make a good deal of sense. Make sure you have a copy of the building code governing your municipality (and a copy of the national building code) if you are planning anything more than a cosmetic renovation* (Inset IV). Furthermore, many states have passed energy conservation codes which may limit the number, size, and glazing of windows, dictate the composition of the exterior walls of an addition, and affect the design and selection of fireplaces, heating systems, and exterior doors.

Be sure to call local and state authorities to determine what codes and restrictions are in effect for renovations and/or additions. Make sure you have the most recent updates to these documents. It is likely that the township you live in will require that you file plans for anything more than a cosmetic renovation (Inset I). You may also have

Getting Ready to Design

35

---

*A cosmetic renovation involves painting, replacing kitchen cabinets, and most repair work.

Although it would be foolish to list the criteria in any one state or city's building code (they often vary from municipality to municipality), there are some items which seem to be common to all codes. Many communities adopted what is called a performance code as their construction guideline. This means that you must meet certain general requirements for construction, rather than follow exact standards for structure, electricity, plumbing, heating, etc. Other municipalities abide by codes that specifically tell you what their requirements are down to the size of every pipe. Generally, the more rural the area, the less strict the code will be.

Here are some general guidelines:

· Every habitable room must have a window. This includes all bedrooms, living and dining rooms, family rooms, etc. Some codes permit unwindowed kitchens (up to a certain size) and bathrooms if proper mechanical ventilation is provided. Check your building code for the minimum window size for light, ventilation, and escape in case of fire and consult your local energy code for the maximum allowable glazing.
· A minimum ceiling height is specified for habitable spaces, usually at least 7'-6", sometimes 8'-0" (except in areas with sloping roofs). Bathrooms, kitchenettes, corridors, and recreation rooms might have a minimum of 7'-0".
· There are often a number of restrictions regarding staircases. In most areas a narrow winding stair will be allowed only as a second stair between floors. The primary stair will have to be of a certain width and not be too steep or too shallow.
· Many municipalities require the use of noncombustible materials in certain or all areas of new construction. Urban ordinances often insist on metal stud partitions and fire-rated gypsum board and doors. Suburban municipalities have rulings that govern the materials used on garage walls, in mechanical rooms, and on roofs.
· Codes often restrict the use of plastic since some plastics are highly combustible or emit toxic fumes when burned. Before using a material that is not traditional, check with your local building department.
· The codes on plumbing and electricity are very specific and must be read in full. Many municipalities will not permit you to do your own plumbing or electric wiring and will insist that this work be done by a licensed professional.
· Chimneys and fireplaces will have a fixed set of codes that must be adhered to. The height of the chimney above the roof will be determined by code. A separate set of codes governs the size, type, location, and support of fuel tanks.

Caution: This is merely a rundown of some of the information usually found in building codes. Read yours carefully!

to file with the local community planning board, the energy conservation board, the Landmarks Commission, and the Environmental Protection Agency. If you have any questions about the legality of what you are planning, it is wise to visit your local building department before finalizing your construction plans. As a matter of fact, it is a good idea to talk to the building department at the very outset of the planning process.

If you live in a rented house or apartment, a co-op, or a condominium, the owner of the building or the board of directors will certainly want to know what you are planning. Most co-op and condo boards of directors require that you have their approval in addition to the usual municipal approvals before any renovation can take place.

STRUCTURAL AND MECHANICAL RESTRAINTS

Any standing building, be it a small detached house or a large apartment complex, has an existing infrastructure of pipes, wires, walls, columns, and beams. Most renovation projects will require cutting into and modifying segments of the building's structural and mechanical systems. Before attempting to put pencil to paper to rough out your design fantasies, take the time to familiarize yourself with the mechanical and structural layouts of the areas affected and the limitations imposed by them. It is better to discover at the outset that your anticipated change is an impossible dream than to find out much later that there is no way of connecting your newly installed toilet to the sewer system. You may even choose to abandon a design scheme that is theoretically possible to construct but too expensive or too disruptive to be worth the trouble.

The structural system may impose significant restraints on your design. If you are anticipating a change that will remove all or part of a wall, be sure that the wall is non-load-bearing or you may find yourself surrounded by rubble. Some parts of the framework, such as the tie beams in the attic and diagonal bracing in the walls, are not as easily identifiable as part of the structural envelope. If you decide to remove a load-bearing wall or any other part of the structural network of a building, you will have to redesign that segment of the structure. This redesign is not for an amateur but should be done by an architect or a structural engineer.

The plumbing system of a building can impose design restrictions as well. For the most part, hot- and cold-water delivery and gas lines do not pose much of a problem. These pipes can be threaded anywhere through the building and can travel relatively long distances against gravity. The waste-disposal pipes are not as easy to deal with, especially in a multistoried building. Waste lines are 3" or more in diameter and run vertically, carrying sewage down to the cellar and odoriferous gases up and out through the roof. A waste line can be tapped on any floor along its route as long as it is large enough to carry the accumulated waste of the bathrooms and kitchens along its line. Since the system relies on gravity (rather than a pump) the horizontal pipes carrying the sewage from the plumbing fixtures (toilets and washing machines) to the vertical stack must be pitched slightly downward to allow the watery waste to flow properly. Because of the pitch of the pipe it is impractical (and sometimes impossible) to locate toilets far away from an existing vertical stack. In a one- or two-story house you may decide to install a new plumbing stack to accommodate a bathroom far removed from the existing plumbing facilities. If you are renovating an apartment on the tenth floor of a high rise, it is almost impossible to install a new stack.

The electrical and heating systems are less critical. It may be expensive to relocate heavy electric appliances or to expand the capacity of the air-conditioning service, but it usually can be done.

In a multistoried building the superintendent is often able to tell you where the main electrical risers, hot- and cold-water pipes, waste lines, and intercom are located. More often than not you will have to investigate for yourself by chiseling small exploratory holes into the suspected areas. You can suspect any wall that is particularly fat, or adjacent to the intercom, or behind the plumbing fixtures, or near the electrical panel box.

Part Two of this book explores in greater detail the structural and mechanical systems of a building and will provide further information on how to locate and identify the various components of these systems and explain how they work. Those chapters should be studied before you get too far into the design process. In addition, we urge you not to rely on the elementary structural and mechanical education provided in this or any other book. Hire an architect or engineer to review your structural plans and consult with a licensed engineer and plumber before lifting a crowbar.

FINANCIAL AND OTHER RESTRAINTS

If anything is likely to rein in your design creativity it is the ultimate price tag of the renovation. To make matters worse, the cost of the total project may be very difficult to estimate in advance. One way to get an idea of what a project is going to cost is to call in a general contractor who has done similar work. This sounds like a good idea but it often backfires. Most contractors are very reluctant to give any estimates at all unless you provide them with very detailed plans and specifications. If a contractor does go out on a limb to give you a price on the basis of your verbal description (or sketchy plans), he is not in any way bound to his "ballpark figure" when you are ready with final drawings. For some reason the price often appreciates considerably between verbal description and hard-line drawings.

Another way to estimate the cost of the renovation is to ask the contractor for square-footage prices. Often a contractor will estimate that a relatively uncomplicated kitchen with few frills will cost so much per square foot and a luxury kitchen will cost so much per square foot. This will not be a very accurate estimate either, since you probably consider your kitchen design to be very basic and simple, whereas the contractor may think it falls into the luxury range.

A third way to estimate the cost of construction before the drawings are completed is to ask around and find out how much similar renovations cost. Let us say you want to replace your kitchen and bathrooms with creations that were inspired by magazine photographs. You have budgeted $15,000 for the renovation and intend to hire a general contractor to do the work. Many of your friends and neighbors have renovated their kitchens and bathrooms and you want to use one of their contractors. If your neighbors paid $60,000 for similar work it is unlikely that your budget of $15,000 is realistic. Perhaps you should reconsider the scope of the project, or consider doing most of the construction yourself.

The best way to get an estimate of construction costs is to give completed drawings and specifications to a general contractor (he will be adding 15 to 25 percent of the construction cost for overhead and profit).

If you are doing the construction yourself, be careful not to bite off more than you can chew in terms of both your finances and your construction skills. It is a depressing experience to live in a home that is in a permanent state of partial demolition because the renovator hasn't the time, the money, or the skills to complete the project.

Another factor that should cause you to pause before demolishing the critical elements of your house or apartment (such as the kitchen and bathrooms) is where you are going to live while all of this is going on. Demolition work of any kind produces a great deal of fine dust that tends to get into everything (even closed closets and drawers). Renovation projects often take much longer than originally anticipated, which means you may be spending a lot of time with the dust and without a kitchen. If possible, find another place to live while the renovation is taking place. If this is unfeasible, be sure not to demolish all of the bathrooms at once. You will be able to set up a temporary kitchen by plugging in a refrigerator and a hot plate, but dirty dishes will have to be washed in the bathroom lavatory.

Some final words of caution: If you are renovating your kitchen or your only bathroom, be sure to order and receive everything needed in advance of demolition. If you are planning to replace windows or remove parts of the roof or exterior walls, schedule the renovation for the summer, when it is likely to be warmest and driest.

5

DESIGNING

THE RENOVATION

The design process is not easy to explain and is even more difficult to teach. Most schools specializing in design teach the subject by briefly outlining theory and then giving students "problems" to solve. The instructors are called "critics" and teach by evaluating the design solutions presented by the student. Since the authors (unfortunately for you) will not be around when you are struggling with your own renovation schemes, we will demonstrate the design process in Chapter 6 by using case studies. The remainder of this chapter discusses design considerations.

Architectural or interior design is an integration of functional criteria with aesthetic ones. The design of a renovation is further complicated by the addition of yet another set of considerations, the existing conditions of the building to be renovated. The best designers begin the chore with a firm understanding of the program (the functional requirements), a feeling for the style or character of the existing house, and the designer's own inherent insight into proportion and spatial flow. The design process takes a good deal of time and concentration. Rarely does a complete design spring spontaneously, full-blown and fully worked out, into the head of the designer. Most often a designer conceives the kernel of a design concept or approach and then spends hours on the details to see if the idea "works." If the concept is a good one, everything should fall into place with a certain amount of ease. If the spaces look "tortured" (odd-shaped rooms, twisted corridors, too much space for circulation), the design concept is rejected and another one tried. There are

often a number of good design solutions to the same design problem. (There are usually an equal number of bad ones.)

Generally the renovation design process begins with the plan of the existing building or apartment. (However, if you are considering an addition to a distinctly styled or historic building, you might want to start with the elevation.) The designer tapes the plan to the drafting board and then tapes a piece of blank tracing paper over it. Most experienced designers then spend at least an hour staring at that blank piece of paper. When inspired, the designer takes a broad marker and makes some sketchy marks on the tracing paper, changing rooms around, removing a partition here, positioning a window there. Often these first attempts are rejected and another piece of "trace" is added on top of the first. This continues for a few frustrating hours until some approach is conceived. At that point the designer uses a scale and drafting equipment to work out the concept.

It is common for a designer to work on layer after layer of tracing paper until the design is worked out to his satisfaction. Conceptual ideas are generally sketched freehand over the existing drawings so that the hand can move as quickly as the mind. Most designers find that the use of freehand lines, instead of hard lines created with straightedge and triangles, early in the design process allows them to design more easily and not get "boxed in" too soon. Once the design has emerged from the several layers of sketch tracing paper the designer switches to a hard-line, measured drawing.

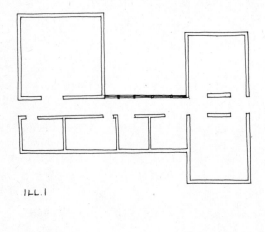

ILL. 1

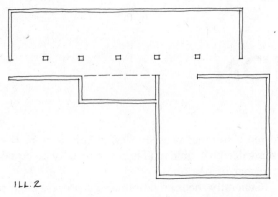

ILL. 2

THE DESIGN CONCEPT

The design concept (or "partee" in architectural parlance) is usually (but not always) an organizational approach. For instance, the designer of a new building might conceive of a linear organization in which the hall is a spine and all of the spaces open along it (Ill. 1). A more sophisticated version of this spinal arrangement has the spine continue through open spaces without walls to define it (Ill. 2). An example of a bad organizational concept is to fit a building into a round plan. Most often the rooms are odd-shaped, the furniture and appliances do not fit right, and the hallways are tortured.

An example of a stylistic partee may be a take-off on the southwestern ranch house, informal and comfortable in approach. These houses are bathed in sunlight and have many overlapping rooms, often in a rambling arrangement. Materials look as if they were taken directly from nature (rather than technically produced) and are often rough in texture. Walls and partitions are constructed of adobe-looking stucco, ceilings are often of wood, and floors are covered in earth-colored Mexican tile. Lines tend to be fluid; there

are few neat creases where corners meet, more often they curve together.

An overall design concept should be the basis for an interior renovation as well. At the outset you should endeavor to develop some organizational or stylistic concept (or both) and stick to it throughout. The concept can be as simple as the selection of a dominant material, such as rough-sawn cedar boards. The material need not be used throughout (as a matter of fact, it would be overbearing if this material was used on all surfaces). In some rooms rough-hewn cedar logs may be used as ceiling beams with cedar boards used as the ceiling surface. The walls in the room can be stucco or plaster. In an adjoining room the wood can be used for doors and window trim. Another room may be fully paneled in the material.

If the house already has a dominant style and the scope of the renovation is small, you must decide either to work within the stylistic confines of the original house or to contrast it. (If you decide to renovate in a style that is in contrast to the dominant elements of the existing building, let this be a conscious decision on your part, rather than the result of a bad design.) If the renovation is a small one you are best advised to stay within the character of the house; otherwise the results may be jarring rather than fresh and innovative.

In the case of a limited renovation, the idea of a house-wide concept may be a luxury that cannot be afforded. A kitchen or bathroom redesign may be limited to pushing out a few walls and moving the tub from one side of the room to the other. But even the renovation of a single kitchen or bathroom should have an overriding concept, if only a color-material concept for the bathroom or an organizational approach to the kitchen.

EXAMINING AND REDESIGNING THE FLOOR PLAN

It should be fairly easy to evaluate your living space if you have occupied it for a long time. You know if the living room is too small, if the kitchen has too little cabinet or counter space, or if the bathtub is not long enough to stretch out in. If you are buying and renovating a new house, the chore may be more difficult. It is important to do a fairly complete evaluation if you intend to do a major renovation. Looking at the house as a whole, rather than room by room, may help you avoid costly mistakes.

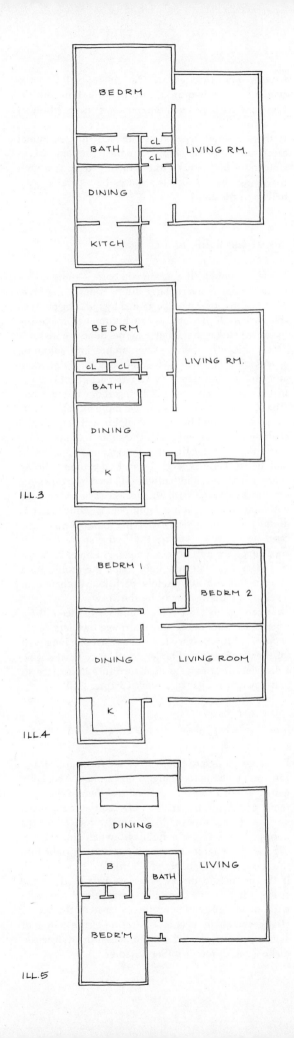

BEDRM

BATH cL LIVING RM.
      cL

DINING

KITCH

ILL.3

BEDRM

cL   cL
BATH

DINING

LIVING RM.

K

BEDRM 1

BEDRM 2

DINING   LIVING ROOM

K

ILL.4

DINING

B   BATH   LIVING

BEDR'M

ILL.5

Begin the evaluation by looking at the circulation pattern.

· Do you have to move through some spaces to get to others? If so, is this traffic flow disturbing to people using the spaces being passed through? Is there any easy way to change the traffic flow (Ill. 3)?
· On the opposite side of the coin, are there any halls or passageways that are useless or redundant? Can you squeeze a badly needed bedroom (Ill. 4) or bathroom (Ill. 5) out of this space? Be moderate in your elimination of hallways, however. You don't want to make the living room or dining room the crossroads of the house. It is one thing to walk alongside the living space to get to the rest of the apartment. It is another thing to have to crisscross it to get to bedrooms or the bathroom.
· Is the entryway large enough? If not, can it be made larger without sacrificing its special quality of being a reception area?
· How does the kitchen, dining room, service entry work? Is the circulation between them easy or do you

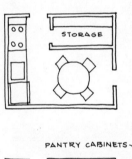

STORAGE

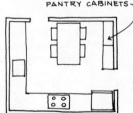

PANTRY CABINETS

ILL.6

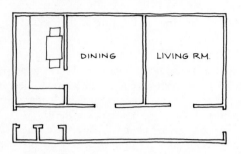

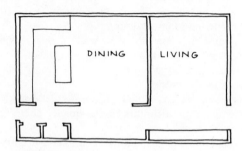

ILL.7

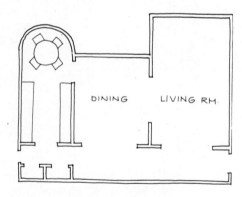

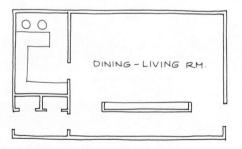

ILL.8

have to pass through an obstacle course? Can the spaces be switched around to ease the flow (Ill. 6)? Can obstructions be removed or new passages opened?

· Is there a good separation between the communal areas and the private areas? Are the bathrooms accessible to the bedrooms without having to pass through the living spaces? Can the spaces be separated by a hallway or a door?

Look at the living room.

· Is it large enough? If not, can you borrow some square footage from an overly large dining room or the foyer (Ill. 7)? Can more space be gained by building out into the backyard? If nothing can be done to make the living room larger, what can be done to make it "look" bigger? Opening wide arches into adjoining spaces is very helpful; so is combining the living room and dining room into one larger space (Ill. 8).

· In the rare event that the living room is too large, what can be done to make it feel more intimate? Platforms and ceilings of various heights will help. Bookshelf-lined walls will make the room more cozy.

· A common problem in some contemporary apartment and house layouts is that the living room, dining room, entry area, and hallway all bleed into one large uncomfortable space (Ill. 9). One is not sure where the hall ends and the living room begins; which part is dining room and which part living room? If this is the case, how can we define the living space without chopping it up into little roomlets? Adding a closet or extending the wall may help shape the room into a more defined entity. A low partition, a change in level, or an archway may be the answer.

· Strangely enough, we have found wall space to be a concern to many house and apartment dwellers. Some people find it necessary to have at least one long wall for the couch and end tables. Wall space need not be a problem. It is easy to float furniture in a space so that no item is against a wall (Chapter 2, Ill. 5).

Now move on to the dining room.

· Is it large enough to house all of the furniture? If not, can you make the room bigger or should you consider getting rid of some of the furniture? Perhaps you can remove part of the partition between the living room and the dining room and construct bifold or pocket doors in its place. On holidays, when the table is expanded for large dinners, it can stretch right into the living room (Chapter 2, Ill. 6).

· If the living and dining areas are part of the same space, what can be done to separate the dining area without visually breaking the expanse of the space? Here a change in level or a lowering of the ceiling or even a large suspended sculptural lighting fixture can make a big difference. (See Chapter 9.)

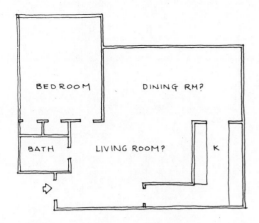

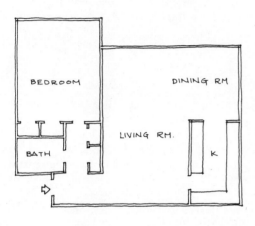

ILL.9

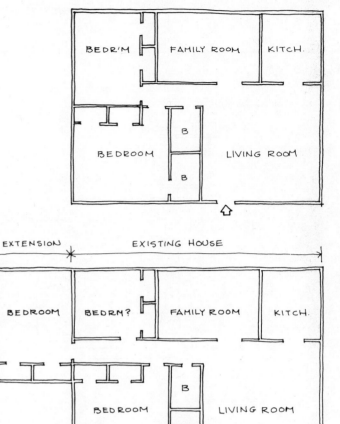

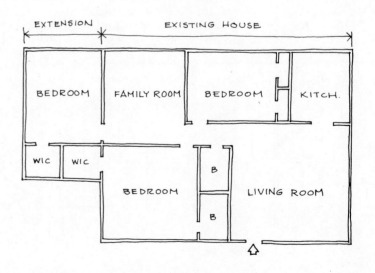

ILL.10

Next look at the bedrooms.

· Are there enough bedrooms to house the family? If not, can you demolish the existing partitions between a few large bedrooms and rearrange the space to form smaller but more numerous rooms (Chapter 2, Ill. 2)?
· If you need another bedroom, can you construct an addition to the house near the other bedrooms? Can the addition be designed so that you need not walk through one bedroom to get to another? You could put a partition dividing the "walk-through" bedroom into part bedroom and part hallway, but that might make the room too small (Ill. 10). If the only location for the addition necessitates walking through one space to get to the new one, consider making the original bedroom into a communal space (such as a family room or playroom) and making the existing family room into a new bedroom (Ill. 11).

ILL.11

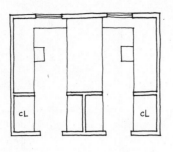

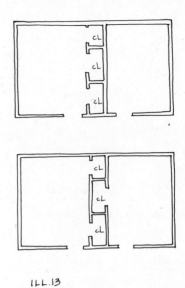

ILL.13

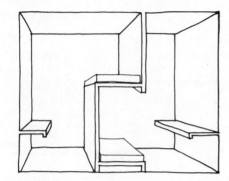

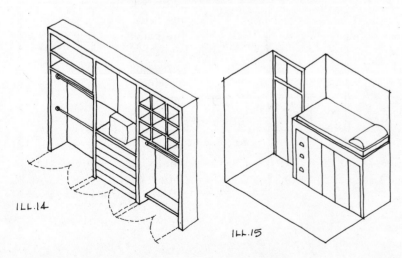

ILL.12

ILL.14

ILL.15

· If there is still a bedroom shortage, consider dividing one bedroom into two. If the bedroom to be divided is not large enough, consider an arrangement that places the beds on top of one another (Ill. 12). The upper bed, in one room, appears to be on a raised platform reached by a short ladder. The lower bed, in the other room, appears to be in a cove with a low ceiling.

· Is there enough closet space in the bedrooms? If there is a closet in the space between two rooms it can be reversed to serve the bedroom it is backing (Ill. 13). A whole wall of closets can be constructed in the bedroom. The closet can be designed to contain hanging rods, dresser drawers, and the TV set (Ill. 14). If the remaining room appears too narrow after the closet

wall is constructed, mirrored doors will make the room appear to be much wider.

· In a very small bedroom consider building space-saving closets on either side of the bed.

· A 4'-6" closet can be constructed under a high platform bed (Ill. 15).

The kitchen deserves special attention.

· The most efficient kitchen arrangement is one in which the major cooking elements (stove, sink, and refrigerator) are arranged in a comfortable triangle. It is best that these elements are spaced far enough apart to have some working counter space between them, but not so far apart as to require a long walk to any one of them. Does your kitchen conform to this general guideline? Is it too large to work efficiently? If so, you may consider a working island (Ill. 16).

· Is the kitchen too small? Can you expand it by borrowing some space from the dining room or mudroom? Many urban apartments have a maid's room adjacent to the kitchen. Can the maid's room be incorporated into the kitchen?

· Is the kitchen efficiently arranged? Can doors or windows be relocated to provide for more counter area or pantry space? Does it make any sense to move the appliances around? If the kitchen feels narrow and small, consider opening it up to the dining room by removing the partition between them. The sense of division between the spaces can be maintained by hung cabinets over the island. The dirty dishes can be partially concealed from guests by a 4'-high divider. (More on kitchens in Chapter 7.)

The bathrooms are next in our evaluation.

· If the bathroom is tiled, any enlargement will probably require a total renovation. If the tub, toilet, and

Entry: The minimum size hall for greeting a guest and taking his coat is 5' × 5'. A gracious entry foyer can be as large as 10' × 10'. Be sure to provide a coat closet adjacent to the entry.

Closets: The minimum depth of a closet is 2'. The length can be whatever you want. A walk-in closet should be about 7' wide to allow for clothing to be hung on both sides. The doors to a closet can be hinged (swinging out), sliding, or louvered. Sliding doors interfere least with furniture placement in the room because they take up no space when they are opened. (See Chap. 2, Ill. 9.)

Hallways: A hall can be as narrow as 2'-6" if it is not much longer than 5' and the ceiling is not too high. It can be as narrow as 3' if it is not much longer than 8'. The hall should be about 3'-6" to 4' wide if it is to run more than 10'. Reasons of practicality and proportion dictate the dimensions of halls. It is difficult for two people to cross each other in a hallway that is 2'-6" wide. Also, a long, skinny hall seems to be oppressive, while the same hall a few feet wider is more comfortable. In addition, the wider hallway can be better lit and can be used to hang art objects.*

Doors: The front door of a house is usually 3' wide. Doors to bedrooms, kitchens, or studies are generally 2'-6" wide, give or take 2". The door to the bathroom is preferably 2'-6", but could be 2' if absolutely necessary.* The same holds true for closet doors on hinges. Most doors come 6'-8" in height, but some are available at 6'-10". Doors can be specially ordered at 7'.

Ceiling heights: The height of the ceiling can vary between 7' (in the oldest Colonials) and 12' or 14' (in the old townhouses). New houses are usually built with ceilings of a minimum of 8' for living areas and a minimum of 7'-6" for bedroom areas. The structure between ceiling and floor can be anywhere between 6" and 1'-6". Ceiling height, like anything else in design, is dependent on a sense of proportions.

Wall thicknesses: The exterior walls of a house constructed from wood are about 7½" thick; the interior partitions, approximately 5" thick. Masonry walls (brick or stone) are about 10" thick. These are approximate dimensions and not necessarily the thicknesses of your walls and partitions.

*Many communities have instituted guidelines to make housing accessible for the disabled. For example, these codes dictate that in new construction, hallways be at least 3'-0" wide and door clearances at least 2'-10". Check your code to see if your building type falls within the code's jurisdiction and if your specific project will require conformance or can be "grandfathered" under the older rulings.

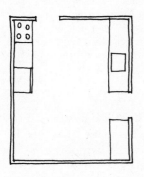

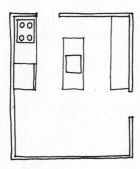

ILL. 16

tile work are in fairly good condition, you may not want to do anything at all in the bathroom. A less expensive face lift could include the replacement of the lavatory with a new cabinet or pedestal sink. New large medicine cabinets can be surface-mounted to the walls for additional storage space.

If you are considering demolishing and reconstructing the bathroom, check to see if you have adequate room for the fixtures you want. A 6'-long tub will not fit on the end wall of a 5'-wide bathroom. Before seeing if you can borrow space from the adjoining rooms, locate the waste line and risers that feed the bathroom. In a one-story house the waste line is easily relocated. In a multistoried dwelling the waste stack runs vertically from roof to basement and is problematic and expensive to relocate. If there are no pipes (or minor feeders) in the partitions, consider relocating the wall to widen or lengthen the bathroom. Sometimes space can be "found" in closets or hallways. (More on bathrooms in Chapter 8.)

Hard-Line Schematics

The hard-line drawings that follow the freehand conceptual overlays are known as the schematics. They are the first set of scaled drawings that show the width of the window openings, the location of the doors, and the exact sizes of the rooms. Schematics are laid out on a piece of tracing paper taped over the drawing of the existing conditions. This process may be best understood by reading the case histories in Chapter 6. These are not necessarily the final design drawings for the house. There are a number of items that must be checked out to see if they "work." Can we get windows that size? Will we have to allow space to accommodate heating, plumbing, and ventilation? Can we fit the kitchen into the space we allotted for it? These questions are answered during the development phase (covered in Part Two of this volume). At that time the plans may be modified somewhat. (See Inset I.)

Designing the
Renovation

45

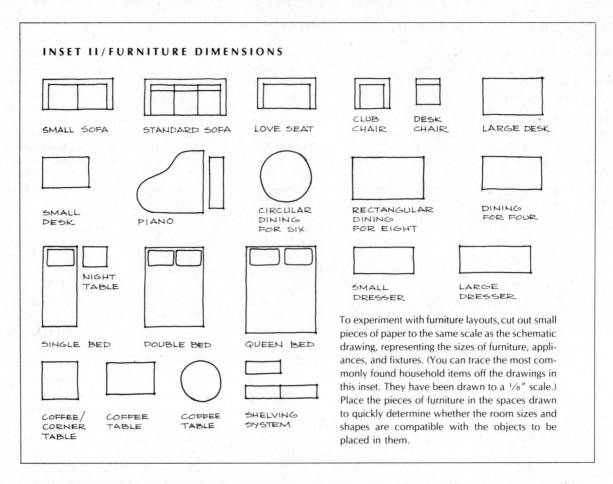

INSET II / FURNITURE DIMENSIONS

SMALL SOFA

STANDARD SOFA

LOVE SEAT

CLUB CHAIR

DESK CHAIR

LARGE DESK

SMALL DESK

PIANO

CIRCULAR DINING FOR SIX

RECTANGULAR DINING FOR EIGHT

DINING FOR FOUR

NIGHT TABLE

SINGLE BED

DOUBLE BED

QUEEN BED

SMALL DRESSER

LARGE DRESSER

COFFEE/ CORNER TABLE

COFFEE TABLE

COFFEE TABLE

SHELVING SYSTEM

To experiment with furniture layouts, cut out small pieces of paper to the same scale as the schematic drawing, representing the sizes of furniture, appliances, and fixtures. (You can trace the most commonly found household items off the drawings in this inset. They have been drawn to a ⅛" scale.) Place the pieces of furniture in the spaces drawn to quickly determine whether the room sizes and shapes are compatible with the objects to be placed in them.

The schematic drawing includes the size of the rooms, the width of the halls, and the placement of windows and doors. Sometimes it is helpful to overlay a furniture plan on the schematic drawing to make sure the furniture fits properly. (See Inset II.)

Elevations

If you are adding a wing to the house, changing the configuration of the windows, or modifying the roofline, you should draw elevations of the building. The exterior elevations will allow you to evaluate your house's new proportions and will serve as "footprints" for the final working drawing. Even if you are not making changes to the exterior of the building, you should draw interior elevations of the kitchen and the bathrooms (and other rooms with intricate details).

Elevations are simple projections of the four sides of the building: front, rear, and both sides. Interior elevations show walls of a room and are particularly helpful if you have windows and a door on the same wall or if you are designing a mantelpiece or are using trim strips. Exterior elevations are laid out by taping the plan to the drafting table slightly above the paper you will be working on. The main lines of the elevation (building boundaries, window and door locations and widths) can be "brought down" using vertical lines. Various heights must be measured directly on the elevation (with care taken that you are working in the same scale as the plan). Interior elevations are drawn in the same way (Ill. 17).

ILL. 17

Materials:

· Cardboard (¹/₁₆″ chipboard, or illustration board, or ¹/₈″ foam core board)
· Matte knife (with extra blades)
· Glue (Elmer's)
· Metal cutting edge
· Cutting board
· Drafting instruments

Exterior model: Begin by drawing the first-floor plan on the cardboard at about ¹/₄″ = 1′-0″ or at the scale of your schematic drawings. Draw and cut all of the exterior walls and make sure they fit around the perimeter of the building. (You will need the elevations for the heights.) Lay the exterior walls back on the drafting table and draw in the windows and doors. Cut out the openings (you can blacken them in with a marker if you are lazy) and glue the exterior walls to the base. Cut and glue the roof to the model. Balconies, porches, greenhouse, and other projections may be added last.

Interior models: A model of the interior floor plan is very helpful in seeing proportion and flow. Draw the floor plan on a piece of cardboard (it is not necessary to cut it out). Draw the exterior walls and partitions to height and cut them out. Be sure that they fit around the perimeter. Put the exterior partitions back on the board and draw in the windows and doors. Cut out the openings and glue the partitions to the base. Then do the same for the interior partitions.

Models

Interior models are worth the effort even if you are renovating only a kitchen. Scale models help you see proportions in a way plans and elevations can't. You will be able to see if the windows are set too high, the door too narrow, the walls too high for the size of the room. Set aside a good chunk of time for the construction of the model, for even a simple project can take the better part of a day. (See Inset III.)

EVALUATING THE EXTERIOR

So far we have concentrated on the interior layout. Keep in mind, however, that a house needs to be looked at as a whole. Many of the choices involving interior planning affect the exterior, and vice versa. Take a walk around the building focusing on its shape and the various elevations.

Begin with the overall shape.

· Are you planning a renovation which includes an extension, porch, deck, or greenhouse? If so, is it going to improve the general massing of the house or make it awkward? Try to keep in mind the scale of the house and its surroundings. Don't plan a deck that is too large for the backyard or an addition that dwarfs the main building (Ill. 18).
· Look at the configuration of the roof. Are you adding a floor or raising the roof to gain additional headroom? The new roof angle should work with the other angles of the building.
· Are you staying within the same roof vocabulary by continuing the same roof angles as those of the existing house? Will using these angles give you the right amount of head clearance? Will they make the house look too tall and bulky?
· Perhaps you are thinking of introducing a new set of roof angles. Should they be steeper or shallower than the existing ones? Are you considering a flat roof? Try to visualize what the new roof or roofs may look like (Ill. 19).
· If you are removing an existing porch, will the house look bare without it?

ILL. 18

Designing the Renovation

47

Next evaluate the elevations with a critical eye to the openings, symmetry, detailing, and materials.

· The overall symmetry of the elevations will have an impact on your renovation options. Are the elevations symmetrical or not? Is the placement of new windows, doors, chimneys, decks, extensions, etc., going to alter this symmetry? Breaking the symmetry by slightly offsetting a window or a door will look more like a mistake than a planned effort (Ill. 20).

· Are you planning more windows? How are they going to look next to the existing windows? Keep in mind the size and proportions of the windows. If you are replacing a large window with a smaller one, will it destroy the harmony of the façade?

· Are you eliminating windows? Try to visualize how the elevation will look with few or no openings.

· What about the type of window? If you are happy with the existing ones, match the new ones to the old. If you are changing the type of window, will it add to or detract from the present style and character of the house? How about the doors? Are you changing their size? We have seen many homes where the original front doors have been replaced with smaller ones.

The result is often an unattractive mismatch of scales. Should you be eliminating doors, make sure the façade does not look as if it's missing something (Ill. 20).

· Is there any trim or other detailing? Will you be keeping it? Could the house use some window and door trim to give it character? New trim around windows and doors should match the old.

· If you are eliminating detail, make sure you are not taking with it the intrinsic charm of the building. Take some time to reconsider that decision.

· What is the material of the exterior walls? New brick or stone should match the original as closely as possible in color and texture. Patches in buildings with wood siding tend to blend in more easily than in masonry buildings. If the building is painted, you need not worry about patches.

· Are you considering putting new siding on the building? If you are changing from shingles to siding, try to assess whether horizontal or vertical clapboards are more in keeping with the original design of the house.

· When building a new extension, will the use of a different facing material enhance the façade? Would you rather keep it within the original materials' vocabulary?

ILL. 19

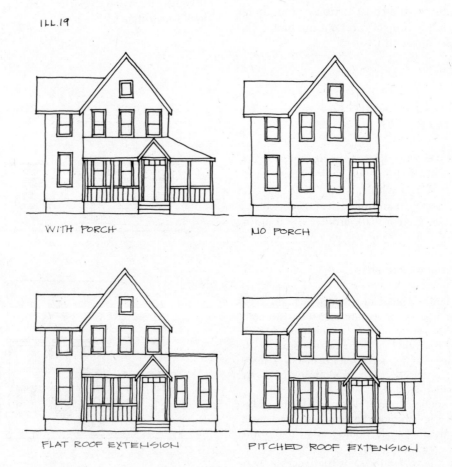

WITH PORCH

NO PORCH

FLAT ROOF EXTENSION

PITCHED ROOF EXTENSION

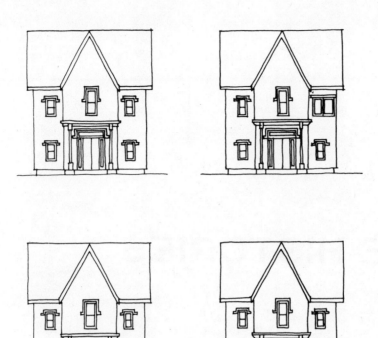

ILL. 20

6

CASE HISTORIES

The following three case histories resolve real design problems through renovation. All of them take into consideration the personal needs of the occupants, the existing conditions of the building, the limitations imposed by the municipality, and aesthetic criteria.

A RENOVATION OF AN URBAN APARTMENT

Jonathan and Toby had been looking for a large apartment in the city for months. They had recently remarried and needed to house four children (two full-time and two for occasional visits), a part-time housekeeper, and a dog. They could not seem to find an apartment with three large and three small bedrooms, but finally found one that came close.

They fell in love with a riverfront apartment with three bedrooms and two tiny (former) maid's rooms (Ill. 1). The apartment had not been remodeled since the building was constructed (in the 1920's) and the kitchen and all of the bathrooms would have to be replaced. Because the apartment needed extensive renovation they would be able to purchase it at a surprisingly low price. The layout of the apartment had some advantages and disadvantages. On the positive side, each of the three main bedrooms faced the river and was bright and well ventilated. On the negative side, however, the family/entertainment rooms of the house had no access to the wonder-

ful river view and received no direct sunlight. (The kitchen, dining room, and the small bedrooms were located on a very dark rear court and the living room faced a narrow side street.) In addition, each of the apartment's three and a half bathrooms was accessible only by walking through a bedroom (Ill. 1). Furthermore, the apartment had a strange layout. The working end of the kitchen was about fifteen feet away from the dining room and there was no room in the kitchen for a small table. The couple decided to buy the apartment on condition that these problems could be resolved by renovation.

The apartment was measured, and plans of the existing conditions were drawn at $\frac{1}{4}'' = 1'\text{-}0''$ (Ill. 1). Some investigation assured them that the structure of the building consisted of steel columns and beams. It was presumed (and confirmed by the superintendent) that the thickened sections of the walls contained the building's columns or the pipe chases for the heating, plumbing, and electrical systems. Since these items could not be removed or relocated, they were darkened on the plan. The thick wall areas near the toilets were assumed to be the location of the waste line. Since these locations were critical for the placement of the kitchen and bathrooms, they were darkened as well.

It seemed obvious that at least one of the riverview bedrooms would have to be sacrificed to open the view to the communal spaces. Two options came to mind: the first made bedroom #3 into the living room and the second converted bedroom #1 into the dining room.

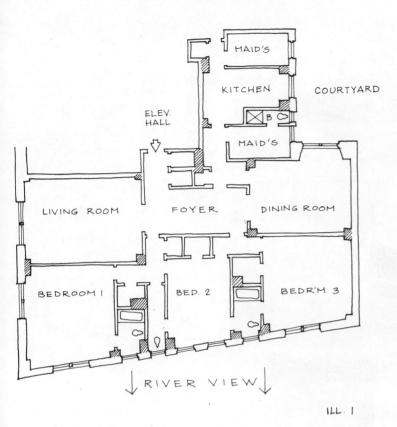

ILL. 1

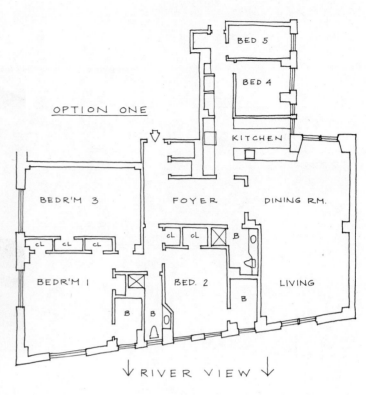

ILL. 2

The first option required the removal of the partition between bedroom #3 and the dining room. An overlay of tracing paper was taped to the plan and the concept was laid out (Ill. 2). The existing living room would become a bedroom, bedrooms #1 and #2 would remain as they were, the maid's room adjacent to the dining room would be converted into a kitchen, the existing kitchen and the remaining maid's room would become small bedrooms. Some doors could be altered to make the bathrooms work better. This plan seemed to meet most of the established criteria. The only problem was an aesthetic one: the foyer would receive even less daylight than in the current arrangement, and the living room—with its magical view—seemed tucked away in a remote corner. This scheme was put aside for a while pending an investigation of the alternative solution.

The second option combined bedroom #1 with the existing living room to form a large living-dining-room complex with river views. An overlay of tracing paper was taped to the plan and a large L-shaped living-dining room was sketched over the existing corner bedroom and living room. The problem with this approach was the location of the new kitchen. At first the couple thought they would leave the kitchen in its original location. This concept was rejected immediately because the kitchen would be too far from the dining room.

A possible solution was to convert the middle bedroom into an eat-in kitchen. The adjacent bathroom ensured that the requisite plumbing was nearby and, as an added bonus, the kitchen would have a lovely view of the river. Yet another overlay was taped to the plan and the new living-dining-kitchen arrangement was sketched out. The remaining rooms were assigned as bedrooms; the two former maid's rooms and the former kitchen and dining room were to be four children's bedrooms (Ill. 3). (It was decided that the housekeeper, only there on some weeknights, would sleep in one of the rarely used small bedrooms.) This seemed to be a very good solution. Only two problems remained. One: which of the two children who made the apartment their full-time home would be assigned the huge former dining room and which child would occupy one of the small back bedrooms? Two: the bathrooms were now in very inconvenient places. Both these problems seemed insoluble. After some deliberation this scheme was rejected for the above reasons and because the couple was reluctant to sacrifice yet another river-view bedroom.

The first option was beginning to look like the leading contender, but the couple decided to give the second option one last shot. They explored

Case Histories

51

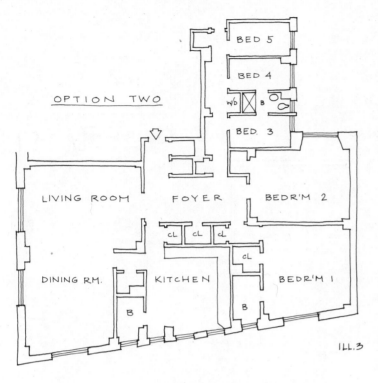

OPTION TWO

ILL.3

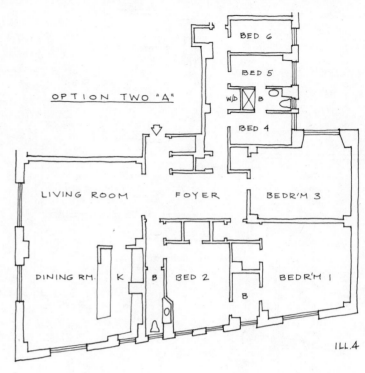

OPTION TWO "A"

ILL.4

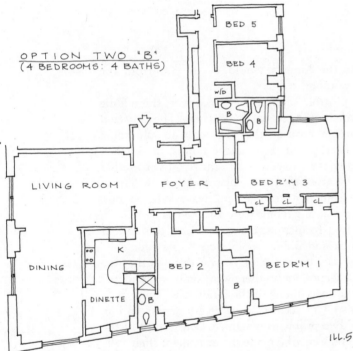

OPTION TWO "B"
(4 BEDROOMS: 4 BATHS)

ILL.5

the possibility of removing the bathroom and closet adjacent to bedroom #1 and making that area into an open kitchen (Ill. 4). This solution actually worked! Bedrooms #2 and #3 would remain as sleeping quarters, the dining room became a bedroom, as did the three rear rooms. They were happy with the living-dining room in that location and suspected that they would be able to see the river as soon as they entered the apartment. Unfortunately, the two-and-a-half-bathroom solution was still awkward.

On the next schematic go-around the couple decided to enclose the kitchen and have a separate dinette for informal dining (photo on p. 67). This decision necessitated demolishing and reconstructing some non-load-bearing partitions, but the expense would be worth the effort. The apartment now had two and a half bathrooms instead of three. It was decided that the narrow bathroom at the rear of the apartment could not be enlarged easily to include a tub and a lavatory. The couple decided to demolish the maid's bathroom and incorporate the space into one of the small bedrooms. After difficult deliberation they decided to sacrifice one of the rear rooms and convert it into an extra-large bathroom. A few overlays later they realized that the allotted space was large enough for two bathrooms, one with access from the rear hall and the other from bedroom #3 (Ill. 5). The schematic design phase was successfully completed.

While drawing the hard-line preliminaries additional details were added: the line of closets between bedrooms #1 and #2, the computer center in the space of the former pantry, a washer-dryer closet, and a wall of built-in bookcases in the rear hall.

AN ADAPTIVE RESTORATION OF A TOWNHOUSE

After a long search, Sarah and John Simon, a professional couple with a young child, purchased an 1880's townhouse in a historic district in New York City. The house had been in the same family for generations and was virtually intact. They loved everything about the house, the woodwork and plasterwork, the fireplaces, the parquet floors, even the old icebox. In plan, the building was a typical Victorian row house with four long and narrow floors. The first floor housed the kitchen and dining room. In addition, this floor had a service entrance and the only access to the backyard. The formal entrance and the traditional front and back parlors were on the second floor. The first and second floors had the nicest details. The third and fourth floors were reserved for the bedrooms and bathrooms.

Although the Simons wanted to modify the house as little as possible, they were aware that their functional requirements were quite different from those of a turn-of-the-century family with live-in servants. To begin with, they needed professional office space. John, a principal in a small interior design firm, was tired of commuting to work and wanted to carve office space out of his new home. The Simons also wished to make the new kitchen and backyard more accessible to the rest of the house. Other considerations were the upgrading of the finishes and electrical system and the provision of additional bathrooms and closet space.

The Simons went to the building department to look for plans and information on the building. Nothing existed on record. They checked zoning ordinances to determine whether an interior design office was permitted in their building. Luckily, because the house was located on a commercial street, office use was allowed. Having no floor plans, the Simons started by measuring the building and drawing plans of the existing conditions (Ill. 6).

With the plans in hand, a number of design options (and limitations) became apparent. The existing kitchen space was so large that the new kitchen could be designed as a combination kitchen–family room with easy access to the backyard. This would allow the formal dining room to remain intact. The service entrance could serve as a mudroom and a place for bikes and provide convenient access to the kitchen, family room, and backyard. Sufficient space would still remain for a half bathroom and washer-dryer. The second-floor parlors would be restored to a gracious living and entertaining area. Two bedrooms and a bathroom would remain on the third floor. If necessary, a small third bedroom and a second bath could be provided at a future date. The top (and least interesting) floor would be reserved for the office suite with its own separate bathroom (Ill. 7).

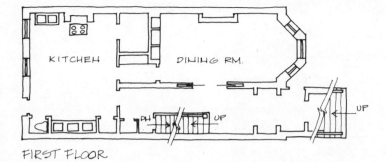

FIRST FLOOR

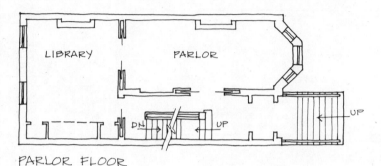

PARLOR FLOOR

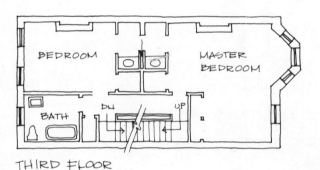

THIRD FLOOR

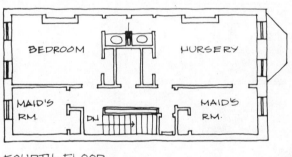

FOURTH FLOOR

ILL. 6

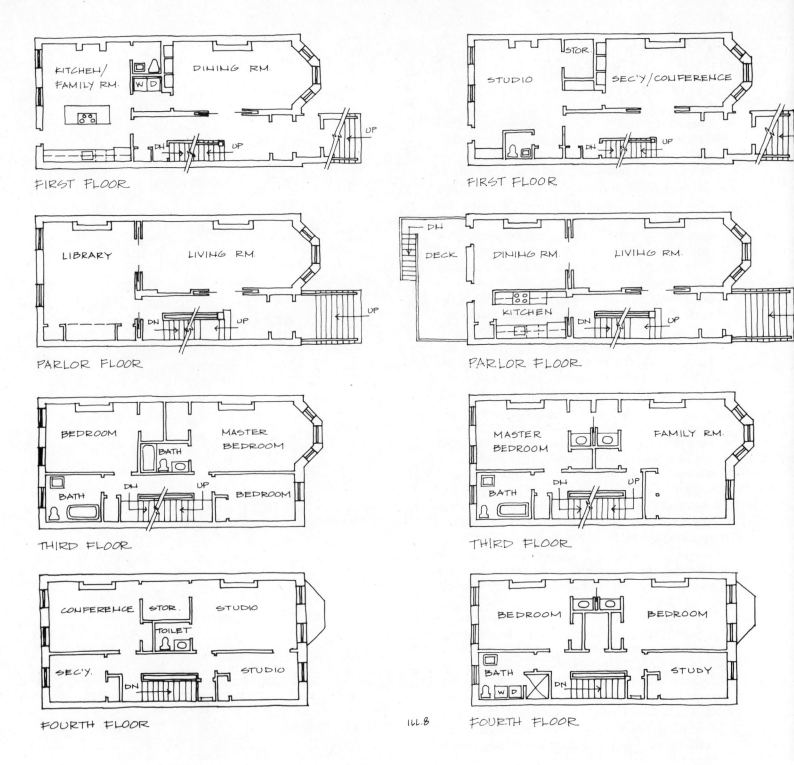

FIRST FLOOR

KITCHEN/ FAMILY RM.

DINING RM.

W D

FIRST FLOOR

STUDIO

STOR.

SEC'Y/CONFERENCE

DN UP

UP

PARLOR FLOOR

LIBRARY

LIVING RM.

DN UP

PARLOR FLOOR

DN

DECK

DINING RM.

LIVING RM.

KITCHEN

DN UP

THIRD FLOOR

BEDROOM

MASTER BEDROOM

BATH

BATH

BEDROOM

DN UP

THIRD FLOOR

MASTER BEDROOM

FAMILY RM.

BATH

DN UP

FOURTH FLOOR

CONFERENCE

STOR.

STUDIO

TOILET

SEC'Y.

STUDIO

DN

ILL. 8

FOURTH FLOOR

BEDROOM

BEDROOM

BATH

STUDY

W D

DN

The major drawback in this scheme was the location of the office. Although the top floor would provide the office with privacy and light, clients and office personnel would have to go through the entire building to get to it. There would be little or no privacy for the family during work hours. Sarah and John took a second look at the house. By using the service entrance as an office entrance, they would gain privacy for the office and the family. The entire first floor could then become office space. The biggest problem with this solution was that the kitchen would have to be moved to another location. The back parlor seemed the most likely candidate. The parlor floor would have a living room in the front and kitchen–dining room toward the back. Access to the backyard could be provided by converting one of the existing windows into a door leading to a deck and staircase.

The existing third-floor layout was not altered.

The Simons would have their master bedroom and family room there. The fourth floor had two small and two large rooms. One of the small rooms would become a combination bathroom—laundry room, the other one a study. The two large rooms would remain as bedrooms (Ill. 8). This solution pleased the Simons. It not only provided them with all the spaces they wanted but also minimized the amount of changes needed in the existing layout.

Having solved the overall space planning, the Simons moved on to designing specific areas. The kitchen was one of their primary concerns. The parlor floor had a wealth of woodwork and detailing which they wanted to retain. The back parlor, where the kitchen would be located, had a fireplace, two large windows, two large closets, and two beautiful sliding doors leading to the front parlor. It was difficult to add a new wall to divide the room in two. Without a wall, there was little or no wall space left for kitchen cabinetry. Sarah and John's first step was to redraw the back parlor plan to a larger scale ($\frac{1}{2}" = 1'\text{-}0"$). This scale allowed them to show all existing moldings and detailing. Over the enlarged plan, they placed a layer of yellow tracing paper, on which they traced everything they wanted to keep (Ill. 9). There was only one length of wall that could be used for cabinetry. They drew in the refrigerator, stove, dishwasher, and sink. There was no room left for any other cabinetry. John suggested getting rid of the two closets in order to get a larger stretch of wall (Ill. 10). This approach would give them more cabinetry, but Sarah felt the room would look incomplete without the closets and woodwork. In addition, she did not like the idea of a kitchen strung along a single wall.

Having decided that the room should remain intact, the only choice left was to create a floating element within the room. It could house one or two of the appliances and give more counter and storage space. This element could also serve as a visual baffle between the kitchen and dining areas. The existing plumbing risers were located in the party wall. It seemed the most logical place to locate the sink and dishwasher. After drawing the sink and dishwasher in plan, they discovered there was still enough space for the refrigerator. Thus the only appliance that would be in the floating unit was the stove. They realized they did not have a lot of storage space and decided to use one of the closets as a pantry (Ill. 11).

With the basic layout in place, the Simons proceeded to look at the kitchen in elevation. They projected lines from the plan and gave them appropriate heights (counters at 36" high and over-

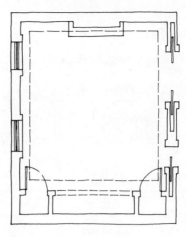

ILL.9

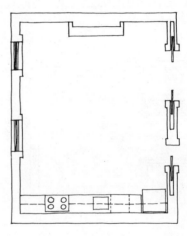

ILL.10

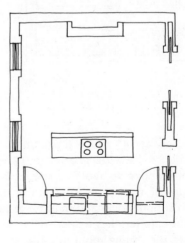

ILL.11

Case Histories

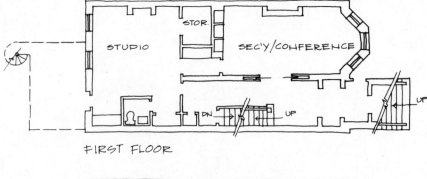

FIRST FLOOR

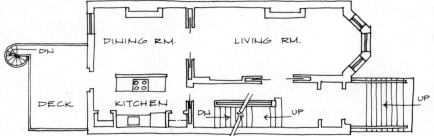

PARLOR FLOOR

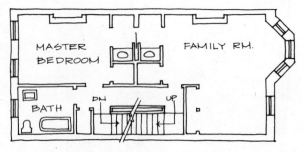

THIRD FLOOR

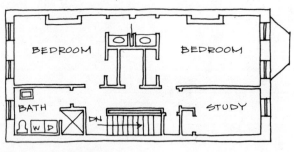

FOURTH FLOOR

ILL. 13

wanted a practical kitchen that would be easy to clean. Plastic laminate seemed the most likely candidate. John was somewhat skeptical about plastic laminate, for he was uncertain how a contemporary material would blend with ornate woodwork. They explored the possibility of wood cabinets, but decided they simply could not afford the type of wood and workmanship that would stand up to what already existed in the room. Not being able to match the existing, they chose to contrast it. The house's architecture would remain intact but the cabinetry additions would be contemporary.

Going back to the plan of the room, they made the window closer to the kitchen into a door to the deck. Zoning regulations dictated a 30' backyard, which left them with a deck 10' in depth. They would have preferred it larger but it seemed adequate. They needed to decide whether the deck should span the whole width of the house or just part of it. Although the entire width seemed preferable because it would give them more room, they realized that such a deck would significantly reduce the amount of light available to the office below. The deck became 14' wide rather than the full 22' (Ill. 13).

There was not much work to be done upstairs. The third floor would remain as it was. Existing sinks were left and used as part of a dressing area (Ill. 13). The fourth floor needed a bit more plan-

KITCHEN ELEVATION

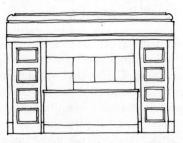

KITCHEN ELEVATION WITH ISLAND

head cabinets at 18" above the counter height). They decided to leave the floating unit low, without cabinets above, to avoid competing with the architecture of the room. To prevent pots and pans from slipping over and in order to hide any mess on the counter, they extended the side of the unit facing the dining room one foot above the counter (Ill. 12).

The next decision concerned materials. Sarah

ILL. 12

ning. The small room in the back became the bathroom since it was directly above the existing bathroom on the third floor. The bathroom did not have to be large. They also realized that by locating the washer and dryer in the same room, they would save themselves a lot of plumbing work. They again redrew the plan to a larger scale and laid out the fixtures: a lavatory, a water closet, and a bathtub. There was only enough space left for either a washing machine or a dryer, not both. They had two choices: either to get an apartment-size washer-dryer, with one unit set on top of the other, or to replace the bathtub with a shower. Since they already had one tub downstairs, they decided it would be better to have the larger appliances and forgo the tub for a shower (Ill. 13).

Finally, there was the office floor. The interior design firm was rather informal in structure. It needed an open layout with lots of drawing tables, a conference area, a space for computer and typewriter, and a separate powder room. As they had done for the other floors, Sarah and John placed tracing paper over the existing plan. They traced those areas they wanted to keep. The old dining room had oak wainscoting, a beautiful fireplace, a marble breakfront, and a bay window. It had to remain intact. The old kitchen, on the other hand, had little left to offer other than crumbling plaster and a linoleum floor. It became apparent that using the front dining room as a conference and presentation room was a good idea. The back area offered wall space for drawing tables and a center section could be carved out for computer and typing facilities. The powder room was located as close as possible to the plumbing risers (Ill. 13).

Sarah and John once again reviewed the overall plan. They had managed to incorporate all their functional requirements without much disturbance to the building. With the preliminary schematic plans at hand, they were ready to proceed with the development of more detailed drawings.

AN ADDITION TO AN EXISTING HOUSE

The Harris-Bankses had designed and built their own house approximately ten years ago. At that time they were not able to build as large a home as they had originally wanted. Instead, they designed an efficient "core" home which satisfied their immediate needs and planned for future expansion. When they built their home they had a young son. Ten years later, their son was twelve

and they had another son, age five. June continued to work as a newspaper editor. Her husband, Murray, a writer, did most of his work at home. It became clear that their two-bedroom house was no longer adequate for their family needs. It was time to expand.

The Harris-Bankses' house was rather compact.

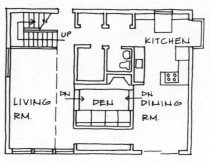

FIRST FLOOR

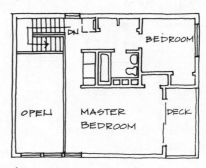

SECOND FLOOR

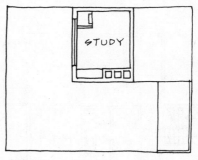

ATTIC

ILL. 14

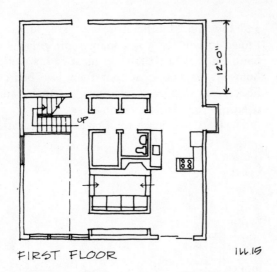

FIRST FLOOR   ILL. 15

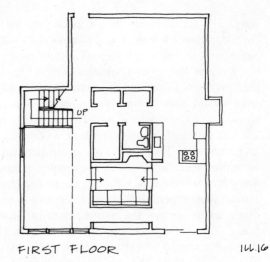

FIRST FLOOR   ILL. 16

SECOND FLOOR   ILL. 17

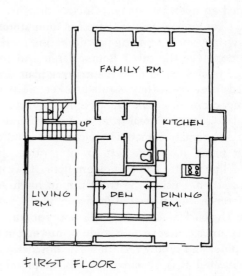

FIRST FLOOR   ILL. 18

FIRST FLOOR   ILL. 19

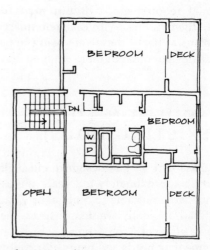

SECOND FLOOR   ILL. 20

It was organized around a central core element which housed the bathrooms and kitchen. The other spaces—the living room, dining room, den, and bedrooms—flowed freely into each other (Ill. 14). This quality was important to June and Murray and they wanted to maintain it in their renovation plans. Their life style, of course, had changed over the years and some of the spaces they had once dreamed of for their expansion were no longer applicable. They did need another bedroom and a family room. In addition, they wanted to enlarge the kitchen and make the half bath downstairs into a full bath. Finally, and in the category of "wish list," they wanted to provide a space for the new grand piano.

Fortunately, the Harris-Bankses had been very methodical in their original design and planning. They were particularly careful about the location of the house on the property. For this reason, there was room for expansion in all directions with no problem in terms of setback requirements. Not having to worry about zoning, June and Murray concentrated on issues such as the view and circulation problems within the house. The nearby pond was seen primarily from the south and west of the house. Both June and Murray enjoyed this view and did not want it disturbed. The combination of the space layout and the roof configuration made expansion to the west rather problematic. The north seemed the most logical direction.

It was time to start the yellow trace overlays. The best location for the family room appeared to be downstairs as close as possible to the kitchen. June drew a rectangular space north of the kitchen extending the full length of the house. She made this space 12' wide since it was the structural module which had been used in their original design. She then moved the entrance door from its existing location to the new outside wall. The space she had just drawn would give them a 12' × 32' family room (Ill. 15). They did not need a room that large. They kept the area closer to the kitchen and cut off the room where the front door to the house would be located (Ill. 16). With the space outline for the first floor laid out, they put down another layer of yellow trace and examined the second floor. A bedroom could be built directly over the family room with access from the top of the stairs (Ill. 17). They liked this scheme because it did not involve changing much of the original house layout.

With some basic decisions at hand, it was time to figure out how the half bath and the kitchen could be made larger. Looking at the half bath, they realized that they could not move toward the den or the mechanical room. Extending toward the kitchen would necessitate reworking of the plumbing and the kitchen cabinetry. Worst of all, the kitchen would lose space. The logical place for enlargement was toward the new family room. They drew lines north and incorporated the existing hallway and closet into the bath area (Ill. 18). There were problems with this solution. Not only would they lose access to the kitchen but they would also lose a good amount of closet space. Perhaps a long line of closets along the north wall of the family room would replace what had been lost to the bathroom expansion (Ill. 18). Although this seemed like a good idea at first, they realized that stealing 2' for closet space from a 12' room would not give them the kind of family room they wanted. They tried placing closets perpendicular to the entrance door. This approach solved the issue of closet space and it also provided the family room with privacy from the entrance (Ill. 19). The pieces were beginning to come together.

A further advantage to the bathroom enlargement was additional wall space for the kitchen. Laying out the new kitchen space, the Harris-Bankses decided to eliminate the eat-in area and extend the kitchen counter on both walls. They would remove the present greenhouse window and install a larger greenhouse in the family room, which could serve as an eat-in area (Ill. 19). The bathroom remained to be laid out. With the lavatory and toilet left in their existing locations, a shower could be incorporated in the new space. The bathroom entrance would be from the entrance hallway (Ill. 19).

It was time to move to the second floor. The new bedroom could easily fit over the family room. The entrance would be at the top of the stairs and there was still room for closet space. They loved the deck in the existing master bedroom, so they decided to include another deck in the new bedroom (Ill. 20).

Happy with their design, the Harris-Bankses looked at the house in elevation. Since they had their old drawings, they simply traced over them and accounted for the new spaces. The south elevation remained the same. The east elevation with the new extension looked rather handsome. They overlaid the north and west elevations (Ill. 21). The house looked different; it no longer had the self-contained quality of the original design. Both from the north and from the west, the new extension looked tacked on. They tried to see what these elevations would look like if the extension ran the full width of the north side. Carrying the existing roof slopes over on the north and west elevations, it became clear that a full-

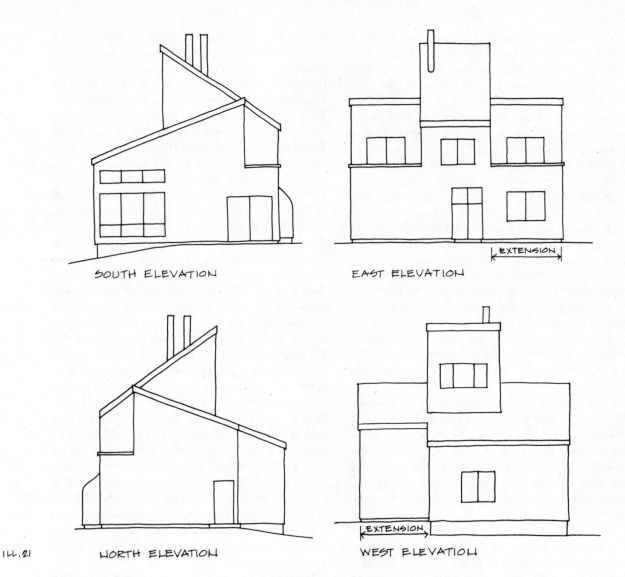

SOUTH ELEVATION

EAST ELEVATION

EXTENSION

ILL. 21

NORTH ELEVATION

WEST ELEVATION

EXTENSION

width extension seemed better integrated into the building (Ill. 22). In addition, they could change the living room's west window to a door and gain easier access to that side of the property.

The Harris-Bankses had to go back to the plans. By making the extension the full width of the house, they now had a space between the front door and the west wall (Ill. 23). The living room could not be extended into this space since the existing stairs were in the way. Perhaps this space could accommodate the grand piano. After giving

it some thought, they decided it was a good idea. June and Murray had always enjoyed the feeling of walking into their double-storied living room. The space for the grand piano would have a ceiling with a pitch similar to that of the living room. Both areas could seem like part of one large open space. They were pleased. The new extension not only satisfied their functional criteria but also offered them the type of spaces and character that they had always enjoyed in their house.

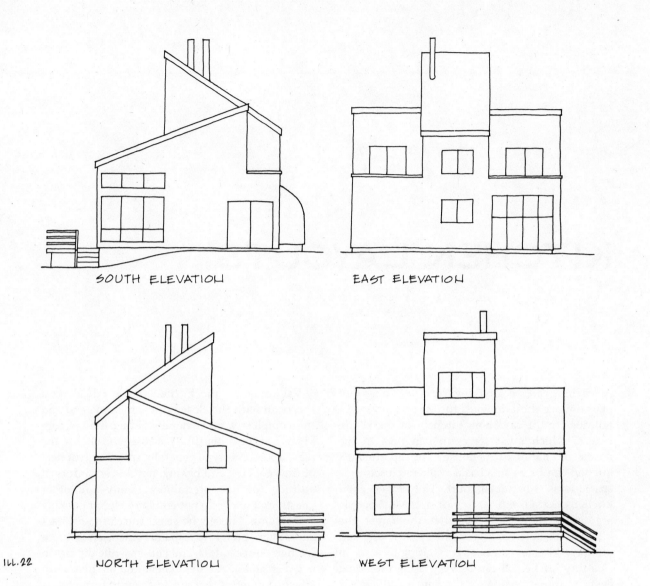

SOUTH ELEVATION

EAST ELEVATION

ILL. 22   NORTH ELEVATION

WEST ELEVATION

ILL. 23

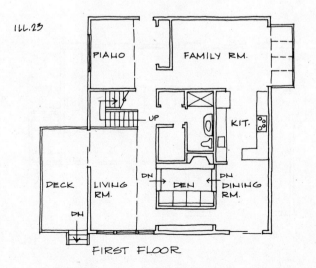

PIANO   FAMILY RM.

UP   KIT.

DECK   LIVING RM.   DN   DEN   DN   DINING RM.

DN

FIRST FLOOR

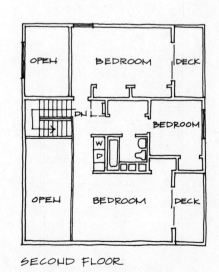

OPEN   BEDROOM   DECK

DN

BEDROOM

W D

OPEN   BEDROOM   DECK

SECOND FLOOR

7

KITCHEN LAYOUTS

A kitchen can be anything from a cabin's hot plate and ice chest designed for the preparation of hot dogs to the cavernous kitchens of the White House, which must serve up banquets to the heads of nations. A house's or apartment's kitchen can be as small as a walk-in closet or as spacious as a handball court. The key to good kitchen design is efficiency, not size. Most people are under the impression that the larger the kitchen, the better. This is a fallacy. A poorly laid out large kitchen can be as frustrating to work in as a tiny kitchen. It can be very tiring preparing even a simple meal in a kitchen in which the refrigerator is twelve or more feet away from the range. The cook has to negotiate numerous round trips between appliances with hands full of milk, onions, and garlic cloves.

Variations on the kitchen theme fall along a spectrum with the closed kitchen at one end and the completely open family-dining-living-room kitchen at the other (Ill. 1). Those who choose the most open prototype generally spend a great deal of time cooking and baking, have a very informal attitude toward entertaining family and other guests, and likely do not employ help for cooking and serving. Those who select the closed utilitarian design prefer to separate themselves from kitchen noises, odors, and clutter while dining. In between are the eat-in kitchens and kitchens with attached dinettes that are adjacent to formal dining rooms (Ill. 2).

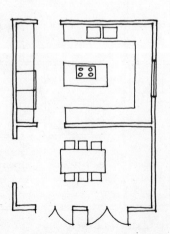

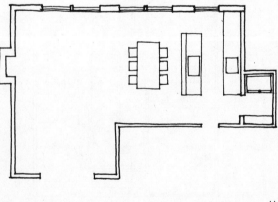

ILL. 1

The original living room of this New York City apartment had to be divided into sitting, dining, and kitchen areas. The mirrored 4 1/2-foot-high partition serves both to conceal kitchen clutter and to reflect the formal mantelpiece on the opposite wall. Renovation architects, Sands and Sperling; photographer, Herman Sands

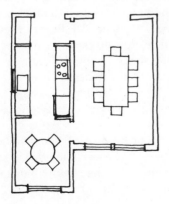

ILL. 2

KITCHEN REQUIREMENTS

Good kitchen design begins with an honest appraisal of the demands that will be made on the kitchen and on the cook. The following questions should be answered before proceeding:

1. Will the meals be elaborate or simple? Elaborate meals seem to require a lot of time and a great deal of room. Good planners who lack both time and space have learned to stage the work required for a large party so that baking is done on Monday (and frozen), casseroles on Tuesday, etc. If the meal must be cooked all at once, it is likely that a number of tasks must be done simultaneously, requiring a lot of counter space. If elaborate meals are prepared only a few times a year, the cook can "borrow" the dining-room table as preparation space or can set up a bridge table in the living room.

In this carriage-house conversion, the kitchen becomes an abstract form within a cylinder played against the overall living and dining room space. Renovation architects, DiDonno Associates

pots and pans, the storage space to accommodate them, and a very large refrigerator and pantry. Cooking for twelve is more time-consuming than cooking for four but does not necessarily require more space if the cook is well organized.

3. How many people will be working in the kitchen at once? We find this to be a critical question. Some kitchens seem to be designed for one cook only. When the dishwasher door is open no one else can work in the kitchen. If cooking is a shared activity, you must plan a kitchen that will accommodate a few cooks at once. Such a kitchen should have a slightly wider space between counters and more than one way in and out.

4. Which appliances do you really need? Again, a very critical question. On the one hand, you don't want to overload the kitchen with expensive, space-consuming appliances you will hardly ever use. On the other hand, you want your kitchen to be flexible.

5. Will you be doing heavy-duty baking on a regular basis? Many home bakers tend to do a week's or a month's worth of baking in a single afternoon. Such a baker has special needs: a large stone pastry board for rolling dough, heavy dough-kneading machinery, multiple ovens for simultaneous baking.

6. What types of cuisine will be cooked in the kitchen? Ethnic cooks may need a whole different set of appliances and equipment. Some cuisines require a great deal of vegetable washing and chopping, which demands multiple sinks and a lot of counter space. French food seems to require pre-cooking in a lot of little pots and pans. These special needs must be considered before planning the kitchen.

OVERALL PLANNING

The very simplest kitchen arrangement consists of a range, a sink, and a refrigerator. Most cooking consultants suggest a triangular positioning for the appliances. This can be accomplished by laying out the kitchen in two parallel bars, in an L shape, or in a U shape. All three of these arrangements will afford counter space around the appliances and should provide enough room for overhead storage cabinets. These layouts work even for the slightly larger kitchen, which may include a dishwasher and double wall ovens (Ill. 3).

In most renovations, of course, the physical configurations of the existing space rather than the requirements of the cook will dictate the size and the shape of the kitchen.

If such meals are prepared on a routine basis, the kitchen should be designed to handle the load. On the other hand, it is foolish to design a restaurant kitchen if you usually broil a piece of fish and steam some vegetables for dinner. Such "show" kitchens are expensive and don't necessarily add to the resale value of the house or apartment.

2. How many people are to be regularly served? If you have eight or ten children, you may not require a super-large kitchen to prepare your family's meals. However, you will probably need larger than usual

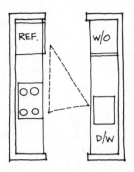

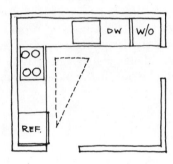

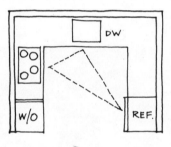

ILL.3

pivot between counters, thus reducing the number of steps required to prepare a meal. This layout loses its efficiency if it is more than 9' wide. An added advantage is that it can be designed with an exit at each end, which makes it useful for two or more cooks.

If the parallel kitchen is to be very long, make sure that the major appliances are not spaced too far apart. The periphery of the kitchen can be used for the broom closet, the double ovens, paper-goods storage, or the cabinet containing the "good" set of dishes and crystal.

The L layout is often used in a large square space that is to serve as an eat-in kitchen. This

To give this large contemporary kitchen a more intimate character, a brick wall with an arch was designed for the range top. It is lit by a decorative soffit that doubles as a display area for crafts. Architects, DiDonno Associates

A parallel-bar layout, once called the Hollywood kitchen, works in a space that is long and narrow. The space must be at least 7' wide (2' for each set of lower cabinets and 3' for the aisle between them)* but can be any length. The rationale of this configuration is that the cook can

*Codes that mandate accessibility for the disabled will require 40" between counters for kitchens that are completely new. (If you are replacing an existing kitchen within already established partitions, this rule may not apply.) Check your building code for other requirements.

layout becomes inefficient if the legs of the L are too long. In this arrangement, as in the one above, keep the major appliances (sink, refrigerator, and range) close to one another.

The U-shaped kitchen is useful if the space is rectangular and between 9' and 11' in width. One end of the space can be utilized for the cooking and the other half for dining.

A rectangular space at least 12' wide suggests an island U arrangement. The three major appliances can be located on each of the sides of the U (Ill. 4). In this layout the island is used primarily for "dry" functions (that is, activities that do not require immediate access to running water) such as slicing, food processing, or kneading dough. When adopting this layout the designer must be careful that the island does not act as a barrier between major appliances. In a modification to this scheme, the sink or the range can be located on the island and the remaining appliances on adjacent legs. The unused leg of the U can be used as a baking center or for the under-counter washer-dryer.

By all means avoid a kitchen layout that has an appliance on each of four walls of the kitchen and a farm-style table in the middle of the space. In this layout the cook is forced to constantly detour around the table when moving from sink to range to refrigerator. This kitchen would work if you had a carousel instead of a table and you were reaching for brass rings instead of onions.

When you are designing a new kitchen in the space of the old one, you may not have very much choice in the layout. If the old space is long and

The ground floor of this brownstone has been made into a large informal kitchen and dining space. Renovation architects, Sands and Sperling; photographer, Herman Sands

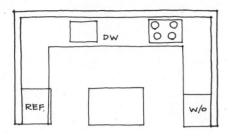

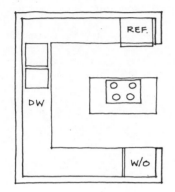

ILL. 4

narrow and you do not wish to (1) widen it by pushing out a wall or (2) relocate it by constructing an addition or (3) enlarge it by incorporating a number of spaces into one room, then your new kitchen will be long and narrow too. But even if the space is to have the same proportions as the old one, you need not feel compelled to keep the fixtures in the same locations. The refrigerator can easily be moved to any location in the room and so can the electric cooktop and ovens. In the case of the latter, be sure to design a route for the ventilation ducts if they are required. Even a gas appliance can be moved since the pipe feeding the oven or cooktop can be concealed in the partition, floor, or ceiling.

Plumbing fixtures are not as flexible. A simple sink requires both hot- and cold-water lines, a

This apartment kitchen was carved out of a bathroom and closet, as described on pages 50 to 52. Renovation architects, Sands and Sperling; photographer, Herman Sands

Here is an abbreviated list of the sizes of the major items included in the kitchen. A more thorough study may be found in Chapter 11. The information below applies to American-made products, which still dominate the appliance market. Many stylish European products are now available. If you intend to incorporate a European product into your scheme, be sure to check its exact size in inches since European manufacturers do not necessarily adhere to our standard modules. (In addition, check the plumbing and electrical specifications of all imported products to make sure they can be hooked up to your electrical and plumbing systems.)

Kitchen counters are always 24" or 25" deep. Most appliances are designed to fit into or adjacent to this 2' counter depth.

Refrigerators are the exception to the above rule. Most are deeper than 2'. Many are as deep as 2'-6". There are a number of companies that make 2'-deep refrigerator-freezers but they tend to be more expensive. Refrigerators come in a variety of widths and heights as well. Be sure to select the refrigerator before firming up the kitchen design. We generally reserve 32" or 36" for the width of the refrigerator when laying out the schematics.

Most ranges (stove top above, oven below) are 25" deep, but some have handles that protrude an inch or more. Ranges are either 24", 30", 36", or 42" wide, with 30" being the most commonly found width. Stove tops are designed to fit into 2'-deep counters and are available in the same widths as ranges.

Double wall ovens are also 2' deep. They come either 24" or 27" wide. Some of the newer imports do not stick to the rules, so research the dimensions carefully.

Sinks are designed to fit into a 2'-deep counter. A good size for a single sink is 25" wide, but sinks can be purchased in a wide variety of sizes ranging from 18" to 30". Double sinks take up more room. Allow at least 30" or as much as 43" (for a triple sink) for the sinks. The most commonly used dimension for a double basin is 33".

Dishwashers fit most neatly into the module. Almost every familiar brand is 24" deep and 24" wide.

Other under-counter appliances, such as garbage compactors, freezers, and wine cellars, come in a variety of widths but generally conform to the 2'-deep module.

There are a few manufacturers that make under-counter washers and dryers. These products may require a 26"-deep counter above them. If you are integrating these units into your kitchen design, make sure that leg of the counter is 26".

---

drain line to remove the waste, and a ventilation pipe to remove odors (see Chapter 18). The water lines are easy to route through walls, floors, and ceilings since the push is nongravitational and the water flows laterally as well as up and down. Drainage systems, on the other hand, are purely gravitational, meaning that the pipe must always pitch downward from the source (that is, the sink). The vent line cannot be (by law) too far from the plumbing fixture. Some apartment dwellers may not be able to position the plumbing fixtures on free-standing islands if they are unable to penetrate the floor systems for the drainage pipes.

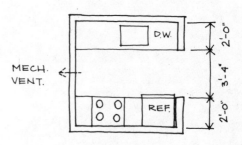

ILL.5

OTHER CONSIDERATIONS

Natural Light and Ventilation

It is nice to have a window in the kitchen. It allows for natural light and ventilation. In some municipalities you are required to provide a window in the kitchen if the kitchen is enclosed. In New York City,* for example, a "kitchen" is a separate room with a window and may be any size. An enclosed, windowless room used for

cooking is called a "kitchenette." The code limits its size to 59 square feet and insists that it be mechanically ventilated (Ill. 5). A windowed, eat-in/live-in kitchen (combining an open kitchen with dining and lounging functions) is usually permitted. Be sure to check your local building code if you are contemplating an interior kitchen.

Another legal consideration is accessibility to the disabled. Many municipalities have adopted rulings specifying minimum widths between counters and other dimensional requirements to allow accessibility to people in wheelchairs. Check with the building department to determine if your renovation is affected.

*Check your code carefully for rulings that dictate allowable sizes and clearances for new and renovated kitchens.

Counter Space

If there is any maxim in kitchen design, it is that you can never have enough counter space. Generous counter space allows you to spread out when working and provides enough work space for several cooks. The only drawback to a lot of counter area is that the cook has a tendency to spread out into new territory rather than clean up after each task. Kitchen counters are typically 24" (or 25") deep. They may be of any length. When planning a new kitchen, make sure you leave enough room in between the major fixtures (sink, cooktop, and refrigerator). A minimum of about 2' of counter on either side of the sink and the stove is ideal. If you can't manage to allocate this much free counter area adjacent to the major fixtures, you will have to compromise. In any case, make sure you leave at least 2' between stove and sink.

The "Look" of the Kitchen

The kitchen is likely to be one of the most expensive rooms in the house and the one that receives the most attention. Most people have some notion of what the kitchen should look like as well as how it should function. These notions range from the open, old-fashioned, "cluttered" country-kitchen look to the sleek, nothing-on-the-counters, shiny-white, modern look. The materials selected for the finishes of the kitchen will determine how the kitchen will ultimately look and feel. It really doesn't matter how the kitchen is configured. A Hollywood kitchen can be made to look warm and cozy or sleek and sophisticated.

8

BATHROOM LAYOUTS

In the past a house with one full bath and a powder room was considered luxurious. Today, many homeowners consider anything less than two bathrooms primitive. For this reason, most renovations on older houses involve the upgrading of existing bathrooms and the addition of new ones. The modern bathroom is not only functional, containing tub, toilet, and lavatory; it is also designed to accommodate relaxation. A lavishly equipped bath may include two or more lavatories, exercise equipment, a bidet, a whirlpool (large enough for two or more), a steam bath, and, sometimes, even a sauna. The bathroom has evolved from outdoor privy to indoor health spa.

The cost of today's bathroom has increased proportionately with its amenities. Although bathrooms were never inexpensive, the construction and finishing of a new or renovated bathroom today is very expensive. To begin with, the fixtures and fittings range from high-priced to extremely high-priced. Their installation involves plumbing work which is either expensive (if you subcontract) or time-consuming (if you do it yourself). Next come the finishing materials. You can choose a simple tile or an outrageous marble, but neither can be considered cheap materials. Masonry installation is also costly and time-consuming. It will be in your best interest to give careful thought to the planning and design of your bathrooms. You will live with the finished product for quite some time.

BATHROOM REQUIREMENTS

At the very least, a complete bathroom needs a toilet, a sink, and a shower or tub. A bathroom also requires plenty of storage space. Cosmetics, medicines, toiletries, hair dryers, curlers, toilet paper, cleaning supplies, etc., need to be kept neatly and readily at hand. Hampers for dirty clothes and storage for clean towels are often included in bathrooms. In addition, you must not forget wall space for accessories such as towel racks, toilet-paper dispenser, tumblers, robe hooks, and toothbrush and soap holders. Having provided for these basic requirements, you must allow for circulation space to get to and from the various fixtures. You should be able to dry yourself or brush your teeth without banging your elbows on the walls. Inset I shows some of the most common bathroom layouts and minimum clearances.*

Bathrooms also need temperature control. People who live in cold climates are very familiar with cold and drafty bathrooms. There are many older homes and apartments with lovely big stained-glass bathroom windows. These windows are wonderful on sunny, warm days but can be rather chilling in cold weather. Allow plenty of room for radiators (preferably under the window)

*Many municipalities have adopted codes requiring that some *new* bathrooms be accessible to the disabled. The requirements for *renovated* bathrooms depend on the extent of reconfiguration and the type of dwelling you are renovating. Check your codes carefully.

The lavatory area of this expanded bathroom was carved out of an adjacent hallway. The portion that now contains the toilet, bidet, and bathtub was the original 5-by-7-foot bathroom space. Renovation architects, Sands and Sperling; photographer, Herman Sands

(see Chapter 19). For particularly problematic spaces, a heat lamp on a timer could provide the extra heat needed at bath time.

Most homes today have a master bath, a children's or second bath, and a powder room. Master bathrooms are the largest, the most complete (in terms of fixtures), and generally the most luxurious. Usually they are equipped with two lavatories, a toilet, a separate shower and tub, and quite often a bidet. All these functions may be accommodated in one or more spaces. In particularly luxurious arrangements, the master bath may be divided into a bathing area and a toilet and sink area. There are master baths with saunas and sunbathing courtyards as part of the overall suite. (For renovators, a well-placed skylight may be the only access to "sun space.") Dressing rooms with or without lavatories are often designed as part of the master bath.

The master bathroom has also become the repository of lots of storage. The old-fashioned

INSET I/COMMON BATHROOM LAYOUTS

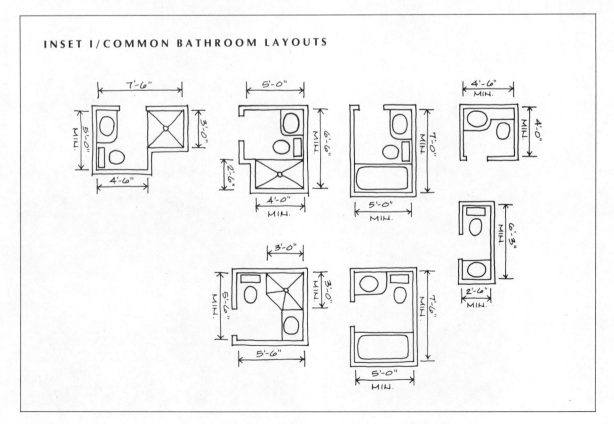

medicine cabinet over the lavatory has given way to exotic storage systems. It seems that every member of the family has his own hair dryer, curler, shaver, toiletries, linens, cosmetics, tissues, soaps, etc., resulting in cabinetry requirements that at times defy reason. Lavatory cabinets with lots of drawers and full-length medicine cabinets become essential to store all these personal possessions. Built-in makeup counters with adequate lighting and storage for cosmetics have also become part of the master-bathroom realm.

The second bathroom in the house usually services the children and an occasional guest. Although a conventional three-fixture bathroom is all you actually need, the use of two sinks is becoming more popular. (Of course, this assumes you have the additional space necessary.) Because this bathroom will be used by several different people, it is a good idea to include separate storage for each person. For example, the vanity can be designed with two separate compartments. You can also include two medicine cabinets and even two hampers to avoid overlapping use (otherwise known as kids fighting over who left what where).

Powder rooms or half baths are generally located near the public areas of the house (meaning living, dining, and kitchen areas). They are used by both family members and guests. Powder rooms can be as minimal as a toilet and a lavatory or can include as much storage as other bathrooms in the house. Because they are used by

In renovating this master bathroom to incorporate an oversized tub, the design goal was to maintain the character of a turn-of-the-century room. The wooden tub surround, the white marble floor and wainscoting, and the traditional cabinetry and detail are all instrumental in achieving this end. Renovation architects, DiDonno Associates

This bathroom takes advantage of the Southwestern climate by opening up on a small private courtyard. Architects, DiDonno Associates

guests, powder rooms are often the place where the fanciest fixtures and finishes are used. Occasionally half baths are combined with laundry facilities (particularly in apartments). The washer and dryer are designed into an alcove with bifold doors to hide them.

Half baths are also a good solution for those with tight spaces. A toilet and a sink could provide a nice amenity in spaces which don't have enough room for a full bath (even at its most minimal standards). Take, for example, a bathless master bedroom. The provision of a half bath will contribute to the overall comfort of the suite. In addition, it will take the pressure off the other bathrooms.

OVERALL PLANNING

It makes good planning sense to approach bathroom design by estimating the number of bathrooms that you need versus the bathrooms that you presently have. If you have lived in your house or apartment for any length of time, you are probably well aware of the inadequacies of your bathroom facilities. If you have a family with growing children, keep in mind that their bathroom usage will change as they get older. It seems to us that a child's bathroom time increases in geometric proportion to his or her age.

On the other hand, you may have just bought your home and may be looking for suggestions. Following are a few questions you can ask:

• How many people does each bathroom service? Do you have enough bathrooms or will they be overutilized? If overutilized, you need to concentrate on adding one or two more or redesigning your existing bathroom layouts for more efficient use. Is it worthwhile to add a new one by expanding into another area or stealing space from an oversized room or closet? If space is at a premium, can you get away with an additional half bath?
• Do you underutilize a bathroom because it is in the wrong location? Is there any way you can make that bathroom more appealing to encourage its use? Can you make the tub bigger, switch to a better shower faucet, add a sink or a radiator?
• Perhaps you have enough bathrooms but they are all too small. You would love to enlarge one of them and make it more comfortable. Is there a hallway or area nearby you can incorporate into the bathroom space? If you are completely locked into the present space, can the layout be made more efficient?
• Are you limited to upgrading what is already there?

If your house or apartment has enough bathrooms for your family's needs, you can afford to customize each bathroom to the family members who will use it. The design process is more complex for those who have less bathroom space than necessary with little or no room for expansion. These bathrooms have to be designed for maximum use and flexibility. A compartmentalized layout may well be the solution when bathroom space is at a premium. This approach separates the bathroom functions into three distinct areas: a sink area, a shower-tub area, and a toilet area. Each of these areas is interconnected by doors which can remain open or closed to allow for privacy as needed (Ill. 1).

Compartmentation can solve a variety of problems. An overused large bathroom can be laid out more efficiently. It can be redesigned as two separate small bathrooms or it can have two separate toilet-sink areas and a common shower-tub area. If space is limited, the design could be modified into two sink areas sharing a bathing and toilet area (Ill. 2). This solution is ideal for families with several children. Hair drying and showering could happen simultaneously, thus minimizing fights over who will be using the bathroom. The biggest disadvantage to compartmentation is that the layout generally takes more space per fixture than a conventional bathroom layout.

ILL. 1

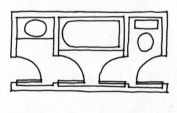

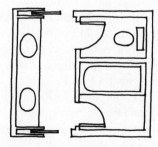

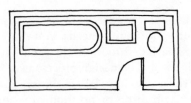

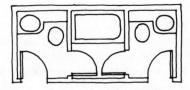

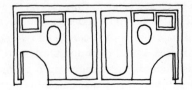

ILL. 2

Another solution to overutilized bathrooms is to provide sinks as part of the bedroom dressing area or even directly outside the bathroom. Interestingly enough, many older homes with only one bathroom have combination lavatory-dressing areas. While at first glance they may seem a waste of space, these sinks are very useful for grooming purposes. Shaving, brushing teeth, and washing can all take place without tying up the bathing and toilet facilities (Ill. 3).

PHYSICAL CONSTRAINTS

As renovators you are most likely confined to locating your new bathroom in the space of the old one. There are a number of physical constraints that limit you in your design flexibility. You have to work with the existing room envelope (ceilings, walls, partitions, doors, windows) and plumbing, heating, and electrical systems.

It may be possible to expand a bath by extending to the outside or by usurping interior space from an adjacent room. If you are renovating a house, you may be able to expand to the outside and create a whole new room extension. The size

of the bathroom is entirely up to you and the zoning laws. (You will have to check minimum side and rear setbacks.) Those who can't expand to the outside of the house or apartment will have to start by looking around for expansion possibilities in adjacent rooms. Can you steal space from a room, hall, or closet? Determine whether the walls or partitions you are thinking of eliminating are structural (see Chapter 16). Find out whether there are any plumbing, heating, or electrical lines hidden in those walls. Electrical and heating lines are relatively easy to move. Plumbing lines are not. A rule of thumb is that behind every plumbing fixture there is a plumbing line. If there is a bathroom directly above the one you are looking at, the problem is compounded. These same plumbing lines are servicing both bathrooms. We advise you not to move the plumbing fixtures around unless it is essential. Apartment building dwellers are advised that, while minor fixture relocation is possible, moving the entire plumbing stack around is close to impossible.

One-story homes with a basement or crawl space directly beneath allow for the greatest flexibility. The basement below provides an area where drainage pipes can pitch freely, while vents can easily be rerouted through the one-story height.

There are times, however, when it is absolutely imperative to relocate one or more of the fixtures. Keep in mind the following order of difficulty. The easiest fixture to relocate is the sink. The reason for this is that the drainage for the sink need not be particularly close to the main waste stack. The tub and shower are second in order of difficulty. The most difficult is the toilet because it needs to be directly connected to the waste stack (see Chapter 18).

ILL. 3

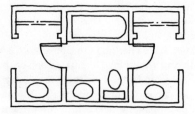

OTHER CONSIDERATIONS

Natural Light and Ventilation

Adequate light and ventilation are important to good bathroom design. Ideally every bathroom should have a window. Not only do windows provide much needed light and ventilation but they also add to the visual amenity of the room. Occasionally, people object to bathroom windows because of the need for privacy—the argument being that blinds, shades, or drapery have to be installed and frequently replaced because of moisture problems. One solution is to locate the windows high up on the wall. When the window location cannot be changed, another solution is to replace clear glass with frosted glass. Skylights are also a popular choice. If you have an interior bathroom, an operable skylight could give you light and air. Most building codes require the provision of ventilating fans for interior bathrooms.

The "Look" of the Bathroom

As architects, we are often asked what the latest bathroom "look" is. The answer is: whatever you like. Bathrooms can be rather attractively designed with sleekly tiled floor and wall surfaces, ample mirrors, and soaking tubs sitting in platforms. They can also be more intimately designed with a minimal amount of mirror space, antique furniture pieces serving as the cabinetry, and a bathtub with legs. While these examples illustrate two design extremes, there are many options that lie somewhere in between. At the risk of repeating ourselves, we believe that the best "look" for your bathroom is the one that makes you feel comfortable.

PART TWO:

DESIGN

DEVELOPMENT

9
DESIGN ELEMENTS

We have discussed in great detail the value of assessing your real needs and the benefits of good functional planning. In addition, we have provided a number of examples to help you reassess and reorganize your space. The following chapter deals with the aesthetics of the space: what you can do to enhance the interior of your home.

Aside from interior decoration, paint, wallpaper, and furniture selection, maximum aesthetic use can be made of every structural and functional element. These design opportunities include the use of natural and artificial light, the introduction of a fireplace or a low partition, and a change in floor level or ceiling height that subtly demarcates one space from the next.

ROOM DIVIDERS

Most of the spaces we are familiar with are divided into rooms by full-height partitions pierced by doors and arches. In recent years it has become fashionable to tear down partitions and convert many smaller rooms into one large, multi-use space. This design strategy has much to recommend it: the larger room has the potential for grandeur as well as greater visual interest, and can accommodate more people at a party. On the other hand, many of these newly created rooms are the unplanned, haphazard by-products of demolition, so completely lacking in architectural definition that it is hard to tell where the hallway ends and the room begins. Sometimes the space is

so amorphous that one is hard pressed to find a good spot for the sofa and easy chair. The worst (or least) designed of these spaces does not provide in any way for visual separation between one functional entity and the next, creating a space that lacks harmony, organization, and intimacy (Ill. 1).

All rooms, both large and small, single or multipurpose, should be defined and well proportioned. By "defined" we mean having some sort of definite or subtle shape. A poorly defined room is one that seems to bleed out in all directions, a shapeless room. Rooms such as bedrooms are usually easy to design because they are small and contained. Large spaces, especially ones that are multifunctional and serve as foyer, hall, living room, dining room, and kitchen, have to be very carefully designed.

An exploration of how most people experience space may be helpful in understanding the design process. When we enter a room, either a friend's living room or the Sistine Chapel, our eye first takes in the room as a whole, its scale and proportions. The experience is immediate and the effect psychological. Our immediate impression of the Sistine Chapel is one of awe. Our first impression of a friend's living room should be one of invitation and comfort. Within a moment, after the initial impression is made, our eye begins to encompass the architectural effects of the space, its balcony, staircase, skylight, mantelpiece, windows, and the like. These larger details create the visual diversity and interest of the room, its intellectual appeal. Last, our eye takes in the finer details, the pattern of the wallpaper, the painting on the wall, the style and color of the furniture. The quality that our eye reads first, the one that makes the first impression, the room's definition and proportion, is of primary importance. No amount of exquisite detailing can save a poorly defined or proportioned room.

In the design process, once the basic shape and proportions of a large room have been established, you can begin designing its larger details, one of which is the subtle definition of smaller, intimate spaces within the larger area.

There are many subtle ways to define the areas within a larger space. One method is the use of different floor levels. The dining area may be located on a platform two steps up from the living area, or, conversely, the lounge area sunk a step or two below the level of the existing floor. The platform construction is not difficult in a renovation since it is easy to build directly on top of the existing floor. The sunken-living-room scheme is more difficult in that it requires the restructuring of the floor system (Ill. 2).

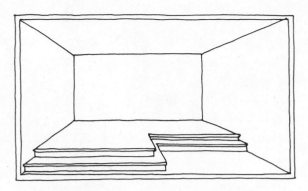

ILL. 2

The living and dining rooms of the first floor and part of a bedroom on the second floor of this split-level house were combined to form a large two-story entertainment area. Renovation architects, Sands and Sperling; photographer, Herman Sands

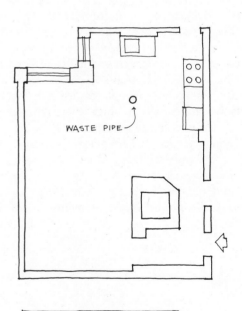

WASTE PIPE

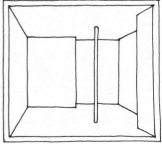

ILL. 1

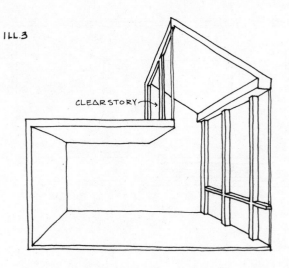

ILL.3

CLEARSTORY →

Another often overlooked means of defining space is a change in ceiling height. If you are lucky enough to have a very high ceiling in your large, multifunctional room, you might define the dining area by lowering the ceiling, or, on the contrary, raising the ceiling over the table (Ill. 3). Likewise, circulation areas may be defined by a dropped ceiling.

Low walls, buffets, and bookcases provide another way to divide the space functionally but not visually. When you are standing in a room containing a waist-high buffet, you see the divider and know where one area ends and another begins. But since the divider is lower than your eye

ILL.4

level, you experience the extended space. A less subtle way to create smaller areas within a larger room is to erect some sort of semi-open divider. A glass-block divider allows light to penetrate from one room to the next. The buffet-book-case-storage wall shown in Illustration 4 can be opened to allow partial visibility or closed to create two distinct rooms.

FIREPLACES

A fireplace adds to the visual drama of a room and, according to recent studies, the installation of a fireplace will dramatically increase a house's resale value. A fireplace not only provides warmth and light in winter; it serves as a room's visual focal point the entire year. In addition, this design element can be used as a divider to define space within a larger room. In a room with a high ceiling, the fireplace can be located at the point of maximum ceiling height so that the long chimney flue will express the verticality of the space. A fireplace finished in a roughly textured material, such as brick, stone, or stucco, can add richness to an otherwise stark room. The visual play between solid and void is emphasized when a fireplace is placed on an exterior wall and is flanked on both sides by panes of glass (Ill. 5).

Built-from-scratch fireplaces are difficult and expensive to construct since they require the skills of an experienced craftsman. Prefabricated and semi-prefabricated fireplaces are easy to install. The semi-prefabricated version consists of the fireplace's internal workings—the firebox, flue, and damper—and can be enclosed in any material, including brick, gypsum board, or marble.

LIGHT

Natural Light

The least expensive means of adding visually to the house is harnessing the energy of the sun. Sunlight, as yet free and untaxed, is available in most parts of the world during most times of the year. Large windows expand the space by letting in the outdoors. Variations in the room's natural lighting can set one area apart from another, giving it a distinct feeling or character. If you have a roof directly over the living room, try to incor-

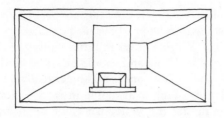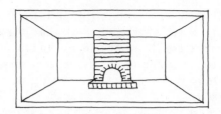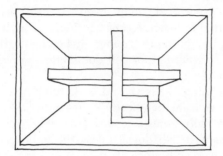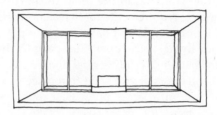

ILL.5

This steel wire and pipe railing, which meets code requirements, was designed specifically **not** to obstruct the river view beyond. Renovation architects, Sands and Sperling; photographer, Herman Sands

porate a skylight or clearstory (Ill. 3). Place the skylight so that it is centered above the sitting area or dinner table. (Remember to use double- or triple-glazed units and/or energy-efficient glass to minimize heat loss in winter and heat gain in summer.)

Adding new windows or expanding existing ones is a way to give an old room a new look. If you have a view, replace a small window with a large panel of fixed glass. (Make sure you have some operable windows in the room to conform to building code requirements for ventilation and egress in case of fire.) If you have a yard or patio outside your living space, open the space to the outdoors by installing a sliding glass door or a few pairs of French doors. If you want to replace your small windows with larger ones, keep in mind that it is easier and less expensive to make them longer than it is to make them wider. Widening the windows necessitates the restructuring of the wall around the window. A far simpler chore is removing the old windows and demolishing the wall beneath the sill. This long, narrow window acts as a visual doorway to the outside.

Artificial Light

Much drama and visual interest can be created with good lighting design. Gone are the days when a single ceiling fixture and a 100-watt bulb were the answer to any lighting problem. We now have tracks, recessed fixtures, low- and high-voltage lighting, special effects to highlight sculpture, and tiny bulbs that make crystal glitter. Residential lighting design is almost a technology in itself, but you don't have to be a professional to design a simple, workable lighting scheme.

The first rule in residential lighting is to avoid the creation of a uniform lighting level throughout the house. Not only is it a dull way to illuminate space; it is functionally incorrect and not very good for your eyes. Different tasks require different levels of illumination. The best light for reading is a source of illumination that comes from over your shoulder or overhead. The lighting source should not be bright, since the pupil of the eye will respond to the brightness of the light source rather than the level of light on the page you are reading, causing eyestrain.

If you are illuminating an area where close work is to be done—a desk, the kitchen counter, a sewing machine, or a piano—try to put the lighting source close to the work surface. A desk can be lighted by a lamp or by long fixtures hidden under the lowest shelf above the desk top.

Similarly, kitchen counters are best lit by fixtures installed under the overhead cabinets.

The old rule of thumb that fluorescent lighting is cold and blue and should never be used in residential applications is no longer really true. Fluorescent tubing is available in many colors, some resembling the yellowish color of incandescent bulbs and some coming very close to matching the color of daylight. Even so, many people are partial to incandescent lighting, and with the exception of under-cabinet kitchen lights, this type of lighting fixture still dominates the residential market.

Dining tables should be lighted directly from above using overhead fixtures either mounted on the ceiling or suspended from it. (Wall sconces cast nasty shadows unless the light is directed upward to bounce off the ceiling.) If the fixtures above the table are at ceiling height, direct the light beam onto the table itself rather than onto the faces of the people sitting around the table. If you are using more than one source of light, organize the light so that there is a soft, general illumination on the table and a narrow spotlight to highlight the centerpiece. Install a dimmer on the switch for added flexibility and enhanced drama. Suspended fixtures are excellent sources of illumination for dining rooms. Lighting experts suggest that you avoid fixtures with exposed bulbs, which cause glare. They recommend that you conceal the source of illumination even to the extent of putting little shades on naked chandelier bulbs.

Living-room lighting is a mix of a number of schemes. Paintings hanging on the walls are best illuminated by ceiling-mounted fixtures located to throw relatively low levels of light directly onto the pictures. General room illumination can be achieved by the use of uplights. Light thrown onto the ceiling is in turn reflected downward to the rest of the room. The objects on the coffee table may be lit by medium-width spotlights. People's faces can be softly lit by table or floor lamps with semi-translucent shades. All of these sources blend together to light the room successfully, creating lighter and darker areas.

The guesswork can be taken out of lighting design by the installation of track lighting. A track mounted to the ceiling allows you to experiment with different light fixtures; for example, low-voltage heads can be used for both wide and narrow spotlighting and fixtures with MR16 lamps can be aimed at china and crystal for bright, glittering light. You can move the heads around and change the bulbs until you get the desired lighting effect. When you mount the tracks, install them about 3' from the walls rather than in the middle of the ceiling; this will prevent glare.

COLOR AND TEXTURE

The use of color in a house is an important consideration.

More than any other aspect of house design, wall treatment is most influenced by current decorating fashion. Every design decade has seen the coming and going of paint-color and wallpaper-pattern trends. Since changing the paint color every few years is a relatively inexpensive alteration, the interior of the house need never look dated. For a long time it had been the practice of architects to paint the interiors of the residences they designed all in white. White interiors bring out the purity of line and form in a well-designed space. In addition, white is a backdrop for selected areas, such as a stair or fireplace, that may be enhanced by the introduction of another color or a rough texture.

Color is often used to set a tone or mood for a room. A study might be treated in rich, muted shades of blue or burgundy. Designers looking for dramatic effect have painted rooms in very dark, glossy brown or even black. Traditionalists follow historical guidelines, using one color of paint on the walls and another, often off-white with a hint of the wall color, on the ceiling and woodwork. Whatever color you choose, keep in mind that lighter values make a room look larger whereas dark colors make it feel smaller and more intimate.

Many fancy painting methods have resurfaced recently, including glazing, faux marble, sponging, distressing, and stippling (see Chapter 10). The effect of all of these techniques is to give the wall surface depth and texture.

There are, therefore, many approaches to decorating and few rigid guidelines. One suggestion we make is that the house be treated as a whole unit with one unifying design concept when it comes to decorative color. This does not mean that you must use the same color in every room. It does suggest that you should consider the house as a sequence or flow of spaces rather than a collection of separate rooms.

Texture can also be manipulated to add visual variety to an area. It is not uncommon to visit a house and be surrounded by "sameness." Wallpaper alone cannot substitute for a range of different materials. Plaster can be smooth in some areas and rough in others. It has been fashionable to apply only the brown coat of plaster and leave it rough and unpainted. There are heavy-gauge papers on the market that are applied to walls and ceilings to give them texture before the paint is applied. One paper has a raised pattern designed to resemble a tin ceiling.

Aside from plaster and paint, the finishing materials most commonly used are carpet and wood, tile and marble. Even these familiar materials can be given new meaning if used in unusual ways. Carpeting may be placed on the floor of a small sitting area, carried over built-in cushioned platforms (to be used for lounging), and laid right onto the walls of the room. Ceramic and marble tiles now are available in a wide variety of textures as well as colors. Ceramic tile floors are made to look like stone, and these stonelike tiles can be used to cover walls as well as floors.

BUILT-IN FURNITURE AND CABINETS

When maximum adaptability is not a requirement, built-in furniture can be a design asset and a space saver. Cleverly designed sleeping, sitting,

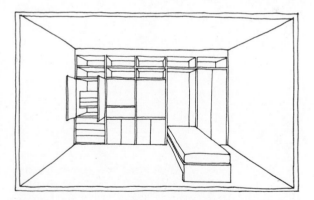
ILL.6

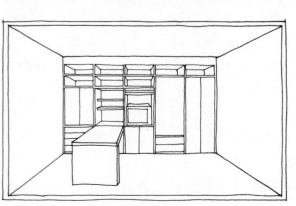

Design Elements
83

working, and storage areas can be integrated into the overall house design. For instance, if a guest room, study, TV room, and sewing area must be made out of the same small space, a storage wall might be designed incorporating all of these diverse elements. The "wall" might contain a concealed, fold-down, Murphy-type bed, a fold-down writing table, and a hidden entertainment area in addition to the usual bookshelves and record cabinets (Ill. 6).

If flexible space is desired, modular wall-closet units on lockable casters can be built and rolled to where they are needed. These portable closets can be used in rows or groupings to act as elements that divide large spaces into smaller ones.

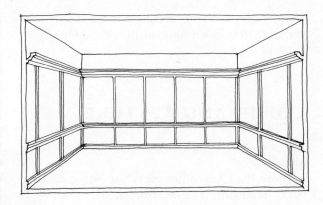

ILL. 7

MOLDINGS AND TRIM

A great deal of interest can be added to a room with the creative use of moldings and trim. Trim is not merely decorative, but serves a very distinct functional purpose. Baseboard, door trim, and crown molding conceal the joints between the walls and floor, door buck, and ceiling, respectively. Chair rails protect the walls from potential scratches made when chairs are pushed back from the table. Projected, exaggerated crown molding can be used to hide light fixtures directed upward to light the ceiling (Ill. 7).

Simple wood molding and trim can be purchased from the lumberyard. Very elaborate architectural sculpture, such as column capitals, friezes, and fancy paneling may be ordered by catalogue or must be custom-carved. Some manufacturers offer elaborate classical molding made out of plaster or fiberglass. These pieces, installed and painted, tend to look very much like woodwork.

Decorative molding can be applied in both traditional and nontraditional ways. Traditional moldings include wainscoting and crown and picture molding. Nontraditional uses for classical details such as column capitals and friezes include their application over doors and as table bases.

10

FINISHING MATERIALS

A vast range of materials qualify as interior finishes. Walls can be plastered, wood-paneled, tiled in marble, or carpeted. Similarly, floors can be covered with anything from brick to rubber. In essence, when it comes to finishing materials almost anything goes. Of course, most of us will have to take into account cost, ease of installation, and functional criteria such as maintenance.

When you select a finish for a part of the house, you must consider the type of activity that will take place in that area and determine the suitability of the material for that use. Many materials that are suitable for one use might fail if subjected to other uses. More than one homeowner has carpeted his kitchen with indoor-outdoor carpet only to discover that although the carpet is tough, it is also extremely vulnerable to stains.

Our discussion of finishes is limited to what we consider the bare essentials. New products are constantly being introduced, each with its virtues and problems. We suggest that you consult Sweet's Catalogue, which can be found in many public libraries. It is an excellent source of information on any new building product.

CERAMIC TILE

The heading of ceramic tile covers a vast range of tile types, the most familiar being the glazed tile used on bathroom floors and walls. Ceramic tile is made out of clay that has been fired in a kiln at very high temperatures. It is an excellent material as far as maintenance is concerned since it is water-resistant and nearly impossible to stain. Its color does not fade and it is hard, tough, and durable. The tiles themselves are very easy to clean. The grout between them, however, can be a cleaning problem if the wrong type is used. Care must be taken to select the right grout for the job; for example, kitchen applications should have grout that is not adversely affected by kitchen grease.

There are two problems with ceramic tile. The first is its cost. As a finish for walls, it is more expensive than resilient tile or gypsum board and paint; when it is used as a floor finish, the reinforced underlayment required often costs more than the tile itself. The second is its installation. Tiles are bonded with adhesive or cement mortar to the wall or subfloor surface. While the placing of the tile on the mortar or adhesive bed is easy, the trimming required to get around openings and fittings (all the piping around the bathroom sink) can be difficult. Unless you have mastered the art of tile cutting, you may spend a lot of time piecing together the remains of shattered tiles. In addition, tile needs a very strong nonresilient surface. The best installations are on "mud," which is 1" or 1½" of Portland cement concrete reinforced with metal mesh applied on top of ¾" plywood or a concrete slab.

Ceramic tile is available glazed and unglazed. Glazed tile is the one most commonly seen in bathrooms, kitchens, and other wet locations. It has a face of ceramic material, which may be glossy, semi-matte, or crystalline. Glazed tiles manufactured domestically generally are available in 4½" × 4½" and 1" × 1" or 2" × 2" squares (mosaic tiles). Various trimming tiles are available for edge and cove conditions. Mexican tiles (which are subject to chipping) and unglazed quarry tile are very porous and must be treated with an appropriate sealant or waxed frequently to prevent staining.

Imported ceramic tile comes in an assortment of sizes, patterns, and colors. The most typical sizes are about 6" × 6", 5" × 10", and 8" × 8" (13 × 13 cm, 20 × 20 cm, etc.), but there is little standardization with these imports. Some of the tiles are made to look like granite in an assortment of colors and some are exquisitely hand-painted in both abstract and traditional patterns. There are also a whole variety of beautiful ceramic trim pieces that can be used with ceramic tile. Be advised, however, when selecting tiles that most of the imported designer tiles do not come with the necessary trim pieces to turn corners. The tile will have to be installed using mitered edges at the corners, a skill that only experienced tile installers have. Furthermore, specialized tiles—for soap dishes, toothbrush holders, toilet-paper dispensers—are almost never available to match imported tiles.

There are so many beautiful designer tiles available that it is difficult to make a selection. Keep in mind that ceramic tiles last almost forever and the bathroom you install today may be the one you have to live with until you either die or sell the house. When selecting tile, be restrained. Don't choose too many patterns and colors to go into one bathroom. Try not to select very fashionable colors. The modish peach-and-maroon bathroom installed in one of the authors' childhood home in the 1940's was considered ghastly in the 1950's and 1960's. Only in the 1980's, when this combination again became fashionable, did the bathroom look *au courant.*

One more admonition: Try to stick to the same tile module for the whole bathroom. If you are using 5" × 10" tiles on the wall, use the same size or 5" × 5" tiles (if this size is available in the series) on the floor. You can use a floor tile on the walls if you wish, but do not use a wall tile on the floor. The wall tile may not be strong enough for floor use or may be too smooth. A highly glossy tile on the floor may become very slippery when wet. You need not choose one tile for the floor and another for the walls. Use the tiles innovatively by taking the floor tile up one wall and applying a coordinating tile on the other three wall surfaces. Similarly, the floor tile can also be used to cover the bathtub platform and the countertop of the lavatory.

Ceramic tile can be used on the kitchen floor and on the counter and/or backsplash. We suggest that you stick to tiles made for countertops if you are considering installing a tile counter. Most domestic brands designed for counter installations feature specialized tiles, such as drip edges and exaggerated corners, which make the counter look and perform better.

A number of materials are used as tile grout. Latex–Portland cement is generally recommended since it is somewhat crack- and stain-resistant and comes in a variety of colors. Silicone and urethane grouts are more stain- and crack-resistant but are not available in all colors and are not recommended as grout for quarry tiles or brick pavers. In any case, a dark grout will look better over the years than one of a lighter color.

MARBLE AND GRANITE

Stone is a beautiful material all around. Types of stone used for flooring include limestone, granite, slate, and marble. Stone floors are used where a durable and attractive material is required. Keep in mind, however, that some stone is easily stained. Another important consideration is its weight. Although the stone used for flooring is cut into very thin tile, it still manages to add up to a substantial weight. Before selecting this material, make sure that the floor system can take the load of the stone flooring.

There are two additional disadvantages to the use of stone: the difficulty of installing it and its high cost. Stone, like ceramic tile, is easy to lay on the mortar bed. Cutting the stone to fit, however, is a demanding and precise job.

Marble is beautiful, hard, and strong and can be used on interior walls or floors. Marble floors should be periodically waxed and used in areas not subject to scratching or acidic action. Marble is available in large slabs that can be used on walls or countertops and in tiles that are generally used for floor applications. Travertine is less dense than marble and has small holes that must be filled with epoxy before the stone is polished. Both are available in 6" × 6" and 12" × 12" sizes. Limestone is available in tiles as well and has a rough, rugged look. One of the advantages of limestone is that the tiles may be used outside as well as for interiors. This allows you to use the same material for a living room and the terrace that it opens onto. Granite, the most durable of the stones, is also available in tiles 12" × 12" and 8" × 8". Granite tiles are available polished or textured, and are about ¼" to ½" thick. Polished granite is almost indestructible and can be used for interior and exterior applications. Flamed granite is not polished and has a rough texture. Since it is porous, it should be sealed. Honed granite has a satin texture that is less glossy than polished granite. Latex–Portland cement grout is often recommended for marble and stone tiles. Larger tiles (2' × 2' or 2' × 4') can be used on wall surfaces if anchored properly.

BRICK

Brick is always an interesting addition to the house. Many a renovator has spent long and painful hours chipping away at the plastered walls to get at the brick wall beneath. The result is well worth the effort. For floors, don't use too porous a brick such as common brick. It is not very durable and will produce a chalky dust as it wears down. Paving brick is a much better choice. With brick as with stone, be cautious of the heavy loads you are putting on the existing structural system and be sure you reinforce the subfloor for brick and other nonresilient flooring materials.

RESILIENT FLOORING

Resilient flooring materials are thin coverings made of various combinations of resins, plasticizers, and fibers in addition to other components. The composition is formed under heat and pressure. This type of flooring is applied to the subfloor with mastic cements and is available in tile or sheet form. Although resilient flooring is not as durable or as easy to maintain as ceramic tile, it is easier to install and lower in cost. In addition, a resilient floor is more comfortable underfoot and reduces noise. The types of resilient flooring available include vinyl, vinyl composition tile, rubber, and linoleum. The tiles are generally 9" × 9" or 12" × 12" squares. The sheets range in width from 36" to 72". The installation of this type of flooring varies with the location of the floor (above or below grade) and the composition of the subfloor (wood or concrete). Because the material is adversely affected by moisture conditions, the selection of resilient flooring and the

adhesive must be carefully researched. Consult your dealer for recommendations.

Genuine linoleum is made from linseed oil, wood dust, cork, and resins, but is no longer manufactured in the United States on a commercial basis. Imported linoleum comes in rolls about 6½' wide or in square tiles. Linoleum has excellent resistance to grease and abrasion. It performs poorly, however, when too much water or alkali detergents are used on it. The constant use of water and strong detergents removes the oil content in the linoleum and causes it to become hard, brittle, and subject to tearing. Vinyl sheeting is often made to look like linoleum, mimicking the old styles and patterns.

Sheet vinyl can be purchased as tiles or in rolls up to 12' wide. Vinyl is very resilient and is highly resistant to abrasion. It is durable and performs well under grease, alkali, and water conditions. Vinyl comes in solid colors and in a number of patterns. Since heel marks show on vinyl flooring and can be a cleaning chore, the multicolored designs and "splattered" patterns are recommended for hiding dirt in heavily trafficked areas. These patterns, although practical, may have a commercial or institutional look and have to be used judiciously.

Solid vinyl tiles are popularly used as residential flooring in the kitchen as well as almost any other room in the house. Alternating a white solid-color vinyl tile with a very dark tile in a checkerboard pattern is a classic installation. Some vinyl tiles are made to look like slate or quarry tile or to resemble brick pavers.

Generally, the more expensive commercial sheets and vinyl tiles are durable. We do not recommend products with only a thin veneer of vinyl over the base material or cushioned flooring. We have found that these products, although inexpensive, do not stand up to kitchen traffic and have to be replaced after a few years.

Vinyl composition tile (VCT) is made of vinyl resins and a variety of fillers. It is relatively low in cost and is used in a number of different commercial installations. VCT can be applied over a concrete slab on or below grade and is resistant to alkalis and grease. This flooring material comes in a variety of sizes and patterns, including tiles that are made to look like ceramic tile, granite, marble, or brick.

Resilient rubber flooring, which has a high-tech look, is durable and offers good resistance to water. It performs well against stains, grease, alkali detergents, and abrasions. Of all the resilient floors, it is probably easiest on the feet and legs and absorbs the most noise. Most rubber flooring comes with raised patterns of dots or squares in a variety of colors, but these projections make the floor more difficult to clean than a smooth floor. The flooring comes in tile-size sheets about 20" × 20". The floor is meant to look seamless but we have found that the seams show after a few years.

CARPETING

Wall-to-wall carpeting has been around for a long time and for good reason. The installation of carpeting directly over plywood subflooring was discovered long ago by housing developers wishing to save themselves the cost of installing the more expensive hardwood flooring. Carpeting does have advantages over other flooring, especially in bedrooms, in that it is both soft and warm on bare feet. In addition, carpeting imparts a feeling of warmth to even the most formally furnished rooms.

Broadlooms, as opposed to area rugs which have a specific design made to fit their rectangular shape, come in many different textures, weights, colors, and qualities. Some are very dense and high-piled, resembling manicured lawns. Others are dense, short, and smooth, resembling velvet. At the opposite end of the spectrum are the Berbers, which look knitted or mat-like. It is important to remember that no carpet, whether of natural or man-made fiber, is made to last forever. All of them will eventually wear down and are susceptible to staining. When selecting carpeting, choose a carpet that you like but one that is suitable for its purpose. A dense low-pile carpet of contract grade is recommended for a young child's room. (Building blocks don't stand up on high-pile carpet.) Choose a very dense carpet for stairs. A high-pile carpet that is not dense will tend to mat down in a few years, especially in heavy traffic areas. It is not recommended at all. Very light-colored carpet shows dirt and will have to be cleaned periodically; very dark carpet shows dust and lint and has to be vacuumed often. Carpet that has been designed to be applied to walls has the advantage of absorbing sound in the room as well as adding a soft texture to the space.

WOOD

Wood floors have traditionally been constructed out of hardwood because of its durability and resistance to wear and tear. Oak has always been and still is a favorite for flooring, but maple, birch, beech, and pecan are also used, among others. Many turn-of-the-century buildings exhibit beautiful oak floors that not only are still in excellent condition but will most likely last for a long time to come.

Wood flooring falls into several types: strip, plank, block, parquet, and acrylic-impregnated.

Strip flooring is one of the most commonly used wood floors. It consists of wood strips ranging in width from 1½" to 2½" and about ¾" thick. The length depends on the available pieces. These strips are blind-nailed to the subfloor in tongue-and-groove fashion every 10" to 12". The lengthwise joints are staggered. (See Chapter 36, Ills. 6 and 7.)

Plank flooring is made up of wood planks of varying widths. Some may be as narrow as 4" or less and others as wide as 12". Some wood plank systems presently available may be applied to the subfloor by means of mastic or adhesive or may be blind-nailed. Check Sweet's Catalogue.

Block and parquet flooring has traditionally been more difficult to construct than either strip or plank flooring. Parquet floors, in particular, required a painstaking amount of work. Thin pieces of hardwood were cut and secured to the subfloor piece by piece, forming an intricate design. (Victorian houses exhibit some of the most extravagant parquet floors.) Fortunately, there are presently available parquet blocks that may be applied as easily as vinyl tile. These parquet blocks come in squares ranging anywhere from 6" × 6" to 19" × 19", and there is a wide range of patterns and types of woods. The blocks are applied in mastic directly to wood or concrete subfloors. (It is inadvisable to apply wood flooring directly on a concrete slab on grade. Changing moisture conditions may damage the floor by causing the wood to swell and buckle.)

Acrylic-impregnated wood flooring consists of 12" × 12" × 5/16" or 2" × 12" × 3/8" strips of solid oak with acrylic and stain forced through the entire thickness of the wood. A special factory-applied process is used to harden the acrylic, resulting in a wood floor designed to be very stain- and wear-resistant. The manufacturers recommend this flooring for heavy-traffic areas. A related product, actually more of a vinyl floor than a wood floor, sandwiches a thin veneer of real wood between two sheets of vinyl, the top vinyl layer being clear. This type of flooring is highly water-resistant and is recommended for kitchens where a wood "look" is desired. Natural cork is available in a similar vinyl product.

Wood can be applied to walls as single wood boards or large plywood panels. The advantage of the wood board over the plywood sheet is its rich texture, which is difficult to match in a highly manufactured product such as plywood. Boards are easier to install in areas with many openings, since they are easier to cut than large sheets. In addition, they give you greater design flexibility. For example, you may install the boards vertically or diagonally, or you may use different-size boards to add further interest.

Plywood panels do not offer such versatility. The advantage of plywood for the amateur is that the installation of the panels is quicker than that of single boards (unless you have a surface with a multitude of openings and notches). Plywood panels are available in interior and exterior grades. They are generally 4' wide and vary in length (8' panels are the most commonly used). Another advantage of plywood is its availability in a variety of exotic woods. Plywood is constructed of a number of thin veneers of scrap wood held together by glue. The outer face of the panel is covered with a paper-thin slice of fine wood. Because of the thinness of this surface veneer, expensive and rare woods can be used at small cost.

You must be aware when buying plywood paneling that not everything that looks like wood is necessarily so. Some of the wood look-alikes are plywood panels covered with vinyl printed with a wood grain. Although the vinyl surface is durable, it does not offer the richness of wood.

One problem with plywood paneling is the horizontal joint. Because panels come in lengths of generally no more than 12', there is a joining problem if the wall surface is any higher than the maximum length of the panel. If you are planning to use plywood paneling, it may be a good idea to inquire about the lengths that the panel comes in while you are still in the design stages.

Raised solid-wood paneling, as found in many old houses built for the wealthy, is mostly custom-made and very expensive. In raised paneling the solid-wood sheets are milled around the edges to create the raised panel, and matching milled trim pieces are placed over the joints between panels. A simulated old-fashioned paneled effect may be created by applying matching wood trim to flush plywood panels in decorative patterns. The effect can be striking if painted. Note, however, that this type of paneling never looks like the real thing.

PLASTER AND GYPSUM BOARD

Traditionally, walls and ceilings have been finished with lath and plaster. Although plaster provides a beautiful texture, it has the serious drawback of being very difficult to apply. If you are renovating a room that is finished in plaster, you may have to hire a professional plasterer to repair the existing walls. If the renovation work is extensive or you don't want to hire a plasterer, much of the new work can be done in gypsum board. If properly done, the new gypsum-board partition and the old plaster wall will be almost indistinguishable.

In most old buildings plaster was applied to lath (thin strips of wood nailed to wood framing with small spaces between the strips to allow keying of the plaster). Today, lath is made either of expanded metal (thin sheets of steel that are slit and stretched to produce openings) or preformed gypsum board (sheets of hardened gypsum covered with absorbent paper to which fresh plaster adheres). Plaster is applied in three coats. The first, called the scratch coat, is troweled onto the lath and then scratched while still wet to create a rough surface to receive the next coat of plaster. The second coat, called the brown coat, strengthens the plaster and presents a smooth surface for the final coat. The finish coat is very thin, about 1/16" thick, and can be troweled smooth or textured. Although all three coats may be applied over gypsum lath, the scratch coat can be dispensed with since the gypsum board provides the rigidity the metal lath lacks.

In a very old house, the plaster walls may be cracked and mottled. It is sometimes difficult to determine whether the cracking is beyond repair or easily fixed. If there are just a few cracks caused by the initial settling of the building or other structural trauma, they can be patched with a mixture of spackling compound and gypsum plaster applied in very thin coats after the cracks have been widened and all loose plaster removed. Sometimes, however, the cracking is caused by the continuing disintegration of the original lath. If this is the case, your spackling repairs may not be permanent. These walls may have to be covered in gypsum board.

The alternative to plaster is gypsum board (also known as Sheetrock, one of its trade names). Gypsum board, like plaster, is used for walls and ceilings. It is a sandwich panel manufactured from powdered gypsum mixed with water and other ingredients which are shaped to form a wide, flat panel. This panel is then covered on both sides with a tough paper. The resulting product is both dense and durable and is resistant to fire and noise. Gypsum board is installed by screwing the panels to the structural studs. The joints between the panels are concealed with tape and spackle to create a smooth, seamless wall. The taping and spackling of the joints is rather tedious and generally requires skill and experience for a smooth job.

Unlike plaster, it cannot be left without an applied finish. Because of the joint work between the panels, gypsum board has to be covered with paint, wall coverings, tile, or other finish. The main advantage of gypsum board over plaster is its relative ease and quickness of installation, both of which make it very appealing to the amateur home renovator. It comes in 4'-wide sheets and the lengths vary from 6' to 16', but it is very difficult to purchase anything other than 8' lengths. The thicknesses range from ⅜" to ⅝". Standard (½"-thick) gypsum board is the most commonly used for residential construction. For a firmer, sounder partition we recommend the use of ⅝" gypsum board, which is heavier than the ½" panels. (The thinner panels are fine for ceilings.) Some home builders elect to install a layer of ½" gypsum board onto a ½" backer board on each side of the studs. Although it is more expensive and time-consuming to install this double layer of gypsum board, the ½" panels are easier to lift than the ⅝" ones.

There are a few different types of gypsum board to meet special requirements. For example, standard gypsum board cannot be installed in areas subject to wetness or on the exterior of buildings. Special moisture-resistant boards are available for use in such areas—for example, bathrooms and kitchens. Another type of board is the backer board, intended for use as a backing material where a double layer of gypsum board is called for. Also available is fire-rated gypsum board, designed for situations where the wall must resist fire penetration for one or more hours. Although not always required by law, we recommend using fire-rated gypsum board around fireplaces, in the garage, and in the mechanical room.

Gypsum board comes with different edge conditions to suit various functions. The edges can be square, beveled, V-shaped, round, or tongue-and-groove. The square-edge board is the most widely used. The edges may also be tapered to provide a smoother and stronger joint. Where different pieces of board meet to form an outside corner, a bead is installed. Beads are metal angles

that can be nailed at the corners, giving you a precise right angle.

Tile backer board is used instead of gypsum board in wet areas such as the walls around showers and bathtubs. Known by various nongeneric names such as Wonderboard and Duroc, it is basically a thin mixture of Portland cement reinforced with vinyl-coated glass fiber mesh fashioned into ½"-thick boards. The cement panels are more resistant to water than moisture-resistant gypsum board and are often used as a substitute for a "mud" (reinforced cement) base for walls that are to receive ceramic tile. Most tile backer board is fire-resistant, comes in various panel sizes, and is recommended only for interior use unless otherwise indicated by the manufacturer.

Paint

Of the applied finishes, paint is by far the most popular. Paints have been developed and improved in the last few years to cover a vast range of applications. They are essentially divided into two types: latex (water-based paints) and alkyds (oil-based paints). Latex paints are preferred by nonprofessional painters because of their ease of application, quick drying time, little odor, and easy cleanup (with soap and water). They are available in different finishes: flat, satin (eggshell), semi-gloss, and glossy. The choice of finishes is dependent on the usage of the surface. For example, in a kitchen, where you may be scrubbing down walls periodically, a semi-gloss or glossy finish will stand up better than a flat one. Flat finishes tend to show marks if abrasive cleansers are used. Keep in mind that the glossier the paint, the more imperfections the surface will show.

Alkyd paints are no longer the hassle they used to be. The new ones are easy to handle. Many of them are advertised as dripless because of their heavier consistency.

Alkyds generally take longer to dry than latex paints and have more of a smell. They are available in the same colors and finishes as latex. Their main advantages over latex paints are their better performance under heavy scrubbing and their tendency not to absorb dirt. Thus oil-based paint is a popular choice in kitchens, in bathrooms, on windowsills, etc.

Both latex and alkyd paints have corresponding primer-sealers. Priming the surface before painting is necessary when the surface is being painted for the first time. The purpose of the primer-sealer is to penetrate and seal the pores of the material and make it ready to receive paint. Primers go on easily and are quick-drying; one coat is usually sufficient. The exceptions are instances where the surface is extremely porous—for example, concrete block.

There is a wealth of paints designed for special applications, such as epoxy enamels for use on surfaces requiring a particularly tough finish, aluminum paints used to inhibit rust, masonry paint specifically designed for use on extremely porous surfaces, and deck and floor enamels.

A recent style in decorating is to make new rooms look old and old rooms look ancient. This trend toward romantic classicism has revitalized some long forgotten painting techniques which can make common gypsum board and plaster look like distressed limestone or aging marble. Most of these effects are achieved by applying one or more paint colors, which have been thinned, over a different-colored background.

"Glazing" is the application of a number of thin layers of paint over a base coat of ordinary paint. The use of several levels of a lighter shade of glaze over a slightly darker undercoat creates a depth of color and a subtle sheen.

"Sponging" is the application of a thinned glaze of paint over a solid-colored background using a natural sponge instead of a brush. When the first layer dries, another layer of a different color is sponged on. This may be followed by still another layer. For depth of color, the first color applied is darker than the subsequent colors. If a soft blending of color is the object, the various levels of glaze are sponged on before the level below is completely dry. Sponging can be accomplished using oil or latex paint. The oil paint gives a crispier look, while the latex paint creates a somewhat softer, more leathery look.

"Stippling" is very similar to sponging in that one thin layer of glaze is applied over a dry base coat of paint of another color and texture. The difference is that the stippling pattern is created by the partial removal of the second coat of paint while it is still wet, partially revealing the base coat. Stippling, which simulates the texture of lemon peel, can be done with a special stippling brush, a sponge, or a sawed-off broom. "Dragging" or "combing" is very similar to stippling except that the pattern is created by combing the still wet second coat with a stiff brush to create long, woodlike grains.

"Ragging" also begins with a dry undercoat of one color and a very thin glaze of another color on top of it. In ragging, the top coat is textured with the use of a crumpled rag which both removes and reapplies the paint at the same time. The result is a little like marble.

"Marbling" is a more complex procedure utilizing most of the techniques listed above in multiple layers. The varying layers may be applied with a brush, sponge, or feather, rubbed off with a rag, or diluted with a sprinkling of solvent.

11

COMPLETING THE DESIGN OF THE KITCHEN

The kitchen is the room most often renovated and we will cover this material in great detail. We have already discussed kitchen layouts in Chapter 7, and by this time you should have a measured drawing of the existing space and some idea as to the best layout for the renovated kitchen. This chapter covers kitchen appliances, storage space, cabinets, backsplash and counter materials, flooring, and lighting.

What goes into the kitchen itself (in terms of appliances, storage space, and the number of square feet of counter area) depends on the cook's needs and budget. There is no end to the gadgets that can be included in a kitchen. Here is a list of the most essential:

COOKING APPLIANCES

If the twentieth century has given us nothing else, it has given us numerous ways to cook an egg. Cooking appliances have become so complex it is difficult for the buyer to make a decision without understanding appliance terminology.

Cooking Fuels

Cooking appliances use either gas or electricity. Common wisdom holds that gas is preferred for the burners because the heat can be increased or decreased almost instantaneously. Many cooks feel that electric ovens have the advantage over the gas varieties in that the temperature can be maintained more uniformly. Gas broilers and grills are generally preferred over their electric counterparts. The authors have cooked with both electric and gas appliances and find that both work well in most situations. Most people do not have a choice of fuels since piped-in gas is not available in most areas (although bottled gas can be used for a cooktop). Cooks in urban areas generally have a choice between gas and electricity and select gas since (in recent years) the fuel costs less.

Electric cooking appliances generally draw more amperage than conventional (non-heat-generating) appliances and a great deal more current than gas-fueled units that use an electric spark to ignite the gas. An all-electric home requires larger electric service than a house with mostly gas appliances. Before selecting one fuel over the other, determine whether you have adequate electric power. Have an electrician evaluate your existing amperage. (Don't add up the numbers on the fuses or circuit breakers; they often give you an inaccurate picture.) If you do not have enough current, you may have to bring up a new line from the cellar. This is often a very expensive proposition and, in fact, it may be untenable, particularly if you live in an apartment house. Your building may not have any additional electricity for you to tap, or your landlord may not want to see exposed conduit snaking through his back halls.

Cooktops

Cooking, meaning boiling, steaming, frying, or sautéing, is done on a cooktop containing two or more burners (heat sources). The cooktop is often a separate unit set into a counter. (When a cooktop is combined with an oven-broiler, the combination is called a range.) The cooktop can be fueled by gas or electricity. Electric burners are called heating elements.

The newest products being marketed include an electric cooktop consisting of solid disk-shaped burners set into a flat panel of heat-resistant glass. Manufacturers claim that this product eases cleaning since drips cannot fall under the heating elements, where they are hard to get at. Another new product, the induction cooktop, looks like a flat sheet of black glass with circles drawn on it. The induction cooktop heats pots and pans by means of magnetic friction and does not heat the cooktop surface at all. Only metal utensils can be used. Manufacturers claim that the unit is safer (in that it is not hot to the touch), very easy to keep clean, and superior to conventional electric burners since temperature changes can be made instantaneously.

Cooktop accessories include a griddle, a rotisserie, and a grill in addition to the standard burners. The griddle is a flat metal plate, often Teflon-coated, which cooks food in the manner of an oversized frying pan. The rotisserie rotates the food on a spit, so that the juices turn with the meat, thus self-basting the roast. The grill sears food by using a somewhat remote high-temperature source located below the grate on which the food is placed. Cooktops come in a variety of nonstandard widths from 30" to about 45", with some models available at 24" and 15".

Ovens

Baking and roasting are done in ovens, which are enclosed units. The traditional oven as we know it is the conventional or radiant oven. It is fueled by either gas or electricity and bakes by heating the air in the oven cabinet. Microwave ovens cook food by using electromagnetic waves and run exclusively on electricity.

Convection ovens use a fan within the oven to circulate hot air around unheated food. Some manufacturers claim that the time needed to cook various poultry and meat dishes is reduced by the use of a convection oven, and that some pies and cakes could be baked at lower temperatures than normally required. Many oven manufacturers produce a convertible convection-radiant oven. At least one manufacturer features an electric convection-microwave convertible oven.

Broiling is generally done in the oven cabinet. Food is cooked by high heat emitted a few inches above the food from either an electric element or gas jets.

The double wall oven might have two radiant oven-broilers or a microwave oven above and a radiant oven-broiler below. Some manufacturers market a double unit with a convertible oven on top and a radiant oven-broiler below. Wall ovens are 24" deep and either 24" or 27" wide. The heights of the double units may vary from one manufacturer to another.

An additional product combines a microwave oven with a vent hood to be located above the range or stove top. (This oven may be a microwave-convection convertible.) More on these below.

Ranges

The basic range contains four burners on top and an oven-broiler below. The unit generally comes either 24", 30", or 36" wide and in various styles, including stainless-steel-and-glass models or enameled finishes in various colors.

A hi-low style of range contains two ovens, one below the cooktop and one suspended above. The top oven may be a conventional oven-broiler or a microwave plus a vent hood.

Commercial Ranges

Many cooks prefer a large restaurant-sized gas range to those available on the residential market. The range is large (often 32" deep) and the finish, although durable, is not as sleek as that of the residential models. Advantages are the additional features available, such as a salamander broiler, high-heat gas jets, greater distance between burners, which allows for the use of wider pots and pans, and enormous ovens. Many commercial ranges have six burners and one or two ovens below.

Combining Cooking Appliances

These cooking appliances can be combined in a number of ways. The simplest configuration is the stand-alone range with its four burners and oven-broiler below. To expand the capabilities of this simple cooking system you may hang a microwave–vent hood from the cabinet above the range.

Many cooks need to bake and broil at the same time and prefer to have two baking ovens in addition to a microwave and broiler. This can be accomplished by using a double wall oven, a cooktop, and a microwave–vent hood, or by installing a double oven (one with a microwave above and an oven-broiler below) in addition to a standard range. Both of these schemes provide the cook with two ovens, two broilers, and a microwave. The advantage of having a range rather than a wall oven is its interior capacity. Range ovens are usually 30" wide, providing a wider interior oven than the wall-hung varieties, whose overall width is either 24" or 27".

Cleaning

Self-cleaning ovens have become almost standard. Almost all electric ovens are available in self-cleaning models. When you choose to clean the oven, the door is locked and a great amount of heat is generated inside the oven that literally burns off grease and spills. A variation on the self-cleaning oven is the continuous-clean oven, which has a Teflon-like surface that tends to slough off grease and spills. The continuous-clean ovens are supposed to continuously burn off oven residue. Many cooks prefer the self-cleaning ovens to the continuous-clean varieties. Most (although not all) gas ovens are available only with the continuous-clean feature, although some have self-cleaning ovens. Since features in all appliances tend to change from year to year, it is best to consult with an appliance dealer who is familiar with a wide variety of manufacturers and models.

Exhaust Vents

Venting is another variable worthy of consideration. The word "venting" (which generally means the removal of smoke or fumes) is used in numerous ways, which often leads to confusion.

Most cooking produces odors and steam that enter the room and are distributed to the rest of the house by normal air circulation. These fumes may be removed by a hood located directly over the burners. This exhaust hood has a suction fan that draws fumes and smoke into the unit and

whisks them away via ducts to the outside. A variation on this ventilation hood is a recycling or ductless variety. This hood draws the fumes into the unit through a filter designed to remove odors and grease. The cleansed air is then released to the room.

These ventilation or exhaust hoods are not to be confused with ovens that require venting. Some wall-oven models require special ducts that remove excess heat, smoke, and odors from the unit directly. Not all wall ovens require venting. Most microwave ovens do not require special venting.

A third use of the word "venting" refers to the elimination of toilet and other plumbing odors. The kitchen sink drainage plumbing will have to be vented by a pipe about 1½" in diameter concealed in the wall (see Chapter 18).

Yet another kind of venting is required (usually by municipal code) for kitchens (and bathrooms) that have no natural ventilation through windows. This vent has a diffuser, fan, and duct system which draws air from the room to the exterior of the building.

Last, your clothes dryer requires a flexible hose to vent moisture (and gas fumes) to the outside.

REFRIGERATION

The modern kitchen requires both refrigerator and freezer. These two functions may come in a single unit or can be separated into two boxes. Typically, refrigerator-freezer combinations come in a number of styles, each in a variety of sizes. The freezer-above/refrigerator-below model has one or two doors. The refrigerator-above/freezer-below model usually has two doors. The side-by-side refrigerator-freezer allows the cook to see what is in the box at eye level. The disadvantage of the side-by-side models (especially in the narrower widths) is the difficulty in storing containers that are wider than the interior width of the cabinet.

Many households, particularly those large in size or in rural areas, require refrigerators and freezers with very large capacity and might select separate units for each.

Refrigerator-freezers do not come in standard sizes. Each manufacturer seems to have his own height, width, and depth criteria. Almost all of the other kitchen appliances (ranges, dishwashers, etc.) are designed to fit the standard kitchen counter width of 24". Most of the popularly priced refrigerators come in depths of 29" or more. When designing the layout of the kitchen, be sure that the door swings clear of the counter on the opposite side. Some manufacturers have a 24"-deep model that looks built-in. The doors are designed to receive plastic laminate or wood panels to match the cabinet doors. These refrigerators tend to be more expensive.

If you are redesigning a kitchen to include your existing refrigerator, keep in mind that your unit may not last more than a few years. It may be difficult to find a new model of the same capacity to fit the allotted space. (This is generally not a problem with modular units such as dishwashers, always 24" wide, and ranges, mostly 30" wide.) Furthermore, consider your future refrigeration needs. You may require a larger unit in a few years. If so, visit an appliance store and obtain the specifications for a larger refrigerator. Design the space for the larger model.

Most freezers are available in frost-free versions, which draw a bit more power than conventional freezers but completely eliminate frost buildup and the need to defrost the refrigerator. Freezers that come equipped with icemakers must have cold-water lines to the unit.

SINKS AND DISHWASHERS

There is nothing as uncomplicated as the kitchen sink, or is there? It comes in stainless steel or enameled cast iron, the latter in a variety of colors. The stainless-steel sink comes in single, double, or triple configurations of various sizes and shapes, with or without adjacent drainboards. Each of these configurations, in turn, comes in various sizes, bowl depths, metal gauges, and steel finishes. You will also have to choose the number of holes (for the faucet fittings) you will require. The enameled sink is available in somewhat fewer options. Both stainless-steel and enameled varieties can be had with accessory baskets and chopping boards that fit over the bowls to make vegetable preparation easier. Most people find a single large sink, about 25" wide (by 22" deep) sufficient. Others prefer two (smaller) side-by-side sinks.

Industrial designers have had a field day with the kitchen faucet. The familiar style of a central faucet and two winglike valve openers is still available. Newer models include a gooseneck faucet or a single faucet with a level that can be moved right and left for hot and cold water. The three-piece set requires a sink with three holes; the single faucet needs only one opening. The remaining openings can be used for other wash-related accessories, such as a spray, a liquid-soap or hand-cream dispenser, and/or an instant-boiled-water device. Most of these accessories are located under the counter, with only the dispenser coming through the hole. An unused hole can always be capped.

A garbage-disposal unit located under one sink has become standard in some areas. Check with the local authorities (if you have city sewage) or with the firm that services your house's waste system to see if a garbage disposal is permitted or advisable.

A water-purification system may be desirable or necessary in many situations. Some filtering systems claim to remove most impurities such as chemicals, asbestos fibers, and dirt. A more powerful model claims to remove toxic chemicals as well. Some systems merely soften hard water or filter out sand and silt.

The dishwasher has become a standard element in any kitchen. This modular unit (always designed to fit into a 24"-wide space under the counter adjacent to the sink) comes in a limited number of styles and with only a few options. The device may or may not scrub pots, preheat water to sterilizing temperatures, or provide an air-dry cycle. A new model of dishwasher is designed to fit directly under the sink, a boon to very small kitchens.

SMALL APPLIANCES

There are a number of small appliances that may be built into your kitchen or pantry. A garbage compactor 12" (or more) wide will compress (and deodorize) a full week's garbage into a 25-pound bag. An electric can opener might ease food preparation.

If you throw a lot of parties, you might consider installing heating ovens so that you or your caterer can heat precooked food. You could also put in an under-the-counter icemaker that will provide you with 25 pounds of ice a day.

A very convenient small appliance is a food center, actually a single motor-driven device that allows you to "plug in" a number of small convenience appliances. The motor is lodged beneath the counter with only a small plate showing on top. The plate contains a connecting device and control switch. The unit is designed to operate a mixing attachment, blender bowl, knife sharpener, fruit juicer, ice crusher, meat grinder, or full-sized food processor. Since they are motorless, the attachments are much lighter than their stand-alone cousins and are stored away in adjacent cabinets. The device is popular since it clears the counter of heavy appliances that are not used often.

A convenient kitchen-related item is the built-in ironing center, a narrow cabinet that holds one or more drop-down ironing boards, an iron, an outlet, and a spotlight.

WASHERS AND DRYERS

Where space is at a premium, especially in an apartment, a kitchen renovation might include the installation of a washing machine and a dryer. These appliances may be stacked one on top of the other in a corner of the kitchen or installed side by side under the counter. Not all manufacturers produce machines designed to fit under the counter. These front-loading models have their controls on the face of the machines rather than on the top. The most popular model is just shy of being full-sized. There are more choices in stackable combinations than there are for under-the-counter installations, most of them front-loading. Some models, designed for small households, are not full-sized and have the dryer suspended on a rack so that the washing machine can be top-loaded. One new model has a tilt-forward washing machine to facilitate top loading.

Most electric and (to our knowledge) all gas dryers must be vented to the outside through a duct pipe. The vent exhausts moisture-laden air to the outside of the house. The dryer must be located not much more than 10' from the outside of the house. (Some municipalities forbid an exhaust outlet that is placed within 8' of a window.) There is an electric dryer that does not require venting. The moisture from the drum goes into a pan at the bottom of the dryer which must be emptied periodically. This dryer can be located almost anywhere in the house.

STORAGE SPACE

Kitchen storage divides into three types: overhead cabinets, under-the-counter cabinets, and full-height closets.

The categories of items to be stored are more numerous. Food items that are frequently used should be stored close to the main kitchen action in overhead cabinets or in a full-height pantry. Items that are being stored for future use, like the extra roll of paper towels or the case of canned tomatoes, may be stored in an area peripheral to the kitchen. Spices should be stored near but not directly over the cooktop since heat might cause them to dry out too quickly. The best-designed spice cabinets are one jar deep. Some cooks prefer to keep the spice jars exposed rather than behind closed doors. Spice racks can be designed to fit on the inside of cabinet doors.

Pots and pans can be stored anywhere convenient to the cooktop. They are best stored at eye level in a full-height cabinet so that the cook does not have to bend to lift heavy pots. Next best is in under-the-counter cabinets on roll-out shelves which eliminate the necessity of poking one's head into the depths of the cabinet. Many cooks prefer to hang pots and pans on hooks adjacent to the range. Be sure not to hang the pots directly over the cooktop, because the exposed pots might be spattered with grease. It is not advisable to store heavy pots in over-the-counter cabinets. A heavy pan may fall off the shelf while you are rummaging around in the cabinet and can cause a good deal of damage.

Everyday dishes and glasses are best stored very close to the dishwasher. These may be located in the cabinets above the dishwasher or in a nearby full-height closet. Rarely used china, serving dishes, coffee urns, and crystal wine goblets can be stored anywhere in the kitchen or in a buffet cabinet in the dining room. Serving trays, cookie sheets, and flat broiler pans are generally stored on edge in a cabinet with vertical dividers. Silverware is best stored in a drawer near the dishwasher. Cooking utensils such as wooden spoons and basters should be in drawers close to the cooktop and/or ovens.

Frequently used small appliances, such as the toaster, toaster-oven, automatic coffee maker, food processor, and the like, are best left on a countertop as close to the breakfast area as possible. Less used appliances, such as the mixer and blender, are often stored in an under-the-counter cabinet. Again, a unit with roll-out shelves is preferable to one with fixed shelves. An innovative storage concept widens the counter to 2'-10" with a tambour or rolltop door enclosing the back 10" where the appliances are located. When planning the kitchen, remember to allocate space for the small-appliance accessories, such as blades for the processor and paper filters for the coffee maker.

Garbage, not really a long-term storage item, must be stored temporarily. Many householders find that a small pail attached to the inside door of the sink cabinet is enough. Most families find this pail to be inadequate. We suggest you install the small pail (for such wet items as eggshells and peelings) and plan on having a larger pail elsewhere. This garbage receptacle can be free-standing and moved where needed or can be built into the cabinetwork. One solution is a garbage "drawer" about 2'-6" high and 18" wide located near the sink. A plastic pail is inserted in the drawer, which can be opened and closed as needed.

Cabinets

Kitchen cabinets can be purchased ready to be installed or can be custom-made. Custom cabinets can be constructed in almost any style or size or to fit any configuration. The advantage of the custom cabinet is that it is made to fit the exact space of the kitchen and there is little wasted space and few "filler" panels. Custom cabinets can vary in height and depth, can be constructed in curved or trapezoid shapes, and can be very innovative in design. If constructed by a master cabinetmaker, the custom cabinet can be made as sturdy and as attractive as premium furniture.

Factory-made cabinets come in a wide variety of styles, prices, and levels of quality and may be less expensive than the custom-made kind (although premium American-made and imported cabinets are about as costly as good custom-made cabinets). If time is a major consideration, you might select factory-made cabinets that are in stock and ready for immediate delivery and installation. Since they are mass-produced, factory-made cabinets can be fabricated with details or finishing materials unavailable to the custom cabinetmaker or too expensive to produce for one kitchen. An added attraction is the wide selection of accessories for the interiors of the cabinets, such as spice and wine racks, corner-cabinet lazy Susans, pull-out and fold-out shelves, wire baskets, and drawer insets. The custom cabinetmaker can make most of these items but custom-made accessories are likely to be very costly.

There is also a line of semi-custom cabinets. These cabinets are made in the factory and, like ordinary stock cabinets, come in standard sizes. However, they are provided with filler strips that can be cut and fit around the standard cabinets to make the installation appear to be custom-built.

Most flush-door cabinets, either custom- or factory-made, are constructed of ¾"-thick plywood or particle board. The faces and edges of the plywood panels are covered in a veneer of either hardwood (such as oak, walnut, teak, or cherry) or plastic laminate (now in a wide variety of brand names, colors, and textures), or laminated with stainless steel, or sprayed with a shiny, durable paint. Flush-door cabinets can have simple metal or wood handles or pulls (or no pulls at all if you are using touch latches). Sometimes the pull is an integral part of the design in the guise of a long wood or metal strip with a carved finger groove. The strips can be mounted horizontally or vertically.

Paneled-door cabinets are generally constructed of a ¾"- or 1"-thick solid wooden frame with an insert of either plywood or glass. The hardwood of the frame and the wood veneer of the plywood inset are selected or stained to match. The wooden frames can have rounded edges and the juncture between frame and inset can be finished with trim pieces. The wooden doors and drawers can be coated with a clear finish showing the natural color and grain of the wood or can be stained slightly or much darker before finishing. The wood can be brushed with a semi-opaque white or pastel stain or can be spray-painted with a completely opaque color.

More elaborate cabinetwork includes brass inlays, molded acrylics, grooved insets, leaded glass, and tambour doors.

Cabinet Hardware

At some point along the line you will have to decide on the cabinet hardware, which includes door and drawer pulls, hinges, and other closure devices. If you are using factory-constructed cabinets, it is likely that the hinges will be part of the finished product, but you may be able to choose the door pulls from a preselected sampling.

Cabinet hinges are either exposed or concealed. The cabinet style that uses exposed hinges has hardwood frames and overlapping doors. The hinges are sometimes decorative and part of the design. The European look in cabinets has a door that completely covers the face of the cabinet and utilizes a concealed European hinge. A third style in hinges is the pivot hinge, which allows the doors to be set in a thin frame. The hinges are barely exposed in the far corners of the doors.

The concealed European hinge has a device that holds the cabinet closed. Mechanical or magnetic catches may be used with the other hinge types. If you do not wish to use door and drawer pulls on the cabinets, you may select a push latch that allows you to open the cabinet or drawer by gently pushing in. This releases the latch, opening the door or drawer a bit. You then manually open it further.

Pulls come in a wide variety of styles, from contemporary to traditional. Most require either one or two holes drilled through the face of the door or drawer. They come in brass, plastic, wood, and stainless steel, in a number of finishes or enameled in various colors.

Childproof latches may be used in addition to the hinges, pulls, and closure devices listed above. They are installed on the inside of cabinet doors to prevent children from getting into lower kitchen cabinets. To open the cabinet, you pull on the knob, partially opening the door. You then insert your hand into the cabinet to release the inside latch.

FINISHING MATERIALS

Counter Materials

We will begin our discussion by answering the most frequently asked question regarding countertops: No, there is no perfect, indestructible material for kitchen work areas. There are many good counter materials but each has its drawbacks.

Plastic laminate (more popularly known by the brand name Formica) is installed by gluing the fraction-of-an-inch-thick material to a ¾" plywood countertop. Laminate comes in a wide variety of colors and in a few subtle patterns and textures. (Some of the less than subtle patterns mimic wood grain.) Manufacturers produce two basic finishes, one shiny (and easily scratched) and the other matte. A third finish, available in limited patterns, is partially shiny. Some patterned laminates have indentations to conform to the patterns; these add to the textural interest of the material. At least one manufacturer features an abrasion-resistant laminate designed for countertops. Plastic laminate is a thin veneer of color applied to a base sheet and is available in three thicknesses. The thickest material is used on horizontal work surfaces, a thinner laminate is used for vertical surfaces such as cabinet doors, and backer board, the thinnest, is generally used on the inside of cabinets or to line shelves. One manufacturer produces a solid-core product that looks like ordinary laminate but is manufactured so that the color penetrates the entire thickness of the material. The main advantage is to eliminate

the dark line of the base material that is visible where ordinary laminated surfaces meet one another at right angles.

Plastic laminate *does* scatch if you cut directly on it, and it *will* stain under some conditions. You should not place hot pots directly on a laminated surface. Cutting boards and hot plates must be used to protect the surface.

Glazed ceramic tile, on the other hand, is stain-resistant and hard enough to cut on. It too comes in a wide variety of patterns, textures, and colors. One manufacturer provides special accessory tiles for counter use, such as tiles with raised-lip edges to limit spills from the counter. The problem with a ceramic tile counter is the grout that fills the spaces between the tiles. The grouted joints are prone to collecting dirt and food particles and stain easily. This problem is reduced somewhat by the use of a dark grout which blends in with the stains. (See Chapter 10 for more information on ceramic tiles.)

Granite and marble are often used on kitchen countertops. Granite is an extremely hard stone and takes a high polish. The polishing process seals the pores of the granite and makes it highly resistant to stains. It is, perhaps, the most durable of the counter materials. Still, you are advised not to cut on a highly polished granite counter since you will scratch the finish. Marble makes a particularly beautiful countertop but it is not stain-resistant and it can be scratched. Both materials are very expensive and must be cut professionally and installed to exact specifications to avoid cracking. (More information on marble and granite can be found in Chapter 10.)

Butcher block is often used so that the counter becomes a continuous cutting board. Although the material will scratch when repeatedly cut on, it can be sanded and refinished every few years. The main drawback to butcher block is that it is porous and can be stained. If the stain has penetrated deep enough, superficial sanding will not remove it. It should be noted that some health authorities no longer permit butcher-block work surfaces in restaurant food preparation areas, because the porous surfaces may absorb bacteria and are difficult to sanitize.

Another category of counter materials comprises composite plastic products designed to resemble stone. The first, well known by the brand name of Corian, comes in a few light colors and a marble pattern. The material should be cut professionally and must be well supported to avoid cracking. It is not stain-resistant but, like butcher block, it can be sanded every few years to eliminate scratch marks. Some manufacturers produce a substance that resembles polished granite. It shares a number of characteristics with Corian. As of this writing it has not been on the market long enough to establish a long track record of performance.

Counter color and texture should coordinate with the cabinets. Wood-patterned laminate should not be used with natural-wood cabinets. (We prefer natural or man-made materials that do not disguise themselves as something else rather than artificial products made to resemble natural ones. We would probably not use plastic laminate in a wood-grain pattern for any surface.) If you have plastic laminate on the doors of the cabinets, you can use any of the above materials for the counters. If you select laminate, you may choose the same color for the counter that you used for the doors or a slightly darker (or lighter) shade or a completely contrasting color. Wood cabinets also work with any of the above counter materials. Be careful in using butcher block with heavily grained wood cabinets. The two heavily patterned materials may look too busy together. Similarly, some ceramic tiles may be too overbearing for wood cabinets with a pronounced grain pattern.

The Backsplash

The wall space between the counter and the upper cabinets is called the backsplash. There are two reasons why some material needs to be put in this space. One, the area behind the counter, especially near the sink, should be protected from water and batter spattering. Second, the gap between the counter and the wall should be closed so that water and food do not fall in the crack. The backsplash is often only a few inches high, but we prefer (for aesthetic as well as practical reasons) to make the splash the full height of the space between counter and overhead cabinet.

An attractive backsplash is one covered in ceramic tile. The tiles can be plain or in elaborate patterns. The countertop can be made of any of the above-mentioned materials as long as you coordinate the tile color and pattern with the color of the counter. If you are using tile on the counter, you are advised to select the same tile or a closely related tile for the backsplash. Plastic-laminated plywood may be used with a laminate counter, and marble or granite backsplashes can be used with their counterparts.

Flooring

The two most commonly used kitchen floor surfaces are vinyl products in tile or sheet form or ceramic tiles. The best argument for a vinyl floor is that it has a more resilient surface than a ceramic floor and is, therefore, easier on the feet. Many people claim that objects dropped on resilient flooring are less likely to break. Also, the vinyl products are less expensive than ceramic tile and easier and cheaper to install. (See Chapter 10 for more details.)

Wood can be used on kitchen floors if it is cared for on a regular basis. The floor should be polyurethaned initially and maintained periodically by lightly roughing the surface and applying an additional layer of polyurethane. The floor should be cleaned by damp mopping. (More on wood flooring can be found in Chapter 10.)

Material Coordination

By this time you will be juggling four materials, one for the cabinet doors, the second for the countertops, the third for the backsplash, and the last for the floors. Generally, when designing the kitchen, the cabinet material, styling, and color are selected first, the countertop and flooring material second, the backsplash material, sinks and faucets, cabinet hardware, and lighting fixtures last. If you are using a cast-iron sink, you will be required to coordinate that color as well. (Paint and wallpaper are fairly easy and less critical since they can be changed more cheaply than the "built-in" materials.) Don't make any final material selections until you have samples of all of the materials in front of you. If you have one strongly patterned material, such as the backsplash tile, select nonpatterned counter material and flooring. You may use the same ceramic tile on floor and backsplash but not necessarily.

LIGHTING

Lighting the kitchen is often, unfortunately, an afterthought. Proper lighting in the kitchen is most important to avoid shadows, glare, dimness, and dark spots—not to mention being unable to see what you have in the pantry. There are two kinds of lighting to be considered in kitchen work areas: general illumination and task lighting. For general illumination, use ceiling fixtures to provide even, medium levels of light so that you can see into overhead cabinets and other shallow storage areas. These fixtures can be incandescent, providing a candlelike light, or fluorescent, providing a whiter-bluer glow. Many people prefer the softer light of the incandescent bulbs (called lamps or A lamps in the industry) in spite of the fact that they consume somewhat more electricity and produce more heat than their fluorescent counterparts. Fluorescent lights produce a shadowless, even light which many consider inappropriate for residential use outside of the kitchen. In recent years fluorescent technology has developed a number of tubes that attempt to imitate sunlight. The colors are much less blue than in traditional fluorescent tubes.

Both types of fixtures can be either surface-mounted to the ceiling or recessed into the ceiling in the space between the joists. The recessed incandescent fixtures are popularly known as high hats and come in versions that take A lamps as well as R-type spots and floods. The recessed fluorescents are not as readily available. Ceiling-mounted fixtures come in rounded domelike shapes or in squares and rectangles. Usually one multilamped incandescent or a single 2-square-foot fluorescent will provide enough general illumination for most kitchens. If the kitchen is particularly long or has side areas or recesses, you may want to use two or more smaller fixtures evenly spaced. Also consider using track lights in the kitchen. Don't forget to place a simple fixture (a plain porcelain socket will do) on the inside of deep pantries and broom closets.

When using incandescent ceiling fixtures, the amount of light can be controlled by using a dimmer or by selecting fixtures that take a spectrum of lamp sizes, say from 75 to 150 watts.

Task lighting provides a more intense light directly on countertops. The source of the illumination, which takes the form of long color-corrected fluorescent tubes or long mini-lamped fixtures, is concealed on the underside of the hung cabinets.

12

COMPLETING THE DESIGN OF THE BATHROOM

Whether you are contemplating a relatively minor cosmetic renovation, a radical change in your bathroom layout, or even creating a new bathroom from scratch, you will have to select new fixtures and materials. It is wise to familiarize yourself with the products available on the market before you crystallize your design decisions.

Regardless of size, all bathrooms have certain items in common: a toilet, a lavatory, and a tub or shower. These fittings need to be evaluated in terms of design, quality, cost, and space requirements.

BATHROOM FIXTURES

Bathtubs

The bathtub is perhaps the single major item in a bathroom. Tubs are available in a wide range of sizes, shapes, materials, and colors. The three principal materials used for bathtubs are enameled steel, cast iron, and fiberglass-reinforced acrylic. Enameled steel is adequate although not quite as durable as enameled cast iron. Acrylic plastics are used for particularly large or unusual shapes, since the material comes in sheet form and is pliable when heated. Most oversized bathtubs (those larger than 36" by 72") are made of fiberglass-reinforced acrylic.

A standard bathtub is a rectangle 32" wide by 60" long. There are some models as narrow as 30"

and as short as 48". For particularly tight spaces, corner bathtubs are available, generally in the range of 34" by 42". Of course, the actual dimensions and design vary with each manufacturer. As a general rule, renovators tend to provide the second bathroom with a standard bathtub if possible within the space constraints.

Master bathrooms are generally equipped with the larger and more exotic models. A popular size is 36" by 72". When space is tight a compromise size is the 36"-by-66" model. There are, of course, much larger sizes, up to 64" by 83". With the increase in size, there is also an increase in available shapes. Ovals are rather popular. Tubs designed for two and even four people are also on the market. These large tubs are almost invariably equipped with whirlpools.*

In the last few years, the demand for tubs with whirlpools has increased substantially. For this reason, manufacturers have developed compact models. There is an efficiently sized model at 32" by 48" which is particularly aimed at renovators. (There are also tubs, specifically designed for renovations, with above-the-floor drainage to facilitate the installation.) Those of you with a bit more space can take a look at more standard sizes, such as 30" by 60" and 32" by 66". The depths and shapes of these tubs are all slightly different. Once you know the specific dimensions that you have to work with, go to the showroom and actu-

*A new swimming tub on the market, about 4' by 12', has a built-in current for swimming in place, the swimmer's equivalent to the treadmill.

ally get into each of the tubs available in that size. We all differ in height and shape, so what one person finds most comfortable might prove back-breaking for someone else. Bear in mind that any bathtub equipped with a whirlpool also has electrical requirements. In addition, an access panel needs to be provided for the motor.

Another popular tub alternative is the soaking tub. These tubs are specifically designed for sitting or reclining and soaking. They are usually round with a built-in bench. The depth is much greater than that of a standard tub (about 30" vs. 15"). If you choose a soaking tub, you may need to build platforms around it for ease of access. The popularity of soaking tubs has been partially responsible for the revival of the old-fashioned bathtub on legs. The basic design has been updated to provide increased comfort. There is an important difference between a platform tub and a soaking tub with three walled sides. A tub designed exclusively for use in a platform cannot be used as a shower-tub combination. A separate shower enclosure needs to be provided elsewhere in the bathroom.

The color selection available for tubs (and for every other bathroom fixture) is extraordinary. The realm of basic white or pastels of thirty years ago is gone. Now there are several grays, beiges, whites, pinks and near pinks, blues, cranberries, browns, blacks, yellows, greens, reds, navies, taupes, and much more. Every year new colors are introduced to accommodate the latest fashions.

Lavatories

The two principal materials used for lavatories are vitreous china and enameled cast iron. They are also available in other materials, such as stainless steel, glazed fireclay, and Corian, a trade name for a man-made composite material (see Chapter 11). In addition to the standard materials, there are lavatories made out of hammered brass, chrome, and painted porcelain. Both vitreous china and enameled cast iron are excellent materials. The smaller sinks are usually made out of vitreous china whereas the larger ones are enameled cast iron. Stainless steel is a good material but its use is more associated with kitchen and utility sinks than with bathrooms. Glazed-fireclay lavatories are not so readily available and they do have limitations in terms of wear and tear. There are some, however, primarily imports from Mexico, which offer a great variety of unique designs and colors. Corian sinks are becoming popular, particularly since they offer an "integral sink" design. This

means that the lavatory is molded together with the countertop, offering a clean surface without joints or edges. It is an attractive cleaning feature.

There are three main types of lavatories: pedestal, countertop, and wall-hung. Pedestal sinks are the traditional favorites and the ones that older homes were equipped with. Because they are free-standing, they make small rooms feel larger. If planning to use a pedestal sink, provide additional shelf storage elsewhere in the bathroom. Most pedestal sinks have little room on their ledges for anything more than soap. Wall-hung sinks were designed later on and emphasized space saving and ease of maintenance. Houses built in the 1940's and early 1950's usually feature wall-hung sinks. From the late 1950's on, the emphasis was placed on countertop lavatories. By installing a sink directly on a countertop a vanity could be provided underneath for storage while getting extra surface space for soaps and other bathroom paraphernalia. Countertop sinks come in two basic designs: self-rimming for over-the-counter installation and rimless for under-the-counter installation. Self-rimming sinks are the most popular. Below-the-counter models are generally used when the counter material is marble or granite. It is interesting to note that while countertop sinks are still the favorite for master baths and second bathrooms, pedestal sinks have again become very popular—this time for use in powder rooms, where storage and counter-space needs are not as great.

Lavatory sizes vary as much as their designs. The most common size for a sink is 19" wide by 17" deep. There are, of course, many other sizes, ranging from 38" by 22" at one extreme to 12"-deep sinks to fit in tight spaces; some are oval, some round, some square. When choosing a countertop sink, keep in mind whether the faucet set is to be mounted on the sink itself or on the counter. This affects the usable space left for grooming. The sink's depth and shape are also important. The deeper the sink, the more comfortable and self-contained it will be. The shallower the sink, the more water will splash onto the counter and floor. In terms of shape, round sinks are perhaps the least efficient. Rectangles and ovals tend to give more usable space and less water overflow.

Lavatories are available in even more colors than tubs. In addition, they also come with patterns, stripes, and designs with color gradations. Some of the new models have nickel and copper finishes (polished or brushed) and there are some that are teak.

If you are replacing the lavatory in your bathroom without changing the rough plumbing, be sure the new sink can be installed with the existing plumbing configuration. Also, if you are replacing a lavatory and are not changing the countertop, be sure the new lavatory will cover all of the existing opening. Should you decide to change the lavatory and not the faucet (or vice versa), be sure they are coordinated. One-hole lavatories must be equipped with a one-hole faucet fitting. Likewise a faucet set with a 4" or 8" spread is designed to fit only on lavatories with this hole spacing.

Toilets

Toilets are made out of vitreous china, which is durable, easily cleaned, and hygienic. There are two types of toilet: the flush tank and the flushometer. Tank toilets are generally found in one- and two-family homes. Flushometer models are used primarily in large apartment buildings. They are noisier than most tank models but have a stronger cleaning action. Tank toilets are designed as either one- or two-piece units. One-piece toilets have the tank integrally designed into the overall shape. These models tend to be the most contemporary in design and also are the most expensive. Because they are at the top of the line, they are designed to have a very quiet flushing mechanism. Two-piece toilets have a separate tank and seat and they are the most commonly used. A variation on the two-piece toilet is the pull-chain "vintage" toilet, which is presently becoming popular for period renovations.

When selecting a toilet, keep in mind the amount of water pressure present in the system. Flushometer-type toilets function well with high water pressure. Low-tank toilets work with moderate pressure. The higher the tank, the easier it is for the flushing mechanism to work, regardless of the water pressure. Toilets are also available in water-saver models.

The size of a toilet varies, particularly the length. The one-piece contemporary designs tend to be long and wide. Their advantage is that they are low. The more traditional two-piece toilets tend to be more consistent in size. A good rule of thumb is to allow for a minimum of 2'-6" in both width and length for the toilet. If you are thinking of replacing your toilet and not enlarging the bathroom, make sure that the new toilet will fit in the bathroom with room to stand in front and for straddling. The new toilets are much larger than their predecessors. There are only a few models on the market that are 25" in length; most are in

the range of 28" to 30" long. In addition, if you are replacing the toilet without changing the rough plumbing, be sure the drainage requirements of the new toilet (called the roughing-in dimension, measured from the rear wall to the center of the pipe in the floor) conform to the existing conditions. (We've seen some ill-matched replacement toilets that were so far from the wall that they looked as if they were standing in the center of the room.)

In terms of colors, toilets come in as wide a palette as tubs and sinks. Generally, however, one-piece models are available in the greatest range of colors, two-piece designs are slightly more limited in color selection, and flushometer toilets have the fewest color options.

Bidets

While Europeans (with the exception of the English) have traditionally included bidets as part of their bathroom design, these fixtures are relative newcomers to the American bathroom. Like toilets, they are made out of vitreous china. The number of bidet designs is rather limited in comparison with other bathroom fixtures. The main reason is that their use has not become mainstream in this country. They are generally left to the realm of master bathroom design in the more expensive renovations. Each manufacturer has three or four models, which usually complement their top-of-the-line toilets in both design and color. They are approximately 14" to 16" wide and 30" long (measured from the wall) including the fittings. Since bidets are generally straddled, with the user facing the wall, 1'-6" should be left clear on either side of the center line.

Bidets come with two varieties of fittings, one that operates like a sink and fills from a nozzle outletting above the rim, the other with a nozzle that sprays upward from the bottom of the bowl. Before making your selection, check the municipal code. The bottom-of-the-bowl model may not be permitted in your municipality. You may be allowed to use this model if you equip it with an anti-siphoning device.

Bathing and Shower Modules

Bathing modules are becoming increasingly popular, particularly for renovation projects. These units consist of an integral bathtub-shower and surrounding wall enclosure. By providing a finished wall surface around the bathing area, these units offer substantial savings in cost and installation time. (Traditional tiling and grouting of walls is completely eliminated.) Bathing modules are made of reinforced fiberglass or plastics. Be aware that their use is not permitted in all localities.

Modules come in basically three different types. There are one-piece units with no seams. They are easy to clean, having no cracks or crevices to collect dirt. These units are best suited for new construction. (If you decide to buy a one-piece module, make sure you have enough clearance to bring it into the space through doors, stairs, elevators, etc.*) Two-piece units are designed in two sections, the lower shower or tub and the upper enclosure. This design offers a good solution to the problem of clearances through the building. A variation on the module is called the bath or shower surround. This plastic surround is designed to coordinate with bathtubs and shower receptors. The wall panels come in five pieces (two end panels, one back wall panel, and two corner panels). The result is a module "look" with the ease of assembly of smaller pieces.

Bathing modules come in a variety of sizes, ranging from the standard 32" by 60" bathtub to a 32" by 36" shower. They are available with several options, such as ledges for soap and shampoo, storage shelves, corner seats, and grab bars, and come in a good number of colors.

Showers

A custom shower consists of a shower pan with a drain and a wall enclosure. The shower pan collects the water and directs it to the drain, preventing water from leaking to the floor structure below. Shower pans have traditionally been made out of lead. Lead, although durable, is heavy and difficult to work with. Plastic pans made of heavy-gauge vinyl are also available. They are easier to work with and are lighter than lead pans. An added bonus is that plastic pans are cheaper. Not all municipalities allow the use of plastic. Check before finalizing your decision.

Ceramic tile is applied over the shower pan and all walls surrounding the shower. Care must be taken to grout the tiles properly. All joints between dissimilar materials should be caulked with silicone. The enclosure has to be kept watertight.

A shower stall should be no less than 30" by 30". A more comfortable size for a shower is 36"

*We know of one unit that was hoisted fourteen stories. The window and its frame had to be removed to get the module in.

by 36". Keep in mind when deciding on the size that you need elbow room and room for bending.

FITTINGS

The number of bathroom fittings presently on the market is rather impressive, with designs ranging from strictly contemporary to period reproductions. In terms of materials, the standard fittings are chrome-plated brass. They are also available in other finishes, such as satin chrome, polished and satin brass, pewter, and even gold. For those interested in ease of maintenance there are washerless fittings. At the very least you will need a faucet set for the lavatory, a bathtub filler, and a shower head. Any and all of these items can be purely utilitarian or extraordinarily luxurious, depending on your budget and general requirements.

Lavatory fittings (faucets) can be either single- or double-handled. Most people tend to choose double handles for the bathroom while leaving the single-lever models for purely utilitarian areas such as the kitchen and laundry room. Sinks come with holes to accommodate the faucets, which are mounted either directly on the holes in the sink or on a metal deck. Faucets can be installed directly on the countertop as well. (This is generally done with under-the-counter sinks.) Faucet handles are available in a vast number of designs from basic metals to Lucite and stones such as marble and onyx. Most lavatories are designed to take either a 4" or 8" spread set or one hole, depending on the spacing of the holes.

Tub fillers are generally available to match the lavatory selection. They are either wall-mounted or deck-mounted. Wall-mounted designs are usually combined with diverters and shower heads. Deck-mounted tub fillers are most often designed for bathrooms that have a separate tub with enough room around it to allow for the deck installation. If using an extra-large tub, be sure to select a tub filler of the appropriate size. Otherwise it may take a very long time to fill the bathtub. In addition, if the deck-mounted tub has a wide rim, you may need an extra-long faucet.

Shower fittings, like tub fillers, come in designs to match those of the lavatory and tub. If you have a preference for a shower head with varying pressure and water jets, make sure that the design you select offers these options. It is sometimes possible to substitute shower heads within the same faucet design. There are models that feature automatic temperature controls which maintain the water at the set degrees during your entire shower. Hand showers are also becoming popular as an additional feature.

FINISHINGS

Accessories

There are a number of accessories that are essential in a bathroom. You need towel bars, towel rings, a toilet-paper holder, and hooks. In addition, you may need soap and toothbrush holders. Many companies offer towel bars, rings, and toilet-paper holders that match some of their more expensive fittings. Many other models are available, ranging from traditional to strictly contemporary. Although most bathroom accessories are made of either metal or porcelain, they are also available in enameled or plastic-covered metals and in Lucite. Towel bars come in lengths of 18" to 24". The other accessories are relatively standard in size. It may be hard to find ceramic fittings to match your tile walls.

Wall and Floor Materials

As with every other aspect of bathroom design, your choice of materials largely depends on the size of your budget. There is no question that you need a water-resistant material next to bathtub and shower walls. The remaining walls and even the floor can be surfaced with pretty much anything you like. We must note, however, that it makes good sense to cover the bathroom floor with a water-resistant surface. In fact, many codes require a ceramic tile floor and base. (For a discussion of ceramic tile, see Chapter 10.)

Lighting

Adequate light is important in a bathroom, particularly at the bathroom sink. In order to shave and apply makeup you need even illumination for your face. The best place to locate the lights is on the wall (rather than the ceiling) directly above the sink. The lights could be at either side of the mirror or at the top of the mirror in a continuous line. If your bathroom is small, this light will probably be sufficient for the entire room. Larger bathrooms may require additional lights. These are often placed directly above the shower or tub.

(Make sure that it is a water-resistant type of fixture.) Often bathroom lights are combined with exhaust vents.

Medicine Cabinets and Mirrors

Medicine cabinets come in many shapes, sizes, and materials. At the very least, a medicine cabinet should have enough room for toothbrushes, combs, prescription drugs, etc. It is also helpful if it is large enough to store hair dryers, shavers, and extra shampoo bottles. The most common size for a medicine cabinet is 18" or 24" wide by 30" long. It is usually placed directly above the sink and has mirror doors. Other locations, such as the walls at either side of the sink or directly above the toilet, are also possible. A vertical (floor-to-ceiling) medicine cabinet can be helpful where width is a problem.

Medicine cabinets can be recessed into the wall or surface-mounted. Their depth should be a minimum of 3½", leaving 3" of clear shelf space inside. Deeper medicine cabinets are even better. A 6"-deep cabinet allows you to store items such as water picks and electric curlers.

Stock medicine cabinets are readily available in bathroom and tile supply stores. Their designs (from traditional to contemporary) vary as much as their prices. These cabinets are usually made out of metal or plastic with adjustable glass shelves. Some come with built-in lights. Custom-designed cabinets are generally made out of plywood or particle board covered with plastic laminate for ease of cleaning. The shelves can be glass or laminate.

Mirrors (whether on the doors of the medicine cabinets or elsewhere in the room) are important to bathroom design. You need a mirror to comb your hair and to shave. A mirror should be placed directly over the sink. The top edge should be at least 6' from the floor. Several lights on the wall directly above the mirror or at either side give you the best illumination. Small bathrooms could be made to feel larger by placing mirrors on several walls. Mirrors placed directly across from a window could brighten even the darkest of bathrooms. Mirrors come in clear, bronze, and silver colorings. The type most often used for bathrooms is 3/16" safety plate glass.

Shower Doors

Shower doors come in three basic styles: folding, sliding, and swinging. Sliding doors are generally used for tub-shower combinations. Folding or swinging doors are installed in shower stalls. The door frame is available in chrome-plated brass, polished and satin brass, anodized aluminum, stainless steel, and even baked-on color finishes. The panels are either plastic, clear laminate safety glass, or tempered glass. They can be clear, bronze, textured, or even have a mirrored finish. Shower-door manufacturers have a wide range of stock sizes and finishes. More unusual sizes or shapes are custom-built. When ordering a custom unit you need to allow approximately six to eight weeks for fabrication and installation.

13

STORAGE SPACES

While houses in the past had little or no closet space, houses and apartments are presently rated in terms of their ability to store our accumulated possessions. We may argue that we buy too much or that we get rid of too little. One way or the other, however, almost every home or apartment dweller inevitably echoes the same complaint: "There's not enough storage space." In the process of renovation, you will most likely be attempting to increase your capacity to store anything from bicycles (new and old) to belts and ties.

Storage can be divided into different categories. The first, bulk storage, is for items such as patio and terrace furniture, snow tires, suitcases, etc. Some of these are used seasonally, other items are being stored for future use, and some are things you simply can't part with. The second category is functional storage. This refers to items that are used on a regular basis, such as tools, toys, clothing, linens, bicycles, gardening tools, etc. While bulk storage can be relegated to a remote room, the cellar, or the attic, functional storage items need to be readily accessible.

BULK STORAGE

We all have pieces of furniture that belonged to someone dear to us, a stereo system that we saved for our kids (but is now outdated), and extra chairs for company. We also have unused tricycles, boxes with paraphernalia from college days,

and gowns that have long been out of style. It is very difficult, if not impossible, to part with any of these items. After all, this is what attics and basements (if they do not flood) are for. Unfortunately, not everybody has an attic or a usable (or unusable) basement. The following suggestions are for those who do not have either cellar or attic or for renovators who are reclaiming these areas as living space.

A separate bulk-storage room is a good alternative to an attic or a basement. Under ideal circumstances, this room should be large and square or rectangular in shape. We all know that this is probably wishful thinking. Even an odd-shaped space could serve if properly organized. A wall of shelves or hooks is always useful to take advantage of the vertical space in addition to the available floor area. Folding chairs and bikes can be hung on hooks high above the floor. It is also important that this room be provided with a door wide enough to allow large items to be brought in and out easily. Finally, try to locate the storage room in an area with easy access. Locating it along a narrow corridor or a twisting stairway could severely limit the size of the items which you could store. Adequate clearance is important when dealing with large pieces of furniture or equipment.

In circumstances where house or apartment space is at a premium, you have to be more creative in finding solutions to storage problems. Look for unused square feet, such as those under the stairs. Is there space along a wide hallway that can be claimed? How about areas where lack of

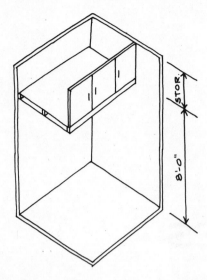

ILL. 1

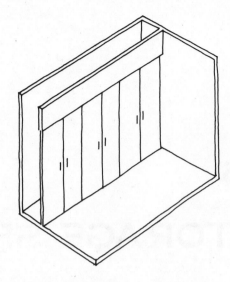

ILL. 2

headroom precludes any other use, such as a crawl space? An old trick often used by apartment dwellers is to steal vertical space. When rooms are very tall, you may be able to provide "dead storage" by lowering the room's ceiling height and providing an access door between the actual and the dropped ceiling (Ill. 1). These spaces are ideal for suitcases and boxes. There are even instances (particularly in lofts and brownstones, where ceiling heights are very generous) in which storage lofts can be designed. For example a 13'-high room could have a partial balcony at about 8' from the floor. This allows plenty of headroom below while leaving a space above of approximately 4' in height for storage purposes.*

Storage walls are another solution. This approach has become very popular, particularly with people who have reclaimed their attics and basements as living space. A storage wall can be created by erecting a new wall a minimum of 3' to 4' in front of the original wall of the room (Ill. 2). The wall is then provided with enough doors to allow every square inch of space to be reached. Many homeowners have found that this solution has not only provided them with sufficient bulk storage but also forced them to organize themselves more efficiently. As a result, everything has a place and is within easy reach when needed.

*Keep in mind that these areas must have sufficient structure to carry the weight of the items being stored.

HOUSEHOLD ITEMS

Household items is a catchall category for every type of storable that needs to be easily accessible. Clothing, shoes, toys, and linens all fall under this heading. In addition, skateboards, bicycles, snow shovels, gardening tools, lawn mowers, etc., should be included. Some of these items need to be within the house or apartment, whereas others must be reached easily from the outside.

Let's begin with the storage of outside items such as strollers, roller skates, sleds, etc., which traditionally have been stored in the garage with lawn mowers, snow shovels, and gardening tools. You may be lucky enough to have a garage large enough to accommodate all of these objects. Owners of garageless homes or apartments have more of a problem. Unless the apartment building offers a separate storage facility, you may have no choice but to store these outside items. A place close to the entrance (preferably the back entrance) adjacent to the backyard or elevator is the best choice. (You don't want your kid to drag a wet sled or a muddy bike right through your house.) This area needs to be relatively large with a wide doorway. (As a general rule, the smaller the space, the larger the doors for ease of access.) Apartment owners often hang their bicycles from hooks on walls or ceilings. This allows two bicycles to be hung next to each other (or above each other) along a wall. The beauty of this solution is that it takes away little of the precious floor space.

Tools

Tool storage is also important. As a renovator, it is likely that you have quite a few of them. Most people see the basement as the logical place for tool storage. (Be aware that a damp basement can ruin your tools.) Basements are not the only sanctuary for tools; they can be stored practically anywhere in the building. One criterion remains important, however. They need to be easily accessible. Tool closets are a good solution. This closet can be as shallow as 18" or as deep as you can make it. It could be efficiently organized with shelving from top to bottom. You'll be surprised at the number of tools, nails, screws, and other paraphernalia that even a 2'-wide tool closet can provide you with.

Cleaning

Vacuum cleaners, brooms, dust mops, etc., need to be stored. The most common location for these items is in or close to the kitchen. Where space is at a premium, you can include a small broom closet in the kitchen for mops and brooms and store the vacuum cleaner and its attachments elsewhere in the house. Don't forget to allocate space for irons and ironing boards.

Toys

The space needed for toy storage is often underestimated, considering the number of assorted toys, games, and small (and not so small) items that children can accumulate. A further complication is that some toys belong to one child and others are to be shared by all the children. Ideally you may have a recreation room or playroom where the toys can be stored. Otherwise you may need to store them somewhere in the children's rooms. We have found that closet space with ample shelving and various-sized bins is a good solution to most toy-storage problems. The shelves can accommodate most board games, coloring books, etc., while the bins offer a place for unusual-shaped items, building blocks, cooking utensils, etc. We have found that shelves between 12" and 18" in depth seem to accommodate most toys. Rather than locking yourself into a specific height for the shelves, an adjustable shelving system with provision for bins is generally the most efficient.

Linens

Linens take up a surprising amount of space. Many small houses and apartments contain a linen closet that hardly accommodates the linen-storage requirements of an average college student (two sets of sheets and two towels). Most families need storage for a few sets of sheets and towels for each family member—not to mention bath mats and rugs. There are also blankets for winter and for spring, comforters and extra pillows, all of which take quite a bit of space. We have found that, where space allows, it makes good sense to provide two separate linen closets. One could be located close to or within the master bedroom. The second closet could service the remaining bedrooms and baths. This arrangement allows each family member to take care of his own linen requirements. Children can find their towels and favorite pillows and comforters without need of adult involvement. Conversely, the parents' linens could be kept in relative order. If you have room for only one linen closet, you can use different shelves for each room and bathroom. Be sure to provide space for toilet paper and guest towels. Linen closets are generally 18" deep. The minimum width should be no less than 2', with shelves approximately every 18" apart.

Storage must also be found for table linens. Tablecloths, napkins, and place mats can be stowed away in a piece of furniture in the dining room if closet space is not available. If space allows, a small closet for table linens is an excellent idea. Quite often, a few drawers for table and kitchen linens are included in the kitchen cabinetry or pantry.

Clothing

Our preference for the way our clothing is stored may be as much a matter of personal choice as the selection of our clothing. Although the requirements for storage of these items are fairly standardized, we have found after years of renovation experience that every person has his own idea as to how best to store his personal belongings. Some people prefer to hang everything from nightgowns to jumpsuits. Others like to keep everything in drawers, providing hanging space only for items like jackets and dresses. Some argue that shelves are more efficient than drawers. The bottom line is that you have to assess how much hanging, drawer, and shelf space best suits your needs.

There are two types of closets: standard and

walk-in. The walk-in closet is preferred by many because it can hold all their clothing items from blouses and shirts to shoes. Walk-in closets can be double- or single-aisled. Double-aisled closets should be a minimum of 6' in width (in very tight conditions you can get away with 5'-6"). Single-aisled closets (which are not very efficient) can be as narrow as 4'-6" (Ill. 3). Wall space not used for hanging purposes can be provided with shelves and drawers to accommodate sweaters, lingerie, shoes, and handbags (Ill. 3). This type of closet should be provided with overhead light.

Standard closets are most commonly found in houses and apartments. They are a minimum of 2' in depth and are usually equipped with one hanging rod and a shelf above. Please note that a depth of 2'-1" to 2'-3" is ideal for a closet of this type. A closet 3' deep is wasteful of space because you can't fit any more clothing into it. The key to taking maximum advantage of this type of closet is to provide it with doors wide enough to eliminate unusable corners. The larger the door opening, the easier it is to gain access to the entire interior. In houses and apartments with particularly high ceilings, shelves can be installed in the high areas for rarely used items (Ill. 4). Fluorescent light strips can be installed directly above the door; they can be switch-operated or provided

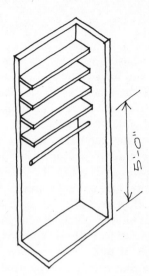

ILL.4

with a mechanism that turns the light on when the door is opened.

There are a few more critical dimensions important to know when planning your closets. Hanging rods are usually installed at 5'. This is a good hanging height for dresses and coats. To make maximum use of the space, two rods can be installed above each other. Measure the clothing you want to hang to determine their vertical spacing. Men's suit jackets require 39", women's blouses require 29". Long dresses, robes, and jumpsuits need to be hung at a minimum of 5'-10" from the floor to avoid dragging. In our experience, an efficient design for closet space has some 5' hanging, with the rest of the closet provided with double hanging. This approach makes maximum use of the available linear feet of space (Ill. 5).

It is not uncommon to have a separate closet space for shoes, pocketbooks, and hats, which need only about 1' in depth. Some people prefer to segregate their dusty shoes from their clothing by providing a separate closet just for shoes. A shoe closet can be as simple as a series of adjustable shelves. This type of shelving gives you the flexibility to make adjustments for different-height heels and boots. Some people prefer to store their shoes on the incline. We have found that this may be a problem with shoes not having a traditional heel, such as sneakers and rubber-soled shoes. It does, however, allow you to store shoes in shallower spaces (Ill. 6).

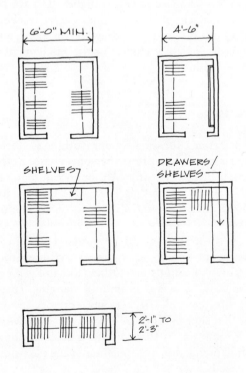

ILL.3

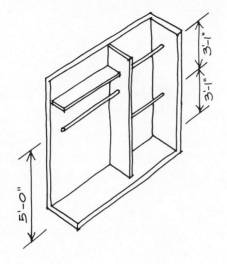

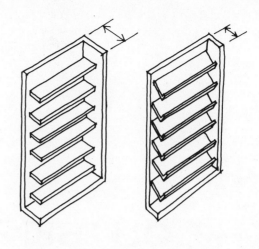

ILL.5

ILL.6

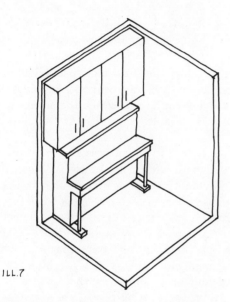

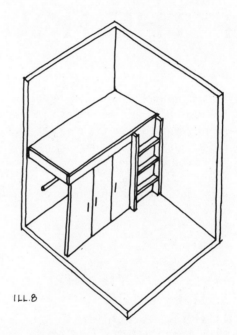

ILL.7

ILL.8

STORAGE STRATEGIES

Some houses and apartments are so small that nontraditional uses must be made of space in order to provide for storage. We once redesigned a two-bedroom apartment into a four-bedroom unit. In order to provide room for the upright piano, we usurped the 5'-wide linen closet. A new, shorter linen closet was built above the piano (Ill. 7). A 4'-wide hallway was redesigned as a 3' corridor with a 1'-deep storage wall containing broom closet, telephone table, mail slots, and book-bag storage.

Beds in the children's rooms can be raised to 4'-6" to provide short hanging and shelf space below if you have the necessary ceiling height. Raising the bed to 6' above the floor provides you with a full-height closet (Ill. 8).

If you are thinking of building a platform above your existing floor, raise it to at least 18" and install a series of trapdoors in the floor. (The doors and hardware can be covered by area rugs.)

One renovator we know even used the 3½" stud spaces in the partitions between rooms to house anything and everything that could fit into the 3½"-deep spaces. His walls were a series of panels operated by touch latches.

If you have very high ceilings, it is more efficient to build a closet over a closet (with full 2'-deep shelves and a separate door) than to have 1' shelves above the hanging. This space is great for dead bulk storage or seasonal items.

In small bedrooms or home offices, storage space can be provided without losing precious floor space by hanging overhead kitchen-type cabinets on the walls as high as possible.

14

THE OUTSIDE
OF THE HOUSE

Renovation can involve not only a building's interior but also its exterior. Some of you may be thinking of adding a porch, a deck, or perhaps even a greenhouse. Others may be more ambitious and be contemplating the addition of one or more rooms to the house. We are including this chapter for those of you who are modifying the exterior of your building.

PROJECTING TO THE OUTSIDE: DECKS, PORCHES, AND GREENHOUSES

A transition from outside to inside is a welcome amenity in any house. The first step is to determine which rooms would benefit most from having access to an outdoor space. An outdoor eating area has been a traditional favorite. This area, be it a porch (open or screened in), deck, or greenhouse, should be within easy reach from the kitchen or dining room. Providing outdoor space next to a family room or den is also desirable. For those who enjoy privacy, a deck adjacent to the bedroom seems a likely choice.

As a general rule, there is no room in the house that would not be enhanced by projection to the outside. The type of outdoor space may vary with the room. For example, you may want to have a screened-in porch for eating, a greenhouse as part of the family room, and a deck for the master

bedroom. Each of these outdoor spaces will offer a different amenity. The greenhouse provides the option of year-round use, while the screened-in porch allows you to be outdoors rain- and insect-free.

The next issue to consider is that of privacy. While openness within the house is limited by every individual's need for privacy from the rest of the family, openness to the outside is affected by the need for privacy from the street and neighbors. Older houses show more evidence of this concern than their newer counterparts. As you walk through older towns and neighborhoods, you will find many houses with front porches. (By the way, the "sitting porch," or veranda, is considered by historians to be an American invention.) These porches serve as buffer zones between what is public and what is private. Someone sitting on his front porch becomes a part of the street life while still being in his separate, semi-private domain. This is not the case when a person sits on the front lawn. Strangers are aware that the lawn is private property. Yet someone sitting or relaxing on his front lawn is a conspicuous element in the street scene. Generally, people will prefer sitting in the backyard, where there is more likelihood of privacy. As architects, we have found that most of our clients have wanted the outside space to be oriented toward those areas of the house most isolated from street and neighbors.

Finally you should take into account orientation to the sun. While a greenhouse with a southeast exposure can be a great asset to a space, one facing due west could be very unpleasant on a summer afternoon. If you have a choice of locations, try to consider which exposure will be more appropriate for your climatic conditions. (See Chapter 19 for·additional information on orientation and the path of the sun.)

Decks

Decks can be constructed out of metal or wood. Wooden decks are more popular, for the simple reason that they are the easiest for the novice to build. There are basically three types of wood that can be used: cedar, redwood, or pressure-treated lumber. Any other wood would tend to rot unless constantly painted. Pressure-treated lumber is the cheapest of the three and for this reason the one most commonly used. It has a greenish tint that is not attractive at first but, fortunately, turns silver in time. Cedar is initially more attractive but more costly. When first installed, cedar is a warm light brown; this slowly turns into a grayish silver. Although cedar does not require an applied finish, we have found that it is most durable and weathers more evenly when protected with a stain (be it transparent, semi-transparent, or bleaching). Redwood is a handsome and durable wood that does not need an applied finish. Because it is presently very scarce, it is the most expensive of the three choices.

Metal decks are more rarely seen since they are more expensive and entail metalworking skills that are not easily acquired. In addition, people often associate metal decks with fire escapes and institutional applications. Not all metal decks need to be unattractive. Perhaps thinking of New Orleans rather than an inner-city tenement can help you visualize the possibilities of designing with metal. Before you make the final decision on using wood or metal, make sure to check with the local building department. There are municipalities in which metal decks are required by law for reasons of fire safety (usually in densely populated urban areas). Metal decks do require maintenance against rust. They have to be painted periodically with a rust-inhibitive undercoat and one or two coats of paint over it.

We have found that combining wood and metal can result in a very interesting deck. Because metal is stronger than wood, a structural framework made out of metal can use much smaller members than one made out of wood. The result is a lighter, more delicate deck. Wood decking can be fitted into the metal framework. It can

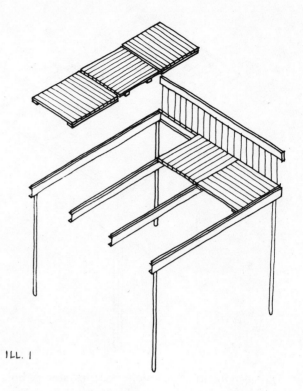

ILL. 1

also be used to cap railings and as treads for the stairs. The introduction of these wood elements provides you with the warmth of wood and the lightness of metal. The result is a very handsome product that accentuates the best qualities of both materials (Ill. 1). An additional advantage to this approach is that this type of deck is often accepted by the building departments requiring metal decks. The logic behind it is that the basic structure is built out of metal with wood serving only as a nonstructural, purely aesthetic element.

Decks can be laid out in many different shapes and sizes. Rectangles and squares are the most popular, since they are the easiest to build. Angles and curves are generally left to the more experienced or the professional builder. Keep in mind that decks should be kept in proportion to the house and to the property surrounding it. We have seen many renovators build enormous decks that have dwarfed their houses in addition to covering most of the available open space. If the deck is up on the second floor or if you have a usable basement underneath, remember that a large deck will block the sunlight for the windows in the lower floor.

A deck is not necessarily better because it is larger. An efficiently designed deck can be more useful and attractive than an overscale one. Decks

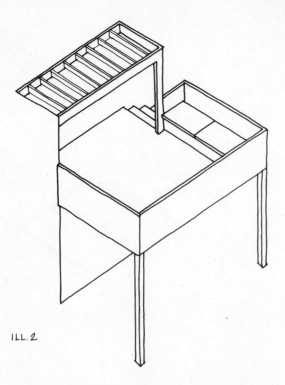

ILL. 2

can incorporate arbors, benches, storage bins, and planters (Ill. 2). An arbor or trellis can offer shade with its rich latticework covered with vines. When space is at a premium, built-in benches give you the extra room you need. Similarly, an arbor can offer you shade and privacy in a densely built area. Storage bins are very helpful, particularly where there is not much room to stow outdoor-related items such as gardening tools.

There are a few basic points that you should remember when designing your deck. Wooden decks need posts which are usually 4″ × 4″. For spans, refer to Chapters 16 and 21. All wood should be kept away from the earth to avoid insect infestation. Metal decks are constructed with Lally columns as the vertical supports; these are usually 3″ or 4″ in diameter. The metal spans (by means of steel channels or beams) can be longer than those of wood. The railing around the deck should be approximately 36″ high. Many codes mandate a minimum of 6″ of space between either vertical or horizontal railings. Those of you with young children should consider the potential hazards of designing widely spaced horizontal elements in the railings. Vertical rails placed at close intervals (about 3″ apart so that a child's head cannot get stuck between supports) are one of the safest designs for children.

Porches

Porches are a more integral part of the building than a deck, for the simple reason that a porch has a roof. This is one of the most attractive aspects of a porch. You can be outside in the rain or under the scorching sun and be protected. A porch can be provided with removable screens. During the spring and fall, the screens can be stored. In the dead of summer when bugs are out en masse, you can install the screens and have a safe haven. Removable glass panels could also be designed to allow the porch to be used during the winter months.

The materials used in the porch will be determined by those used in the rest of the building. Most likely the porch, like the house, will be built out of wood. The type of wood would be similar to that of the house and would be painted or stained to match. In planning a porch keep in mind its proportions. The porch should not dwarf the house but rather should complement it. Similarly, the roof of the porch should be designed to enhance the lines of the existing roof.

Greenhouses

In the past greenhouses were used primarily by people who enjoyed gardening or raising house plants. Now they are quite popular for other purposes. A greenhouse is often installed as an extension to a room in the house and is a welcome addition to a playroom, dining area, sitting room, or even a bathroom. A greenhouse may also be used in place of a corridor to connect two spaces. The primary advantage of a greenhouse is that the all-glass enclosure lets in light and serves as a means of bringing the outdoors in. Unlike an open porch or deck, greenhouses can be conditioned so that the space can be used year-round. In addition, if the greenhouse is properly oriented it can become a source of passive solar heat for the house (see Chapter 19). All of these benefits can be gained at relatively low cost.

Greenhouses can be framed in wood or purchased ready-assembled. We do not recommend getting involved in the framing of a greenhouse since it is a rather painstaking process. The glazing needs to be cut to size and fit very carefully into the framework. To avoid water penetration, joints need to be tightly sealed with caulking or glazing compound or gaskets. In addition, you have the problem of sweating or condensation. (This occurs when warm, moist air comes in contact with cold glass.) All of the above spell a labor-intensive and problem-ridden process that can easily be avoided by buying a manufactured greenhouse. In the process of improving their product, manufacturers have solved many of the problems related to water leakage and condensation control which are inherent in greenhouse design.

Prefabricated greenhouses are made of modular components. These modules or bays are approximately 2'-6" in width. The length can be customized by the number of bays that you choose. In widths, the bays range from 3' at the narrowest to 15' at the widest. In terms of height, greenhouses are available in models of one, two, and more stories. Greenhouse companies keep their most popular models in stock. These usually range from 3' to 13' in width, from three to ten bays in length, and are one or two stories high. When ordering a greenhouse, you will be asked the number of gable ends you need—that is, whether you need a greenhouse with one glass end wall, two glass end walls, or none at all (Ill. 3). The number of gables (or lack of them) depends solely on your specific design.

The two principal components of a greenhouse are the structural framework and the glazing. The frame can be made out of metal (generally anodized aluminum) or wood. Metal greenhouses offer ease of maintenance at a relatively low cost. In addition, the slender metal components give these greenhouses a light and airy look. For those who object to the "industrial" look of metal, laminated-wood greenhouses are also available.

The wood framework, although heavier, offers the warmth inherent in the material. On the downside, wood, by its very nature, requires more maintenance and is generally higher in cost. If you decide on a wood greenhouse, we recommend you use those made out of cedar since they tend to be more durable.

The type of glazing that you choose is also important. Greenhouses can be single-, double-, or triple-glazed. Single glazing means that there is one layer of glass between you and the outside. Double glazing gives you two layers of glass with an air space sandwiched in between. Triple glazing has three layers of glass and two air spaces. Single glazing is subject to condensation problems. For this reason, we recommend single glazing only for those of you who intend to use the greenhouse solely for gardening. Double glazing eases condensation significantly and it is the one we recommend. Triple glazing is even more efficient but it is more expensive. As a general rule, greenhouses come equipped with tempered safety glass. In terms of color, the most popular is the clear glass. Bronze and silver glass are optional.

There are a number of accessories available for your greenhouse. For ventilation, you can get awning windows or louvered vents. The greenhouse can have single, French, or sliding doors installed in one or both gable ends. Issues of insulation, privacy, and sun control are addressed with a variety of devices. There are insulated shades and window quilts which offer all of the above. Some types are motorized to facilitate raising and lowering. In addition, there are pleated translucent shades and mini-blinds which allow privacy and shading.

EXTERIOR FINISHES AND WEATHERPROOFING

Those renovators who are building extensions to their homes or moving windows around should be versed in the various materials available for completing the exterior. If you are patching the existing exterior, you will want to match the material exactly. Those of you who are adding an extension will find the choice of exterior finishes dictated primarily by the materials already on the house. Combinations of different materials are also possible but should be carefully evaluated in terms of both aesthetics and maintenance. For example, if your existing house is constructed of brick, it may be easier and aesthetically more interesting to finish the addition in clapboard rather

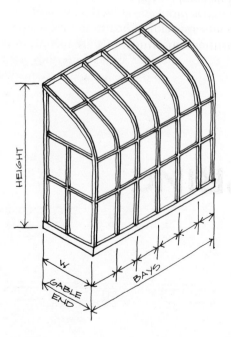

ILL. 3

than brick. First, if the existing brick is old, it is unlikely that you will match the color (and sometimes even the size). It may take years for your new brick addition to develop the patina of the existing house. Second, wood siding is easier and less costly to install. There are historical precedents for wood additions to brick main houses and so the combination will not be out of context. (A brick extension on a wooden house is another matter.) If you have an all-brick house and want to continue using brick, you should be careful to match, as best you can, the existing brick in color and texture. Wooden houses are easier to deal with, particularly if they are painted. Although this is not a general rule, houses with a painted finish should have painted extensions and buildings that have wood-stain siding should have stained extensions. A rudimentary knowledge of roofing, waterproofing, and weather stripping is also important. After all, the last thing you need after going through the trouble of a renovation is a leaky roof.

Exterior Wall Finishes

There are many ways in which exterior walls may be finished. Exterior finishing materials may be categorized into natural and "other." The authors must admit a strong prejudice for natural materials, which include all of the wood products, stone, and brick, over "others," which include aluminum and vinyl-coated metal siding. This prejudice stems from the fact that the natural materials look like what they are supposed to be—that is, wood boards look like wood boards, brick looks like brick, and so on. The other products disguise themselves as something that they are not. Aluminum is made to appear to be wood boards; plastic is cast to resemble random stone or slate. There are a number of advantages to these products, including the fact that they are maintenance-free and in some cases cheaper than what they imitate. Be that as it may, we will not elaborate on these materials. If you are eager to use them, it is easy enough to find information on their advantages and cost.

In choosing among the large number of exterior finishes available, you should consider color, pattern, material, texture, and direction of emphasis (either horizontal or vertical). In addition, there are the not so small considerations of price and ease of erection.

Wood

Horizontally applied siding comes in a number of styles. Two of the most popular are clapboards and beveled siding (Ill. 4). When siding is applied horizontally, the long horizontal shadows cast along the wall emphasize the length of the house. Had these same boards been applied vertically, the emphasis would have been on the height of the building. Traditionally clapboards are painted, but they need not be. Beveled-siding boards come in lengths up to 12'.

Vertically applied siding comes in tongue-and-groove boards and in board-and-batten patterns. Tongue-and-groove boards are manufactured to form a lock-and-key joint where they abut one another (Ill. 5). In the board-and-batten style the

ILL.4

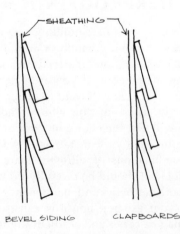

BEVEL SIDING   CLAPBOARDS

ILL.5

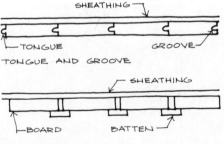

TONGUE AND GROOVE

BOARD AND BATTEN

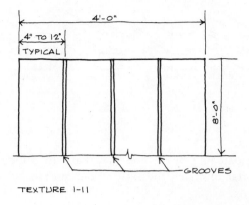

TEXTURE 1-11

ILL. 6

board-and-batten style and a panel that has a vertical indentation every 12", which is called texture 1-11 (Ill. 6).

Before deciding on an exterior finish for your extension, consult Sweet's Catalogue, the various construction magazines, the house and garden periodicals, and the folders at the lumberyard. There is a wealth of advertising literature on exterior siding.

Brick

There are many types of brick. Some are marketed for great strength, some for unique color, and others for unusual size. Bricks are made out of clay that is either dug from underground tunnels or stripped from the surface of the earth. Essentially, the raw clay is dried, crushed into a fine powder, and mixed with water to a mud consistency. The clay is then molded into units, dried in ovens, and finally baked in high-temperature kilns. This is the age-old procedure for manufacturing the bricks you might come in contact with. Bricks are named according to the clay they are made from (fireclay or otherwise), the kind of method used in shaping the units (sand- or waterstruck), the care taken in the manufacturing procedure (face brick or common), the built-in strength, or the finish applied to the face after the initial firing (glazed brick).

It is likely that you will be working with face brick. This type of brick is similar to common brick but is manufactured with greater care given to color and texture. The range of colors presently available is very large. Many brickyards also carry used bricks. This is of particular value to renovators trying to match existing brick.

In selecting your bricks, make sure that you are buying the appropriate grade. SW (severe weather) brick is for exterior construction in climates that combine wetness with temperatures below freezing. The second grade, MW (moderate weather), is for exterior use in dry climates that might be subject to freezing temperatures. The third classification, NW (no weather), is for interior use.

Brick comes in many sizes and shapes (Ill. 7). The standard brick size (which includes the bricks described above) is 2¼" high by 3¾" wide by 8" long. If you are matching brick, make sure to bring one along to the brickyard. It is important to consider the type of bonding you will use, the bonding material, its color, the width of the joints, and the method that will be used by the mason to "strike" the joints (Ills. 8 and 9). If you

boards are usually side- and square-cut. Because they have a tendency to expand and contract depending on the weather, they cannot be laid out tightly side by side. A small expansion joint is left between the boards, which is then covered up by a narrow batten strip (Ill. 5). Vertical siding can be painted, stained, or treated with a preservative and left to weather naturally.

Shingles are another category of siding materials. They are a little more time-consuming to install than either vertical or horizontal boards. They come in a variety of sizes, colors, and materials (from wood to fiberglass-asphalt strips). The most expensive are hand-split wood shingles; their heavy texture lends a rustic look to the house. Factory-made cedar shingles are attractive and can be left in their natural state to weather.

Plywood exterior panels are rather popular. They are easy to erect and because of their size involve a good deal less work than other siding. An additional advantage is that the exterior plywood panel can be nailed directly to the studs, thus eliminating the need for sheathing altogether. The panels come in widths of 4' and lengths of 8', 9', and 10'.* If the exterior plywood panel is to be applied directly to the studs without sheathing and is to act as structural bracing as well as finishing, it should be a minimum of ¾" thick. There is a large selection of colors and patterns in plywood siding. The most popular are the

*If one or more sides of the house are taller than the height of the sheet of plywood siding, you may reconsider your decision to use plywood siding. Although the vertical joint between panels is easy to mask, the horizontal joint will be obvious. In addition, the horizontal joint may require metal flashing, which might detract from the appearance of the wall.

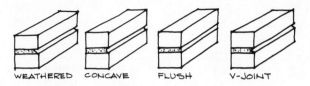

WEATHERED CONCAVE FLUSH V-JOINT

ILL.9

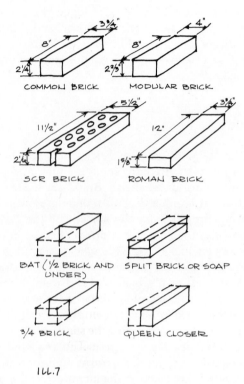

COMMON BRICK   MODULAR BRICK

SCR BRICK   ROMAN BRICK

BAT (½ BRICK AND UNDER)   SPLIT BRICK OR SOAP

¾ BRICK   QUEEN CLOSER

ILL.7

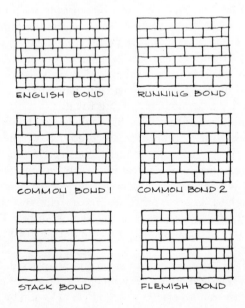

ENGLISH BOND   RUNNING BOND

COMMON BOND 1   COMMON BOND 2

STACK BOND   FLEMISH BOND

ILL.8

are patching brick, you may have to color the mortar to match the existing old mortar.

Stone

Although stone is a most beautiful building material, it would be irresponsible of us to recommend your undertaking a project that includes stone construction. The material is hard to find, expensive, tricky to cut, heavy to haul, and time-consuming to lay. There are renovators who may already have stone or partially stone buildings. Our recommendation is to get a good mason. If you live in a landmark neighborhood or in an area where there is a Landmarks Commission, give them a call. They usually have a list of approved contractors whom they recommend.

Roofing

Roofing materials come in two major categories, and which one to choose depends on the slope of your roof. Built-up roofing is most generally used for "flat"* and low-sloped roofs. This type of roofing provides watertight protection for the roof that does not drain rainwater and snow quickly. Pitched roofs, on the other hand, shed water and snow quickly and provide a scalelike protection.

We will begin the discussion with the sloped roof using wood shingles. Wood shingles and shakes are an extremely attractive roof finish. The shingles, be they cypress, redwood, or cedar, machine-finished or hand-split,† provide natural water resistance with their own resins and oils. Shingles are graded no. 1 and no. 2. They are cut in standard lengths of 16", 18", and 24" and are

*There is no such thing as a truly flat roof. What is called a flat roof actually has a slight pitch to allow for water drainage.
†Split shingles, more commonly known as shakes, are sawed from hardwood. Because they vary considerably in thickness, in width, and even in color, a shake roof or wall adds a good deal of texture and character to the house.

bundled in random widths for purposes of design texture. The shingles come tapered and in a variety of thicknesses. Thickness determines how the shingles are laid, since they are overlapped one on the other. Usually one bundle of shingles will cover 100 square feet of roof. The disadvantages of the material are that it is combustible and relatively expensive. There are, however, some roofing systems using wood shingles that have been given a high fire-resistance rating.

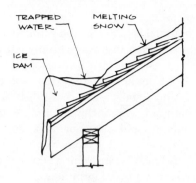

ILL.11

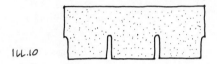

ILL.10

Asphalt shingles come either in strip form or as individual shingles (Ill. 10).* The shingles are composed of felt (rag, wood, or mineral fiber) that has been saturated with asphalt and coated on one side with granules for color and texture. The strips come in 12" × 36" pieces that are scored to look like individual shingles. Strip shingles are laid over asphalt-saturated felt and have a high fire-resistance rating.

Fiberglass-asphalt shingle strips are highly resistant to fire, rot, and decay. This type of material is applied over a layer of roof felt for roofs with a slope of at least 4" in 1'. For slopes between 2" and 4" in 1', two layers of felt are required with a layer of hot-mopped asphalt between them.

Roofing tiles, popular in Europe, are not commonly used here, because of their excessive weight (which necessitates structuring the house to accommodate the roofing material) and their high cost. The tiles consist of baked unglazed clay and come in a variety of orange-red and green-gray shades.

Slate roofs, often seen on older houses, are increasingly rare. The primary reason is the high cost of both material and labor. Like clay tile, slate is very heavy and the roof structure must be strengthened to support it.

Flat or low-sloped roofs require watertight roofing comprised of bituminous substances. In built-up roofing, layers of felt and bitumen are alternated to form a seamless, waterproof, flexible membrane that protects the roof from water. The bitumens keep the felt watertight, and the felts provide support for the bitumens, which would otherwise crack under the heat of the sun.

Steep roofs finished with wood shingles often do not require felt at all because of the fortunate tendency of the shingles to shed water quickly. The lower five or six rows of shingles should, however, receive the protection of some roofing paper to prevent what is called the ice dam effect (Ill. 11). The ice dam is created by an accumulation of melting snow at the periphery of the roof a few days after a snowfall. The snow slides to the edge of the roof and is melting. The temperatures fall and the melting snow turns to ice. If more snow should fall, this ice dam will prevent the new accumulation from sliding off the roof. When this second layer begins to melt, the water will be backed up behind the dam and may make its way through the shingles to the sheathing.

Flashing

Flashing consists of long, thin sections of sheet metal or flexible sections of a waterproof membrane material that are placed where two different building materials are juxtaposed. Its purpose is

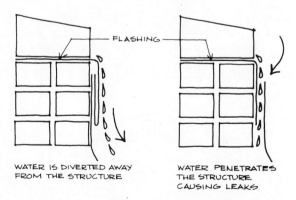

WATER IS DIVERTED AWAY FROM THE STRUCTURE

WATER PENETRATES THE STRUCTURE CAUSING LEAKS

ILL.12

*The strips make the roof installation much simpler than it would be using individual shingles.

The Outside of the House

119

to prevent water from entering the joint. The flashing material is laid over the gap between the two materials and prevents driving rain from penetrating by diverting it away from the structure (Ill. 12). Common locations that will require careful flashing details are at roof ridges and valleys, at the point where the chimney meets the roof, at window and door openings, and where the roof is penetrated by pipes, vents, skylights, etc. Be careful to provide flashing where an extension intersects the existing building.

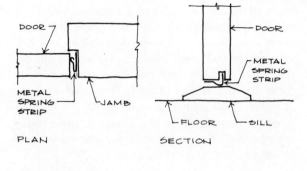

Weather Stripping

Wood, metal, and other materials have a tendency to expand in warm or moist weather and to contract in colder, drier air. This presents an interesting dilemma when it comes to doors and the infiltration of cold air in winter. In the summer, the moisture in the air tends to swell a wooden door, so that it might occasionally stick in its frame. On the other hand, in the winter, when we would prefer an airtight joint between the door

and its frame, the door shrinks, causing a gap that allows cold air to infiltrate. This problem is easily rectified for doors by installing metal spring strips around the doors to prevent infiltration (Ill. 13). The bent piece of metal is tensioned so that it is "open" in the winter, when the gap is the widest, and it is "closed" in the summer, when the door presses against the frame.

15

WINDOWS, DOORS, HARD-
WARE, AND SKYLIGHTS

WINDOWS

Windows can be a major part of a house or apartment renovation project. Some renovators will limit their window changes to the removal of the old windows and the installation of new ones in the same rough openings. You may be considering replacing your old windows for a number of very valid reasons: your single-glazed windows are losing too much heat and you wish to replace them with double-glazed units with special glazing, your existing wooden sash has rotted beyond repair, your windows have been painted so many times that they are glued shut, or the wood of the existing frames and sashes has shrunk, allowing cold air to infiltrate between the broad cracks.

Aside from these practical considerations, you may decide to replace or relocate windows for purely aesthetic reasons. You may not care for the style of the existing window, preferring a casement to double-hung window or French doors to those of sliding glass. It may be that the existing windows are poorly located, offering you an exceptional view of the storage shed from your chair near the fire but requiring you to stretch your head out the window to see your duck pond. Or the existing windows are so small that you can see only a fraction of the potential view, and what's more, the room does not get enough natural light.

If you live in an urban apartment house, it may be difficult or impossible to enlarge a preexisting window or to install a window where there was none before. Some of the difficulties stem from the ownership of the building. If you live in a condominium or a cooperative building, the board of directors probably has jurisdiction over the exterior aesthetics of the building and may not allow you to install a window that does not conform to its guidelines. In addition, many municipal building codes impose restrictions on the size and the location of windows. Some municipalities mandate a minimum window size for reasons of ventilation, while at the same time insisting on a maximum allowable size for reasons of energy conservation. Some codes require that each room have at least some windows that are operable even if there is adequate mechanical ventilation and that the operable part of the window open wide enough to permit an adult to escape in case of fire. Many codes do not allow the placement of windows on a property-line wall (other than the street elevation). Be sure to check your municipality's codes, the local energy laws, and your building's bylaws before planning to replace, enlarge, reduce, relocate, or eliminate your existing windows.

Another factor that may discourage you from enlarging an existing window opening or penetrating a blank wall is the cost of the project, which will entail the expense of restructuring the surrounding wood-frame or masonry wall. As we have mentioned before, it is relatively easy to lengthen an existing window opening by removing material beneath the sill. Widening a window in a wood-frame building requires removing and replacing the lintel (the wood member that supports the frame above the window) as well as the vertical supports on either side of the opening. Similarly, the wood or steel lintel over an opening in a masonry wall must be replaced if a wider window is to be installed. Both cases may call for delicate construction maneuvers, including the temporary jacking of the upper portion of the building while the lintels are being replaced.

With these pros and cons on window relocation in mind, we will offer some hints on the placement and selection of windows. First determine what you wish to look out at (or, conversely, what you wish to avoid seeing). Next determine the placement of furniture in the room. Be sure to make the windows big enough and low enough so that when you are sitting you can see more than the sky; also make sure the window extends high enough so that you can see out when you are standing up. If you want to allow light into the room but do not wish to look into your next-door neighbors' window, you can purposely place windows high on the wall. Although these factors may seem obvious, they are often overlooked in both renovation and house design.

In addition, when designing a wall of windows, be careful not to locate the mullions (the vertical or horizontal separations between sections of

glass) where they will block the view. A grave error of this kind was made by the renovators of a summer house facing a spectacular bay view. They replaced some small double-hung windows with a wall of windows that combined three nonoperable fixed windows with three awning windows below. When a person is seated on the couch that faces the bay, his view is bisected by the horizontal mullion, which, unfortunately, coincides with the horizon line where sea meets sky (Ill. 1). The window renovation might have been handled better if the ventilation windows were positioned above the fixed panes, or if two long casement windows were placed at the sides of one or more floor-to-ceiling fixed windows.

Since windows offer such great design opportunities, you may be tempted to remove whole walls (and even the roof of the house) and replace these areas with glazing. Be sure to temper your light obsession with the realities of climate and the knowledge that glass loses heat at a much faster rate than an insulated exterior wall. Replacing lost heat is very costly and you should keep this in mind when determining the sizes of windows and skylights.

Insulating Glass

Because glass loses heat at such a rapid rate, a great deal of research has gone into producing a window that limits the heat loss without obstructing visibility. The result is a double-glazed window unit that is mass-marketed under a number of trade names. Essentially, the unit contains two thicknesses of sheet glass separated by an air space. The space between the sheets of glass is dehydrated and then sealed. The drying out of the air in the space prevents the development of condensate that would obstruct visibility. Many manufacturers include a third sheet of glass, a storm sash, but this added protection does not cut the heat loss by a proportionate amount. Another way to reduce the heat loss through glass is by the use of insulated curtains or shutters which are closed at night or when the room is not in use.

A new glazing option is being marketed under a number of names, such as low-E glass. An invisible metallic coating is used that provides greater energy efficiency. This glazing option is particularly effective for those people in hot climates who want to restrict the radiant heat entering the window without reducing light. Most window manufacturers combine this new glazing feature with the insulating value of double-paned glazing.

ILL. 1

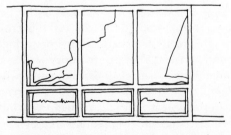

VIEW

VIEW FROM SOFA

Window-Frame Materials

Residential window frames come in three basic materials: wood, plastic-coated wood, and metal. The plain wooden windows (made of ponderosa pine) are the most commonly used. Wood is a very fine insulator, and so the wooden windows are weathertight as well as handsome. The only disadvantage of this moderately expensive frame is that it must be maintained. A redwood frame may be stained and creosoted with the rest of the house or it may be painted. The stock pine windows, however, are usually painted, but can be left untreated on the interior. In most climates the trim (the exterior side of the window frames) will need treatment only once every four or five years. Houses located near salt water will require more frequent care.

Some wooden windows are manufactured with the exposed wood sections sealed with a rigid vinyl or metal covering. In addition to eliminating "sticking" windows, this coating ends the need to paint the frame and sash. Although these windows are higher in price than the plain wooden frames, the extra cost might be justified in some climates (Ill. 2).

Metal windows do not require painting. They also do not have the tendency of wooden windows to swell with moisture in the summer and stick in their frames. Metal in itself is a great conductor of heat, and solid-metal frames lose a great deal of heat through conductivity. There are many metal windows on the market, however, that offer excellent insulation. The hollow metal frames are filled with rigid insulation and are weatherproofed with metal and vinyl strips. Most replacement windows on the market are constructed of aluminum with a baked-on finish that requires no maintenance.

When you purchase a window from the lumberyard or from a local representative of one of the major window manufacturers, you will be buying the entire frame and sash, complete with glazing and hardware. The window will be ready to install; all you have to do is provide the rough opening in the wall. The manufacturer's literature will include all the available stock sizes and types. Be sure to have current catalogues on hand before selecting windows. (Check that the frame thickness conforms to the thickness of your wall.) In addition to the glazing options available (either single, double, or triple sheets of glass) and the frame material (wood, coated wood, or aluminum), you must select the appropriate type of window (double-hung, sliding, casement, or fixed).

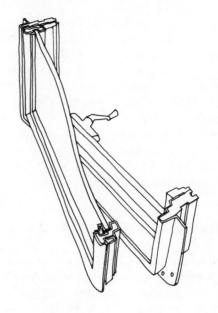

ILL. 2

Window Operation

The various window frames are named for the method by which they may be opened and closed—the single exception being the fixed window, which cannot be opened. The movable members of the window frame are referred to as its sash. The fixed perimeter members are its frame. The various categories of window sash are identified below (Ill. 3).

The casement window is hinged on its vertical side and can be opened and closed by turning a crank. Casements are available as single units, in pairs, or in multiples. Some prefabricated bay-window units come as a fixed pane of glass flanked by two casements.

Awning windows are similar to the casements but are hinged on top and open horizontally. The windows open outward, offering some rain protection when open. Although awning windows can be used by themselves, they are often grouped under (or over) large fixed panes of glass.

The hopper window is similar to the awning window except that it is hinged at the bottom.

Double-hung windows are the most traditional style available and were used in our oldest American houses. The window sashes are mounted on two sets of vertical tracks installed on the frame. The sashes move up and down past one another to open or close the window. In the large older versions of the double-hung window, the weight of the sash was offset by a counterbalance system hidden inside the window frame. In the contemporary version of the window, the sash is held in place by a spring system designed to facilitate the removal of the sash for easy cleaning. Unfortunately, these new windows do not employ counterweights.

Sliding windows are similar to the double-hung windows in that the window is mounted on a set of tracks. In this case the windows move horizontally instead of vertically.

Multipaned Windows

Windows on historic houses have small panes of glass separated by narrow muntins. Small panes rather than large sheets of glass were used, not for aesthetic reasons, but because glass manufacturers had not yet developed the technology of plate glass. The popularity of multipaned windows en-

dured long after technology was able to deliver large sheets of plate glass, and both styles of window are still being manufactured. When insulated glass was developed, window manufacturers continued to produce single-glazed small-paned windows but did not construct a double-glazed version. (One would guess that the thicker windows did not look right in the thin muntin tracery.) Instead, the major manufacturers developed a lightweight plastic inset which fits over a large panel of glass in almost any size or style of standard window. The plastic inset mimics the tracery of the small-paned window, but is really a poor substitute. If double-glazed small-paned windows are a must, there are manufacturers who will custom-make the windows (and doors) for you. Be advised that the muntins between the double-glazed panels may be much thicker than the narrow muntins that support single thicknesses of glass. What's more, the windows, being custom-made, are more expensive.

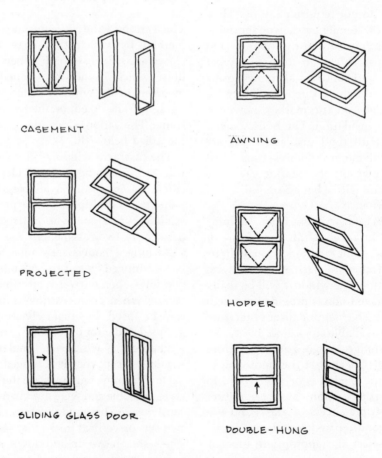

CASEMENT

AWNING

PROJECTED

HOPPER

SLIDING GLASS DOOR

DOUBLE-HUNG

ILL.3

Sliding Glass Doors

Sliding glass doors are like sliding windows in that they move horizontally on twin sets of tracks. The doors come in a variety of widths starting with two-paneled doors about 5' wide with one fixed panel and the other operable. Sliding doors are also available in triple units up to 12' wide. In the triple varieties, the center section is operable and the two flanking sections are fixed.

DOORS

If you are thinking about a new front door, check the codes to determine if there are any limitations in location, size, or materials. For instance, if you live in an apartment house, you will probably be required to install a fire-rated metal door between hall and apartment. The door will have to swing in so as not to block the corridor. In addition, check the codes before permanently removing any doors to the outside. Some codes mandate at least two means of egress from an apartment or house. It is tempting to convert the mudroom into a shelf-lined pantry, but be sure you have a legal alternate means of egress in case of fire if you intend to block the existing door.

In addition, many municipalities require that both exterior and interior doors be wide enough to provide access for a wheelchair. Check the building codes to determine if your renovation must be accessible to the disabled and what other requirements must be met.

Doors can be classified by the way they are opened, the materials they are constructed from, and/or their design.

Exterior Doors

Doors that separate the inside of the house from the outside are generally made of solid wood. Panel doors are constructed of wood sections about 1¾" thick called stiles, which frame indented, thinner wood panels. Many panel doors have tempered glass sheets in place of wood panels in the stiles. French doors are constructed like windows, containing wood stiles on all four sides and muntins separating the glass inserts. Most French doors are manufactured either with single sheets of plate glass or with tempered glass (a manufactured product that makes glass stronger and more resistant to shattering). It is possible to order custom-made French doors with insulating glass in place of regular glass.

Wooden solid-core flush doors are smooth-faced and are manufactured by gluing two veneers of wood to solid wood blocks or bonded wood chips. Metal doors are made of pressed sheets of metal filled with rigid insulation material. Metal doors have the advantage of not expanding and contracting with the temperature changes as do wooden doors. Except in the mildest climates, all exterior doors should be weatherproofed with thin strips of metal and insulating material to prevent the infiltration of cold air and wind-driven rain (see Chapter 14).

Interior Doors

Doors used inside your house or apartment may be either hinged, folding, sliding, pocket, or accordion-pleated (Ill. 4). The hinged door is most commonly used between rooms and on closets. Solid-core flush doors are recommended for use between rooms for their greater durability and sound-insulating qualities. Hollow-core flush doors, consisting of an interior of honeycombed wood strips covered by a veneer of plywood, are recommended for closets, but can also be used between rooms. Paneled doors, consisting of thin solid pieces of plywood framed by heavier members, are recommended for closets and between rooms where a more traditional look is desired.

Bifold doors are folding doors and are often used for closets because they permit a large opening to be exposed while using a minimal amount of floor space. Each door has a hinge in the center and slides on a track. The individual panels are usually hollow-core flush doors, but can be solid, paneled, or louvered.

Sliding doors are also often used for closets. The doors do not take any room from the space they are opening into and therefore are preferred to folding doors if space is at a premium. They are hung from a metal track screwed into the upper frame. The doors are arranged on a double track so that they slide past each other.

Pocket doors are hollow-core, solid-core, or paneled doors that are mounted on a track and are designed to slide into a concealed pocket in the wall. The doors are completely hidden when open, making the archway between two rooms look permanently open. Pocket doors are extremely useful in situations where a hinged open door would take up a lot of needed space or would block traffic flow. They are very handy for rooms that will require privacy only occasionally,

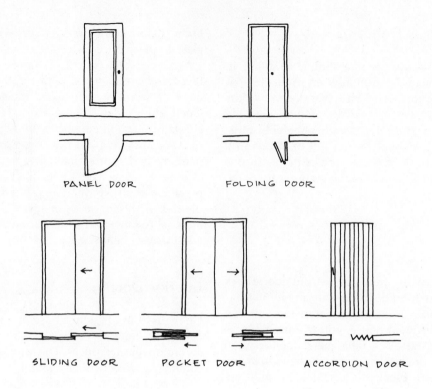

PANEL DOOR   FOLDING DOOR

SLIDING DOOR   POCKET DOOR   ACCORDION DOOR

ILL.4

such as a family room that will be used as a guest room every so often. Two pocket doors can be used in the opening that separates the living room from the dining room if one of those rooms must be used on occasion for quiet pursuits. If you are considering pocket doors, be sure that the walls on either side of the doors are at least as wide as the doors. Many hardware manufacturers have special prefabricated assemblies for pocket doors so that the wall thickness need not exceed the usual 4¾" (3½" for the stud thickness and ⅝"-thick gypsum board on each side).

Accordion doors are not often seen in residences, but sometimes can be put to good use. They are used in the same general situations where pocket doors would be used. Although not as handsome as pocket doors, accordion doors are considerably less expensive and can be used in locations where the wall space required for the pockets does not exist.

Although doors can be obtained in a variety of materials, wooden doors are the most commonly used in residential architecture. Doors for interior purposes, such as closet doors, do come in metal and in vinyl-coated aluminum varieties, but we

do not recommend them because the metal is too thin and flimsy. One good bang can change its shape or mar its appearance.

Most doors are 6'-8" high and come in a variety of standard widths. The front door is usually 3' wide and 1¾" thick. The doors that separate rooms are 2'-6" wide and 1⅜" thick. It is not unusual to design the door to the bathroom to be 2' wide, but it is not recommended, since the opening is too small.*

Doors, both interior and exterior, may be bought "pre-hung," which means that the door-frame and hinges are preassembled. These doors, although more expensive, save a good deal of labor. They are particularly advantageous for exterior doors because they come weatherproofed, which is a tricky operation to do yourself.

Garage Doors

The most commonly used garage door is the over-head type composed of several hinged sections

*Check code requirements for minimum door widths.

that roll up to the ceiling on tracks. The doors may be operated manually or by a remote-control device that opens the door without your having to leave the car. The doors come in heights of 6'-6" and 7' and are usually 1⅜" thick. A single-car garage may be equipped with a door that is 8' or 9' wide. Double doors are 16' wide. Although they are available in both wood and metal, we prefer the wooden doors.

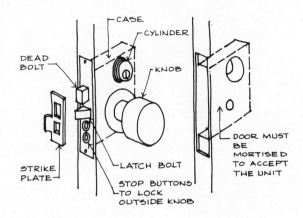

ILL.5

HARDWARE

Hardware includes locks, latches, and hinges. Because the hardware is such a visible and integral part of the renovation, it is important to select these items for their appearance as well as for their functional qualities. Most lumberyards and hardware stores have a complete collection of finish hardware, doorknobs, and latches and should provide a sufficient selection. If you are looking for unusual hardware, try the specialized magazines as well as Sweet's Catalogue for advertisements and manufacturers' literature. Much of the hardware can be obtained through mail order.

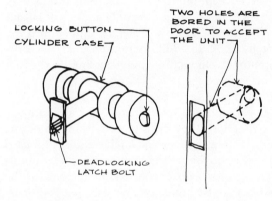

ILL.6

Hinges

Doors swing on hinges in order to open or close. A hinge is made up of two leaves, which are joined together by a pin. They are available in several types. Some hinges are completely concealed, others are totally exposed, and there are still others in which only the pin is visible (butt hinges). A mortised hinge is one in which the leaves are notched into the wood. When the leaves are visible, it is called a surface hinge.

Wrought steel, brass, bronze, and stainless steel are some of the materials in which hinges are available. Stainless steel provides the strongest, most durable, and most corrosion-resistant hinge at a relatively high price.

In terms of size, hinges vary from 2" to 6". The size is relative to the weight and the thickness of the door. Hinges are generally mounted on doors 5" from the head and 10" from the floor. Should a third hinge be necessary, it is placed at the center point between the top and bottom one.

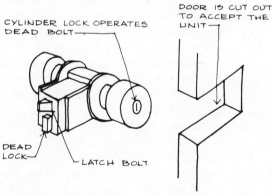

ILL.7

Locks and Latches

Locks and latches are used to hold doors in place and provide security. When a door is closed, the

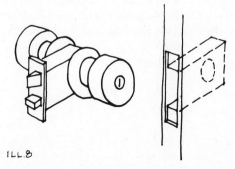

ILL.8

latch automatically slides into position. The locking device is called a bolt. It may be manually operated (dead bolt) or be set automatically (latch bolt). Locks and latches are often combined into one unit.

The most common locks and latches used in residential construction are of the mortised and bored-in type. ("Mortised" and "bored-in" refer to the method of installation.) In the mortise type, the unit is concealed in the edge of the door. Its installation involves carving a hole in the core of the door into which the unit will fit (Ill. 5). The bored-in type (whether cylindrical or tubular) is easiest to install, requiring only the boring of two holes (Ill. 6). One other type of lock and latch deserves mention: the unit lock. This lock is very simple to install, requiring only a notch or cutout in the door. The unit is merely slipped into the notch (Ill. 7). In addition, unit locks are factory-assembled, eliminating much fussing on the job. Mortise-type integral locks and latches may also be purchased factory-assembled (Ill. 8).

Lock and latch mechanisms vary according to the functions they must serve within the house. For example, the lock and latch combination used in a bedroom or bathroom door is not the same as that used for a closet door. While the one for the bedroom or bathroom will need a latch bolt operated by a knob from either side and should be capable of being locked or unlocked by a push button or a turn from the inside, the closet will only need a latch bolt that is operable at all times by a knob on either side. Care must be taken to select the right mechanism for the specific job.

For added security you may consider installing a dead bolt in addition to the combined lock and latch on your exterior door. A dead bolt consists of a shaft of high-strength steel installed on (or in) the door that slips into an armored strike plate on (or in) the doorframe. A dead bolt is more difficult to "pick" than a latch. There are more sophisticated locks on the market if you require greater security. Check manufacturers' literature or talk to your hardware merchant.

It is a good idea to purchase all of your locks and dead bolts from the same manufacturer and supplier so that all can be keyed alike. This eliminates the need to carry around several different keys.

Locks and latches are available in a wide range of materials, including stainless steel, brass, bronze, and aluminum. The visible components, such as knobs and lever handles, may be obtained in a variety of finishes and designs ranging from bright to satin and from contemporary to traditional.

SKYLIGHTS

Skylights, originally used to light the interior space of factories, are popular for residential use. The skylight allows for the dramatic introduction of natural light into any room in the house that is directly under the roof. A skylight may be constructed by simply framing glass between the rafters or roof joints. This kind of skylight, although inexpensive, is difficult to waterproof. Care must be taken to properly construct the skylight so that water is shed from it and does not collect around the edges where it can leak. The best bet for a renovation or a new extension is a prefabricated skylight, shaped like a pyramid or dome. It is easy to install and is usually leakproof. The bubbles are available in many sizes. These units come complete and are designed to shed water. All that must be provided is the rough opening (Ill. 9). In addition, there are skylights that can be opened for ventilation and varieties that have built-in fans and shading devices.

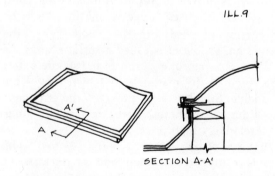

ILL. 9

SECTION A-A'

PART THREE: TECHNICAL DECISIONS

16

STRUCTURAL PRINCIPLES

No renovation beyond the most superficial should be attempted without a sound understanding of structural principles. One enthusiastic renovator we know did a beautiful remodeling of his parents' basement recreation room which included the removal of an ugly Lally column that stood in the center of the space. It did not take long for him to recognize his structural error; luckily his parents were not home at the time of the collapse. The discussion below will not qualify you (by any stretch of the imagination) to practice engineering (which would be foolish and illegal). It will, hopefully, provide you with some basic structural tenets and some idea as to when to consult a professional.

We have found that most people have only a vague idea of what makes a building stand up. Most people know (with the exception of the young man cited above) that you can't remove a "structural wall" without dire consequences, but few laypeople have any idea of how to identify a structural wall from one that is non-load-bearing. Many people we have talked to are under the erroneous impression that only the outer walls of a building are structural and that all of the inner partitions* merely divide the space into rooms. Others, on the very conservative side, think that all partitions are structural and refuse to consider the removal of anything that resembles a wall.

The structure of a small house or apartment building employs the same basic principles as the megastructure of a skyscraper. In the attempt to gain insight into how any building works, it is more valuable to think of the various structural components as working together to transfer loads downward to the ground rather than to consider them as holding something up. When dealing with buildings, one of the essentials to keep in mind is structural continuity. This kind of continuity applies to human anatomy as well. Our body skeleton carries the weight of our various organs and tissues from one bone to the other until the entire load is transferred through our feet to the ground. Similarly, the loads on a building, both inherent (dead loads: the weight of materials) and applied (live loads: people, furniture, and snow), must be transferred through the various horizontal, vertical, and diagonal structural members to the foundations and from there to the ground (Ill. 1).

A building consists of three main structural systems that interrelate to transfer the loads downward. The horizontal system includes the floors and flat roof which directly receive the weight of people, furniture, snow, and rainwater and transfer that weight to the vertical supports. The vertical supports are either columns, walls, or partitions that transfer the loads vertically to the foundations. The foundations serve two purposes: to transfer the building loads to the ground and to anchor the building (Ill. 2). (A diagonal

*We will use the term "wall" for the divider between the interior of the building and the outside. A "partition" is defined as a floor-to-ceiling divider separating one interior space from another. Both walls and partitions may be either structural or nonstructural.

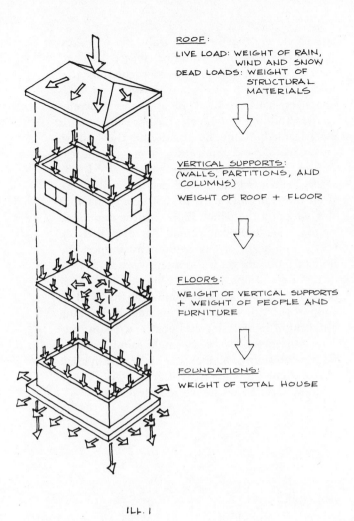

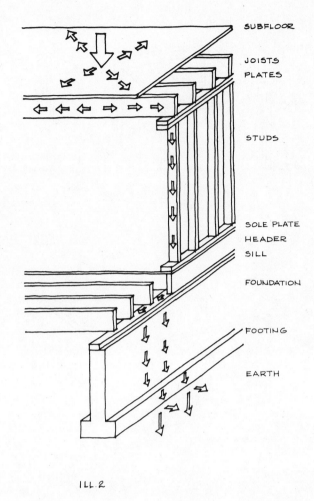

ROOF:
LIVE LOAD: WEIGHT OF RAIN,
              WIND AND SNOW
DEAD LOADS: WEIGHT OF
              STRUCTURAL
              MATERIALS

VERTICAL SUPPORTS:
(WALLS, PARTITIONS, AND
  COLUMNS)
WEIGHT OF ROOF + FLOOR

FLOORS:
WEIGHT OF VERTICAL SUPPORTS
+ WEIGHT OF PEOPLE AND
FURNITURE

FOUNDATIONS:
WEIGHT OF TOTAL HOUSE

ILL. 1

SUBFLOOR
JOISTS
PLATES
STUDS
SOLE PLATE
HEADER
SILL
FOUNDATION
FOOTING
EARTH

ILL. 2

roof transfers loads both vertically and laterally; this presents its own set of problems.)*

VERTICAL SUPPORTS

There are a number of ways to structure a simple building: you can frame it with columns and beams, you can use load-bearing walls to support the floors, or you can construct the building using light-frame construction methods, which in essence combine the other two systems. The Empire State Building in New York is of steel-frame construction. In that structure and in thousands like it of smaller stature, the loads of the building are

*In geographic areas where earthquakes are a threat, walls, floors, and foundations must be designed to resist these lateral vibrations. Seismic design is not discussed in this book.

transferred through the steel frame downward, much as a person's weight is carried to the ground by the body's skeleton. The floor loads are transferred through beams to girders to columns and down through the columns to the foundations. The walls act to enclose the building, are nonstructural, and are referred to as curtain walls. A small house could be constructed using exactly the same principles if framed with lightweight steel components or timber, a method known as post-and-beam construction. Most high-rise apartment buildings (more than six stories) and many shorter multiresidences are constructed by means of this point-support system using either steel or reinforced-concrete columns and beams (Ill. 3).

A small warehouse with masonry walls is structured on the principle of the load-bearing wall. Some of the walls and partitions of this building do more than enclose space for reasons

Structural
Principles
131

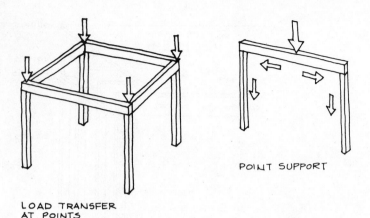

POINT SUPPORT

LOAD TRANSFER
AT POINTS

ILL. 3

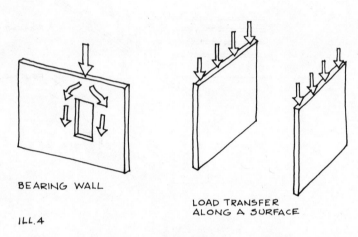

BEARING WALL

ILL. 4

LOAD TRANSFER
ALONG A SURFACE

spaced closely together. The walls and partitions consist of studs (mini-columns) spaced 12″, 16″, or 24″ apart instead of heavier columns that might be spaced 6′ or 8′ apart in wood post-and-beam construction, 12′ to 18′ apart in a concrete-frame building, or even farther apart in a steel-frame building. By positioning the studs so close together and connecting them with sheathing for bracing (usually sheets of plywood), the wall is converted into a load-bearing wall (Ill. 5). If all the walls and partitions are constructed in this way and the penetrations for the doors and windows are limited and small (narrower than 6′), there is no need for any columns to support the floors or roof above. If the interior space is large, or if the partitions are inconveniently placed for load-bearing purposes, columns can be used to support the structure above, making the building a hybrid of light-frame and post-and-beam construction methods. Most single-family houses with wood siding and many houses faced in brick utilize light-frame construction. So do many small suburban row-house complexes.

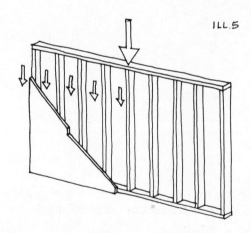

ILL. 5

HORIZONTAL SUPPORTS

In the vertical support system of the house, especially in walls and short columns, loads are transferred mostly through compression—that is, the molecules or fibers in the column are being compressed or squeezed together. Most structural materials are strong in compression, meaning that they can carry a great deal of load while being squeezed, but to varying degrees are weak in tension (stretching) (Ill. 6). Both of these stresses occur when a structural member is positioned horizontally. When a beam is placed between two supports and is loaded, it is said to be subjected

of privacy and the need to hold heat in winter. These walls and partitions transfer the weight of the floors and roof to the foundation all along the length of the walls. Since the bearing wall or partition acts as a unit to transfer the loads, there is a certain limit to the number of openings (such as windows and doors) that can be placed in it (Ill. 4). When the penetrations in a wall become so large that the wall can no longer act structurally as load-bearing, other arrangements are needed for the transfer of the weight. In such cases, the loads are distributed through lintels (acting as beams), which transfer them to point supports—that is, columns. Many small apartment buildings and urban row houses are based on the load-bearing wall system and so is the solid-brick or stone single-family house. Some very old apartment houses are hybrid in construction in that most of the structure is carried by load-bearing walls with the exception of a few rows of columns placed in locations where bulky walls are undesirable.

In a building of light-frame construction, the house is framed using slim structural members

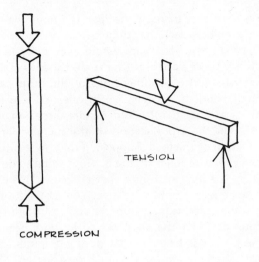

TENSION

COMPRESSION

ILL. 6

weight across the gap. (We are assuming, of course, that he is a tightrope walker.) He would probably decide that a tree trunk 4″ in diameter would do the trick. Were the gap increased from 5′ to 15′, he might question whether a 4″-diameter log (assuming he could find one long enough) would be able to support his weight across the longer span. Presented with this problem, he would probably turn around and look for a log thicker than 4″. He suspects, correctly, that the 4″ log would bend or perhaps would even snap in two if he attempted to walk on it (Ill. 8).

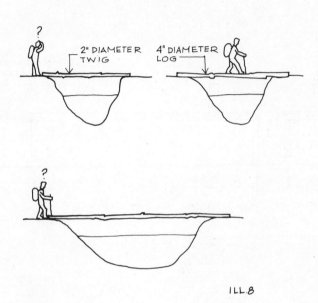

2″ DIAMETER TWIG

4″ DIAMETER LOG

ILL. 8

to "bending" stresses (a combination of compression and tension). The beam gives, or deflects, under the weight. If we concentrate on what is happening somewhere in the middle of the deflecting beam, we will see that the uppermost molecules in the member are being compressed, whereas the lower molecules are being stretched, or placed in tension (Ill. 7). The tension stresses are greatest at the bottom of the section and decrease toward the center. The compression stresses are greatest at the top of the beam and decrease toward the center. The centermost molecules (those running along an imaginary line called the neutral axis) are not subjected to any stresses at all. Because of the dual stresses (tension and compression) that occur in horizontal structural members when subjected to bending, they require different structural analysis than do short vertical supports, which are generally subjected only to compressive stresses.

Let us suppose that a hiker has to cross a stream that is 4′ or 5′ wide. He would know that a long twig about 2″ in diameter would not support his

Whether we realize it or not, most of us have some basic knowledge of the tenets of structural design. In the example just given, the hiker knew that the dimensions of the structural member required to bridge the gap were dependent on the length of the span and the loads to be supported. In fact, even highly sophisticated structural problems that involve spanning between supports can be reduced to four variables:

1. The span—the distance between the supports and how the member is connected to its supports.

2. The loads to be carried—how much weight, where it is concentrated, and for how long.

3. The cross-sectional dimensions of the structural member—the thickness and shape of the cross section of the member.

4. The material being used—its strength, characteristics, ability to withstand the stresses it is being subjected to.

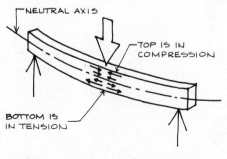

NEUTRAL AXIS

TOP IS IN COMPRESSION

BOTTOM IS IN TENSION

ILL.7

Structural Principles

133

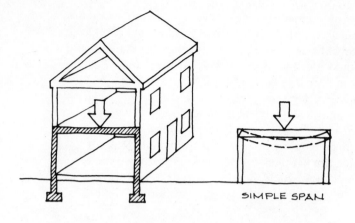

ILL. 9

SIMPLE SPAN

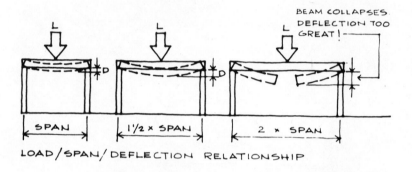

BEAM COLLAPSES. DEFLECTION TOO GREAT!

LOAD/SPAN/DEFLECTION RELATIONSHIP

ILL. 10

The Span

The word "span" means the distance between supports. The most common span in residential architecture is the "simple span." This refers to a horizontal member (a plank, joist, beam, or girder) that is supported at both its ends by either walls or columns. The ends may be secured to the supports in some way, but the connection is not rigid enough to prevent slight movement (or rotation) (Ill. 9). When a simple span is loaded (that is, when weight is put on the beam), it tends to give somewhat under the weight. This giving, or bending (the combination of tension and compression), causes the beam to become slightly distorted. We use the term "deflection" to describe the amount of distortion (Ill. 10). In the case of the hiker, the distance between the supports was increased from 5' to 15' without any increase in the thickness of the cross section of the log or in the load that it would have to bear. This increase in the span would cause the member (the log) to deflect even more (under its own weight). Were

you to further increase the span (without changing the cross-sectional dimensions of the spanning member), the beam would eventually fail.

Since these variables (the span, the loads, and the cross-sectional dimensions of the beam) are interdependent, an increase in one of them (in this case, the span) would require either an increase in the cross section of the member or a reduction of the load. Supposing that these alternatives are impractical, the obvious thing to do is divide the long span into shorter spans. This can be done in a number of ways. The first solution is to erect additional supports and to bridge the spans between the supports with short beams. These simple beams, with nonrigid joints, are most often seen in wood-frame construction. The second method is to use one continuous beam across all of the supports. This would reduce the deflection in any one span and would be the more efficient solution (Ill. 11). Another way to obtain the structural benefits of a continuous beam without the problems of importing an extraordinarily long girder to the construction site is to be sure that the joints that tie the beams to the columns and to each other are rigid (nonrotating).

The simply spanned beam, one that spans from one support to the other, is commonly used in residential architecture and is perfectly adequate in most cases. We don't often see long continuous beams in ordinary house construction. Very long milled sections are unusual and expensive; the longest section you are likely to find without special ordering would be about 22'. Laminated beams (manufactured structural members that are produced by pressure-gluing short, thin wood strips together) are expensive both to purchase and to move to the site. Likewise, rigid connections are not often used in wood-frame construction. It is possible, however, to build up a long continuous beam out of lengths of 2"-thick lumber. (See Chapter 29, Ills. 3 and 4.) All welded steel connections are considered rigid connections, and any poured-in-place concrete frame is by definition a rigid frame.

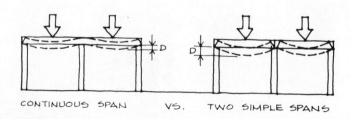

CONTINUOUS SPAN   VS.   TWO SIMPLE SPANS

ILL. 11

THE CANTILEVERED SPAN: There are instances where the design of a building calls for an overhang or balcony, eliminating the end support of the beam. In this situation the beam is cantilevered. The structural member will have two supports, but only one of these will occur at the end. The other support occurs somewhere along the length of the beam. When the end of the cantilevered portion is loaded, the effect is like a seesaw. The downward motion at the cantilevered portion must be opposed by a downward force at the beam's opposite end. Otherwise, that end will go up like the end of a seesaw. A wall or other similarly heavy weight applied at the noncantilevered end will act to balance the beam. Otherwise, the connection between the beam and its end support will have to be made very strong (Ill. 12).

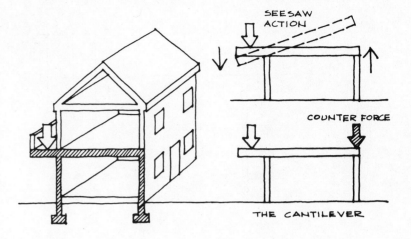

ILL. 12

LOADS

A beam's primary function is to carry the loads applied along the length of its span to its supports. Three crucial questions about the loading of a beam must be answered: How much weight must the beam carry? For how long? Is the load concentrated at any one point or is it evenly distributed along the beam's length? If the load is evenly distributed along the length of the span, every inch of the member is put to work supporting the weight applied to it, in addition to transferring the weight to the nearest support. The same total load applied at a single point causes different problems. If the load is applied at or near midspan, the bending and consequent deflection will be greater (Ill. 13).

The length of time the load will be sustained is an important consideration as well. A wood member might be fine to support an enormously heavy load for a few minutes or even as long as a week. It will bend a bit under the load and deflect to some extent, but if the load is removed it will come back to its original shape. If the load is kept there for as long as a year, strange as it may seem, the material gets fatigued. When the load is removed, the member will not assume its original shape.

The magnitude of the loads to be carried is the decisive factor in the design of a beam. The greater the load on a beam, the greater the bending stresses, and the greater the danger of the beam failing. If the loads are too great for the beam, it will fail (Ill. 14). Presented with a large load and a fixed span, the only variable left is the cross-sectional dimensions of the structural member.

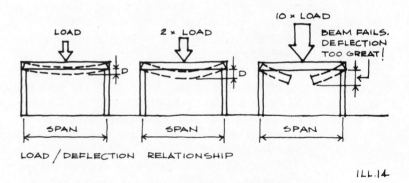

EVENLY DISTRIBUTED LOAD VS. CONCENTRATED LOAD

ILL. 13

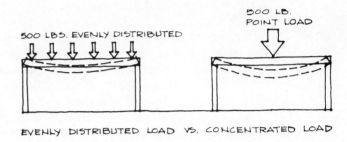

LOAD / DEFLECTION RELATIONSHIP

ILL. 14

ILL. 15

CROSS-SECTIONAL AREA = DEPTH × WIDTH

Structural
Principles

135

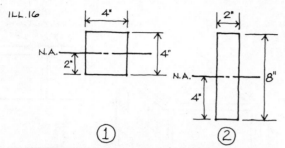

ILL. 16

BOTH SECTIONS 1 AND 2 HAVE A CROSS-
SECTIONAL AREA OF 16" SQUARE.
THE 2"x8" IS MORE EFFICIENT SINCE
IT PLACES MORE MATERIAL FURTHER
AWAY FROM THE NEUTRAL AXIS.

Cross-Sectional Dimensions

The cross section of a structural member refers to the shape and area of a cut perpendicular to its length. When we speak of cross-sectional area, we refer to the amount of material in the cross section (Ill. 15). In a rectangular section this would be the width times the depth of the cross section. If we speak of the shape of the section, we are talking about its proportions. It is a fact that a rectangular member when placed on its edge (long side vertical) will be able to span a longer distance and support a larger load than if it was placed on its flat side. Actually, the strength of a structural member is not so much dependent on the amount of material in the cross section as it is on the depth of the section. The most efficient section has most of its material (cross-sectional area) furthest away from its neutral axis. In doing this it is putting the most resistance where the stresses (compression and tension) are the greatest, at the top and the bottom of the section. Where the stresses are at their smallest (near the neutral axis), there is need for little material (Ill. 16).

ILL. 17

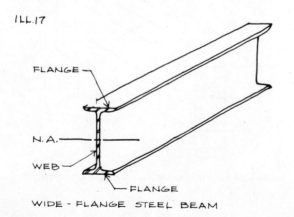

FLANGE

N.A.

WEB

FLANGE

WIDE - FLANGE STEEL BEAM

The wide-flange steel beam economically responds to this basic principle. The member is designed in such a way as to put the most steel where it is needed, at the top and the bottom, to counter the bending stresses (Ill. 17). The same principles apply to wood, but it is wasteful and expensive to cut wood in the wide-flange shape. Instead, wood is cut into rectangular sections of narrow width and large depth. Were timber to become as precious and costly a resource as steel, we might see lumber mills cutting more economically designed members. (Interestingly, some manufacturers are producing composite joists made out of plywood and lumber that closely resemble I-beams in shape.)

ILL. 18

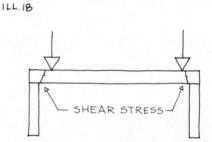

SHEAR STRESS

A beam carrying a load across a span is subjected to a combination of stresses (or intensities of strain). The stress at the *ends* of the beam, where it is attached to the columns, is called shear. Shear stresses can be described as ripping in opposite directions (Ill. 18). Bending stresses (Ill. 7), the combination of tension and compression, are greatest at the *center* of the beam span when the beam is uniformly loaded throughout.* It is important to know where these major stresses occur in a beam and how they affect its strength. As a general rule, you do not want to disturb the beam at a location where the stresses are greatest. For a uniformly loaded simple span beam, the shear stresses are greatest at the ends of the beam and zero at the center of the span, and the bending stresses are greatest at the center of the span and zero at the ends. For this reason, if you *must* drill a small hole through a beam, you should drill the opening along the neutral axis, toward the center of the span.

In the design of joists, beams, and girders, the interrelationship among span, load, and the structural member's cross-sectional dimension need to be evaluated to produce a satisfactory solution.

*Bending stresses in continuous beams and in rigid frames are more complex.

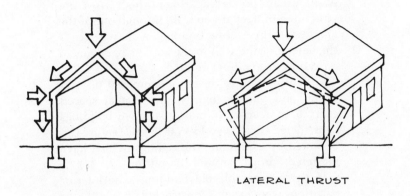

LATERAL THRUST

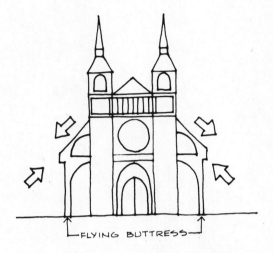

—FLYING BUTTRESS—

ILL.20

ROOF STRUCTURE

A flat roof acts exactly like a floor and is structurally designed as a horizontal component system. Sloped roofs, on the other hand, present their own problems. If the roof is sloped (over 20 degrees), it begins to differ from a strictly load-transferring horizontal component. The sloped roof transfers the load diagonally. This diagonal thrust must be broken down into a vertical and horizontal component in order to design for its proper support. The vertical component is supported by the walls (or beams to columns). The horizontal component, or lateral thrust, must be accounted for as well; otherwise, there is a tendency for the roof to push the walls outward (Ill. 19).

This outward thrust could be accommodated by placing a buttress against the outer walls. That is the way the lateral thrust of the nave in the Gothic cathedrals was countered (Ill. 20). Buttressing, however, is clumsy and unwieldy. The thrust could be countered by tying the rafter ends together using a steel chain or a piece of timber. This section is in tension—that is, it is being pulled or stretched. The most common solution in houses is to use a wood section as a collar beam or as ceiling joists to tie the rafter ends to each other, thereby countering the thrust (Ill. 21).

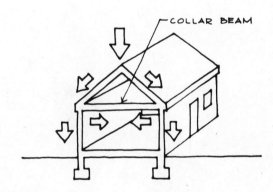

—COLLAR BEAM

ILL.21

HOW IS YOUR BUILDING STRUCTURED?

The following is a synopsis of the various building types. Your house or apartment building should fall into one of the categories.

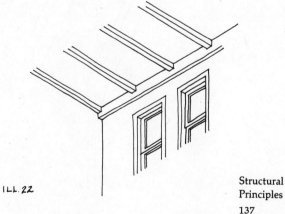

ILL.22

Structural
Principles

137

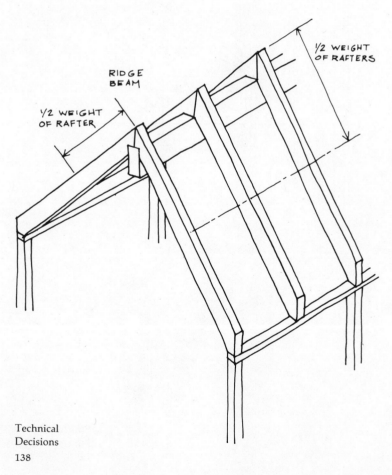

ILL. 23

RIDGE
BEAM

½ WEIGHT
OF RAFTER

½ WEIGHT
OF RAFTERS

ILL. 24

Apartment Buildings

Most urban prewar apartment high rises are structured in steel. If you walk through one of the apartments in such a building, you will see a thickening of the wall in the corners of rooms in a rhythm (or module) of 12' × 20' or 20' × 20'. The floor system is generally composed of steel beams and purlins (lightweight beams) spaced every 6' to 8' apart. In most apartment buildings constructed before World War II, this feature can be noted by examining the ceilings, which have plastered "drops" around the purlins (Ill. 22).

In these venerable old buildings, the interior partitions were usually constructed of 3"-, 4"-, or 5"-thick gypsum block, which is a lightweight, fire-resistant material that tends to crumble when cut into. Three coats of plaster—a brown, scratch, and finish coat*—were applied to the block wall. The partitions and, to some extent, the ceilings are solid. This means that you will have to channel into and then replaster the partitions should you add electric outlets, switches, or pipes.

Most postwar apartment buildings were constructed of poured-in-place concrete beams and columns. The floor structure consists of a poured-concrete slab 6" or more thick. The finished flooring was applied to the top of the slab, and plaster (or in some cases just paint) was applied directly to the bottom of the slab as the ceiling. The partitions in these buildings are usually metal stud and gypsum board (Ill. 23).

The oldest urban apartment buildings, generally no taller than six to eight stories, have solid-masonry load-bearing walls and wood-joist floor systems. It is often difficult to determine the structure of the building without probing the ceilings and partitions. Buildings of this genre usually have some very thick partitions and some thinner ones. The wood joists generally span between the thicker partitions, which are load-bearing. In a load-bearing building, it is critical that you not accidentally remove a load-bearing partition or cut into the joists of the floor system.

Wood-Frame Houses

Both the earliest and most modern wood-frame houses are based on a system called post-and-beam construction. This system is somewhat sim-

*The brown coat is composed of cement plaster, lime, and water. The scratch coat is similar to the first but is heavily scored (scratched) to receive the last coat. The plaster that is applied as a finish is called the white coat.

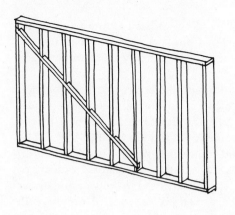

ILL. 25

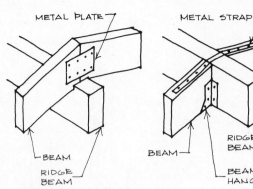

METAL STRAP — | METAL PLATE — | METAL STRAP —

BEAM

RIDGE BEAM

BEAM

RIDGE BEAM

BEAM

RIDGE BEAM

BEAM HANGER

ILL. 27

ilar to the steel-frame model, using relatively heavy lumber at wide intervals to transfer loads from roof to foundations (Ill. 24). Posts may be 4″ × 4″ or 4″ × 6″ in cross section and spaced 6′ to 8′ apart. Floor beams and roof rafters are often 4″ × 12″ or more in cross section and are spaced 4′ to 8′ apart. The floor and roof are structured with planks that are about 2″ thick. In the early days of heavy timber construction, care was taken to ensure the rigidity of the heavy frame by providing diagonal bracing (Ill. 25). Originally the connections were made with wooden pegs (Ill. 26). Today, these connections are made with steel timber connectors; nails are just not strong enough to hold the connections for post-and-beam construction (Ill. 27). The advantage of the

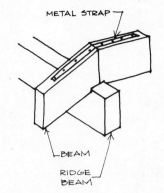

ILL. 28

ROOF

JOISTS

CONTINUOUS STUDS

JOISTS

FOUNDATIONS

SUBFLOOR

THE BALLOON FRAME

ILL. 26

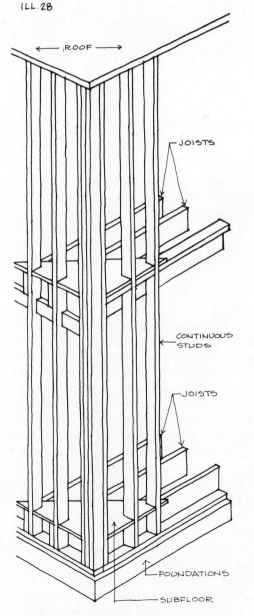

Structural Principles

139

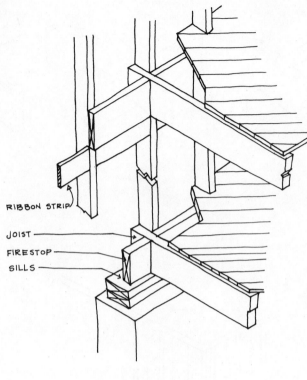

RIBBON STRIP
JOIST
FIRESTOP
SILLS

THE BALLOON FRAME   ILL. 29

fragile for a building, utilized a number of light-weight wood sections spaced inches apart instead of heavy timbers spaced many feet from one another (Ill. 28).

The predominant characteristic of the balloon frame is the use of 2 × 4 mini-columns (studs) that run vertically from the foundation to the roof. The frame is not rigid in itself (it will not be able to stand up at right angles in a windstorm) but requires the addition of diagonal bracing or plywood sheathing to keep it from swaying under pressure. This method of construction is still

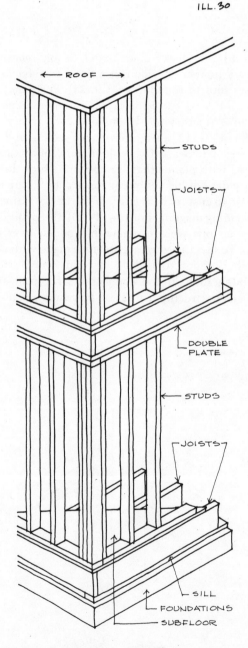

ILL. 30

ROOF
STUDS
JOISTS
DOUBLE PLATE
STUDS
JOISTS
SILL
FOUNDATIONS
SUBFLOOR

THE PLATFORM FRAME

post-and-beam frame today is to open the exterior walls for very wide windows and to allow for a feeling of openness on the interior.

Light-frame construction differs from the heavier-frame systems in that it uses much thinner and lighter structural members, usually not more than 2" thick. These studs (2 × 4's for the interior partitions and 2 × 6's for the exterior walls), joists (2 × 10's, 2 × 12's), and rafters (about the same sizes as the joists) are spaced 12", 16", or 24" apart. The framing members are nailed together and are braced by applying ¾"-thick plywood sheathing over the outside frame. This lightweight-framing method works almost like a load-bearing wall rather than a point support. Currently, two light-framing methods are used for residential construction: the balloon frame and the platform (or western) frame, the latter being the most popular of the two.

The balloon frame was invented in the 1830's and has been used for over 150 years. This system was designed in the Midwest just after the inventions of machine-made nails and the water-powered sawmill. The balloon frame revolutionized the house construction industry since it required only two or three workers to erect the frame and reduced its cost by almost 50 percent. This system, disparagingly labeled "balloon" by its earliest critics, who thought the frame was too

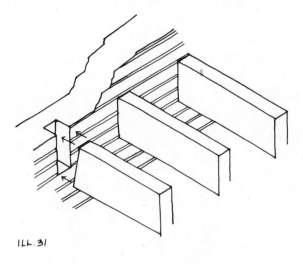

ILL. 31

being used today for two-story houses faced with masonry or stucco, since there is less overall shrinkage in the frame that might cause cracks in the stucco.

The easiest way to determine if your house is a balloon frame is to remove a small portion of the exterior siding in an area between the first and second floors. The studs are two stories long in a balloon frame, and the joists are nailed directly to them. If your house is two or more stories high and is finished in stucco, chances are the structure is balloon frame (Ills. 28 and 29).

The simplest method of wood-frame construction is the platform frame (Ill. 30). In this method, the builder constructs the entire subfloor before beginning the walls. In doing so, the worker has a flat and safe surface on which to build the wall sections. These sections are usually constructed horizontally on the floor with studs that are only one-story high and are then tilted up into place, temporarily braced, plumbed straight, and nailed to the subfloor. This system is the easiest to construct and will be the one discussed in the chapter on framing the extension.

The interior partitions in all wood-frame construction consists of wood studs (although some builders are using metal studs now) covered with either plaster (in the old houses) or gypsum board (in houses built after World War II). In either case, you can pretty much depend on the partitions being hollow and easily modified. Most wood-frame houses, whether sided in wood or

trimmed with a small amount of brick, are structured as platform frames. This method requires the least amount of cutting and is easiest to construct whether you are an experienced carpenter or a novice.

Garden Apartments and Low-Rise Apartment Buildings

Many apartment buildings located outside of the city and not more than three stories tall are built using platform-frame construction and sided with wood or with brick. The interior partitions are either wood or metal studs covered with either gypsum board or plaster. Some of the turn-of-the-century walk-up urban buildings are structured with masonry load-bearing walls with wood-joist floor systems.

Townhouses and Brownstones

Most attached housing is based on the structural principle of the load-bearing party wall. Most older buildings have masonry party walls; newer buildings are framed in fine-rated metal stud assemblies. Walls between the units support the floors, consisting of wood beams (or joists) that span between the walls, supporting planks (or plywood) (Ill. 31). The end walls of the house are generally non-load-bearing (except that they carry their own weight) and serve to separate the inside from the outside. If the townhouse is less than 16' wide, it is likely that the beams that span between the party walls do so without any intermediary support.*

The interior partitions may be composed of either studs, lath and plaster, or studs and gypsum board, depending on when the building was built.

*Some wide, old brownstones (say, over 19' wide) have a "prop" wall, an intermediary supporting partition that runs parallel to the long side walls, even though the joists run continuously from party wall to party wall. If you are considering removing anything that may be a prop wall, be sure to consult an architect or structural engineer.

17

STRUCTURAL

BUILDING MATERIALS

This book has three chapters on materials. The first, Chapter 10, deals with visible, finishing materials for the interior of the house, such as ceramic tile, parquet floors, and linoleum. Chapter 14 deals with exterior finishing materials, such as roofing shingles and wood siding. This chapter covers the unseen materials used for the structural parts of your renovation, such as metal studs, wood beams, and concrete. The sections on lumber and metal studs would be useful to most renovators since almost all of you will be involved with reworking some partitions and the easiest way to construct a partition is out of wood studs and gypsum board. The sections on concrete and concrete block (for foundations and load-bearing walls) have been included for renovators who are considering an addition to the house.

Generally, you can choose which structural materials you prefer to use, wood or metal studs for the walls, concrete or concrete block for the foundations. Be aware, however, that your choice of materials may be limited by various codes and covenants. For instance, if you are renovating your urban condominium, the city's building code may require that you use a fire-rated material such as metal studs and joists or lightweight concrete block (once known as cinder block) instead of wood structural members.

STRUCTURAL WOOD

Most of the houses in this country are structured in wood. This fact may not be immediately evi-
dent since many American houses are sided in brick, stucco, or aluminum applied to a wood frame. Lumber has always been the popular choice because it is inexpensive, readily available, easy to cut and nail, and relatively lightweight. The major drawbacks of this material are its tendency to decay when subjected to adverse conditions, to shrink and expand depending on its moisture content, as well as its combustibility and its edibility—by termites, that is.

Wood is almost always cut from the tree lengthwise, parallel to its long, sinuous fibers. It is strongest in this direction. Standing upright on a slim trunk, the living tree carries the weight of its branches, leaves, fruit, and the added loads of snow and wind (Ill. 1). Wood is strong in compression, which means that it can carry a lot of weight. Long vertical pieces of lumber act as columns or mini-columns (called studs) and carry the entire weight of the second floor and roof down to the foundation (Ill. 2).

Very often the tree is subjected to high winds, which cause it to bend. Wood's ability to bend (and not to fail under these stresses), to regain its original shape when the pressure is removed (its elasticity), and to resist completely succumbing to the bending forces (its stiffness) makes it a very good material to use horizontally as well as vertically. When a board is placed on its narrow side and made to span two supports, it is subjected to such bending stresses. The long sinews in wood, its fibers, resist these stresses (Ill. 3). (See Chapter 16.)

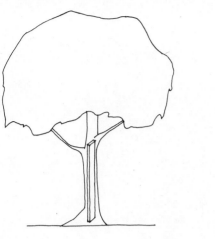

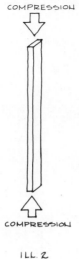

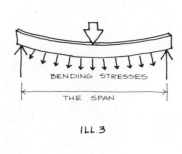

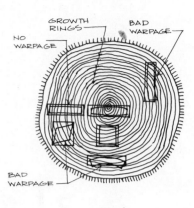

ILL.1

ILL.2

ILL.3

ILL.4

KILN-DRIED VERSUS ''GREEN'' LUMBER: The living tree consists of about 55 percent moisture. When the tree is cut down (thus becoming deadwood), it loses its natural juices and shrinks. Often, the moisture content of the lumber is removed artificially by the mills in drying ovens called kilns. Ideally, the moisture should be about 19 percent for wood that is to be used structurally. Why is the moisture content so important? If the lumber is used ''green'' (straight from the tree without being dried out), it will dry in time and in doing so will shrink quite a bit, while other building materials such as tile, glass, masonry, gypsum board, etc., will not. Joints that were previously tight will become loose; nails will become exposed, doors and windows will leak air. At the other extreme, if wood is oven-dried to remove all of its water, it will have the tendency to absorb moisture from the air in great quantities. The swollen wood would cause doors and windows to stick in hot, humid weather. In simplistic terms, wood swells and shrinks only slightly parallel to its grain (in its length), but does tend to swell and shrink perpendicular to its grain (across its trunk).

Because there is little shrinkage along the length of stud and a much greater degree of shrinkage in its cross section, the balloon frame (using long studs from sill to roof) is used when stucco or masonry facing material will be attached to the structure. These materials are relatively brittle and would crack if exposed to dimensional changes in the framing. The platform frame shrinks and expands in its length because of the floor framing elements used between the studs. Wood siding has the flexibility to accommodate these minor and invisible dimensional changes and can be used in conjunction with the platform frame.

When wood shrinks unevenly it warps. The amount and kind of warpage that occurs in a board depends on the original moisture content of the wood and how it is sliced from the tree trunk (Ill. 4). If you look at the end of a ''green'' board you will see part of the annual ring pattern of the trunk of the tree and you may be able to predict whether the board will warp when it dries. This may not be the most practical approach to the purchase of a major quantity of wood. If you purchase kiln-dried lumber, on the other hand, it is unlikely that the boards will warp.

Lumber

The term ''boards'' usually refers to pieces of wood that are less than 2" in depth, whereas ''lumber'' is wood cut into standard structural sizes and is generally 2" to 5" in depth. The ''nominal'' (rough) size is what it is called at the lumberyard and on architectural drawings (2 × 4, 2 × 6). The actual, dressed dimensions of the lumber you take home are smaller (a 2 × 4 will be ½" smaller in two dimensions). The reduction in size of the lumber dimensions is justified as part of the milling process that standardizes lumber sizes by planing all four surfaces to a smooth uniform product. You pay for the nominal size but buy the actual member. Kiln-drying, which also plays a part in diminishing the size of the lumber, reduces the shrinkage that may take place in the finished house. The reductions in dimensions have been standardized, so that a 2 × 4 will

INSET I/NOMINAL AND DRESSED SIZES OF SOFTWOOD LUMBER

(These are the "actual" dimensions for the following "nominal" sizes. When you purchase a 2 × 4, the actual lumber you go home with is 1½" × 3½".)

		Nominal	Actual (dry)	Green
Boards	(up to 12" wide)	1"	¾"	
		1¼"	1"	
		1½"	1¼"	
Lumber	(thickness: 2", 3", 4";	2"	1½"	1⁹⁄₁₆"
	width: up to 12"	3"	2½"	2⁹⁄₁₆"
	and over)	4"	3½"	3⁹⁄₁₆"
		6"	5½"	5⅝"
		8"	7¼"	7½"
		10"	9¼"	9½"
		12"	11¼"	11½"
		over 12"	less ¾"	less ½"
Timbers	(5" thick and over)	5" and larger	less ½"	less ½"
Decking	(tongue-and-	2" (thick)	1½"	
	groove boards)	3"	2½"	
		4"	3½"	

NLGA RULE NO. 1 S-GRN HEM-FIR — PL 73 — ILL. 5 (handwritten notation)

always be exactly 1½" by 3½", and a 1 × 12 will always measure 25/32" × 11¼". Inset I gives the actual dimensions of the most common nominal sizes. The length of the board, by the way, is not affected. When you buy a 14'-long board it should measure 14'.

Lumber is sold in lengths up to 24'. Although you can have lumber cut to any size (under 24'), it is more efficient to use it in the standard lengths in which it is sold—less waste, less labor. Yard lumber is commonly sold in lengths of 8', 10', 12', 14', and 16'. Lumber longer than 16' may be difficult to find and/or more costly. Lumber longer than 24', whether cut from one piece or laminated,* is very expensive and should not be needed for residential construction. It is a good idea to plan the joists in modules of 2' so that you will not have to cut longer sections down.

TYPES AND GRADES OF LUMBER: Many kinds of wood are used for construction purposes and each variety of tree is divided further into grades depending on the quality of the sample cut. Wood is classified as either softwood or hardwood (misleading terms, because they have absolutely nothing to do with the strength of the timber). Softwoods are cut from conifers, trees that have

needles, also known as evergreens. Commonly used conifers are pine, Douglas fir, and hem-fir. Softwood is generally used for structural purposes, such as framing, but has also been used for finished flooring and furniture. Hardwood comes from deciduous trees (those that lose their leaves in winter) and is very dense. Hardwoods such as maple, mahogany, oak, and fruitwood are used for finished floors and fine furniture.

Structural softwood is generally divided into classifications and grades depending on its strength, likely use, and imperfections. Lumber is classified into two major categories: *stress-graded lumber* and *yard lumber*. Stress-graded lumber is used for long span beams where the loads are large and have been carefully calculated. These beams are usually supplied to developers directly from the mill and are rarely seen in lumberyards. Yard lumber—used for light framing—is readily available and is divided into the following subcategories: *select-structural,* the best of the lot, is clear—that is, without knotholes, bark, splits, or other defects; *construction* (also called no. 1) is mostly clear; *standard and better* (no. 2) has firm knotholes that should not affect its overall strength; and *utility* (no. 3) covers whatever is left that can still be called lumber. Select-structural and construction grades are used for beams and joists. Standard and better is used for studs. The strength of the joist is related to both the type of tree and its grade. A no. 1 joist cut from Douglas

*Laminated means that several thin layers of wood are bonded together to form one solid piece.

LUMBER CUT FOR HORIZONTAL USE

Joists: Usually 2″ (nominal) in thickness used to directly support floor or ceiling, and supported in turn by a larger horizontal member (beam or girder) or a bearing wall. Joists are generally spaced at small, regular intervals, such as 12″, 16″, or 24″ on center.

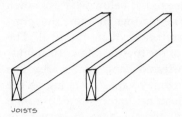

JOISTS

Beams: Larger (in cross section, not necessarily in length) than joists. Used to support joists and transfer their loads to vertical supports (or to girders).

Girders: Similar to beams, only larger in cross section.

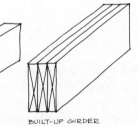

BEAM   BUILT-UP GIRDER

Planks: 2″ in thickness (could be 3″ or 4″). Used as flooring, roofing, or decking, directly over and supported by beams.

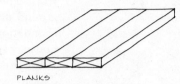

PLANKS

LUMBER CUT FOR VERTICAL USE

Posts: Vertical supports, usually short.

Columns: Vertical supports, longer than posts. Used to transfer horizontal loads down to the foundations.

Studs: Mini-columns. A series of slender structural members placed at small, regular intervals as the supporting elements in load-bearing wood walls and partitions.

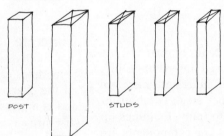

POST   STUDS

COLUMN

LUMBER CUT FOR DIAGONAL USE

Bracing: A piece of lumber applied to the frame on the diagonal to stiffen the structure.

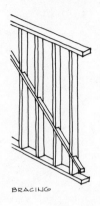

BRACING

Bridging: Used in an "X" pattern between the joists to stiffen the floor.

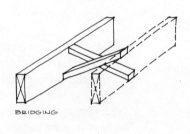

BRIDGING

---

fir will be stronger than one similarly graded cut from hem-fir.

Each piece of yard lumber bears the stamp of the manufacturer, giving its brand name, the code for the mill location, the tree from which it was cut, its grade, and its moisture content (Ill. 5). The stamp may indicate the suggested usage as well, such as "stud." Most lumberyards will stock only a limited selection of tree types and grades (Inset II).

LIGHTWEIGHT METAL FRAMING

The channel-shaped light steel sections used in lightweight metal framing resemble wood studs and joists more than they do heavier steel girders and columns (Ill. 6). As a matter of fact, light

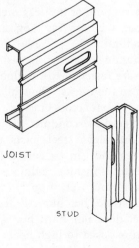

JOIST

STUD

ILL.6

Structural
Building
Materials

145

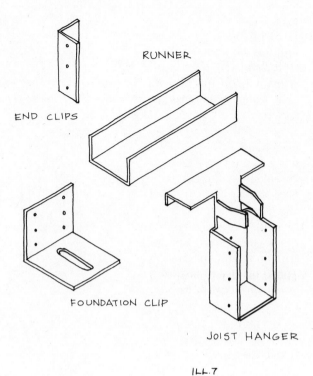

END CLIPS

RUNNER

FOUNDATION CLIP

JOIST HANGER

ILL. 7

metal sections are a substitute for lumber and the two materials are often used interchangeably. Lightweight structural steel studs and joists are made of galvanized* or primed steel. These structural components are used to frame buildings up to four or five stories high. The components are screwed together using clips, straps, and anchors where required or can be welded (Ill. 7). In addition, "nonstructural" lightweight metal studs are available for use in non-load-bearing walls and partitions. The gauge of the metal indicates whether it is structural or not: 24g metal framing is nonstructural, whereas 14g, 16g, and 18g are generally structural.

The wall framing systems consist of runner channels that are fastened to the floor and steel studs screwed to the tracks. The wall studs have openings in the web for cross bracing and the easy passage of electrical conduits or horizontal plumbing. Lightweight steel joists come in a number of sizes and can be cut to the desired lengths. Accessories include endpieces for framing, joist hangers, and web supports. Steel framing is incombustible, but like all steel it is not fireproof. Steel does not burn but will lose its strength when exposed to high heat.

*Galvanizing: the application of a zinc coating to steel as a means of preventing corrosion.

CONCRETE AND CONCRETE BLOCK

If you are constructing an addition to the house, you will need to know about concrete and concrete block for the footings and the foundation work. The foundations of a building root it in the ground and transfer its loads to the earth. The foundations are a continuation of the walls of the house deep into the ground below what is known as the frost line.* The footings sit under the foundation wall and are wider than the wall. The width or "spread" of the footing allows the building loads to be transferred along a wider area. The width of the footing may vary depending on the magnitude of the load being transferred through the foundation wall and the bearing capacity of the soil. (The classic example is how snowshoes transfer your weight to the snow over a large surface area.) Foundation walls can be constructed of reinforced poured concrete or concrete block. Footings are always constructed of poured concrete.

Concrete

Sometimes called man-made stone, concrete has all the characteristics of the original—durability and compressive strength. In addition, it can be cast into any shape and reinforced with steel rods to increase its tensile strength. Concrete consists of the following ingredients in varying proportions determined by the desired strength of the resultant product, its appearance, and weather conditions: fine aggregates (sand), coarse aggregates (crushed stone), Portland cement, and water.

Portland cement is a combination of various minerals (primarily lime, iron, alumina, silica, etc.) which are mixed and fired in a kiln. The final mixture, when combined with water, forms a paste. This paste cures into a very hard mass. Type I Portland cement is the most commonly used.

Water, when mixed with Portland cement, triggers a chemical reaction (called hydration) that causes the cement to set. The amount of water used in a batch of concrete is critical. Enough water must be used to produce the chemical reac-

*The frost line is the depth at which the moisture in the soil will not freeze. This depth varies from climate to climate. Since water tends to expand when frozen, icy soil under the foundations can cause the entire house to heave unevenly, causing enormous structural damage.

tion and to make the concrete workable when fluid. Too much water weakens the concrete to a significant degree. Proportions of water to cement vary according to the nature of the job.

The aggregates determine the weight of the concrete. For the most part, sand is used to fill in the voids between the coarser aggregates. Most lightweight aggregates are nonstructural. Mineral feldspar, for example, is used in construction applications requiring less heavy concrete or to insulate steel against fire. The resultant product is comparatively weak.

The mixing of concrete is very tricky. Since so many things can go wrong, weakening or contaminating the concrete, we don't recommend that you mix your own. (If you need only small amounts for noncritical applications, purchase a bag of dry mix and follow the directions on the bag.) If you need enough concrete to pour footings and/or foundation walls, we suggest you purchase ready-mixed concrete delivered by mixing truck. Ready-mixed concrete has a number of benefits other than sparing you a tedious job. The manufacturing process assures you a mixture of uniform quality and guarantees strength. In addition, a truckload of concrete allows you to pour continuously (without pausing to make a new batch), which results in a better-looking, more watertight product.

Concrete, which is very strong in compression but weak in tension, can manage compressive stresses by itself but does not hold up very well under stretching and bending (tensile) stresses. To compensate for this, concrete is often combined with steel to withstand bending and produce a more efficient and much stronger material; this is known as reinforced concrete. Steel bars are embedded in the concrete. The concrete then carries the compressive load while the steel (an excellent material in tension) takes care of the tensile stress. Reinforcing steel bars are placed in the areas where there will be tension (Ill. 8). Rein-

forcement is almost always used in the lower portion of the simply supported horizontal beam, where most of the "stretching" occurs.

Concrete must be poured into formwork that is constructed and braced before the concrete is mixed. Erecting formwork is not easy since it involves carpentry work and great care. Forms have to be well constructed and strong enough to sustain the weight of the concrete. In addition, they should be easy to remove when the concrete has hardened. The construction of formwork is not recommended for the beginner. The cost of lumber for the formwork must be added to the cost of the foundations. In some areas of the country the rental of metal formwork may be a viable option.

Concrete Block

Concrete block can be used to construct load-bearing walls and foundation walls. There are a number of different kinds of concrete block, some for construction purposes only and others with a decorative, textured surface which make an attractive wall as well as a serviceable one. Concrete block is a manufactured product made up of the same components as concrete. The mix proportions and the curing process are closely regulated, resulting in a product of uniform quality. A concrete-block wall is less expensive to construct than a brick wall.

Block comes in a number of sizes, shapes, and classifications. Grade N blocks are used for exterior walls and for foundations, whereas S blocks should be used only for interior partitions that will not be subject to freezing. Grade I block is a low-moisture block meant primarily for very dry areas, and grade II is designed for most locations. NII is an all-purpose block. Among the many shapes and sizes available, the stretcher block (nominal size: 8″ × 8″ × 16″, actual size: 7⅝″ × 7⅝″ × 15⅝″) is most often used, but the block size will vary according to structural requirements. Corners and double corners (or pier blocks) are used in conjunction with the stretcher blocks for end conditions (Ill. 9).

Concrete block is rated according to strength, ranging from solid load-bearing block for jobs where heavy compressive strength is required to hollow non-load-bearing block for use as non-load-bearing partitions. The most commonly used block, however, is the hollow load-bearing block, since it offers a great range of uses and is most readily available. It has a good capacity for carrying compressive stresses, in addition to being

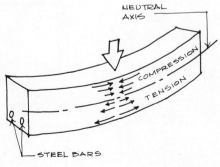

ILL. 8

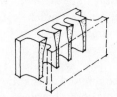

Because the cores in the block are tapered, one face has smaller cavities than the other and, therefore, more concrete-bearing surface. In order to get maximum bonding with the mortar, the side with the smaller cores should always face up.

ILL. 9

STRETCHER BLOCK

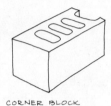

CORNER BLOCK

DOUBLE CORNER OR
PIER BLOCK

lightweight and coming in a wide range of shapes and sizes. Hollow blocks are either two- or three-cored, each kind having slightly different physical properties. Two-cored units have larger holes than three-cored ones and are consequently lighter and cheaper. The air spaces between the block faces have some insulating quality in themselves, but they can be filled with insulating material or concrete or grout. Three-cored blocks are stronger than the two-cored variety and are better suited for foundation walls. The cores in concrete block are tapered so that one side of the block has smaller openings than the other. Blocks are laid with the smaller cores up to provide a bed for the mortar (Inset III).

18

PLUMBING DESIGN

Most people embarking on a renovation would like to forget about plumbing. Plumbing is not glamorous or exciting. Unlike carpentry, it is hidden within the walls of the house. No one will ever admire it. People will merely assume it is there and will be inconvenienced if it does not operate properly. Like it or not, a renovator has to come to terms with plumbing, whether to properly plan extensions to the system or to resolve existing problems.

In this chapter we attempt to demystify plumbing by examining the various components that make up the system. The cycle of bringing water in, through, and out of a house breaks down into three basic phases. The starting point is the source of water, be it a municipal water main, a private well, or another source. Next there must be a distribution system inside the house which makes the water accessible to the various fixtures and faucets, to the hot-water heater, and to the heating system (if applicable) in the building. Finally, the used water and any waste have to be drained and disposed of by means of a sewage disposal system.

Before moving ahead to explain the components of a plumbing system, a few words of advice are in order. Although the plumbing system in a house is relatively simple to understand, its actual design and installation are far from easy tasks. Pipes are heavy and cumbersome to handle and the connection work is sometimes tricky. Leaky connections can damage walls, floors, and fancy finishes. Because faulty plumbing installations can be a health hazard, most communities require a license to do plumbing work. We believe it is wiser to hire a plumber. Those of you who live in apartments are cautioned even more strongly. Keep in mind that you have people living all around you. Any mishap or inconvenience will affect not only you but your neighbors as well. For this reason, in addition to the requirements of the building code, the co-op board or management agent will probably not allow work by anyone other than a licensed plumber. Perhaps your talents would best be used in hooking up fixtures once the pipes are installed, if the codes permit it. Be sure to consult all codes and the appropriate building officials before going ahead with any aspect of the design or installation of the system. Even if you do hire a plumber, it is helpful to have an understanding of how the system operates and what materials can and should be used.

GETTING WATER TO THE FIXTURES

The primary function of the water supply system is to make water available to the various fixtures in the house. It consists of a water supply main, a water heater, hot- and cold-water pipes, valves, air chambers, and a meter (pumps and storage tanks are required for private systems).

Water is pushed into the fixtures by either gravity, street pressure, or circulating pumps. Municipal mains get the necessary pressure by

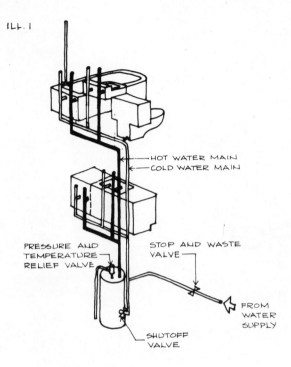

ILL. 1

HOT WATER MAIN
COLD WATER MAIN

PRESSURE AND
TEMPERATURE
RELIEF VALVE

STOP AND WASTE
VALVE

FROM
WATER
SUPPLY

SHUTOFF
VALVE

gravity since reservoirs are situated at high altitudes or water is stored in water towers. In private systems where cisterns are used, the water pressure is obtained by means of a circulating pump. In well systems the joint effort of a well pump and a storage tank supplies the necessary pressure. The pump pulls the water out of the well and into the tank. Once there, the compressed air in the tank pushes the water out of the tank and into the supply main.

The water supply main (the pipe bringing the water from the source to the house) is a very important component of the system since any problems in the main could potentially cut off the water supply. In cold climates, the main is always located well below the frost line to avoid any danger of the pipe freezing and bursting. Make sure this is the case at your house.

Upon entering the building, the supply main (like a tree) branches out to reach the fixtures and supply them with hot- and cold-water service. Any special provision, such as water-softening treatment or installation of a water meter, occurs at this point, before the main has been subdivided (frequently softening equipment is installed in the hot-water supply). Afterward, the main supply line is divided into a hot- and a cold-water main. The hot-water main is connected to an electric, oil, gas, or solar water heater, where the water is brought up to a higher temperature (Inset I). (Houses using hydronic—that is, steam or hot water—heating may utilize the boiler as

the heating medium.) Once the water is heated, the pressure in the pipes directs it to each fixture branch pipe via intermediary branch lines and risers (Ill. 1). These lines are hidden by snaking them through walls, floors, and ceilings.*

The cold-water system, on the other hand, bypasses the water heater. It branches out in parallel with the hot-water supply into intermediary pipes, risers, and fixture branch pipes until each fixture is reached.

Integral parts of the cold- and hot-water supply systems are the valves for the regulation of the flow of water. Some valves can be gradually opened or closed to get the desired quantity of flow. Other valves are designed to completely close off the flow or open it to full capacity. Shutoff valves such as these are installed throughout the system to isolate sections and facilitate repairs. For instance, a shutoff valve is provided in the water supply main and on both sides of any meter before it branches out into hot- and cold-water mains. They are also installed at each fixture branch pipe and horizontal branches leading to the kitchen and bath. The main cold-water shutoff may be outside the house, in a pit or box, depending on utility company requirements.

Valves are also instrumental in the drainage of the water supply system. Houses situated in cold climates need to have their water supply system totally emptied if they are to remain unheated for a period of time during the winter. Otherwise, freezing water inside the pipes can cause severe damage to the system. To facilitate drainage, all the horizontal branch pipes are pitched toward one or more drain valves. (Pipe hangers are used to adjust pipes to the correct pitch.)

Water pipes can be noisy. You may have heard a loud bang (water hammer) while quickly closing a faucet. This is caused by water pressure and can be corrected by installing an air chamber in both the hot- and cold-water supply at each fixture. In spite of the fancy name, an air chamber is simply an extra run of pipe located at each fixture (Ill. 2). The extra length of pipe is filled with air. Water can get into it only by compressing the air. The compression in turn provides a cushion to prevent the bang. A device called a petcock may be in-

*Another approach to the standard hot-water system is to provide a continuous hot-water circulation by cycling water back to the heater. The purpose of recirculating the unused water is to prevent it from cooling off while standing in the pipes near the faucet. Instead, it flows back into the heater, allowing the fixture branch pipe to receive new hot water. This system is more expensive but in a large house it provides hot water on demand.

A water heater is a heat transfer mechanism by which cold water is brought up to a higher temperature. The heat can be generated electrically or by means of oil or gas firing. Houses with hydronic heating systems may use their boilers as the heat source.*

Solar collectors offer another method for heating water. There are many systems commercially available which will supply between 40 and 100 percent of a house's requirements. The extra components of a solar system involve south-facing collectors of between 30 and 100 square feet in area, circulating lines, a storage tank, a pump, and connections to tap into the conventionally powered hot-water heater. The angle of the collector is calculated by adding 5 degrees to the latitude (number of degrees above the equator) of your house.

Besides the difference in the method of heat generation, water heaters can be of the tank or tankless type. Tankless heaters are utilized on small compact houses. Tank-type heaters, on the other hand, are employed to have a large amount of water quickly available and assure a better supply of hot water at all times. Another advantage of tank-type heaters is that the size of the heater itself may be reduced because there is always a supply of water in the tank.

SIZING A TANK-TYPE HEATER

The size of the water heater needed varies according to the hot water used per person per day. Water consumption per person may range from 20 to 100 gallons per day (gpd). These variations take into account the use of water-consuming appliances such as dishwashers and washing machines. For our calculations, we'll use a comfortable 100 gpd, projecting the use of a dishwasher and washing machine. You should keep in mind, however, a few tips which will reduce your hot-water requirements. Use spray-type faucets and short or insulated runs of pipe. In addition, washing machines, dishwashers, and other water-consuming appliances should be run at peak capacity. By following these suggestions, you can reduce the 100 gpd per person figure by two-thirds.

To calculate the size of the heater, a few points must be kept in mind. First, it has been estimated that the peak hot-water demand in residences occurs within a four-hour period. This maximum hourly demand, however, represents only about one-seventh of the total daily demand. Second, a tank large enough to hold one-fifth of the daily hot-water requirements is recommended. Keep in mind that the figure representing the total tank capacity is deceiving, since when more than 70 percent of the tank's volume is drawn, the water starts to cool. For this reason, the tank's total capacity is multiplied by a factor of .70 in order to arrive at a net capacity (in other words, to find out how much hot water it will realistically supply).

The calculations follow. Let's assume a family of five.

1. Determine the total daily hot-water requirement: 5 people × 100 gpd per person = 500 gpd total demand.

2. Determine the maximum hourly demand: 500 gpd (total demand) × $\frac{1}{7}$ (maximum hourly demand factor) = 71.4.

3. Find out the amount of water needed to satisfy the four-hour peak load: 71.4 (maximum hourly demand) × 4 = 285.6 gallons.

4. The tank's capacity should be one-fifth the total daily requirement: 500 gpd (total daily requirement) × $\frac{1}{5}$ = 100 gallons.

5. Determine the tank's net volume: 100 gallons (total volume) × .70 = 70 gallons.

6. Since the water needed to satisfy the four-hour peak load is 285.6 gallons and the net capacity of the tank is 70 gallons, there are still 215.6 gallons of water (285.6 − 70) that the water heater must heat.

7. To find out the heater's hourly output, divide 4 (peak hours) into 215.6 gallons of water which remain to be heated:

$$\frac{215.6 \text{ gallons}}{4 \text{ peak hours}} = 53.9 \text{ gallons per hour (gph)}.$$

In order to satisfy the house's hot-water requirements, the water heater in the example must be able to produce 54 gallons of hot water per hour.

*This particular type of water heater can be of the internal or the external type: internal is where the heating mechanism is literally immersed in the boiler; external is where it sits outside the boiler but receives hot water from the boiler as the heating medium.

---

stalled in the air chamber to recharge it with air. In addition to air chambers, there are mechanical shock absorbers; these provide a more sophisticated and efficient solution to the problem of water hammer.

Supply Pipe Materials

There are numerous materials available for supply piping. If you are lucky, your house will have copper supply piping (more correctly called tubing) from top to bottom. Other materials that you may find are lead, galvanized steel, brass, and, in new homes, even plastic (Inset II). Should your house have lead piping, there is only one solution: it needs to be replaced. Lead pipes may leach poisonous substances into the water. Each of the other materials poses different problems in terms of durability and joinery.

Piping materials can be rated in terms of corrosion resistance, method of connection, cost, and acceptability by the various codes. Materials range from plain or galvanized steel to cast iron, brass, copper, and plastic. To further complicate matters, the selection of one material alone does not solve all your problems. Codes sometimes specify one material for the water supply system, another one for the drainage system or for a particular section of each system. Occasionally they

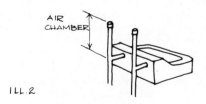

ILL. 2

stipulate that certain materials may not be used at all. What might prove to be a very good choice for water supply pipes might not be so efficient for drainage, or vice versa. In essence, the problem is not simple. We have tried to narrow down the choices by rating the materials in terms of performance, corrosion, and ease of installation. (Needless to say, if the code says otherwise, it wins.) In addition, consideration must be given to the problem of joining different supply pipe materials within one installation.

There are many ways of joining pipes: threading, soldering, brazing, caulking, gluing (or cementing), and mechanical connections. The most commonly used methods are threading, soldering, and gluing. Threading is a tedious and difficult job, involving cutting a length of pipe, fitting a threader into the pipe, turning it until enough thread has been cut, screwing the pipe into the fitting, and applying a compound or joint tape. A solder joint, on the other hand, involves only cutting, slipping on the fitting, and soldering the connection. An entire assembly of pipes can be set without turning any of the parts. Although neither one of these two can be considered elementary procedures, soldering is easier than threading. This is very important when you consider how many connections you have to make. Steel and brass pipe require threaded connections. Plastic pipe is the easiest to assemble, merely requiring cutting and applying a cement. The biggest drawback, however, is that once the pipes are glued together they cannot be taken apart.

In terms of corrosion resistance, copper and plastic rate better than plain or galvanized steel, iron, or brass.* Plastic piping is presently widely available. Its great ease of installation, low cost, light weight, and self-insulating qualities make it a very attractive choice. Its use is still sometimes restricted by code because of its possible health hazards. (Controversy still exists as to its poten-

tial toxicity.) Many codes do not allow its use, particularly for the water supply system.*

Copper is a very popular choice and the one we recommend in particular for the water supply system. It is not subject to attack by acids or corrosion and is therefore more durable. In addition, it comes in both rigid and flexible form. Because it requires solder joints rather than threading, it is relatively simple to assemble. It is more expensive than either ferrous or plastic piping, but it is cheaper than brass. In addition, it is widely accepted by building codes.

Connecting New Pipe to Old

Connecting to the existing piping is a tricky maneuver. If your existing pipes are galvanized steel, you may find that when you try to cut into them to make a connection they appear to disintegrate, particularly at the threads. We have often found in renovation work that whole sections of galvanized steel piping, although seemingly in reasonably good condition, fall apart when new plumbing pipes are being attached to them. The best solution is to replace them all. If you live in an apartment, this may not be an option. You would be best advised, however, to have all the pipes replaced within your apartment and all the way to the building riser which supplies your

*Red brass is an exception, offering excellent corrosion resistance. It is alloyed with copper, and although it is almost pure copper, it is correctly called brass.

*The use of PVC and other plastic piping materials has long been a source of controversy. Potential health hazards were originally raised in terms of the inhalation of PVC fumes by workers in the plastics industry. In addition, it has been suspected that minute amounts of PVC may "leak" from PVC bottles into the contained liquid. (This suspicion was responsible for the FDA ban on the use of PVC in liquor bottles and food containers.) In the event of a fire, plastic piping and tubing can become a source of hazardous fumes. A wide range of plastics is currently being used for piping, including PVC. This plastic piping comes with ratings for various uses, including heat resistance, pressure, and even potable water use. We do not recommend the use of plastic for the water supply system. Should you decide (and are allowed by code) to do so, make sure to research the material thoroughly.

apartment. Discuss this in advance with the building manager or superintendent.

A further consideration in renovation is joining dissimilar materials. Joining ferrous to nonferrous pipes results in galvanic action. For this reason, whereas connecting copper to red brass is not a problem, connecting galvanized steel to copper or brass will leave you with a problem-ridden installation. There are instances, such as in the case of an apartment building, where even if you replace all the piping within your apartment with copper, you still may need to hook up to a main supply riser made of steel. Special fittings or adapters designed for this purpose are available.

Pipe Sizing

The sizes of pipes vary according to their function within the system and the amount of water they must carry. The principle is well illustrated in the structure of a tree: the farther away from the trunk, the smaller the branch. A branch pipe bringing water to a sink carries less water than the main that supplies the entire bathroom and is, therefore, smaller in diameter.

The sizes of pipes necessary for one- or two-family houses are rarely calculated. The required sizes are often outlined by codes or by tried-and-true rules of thumb. If you live in an apartment building, you have to use the building's guidelines (which would have been dictated by the building code). For preliminary design purposes, we have compiled a list of the most common sizes used for supply copper tubing in residential work. (Keep in mind that pipe sizes vary according to the material used.) Consult your local building code before finalizing the sizes. Do not make these sizes any smaller unless you want to hear humming in the pipes or have low water pressure. Making the pipes larger than required does not hurt.

WATER SUPPLY PIPE SIZES

Supply main: 1"
Hot- and cold-water mains: 1"
Intermediary branches: 3/4"
Branches to each fixture: 1/2"

Pipe Fittings

In their run through the house, pipes have to change direction, branch into other pipes, reduce large pipes into smaller ones, and so on, while at the same time permitting the uninterrupted flow

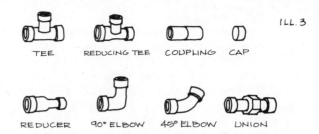

ILL. 3

TEE   REDUCING TEE   COUPLING   CAP

REDUCER   90° ELBOW   45° ELBOW   UNION

of water. Pipe fittings are provided for this purpose. They can be soldered, threaded, or specially designed, as in the case of plastic or cast-iron piping. It all depends on the material you are using. Copper piping is connected by means of soldered fittings (Ill. 3).

How to Modify and Map Out the Water Supply System

1. Start by determining the material of the existing piping (Inset II). If you have galvanized steel or lead, plan to replace all the piping. Those with copper or brass piping need be concerned only with extending or modifying the existing system to accommodate the renovation plans. Should the supply pipe be plastic, you must investigate issues of code compliance and potential health hazards.

2. Check the water pressure. There are various problems that can result in low water pressure. The town may have a recurrent problem with the water pressure. Talk to the local authorities. There may be other culprits. The main supply pipe into the house may be too small. It should be at least 1" in diameter. If the supply pipe is large enough, then the problem may lie with the pipes within the building. They could be too small, might be kinked, or have deposit buildup. Lack of water pressure in houses connected to a well may be the result of a worn-out pump or lack or water in the well. A well pump running excessively is often a sign of trouble.

3. Is your existing hot water heater large enough to handle your present load? Does it have enough capacity to meet the additional demands you are planning for your plumbing system? Investigate the advantages of going to a larger size.

4. Check to see if the existing water drainage system is vented. (It is not uncommon for older buildings to have unvented piping.) If it is not vented, you must include the venting of these pipes in your renovation plans.

5. Make sure that the existing pipe sizes meet code requirements. You may have to increase the size of some pipes.

Plumbing Design

153

6. Take a look at your preliminary plans and examine the locations of the proposed bathrooms, kitchen, laundry room, and any other area requiring plumbing. Are they efficiently arranged? Can they be moved closer? Can they share a "wet" wall by being back to back or by being stacked? It should be evident at this point why grouping fixtures together facilitates the design and installation of a plumbing system. The closer the fixtures, the shorter the pipe runs and therefore the less work and expense. In addition, when the distances between baths or other plumbing fixtures are excessively long, the code may require that you install a circulating hot-water line.

7. Keep in mind that, with the exception of basements (where pipes may be left exposed), pipes are usually concealed inside walls, floors, and ceilings. Wherever you require a new pipe or are replacing an old one, all these finishes need to be ripped apart and later patched and repaired. However, nothing prevents running exposed piping if the aesthetics are not displeasing to you.

8. Show all the fixtures on the plan and provide each one of them with a hot- and a cold-water supply pipe (as required). You can indicate the pipes as circles in the wall next to the fixture (Ill. 4).

9. Make provision for valves throughout the system. Keep in mind that check valves are required in both the cold- and the hot-water lines to dishwashers and washing machines.

10. Establish the shortest route that the hot- and cold-water pipes must travel in order to reach the supply main and the water heater or boiler. In order to do this, examine the available walls, floors, and ceilings through which the pipes can run. Consider the structural elements within the walls and floors (studs, joists, etc.). Make sure that the pipes work with them rather than disrupt them.

DRAINAGE

The used water together with any waste it has collected has to be led out of the house and into a disposal system (be it a municipal sewer main or a private sewage system). This is the function of a drainage system. In addition to getting rid of the waste, the drainage system has to provide an exhaust for harmful and smelly gases generated by the waste. Two interlocking networks are provided for this purpose. The first is a network of pipes that carries all waste from each fixture to the sewage disposal system. The second is a venting system in parallel with the drain piping that allows gas to be exhausted to the outside while letting air in (Ill. 5).

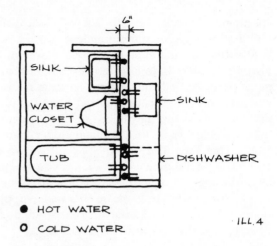

HOT WATER
COLD WATER

ILL. 4

The drainage system operates very much like the water supply. Waste from the fixtures drains to the waste pipe and is discharged into an intermediary branch line, which picks up waste from fixtures located on the same floor or in the same area. In order to reach the basement, the waste is channeled to a vertical pipe (soil stack) that runs the full height of the building (from the basement to the roof). The purpose of a soil stack is to receive the waste from all intermediary lines and transfer it to the house drain, which is the link between the drainage and the disposal system (Ill. 5). The soil stack carries both solid and liquid waste. In large installations or where the distance between some fixtures and the soil stack is too great, a secondary stack called a waste stack is provided (Ill. 6). In apartment houses there are sometimes two stacks, a 4″ soil stack for toilets and a 3″ waste stack for service sinks. Houses may need two stacks where kitchens and bathrooms are remote from each other.

Unlike the water supply system, which functions by means of pressure, the drainage system relies completely on gravity. For this reason, all waste pipes are either vertical or have a downward pitch (⅛″ per 1′ to ¼″ per 1′). In addition, drainage pipes have a large cross-sectional area to help prevent solid matter from accumulating and clogging the pipes.

The venting system is an integral part of the drainage system. The soil stack, which is the main artery for drainage, becomes the "lungs" for the vents. It serves this purpose by being open at the roof (Ill. 5). This opening allows air into the soil stack (referred to as the stack vent once it extends over the highest fixture) at the same time that gases are exhausted, preventing suction and gas accumulation in the pipes. In addition to the soil stack, a fresh-air inlet is sometimes provided at or near the house trap.

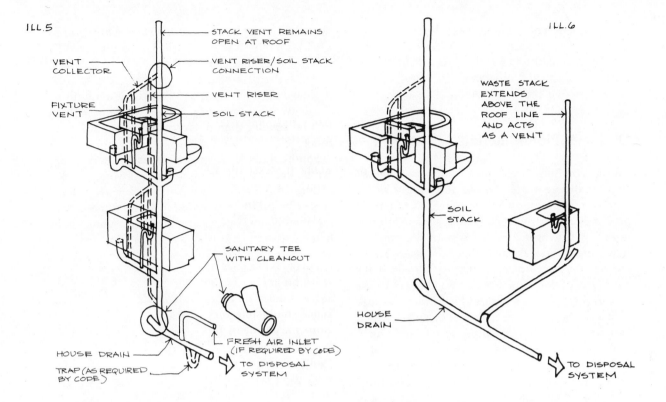

ILL.5

STACK VENT REMAINS OPEN AT ROOF

VENT COLLECTOR

VENT RISER/SOIL STACK CONNECTION

VENT RISER

FIXTURE VENT

SOIL STACK

SANITARY TEE WITH CLEANOUT

HOUSE DRAIN

TRAP (AS REQUIRED BY CODE)

FRESH AIR INLET (IF REQUIRED BY CODE)

TO DISPOSAL SYSTEM

ILL.6

WASTE STACK EXTENDS ABOVE THE ROOF LINE AND ACTS AS A VENT

SOIL STACK

HOUSE DRAIN

TO DISPOSAL SYSTEM

Although the soil stack is the main source of air, it is difficult for air to find its way to all the fixtures unless each is provided with a branch vent. Branch vents are pipes carrying nothing but air that lead from each fixture to a vent collector. In compact installations, the collector hooks up to a vent riser. The connection between the vent riser and the soil stack occurs above the level of the highest fixtures, where the soil stack becomes the stack vent (Ill. 5). In large installations or where distances between the vent riser and the soil stack are too great, the riser is led directly to the roof, becoming a direct ventilation source—it is common in houses for a bathroom and the kitchen sink to have a separate vent (Ill. 6).

To further prevent gases from entering the house, traps are provided at each fixture. A trap is the U-shaped pipe you always see under sinks. Every fixture has a trap but most of them are hidden within walls, floors, or the fixtures themselves. The trap literally traps water in the U. The water acts as a seal against sewer gas and drainage pipe odor penetration (Ill. 7). Venting is essential to the proper functioning of the traps. When there is no air in the drainage system, suction (siphonage) can take place. Siphon action can draw the water out of the trap, breaking the seal and leaving an open path for gases to enter the building or room.

Cleanouts are also important to the drainage

system. They are openings in the pipes that give access to the interior of the system and are valuable in the event of clogging or other problems. The number of cleanouts varies according to the complexity of the piping network or as required by code. A cleanout plug, however, is always required at the bottom of the soil stack—before it turns into the house drain (Ill. 5). A rule of thumb is to provide cleanouts at every change in direction and in sufficient number to make the entire drainage system accessible for cleaning.

Other components such as a house trap and a separate fresh-air intake are sometimes included. The house trap (a trap in the house drain) has been a source of controversy. There are those who feel that although it provides further insurance against gas penetration from the disposal system, it may interfere with the efficient outflow of

ILL.7

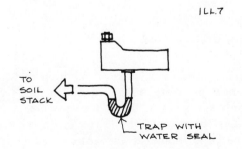

TO SOIL STACK

TRAP WITH WATER SEAL

waste. Check your code to see whether it is required in your locality or not. A fresh-air inlet is usually included whenever a house trap is provided, and omitted otherwise. Its purpose is to allow fresh air into the system.

Drainage Pipe Materials

The criteria for the selection of drainage pipes are slightly different from those for supply pipes. Like supply pipes, drainage piping has to handle problems of corrosion and facilitate installation. It does not, however, have to sustain the pressure that supply pipes do and toxicity considerations are not relevant. Instead, it must allow for the easy flow of sometimes bulky waste. Due to the lack of pressure, its walls can be thinner. Because of the waste, its diameter should be larger. When you are buying drainage pipe, specify it as such. The thinner-walled piping will be a bit cheaper and lighter than that used for supply lines.

Copper, plastic, and cast iron are the three most widely used materials for drainage piping. (Many codes specify cast iron as the only acceptable material, especially where drainage piping is buried.) Although cast iron costs less than copper, it is much heavier to support. In the past the technique for connecting cast-iron piping was rather complicated. Fortunately, a new joining system for cast-iron piping is now available. These no-hub couplings consist of a neoprene section protected by a thin metal ring. They are much easier to install than the traditional connections. Their use may be restricted in some locations. Copper tubing has been widely used for drainage systems. Its essential characteristics have already been described on page 152. Plastic piping is an economical and work-saving option. Although many codes do not accept plastic in the water supply system, they allow its use for drainage lines. Plastic resists corrosion, is lightweight, and is simple to install. Unless the code requires otherwise, we recommend plastic tubing for the drainage lines. On the debit side, plastic pipes are noisy.

Pipe Sizing

Because they carry waste in addition to water, drainage pipes are larger in diameter than water supply pipes. In addition, the system operates completely on gravity. The area of the pipes has to be large enough to prevent any waste from getting stuck and clogging the system. Con-

versely, too large a pipe (or too steep a horizontal pitch) is not desirable since the liquid will run off, leaving solid matter behind.

As in the case of the supply lines, the size of drainage pipes is relative to their function within the network. Obviously, a pipe draining a sink will be smaller than one carrying waste out of a toilet.

Following is a list of widely used dimensions for copper and plastic tubing in residential work. (Those of you in apartment buildings need to check the building standards.) These dimensions are merely indicators; always check your code first.

DRAINAGE PIPES

	Copper	Plastic
House drain	4″	4″
Soil stack	4″	4″
Drains in kitchen	2″	2″
Drains in toilet	4″	4″
Sink and bathtubs	1½″	1½″

VENTING PIPES

All vents	2″	2″

Pipe Fittings

The type of fitting in the drainage system varies from that of the supply system because it serves a different function. Fittings are needed not only to connect the different branches within the network but, more important, to permit maximum ease of flow of the sewage out of the building.

To prevent any waste from being trapped at turnings, connections between branches and the main stack are gentle curves rather than sharp

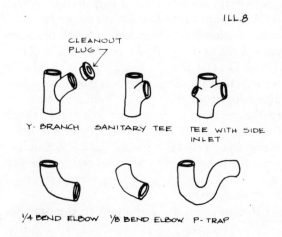

ILL. 8

CLEANOUT PLUG

Y-BRANCH   SANITARY TEE   TEE WITH SIDE INLET

¼ BEND ELBOW   ⅛ BEND ELBOW   P-TRAP

angles. (Angles are generally greater than 45 degrees with the horizontal; 90-degree angles are not permitted.) In addition, the fittings are designed with no protrusions on their inside diameter (Ill. 8).

How to Modify and Map Out the Drainage System

1. Take a look at the existing drainage piping. If the pipes are galvanized and show signs of rusted joints, they will require significant replacement. Those who have old cast-iron piping should give it a gentle tap (not too hard or it may break). If the walls sound thick and solid, they should be fine. Keep in mind that when connecting different materials (for example, cast iron to plastic) you need special no-hub fittings designed for this purpose.

2. Check to make sure that the drainage system is vented. If unvented, a venting system must be planned for.

3. Determine whether the existing drainage pipes are of adequate size (they should, at the very least, meet code requirements). If they are undersized, include their replacement in your renovation plans.

4. Check to see if there is a house trap, and whether or not it is required by code.

5. With your preliminary plans at hand showing the location of all the bathroom, kitchen, and laundry fixtures, proceed to draw a riser diagram. (This plan should also include the hot- and cold-water supply requirements.) A riser diagram is a section/elevation view of all the plumbing fixtures. This diagram allows you to visualize all the components necessary in the drainage system (drains, vents, stacks, etc.). It also serves as a checking device at the end of the planning stage (Ill. 9).

6. Provide each fixture with a drainage pipe. Remember that horizontal drainage pipes generally run in the floors (Ill. 10).

7. Provide each fixture with a vent. Vents are usually within the wall (Ill. 10).

8. Establish the best route to bring the branch vents into the existing soil stack. In renovations where the runs are too long, providing a secondary "waste stack" to handle the new fixtures may be the best solution. Keep in mind that waste stacks, like soil stacks, must run vertically through the entire house. Check for available walls where it can run (Ill. 10).

9. Draw branch lines indicating the best and shortest run for each branch drain to the soil or waste stack. Try to keep bends to a minimum (Ill. 10).

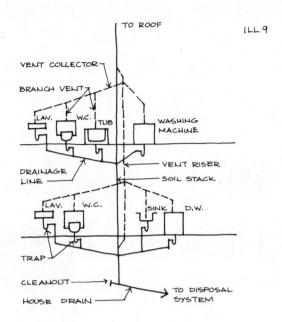

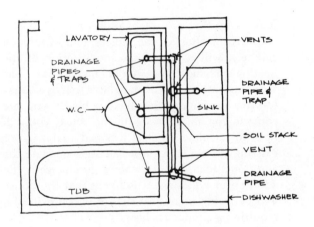

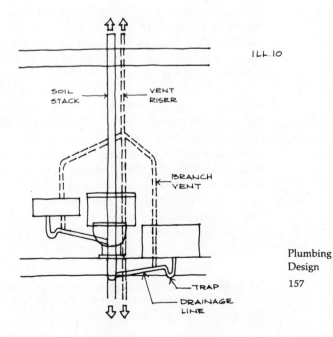

Plumbing Design

157

19

HEATING DESIGN

It is likely that any renovation project you are considering, short of the replacement of kitchen cabinets, will require some modification of the heating system. If you are demolishing and constructing partitions, you may have to move radiators or reconfigure the ducts a bit. If you are constructing an extension to the house, you will have to calculate the heat loss and analyze your existing system to see if it can accommodate the additional load. Even if your only change is the addition of windows, it is likely that the house will be losing more heat than it was previously, requiring a similar analysis.

If you are constructing an addition to the house, or are adding a significant number of square feet of window to a particular room,* you must decide if it is more efficient to increase the size of your existing central system or to install separate, room-size units to supplement it. In renovations where modifications to the exterior shell are extensive, or in cases where the existing heating system is inadequate to begin with, you may decide to replace your central system.

In this environmental design chapter we will discuss these modification options so that you can analyze your situation and come up with a direction. We recommend, however, that you consult with a mechanical engineer or with a heating-and-cooling consultant (often provided as a free service by the company that supplies your fuel) before making any changes.

HEAT LOSS AND GAIN

Human beings can adapt to a wide range of temperatures and humidities (given adequate clothing) but are "comfortable" only when the surrounding air is within a relatively narrow range of temperatures. In winter a building's heating system must supply heat to raise the temperature of a room to the desired level. At this point, ideally, the heating system should go off and stay off. This is never the case, however, since heat is constantly being lost to the outside. (Sometimes, even in winter, the house can pick up heat from the sun through south-facing windows. Generally, in northern climates more heat is lost than is gained.) In order for the mechanical system to maintain a constant comfortable temperature inside, it must replace the heat (measured in Btu's*) being lost to the outside. The amount of heat lost is dependent on (1) the difference between the interior temperature and that outside, (2) the amount of surface (walls, roofs, etc.) in

*Be sure to consult your state's energy conservation code for new or renovated construction to see if it allows the extent of glazing you wish to incorporate in your redesign.

*A Btu (British thermal unit) is a measure of the quantity of heat. One Btu is the amount of heat necessary to raise the temperature of one pound of water one degree F.—roughly the equivalent of the amount of heat given off by one wooden match. Heat loss is measured in Btuh's, the amount of Btu's per hour.

There are still a number of houses that have never been insulated. In addition, there are many houses whose insulation has been rendered ineffective by moisture trapped in the wall or other conditions. One telltale sign that the walls contain little or no insulation is the buildup of condensate on the inside walls of a heated room. If the interior walls are cold, any moisture in the room (from a kettle, perhaps, or a long-running shower) will condense and make the walls wet. One way to determine if the walls are insulated is to make a test hole in a suspicious place; another is to have the house photographed in the winter with infrared film. The photographs actually show the flow of heat from gaps in the insulation and cracks.

Loose-fill insulation is primarily used on buildings that have already been constructed. The loose particles, or granules, are poured or blown into the cavity of the wall. A 4" cavity between the inner and outer walls filled with loose insulation may have four times the insulation value as a wall with an empty cavity. Be sure that the insulation material that is pumped into your walls is noncarcinogenic and is fireproof. Since the insulation must be blown into the wall to fill every void, we suggest you hire a professional who has the right equipment. If you do the work yourself, wear a mask.

Rigid insulation, which may be placed in the wall or on its surface (making it an option for use in renovation), is manufactured in varying thicknesses ($1/2$" to 6") and materials and can be used to insulate walls, roofing, and foundations or as a combination sheathing-insulating material. Most rigid boards are made of expanded polystyrene, fiberglass, and urethane.

For any new construction, such as an addition to the house, we advise using batt insulation. Batt insulation is flexible and is sold in blankets or rolls about 15" wide. These strips are designed to fit in between the stud spaces, and come in thicknesses of 2", $3 1/2$", $5 1/2$", $6 1/2$", and up to 13". Batt insulation consists of mineral, rock, slag, or glass wools. The puffed material is secured between two layers of semi-flexible material (such as paper) to form batts, which are either stapled or taped to the studs. Some batts come with a vapor barrier attached for condensation control. The batts are installed with the vapor barrier facing the warm side of the space, generally the interior.

Reflective insulations work on the principle that the surface of a highly polished and shiny substance (usually aluminum foil backed with heavy paper) will reflect up to 90 percent of the radiant heat. The system must have an air space of at least $3/4$" in front of the reflective material for it to work. Very often the foil is double-sided, which increases its insulating value. The foil works to reflect the heat from the interior of the house back into the house, and is effective to a limited degree in areas that do not get too cold. The principle of reflective insulation works most efficiently when the reflective properties of aluminum foil and its additional property of being an excellent vapor barrier are combined in the foil that is attached to a blanket-type insulation.

---

contact with the outside, (3) the resistance to heat transmission of materials used in the construction of the exterior walls, and (4) the amount of infiltration of cold air due to loose fits in the window sashes and doorframes and unsealed joints.

In order to determine heat loss it is necessary to quantify the four variables listed above:

1. The design temperature differential is the difference between the desired indoor temperature (usually 70°F.) and the usual low temperature for the geographic area of the house. The lowest temperature ever recorded for the area is not the one used in this calculation since this low temperature may occur only rarely. When the temperature of the air dips below the design outdoor temperature, the house temperature drops only a few degrees, which is considered tolerable since it happens infrequently. Table III-C gives the low temperatures of many United States cities.

2. Determining the amount of surface in contact with the outside will require the calculation of roof, wall, and glazed surface areas. These calculations must be made separately since each of these composite materials has a different rate of heat loss. For instance, a 100-square-foot section of well-insulated roof will lose heat at a much slower rate than a window of the same size.

3. The materials used in construction of the exterior walls and roof are of primary concern in economical heat design. Some materials transfer heat better than others. In general, the more dense a material, the better it is as a conductor; the less dense, the better it is as an insulator. Metals, being very dense, are excellent heat conductors and for this reason are used for pots and pans. Solid wood resists the transfer of heat much better than metal. Most valuable for its heat-transfer resistance is air that is trapped in tiny pockets in blown or woven glass or plastics.

Insulating materials (Inset I) and composite wall sections are measured by either their R or their U values. An R value is the measure of a homogeneous material's resistance to the flow of heat. The higher the R value, the less heat is transmitted through a material, the better that material is as an insulator. Walls and floors, however, are constructed of more than one material, each having its own R value plus pockets of trapped air, which has some insulation value. The U* value (which is used for composite wall sections and not for any single material) measures the amount of heat that actually gets through an assembly of materials. Since the U factor measures the amount of heat that leaks through a

---

*The U factor is the overall coefficient of heat transfer. Thus if a wall has a U factor of .3, $3/10$ of a Btu will be transferred through one square foot of the wall to the outdoors every hour for every one degree of temperature difference between the outside and the inside.

wall, the higher the U factor, the more heat lost, or conversely, the lower the U value, the better the composite material is as an insulator. The U value is the reciprocal of the total resistance. If you have the R values of some materials and want to compare them with an assembly for which you have only the U value, you may use the formula $U = 1/(R + R + R . . .)$.

In order to understand the importance of insulation in all exterior construction, review the following example of a typical frame exterior wall consisting of studs, siding, sheathing, and gypsum board and the same wall with 2" of batt insulation between the studs. The uninsulated wall has a U factor of .32, whereas the insulated wall has a (lower, therefore better) U factor of .10. Were the insulation 3½" thick and of a certain type, the U factor would be .08, indicating that the well-insulated wall has four times the insulation value of the plain wall. Most new construction in northern parts of the United States uses 2×6 studs so that 5½"-thick insulation can be used instead of the 3½" variety.

The number and sizes of penetrations in the wall made for windows and doors are of great importance in the calculation of heat loss, for two reasons. First, glass loses heat at a far greater rate than most other construction materials, and second, there is often infiltration around the window sashes and doorframes. The quality of the window or door, the type of glass or door panel, and the direction faced are crucial to the design of the heating system (and the cooling system, which we will not discuss here).

Windows and doors, no matter how well insulated, have significantly higher (therefore worse) U values than insulated walls. In fact, at least ten times more heat is lost per square foot through a single sheet of glass than through a well-insulated wall. Heat loss can be reduced by using a specially made thermal window unit, which consists of two (and sometimes three) sheets of glass separated by sealed air spaces. Furthermore, window units with a new type of metallic coating bonded to glass are available. The manufacturer of these windows claims that the coating reduces the transmission of radiant heat, allowing most of the low winter's sun into the room but keeping most of the radiant heat from escaping to the outside. Even with these refinements, glazed surfaces lose heat faster than insulated walls. Windows, therefore, should be planned carefully.

A further argument against the indiscriminate use of glass and placement of windows is the infiltration of air into the building through cracks in operable window frames. The cold air forced into the house by the wind must be heated. (Fixed windows that are well caulked and sealed do not significantly increase infiltration.)

Almost all states have energy conservation codes that set guidelines and restrictions regarding wall insulating materials and glazing. Generally, the codes require that you limit the overall heat loss from a building. If you have only 2" of insulation in the walls and plan to use single-glazed windows, you will have to restrict the number and size of the windows. On the other hand, if you have well-insulated walls and plan to use low-heat-transmitting glazing, it is likely that you will be able to install larger windows.

Heat gain is as important in the environmental renovation of the house. The same good U values of the composite walls and roof that serve to keep the heat inside in the winter will be effective in keeping the heat out in the summer. Windows, on the other hand, pick up heat in different ways and must be calculated differently when it comes to heat gain. As a matter of fact, properly placed windows can be an advantage in the winter by picking up much needed heat during the day by means of solar radiation to supplement the fuel-burning system (Inset II). When it comes to heating through solar energy, direct sunlight is of great value, although the amount of heat radiated through any one window during any particular time is difficult to measure. Those same windows that serve as a source of heat when the sun shines become a liability at night as heat is lost through the glazed surfaces and during the summer when unwanted heat radiates through the glass (Inset II).

If you are thinking of adding or relocating windows, a number of variables should be evaluated. One of them, of course, is the potential heat loss from the window. This, however, should not be your only criterion. We think that any potential view should receive highest priority. We have seen quite a number of houses that face away from the lake because the builder followed (what he thought to be) a cardinal rule: that one never places windows on the north side. If you have a view, enjoy it. Put a nice big window on that wall, make sure it is the most resistant to heat transmission available on the market, and pay the slightly higher fuel bill on the assumption that the money is well spent. If you don't have a great view in any one direction, locate most of the windows on the south side of the house. The house will be bright in most seasons. To protect the windows from excessive summer heat gain, design some exterior screening (deciduous trees or roof overhangs) or install interior shades. As a third priority, try to avoid an unprotected western orientation for the living room and dining room, since the glare from the setting sun may make that exposure untenable on late afternoons. Last, if you don't have a vestibule to minimize heat loss when an exterior door is opened, try to locate the door out of the wind, in an alcove, or on the less windy face of the house.

HEATING SYSTEMS

When we refer to a heating system we identify it by (1) the fuel that it burns and (2) the medium by which the heat is circulated through the house. For example, you may have a gas-fired/hot-water system or one that is oil/forced air.

There are primarily three major fuel types (if you don't count the sun or wood): oil, natural gas, and electricity. It is hard to say definitively which is more or less expensive, since the comparative prices of these fuels keep changing over the years. In most areas oil and gas cost about the same and electricity is much more expensive.

Household distributing systems can be divided into two major categories: direct and central. Direct heating consists of room-size units usually powered by electricity. Generally, central heating systems are fueled by gas, oil, or electricity.

Direct Systems

The unitary, or direct, heating system uses individual electrically driven units in each room. In this system a single electric wire connects to the heating unit and provides heat for that room only. For the most part, these systems produce heat generated by the energy lost in the resistance of the wires in the unit. The room units can be mounted high or low on the wall or can surround the perimeter walls as baseboards. Baseboard

electric resistance systems are relatively inexpensive to install and are not excessively expensive to operate if the room is very well insulated and therefore has little heat loss.

Many houses built or renovated in the 1950's and 1960's have ceiling panels containing resistant heat coils which radiate heat downward or heating coils installed in a concrete floor slab that radiates the heat upward. Floor and ceiling radiating systems are expensive to install, somewhat less fuel-efficient, and slow to respond to temperature changes.

The heat pump can be purchased as a room-sized unit or as a component of a central distributing system. It should be considered only if you require both heating and cooling and if your winters are not too severe. The electrically powered heat pump is a refrigeration compressor in which the condenser and evaporator can be interchanged to provide both heating and cooling. In the winter, the heat pump picks up heat from the outside air to heat the interior. In the summer, the process is reversed; the heat in a room is directed to the outside. The heat pump generally consumes less electricity than conventional electric resistance units. The heating process, however, is most efficient if the outside air is above freezing. At temperatures lower than 28°F. the pump works less efficiently to extract warmth from the air and an auxiliary heating system (such as electric resistance heat) is required. Most heat pumps have electric resistance coils built into the units which are thermostatically triggered when the temperature drops below a certain point. (See page 168 for the newest energy-efficient heat pump models which operate at lower temperatures.)

Central Systems

The central systems consist of the heating (or cooling) generating plant and the distribution system.

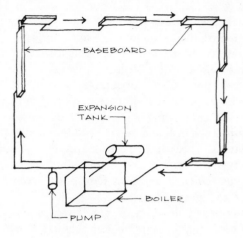

BASEBOARD

EXPANSION TANK

BOILER

PUMP

ILL. 1

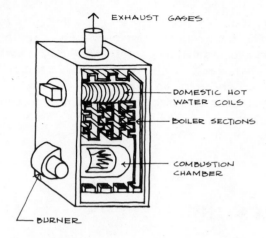

EXHAUST GASES

DOMESTIC HOT WATER COILS

BOILER SECTIONS

COMBUSTION CHAMBER

BURNER

ILL. 2

A hot-water system generally consists of a burner, either gas or oil (and with oil you will need a fuel storage tank), and a boiler. If you are using electricity, an electric hot-water boiler can be used which contains immersion heating elements. The heated water is distributed through pipes to convectors or radiators.

A forced-hot-air system consists of a fossil-fuel burner (oil or gas) and a furnace, or an electric furnace. Forced-air systems are sometimes fueled by one large heat pump (with resistant heat backup) instead of a furnace (see the paragraph above on heat pumps). Blowers push the conditioned air through ducts to supply registers in the rooms. A return-air system of some sort is required. This can take the form of a simplified system of ducts more or less paralleling the supply ducts, or in small houses there can be a plenum that is formed between the ceiling and the attic.

HOT-WATER SYSTEMS: In a hydronic (hot-water or steam) system, water is the medium that carries the heat to the individual rooms of the house. The water is heated centrally and is distributed through hot-water pipes to radiators or convectors (Ill. 1).

Either gas or oil is burned in a cast-iron or steel boiler generally of the water-tube variety (Ill. 2). The basic system consists of a burner, the boiler, a water main (a single water pipe designed in a loop), a number of fittings to join the pipe segments together, baseboard units, a thermostat to regulate the heat, a pump to push the water through the circuit, and an air-cushion tank (an expansion tank) to accommodate the expanded volume of heated water in the circuit without bursting pipes or fittings. A refinement of this

simple loop system is one that uses two pipes; this allows you to modulate the heat in individual rooms.

Many boilers are designed to heat the domestic water (used for showers, etc.) in addition to the water that is circulated to the baseboards. (Check to see if your state's conservation code allows the use of this kind of boiler.) Boilers that provide domestic hot water have an additional set of coils passing through the body of the boiler. The heat generated by the burner heats both sets of coils. The advantage of this system is that it is very efficient and fuel-saving in the winter when the boiler is always working. It is much less efficient in the summer when the entire boiler must work just to heat domestic hot water. A further disadvantage is that the boiler must be sized at a Btuh level large enough to provide for both needs. Furthermore, at times of peak demand, the boiler may not be able to heat the water fast enough to adequately provide enough hot water for a series of showers. This can be rectified by having a hot-water storage tank near the boiler. A recommended method of providing domestic hot water is to have a separate hot-water heater/storage tank fueled by electricity, oil, or gas.

If you have hot-water heating, it is likely that you have a series-loop baseboard system since it is the one most commonly used in small houses. The system consists of one pipe that carries hot water from the boiler through each of the baseboards around the perimeter of the house. The hot-water pipe circles the house and returns to the boiler (Ill. 1). Since the pipe goes through all of the baseboards in its loop about the house, the system can be adjusted or modulated only slightly in the individual rooms by means of dampers. The water is at its hottest when it leaves

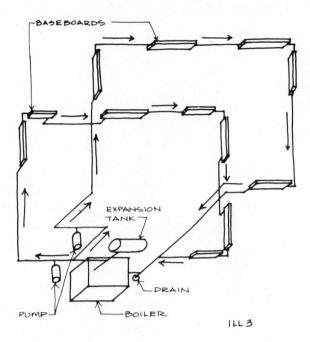

ILL.3

ters. If heating is required, the furnace is tapped. If cooling is called for, a heat exchanger (blower unit) and a condensing unit are used. Optional features can include different types of filtration systems and humidification.

The advantage of this kind of system over the hot-water heater is that, in addition to heating, the same ducts can be used to cool, ventilate, humidify, dehumidify, and clean air by removing dust, cooking and smoking odors, and allergenic substances. Many people choose air systems because of the filtration options. The filters can remove dust and pollen from the air, making life more comfortable for people with allergies.

the boiler and is cooler at the end of its loop (having lost much of its heat to the rooms in its travels). A single thermostat controls the room temperature for all the rooms in the series. To keep the loops short, the system often is divided into two separate loops, each one controlled by its own thermostat, and is considered "zoned" (Ill. 3). Separate loops for the different floors or wings of the house are required by most energy conservation codes.

Many old houses, apartment buildings, and brownstones are serviced by steam systems. Steam is produced in a boiler and is distributed to the radiators by pipes. Most domestic systems are one-pipe systems. The pipe that delivers the steam carries the condensate back to the boiler. (The knocking often heard in the walls of old houses occurs when incoming steam in improperly sloping pipes traps the cooler condensate and causes it to hit the pipe at the tees and elbows.)

FORCED-AIR SYSTEMS: In the forced-air system the air is conditioned at a central location, pushed by blowers through ducts to each room of the house, and released through outlets (registers in the walls or floor) into the space. An additional register in the room (or in the corridor outside the room) draws in air and returns it to the conditioning plant.* This process is referred to as the conditioning cycle. The components of all forced-air systems include a blower, ductwork, and regis-

*Large houses generally have a system of return air ducts that parallel the supply ducts. Small buildings often use the halls or the basement as return air plenums.

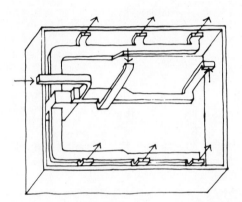

ILL.4

TRUNK SYSTEM

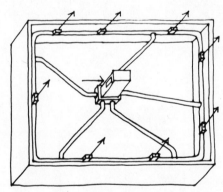

PERIMETER LOOP SYSTEM

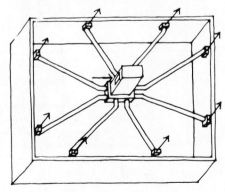

RADIAL DUCT SYSTEM

Heating Design
163

INSET III/CALCULATION OF HEAT LOSS

(Calculate separately for each room. Use Table III-A for calculations.)

1. Determine the gross wall area that is exposed to the outside or to unheated spaces (such as the garage or attic). The exposed walls of closets adjacent to livable rooms must be taken into consideration as well.
   Gross wall area = length of wall × height.

2. Measure windows and doors and determine the total area of glass per room, and the total area of doors going to the outside (or unheated spaces).

   Measurements for windows are taken from the outside of the sash. Doors are measured by the size of the actual door.

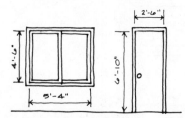

3. Determine net wall area exposed to the outside. Net wall area = gross wall area − total window and door area (for the room).

4. Determine ceiling area if the space above is unheated. (If there are heated rooms above, this step can be omitted.) Ceiling area = length of room × width.

5. Determine floor area if exposed to unheated space (basement or crawl space below).

6. Determine room volume (= length × width × height).

7. Using Table III-B (Heat-Loss [U] Factors) determine U factors for walls, windows, ceilings, and floors exposed to the outside.

8. Determine design temperature difference using Table III-C. The design temperature difference is equal to the difference between the desired indoor temperature (usually 70°F.) and the usual low temperature for the area where the house is to be built. The lowest temperature ever recorded for the area is not the one used in this calculation since this low temperature occurs only rarely. (When the temperature of the air dips below the design outdoor temperature, the house temperature drops only a few degrees, which is considered tolerable since it happens infrequently.) Table III-C records outdoor design temperatures for different parts of the United States.

9. Calculate area × U factor for each room component (walls, windows, doors, ceilings, and floors).

10. Determine infiltration factor for window type using Table III-D.

11. Calculate room volume × infiltration factor.

12. Determine total heat loss per room by adding the area × U factors and the volume × infiltration factor; multiply this total by the design temperature difference.

13. Add total heat loads of each room to determine total house heating loss.

TABLE III-A: HEAT-LOSS CALCULATIONS

Room	Length of Exposed Wall	Height of Room	Gross Wall Area (Sq. Ft.)		Windows		Door	Walls	Floor	Ceiling		x Temp. Diff.	Room Heat Loss
					#1	#2							
				Net area (A; sq. ft.)							Vol. (V; cu. ft.)			
				U*							F†			
				A × U							V × F			
				Net area							Vol.			
				U							F			
				A × U							V × F			
				Net area							Vol.			
				U							F			
				A × U							V × F			
				Net area							Vol.			
				U							F			
				A × U							V × F			
				Net area							Vol.			
				U							F			
				A × U							V × F			

*U: Heat-loss factor; see Table III-B
†F: Infiltration factor; see Table III-D

TABLE III-B: HEAT-LOSS (U) FACTORS

BLANKET

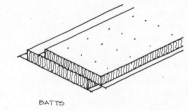

BATTS

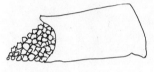

LOOSE FILL

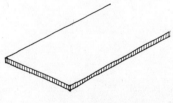

RIGID

				U Factor
Glass	Single sheet	by itself		1.13
		with storm sash		.56
	Double-glazed	¼" air space		.61
		½" air space		.55
		with plastic coating on frame		.52
	Double-glazed with storm sash	¼" air space		.46
		½" air space		.38
Doors	1" thick			.64
	1½" thick			.50
Wood-Frame Walls	2 × 4 wood (or metal) studs,	no insulation		.25
	16" o.c., wood (or metal)	batt or loose insulation:	R-8	.09
	siding, wood sheathing, drywall,		R-11	.08
	vapor barrier		R-14	.07
	2 × 6 studs, same construction		R-8	.09
	as above		R-11	.07
			R-19	.05
Frame with Brick Veneer	2 × 4 wood or metal studs, air space + sheathing (or 1" rigid insulation), vapor barrier, drywall		R-8	.09
			R-11	.07
			R-19	.06
Brick and Block	Face brick, air space	as described		.12
	8" 80 lb./cu. ft. concrete	with rigid insulation	R-3	.09
	block, core insulation		R-8	.06
			R-11	.05
Brick Wall	8" solid wall	interior unfinished		.50
		plaster on masonry		.46
		1" furring space filled with insulation, drywall		.20
Pitched Roof	Asphalt (or wood) shingles on rafters with ½" sheathing	no insulation		.53
		2" rigid roof insulation on 1½" wood planks		.12
		batt or loose fill insulation, vapor barrier, and gypsum-board ceiling:	R-11	.08
			R-19	.05
			R-22	.04
			R-30	.03
Ceilings	(unheated attic space above)	gypsum-board ceiling only		.78
		4" insulation		.07
		+ subfloor		.06
Wood Floor	Over crawl space, subfloor, and hardwood floor	no insulation		.15
		4" insulation		.04
	Over exposed space	no insulation		.39
		4" insulation		.06

RESISTANCE (R VALUES)
OF INSULATING MATERIALS

(This table is primarily for the purpose of demonstrating the comparative values of different insulating materials and not necessarily for the purpose of calculating heat loss. Table III-B lists the composite U values for walls and roofs and has been designed for heat-loss calculations.)

	R
Air spaces:	
without reflective material, ¾" to 4"	.92
one-side reflective material	2.17
aluminum foil both sides	2.64
Batts and blankets: all materials	
2" thick	7.64
3½" thick	11
Loose fill:	
rock, mineral, or glass, 3⅝" thick	12.08
Rigid board:	
fiberglass, 1" thick	4.4
Insulation-board sheathing:	2.06
Concrete block (cinder):	
8" thick	1.66

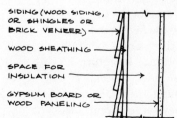

SIDING (WOOD SIDING, OR SHINGLES OR BRICK VENEER)

WOOD SHEATHING

SPACE FOR INSULATION

GYPSUM BOARD OR WOOD PANELING

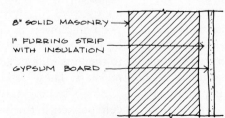

8" SOLID MASONRY

1" FURRING STRIP WITH INSULATION

GYPSUM BOARD

TABLE III-C: OUTDOOR DESIGN TEMPERATURES (DEGREES FAHRENHEIT) FOR SOME CITIES IN THE UNITED STATES

City	°F	City	°F	City	°F
Birmingham, Alabama	21	Des Moines, Iowa	−5	Bismarck, North Dakota	−19
Mobile, Alabama	29	Topeka, Kansas	4	Cleveland, Ohio	5
Fairbanks, Alaska	−47	Lexington, Kentucky	8	Tulsa, Oklahoma	13
Flagstaff, Arizona	4	New Orleans, Louisiana	33	Salem, Oregon	23
Tucson, Arizona	32	Portland, Maine	−1	Pittsburgh, Pennsylvania	5
Little Rock, Arkansas	20	Baltimore, Maryland	13	Providence, Rhode Island	9
Sacramento, California	32	Boston, Massachusetts	9	Columbia, South Carolina	24
San Diego, California	44	Detroit, Michigan	6	Rapid City, South Dakota	−7
San Francisco, California	40	Minneapolis, Minnesota	−12	Nashville, Tennessee	14
Denver, Colorado	1	Jackson, Mississippi	25	Dallas, Texas	22
Hartford, Connecticut	7	Columbia, Missouri	4	El Paso, Texas	24
Wilmington, Delaware	14	Billings, Montana	10	Houston, Texas	32
Washington, D.C.	17	Omaha, Nebraska	−3	Salt Lake City, Utah	8
Miami, Florida	47	Las Vegas, Nevada	28	Burlington, Vermont	7
Tallahassee, Florida	30	Reno, Nevada	10	Lynchburg, Virginia	16
Atlanta, Georgia	22	Concord, New Hampshire	−3	Seattle, Washington	27
Savannah, Georgia	27	Trenton, New Jersey	14	Charleston, West Virginia	11
Boise, Idaho	10	Albuquerque, New Mexico	16	Green Bay, Wisconsin	−9
Chicago, Illinois	−4	Buffalo, New York	6	Casper, Wyoming	−5
Springfield, Illinois	2	New York, New York	15		
Indianapolis, Indiana	2	Charlotte, North Carolina	22		

TABLE III-D: INFILTRATION FACTORS FOR WINDOWS AND DOORS

Rooms with Windows and Doors	No Weather Stripping nor Storm Sash	With Weather Stripping or Storm Sash
on 1 side only	.018	.012
on 2 sides	.027	.018
on 3 or 4 sides	.036	.027

The most common residential distributing systems include the trunk system, which is a central plenum adjoining the furnace with small feeder lines coming off it; the radial system, with all ducts radiating out of the central location and leading directly to the outlet registers; the perimeter loop, which combines the radial concept with a loop system that surrounds the perimeter of the house. The latter system is used primarily in a slab on grade (a concrete floor that rests directly on the earth). The circulating warm air through the perimeter loop warms the concrete slab (Ill. 4).

The size and layout of the ductwork are critical to the even distribution of hot air. Ducts that are too small or make too many bends will cause problems with the delivery of heat, the balancing of the system, and noise caused by vibrations. Dampers in the ducts control the amount of heat delivered to the individual rooms. If you are not using a particular room, you may want to close the damper. One way to balance a system is to size the ducts so that the right amount of heat is delivered to each room. Another way is to use dampers that are opened to the right aperture to allow the needed amount of hot air to flow through. Generally, you fully open the dampers in ducts feeding rooms far from the furnace and partially open ducts in rooms close to the heat source or on the lower floors (remember: heat rises). In any duct layout try to avoid changes in direction. Bends in the ducts reduce the flow of air and cause vibrations.

A variation on forced-air heating is the gravity warm-air system in which ducts, without fans, are used for supply air. This system does not depend on blowers to distribute the heat, but works on the principle that hot air rises. Cooler air falls to the lower floor and is "captured" by return-air registers. These very old-fashioned systems still work to some extent, although there are often cold pockets in the houses they serve. (Some very old houses have no ducts at all. The heated air is released through large registers on the bottom floor of the house and naturally flows upward.)

SYSTEM MODIFICATIONS

After studying how your existing system works, you will have to decide what, if anything, you are going to do with it. If you are renovating a house, there are three approaches to the modification of the heating-and-cooling system:

If the renovation is a very minor one, you may decide to leave the heating system alone (unless, of course, the system is inefficient). If you are adding windows, calculate the heat loss (Inset III) to determine if you need auxiliary heat. Chances are that the replacement windows are better insulated than the (smaller) ones you are removing and the heat loss will be about the same. You may have to add or move a hydronic baseboard or an air diffuser. This is not very difficult and is covered in Chapter 34. If you are adding a room or a wing to the house, or if you are adding significantly to the glazing, you must do a heat-loss analysis (Inset III) to determine how much your existing system will be taxed. If the system was overdesigned to begin with, you will only have to modify the distribution system. If the system will be overtaxed (or if it is too small for existing needs), you have to decide whether to replace the existing central boiler or furnace with a larger one or to use individual room-size units to make up for the increased heat loss.

In evaluating these alternatives you must take into consideration cost, the kind of house you have, and your construction skills. It is least expensive and not too difficult to add or move a radiator if your pipes or ducts are easily accessible in a basement or attic. In an apartment, the ducts or pipes might be a little harder to get to, but at the very worst you can run them along the ceiling and encase them in gypsum board. If you have more heat loss than your central system can handle, it may be more efficient to use an electric resistance heater (if there is electrical capacity to spare) than to both replace the furnace (or boiler) and modify the ducts (or pipes).

DESIGNING FOR UNIT HEATERS: If you are adding a single room to your house and do not want to modify the existing system, calculate the heat loss of the new room and purchase a through-the-wall unit for heating and cooling or an electric resistance baseboard that will provide enough heat to cover the loss.

If you are adding windows and are not sure if you are overloading the existing system, calculate the heat loss for the entire house and see if it matches the capacity of the existing boiler or furnace. If it doesn't, you may be able to use unit heaters to make up for the additional heat loss. The best way to do this is to use the unit heater in the part of the house that is now the coldest or most remote (heat carried in pipes and ducts is reduced when made to travel a very long distance), but not necessarily in the area with the new windows. Here you can increase the size of the baseboards or open the dampers to allow in more hot air. Calculate the heat loss for the entire house and subtract the heat capacity of the boiler or furnace. The difference is the amount of heat that has to be provided by unit heaters. If there is a remote, cold room in the house (with a door), calculate the heat lost from that room. If it more or less matches the difference previously calculated, purchase a unit that will heat that room and remove the room's radiator or register.

MODIFYING A HOT-AIR SYSTEM: There are two considerations in the modification of the hot-air system: the size of the furnace and the distribution system. If the heating plant is not large enough for the needs of the renovated house, you will have to purchase a new furnace or make up the difference with unit heaters (see the paragraph above). If your renovation increases the heat loss of a particular area, you will probably have to modify the distribution system. If the new space is along the path of an existing duct of a trunk system, open the duct and add a diffuser. You will probably have to rebalance the system by adjusting dampers along the trunk and by adjusting the amount of hot air that enters the trunk from the furnace. If the new room is enclosed, you will have to worry about return air. If the return-air system is unstructured (the air drifts back to the furnace through the hall), install a vent in the door or undercut the door by about an inch.

If you are installing new or additional ducts in an old house, it may be difficult to bury the ducts in existing plaster walls and ceilings. It may be easiest to run the ducts through existing closets or along existing partitions (and fur them out with new gypsum board) so as not to disturb the plasterwork or parquet flooring. Try to plan the installation so that all horizontal runs are made in the cellar and the vertical runs in closets.

MODIFYING A HOT-WATER SYSTEM: If you are modifying a series-loop system you can easily cut into the system at any point and add more

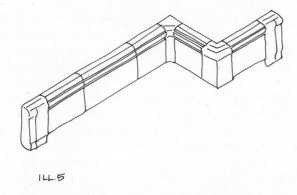

ILL. 5

baseboard. You must consider, however, whether the boiler is generating enough hot water to heat the entire line. To make sure the boiler is large enough for the modified house, calculate the heat loss (Inset III) and match this figure to the one on the boiler. If the heat is zoned, calculate the heat loss for the zone that is being modified. You will also have to check to see if the tubing going through the baseboard will carry the zone's load. (If the existing tubing is too small for the new load, you have to consider changing all of the baseboards and pipes in the loop, or dividing the circuit into two separate loops, or using an electric heater.) Decide where the new baseboard will be located. The baseboard works best (by stopping down drafts) when placed under a window.

Next, select the baseboard (Ill. 5). You must have the manufacturer's literature in order to select baseboards, since you need the actual rating for each linear foot of baseboard, which differs from one manufacturer to another. The sample in Illustration 6 can be used as an example. To select a baseboard you will have to know the water flow in gallons per minute (gpm), which is calculated by dividing the heat loss (Btuh) for the circuit by 10,000. (Use the 4 gpm rating only when the flow is known to be over 4 gpm; otherwise use 1 gpm.) The hot-water rating must also be known; 200 degrees is commonly used in domestic systems.

When you have the baseboard rating, you can calculate the length of the baseboard for each room by using the following formula:

$$\text{the length of baseboard per room} = \frac{\text{room heat loss}}{\substack{\text{rating of the baseboard} \\ \text{in Btuh per linear foot}}}$$

Energy-Efficient Boilers, Furnaces, and Heat Pumps

You may be replacing your heating plant as part of your renovation. Aside from the conventional boilers, furnaces, and heat pumps, new technologies have been developed by the heating industry to burn fuel more effectively and thus to conserve energy. These new heating appliances are smaller and lighter than older models, lose less heat, and produce less exhaust. We recommend that any boiler or furnace you are purchasing be sized and installed by a professional heating firm since improper installation of the unit and its exhaust system can be very dangerous. We are even more emphatic when it comes to some of the new units listed below which have very delicate controls. Choose a unit that has a good safety record and have it installed by someone recommended by the supplier.

CONDENSING FURNACES AND BOILERS: Condensing furnaces (there are some condensing boilers on the market, but the majority of appliances available are gas-fired furnaces) may be 10 percent more efficient than conventional units (some manufacturers claim that their models are 20 percent more efficient). This technology, which produces a cool exhaust, operates on the following principles: First, a larger heat exchanger produces cooler gas. The heat that would ordinarily go up the chimney as waste is now saved. Second, gas (natural or propane) when burned produces waste gas that contains a great deal of

HOT WATER RATINGS*
(BTU PER HR. PER LIN. FT. WITH 65° ENTERING AIR

	HOT WATER RATINGS (BTU/HR.)										WATER FLOW	PRESSURE DROP
	160°	170°	180°	190°	200°	210°	215°	220°	230°	240°		
3/4" NOMINAL COPPER TUBING	450	510	580	640	710	770	810	840	910	970	1 GPM	47
	480	540	610	680	750	810	860	890	960	1030	4 GPM	525

* TO BE USED FOR PRELIMINARY DESIGN ONLY

ILL. 6

water vapor. The condensing furnace lowers the temperature of the gas to below the dew point, which causes the vapor to precipitate into water. The heat of vaporization yields almost 1,000 Btu's of heat for every pound of water that is condensed. A happy consequence of less and cooler exhaust gas is the elimination of the need for the standard flued masonry chimney. Many of these systems need only a 3"-diameter PVC exhaust pipe. The condensing appliances, although more fuel-efficient, are more costly than conventional furnaces. This additional expense is attributed to the fan that is required to vent the unit, the drainage line needed to remove the condensate, and the corrosive-resistant materials required in the construction of the unit.

PULSE BURNERS: The first condensing units developed were the pulse burners, which burn a controlled mixture of fuel and air in small explosions. A drawback of the original pulse units on the market was the increased noise and vibration created.

FAN-DRIVEN BURNERS: Most gas burners operate using natural draft, which often provides more air than needed to support combustion. Fan-driven burners use less air for combustion and are more efficient. The burners come with either fans that blow fuel and air into the combustion chamber (forced-draft burners) or fans installed at the exhaust end (induced-draft burners).

DOMESTIC HOT-WATER COILS: Many conventional systems have coils integrated into the boiler to provide for domestic hot water. These tankless systems, although desirable since they save the initial cost of a separate hot-water heater, are considered energy-wasting because they require use of the boiler every time domestic hot water is desired, even in the summer months, when general heating is not needed.

However, modifications of boiler technology have made the integration of hot-water coils both economically feasible and fuel-conserving. Today's new boilers are packaged with a remote, well-insulated hot-water storage tank which eliminates the need for the boiler to constantly switch on and off.

NEW HEAT PUMPS: Recent improvements in heat pumps have made the units about 35 percent more efficient, according to manufacturers' claims (and while these models are still new on the market, about 40 percent more expensive). Conventional heat pumps have single-speed motors which cycle on or off, requiring a surge of electric power each time. The new heat pump achieves its efficiency by varying the speeds of the electric motors and compressor. In addition, these units reduce fuel consumption during the summer by converting the heat extracted from the interior of the house and using it to produce domestic hot water. (The manufacturer advises you, however, to have a backup hot-water heater for domestic hot-water requirements in the winter.)

AUTOMATIC FLUE DAMPERS: When the furnace (or boiler) is not working, a lot of the heat left in the unit is lost up the chimney. An automatic flue damper closes the flue when the burner goes off and opens it again when the system goes back on.

SOLAR STRATEGIES

It may be wise to remove part of the southern wall of the house and install a greenhouse (or at least a very large window) to take advantage of some of the passive* solar strategies that have been developed in the last decade.

Direct Gain

The most straightforward of the solar strategies is the direct-gain method, which consists of using large expanses of glass on the south side of a building. The sun's radiant heat enters through these glazed areas and provides warmth to the space within (Ill. 7). In this method, as in all of the passive systems, solar radiation passes through the glass in short waves, the form that light energy takes. When these short light-energy waves come into contact with a surface of any kind (walls or floors), they are absorbed and radiated as long heat waves. Since these longer heat waves

*There is a big difference between "passive" and "active" solar systems. An active solar heating system gathers the sun's heat in roof-mounted collectors and can produce either hot water or hot air to be circulated through the house via conventional pipes and ducts. So far, active systems have not proven to be very cost-effective, and are not widely used. First, active systems are costly and cumbersome, calling for a roof that faces directly south in addition to a large storage area of water tanks or rock to hold accumulated heat. Second, the cost of installation is high, aggravated by the fact that a duplicate, conventional backup system must be installed since the sun does not shine all day, every day. Passive systems are less complicated and less expensive.

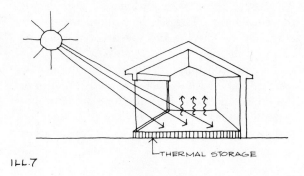

THERMAL STORAGE

ILL.7

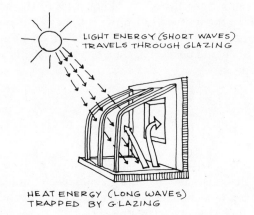

LIGHT ENERGY (SHORT WAVES)
TRAVELS THROUGH GLAZING

HEAT ENERGY (LONG WAVES)
TRAPPED BY GLAZING

ILL.8

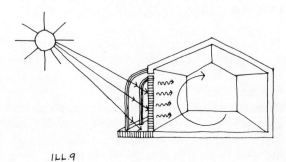

ILL.9

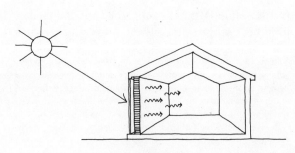

ILL.10

cannot be transmitted through the glass, they are trapped within, heating the space.

To reap the maximum benefits from the daytime solar gain, this heat should be stored for later use. For this purpose materials that can hold large quantities of heat for as long as possible are used. Stone and similar masonry building materials can retain heat for long periods of time and are called thermal mass. Heat that is stored in thermal mass slowly radiates back into the space and—with the exception of a small amount of heat lost through the glass by conduction—is trapped within. Double glazing and high-performance glazing only slightly reduce the amount of radiant heat being transmitted into the house, but do reduce the amount of stored heat lost through conduction. The most logical location for the thermal mass is in the floor adjacent to the windows. A concrete slab, 6" thick or more, covered with brick pavers, slate, or ceramic tile, is effective if the floor is not covered with carpeting or upholstered furniture.

The major drawbacks of any solar-energy system apply to this one as well. It cannot be depended on as the sole heating system since there are long periods of time when the sun does not shine. In addition, large expanses of glass lose heat at a ferocious rate and should be shuttered with insulated panels or quilted drapes when it is cold and dark. Finally, in the summer the window should be shaded and the room well ventilated to prevent overheating.

Sun Spaces

The sun space or greenhouse (a completely glazed, south-facing room with a thick masonry floor) is a refinement on the direct-gain system. The wall between the building and the sun space (there must be a wall, otherwise the "greenhouse" is nothing more than a large window) may be of glass or any other construction. Heat, in its short waves, enters the greenhouse and is temporarily stored in the floor's thermal mass. Windows and doors between the house and the greenhouse are left open to allow heat from the floor to flow into the house by convection air currents (Ill. 8). When the heat in the floor is dissipated, the windows are closed. In the hot months, sun shades are lowered over the glass and ventilation panels are left open to cool the sun space and its floor.

In a further refinement, the wall between the main building and the greenhouse is constructed as a thermal mass—that is, of stone, brick, concrete, or adobe (Ill. 9). The result is a house with a double-layered façade. The thermal wall is painted black on the greenhouse side to allow absorption of the maximum amount of heat. The heat stored in the mass radiates to both sides of the wall. Air currents, circulating inside the house, pass close to the wall, are heated, and distribute warm air to the rest of the room. The system can be "shut off" by shading the glass, by ventilating the sun space, and/or by placing insulation panels on the outside face of the thermal wall.

Thermosyphoning

This method is very similar to the one above but takes up less room. The southern façade of the house is covered with large areas of glass. A wall is built directly behind the glass with an air space of about 4" between the two surfaces (Ill. 10). The wall is generally built of heavy masonry, but could also consist of water containers. The outside surface of the wall is painted a very dark color to allow maximum heat absorption.

Thermosyphoning provides heat in two ways. The first is through the thermal mass of the wall. The stored daytime heat is available for slow radiation into the house in the evening. As an added bonus, the wall thickness (generally 12") slows down heat transmission during the daytime hours when the sun may be too hot. (It takes about six hours for the heat to travel the full depth of the wall.) The second way involves the narrow air space between the thermal wall and the glazing. During the day the sun penetrates the glass, heating the air space. Four operable vents are placed at the top and bottom of the wall. One set is inserted in the glazing and one set in the thermal wall. On cold, bright days, the vents in the glass are closed and the ones in the masonry opened. Cool air circulates by gravitational flow (or is pushed along by fans) through the bottom vent from the house into the air space. Heated air then rises through the air space and flows through the top vent into the interior space. If the room gets too warm, the vents in the wall can be closed. At night, when the sun no longer shines, all vents are kept closed. On warm nights all vents are left open to ventilate the interior space. In the summer shading can be placed over the exterior glazing. One answer to modulating the heat is a system that blows insulating Styrofoam balls into the air space.

20

ELECTRICAL DESIGN

The basic electrical requirements of an average home have increased steadily over the years. As a general rule, the older the building, the less electrical power it was supplied with. For this reason, most renovations involve some form of electrical work. This can range from a new electrical service and distribution system to merely adding a few outlets. We do not (and cannot) claim to be experts in this field. What we attempt to do in this chapter is to give you some background on electrical theory by explaining the system's principal components. The aim is to help you to understand the basic criteria involved in the design of your house's electrical system.

While it may be inaccurate to say that electrical work is difficult, we can rightfully say that it is potentially hazardous. A faulty electrical installation could be the cause of fire or personal injury. We discourage anyone (other than a licensed electrician) from doing his own electrical work. We are not alone in our advice. There are numerous areas in which the building code will not allow you to do your own electrical work. Furthermore, some insurance companies may charge you higher rates when they find out you were your own electrician.

One way to solve this problem is to hire a licensed electrician to handle the overall job with you working as one of his helpers. Such an arrangement will offer the assurance that a qualified professional is in charge while still allowing you to be an integral part of the renovation crew.

CORE COMPONENTS

Electrical Circuits

When you turn on a lamp, you trigger an intricate series of events. Electrical energy, composed of moving particles called electrons, starts flowing from the generator (at your local power company) to the lamp via a system of wires. The flow of electrons (current) from the source to the lamp constitutes a simple electrical circuit (Ill. 1).

This circuit may be compared to the water supply cycle in a plumbing system—with one important difference. Whereas in the plumbing system the water comes from the source through the pipes to the fixtures and is later drained and disposed of, in an electrical circuit two terminals are needed to induce the current flow. The electron flow must "return" to its source to complete an electric circuit. The reason for this is that electrons are negatively charged particles that flow or move because there is a higher positive electric charge at one terminal than at the other. The circuit therefore starts at the source, goes to the appliance, where the power is consumed, and ends at the source (Ill. 1).*

Switches

The switching device you use to turn the lamp on is designed to open or close the circuit. When the

*To simplify matters, we will assume we are dealing with direct current (DC).

switch is in the "off" or open position, the current flow is interrupted. The circuit is "broken" and there is a gap in the current path. No current is allowed to flow and the light will be out. When the switch is in the "on" or closed position, the reverse takes place (Ill. 2).

Switch arrangements vary in their complexity. There are instances in which you may want to turn on the light at one location and turn it off later from another location. A "three-way" switch arrangement, designed to open or close the circuit from two different locations, can do this (Ill. 3). "Four-way" switch arrangements are also available for control of a single light from several locations.

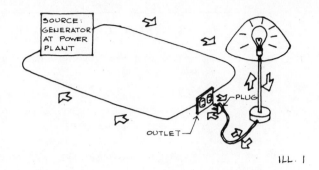

ILL. 1

Outlets

Outlets are devices within the circuit where electric power is made available. They include receptacles, ceiling outlets, and sockets. In the simple circuit previously described, a floor lamp becomes part of the circuit by being plugged into a receptacle. It draws power from the circuit via the receptacle by contact between the wires in the plug and those in the receptacle. The receptacle itself consumes no power. Receptacles are most commonly seen in duplex form—that is, with provision to accommodate two plugs. Quad receptacles for four plugs are also available (Inset I).

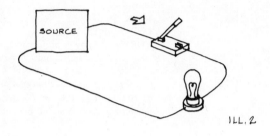

ILL. 2

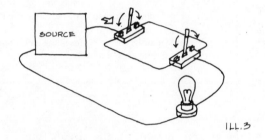

ILL. 3

UNITS OF MEASURE

Your monthly electric bill states the number of kilowatts (or thousand watts) consumed by the house's electrical system. The monthly charge is based on a rate per kilowatt-hour. If you take a look at the appliances you presently own, you will see that they are also rated in watts: a light bulb may be 30, 60, or 100 watts, a toaster 1,200 watts, and a radio 150 watts. These ratings mean that these appliances need that specific number of watts to operate properly.

Watts are a measure of electric power flowing through a circuit at a given time. They are a function of the current flowing in the circuit (measured in amps) and the "push" needed to get the current from the source to the appliance (measured in volts). Watts = amps × volts, or $W = A \times V$. For example, let's say you have a washing machine requiring 700 watts and 115 volts to operate. You will need $W = V \times A$, or $W \div V = A$—that is, 700 ÷ 115 = 6.08 amps—for the washing machine to function properly.

The utility company that serves you will determine the voltage you receive, be it 115/230, 120/240, or 125/250.* The amperage (the amount of current quantity) available to you is dependent on the capacity of the "service entrance" that you already have or that you request from the power company. As a general rule, the older the house, the less amperage is available to it. It is not uncommon to find large turn-of-the-century houses which have a service entrance of 50 amps (some-

times even less) or an apartment with 35 amps. The service entrance is the place where the cables from the power company enter the building for distribution to the various circuits. The incoming power (or entrance capacity) from these wires and the related fuses or other safety devices must be sufficient to feed all the house fixtures and appliances with an adequate amount of electrical energy and allow room for growth. To plan the electrical capacity needed in your renovation, you must determine the amount of electrical power (watts) you need and divide by the available voltage. This gives you the desired amperage capacity. Compare this figure with the amperage at the service entrance. For a renovation, you will probably need more than you now have (Inset II).

Apartment buildings are more complicated to deal with. Each apartment is allocated a certain amperage as its total "service." This, in turn, is tied to the main service entrance to the building. If you require additional power, you need to find out whether the building can make this power available to you. If not, you may have to bring a new service into your apartment by means of a new electrical "riser" or "feeder" from the cellar.

*To find out the exact voltage in your area check with the power company. All areas are subject to periodic minor voltage variations, mostly voltage reductions, as a result of changes in current demand. These voltage reductions, if major or prolonged, are referred to as brownouts.

People in upper-floor apartments and in penthouses will require the longest and therefore the costliest runs.

THE THREE-WIRE SYSTEM

The electrical devices in contemporary houses range from a clock, requiring 2 to 8 watts, to an electric range, which may consume up to 14,000 watts. Because the variation is so great and the demand for power has increased, a three-wire system has been devised. With this system, two different voltages are made available: one relatively low voltage (115, 120, or 125 volts) for devices using little power and a higher one (230, 240, or 250 volts) for high-wattage appliances.

The operation of a three-wire system is not difficult to understand. Three cables from the power company are brought into the house and connected to a single meter. They are then brought into the service entrance panel for distribution to the various circuits. Either voltage can be obtained at the service entrance. The three incoming wires are generally black, red, and white. The black and red wires are called hot wires; the white one is the neutral. (Don't be misled by the "hot" and "neutral" terminology; they are all equally dangerous.) The hot wires are each connected to a 115-volt generator, while the white neutral is connected to both generators (Ill. 4).* When the wires in a circuit are connected to the neutral and one hot wire, they are hooked up to one generator (or one generator "winding"). The voltage being supplied is 115 V + 0 V = 115 V (Ill. 5.). When the circuit is connected to both hot wires, each of which is connected in turn to a separate generator (or to two separate generator "windings"), the resulting voltage is 115 V + 115 V = 230 V (Ill. 6). Devices in the circuit connected to one hot wire and the neutral will receive 115 volts; those connected to both hot wires (and not to the neutral) will receive 230 volts. Thus, by a choice of wires either voltage can be obtained, according to the rated voltage of the appliance. Circuits handling the heavy-wattage equipment such as an electric stove will most likely be supplied at 230 volts, while those circuits feeding lamps and other small appliances will be supplied with 115 volts.

Owners of older homes will probably find that the incoming service to their building is a two-wire system. This provides only 115 volts, which is not sufficient to operate high-voltage appliances such as air conditioners. Plan for a new three-wire system in your renovation.

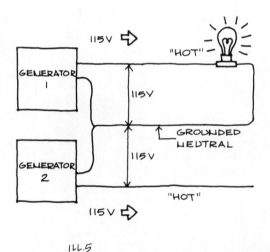

ILL. 4

ILL. 5

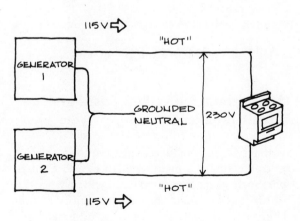

ILL. 6

*We are discussing supplies of 115 and 230 volts in our examples throughout; 120 and 240 volts are also supplied by some utility companies.

Electrical Design
175

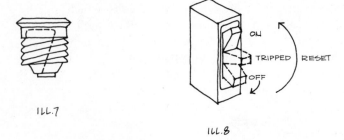

ILL.7

ILL.8

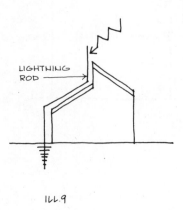

LIGHTNING
ROD

ILL.9

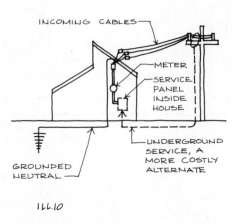

INCOMING CABLES

METER

SERVICE
PANEL
INSIDE
HOUSE

UNDERGROUND
SERVICE, A
MORE COSTLY
ALTERNATE

GROUNDED
NEUTRAL

ILL.10

SAFETY DEVICES

Overcurrent Protection: Fuses and Circuit Breakers

At times we may inadvertently overload a circuit by connecting too many appliances and fixtures to it. Such an accidental overload will increase the heat in the wires and thus the possibility of fire. Safety devices—either fuses or circuit breakers— must be provided to limit the amperes to a predetermined number, in somewhat the same manner

that safety valves keep in check the pressure and temperature in a plumbing system.

You are undoubtedly familiar with the location of the fuse or circuit breaker box in your house or apartment. Most likely you have replaced a blown fuse or reset a circuit breaker at one time or another. A fuse consists of a short length of metal wire with a high resistance to current and a relatively low melting point. As long as the current flowing through the circuit is below a predetermined amperage, the metal in the fuse will carry it with no problem. When the amperage exceeds the rated preset level, the metal will melt because of the heat generated by the excess amperage, thereby breaking the circuit. Some fuses combine a slow action for low overloads with instant action for high overloads. Whenever you try to draw more power from a circuit than it can deliver (for example, if you turn on a stereo, a color TV, a blower, an air conditioner, a typewriter, an iron, and all the lights on one circuit all at the same time), you will blow a fuse. Fuses are rated according to the maximum amount of amperage they can carry—15 A, 20 A, 30 A, and so on (Ill. 7).

A circuit breaker operates as a switch. Whenever more current flows than the breaker is designed for, it automatically opens up, breaking the circuit and stopping the current flow. Circuit breakers are preferred over fuses because they are safer and, unlike fuses, they can be reset and reused. A blown fuse must be replaced with a new one. It makes good planning sense to replace your present fuse box with circuit breakers (Ill. 8).

Overvoltage Protection: Grounding

Grounding is the provision of an escape route for leakage of electrical current. It is a mandatory code requirement. When you install a lightning rod, its purpose is to direct the electric charge via a separate path away from the house to the surrounding earth (Ill. 9). Similarly, when you ground the electrical system you are providing an alternate path by which the leakage of fault or "short circuit" current can be more safely discharged. This is customarily done by connecting one of the wires in the system (the neutral) to the earth by means of a wire leading to the metal water service entry pipe in the house or a metal rod driven in the ground (Ill. 10).* The grounded

*The metal cold-water service is customarily used for the main building electrical ground connection. Where a plastic cold-water service is used, a ground rod is needed.

neutral (white) wire is never interrupted by a switch, fuse, circuit breaker, or any other device.

In addition to grounding the entire system, all appliances should be grounded. The reason for this is that a defective appliance can have exposed live voltage on its metal parts. In other words, the electricity-carrying equipment within the appliance (normally insulated from the casing) can accidentally come in contact with the casing, establishing an electrical circuit and making the casing electrically "live" to the touch. Should you touch the casing, you may become part of the circuit, carrying current through your body to the ground (Ill. 11). To avoid this danger, codes have traditionally specified that all devices with motors, as well as heavy electricity consumers, such as electric ranges, water heaters, clothes dryers, and bathroom heaters, be grounded by means of grounding-type receptacles (Ill. 12). These receptacles have provision for an additional circular prong. This third prong connects the appliance casing to the grounded wire in the distribution wiring system.* Fixtures such as refrigerators, freezers, and dishwashers come equipped with a three-prong plug. Minor appliances like radios or televisions that do not have a three-prong plug can also be connected to three-prong receptacles, since they are designed for use with either receptacle. Grounding-type receptacles are now usually required by local codes throughout the entire installation.

In addition to system grounding and special appliance grounding, the entire wiring system (regardless of type) must be continually grounded throughout. The purpose of this is to automatically ground fixtures when they are connected to the outlet. More on this follows in the section on wire types.

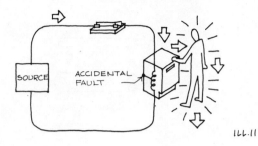

ILL. 11

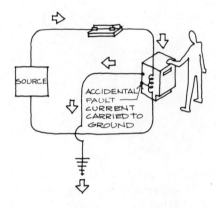

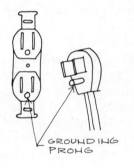

GROUNDING PRONG

ILL. 12

Ground-Fault Protection: Ground-Fault Circuit Interrupters

To further protect you from the danger of shock or fire, ground-fault circuit interrupters (GFCI or GFI) now must be included in your electrical system in selected locations such as bathrooms. A GFI is a device designed to open the circuit and stop the flow of current in the event of a fault or an unwanted flow of current to the ground from an exposed wire or "live" part. The latter may

occur as the result of accidental contact between a hot wire and a grounded conduit, the armor of a flexible armored cable, a grounding wire, or the casing of a motor or appliance. The current flowing as a result of a ground fault is often too small to blow a fuse or trip a circuit breaker, but is large enough to give a shock or start a fire.

Although three-prong plugs and three-wire cords properly installed to grounding receptacles should reduce these dangers, the possibility remains that the cord or plug may be defective.

Some GFI's available offer protection to an entire two-wire system,* whereas others protect

*Older wiring systems did not provide the third-prong ground connection for every appliance. Newer systems, using three-prong plugs, do provide a ground connection for each appliance.

*A GFI will not protect a two-wire circuit that is part of a three-wire supply system having two hot wires with a common neutral.

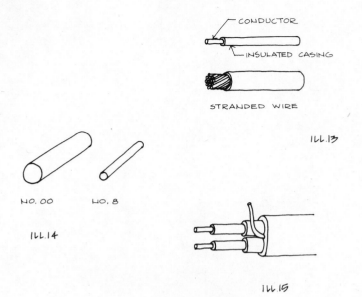

CONDUCTOR
INSULATED CASING

STRANDED WIRE

ILL.13

NO. 00   NO. 8

ILL.14

ILL.15

only a single receptacle. Keep in mind that the GFI's maximum amperage rating has to be the same as that of the circuit or receptacle it protects, but unlike a fuse or a circuit breaker, it will trip on lower fault currents than its rated carrying capacity.

The National Electrical Code (NEC) requires, among other things, the installation of GFI's in all outdoor 115 V, 15 A, and 20 A outlets and in all 15 A and 20 A receptacles at construction sites. In addition to those locations, the code also requires GFI's to be installed in garages and bathrooms where appliances are used close to grounded plumbing.* Countertop outlets closer than six feet to the kitchen sink must also be provided with GFI's. It is likely that future NEC editions will require an even greater use of GFI's.

WIRES

Wires provide the path through which electric current travels. They consist of a copper conductor (aluminum and copper-clad aluminum are also available but are not recommended) wrapped in an insulating layer of plastic compound or rub-

*The neutral (white) wire in the electrical system is grounded by connecting it to the earth via a wire leading to the metal water supply pipe in the plumbing system. In the event an exposed wire in an appliance causes the case or any exposed part to have "live" voltage on it, if you touch the case and a faucet or another part of the plumbing system, you'll be completing the circuit from the fault to the plumbing and carrying current through your body.

ber. Aluminum conductors have been forbidden by code in some localities (Ill. 13).

Wire Sizes: Ampacity

Wires offer resistance to the flow of current. The energy lost by this resistance translates itself into heat. The greater the current flow (amperage) in the wire, the greater the resistance encountered and therefore the greater the heat that is generated. As the heat increases, the chances of the insulation breaking down, and consequently the possibility of fire, increase. For this reason, it is extremely important to limit the amount of amperage that a wire can carry.

The ampacity, as the current-carrying capacity of a wire is called, is dependent on its size and on the type of insulation. The larger the wire, the more amperage it can carry with less resistance. A most peculiar aspect of wire sizing, leading to much confusion, is the fact that the smaller the circumference of the wire, the larger the number it is assigned. For example, size 00 wire is approximately 3/8" in diameter, whereas size 8 wire is only about 1/8" (Ill. 14). (This size represents the diameter of the copper conductor and does not include the insulating casing around the wire.) Wire sizes range from large ones, size 0000 (4/0), which is about 1/2" in diameter, to minuscule ones, size 40. Table A lists the ampacity of copper wires commonly used in residential work.

According to the NEC, a circuit is not rated exclusively according to the ampacity of its wires but is also rated according to the fuse or circuit breaker protecting the circuit. For instance, a no. 12 wire rated for an ampacity of 20 amps can carry that capacity only if the circuit it serves is

TABLE A*
(to be used for preliminary
selections only)

Wire Size	Ampacity
14	15
12	20
10	30
8	40

*This table is included as an illustration of ampacities for preliminary design purposes. Since the NEC is periodically revised, check the most current edition for specific values.

protected by a 20 amp fuse or circuit breaker. Should the circuit have only a 15 amp fuse or breaker, the wire and the circuit ampacity will be reduced to 15 amps.

ILL.16   ILL.17

Wire Types

For ease of installation, two or three wires are grouped together to form a cable. Two-wire cables have one white neutral and one black hot wire. Three-wire cables have one white neutral and one black and one red hot wire.

The two most commonly used types of cables for residential work are non-metallic-sheathed cable and flexible metal-armored cable, each with a different cost, method of installation, and acceptability by code. Conduit (both rigid and thin-walled) is yet another alternative but is usually not required for new residential construction (unless called for by code or it is to be used for surface wiring or some other special condition).

Non-metallic-sheathed cable, generally referred to by its trade name, Romex (Rx), is available in type NM for use in dry locations and type NMC for damp (although not permanently wet) locations (Ill. 15). (NM and NMC are National Electric Code designations.) This cable is cheaper than metal-armored cable and is easy to install, requiring no special tools. It is, however, more vulnerable to damage. Type NM consists of two or three wires covered with a flame-retardant and moisture-resistant plastic jacket. In addition to flame retardancy and moisture resistance, type NMC is fungus- and corrosion-resistant. Both its wires are embedded in solid plastic. An additional uninsulated wire is also present for grounding purposes. This wire is carried from outlet to outlet to provide a continuous ground. Although non-metallic-sheathed cable is very popular, some codes do not allow its use, favoring armored cable instead.

Flexible armored cable (usually referred to by its trade name, Bx) is most commonly available for residential work in type AC. (AC is the National Electrical Code designation.) This type, which is restricted to dry locations, consists of two wires, normally plastic-insulated, bound together with tape or braid. The wires, in turn, are covered with a spiral galvanized-steel armor. Like non-metallic-sheathed cable, it uses an uninsulated copper wire for grounding (Ill. 16). The metal casing is grounded to every electrical device, metal box, or cabinet (see page 315, Inset II). Many codes prefer this type over nonmetallic-sheathed cable (Romex) because it offers greater

protection against accidental grounds and against physical damage. It is, however, more difficult to install and generally more expensive.

Neither nonmetallic-sheathed cable nor armored cable is suitable for underground installation. Check your local code for recommendations on cables to be installed in such special conditions.

A few words on cable sizes. The size of a cable is referred to first by the size of the wire, say no. 12, then by the number of wires. For example, a 12-3 cable will be one with three no. 12 wires. A 12-3 cable with ground will have in addition a grounding strip or wire.

Conduit is still another wiring method which, although not generally used for residential construction, deserves special attention. Conduit is essentially a steel or plastic pipe (or tube). Wires are not originally inside the conduit when you buy it; they are pulled through once the conduit has been installed. Metal conduit is available in rigid or thin-walled forms. It is hard to install, not necessarily because of cutting and connection work but because it is difficult to bend. It is, however, a very safe wiring system, and is generally required for large jobs (almost always required in commercial, industrial, or institutional work), in surface wiring of old installations, and certain other special conditions (Ill. 17).

MODIFYING THE EXISTING ELECTRICAL INSTALLATION

Start by becoming thoroughly familiar with your local electrical code. Most likely, unless you are building in a heavily built-up area such as New York City, which has its own, quite strict code, you'll be required to follow the National Electrical Code. Many localities have adopted the NEC as their guideline for construction. Others have amended it to incorporate local conditions.

A few words about the NEC. The primary goal of this code is safety. We point this out for two reasons. The first is to emphasize that not following the code will lead to an unsafe installation;

any deviation is both unwise and illegal. The second is to point out that its requirements are those needed for minimum safe conditions. Improving on minimum recommendations by providing larger service entrances and wire sizes and more circuits than required will give you a better installation with more room for expansion. Keep in mind that the use of electricity has increased drastically in the past and will probably continue to do so in the future.

Another recommended, although not essential step to take before designing the system is to contact the company that will provide you with fire insurance. Find out if any variation in the methods, materials, or design you are planning might make a difference in future insurance rates.

The Size of the Service Entrance

Find out the capacity of your present service entrance. In very old homes and apartment buildings, this is not an easy job. The boxes are not clearly marked and are often hazardous. It makes good sense to hire an electrician. He can take a look at the service entrance panel and advise you as to its capacity and condition. He should also check to make sure that the system is properly grounded. If the system is not grounded, it has to be grounded. The older the building, the more likely the service entrance will need upgrading. If your service is presently a two-wire system, it will probably have to be brought up to a three-wire system to meet code.

The NEC has traditionally specified a minimum service entrance of 100 amps and three-wire service for a single-family house. Inevitably this requirement will be increased with future code revisions. Bear in mind that the NEC deals with minimum safety requirements; it does not take into account possible expansion of the house. Make sure that your service entrance has sufficient capacity not only to handle your present renovation but also for future growth. Some codes already require a minimum service entrance of 200 amps. We recommend a service of no less than 150 amps and preferably 200 amps (Inset II). The additional amperage will provide sufficient spare power to allow for growth, such as the installation of a central air-conditioning system at a later date. If you are planning to have electric heat, the minimum service will have to be 200 amps. (To enlarge the service of an existing residence, your electrician must work with and get approval from the utility company.)

Evaluate the Condition of the Wiring

In the past, electrical wiring was insulated with paper, cloth, or rubber. This insulation will dry out and become brittle over the years, resulting in a hazardous electrical condition. All electrical wiring with dry or brittle insulation needs to be replaced. A licensed electrician is the person best qualified to evaluate the condition of the wiring.

Determine an Adequate Number of Circuits

Electrical outlets are grouped together into various circuits, each circuit protected by its own fuse or circuit breaker. Providing the premises with several different circuits decreases the possibility of overloading any one of them. Your local code will indicate the minimum number of circuits that may be installed. This figure is generally based on the floor area of the house.

Start by determining how many circuits you presently have. One way to approach this is to make a diagrammatic sketch of every room or area of your house or apartment. Indicate every electrical device in each room. This includes light switches, outlets, lights, appliances, etc. (See "Drawing the Electrical Plans," pages 182–184, for the symbols and the procedure to follow.) Turn the switches on and off to determine which device they control, and draw a line between those on the same switch and on the same circuit.

The next step is to go to the service panel and assign a number to each circuit (each fuse or circuit breaker represents a circuit). From this point on you will need the help of a friend with a good pair of lungs or a set of walkie-talkies. One person will remove the fuses or flip the breakers while the other turns on lights and appliances and tests outlets to see whether they are on or off. Each electrical outlet should be given the number of the fuse or breaker that controls it. You should also note the number of outlets in any one circuit and whether they service small appliances, special appliances (such as electric ranges or air conditioners), or general outlets and receptacles.

There are three types of circuits: the general (or lighting) circuit, the small-appliance circuit, and the special circuit. The general circuit includes not only permanently installed devices such as ceiling fixtures but also receptacles for floor and table lamps and other minor appliances like radios and vacuum cleaners. The figure used by the NEC to estimate the total load of the general circuit is 3 watts per square foot of floor area. To arrive at the number of general circuits, use the following calculation. A 2,500-square-foot house will require 2,500 $\times$ 3 or 7,500 watts as the total load to be carried by the general circuits. If the house is wired with no. 12 wire having an ampacity rating of 20 amps and a voltage of 115 volts, the load-carrying capacity of each set of wires will be W = A $\times$ V, or 20 amps $\times$ 115 volts = 2,300 watts.* To find out how many circuits are needed to successfully deliver the required 7,500 watts, divide the total watt load (7,500) by the wattage that a pair of no. 12 wires can carry (2,300). It follows that 7,500 $\div$ 2,300 = 3.26 required circuits. Since it is impossible to install a fraction of a circuit, four circuits will be provided. Keep in mind that the code is dealing with minimum safety figures. Together with the requirement of 3 watts per square foot, the NEC makes a recommendation (not a requirement) to install one circuit per 500 square feet of total floor area. Using this figure will give you five circuits for the same 2,500-square-foot house. Going one step further and providing one circuit per 400 square feet will give you even greater flexibility and make allowance for future needs. According to that figure the same house will be equipped with 6.2 or seven circuits. (Use an eight- or twelve-circuit panel.)

Follow this procedure to determine the number of circuits that your house should have (including additional square footage that may be part of your renovation plans). Compare the result with the existing number of circuits. Most likely you will have to add or extend the present circuits. Some codes do not allow extending circuits from existing boxes. Be sure not to exceed the circuit's capacity or the ampacity of the wire or of the circuit breaker. It is considered good practice to supply no more than six outlets per 15 A circuit and eight outlets per 20 A circuit. Check the NEC and your local code to see if they offer different guidelines. Count the number of outlets serviced by each circuit. If they exceed the code requirements, take some off the circuit.

General circuits cannot handle the heavy loads required by small appliances such as toasters, blenders, coffee makers, and portable microwave ovens. Although not permanently installed, these appliances need a greater amount of electrical energy for their operation. Have you ever noticed how the lights dim when the toaster is in use? That is an indication that the circuit does not

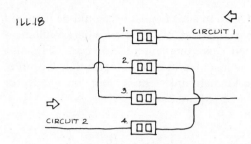

ILL.18

have as much capacity as it should have. Small-appliance circuits are designed to handle such loads. These circuits are strictly for portable appliances; no permanent appliances or lighting outlets may be installed on them.

Look back at your survey to see if in fact you presently have any small-appliance circuits. Your renovation may involve extending or adding to them. Those who don't have small-appliance circuits must include them in their renovation plans. The NEC calls for a minimum of two small-appliance circuits, each equipped with no. 12 wires and protected by a 20 amp fuse or circuit breaker. (Each of these circuits will have a capacity of 20 amps $\times$ 115 volts, or 2,300 watts.) When installing the outlets, it is wise to connect alternate outlets to alternate circuits. In other words, if you have four small-appliance outlets in a row, connect the first and the third to one circuit and the second and fourth to the other, further reducing the possibility of an overload. Do the same with two or more circuits in the same room (Ill. 18). Check your local code for its specific requirements.

Although not required by some codes, it is good practice to provide new installations with individual dedicated circuits for permanently installed appliances requiring heavy power loads such as electric ranges, water heaters, dishwashers, clothes dryers, or any appliance with a power rating over 1,000 watts. This will include permanently connected motors with a rating of $\frac{1}{8}$ horsepower or more (for an oil burner, furnace blowers, water pump, etc.). These circuits will be either 115 volts or 230 volts depending on the appliance voltage rating. Wiring of a sufficient amperage should be designed for each—30, 40, or 50 amps or as required.

Determine the Locations Requiring GFI's

Take a look around. All outdoor and bathroom receptacles (existing or new) should be replaced

*We recommend no. 12 wire of 20 amp capacity as the minimum wire size for general circuits.

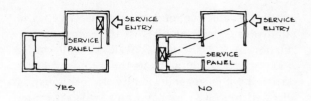
with GFI's. In addition, GFI's should be installed in the garage and any location where appliances are used close to plumbing fixtures. GFI's also must be installed in countertop outlets within 6' of the kitchen sink. Check your local code for additional requirements.

Drawing the Electrical Plans

Take your plans (including both new and existing conditions) and trace onto a clean sheet of paper the walls and partitions of the house, including all openings for doors and windows. In addition, be sure to indicate the location of all special appliances in the kitchen, laundry room, workshop, utility room, and any other area requiring them. Draw the location of the service panel.

To prepare a workable set of electrical plans, the following components, both new and existing, should be shown and identified:

- Wall outlets
- Ceiling outlets
- Switches
- Small-appliance outlets
- GFI outlets
- Special-appliance outlets such as air conditioners or stoves
- Circuits

THE SERVICE PANEL: The service panel should be located very close to the point of entry of the incoming cables from the power company. The reason for this is that until these conductors arrive at the main lugs or disconnect switch (in the service panel), the service entrance cables are without overcurrent protection. As a fire and safety precaution, the length of unprotected conductor must be kept to a minimum. Maximum allowable distances vary with the different codes, and sometimes they are not even specified. In any case, make sure that the length of unprotected conductor is kept in accordance with the NEC.

It is often illegal and may be hazardous for a service panel to be located in a highly combustible area. Ideally, service panels should be easily accessible and have plenty of working space around them (Ill. 19). If your existing panel is in an illegal or hazardous location, it should be relocated.

LOCATE THE WALL RECEPTACLES: Draw the location of the existing wall receptacles in your plans. Check your local code to see whether it includes maximum distance requirements between receptacles. The NEC states that no point along a floor line shall be more than 6' from an outlet in that space. Few appliances or fixtures, however, come with 6'-long cords, so you should consider placing at least one receptacle and possibly two on each wall of each room. Look at the existing receptacles. If there are too few, or there is only one on a long wall, add more receptacles. Provide enough receptacles to allow for flexibility of furniture and appliance arrangement. For example, locate wall outlets on each side of a bed. You may otherwise find yourself using an extension cord every time you change your favorite

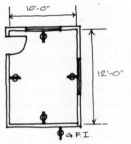

ILL.20   WALL RECEPTACLE

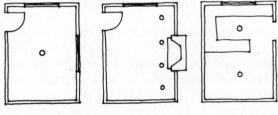

ILL.21   O CEILING OUTLETS

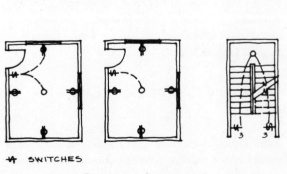

SWITCHES

ILL.22

reading spot. Extension cords, in addition to being a hassle, are unsafe and unsightly (Ill. 20).

At this point also include any weatherproof receptacles you may want to add to the exterior of the building. Make sure to indicate them as ground-fault circuit interrupters. While working on the exterior of the building, locate outlets for outdoor lights, motion/security light sensors, etc.

LOCATE THE CEILING OUTLETS: Indicate in your plans the existing ceiling outlets (if any). Do they provide you with adequate light? Are you planning to replace some of the lights with ceiling fans? Perhaps the best approach to the lighting problem is to study the types of activities that are to take place in these areas. Is the present light source adequate to handle these activities? Do you need supplemental or task lighting? If you are planning a new room or redesigning an existing one, is it going to be lit by means of floor or wall lamps or from an overhead source? Would one light source, centrally located, be sufficient or do you need more lights to obtain proper illumination levels? Do you want a central outlet or would you rather highlight an area or element in the room such as a fireplace? Do you have a light switch at the entrance to give light when you come in? How about a high wall outlet for a favorite picture light? By answering these questions you can determine how many (if any) ceiling outlets you need (Ill. 21).

LOCATE THE SWITCHES: Examine each room or area and determine whether the existing switching is sufficient or whether you need more. There are areas that require switches from more than one location. Stairs, for example, should have a three-way switch at either end of the run. You already know your existing path of travel in order to turn lights on and off. Would you benefit from adding switches or converting some existing switches into three-way switches? Consider the possibility of having one or more wall outlets connected to a switch. This way, if the living room is lit exclusively by floor and table lamps, you do not have to move all around the room to turn them on and off; you can instead control them from a single switch. Check that each of your ceiling outlets is controlled by a switch. The most convenient location for switches is on the latch side of the door.

To indicate which outlets are connected to which switches, draw a dotted line between the outlet and the proper switch. In addition, indicate whether it is a one-pole or a three-way or four-way switch (Ill. 22).

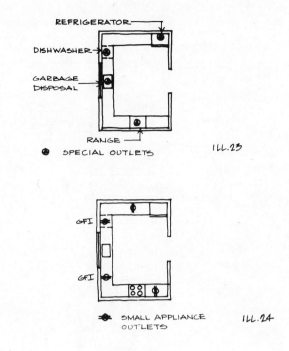

ILL. 23

ILL. 24

LOCATE THE SPECIAL CIRCUITS: Kitchens, laundry rooms, workshops, utility rooms, etc., all deserve careful attention because of the concentration of appliances requiring special circuits. All such appliances (new and existing ones) should be shown in your drawing to remind yourself of the special outlets you need to provide. Give each one an outlet, noting next to it the exact power requirement. Consider installing a dedicated heavy-duty outlet for an air conditioner below or to the side of each living-room or bedroom window (Ill. 23).

LOCATE THE SMALL-APPLIANCE OUTLETS: Indicate in your plans any existing above-the-counter outlets in the kitchen and laundry room. The NEC requires a minimum of two small-appliance circuits. If you have only one, you need to add a second one. Assess if you have a sufficient number of outlets to service portable appliances such as blenders, coffee makers, irons, etc. (Ill. 24).

INDICATE THE CIRCUITS: Indicate the existing circuitry by drawing a solid line between all the outlets connected to one circuit. Give each circuit a number. If you are adding or modifying a circuit, draw a slash line over the circuitry lines to be modified (Ill. 25). With a solid line indicate the new circuits. Keep in mind each circuit's maximum capacity; for example, a 15 A $\times$ 115 V circuit has a maximum capacity of 1,725 watts. If

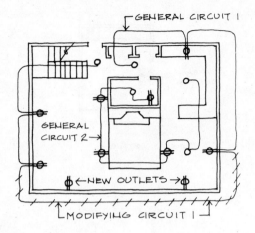

GENERAL CIRCUIT 1

GENERAL CIRCUIT 2 →

← NEW OUTLETS →

MODIFYING CIRCUIT 1

ILL. 25

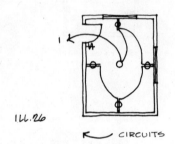

ILL. 26

CIRCUITS

the wattages of the appliances to be installed in any one circuit exceed the circuit's capacity, split it up into two or more circuits as needed. Check yourself by adding up the power required by each of these appliances and comparing it with the circuit's maximum capacity.

Splitting up circuits not only will prevent overloading but will give you usable outlets in each room should one of the circuits go dead. Provide the refrigerator and freezer with one circuit each. When they share a circuit with other appliances, you run the risk of being stuck with a lot of spoiled food if something in the circuit goes wrong and causes the circuit breaker to trip.

Once the circuits are established, each one is given a number. The drawing of the room with all outlets, switches, and circuitry included should look something like Illustration 26.

LOCATE MISCELLANEOUS DEVICES: It is at this point that the location of doorbells, the intercom system, and any other special electrical devices should be included.

21

THE STRUCTURAL FLOOR:

ITS DESIGN OR RENOVATION

The authors firmly believe that you should know something about structures before tampering with the bones of your building. We have heard too many stories of buildings that have collapsed around the ears of novice renovators who attempted surgery on the body of their buildings without having studied structural anatomy. The old adage "a little bit of knowledge is a dangerous thing" does not necessarily apply here. We hope that a little bit of structural knowledge, at the very least, will engender a respect for the complexity of structure and that you will be wise enough to hire an experienced carpenter if you are not sure you can handle a particular procedure. If you are designing the floor system for the extension or if you are planning to cut an opening into your existing floor, be sure to have an architect or structural engineer review your structural plans and calculations.

We have included the following four chapters primarily for those of you who are planning to construct an addition to your house. The chapters are critical, however, for all renovators who are planning to make even minor modifications to the floor structure, walls, roof, or foundations of the existing house. Many novices are unaware that any penetration of these areas may affect the integrity of the structure. For instance, even the addition of a skylight may require a modification of the roof structure and, while still in the design stages, you should have an understanding of how roofs work. Apartment renovators will probably be able to skip the chapters on roofs and foundations but will need the one on walls since it explains partition construction. The chapter on floors is critical if you are combining two apartments to make a duplex and have to cut into the floor to install a stair, add a partition, or put in a bathtub.

DESIGNING THE FLOOR OF THE ADDITION

Although buildings are constructed from the foundations up, it is easiest to design the structure by considering the floor system first, the walls next, the roof third, and the foundations last. It is difficult to make decisions about the foundations without knowing how you are going to frame the floor, where you are going to locate the load-bearing partitions, and how the roof is going to work. On the other hand, you can't finalize any aspect of the structural design until you have considered all aspects. This makes the design process complicated since it does not fall into a neat step-by-step order. If you are constructing an extension, we suggest that you read about all of the parts—floors, walls, roofs, and foundations—before making any decisions or calculations. (Read the construction chapters in Part Four of this book as well.) When you have an overall understanding of the process, return to this chapter and design the floor system.

Most houses built since the 1950's use the platform floor system of construction since it is the easiest to build. We advise you to use this method

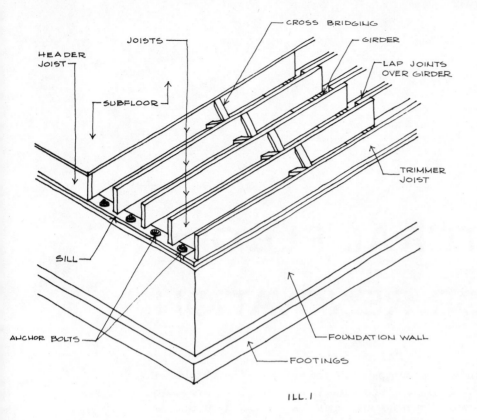

CROSS BRIDGING

JOISTS

HEADER JOIST

GIRDER

LAP JOINTS OVER GIRDER

SUBFLOOR

TRIMMER JOIST

SILL

ANCHOR BOLTS

FOUNDATION WALL

FOOTINGS

ILL. I

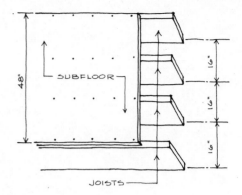

SUBFLOOR

4'-8"

16"

16"

16"

JOISTS

ILL. 2

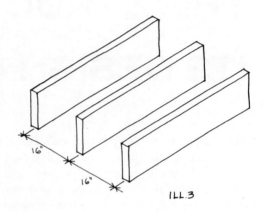

16"

16"

ILL. 3

ILL. 4

when constructing your extension for much the same reason.

It is easier to understand the design of the floor system if you have a clear understanding of how the floor system works. In its simplest terms, each component of the floor acts to transfer the weight placed on it to the foundations. The floorboards receive the live loads and transfer that weight plus their own weight to the joists. The joists add their own structural weight and transfer the loads to the girders or beams, which in turn transfer the loads to the vertical supports or directly to the foundations. Eventually all of the live and dead loads are transferred by the foundations' footings to the ground. The trick is to get the loads transferred evenly to the ground without putting undue stress on any of the components. A poorly designed floor will sag, squeak, or, at worst, fail.

Laying Out the Platform Floor

The platform floor is exactly that, a platform. It consists of a subfloor (the finished floor is laid much later, after the danger of its being ruined by rain, cement droppings, paint, etc., has passed), which is nailed to the floor joists. The subfloor is usually made of sheets of plywood. The floor

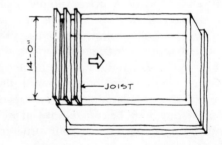

14'-0"

JOIST

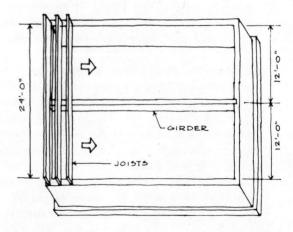

24'-0"

12'-0"

12'-0"

GIRDER

JOISTS

joists are long, slender horizontal members spaced either 12", 16", or 24" o.c. (Ill. 1).*

These joists span between supports. Both supports could be continuous foundation walls, or if the span is too long, the joists will span between a foundation wall and an intermediate girder (Ill. 4). In the case of an addition to an existing house, the joists will be supported by two new foundation walls or one new foundation wall and the side of the existing house (with or without intermediate supports) (Ill. 5).

If foundation piers are used instead of a continuous foundation wall, the joists will span from a perimeter girder to an intermediate girder (Ill. 6), or in the case of an extension, from the existing house to an intermediate or perimeter girder.

Floor joists are the lightweight horizontal members that carry the subfloor. Joists are easily differentiated from beams and girders† in that they are always spaced closely together.

In a house with continuous foundation walls the joists frame into a member called the header (Ill. 1). If the house sits on piers, the joists frame either into a header or directly into the girder. The header is usually the same size (the same cross-sectional dimensions) as the joists. It is used as a nailing surface for the joists (giving them added rigidity) and also serves to enclose the space and to keep out unwanted animals and drafts. The end joist that sits on the foundation wall parallel to the run of the joists is called the trimmer joist. It closes off those ends of the house and carries the end load of the floor and the wall.

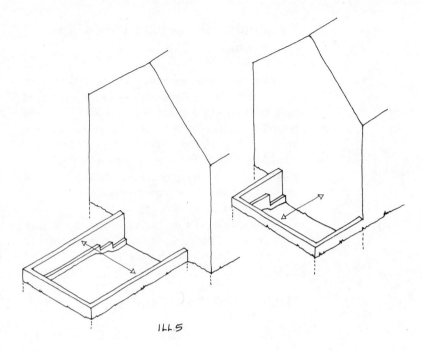

ILL. 5

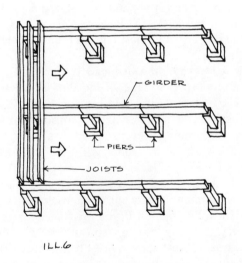

ILL. 6

---

*Why the 12", 16", or 24" spacing? This spacing is used for studs, floor joists, and roof rafters. It is a modular unit derived from the standard sheet size of most sheathing, subflooring, paneling, and plywood, which is 4' × 8'. Four feet is equal to 48", which is evenly divided by 24" (into two segments), 12" (into four segments), or 16" (into three segments). Any of these spacings ensures that the 4' × 8' sheets have a nailing surface at each end (Ill. 2).

Historically, this spacing derives from the fact that in England firewood was cut to 16" lengths (to fit into a fireplace constructed of 8"-long bricks). This firewood was often split into lath strips to support plaster. The wood uprights that supported the lath were then spaced 16" apart.

The "o.c." refers to "on center," meaning that the distances between structural components are to be measured from the center line of one joist to the center line of another (Ill. 3).
†Beams and girders are heavier structural members and are harder to tell apart. Generally, a girder is heavier than a beam, meaning that it either spans a wider gap or carries a heavier load or supports beams. In buildings that have joists, beams, and girders, the joists carry the direct floor loads, transferring these loads to the beams, which transfer the loads to the girders, which transfer the loads to the vertical supports or to the foundations. Few house designs require both beams and girders. We will call the intermediate support for the joists the girder.

Both the headers and the trimmers sit on a mud sill (pressure-treated to resist rot and insects), a wood board generally a 2 × 6 or 2 × 8, which lies directly on top of the foundation wall and is secured to it with anchor bolts. The remaining structural element of the floor system is the bridging. The bridging (cross or solid) helps make the floor more rigid. The bridging holds the joists in straight, reducing the potential movement in the floor. A well-designed and well-constructed floor should not creak. Although a tiny bit of resilience is tolerable, if not actually desirable, a creaky floor is not.

Designing the Framing Plan of the Extension

It is likely that your extension will abut the house on one side. If the extension is longer than it is narrow, and its long side is perpendicular to the house, it makes sense to run the joists between your new foundation walls (or new girders supported by piers). If the length of the extension is parallel to the adjacent wall of the house, it makes sense to run the joists from the existing house to the new foundation wall (Ill. 5). If you are going to frame the joists into the existing wall so that the new and existing floors will be level, plan to frame into the existing header or trimmer.

Determining Loads and Spans

The design of the floor system is determined by the loads on the floor, the distance the beams and joists must span, and the strength of the lumber you are going to use. Knowing all of these factors, you can specify the dimensions, spacing, and length of the joists and beams.

Building codes in most regions require that for single-family residences the first-floor framing be designed to support a live load of 40 pounds per square foot (psf) and the second-floor framing be designed to support a live load of 30 psf. This means that you must design the floor so that it can carry 40 pounds on every square foot of space. (Picture a 10' × 10' room with 100 little kids jammed into it.) Our design chart (Table A)* is based on the 40 psf design requirement. The 40 psf requirement covers normal household furniture, including pianos. If you are considering installing anything heavier, consult the building department. Most garages must be designed for a 50 psf load, but you would use a reinforced-concrete slab and not wood for the floor. (It is unlikely that your code allows a wood floor in the garage.)

The design span is determined by the floor plan of the extension. If the extension is to be less than 16' wide, you may be able to span from founda-

tion wall (or girder) to foundation wall (or girder) without needing any intermediate supports. If the extension is over 18' wide, you will need an intermediate support, which will reduce the span by half (Ill. 6). There are borderline cases. For instance, if the extension is 18' wide, you could specify floor joists that are 18' long, but your floor might have too much bounce in it. For the borderline cases we recommend breaking the span in two. In addition, lumber over 14' long might be difficult to come by. The length of your joists and girders might be determined by what is available in the local lumberyards.

Selecting the Joists

The design of the floor joists is made relatively simple by the availability of joist charts, which are a compilation on one page of all the necessary mathematical calculations. All that is left for you to do is to feed the charts the required span of the joists and the type of lumber you will be using. The chart identifies the cross-sectional dimensions of the appropriate structural member.

As an example, assume the extension is 24' wide. (The width, remember, is the shorter dimension. If your extension is 14' × 24', the width is 14'. The joists are designed to span the shorter distance.) We decide that the 24' span will be broken into two spans of 12' each. Therefore, the joists will span 12' (Ill. 8). (If your extension is less than 16' wide, you can span from foundation wall to foundation wall and eliminate the intermediate girder support.) Our first choice for the lumber is Douglas fir, but we discover that it is out of stock. We choose hem-fir (not as strong, but good enough for our purposes) and decide to use no. 1. As a general rule, architects and contractors select stronger materials for horizontal structural members, such as joists and girders, which are subjected to bending stresses. Vertical structural members, such as columns and studs, are subjected to compression stresses, which are less critical. It is not uncommon for a contractor to use no. 1 grade for the joists and no. 2 grade for the studs.

Going to the simplified joist table (Table A), designed specifically for a live load of 40 psf, we read down the left-hand column and find hem-fir (north) no. 1. The numbers in the boxes are the span designations in feet and inches. Reading across the line from left to right we pass 10'-6", etc., and stop at a number that is longer than our 12' span, which is 12'-7". We look up to the top of the column to learn that the structural member

*The tables provided in this book are for preliminary design purposes only and should not be used for final selection of structural sections. Since each municipality follows its own codes and standards, what is valid in one community may not be valid in another. In addition, the calculations in these tables (and all tables in this book) are based on the strengths of lumber that is "stress-graded." Since the lumber available in the lumberyards is not stress-graded, when using the tables in this book assume that the lumber is no. 3 grade for making your preliminary selections.

Species	Grade	2 × 6		2 × 8		2 × 10		2 × 12	
		Joist spacing (inches)							
		12	16	12	16	12	16	12	16
		Maximum allowable span (feet-inches)							
Coast sitka spruce	select structural	10-11	9-11	14-5	13-1	18-5	16-9	22-5	20-4
	no. 1 & appearance	10-11	9-9	14-5	12-10	18-5	16-4	22-5	19-11
	no. 2	10-3	8-11	13-7	11-9	17-4	15-0	21-1	18-3
	no. 3	7-9	6-9	10-3	8-11	13-1	11-4	15-11	13-9
Douglas fir, larch (north)	select structural	11-2	10-2	14-8	13-4	18-9	17-0	22-10	20-9
	no. 1 & appearance	11-2	10-2	14-8	13-4	18-9	17-0	22-10	20-9
	no. 2	10-11	9-11	14-5	13-1	18-5	16-9	22-5	20-4
	no. 3	9-3	8-0	12-2	10-7	15-7	13-6	18-11	16-5
Eastern hemlock-tamarack (north)	select structural	10-0	9-1	13-2	12-0	16-10	15-3	20-6	18-7
	no. 1 & appearance	10-0	9-1	13-2	12-0	16-10	15-3	20-6	18-7
	no. 2	9-6	8-7	12-6	11-4	15-11	14-6	19-4	17-7
	no. 3	8-7	7-5	11-3	9-9	14-5	12-5	17-6	15-2
Hem-fir (north)	select structural	10-6	9-6	13-10	12-7	17-8	16-0	21-6	19-6
	no. 1 & appearance	10-6	9-6	13-10	12-7	17-8	16-0	21-6	19-6
	no. 2	10-3	9-4	13-6	12-3	17-3	15-8	21-0	19-1
	no. 3	8-3	7-2	10-11	9-5	13-11	12-0	16-11	14-7
Ponderosa pine	select structural	9-9	8-10	12-10	11-8	16-5	14-11	19-11	18-1
	no. 1 & appearance	9-9	8-10	12-10	11-8	16-5	14-11	19-11	18-1
	no. 2	9-6	8-7	12-6	11-4	15-11	14-5	19-4	17-7
	no. 3	7-7	6-7	10-0	8-8	12-10	11-1	15-7	13-6
Red pine	select structural	10-0	9-1	13-2	12-0	16-10	15-3	20-6	18-7
	no. 1 & appearance	10-0	9-1	13-2	12-0	16-10	15-3	20-6	18-7
	no. 2	9-9	8-6	12-10	11-2	16-5	14-3	19-11	17-4
	no. 3	7-5	6-5	9-10	8-6	12-6	10-10	15-3	13-2
Spruce-pine-fir	select structural	10-6	9-6	13-10	12-7	17-8	16-0	21-6	19-6
	no. 1 & appearance	10-6	9-6	13-10	12-7	17-8	16-0	21-6	19-6
	no. 2	10-0	8-8	13-2	11-6	16-10	14-8	20-6	17-9
	no. 3	7-7	6-7	10-0	8-8	12-10	11-1	15-7	13-6
Western cedars (north)	select structural	9-6	8-7	12-6	11-4	15-11	14-6	19-4	17-7
	no. 1 & appearance	9-6	8-7	12-6	11-4	15-11	14-6	19-4	17-7
	no. 2	9-2	8-4	12-1	11-0	15-5	14-0	18-9	17-0
	no. 3	7-9	6-9	10-3	8-11	13-1	11-4	15-11	13-9
Western white pine	select structural	10-3	9-4	13-6	12-3	17-3	15-8	21-0	19-1
	no. 1 & appearance	10-3	9-4	13-6	12-3	17-3	15-8	21-0	19-1
	no. 2	9-8	8-4	12-9	11-0	16-3	14-1	19-9	17-1
	no. 3	7-5	6-5	9-10	8-6	12-6	10-10	15-3	13-2

*To be used for activity floors.

made out of no. 1 hem-fir that can span 12'-7" with a live load of 40 psf is a 2 × 8 joist spaced 16" on center. If we examine the line further, we see that the same 2 × 8 joist would span as much as 13'-10" if it were spaced 12" on center. Obviously, we would require more joists for this spacing and our lumber bill (and labor) would be greater. Besides, the 16" spacing will do the job.

If our design span was 13'-6", we could use 2 × 10's at 16" o.c. (good for a 16' span) or 2 × 8's at 12" o.c. To determine which is more economical, add up the number of joists you will need and multiply it by 14'. (Remember that lumber is often sold in lengths that increase in 2' intervals.) You will have to pay for the 14' joists, but you may need the extra length to overlap the girder. Multiply this figure by the cost of the joists per square foot. Compare the price of the 2 × 8's with

The Structural Floor: Its Design or Renovation
189

It is not necessary to frame the house completely in lumber. Steel beams and girders can span longer distances with less chance of bending than can wooden beams, and are therefore often used in place of heavy wooden girders in the framing of floor systems. A 6"-deep steel section can substitute for a wooden member 14" deep, thus saving headroom. The table gives the allowable loads for steel beams and it indicates two types of steel sections. The well-known I-beam is designated on the table as an S section. The W designation refers to a steel section with wider flanges than the I section (Ill. I-1). Illustration I-2 shows framing details.

TABLE I-A: SAFE LOADS (IN POUNDS) FOR STEEL BEAMS AND GIRDERS
(for preliminary design purposes only)

| | Spans | | | | | |
Shapes	10'	12'	14'	16'	18'	20'
S 6 × 12.5	8,700	7,300	6,200			
S 6 × 17.25	10,400	8,700	7,400			
S 7 × 17.5	13,300	11,100	9,500	8,300		
S 8 × 18.4	17,100	14,200	12,200	10,700	9,500	8,400
S 8 × 23	19,300	16,100	13,800	12,000	10,700	9,600
W 8 × 17	21,000	17,000	15,000	13,000		
W 10 × 21	33,000	28,000	24,000	21,000	18,000	15,000

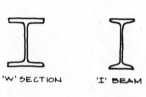

'W' SECTION   'I' BEAM

ILL. I-1

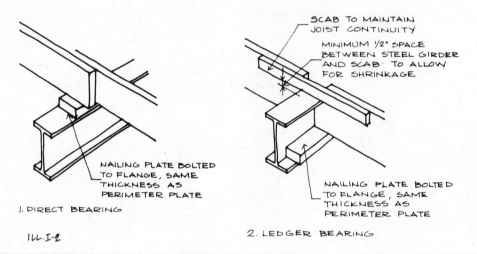

NAILING PLATE BOLTED TO FLANGE, SAME THICKNESS AS PERIMETER PLATE

1. DIRECT BEARING

ILL. I-2

SCAB TO MAINTAIN JOIST CONTINUITY

MINIMUM 1/2" SPACE BETWEEN STEEL GIRDER AND SCAB TO ALLOW FOR SHRINKAGE

NAILING PLATE BOLTED TO FLANGE, SAME THICKNESS AS PERIMETER PLATE

2. LEDGER BEARING

that of the 2 × 10's. There are other considerations: the 16" spacing will require less labor and the 2 × 10 floor will be firmer than the floor with joists that are not as deep.

Designing the Girder

The girder is used as the intermediate support between foundation walls or, if you are using foundation piers instead of a continuous wall, to span between the piers. The girder must be strong enough to carry the weight of the joists, which carry the weight of the floor system, as well as the partitions resting on it and the live loads.

We design the girders by trial and error. We make some tentative design decisions based on our 24'-wide extension. We have already divided the span into two parts of 12' each which the joists will span. As an example, let us say the extension is 32' long, which is much too long a span for the girder. A rule of thumb for girder design suggests 10' as the maximum practical

span for a wood girder. We could make the span longer if we are willing to use a very deep built-up section. If we divide our 32' length into three parts, we get spans of 10'-8" each. If we divide the length into four parts, we get short spans of 8'. How we divide the girder will determine how many foundation piers will be needed. We will evaluate both of these choices to determine which division is best (Ill. 7). If we need a very long girder we may turn to steel (Inset I).

In order to determine the cross section (size) of the girder, we must evaluate how much weight it will be supporting. First we must determine which portion of the floor will be supported at the perimeter of the house and which must be supported by the girder. We have sketched our potential floor-framing plan in Illustration 8. Under the drawing is a section through that plan at the point indicated by the lines with the arrows at the ends. (A-A' identifies the section and shows exactly where on the plan the cut was taken.)

We will analyze the requirements for four spans of 8' each first. Since the joists are spanning the north-south (assuming north to be at the top of the page), it is obvious that the east and west perimeters of the building need to support only the weight of the walls above them. The center girder supports half the weight of the floor joists, as indicated on the framing plan (Ill. 8) by the shaded portion. If the total floor is 24' wide and the girder is placed midway between the north and south perimeters of the building, the girder will be supporting half of each of the 12' spans—that is, a total of 12' of width. If we isolate the part of the floor system directly supported by the girders, we can add up the loads that will be placed on it.

Live loads are the first consideration. Since we are designing a one-story extension, we are required to design for a minimum of 40 psf. The dead loads (the weight of the materials in the joists, subfloor, finished floor, etc.) are about 10 psf (Inset II). The total live loads and dead loads are 50 psf. The load on the floor segment can now be calculated: 50 psf × 12' × 8' = 4,800 lbs.

If there are load-bearing partitions that rest either on the girder or on the section of floor that the girder supports, these loads must be considered too, as they will be taken on by the girder. The next calculation requires us to guess the weight of the girder itself. Since we don't know what the girder will be, we will assume a girder that is 4 × 10. We consult Table II-A for the weights of the various structural members. The 4 × 10 weighs 9 lbs. per linear foot: 9 lbs × 8' = 72 lbs.

To complete the calculations:

Add up the live and dead loads:	4,800
Add the dead load of girder segment:	72
Add the dead load of a non-bearing partition: 12' long × 9' high × 8.2 psf (The roof is supported by the peripheral walls and not by the girder.)	885
Total load:	5,757

Table B (on the following page) will give us the proper girder for the given loads. For the 8' span we may use a 4 × 10, which is good for up to 6,820 lbs. Since this is such a light member, we should try the calculations for the 12' spacings and compare the two. We don't know an easier way to design girders. We leave you with this advice: When in doubt, overdesign.

Framing the Joists to the Girder

Joists can be framed into a girder in one of three ways depending on the framing situation. The

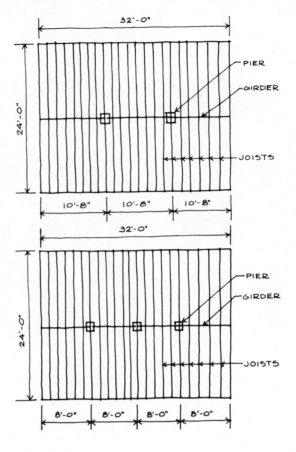

ILL. 7

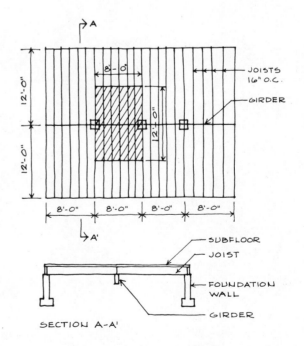

ILL. 8

The Structural Floor: Its Design or Renovation

191

When calculating loads, both live loads and dead loads must be accounted for. Table II-A gives the weights of various building materials and composite structural items. Most of the listings are per square foot, which means that if you are trying to determine the weight of a 2 × 4 stud wall with ½" gypsum-board walls on both sides of the studs, you would multiply the weight of the wall per square foot (8.2 lbs.) × the dimensions of the wall (let us say, 8' high by 12' long) = 787.2 lbs.

TABLE II-A: DEAD LOADS
(to be used for preliminary design purposes only)

		Pounds per square foot
Walls	wood stud wall: ½" gypsum board, both sides	8.2
	4" lightweight concrete-block wall	20.0
Floors	plyscore	1.5
	hardwood flooring	4.0
	joists with hardwood floor and plyscore subfloor:	
	2 × 6	10.5
	2 × 8	11.5
	2 × 10	12.0
	2 × 12	12.5
Roofing	shingles:	
	wood	2.5
	fiberglass-asphalt strip	2.5
	plywood sheathing	1.5
Windows	For windows and sliding glass doors constructed of wood frame and double glazing (insulating glass) use 3.5 psf for approximating purposes	3.5
Ceilings	½" gypsum board	2.1
Roof Plank	2" thick	5
	3" thick	8

(The following are *not* in pounds per square foot):

		Pounds per linear foot
Beams and Girders	4 × 8	7.2
	3 × 10	6.6
	4 × 10	9.1
	4 × 12	11.0
	6 × 10	13.8
	4 × 14	13.0
	6 × 12	16.7
Stairs	Weight for a complete simple stair about 3' wide: 300 lbs.	

TABLE B: SAFE LOADS (IN POUNDS) FOR WOOD BEAMS AND GIRDERS
(to be used for preliminary selections only)

			Spans				
Size	6'	7'	8'	9'	10'	11'	12'
4 × 8			4,250	3,780	3,400	3,090	2,830
4 × 10			6,820	6,060	5,450	4,960	4,540
6 × 10	11,357	10,804	9,980	8,887	7,997	7,520	6,890
6 × 10 built-up	10,068	9,576	8,844	7,878	7,086		
6 × 12			13,300	12,900	12,100	11,000	10,100
8 × 12			18,100	17,500	16,500	15,000	13,800
4 × 14			10,900	10,400	10,100	9,840	9,180
4 × 16			13,300	12,600	12,100	11,700	11,500

most common method is to lap the joists over the girder, nailing the joists to each other and to the girder (Ill. 9). The advantage of the lap joint is that the joists do not require absolutely precise measuring and cutting. The disadvantage is that it steals a lot of potential headroom from the basement or crawl space. The second method is to butt the joists end to end over the girder and to use metal ties to connect them to each other and nails to join them to the girder. The advantage of this method is ease in joist layout. (The joists are now laid in straight and not staggered lines.) The disadvantage is that the joists must be cut precisely to size. The third method resolves the headroom problem by hanging the joists to the girder so that the top of the girder and the top of the joists are on the same plane. This can be accomplished with metal joist hangers designed for this purpose.

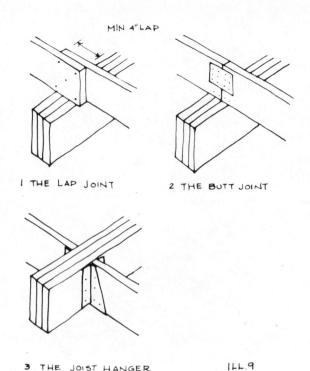

1 THE LAP JOINT   2 THE BUTT JOINT

3 THE JOIST HANGER   ILL. 9

Framing the Joists and Girder to the Foundation Wall

Joists are framed into a continuous foundation wall by nailing the ends of the joists to both the mud sill and the header (Ill. 10). The intermediate girder is supported on the extreme ends by the foundation wall. If you are using the joist lap or butt methods, the girder will join the foundation wall at some point a few inches below the top of the wall. In this case the girder is framed into a "pocket" that was made when the foundation wall was constructed (Ill. 11). Even if you use the joist hanger method, it is likely that the girder will need a small pocket in the foundation wall. (Its depth is usually a few inches greater than the joists.) Whatever method used, be careful to coordinate the heights of foundation wall, foundation piers, girders, and sills to ensure that the joists are perfectly level when joined to both sill and intermediate girder.

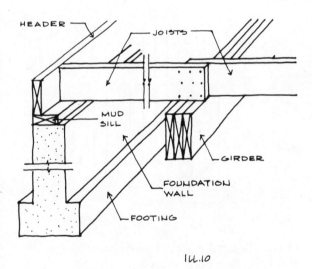

HEADER
JOISTS
MUD SILL
GIRDER
FOUNDATION WALL
FOOTING

ILL. 10

Stabilizing the Floor with Bridging and Subflooring

The joists are held in position, to some extent, by being nailed to the headers or joined to the girders. The joists are further stabilized by diagonal or solid pieces of lumber nailed between them, called bridging. In addition to its value in keeping the joists straight, the bridging helps in the distribution of a concentrated load to the other joists. Cross bridging (Ill. 12) joins the joists by means

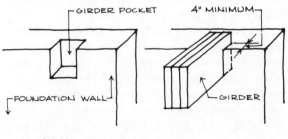

GIRDER POCKET   4" MINIMUM
FOUNDATION WALL   GIRDER

ILL. 11

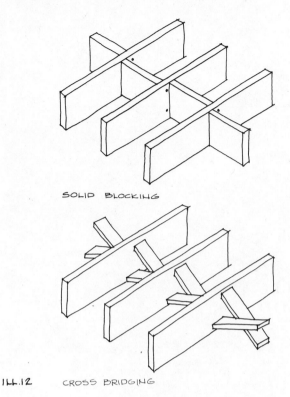

SOLID BLOCKING

ILL. 12   CROSS BRIDGING

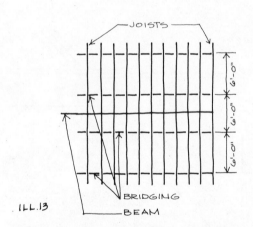

JOISTS

6'-0"
6'-0"
6'-0"

ILL. 13   BRIDGING
BEAM

may have boards that were nailed on the diagonal to the joists as subflooring. The subfloor, bridging, and joists are nailed tightly together to form a structural unit that acts to resist stresses and transfer loads. In addition, the subfloor serves as a platform on which the wall units may be constructed. The finished floor is not installed until much later.

MODIFYING THE FLOOR SYSTEM OF A PLATFORM FRAME

This section covers framing conditions that are likely in the design of the extension's floor system. In addition, it covers framing modifications that must be made to the existing house as a result of the renovations. Before modifying the floor of an existing house, you will have to determine the layout of the existing joists. For modifications of the first floor, go down into the basement or crawl space and draw the framing plan to scale. If you are making changes to the second floor, you may have to remove a small portion of the first-floor ceiling to determine the way the joists are running as well as their depth and spacing. The thoroughness of this analysis depends on what you are planning to build above the floor. You will need an exact framing plan if you are framing an opening for a stair. If you are adding lightweight partitions for a closet, you may not need to be all that cautious. On the other hand, if you are planning to put an oversized Jacuzzi midspan on the second floor, you will probably have to reconstruct whole segments of the second-floor framing system.

Framing under a Partition or Bathtub

The floor under a partition or a bathtub must be reinforced in order to carry the added load. When the partition or tub runs parallel to the run of the joists, the joists are simply doubled beneath it (Ill. 14). If the partition running parallel to the joists is to carry plumbing, it is necessary to create a space through which these lines will pass. The floor joists are doubled and separated a few inches (they are placed to straddle the plate of the partition above). Solid bridging is nailed between them every 16" so that the two joists will act in unison (Ill. 15).

If the partition runs perpendicular to the joists, some say there is no need for added reinforce-

of two diagonal pieces of wood, usually 1 × 2's that cross each other in an X pattern. Metal cross bridging is available that eliminates the cutting and simplifies the nailing. Solid bridging uses pieces of lumber the same dimensions as the joists. The pieces are measured, cut, and nailed solidly into place. A row of bridging joins the joists every 6' to 8' (Ill. 13).

The final floor of the house will have two layers: the subfloor, or the rough floor, and the finished floor, which may be of wood planks, parquet squares, tile, or carpet. The subfloor is constructed immediately after the joists are secure and the bridging in place. It generally consists of 4' × 8' sheets of plywood, ¾" thick, nailed to the joists in a basket-weave pattern. Some old houses

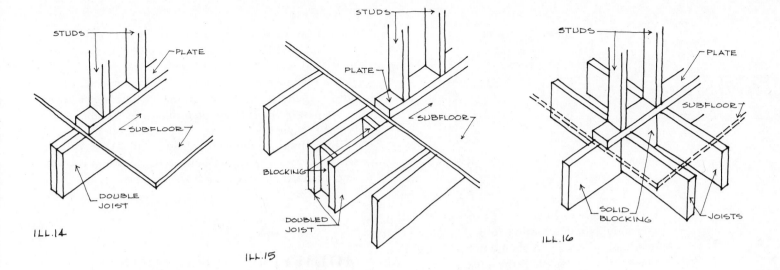

ILL.14

ILL.15

ILL.16

ment. Conservative carpenters recommend solid blocking between the joists directly beneath the partitions (Ill. 16). In the case of a load-bearing partition or an oversized bathtub running perpendicular to the joists, it makes sense to be cautious and double every other joist.

Framing an Opening

You will need to frame an opening for a stair, a fireplace flue, or a fireplace foundation. No matter which way the joists run, parallel or perpendicular to the opening, some of the joists must be cut and, thereby, "crippled." Generally, the crippled joists are supported by a doubled or tripled header which is framed into doubled or tripled trimmer joists (Ill. 17). The opening is thus framed by a box made of doubled headers and trimmers. If the opening does not line up with the spacing of the joists, it might even be necessary to throw in an extra joist or two (Ill. 18).

Framing a Cantilever

A cantilever is an overhang or projection which is supported on one side. Large bays, porches, and balconies can be designed as cantilevers. It is relatively easy to incorporate a cantilever in the design of an extension. On the other hand, because of the nature of its framing, it is very difficult to add a cantilevered element to a house that is already built.

A cantilever is actually an extension of the floor system, rather than an element added on at the end. The joists that support the cantilevered portion must be extensions of the joists of the adjacent floor system. Because the cantilever must be

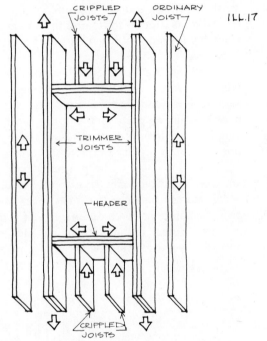

ILL.17

ARROWS INDICATE HOW THE LOADS ARE TRANSFERRED

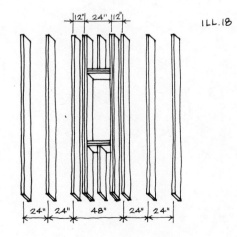

ILL.18

The Structural Floor: Its Design or Renovation

195

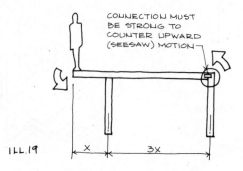

ILL. 19

CONNECTION MUST
BE STRONG TO
COUNTER UPWARD
(SEESAW) MOTION

combat both the gravitational force of the ordinary floor and the upward tendency of the cantilever (Ill. 20).

In a case where the extension's joists are running perpendicular to the cantilever, you must revise part of the framing plan to ensure that the projecting portions of the joists are counterbalanced by three times their lengths (Ill. 21). Essentially, we have a condition similar to framing an opening, in that we are left with crippled joists.

fully counterweighted by the structure behind it, you should limit its width to 6' to 8'. The part that overhangs the support should not be longer than one-fourth the length of the adjacent (fully supported) part (Ill. 19). The noncantilevered end must be either counterweighted or firmly anchored to its support to counter the upward tendency that is produced when a load is placed on the overhang.

If the cantilever occurs parallel to the run of the joists, this rule is easily applied. The regular joists are merely extended so that they span the length between the supports and also the cantilevered length. A header is placed at the end of the projection to supply rigidity to the joists. The trimmer joists on the sides of the projected portion are doubled. Solid blocking (short pieces of lumber) is constructed between the joists (over the support) to maintain structural integrity. It is important to connect the nonprojecting ends of the joists to the girder using metal framing anchors to

MODIFYING A BALLOON-FRAME HOUSE

If you are renovating a house that is more than forty years old, or if the house is stuccoed and multistoried, there is a good chance that it is a balloon frame. Illustration 30 in Chapter 16 covers framing details for the balloon as seen from the inside of the building (see also Chapter 16, Ill. 31). Adding a joist for a partition or a bathtub may be a little difficult. If you are trying to double a joist under a midspan weight and you can't get the new joist to rest on the sill, bolt the new joist to the existing one to reinforce it. (Remember that the main stresses on the joists will be bending stresses at midspan rather than the shear stresses at the end supports.) If you are thinking of extending your existing balloon-frame house, use

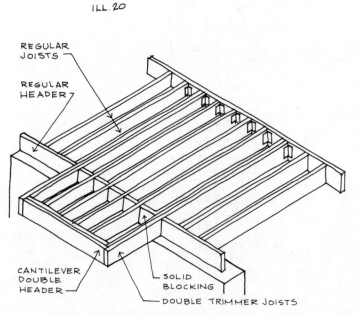

ILL. 20

REGULAR JOISTS

REGULAR HEADER

CANTILEVER DOUBLE HEADER

SOLID BLOCKING

DOUBLE TRIMMER JOISTS

CANTILEVERED PORTION IS PARALLEL TO THE RUN OF THE JOISTS

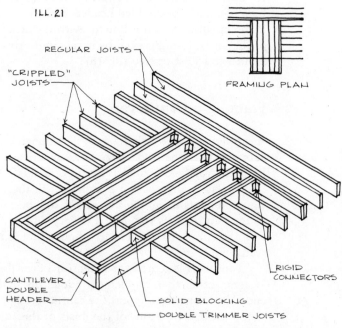

ILL. 21

REGULAR JOISTS

"CRIPPLED" JOISTS

FRAMING PLAN

CANTILEVER DOUBLE HEADER

SOLID BLOCKING

DOUBLE TRIMMER JOISTS

RIGID CONNECTORS

CANTILEVERED PORTION IS PERPENDICULAR TO THE JOISTS

the platform frame for the extension. Balloon-frame construction requires fire stops between floors. Be sure not to remove the existing ones.

MODIFYING CONCRETE-SLAB FLOORS

Many apartment buildings are constructed using a slab called a flat plate, which is about 5″ to 10″ thick and reinforced with steel rods and wire mesh. There are no beams in this system and the bottom of the slab is the ceiling of the floor below. Generally, there is a good deal of special reinforcement at the points where the slab is joined to the column. We are reluctant to give you advice on how to cut into the slab for an opening. We suggest that you consult an architect or a structural engineer. Depending on the location of the hole and its size, the opening may or may not need special reinforcing. In addition to the structural problems, there may be plumbing and electrical lines buried in the slab that may be disturbed.

22

WALL AND PARTITION
DESIGN AND MODIFICATION

The design of the walls and partitions* (even if they are load-bearing) will not take us into mathematical tables since the structural criteria are not as critical as those for floors.

Walls and partitions are subjected to gravitational loads, which are compressive, and most structural materials are very strong in compression. Be that as it may, it is important to understand how these vertical supports work if you are thinking of adding, removing, or modifying a wall, partition, or, especially, a column.

The load-bearing vertical supports of a building transfer the roof and floor loads down to the foundations. For the most part, the stresses on a wall or column are mostly compressive. In some situations, vertical supports, especially columns, are subjected to bending stresses. Different structural materials respond in different ways to the various stresses. Unreinforced concrete is very strong in compression but extremely weak in tension, as in bending. We must reinforce these walls and columns with steel bars if we expect any bending stresses. Masonry, as in brick, concrete block, or stone, is a very strong material when the stresses are compressive. You are probably most familiar with load-bearing walls that are constructed of double-thick brick or brick and concrete block. These walls are very good in compression, but will crack if subjected to bending stresses, such as the uneven settling of the foundation. Wood, on the other hand, although

not as strong as concrete in compression, can assume a great deal of bending stress. A variation of the load-bearing wall is the wood-frame stud wall.

WOOD STUD WALLS AND PARTITIONS

Essentially, there is little difference in appearance between the load-bearing and non-load-bearing partitions and walls. They are both constructed of 2 × 4's or 2 × 6's* (which are actually 1½" × 3½" or 5½" in cross section) spaced 16" o.c. Partitions that are not load-bearing use studs that are at least 3½" deep for stability. In some circumstances, as in the stub wall between closets, shallower studs (2 × 3's) or 2 × 4's set sideways are used to save space. But these thin partitions, even if non-load-bearing, are never used in trafficked areas where they may be leaned against.

Exterior stud walls used in platform-frame construction are built after the floor below has been completed. The structural elements of the wall are the studs and the sheathing. The non-structural elements consist of the insulation and condensation-controlling elements, the interior wall finish, and the exterior siding.

The outside walls consist of 2 × 4 or 2 × 6

*Walls separate the inside of the house from the outside. Partitions separate one interior space from the other.

*The 2 × 6 stud allows for more insulation in the exterior walls.

studs which are approximately 8' long positioned vertically between the sole plate on the bottom and the double plates on the top (Ill. 1). Plywood sheathing (generally ½", ⅝", or ¾" thick) is an important structural element since it is needed as bracing. Many of the old, pre-plywood houses have diagonal bracing that has been "let in" to notches made in the studs (see Chapter 16, Ill. 27). The sheathing also acts as a skin which, to some extent, allows for the spreading of the load from one stud to the adjacent studs.

Studs are traditionally spaced 16" on center, but can be spaced 12" or 24" apart if conditions warrant. (The 24" spacing is often used in houses with 2 × 6 studs.) The stud spaces in the walls of houses in mild climates are filled with 3½" of insulating materials. Houses built in northern climates have 2 × 6 studs and 5½" insulation. The most commonly used insulation is the blanket variety available in 15"-wide rolls, which comes with and without a vapor barrier and is designed to fit snugly in between the studs. Many old houses have 2" of insulation or no insulation at all. If your house lacks insulation and you live in a climate that requires the house to be either heated or cooled, you should add insulation (see Chapter 19).

Interior partitions, whether load-bearing or not, are either 4½" thick (for walls with ½" of gypsum board on each side of the studs), 4¾" thick (for ⅝" gypsum board), or 5½" thick (for walls with ½" of backer board and ½" of gypsum board on each side). Exterior walls are about 6" to 8" thick (counting the stud, ⅝" interior gypsum board, ½" sheathing, and about 1" of exterior siding). Since the exterior siding and sheathing extend over the edge of the foundation wall (Ill. 2), the thickness of the exterior wall, as measured from the edge of the foundation to the inside of the room, is only 6⅛" (or 4⅛").

REMOVING PARTITIONS

Many of you may be considering the removal of a partition to combine two or more rooms. If the partition you remove is nonstructural, you will probably not have to reinforce the structure. On the other hand, if the partition is structural, it will probably have to be replaced with a beam and, perhaps, one or more columns. The removal of any wall or partition is so very critical to your safety and to the integrity of the structure that we strongly advise you to consult with an architect or structural engineer before taking any action. The

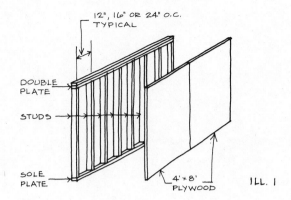

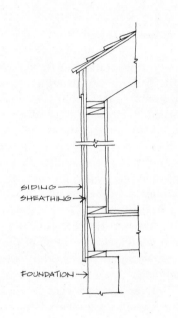

following discussion on how to determine whether or not a partition is structural, or how to design the replacement girder and columns, should not be considered a substitute for this professional's advice.

It is sometimes difficult even for a professional to be absolutely sure if a partition is load-bearing. First, you may have to make a hole in the ceiling under the upstairs floor to determine the direction of the span of the joists. If the joists above the partition are running parallel to it, it may suggest that the partition is non-load-bearing (unless, of course, it is propping up the extra load of a bathtub). If the joists are running perpendicular to the partition, and their ends are resting on it, it is very likely that the partition is load-bearing (Ill. 3). When in doubt, trace the partition down to the basement or the cellar. If there is a partition or line of columns under the partition in question (especially if the basement supports are not needed

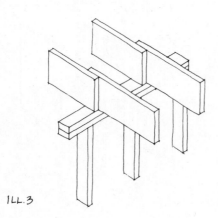

ILL.3

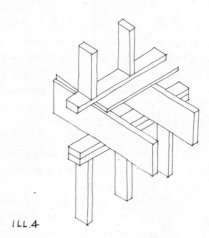

ILL.4

functionally to separate rooms), you may suspect that the partition is load-bearing.

Sometimes a partition that is perpendicular to the joists is non-load-bearing and sometimes it is partially load-bearing. If the span is short, under 20', and the joists go over the top of the partition but do not end there, it is difficult to tell if the partition is completely extraneous to the structure or if it serves as a "prop wall" (Ill. 4). The prop wall is commonly seen in a brownstone row house. It is the partition between the parlor and the front foyer. However, not all of the partitions between parlor and foyer are prop walls. Some are completely load-bearing, and some are non-load-bearing and can be removed. In the case of a brownstone, you learn a lot about its structure by tracing it from cellar to roof. If you are considering removing any old townhouse partition that runs parallel to the long lines of the building, consult an architect or engineer. He or she is likely to go down into the cellar and see if there is a masonry wall or a line of columns directly under that partition. If there is, and the line of support can be traced up to the partition in question, the partition should not be removed without providing some other support for the floor system above it.

In an apartment building taller than eight stories (with some few exceptions) you can be relatively sure that the building's structure is a steel or reinforced-concrete frame and that all of the partitions are non-load-bearing. Old apartment buildings up to seven or eight stories are often constructed of masonry load-bearing walls and wood-joist floor systems. In this type of building about half of the partitions are load-bearing. If you are living on the second floor, it is likely that the partition between the bedroom and the living room is supporting the floor systems of all of the bedrooms and living rooms above you. It is best

not to remove that structural wall even if you would add a steel beam in its place. If the building is old, there may be a lot of cracking and resettling above the new beam that may cause many of your neighbors a great deal of distress. Evaluating the structure of old buildings can be tricky. There are a number of apartment buildings that have both load-bearing walls and some lines of columns.

In addition to structural considerations, there should be no chimney flues or any major plumbing, electrical, intercom, or cable TV lines in the partition to be removed.

GIRDERS AND COLUMNS

If you want to open one space into another and remove a load-bearing partition, have an architect or engineer evaluate the situation. He or she is likely to suggest that you use a girder* spanning between two columns to support the floor joists above. The columns might be designed to be free-standing or they might be enclosed as part of an adjacent partition. Columns are generally constructed out of wood, steel, or reinforced concrete, or are Lally columns, which are hollow steel shafts filled with concrete. In private residential construction, wood is by far the most popular choice.

When designing columns, two sets of criteria must be met: first, the column must be strong enough to hold up its load (that is, it must resist the compressive stresses applied to it), and second, it must also have adequate thickness to

*The procedure for selecting the girder is exactly the same as the one described in Chapter 21.

P = Maximum allowable axial load in pounds
P/A = Allowable axial stress for buckling in psi (pounds per square inch)

Nominal size	A Sq. In.	8' P/A	P	9' P/A	P	10' P/A	P	11' P/A	P	12' P/A	P	13' P/A	P	14' P/A	P
4 × 4	13.14	752	9,890	595	7,820	482	6,330	398	5,230	335	4,400	286	3,750	246	3,230
4 × 6	19.94	752	15,000	595	11,900	482	9,610	398	7,940	335	6,670	286	5,680	246	4,900
4 × 8	27.19	752	20,500	595	16,200	482	13,100	398	10,800	335	9,100	286	7,750	246	6,680
4 × 10	34.44	752	25,900	595	20,500	482	16,600	398	13,700	335	11,500	286	9,820	246	8,470
4 × 12	41.69			595	24,800	482	20,100	398	16,600	335	13,900	286	11,900	246	10,200
4 × 14	48.94					482	23,600	398	19,500	335	16,400	286	14,000	246	12,000
4 × 16	56.19					482	27,100	398	22,400	335	18,800	286	16,000	246	13,800
6 × 6	30.25							917	27,700	806	23,300	655	19,900	568	17,100
6 × 8	41.25									806	31,800	655	27,100	568	23,300

withstand possible buckling (which subjects it to bending stresses).

In light-frame wood construction, it sometimes isn't even necessary to calculate the cross-sectional dimensions of a column needed to support a relatively light compressive load, if the column is not much taller than 8' and is enclosed in a wall. As a rule, an enclosed wood column with a 4 × 8 cross section will support a portion of one story and the roof of a house above it if the column is short and, therefore, not subjected to bending. But have your individual situation evaluated by an expert.

As in designing girders, the span of the column, which is its unsupported length, is critical. If the column is long and thin, and eccentrically loaded, it will tend to buckle along its slimmest axis (Ill. 5). If the load on the column is applied centrally (along its neutral axis) and evenly, the stresses on that column are purely compressive. If the loads are applied off center or unevenly (even as little as a quarter of an inch), the column may bend or "buckle" slightly. In wood-frame construction it is very difficult to control the loading and subsequent bending on the column. Even if you are very careful to center the load on the column, the lumber itself might contain an invisible defect which unbalances its load-carrying capacity.

To make sure that the column selected (using the above rule of thumb) will not buckle, subject it to a simple mathematical test. The length in inches of the column is divided by the depth in inches (its smallest dimension). The result of this equation must be less than 50. If it is not, the depth of the cross section will have to be increased. Table A integrates both sets of criteria.

Procedure for Column Design

Remember when designing columns that the loads are cumulative. That is, if a column is to be installed on the lowest floor, loads from the top of the building downward must be calculated.

1. Establish all loads on each section (floor to floor) of the column separately. Multiply the live load (L.L.) as established in the code by the floor area supported by the column. For the dead load (D.L.) include the weight of the materials used in the flooring system (joists, subfloor, finished floor) plus the weight of the partitions (Ill. 6).

2. Working from the top down, determine the loads accumulated on the lowest column section. (Add all of the floor loads.) This gives you P, the axial load in pounds. In Table A, look under the heading corresponding to the height of the column for that section of column only—not for the whole length

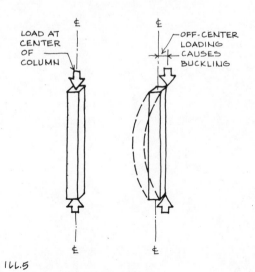

LOAD AT CENTER OF COLUMN

OFF-CENTER LOADING CAUSES BUCKLING

ILL.5

Wall and Partition Design and Modification
201

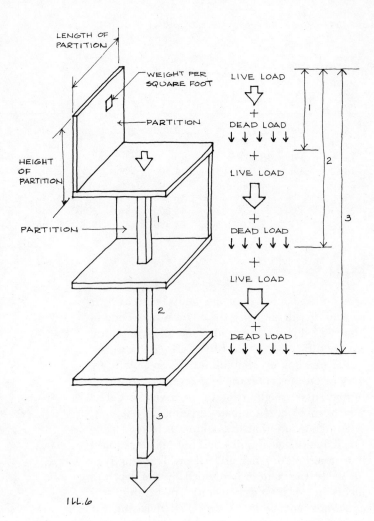

LENGTH OF PARTITION

WEIGHT PER SQUARE FOOT

PARTITION

HEIGHT OF PARTITION

PARTITION

LIVE LOAD

+

DEAD LOAD

+

LIVE LOAD

+

DEAD LOAD

+

LIVE LOAD

+

DEAD LOAD

ILL. 6

from basement to roof; you want the unattached length only. Read down to a number greater than load P previously calculated. Read left to determine the nominal dimensions and the cross section. Make sure that the P/A for the chosen section and column height is less than that recorded in the table.

Example: The axial load P for the lowest section of a column on a two-and-a-half-story house is 15,000 lbs.; the column height is 14′. Check Table A. Read down under P in the 14′ column. Stop at a number greater than 15,000 lbs. Look to the left. Nominal size of the section is 6 × 6. The area of the 6 × 6 is 30.25 square inches. Check:

$$P/A = \frac{15,000}{30.25} = 496$$

Check against the maximum P/A allowed (just to the left of the maximum allowable load for that height column), which in this case is 568.
496 < 568.
Use a 6 × 6.

Have an architect or engineer review your calculations before proceeding further.

23

DESIGNING OR MODIFYING THE ROOF

There are four probable renovation approaches that would result in the modification of your roof's profile: (1) the penetration of the roof for skylights, (2) the construction of an extension to the original house, (3) the inclusion of porches, verandas, or other overhangs, and (4) the addition of another story onto the house.

With the exception of the skylights, all of these modifications must be structured as if they were new roofs. The most important consideration in the structural design of the roof, as in the design of floor and wall framing, is the transfer of loads from one structural member to another. In addition to the dead loads (the weight of roofing materials), the roof is expected to carry live loads, which in this case are the weight of accumulated snow and the lateral pressures of wind and wind-driven rain. Because the weight of accumulated snow is so great in northern climates, roofs often are designed with slopes that shed the piles of snow. Flat roofs in snowy climates must be designed to carry greater live loads.

Keep in mind that in addition to structural and aesthetic considerations, there are a number of legal imperatives. Check with the zoning authorities to see if there are height (or style) restrictions for the roof. Check with the building department to see if they require you to use fireproof structural or finishing materials and to determine the roof's design loads. If you are thinking of building on top of an apartment house in an urban neighborhood, you will have to clear it with at least a half dozen authorities.

Roof design, even for a small extension, requires some education in structures. Also, the roof, being exposed to the elements, presents a more complex design problem than the structural design of the house's interior floor systems. The criteria for roof design vary considerably from one geographical area to another. Some areas of the country are subject to occasional earthquakes, tornadoes, and gale winds, not to mention the more ordinary problems of heavy rain and snowfall. Therefore, we urge you to consult an architect or structural engineer for any new roof or for the modification of an existing roof. The instructions and tables included in this chapter are to serve for preliminary design purposes and are not to be used so that you can design your own roof.

THE FLAT ROOF

No roof, not even a "flat" roof, is ever designed to be perfectly level. The roof is always pitched to a drain that carries water down through the house or through drainpipes along the exterior walls to a dry well or storm sewer. It is never a good idea to allow water or ice to accumulate on a roof. In the first place, water is heavy and its weight may stress the roof beyond its structural capacity. Second, a large, standing pool of water may cause seepage to the interior below if the roof member is any less than perfect.

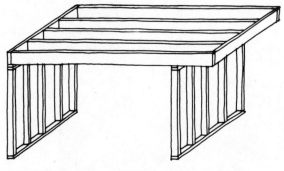

JOISTED FLAT ROOF SUPPORTED BY STUD WALLS

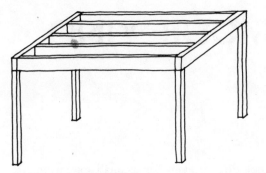

JOISTED FLAT ROOF SUPPORTED BY POST AND BEAM

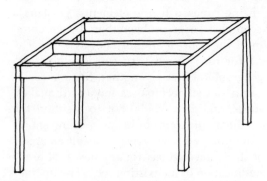

ROOF BEAMS SUPPORTED BY POST AND BEAM

ILL. 1

Framing the Flat Roof for an Extension

For the most part the flat roof is structured like a floor with some degree of variety. A flat roof may or may not have an overhang. The beams and joists can be concealed by a ceiling, or exposed to reveal the structure. The roof can be constructed of joists and beams or can be of the post-and-beam variety (see the section on plank-and-beam construction, page 210).

The flat roof is framed as if it were a floor system (Ill. 1). Review the procedure for the framing and sizing of structural members in Chapter 21. Openings for the chimney and skylights are framed as you would frame an opening for a stair.

Building codes must be consulted to determine the live loads to be used for the design of the roofing in your particular weather zone. These loads will vary considerably from one section of the country to the other. Because the roof is flat, and must support snow loads as well as the ceiling, the built-up roofing, and whatever mechanical pipes and ducts are hung from it, the loads are likely to be greater than those used for an interior floor system or for a pitched roof. The absolute minimum design live load for a roof in a climate not exposed to snow, earthquake, or major winds is 20 pounds per square foot (psf). To this basic figure you must add the snow and wind loads for your area and the dead loads for the roof's plywood sheathing and the membrane materials. If the live and dead loads for a flat roof in your area are under 40 psf, you may use Table A for the preliminary selection of the joists. Framing details for flat-roof construction are similar to those used in floor construction. Refer to the illustrations in Chapter 21 for framing details. When designing the roof, keep in mind that the roof must slope about 1/4" per 1' to drain water. Roofing details and end conditions can be found in Chapter 31.

Roofing Insulation

It is likely that the roof will be insulated. Flat roofs can be insulated both under and over the deck surface. Traditionally, insulated batts, at least 8" thick and with a vapor barrier, are stapled

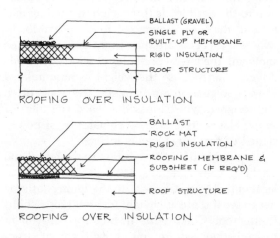

BALLAST (GRAVEL)
SINGLE PLY OR BUILT-UP MEMBRANE
RIGID INSULATION
ROOF STRUCTURE

ROOFING OVER INSULATION

BALLAST
ROCK MAT
RIGID INSULATION
ROOFING MEMBRANE & SUBSHEET (IF REQ'D)
ROOF STRUCTURE

ROOFING OVER INSULATION

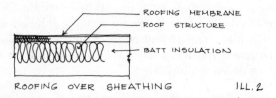

ROOFING MEMBRANE
ROOF STRUCTURE
BATT INSULATION

ROOFING OVER SHEATHING   ILL. 2

between the roof joists. A bit of an air space should be left between the batts and the deck to allow any seeped moisture to dissipate. Rigid insulation in the form of boards (usually composed of a sandwich of foam plastic, fiberglass, and other materials) may be installed above the roof deck with the roofing membrane applied on top of it. The boards must be rigid enough to hold the occasional weight of workers on the roof. A roofing concept rarely seen in small residential buildings places the rigid insulation (usually in the form of polystyrene foam board) above the roofing membrane. The light panels must be weighted down by a heavy layer of gravel to keep them from blowing away and to protect them from the sun's decaying rays. This sometimes adds considerably to the weight of the roof (Ill. 2).

Roofing Membranes

The roofing membrane is the waterproof skin that protects the inside of the house from water penetration. This skin, which must seal the house completely, has to be flexible so as to expand and contract with the thermal expansion and contraction of the other structural materials, and must be able to withstand the freezing effects of winter as well as the blistering heat of the sun. Most of the membranes described below are not made to stand up to regular pedestrian traffic. If you want to use your roof as a deck, you will have to add a traffic deck above the membrane.

The traditional roofing membrane is a "built-up" roof consisting of multiple (three to five) layers of asphalt-impregnated felt, with hot moppings of coal-tar bitumen between the plies of felt. A five-ply built-up roof has a dead load of about 5 psf. Some designers add a layer of aggregate to the surface to protect the membrane from the sun.

Recent technological developments have produced new materials with the required characteristics listed above. Cold compounds of asphalt and other materials may be used in place of the hot bitumens in built-up roofing. These mastics are usually brushed on. Recently sheeting materials have been used and are known as single-ply roofing. These highly elastic membranes are made of polyvinyl chloride, synthetic rubber (neoprene or ethylene propylene diene monomer), and other sheeting. Modified bitumen sheets have seams that are joined by welding either with a blowtorch or chemically. Some of these sheeting materials require aggregate protection and some do not.

If you want to use the roof as a play deck, you will have to install a decking material over the roofing, being very careful not to rip the membrane. One system used is an open-jointed paving block that is laid over the membrane. Water is allowed to fall between the blocks down to the drain. These blocks are particularly valuable if you must repair the roof at any future date, since they are easy to move and stack. The blocks add considerably to the dead load of the entire structure and their weight must be considered in any design calculations. Many roofing material companies will not guarantee their roofs unless their instructions for traffic protection are adhered to strictly.

Adding a Small Overhang or Porch Extension to a Flat Roof

Illustration 3 shows you how to frame an overhang for a new roof. If you want to add a cantilever overhang to an existing roof (say, to protect a door), you will have to cut back into the existing roof (see the section on framing a cantilever in Chapter 21). If it proves to be impractical to restructure the roof to provide for a cantilever, rethink your concept. It may be more economical to use the house to support one side of the extended roof, and columns to support the far side. For flashing details (to ensure that the intersection of the roofs is watertight), see Inset I, Chapter 31.

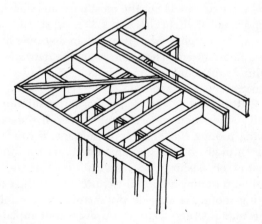

FLAT ROOF FRAMING CORNER DETAIL

ILL. 3

Designing or
Modifying
the Roof

205

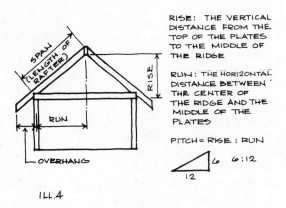

RISE: THE VERTICAL DISTANCE FROM THE TOP OF THE PLATES TO THE MIDDLE OF THE RIDGE

RUN: THE HORIZONTAL DISTANCE BETWEEN THE CENTER OF THE RIDGE AND THE MIDDLE OF THE PLATES

PITCH = RISE : RUN

6:12

ILL.4

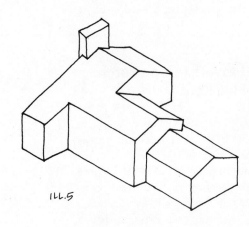

ILL.5

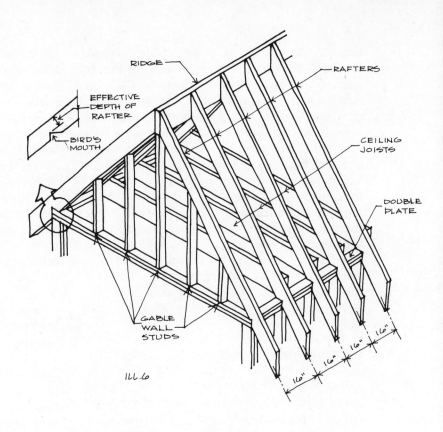

ILL.6

Penetrating an Existing Flat Roof for a Skylight

A number of things must be taken into consideration when adding a skylight to a flat roof. The first is a structural consideration: how is the opening to be restructured? For the most part, an opening for a small skylight (let us say 2' × 4') should be no more complicated to frame than any opening in a floor system. The "hole" must be reinforced with doubled headers and trimmers as detailed in illustrations on page 195.

Cutting through the vapor barrier, insulation, and roofing membrane is a bit trickier. If the existing roofing is a built-up membrane, it can be cut through and the skylight added (use the kind that is self-flashing). Mop on additional layers of built-up roofing around the entire area. If the existing roofing is a single-ply membrane, consult the manufacturer before you even contemplate cutting through the membrane. Each material has its own adhesives and idiosyncrasies.

The vapor barrier and insulation should present no problem if they are the traditional between-the-joists kind. Just be sure that the vapor barrier is continuous and completely covers the insulation. For a roof with insulation boards above the structural deck, purchase a self-flashing skylight with a relatively high curb. Consult with both the manufacturer of the roofing system and the manufacturer of the skylight before making the installation.

PITCHED ROOFS

The pitched roof is ubiquitous in most parts of the country. Originally imported from Northern Europe to New England because of its ability to quickly shed rainwater and snow, the pitched roof can be seen in houses all over the United States. If your existing house has a pitched roof, it is likely that your new extension or new porch should have a roof with a similar slope, for stylistic if not purely technical reasons.

Technically, the angle of roof slope determines the amount of waterproofing required on the roof. The steeper the pitch, the quicker rain and snow are discarded, the less waterproofing is required. In addition, a steep roof can be designed for a smaller live load (mostly since snow loads will not accumulate). The slope of the roof can be analyzed by comparing the rise to the run (Ill. 4).

If the run of the rafter is 10' horizontally and the rise is 5' vertically, then the slope is 1 to 2 or, expressed in inches, 6" to 12" (or about a 27° slope).

If you are planning a new extension to an existing house, the correct angle of slope for the roof should be determined more on the basis of aesthetics than on snow loads. If you want the extension to blend in with the existing house, it may be best to slope the new roofs at the same angle as the existing ones (Ill. 5). You don't, of course, have to make the new roof at the same pitch as the existing roof, as long as the new roof is proportionately in keeping with the existing roofline. It always helps to construct a model of the existing house and the extensions.

There are two different kinds of pitched roofs: one with an attic and one without. The difference between them involves more than the availability of storage space. The roof with an attic is structured very differently from one without an attic. If you are thinking about removing the attic in your house to create a cathedral ceiling effect, you may have to reconfigure the house structurally. (Review Chapter 16, Ills. 20–22.)

The Pitched Roof with an Attic

The pitched roof with an attic is usually constructed using lightweight structural members, 2" wide, to create a stable triangular structural element (Ill. 6). The rafters support the weight of the roof and are supported in turn at the sills on either side of the house. The rafters lean in on one another and in that way transfer their loads like two people leaning back to back. The central ridge holds the rafters in line but is not really structural since it does not take on the weight of the rafters. This leaning-in arrangement creates a lateral (sideways) thrust on the walls pushing them outward, which is counteracted by the ceiling joists that act as ties to hold the building together. If, during the course of renovating, you remove the ties, it is likely that the roof will collapse (Ill. 7).

Designing a Light-Framed Pitched Roof with an Attic

To structure the roof, draw a plan and section of the roof and ceiling at ½" scale and the plan of the top floor of the extension (showing the double plates of the load-bearing walls and partitions). A section through the designed roof is drawn and its exact pitch is measured. This section helps deter-mine the actual length of the piece of lumber to be used as a rafter (the span of the rafter plus the overhang). Ceiling joists are selected using Table A* on the following page. (This table is based on a live load of 30 psf, which is the design live load for an attic to be used for living. If the attic is to be used for light storage only, a design live load of 20 psf can be used.) The ceiling joists are usually framed with the same spacing as the rafters, to simplify framing and nailing.

The sizing of the rafters is dependent on the amount of annual snowfall and the pitch of the roof. The steeper the roof, the lower the design load. Tables B and C cover the design of roofs with pitches of over and under 3 in 12, respectively, on the assumption of a 20 psf and a 30 psf live load. Check with your building department to determine the snow live load for your area and the reduction coefficient for the amount of your roof pitch. Tables B and C can be used as guidelines if the design loads conform to (or are less than) the ones provided for in our tables. The procedure for rafter selection is exactly the same as that outlined for joists in Chapter 21. In this case, however, the "span" is the horizontal projected length of the rafter between supports (that is, between the plates on one side and the ridge on the other, Ill. 4).

The ridge itself is usually constructed of a 2"-thick section that is about 2" deeper than the rafter sections to simplify framing. Since it is non-structural, the span of the ridge is not an important consideration. The roof is sheathed in ¾" plywood (exterior grade), which adds rigidity to the structure.

The triangular walls at the ends of the gable (Ill. 6) are constructed out of studs in much the same way as the wall sections outlined in Chapter 22. This attic space may be insulated in one of two ways. The space between the ceiling joists can be stuffed with insulation or, in the case of a heated attic, by insulating the spaces between the rafters and in between the studs of the end walls. It is important to install large louvers with powerful fans in the end walls of the attic to dissipate the heat that can build up under the roof in the summer.

*These tables are supplied for preliminary design purposes only and are not to be used for final selection of rafters or ridge beams. Be advised that the lumber referred to in the tables is "stress-graded." The lumber available to you in lumberyards is not stress-graded. Therefore, when using the tables in this book, assume that the lumber is no. 3 grade to get your preliminary sizing. Most municipalities adhere to strict building codes and use their own guidelines.

(to be used for preliminary design only)

Species	Grade	2 × 6		2 × 8		2 × 10		2 × 12	
		Joist size (inches)							
		Joist spacing (inches)							
		12	16	12	16	12	16	12	16
		Maximum allowable span (feet-inches)							
Coast Sitka spruce	select structural	12-0	10-11	15-10	14-5	20-3	18-5	24-8	22-5
	no. 1 & appearance	12-0	10-10	15-10	14-4	20-3	18-3	24-8	22-3
	no. 2	11-6	10-0	15-2	13-2	19-4	16-9	23-6	20-5
	no. 3	8-8	7-6	11-6	9-11	14-8	12-8	17-9	15-5
Douglas fir-larch (north)	select structural	12-3	11-2	16-2	14-8	20-8	18-9	25-1	22-10
	no. 1 & appearance	12-3	11-2	16-2	14-8	20-8	18-9	25-1	22-10
	no. 2	12-0	10-11	15-10	14-5	20-3	18-5	24-8	22-5
	no. 3	10-4	9-0	13-8	11-10	17-5	15-1	21-2	18-4
Eastern hemlock-tamarack (north)	select structural	11-0	10-0	14-6	13-2	18-6	16-10	22-6	20-6
	no. 1 & appearance	11-0	10-0	14-6	13-2	18-6	16-10	22-6	20-6
	no. 2	10-5	9-6	13-9	12-6	17-6	15-11	21-4	19-4
	no. 3	9-7	8-3	12-7	10-11	15-1	13-11	19-7	16-11
Hem-fir (north)	select structural	11-7	10-6	15-3	13-10	19-5	17-8	23-7	21-6
	no. 1 & appearance	11-7	10-6	15-3	13-10	19-5	17-8	23-7	21-6
	no. 2	11-3	10-3	14-11	13-6	19-0	17-3	23-1	21-0
	no. 3	9-3	8-0	12-2	10-6	15-6	13-5	18-10	16-4
Ponderosa pine	select structural	10-9	9-9	14-2	12-10	18-0	16-5	21-11	19-11
	no. 1 & appearance	10-9	9-9	14-2	12-10	18-0	16-5	21-11	19-11
	no. 2	10-5	9-6	13-9	12-6	17-6	15-11	21-4	19-4
	no. 3	8-6	7-4	11-3	9-9	14-4	12-5	17-5	15-1
Red pine	select structural	11-0	10-0	14-6	13-2	18-6	16-10	22-6	20-6
	no. 1 & appearance	11-0	10-0	14-6	13-2	18-6	16-10	22-6	20-6
	no. 2	10-9	9-6	14-2	12-6	18-0	15-11	21-11	19-5
	no. 3	8-4	7-3	11-0	9-6	14-0	12-2	17-0	14-9
Spruce-pine-fir	select structural	11-7	10-6	15-3	13-10	19-5	17-8	23-7	21-6
	no. 1 & appearance	11-7	10-6	15-3	13-10	19-5	17-8	23-7	21-6
	no. 2	11-0	9-9	14-6	12-10	18-6	16-4	22-6	19-11
	no. 3	8-6	7-4	11-3	9-9	14-4	12-5	17-5	15-1
Western cedars (north)	select structural	10-5	9-6	13-9	12-6	17-6	15-11	21-4	19-4
	no. 1 & appearance	10-5	9-6	13-9	12-6	17-6	15-11	21-4	19-4
	no. 2	10-1	9-2	13-4	12-1	17-0	15-5	20-8	18-9
	no. 3	8-8	7-6	11-6	9-11	14-8	12-8	17-9	15-5
Western white pine	select structural	11-3	10-3	14-11	13-6	19-0	17-3	23-1	21-0
	no. 1 & appearance	11-3	10-3	14-11	13-6	19-0	17-3	23-1	21-0
	no. 2	10-10	9-4	14-3	12-4	18-2	15-9	22-1	19-2
	no. 3	8-4	7-3	11-0	9-6	14-0	12-2	17-0	14-9

The Pitched Roof without an Attic

The pitched roof without an attic can be structured as a light-frame or (more likely) can be designed for plank-and-beam construction. (It is possible to mix the two systems. Often a house has a platform-frame floor system, a combination of stud walls and columns, and a plank-and-beam roof.) If you are using a light-frame roof, you will have to design tie beams or collar beams at inter-vals to counteract the lateral thrust (Ill. 7). Plank-and-beam (also called post-and-beam) differs from light-frame construction in that it consists of structural members that are heavier than studs and joists and are spaced at greater intervals than the usual 16" on center. Generally the rafters are about 3" (or 4") by 10" or more and are spaced 4' to 6' apart. The planks are about 2" thick and span between the rafters (Ill. 8). Because the structural members are heavier than in light-frame con-

(to be used for preliminary design only)

Species	Grade	Rafter sizes (inches)							
		2 × 4		2 × 6		2 × 8		2 × 10	
		Rafter spacing (inches)							
		12	16	12	16	12	16	12	16
		Maximum allowable span (feet-inches)							
Coast Sitka spruce	select structural	11-1	10-0	17-4	15-7	22-11	20-6	29-2	26-2
	no. 1 & appearance	11-1	9-9	16-5	14-2	21-7	18-9	27-7	23-11
	no. 2	10-3	8-10	15-0	13-0	19-10	17-2	25-3	21-11
	no. 3	7-8	6-8	11-4	9-10	15-0	12-11	19-1	16-6
Douglas fir-larch (north)	select structural	11-3	10-3	17-8	16-1	23-4	21-2	29-9	27-1
	no. 1 & appearance	11-3	10-3	17-8	16-1	23-4	21-2	29-9	27-1
	no. 2	11-1	10-0	17-4	15-4	22-11	20-2	29-2	25-9
	no. 3	8-11	7-9	13-6	11-9	17-10	15-5	22-9	19-8
Eastern hemlock-tamarack (north)	select structural	10-1	9-2	15-11	14-5	20-11	19-0	26-9	24-3
	no. 1	10-1	9-2	15-11	14-5	20-11	19-0	26-9	24-3
	no. 2	9-7	8-8	15-0	13-8	19-10	18-0	25-3	22-11
	no. 3	8-4	7-3	12-5	10-9	16-5	14-3	20-11	18-2
	appearance	10-1	9-2	15-11	14-5	20-11	19-0	26-9	24-3
Hem-fir (north)	select structural	10-7	9-8	16-8	15-2	22-0	19-11	28-0	25-5
	no. 1 & appearance	10-7	9-8	16-8	15-0	22-0	19-10	28-0	25-3
	no. 2	10-4	9-3	15-8	13-7	20-8	17-11	26-5	22-10
	no. 3	7-11	6-10	12-1	10-5	15-11	13-9	20-4	17-7
Ponderosa pine	select structural	9-10	8-11	15-6	14-1	20-5	18-6	26-0	23-8
	no. 1 & appearance	9-10	8-11	15-6	13-11	20-5	18-4	26-0	23-6
	no. 2	9-7	8-8	14-6	12-6	19-1	16-6	24-4	21-1
	no. 3	7-5	6-5	11-1	9-7	14-8	12-8	18-8	16-2
Red pine	select structural	10-1	9-2	15-11	14-5	20-11	19-0	26-9	24-3
	no. 1 & appearance	10-1	9-2	15-8	13-7	20-8	17-11	26-5	22-10
	no. 2	9-10	8-6	14-3	12-4	18-10	16-3	24-0	20-9
	no. 3	7-5	6-5	10-10	9-5	14-4	12-5	18-3	15-10
Spruce-pine-fir	select structural	10-7	9-8	16-8	15-2	22-0	19-11	28-0	25-5
	no. 1 & appearance	10-7	9-7	16-1	13-11	21-2	18-4	27-0	23-5
	no. 2	10-0	8-8	14-8	12-8	19-4	16-9	24-8	21-4
	no. 3	7-6	6-6	11-1	9-7	14-8	12-8	18-8	16-2
Western cedars (north)	select structural	9-7	8-8	15-0	13-8	19-10	18-0	25-3	22-11
	no. 1 & appearance	9-7	8-8	15-0	13-8	19-10	18-0	25-3	22-11
	no. 2	9-3	8-5	14-7	12-8	19-2	16-9	24-6	21-4
	no. 3	7-6	6-6	11-4	9-10	15-0	12-11	19-1	16-6
Western white pine	select structural	10-4	9-5	16-3	14-6	21-6	19-1	27-5	24-5
	no. 1 & appearance	10-4	9-3	15-8	13-7	20-8	17-11	26-5	22-10
	no. 2	9-7	8-3	14-1	12-2	18-7	16-1	23-8	20-6
	no. 3	7-3	6-3	10-10	9-5	14-4	12-5	18-3	15-10

struction, you will have to use timber connectors instead of nails (see Chapter 16, Ill. 29).

The major structural feature of the plank-and-beam roof is that the ridge is actually a beam and is designed to take on and transfer the loads from the rafters. The cross-sectional dimensions of the ridge beam, which must be calculated as with any other beam, are determined by its span and loading. If the ridge is designed as a beam, it bears the full weight of the load of the rafters. This load is transferred to the columns and there should be no roof-generated lateral thrust exerted on the walls (Ill. 8). When designing the ridge beam, remember that it must be supported fully by columns or buttresses, either free-standing or buried in the walls. Even so, if the ridge beam is to be more than 15' long (supported or unsupported), to ensure stability two or more collars are used to tie the roof back (Ill. 7).

If you plan to construct a new extension to the

Designing or
Modifying
the Roof
209

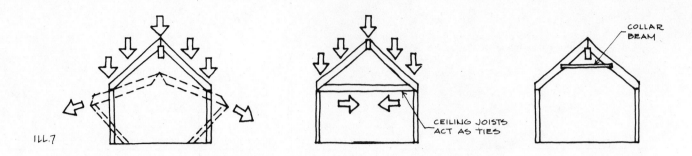

ILL.7

CEILING JOISTS
ACT AS TIES

COLLAR
BEAM

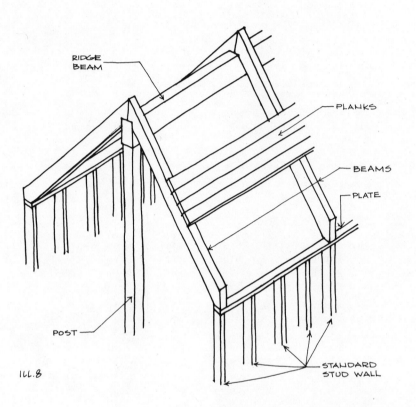

RIDGE
BEAM

PLANKS

BEAMS

PLATE

POST

STANDARD
STUD WALL

ILL.8

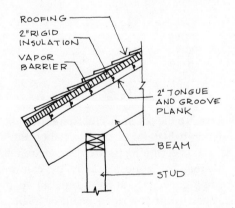

ROOFING

2" RIGID
INSULATION

VAPOR
BARRIER

2" TONGUE
AND GROOVE
PLANK

BEAM

STUD

ILL.9

house with a plank-and-beam roof, you may want to take advantage of the soaring effect of a cathedral ceiling. If you plan to nail a gypsum-board ceiling to the bottom of the rafters, you can insulate the space between planks and ceiling with batts of insulation. As it happens, you may wish to expose the handsome structural elements, the planks and rafters. If so, have rigid insulation installed above the planks (Ill. 9). It should be noted that some architects consider the 1½″ or more of wood in the thickness of the planks to be enough insulation. This may be adequate if your winters and summers are not too intense, but be sure to consult the energy conservation codes.

Designing a Plank-and-Beam Roof

Draw a framing plan of the roof. Use a large scale such as 1½″ = 1′-0″. Make sure that the ends of

(to be used for preliminary design only)

Species	Grade	Rafter size (inches)							
		2 × 6		2 × 8		2 × 10		2 × 12	
		Rafter spacing (inches)							
		12	16	12	16	12	16	12	16
		Maximum allowable span (feet-inches)							
Coast Sitka spruce	select structural	13-9	12-6	18-2	16-6	23-2	21-1	28-2	25-7
	no. 1 & appearance	13-6	11-8	17-9	15-5	22-8	19-7	27-7	23-10
	no. 2	12-4	10-8	16-3	14-1	20-9	18-0	25-3	21-11
	no. 3	9-4	8-1	12-4	10-8	15-8	13-7	19-1	16-6
Douglas fir-larch (north)	select structural	14-1	12-9	18-6	16-10	23-8	21-6	28-9	26-1
	no. 1 & appearance	14-1	12-9	18-6	16-10	23-8	21-6	28-9	26-1
	no. 2	13-9	12-6	18-2	16-6	23-2	21-1	28-2	25-7
	no. 3	11-1	9-8	14-8	12-8	18-8	16-2	22-9	19-8
Eastern hemlock-tamarack (north)	select structural	12-7	11-5	16-7	15-1	21-2	19-3	25-9	23-5
	no. 1 & appearance	12-7	11-5	16-7	15-1	21-2	19-3	25-9	23-5
	no. 2	11-11	10-10	15-9	14-3	20-1	18-3	24-5	22-2
	no. 3	10-3	8-10	13-6	11-8	17-2	14-11	20-11	18-1
Hem-fir (north)	select structural	13-3	12-0	17-5	15-10	22-3	20-2	27-1	24-7
	no. 1 & appearance	13-3	12-0	17-5	15-10	22-3	20-2	27-1	24-7
	no. 2	12-11	11-2	17-0	14-9	21-8	18-9	26-5	22-10
	no. 3	9-11	8-7	13-1	11-4	16-8	14-5	20-3	17-7
Ponderosa pine	select structural	12-3	11-2	16-2	14-8	20-8	18-9	25-1	22-10
	no. 1 & appearance	12-3	11-2	16-2	14-8	20-8	18-9	25-1	22-10
	no. 2	11-11	10-3	15-8	13-7	20-0	17-4	24-4	21-1
	no. 3	9-1	7-11	12-0	10-5	15-4	13-3	18-8	16-2
Red pine	select structural	12-7	11-5	16-7	15-1	21-2	19-3	25-9	23-5
	no. 1 & appearance	12-7	11-2	16-7	14-9	21-2	18-9	25-9	22-10
	no. 2	11-9	10-2	15-5	13-5	19-9	17-1	24-0	20-9
	no. 3	8-11	7-9	11-9	10-2	15-0	13-0	18-3	15-9
Spruce-pine-fir	select structural	13-3	12-0	17-5	15-10	22-3	20-2	27-1	24-7
	no. 1 & appearance	13-2	11-5	17-5	15-1	22-2	19-3	27-0	23-4
	no. 2	12-0	10-5	15-10	13-9	20-3	17-6	24-8	21-4
	no. 3	9-1	7-11	12-0	10-5	15-4	13-3	18-8	16-2
Western cedars (north)	select structural	11-11	10-10	15-9	14-3	20-1	18-3	24-5	22-2
	no. 1 & appearance	11-11	10-10	15-9	14-3	20-1	18-3	24-5	22-2
	no. 2	11-7	10-5	15-3	13-9	19-5	17-6	23-7	21-4
	no. 3	9-4	8-1	12-4	10-3	15-8	13-7	19-1	16-6
Western white pine	select structural	12-11	11-9	17-0	15-6	21-9	19-9	26-5	24-0
	no. 1 & appearance	12-11	11-2	17-0	14-9	21-8	18-9	26-6	22-10
	no. 2	11-7	10-0	15-3	13-2	19-5	16-10	23-8	20-6
	no. 3	8-11	7-9	11-9	10-2	15-0	13-0	18-3	15-9

the ridge beams are properly supported by free-standing columns or columns buried in the end walls. Limit the span of the ridge beams to no more than 16'. Keep the "run" of the rafters (the horizontal distance between supports) short, under 14'. Also make sure that there are no uninterrupted, large expanses of glass under the load-bearing wall where the rafters come down. See the "Framing Plan" illustration under Table D.

Determine the slope of the roof by drawing a section through the plan. The "span" of the rafter can be determined by scaling the drawing or by using the right-triangle method of $a^2 + b^2 = c^2$. The span of the rafters (the actual length of the section between supports) should be under 18'. See the "Ridge Beam Sections for Plank and Beam Construction" illustration under Table D.

Decide on the rafter spacing. Tongue-and-groove planks 2" thick are good for spans of up to 8'. We have designed our charts for either 6' or 8' spacings. If your room is 16' long, you can have two spacings (one line of rafters) at 8' apart. De-

Designing or
Modifying
the Roof
211

TABLE D: ROOF BEAMS (RAFTERS) FOR PLANK-AND-BEAM CONSTRUCTION
(to be used for preliminary design only)

Rafter spans	10'		12'		14'		16'		18'		20'	
Plank spacing	6'	8'	6'	8'	6'	8'	6'	8'	6'	8'	6'	8'
For L.L. of 20 psf or less												
Stress grade												
f = 900	4×8 2/2×8	3/2×8 2/2×10	3/2×8 2/2×10		2/2×12 3/2×10	4/2×10 2/3×10 6×10	2/3×10 6×10	8×10 3/2×12	4/2×10 3/2×12		6×12 2/4×12	
f = 1,200	3×8 2/3×6	4×8 2/2×8	3×10 4×8	3/2×8 2/3×8	2/2×10 4×10	3/2×10 2/2×12	3/2×10 3×12	6×10 2/3×10	3/2×10 4×12	4/2×10 3/2×12	3/2×12	6×12
f = 1,500		3×8 2/3×6	2/2×8	3×10	3×10	2/2×10	2/2×10 4×10	2/2×12 3/2×10	2/2×12	6×10 2/3×10	4×12	3/2×12
For L.L. of 20–30 psf												
Stress grade												
f = 900	3/2×8 2/2×10	2/4×8	2/4×8 3/2×10	2/3×10	2/3×10 6×10	2/4×10	2/4×10 3/2×12	4/2×12	4/2×12 2/4×12	5/2×12 2/4×12	2/3×14 2/4×12	10×12 4/3×12
f = 1,200	4×8	3/2×8 2/2×10	2/2×8	3/2×10 2/4×8	3/2×10	2/3×10	4×10 6×10	2/3×12 3/2×12	4/2×12 3/2×12	4/2×12 2/4×12	8×12 6×12	8×12 2/4×12
f = 1,500	3×8 2/3×6	4×8	2/2×8	2/3×8 2/2×10	2/2×10	3/2×10	3/2×10 2/2×12	6×10 4/2×10	2/3×10 4×12 6×10	2/3×12 3/2×12 8×10	3/2×12	2/3×12 6×12 4/2×12

INSTRUCTIONS FOR THE USE OF TABLE D

See illustrations below.

The above table is designed to simplify the selection of beams or rafters to be used in flat-roof framing (post-and-beam) or for pitched-beam roofs (as rafters).

SPAN: Considered to be from support to support. If the roof is flat, it is the horizontal distance between supports. If the roof is pitched, it is the actual length of the section between supports.

SPACING: Either 6'-0" or 8'-0" is the dimension between the beams (rafters). It is the span of the planks.

L.L.: Either 20 psf or less, or between 20 and 30 psf should cover most code requirements.

f: The fiber stress in bending for the particular wood being designed for.

2/3 × 6 indicates a built-up section using two 3 × 6 sections.

Douglas fir	no. 1 select	f = 1,900
	no. 2 construction	f = 1,500
	no. 3 standard	f = 1,200
hemlock, eastern	no. 1 select structural	f = 1,300
	prime structural	f = 1,200
	common structural	f = 1,100
	utility structural	f = 950
hemlock, west coast	select structural	f = 1,600
	construction	f = 1,500
	structural	f = 1,200

Deflections were not considered in compiling this table. Since there are hardly any stiff wall-finishing materials (for example, plaster) in common use today, deflections of only fractions of an inch would not be harmful to the building or its inhabitants.

For rafter lengths of less than the 2' increments use the higher span. That is, if you have a span of 10'-11", use the span tables for 12'-0".

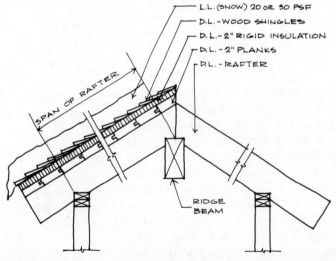

RIDGE BEAM SECTIONS FOR PLANK AND BEAM CONSTRUCTION

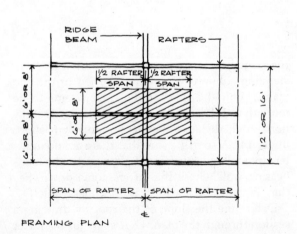

FRAMING PLAN

termine the stress capabilities of the lumber you are using by consulting the chart in the instructions for the use of Table D.

Determine the live load requirements by checking the building code for your locality. Table D is based on L.L. of 20–30 psf, which should satisfy the requirements for most areas of the country. (Areas in the northern regions of the United States may require a greater live load as a reflection of the area's greater snow accumulation. Verify.)

With the input from all of the steps above, use Table D to determine the size of the rafters.

Use Table E for the preliminary selection of a ridge beam (if your live load is not more than 30 psf). This table has been greatly simplified for the purposes of this book and is keyed to Table D.

The simplification of the charts and tables makes the design procedure appear to be less complex than it actually is. Once again, since the structural design of the house is so important to the future safety of its occupants, you must consult with an architect or structural engineer before constructing a roof. In most areas it is required by law. If your spacings, length of ridge beam, quality of lumber, or snow loads don't conform to our tables, you will not be able to use them even for preliminary design purposes.

Roofing shingles, insulation, condensation control, and flashing are covered in Chapter 19.

TABLE E: RIDGE-BEAM SECTIONS FOR PLANK-AND-BEAM CONSTRUCTION
(to be used for preliminary design only)

For ridge spans of either 12' or 16'

For L.L. of 20 psf

Span of rafter	Ridge span = 12'		Ridge span = 16'	
	f = 1,200	f = 1,500	f = 1,200	f = 1,500
10'	3-2 × 10 4 × 12 6 × 10	4 × 10	8 × 12 6 × 14	6 × 12
12'	4 × 12 3-2 × 10 6 × 10	4 × 12	10 × 12	4 × 16
14'	4 × 14	4 × 12 6 × 10	10 × 12	8 × 12 6 × 14
16'	4 × 14 8 × 10	6 × 10	12 × 12 6 × 18	10 × 12
18'	6 × 12	4 × 14 8 × 10	6 × 18 10 × 14	10 × 12 6 × 16
20'	4 × 16	4 × 14	10 × 14 .	6 × 18
		For L.L. of 30 psf		
10'	4 × 14	4 × 12	8 × 12	6 × 12
12'	4 × 14	6 × 10	10 × 12 6 × 16	4 × 16
14'	4 × 16	4 × 14	6 × 16 8 × 14	10 × 12
16'	4 × 16 6 × 14	4 × 14	6 × 18	10 × 12 6 × 16
18'	8 × 12 6 × 14	4 × 16	6 × 18	6 × 16 8 × 14
20'	6 × 14	4 × 16	8 × 16	6 × 18

24

FOUNDATION DESIGN

This chapter on foundations is aimed at those of you who are planning an extension. Foundations are the structural elements that transfer all the loads (including the structural weight of the house) to the surrounding ground, giving the house stability and permanence. They literally root the house to the soil (Ill. 1). A sound foundation is crucial to the project. For this reason, it is important to have a good understanding of how foundations work.

Foundations can take many forms. Early Colonial buildings were constructed on top of a few flat stones, which served to isolate the building from the ground and prevent the wood from rotting. The settlers soon learned that this method did not provide them with a stable house. Either bad storms and uneven settling ripped the house from the ground or the walls were destroyed by rotting. Very few, if any, of these houses remain. Another type of foundation is seen in fishermen's houses in New England's coastal towns; these homes are built over the water resting on wooden piles—the only way in which a house could be secured to the underwater bedrock.

Because foundations are a crucial component of the structure continuum, it is important to study how they transfer the house loads into the surrounding ground. There are two basic types of loading conditions: point loads and uniformly distributed loads. A pole vaulter making his jump clearly illustrates both of these principles. While preparing to jump, he runs, grabs on to the pole, and places his entire weight on it. His weight is being transmitted to the ground at only one point. Once he completes the jump, he comes to rest lying flat on a mat. The ground now receives his weight at many points along this mat; it is being transmitted uniformly (Ill. 2). Similarly, foundations can transmit loads to the ground at points or uniformly.

In addition, the design of the foundations and the selection of materials are determined by the type of soil on which the house is built, the topography of the site, the nature of the house (a year-round house vs. a vacation cabin), and the availability of materials and labor.

Foundations are relatively simple to design when compared to roofs or floor systems. Nonetheless, there are so many different kinds of subsurface conditions (all underground where it is impossible to see them) and other variables that you are advised to seek out the help of an engineer when designing foundations.

Foundations may be classified into three basic types: continuous foundations, piers, and piles. The most often used of the three is the continuous foundation wall. The wall, completely or partially buried in the earth beneath the house, follows the perimeter of the house and rests on a continuous base called the footing. The loads of the walls, floors, and roof are uniformly distributed along the foundation walls. These walls, in turn, evenly transfer all the loadings to the surrounding earth. Continuous foundation walls are usually built of concrete poured into formwork or of concrete blocks (Ill. 3). Many historic houses may have

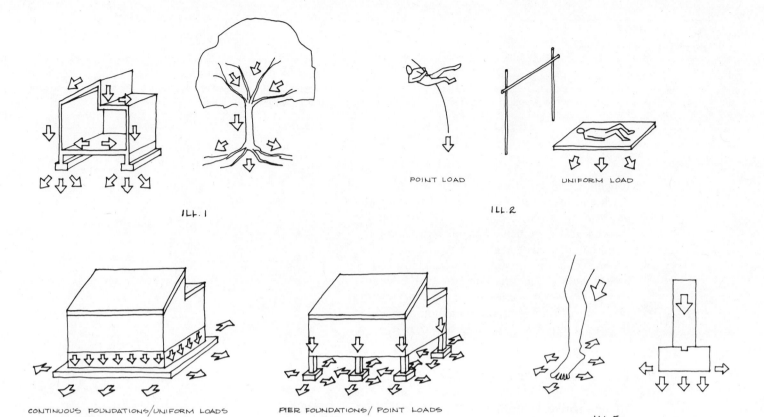

ILL. 1

POINT LOAD   UNIFORM LOAD

ILL. 2

CONTINUOUS FOUNDATIONS/UNIFORM LOADS

ILL. 3

PIER FOUNDATIONS/ POINT LOADS

ILL. 4

ILL. 5

stone foundation walls. These walls, although beautiful, are extremely labor-intensive and difficult to replicate.

Piers and piles are essentially fingers gripping the ground, holding the structure in place and transmitting loads to the ground at various points. Piles (used mostly for construction in wetlands or marshes) are driven, or hammered, into the earth. They are commonly made out of chemically treated tree trunks. Piers, like continuous foundations, are built on normal soils and are cast or laid in place rather than driven. They are usually constructed of poured concrete or masonry block (Ill. 4).

FOUNDATION TYPES

Continuous Foundations

Continuous foundation walls are the best choice in the majority of cases and most likely are used to support your existing house. (They are suited to all soil types and terrains with the exception of marshlands, water, and very steep slopes.) Continuous foundations distribute the loads evenly to the earth. In addition, foundation walls help insulate the floor from drafts and serve to hide and protect the electric, heating, plumbing, and gas lines.

Continuous foundations are built in two separate stages: first the footing and then the wall. The footing (like its namesake) distributes the weight of the structure over a larger area of earth. The spreading of the foundation at the bottom puts more earth directly under the weight, which offers more resistance to the downward push (Ill. 5). Footings are always constructed out of poured-in-place concrete. The foundation wall which rests on the footing may be constructed of poured concrete or concrete block. The height of the wall itself is determined by the depth of the frost line (see Inset I) and whether or not there is a basement or a crawl space.

The choice between poured concrete or concrete block is contingent on whether your extension is to have a full basement or a crawl space. A poured-in-place concrete wall, constructed

Foundation
Design
215

INSET I/FROST LINE

Frost line is the depth to which frost penetrates and freezes the ground. Foundations placed above this line are in danger of cracking as the ground beneath them expands and moves due to freezing. Local codes will advise you of the depth of frost penetration in your particular area. The National Building Code requires foundations to be located at a minimum of one foot below the frost line.

properly, will be stronger and is less likely to crack and leak than a block wall. The work and expense involved, however, are considerable drawbacks. Concrete block is much easier to work with than poured concrete and, in addition, is less expensive. If you are not considering a full basement (and we do not recommend a full basement for your extension—see Chapter 27), block is the best choice. Steel reinforcement should be added to both footings and concrete-block walls.

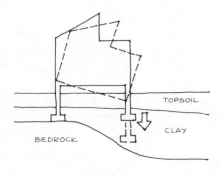

ILL. 6

Pier Foundations

An alternative to continuous walls, pier foundations save time, labor, and money. They are particularly suitable for steeply sloping terrain or where excavation should be kept to a minimum. A word of caution: In cold or temperate climates the exposed plumbing lines underneath the floor are in danger of freezing. In addition, the heat loss through the floor is significant (unless you insulate the floor very well). Pier footings would be suitable for those renovators planning porch extensions, or extensions where plumbing lines (if any) can be routed through the existing basement. They are also applicable for summer homes (where plumbing lines are drained of water during the winter) or in warm areas not subject to freezing temperatures. The other problem of pier footings is uneven settling. All piers must rest on a similar soil bed to avoid uneven settling and subsequent cracks in the structure of the house (Ill. 6).

Piers are most commonly constructed of treated wood, poured concrete, or concrete block, and vary in shape from a simple column to a column resting on a footing (Ill. 7). Treated-wood piers are good for light-frame buildings such as bungalows or toolhouses. They are not as durable as masonry piers and eventually will have problems of rot and decay. Many building codes do not allow their use for house construction. We do not recommend them. Masonry piers, on the other hand, whether constructed of poured concrete or

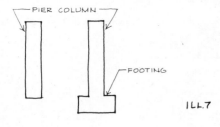

ILL. 7

concrete block, offer more stability and are not subject to rotting.

Poured-in-place concrete piers are stronger than their concrete-block counterparts. This is due to the homogeneity of concrete as a material. They do, however, require more labor and are more expensive. The expense is due to the fact that you must purchase both the lumber for the formwork and the ready-mixed concrete. One way to simplify the labor involved in poured-in-place foundations is to use spiral cardboard forms (also referred to as Sono-Tubes, a brand name). These forms come in many diameters and are placed over the footings. A tie between the footing and the pier is provided by means of vertical reinforcing bars. These tubes must be braced with lumber before the concrete is poured.

Concrete-block piers are relatively simple and inexpensive to build. Blocks are easy to handle and can be stored on the site, eliminating the problem of having to build all piers on the same

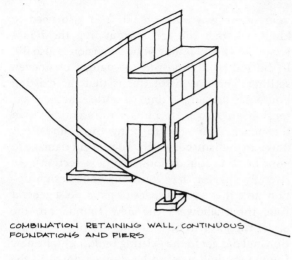

COMBINATION RETAINING WALL, CONTINUOUS FOUNDATIONS AND PIERS

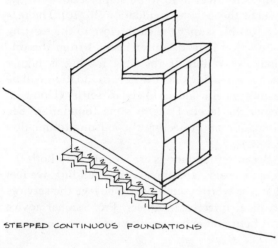

STEPPED CONTINUOUS FOUNDATIONS

ILL.8

day (as in the case of poured concrete). Building with concrete block can be a one-person job. Reinforce the pier with steel bars and fill the holes in the block with cement mortar.

If you are building piers with footings, you will have to purchase footing lumber and pour concrete. (Check to see if the company sells that small a quantity of concrete.) The formwork for footings, however, is very simple. Although this type of pier requires more work than a simple column pier, it will give you a considerably better distribution of loads and consequently a more stable structure. Your job can be simplified by pouring the footing and then building the pier itself out of concrete block.

Pile Foundations

Piles are particularly effective for building on marshlands or in water. They can be constructed of treated wood, poured concrete, or precast concrete. (In large-scale construction steel beams are used, but this is far too sophisticated for small-scale residential work.) Treated-wood piles are widely used for beach houses. Poured or precast concrete piles are also used, but although more durable, they are considerably more expensive. Driving or casting piles is not easy and requires heavy machinery to drive the wood or precast concrete piles into the ground or to drill the holes for pouring concrete. If your extension requires such a foundation, hire a company that specializes in driving piles.

Variations

One of the likeliest variations is that subsurface conditions may vary from one corner of the house to another. A licensed professional engineer who specializes in subsoil investigations should be consulted. He or she will do test borings of the soil to determine its bearing capacity.

We have limited our discussion to simple pier, pile, and continuous foundations. There are, of course, numerous variations and combinations of these (Ill. 8). It is likely that your extension may have a different type of foundation than the main house. For example, a house can have a partial full basement to enclose the boiler while the rest of the building sits on a crawl space or piers. Continuous foundations can be stepped when built on sloping ground to facilitate excavation. Combinations of continuous and pier foundations are also possible. On steeply sloping sites, one of the foundation walls might serve as a retaining wall. (This involves a more complex design procedure. We suggest that, if faced with this condition, you consult a professional as insurance against costly errors.) While making design decisions, keep in mind the benefits and drawbacks of each type of foundation. Try to keep the construction work as simple as possible.

DESIGNING THE FOUNDATIONS

The size and depth of the foundations are directly related to the bearing capacity of the soil, the house loads, the underground water table, and, in cold and temperate climates, the frost line. Since the loads on residential design are light, foundation sizes are rarely determined mathematically.

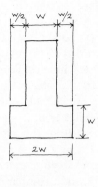

ILL. 9

In many areas, the local building code will tell you the sizes required depending on the house design and the type of soil you are dealing with. In addition, since you are working with an existing house, you already know the size of the existing foundations. Unless the house is settling badly, the foundations are cracked, or the subsoil conditions vary significantly, the size and depth of the existing foundations are probably adequate.

In the event that your local code has no requirement for foundation sizes or there is no local code, the following are some helpful guidelines. Since the width of the foundation wall is related to the wall directly above, it would vary from approximately 10" to 12". For instance, in wood-frame construction, the outside walls will generally vary between 6" and 7" wide; therefore a width of 10" will be adequate for the foundation wall. (We do not recommend anything less than 10" since the foundation wall has to be able to sustain the pressure from the surrounding earth.) In the case of a brick-bearing wall, which is wider, you will most likely need a 12" foundation wall.

A good rule of thumb for sizing footings is to make the footing width twice the width of the foundation wall and its depth the same as the width of the foundation wall. For example, if the foundation wall is 12" wide, the footing should be 24" wide and 12" deep (Ill. 9). (In poor load-bearing soils such as clay, footings carrying heavy loads may have to be made wider in order to spread the load over a larger area.)

Foundation depth depends on whether you have a basement or a crawl space, the distance to suitable bearing soil, the frost line, and the underground water table. The bottom of the footing should be above the water table to avoid leakage problems and at least 1' below the frost line. (Consult your local code.)

It is important that you find out whether or not

your house was built on fill. You also need to know whether the soil surrounding the house where you are planning your extension is also fill. If the soil is fill, you run the danger of uneven settling. The reason for this is that the existing house has had ample time to settle. The new extension will also settle, but at a different rate than the house. You need to bring the foundations down to undisturbed earth. To prevent damage to your existing foundations (see next section), we strongly suggest that you limit your design options to either a crawl space or piers. As a general rule, the shallower* the new foundation, the easier the job will be (in terms of both construction and danger to the existing building). The new foundation will need to be stepped down to the level of the existing foundation (Ill. 10). The reason for this is that the earth close to the existing foundation is made up of backfill from the original excavation. If the new footing is higher than the existing one, the new foundation will be resting on fill and is likely to settle. (Don't go below the level of the existing foundation! See discussion on protecting the existing foundation below.)

Because foundations are so critical to both the new extension and the existing building, we feel that it is worth your while to engage the services of an architect or engineer. Professional advice will help you avoid costly mistakes.

Protecting the Existing Foundation

Foundations often fail when the earth around them is disturbed. Take every precaution to ensure that the existing foundation will not be disturbed when the new ones are built. Recently there were two building collapses in New York City. In both cases, there was excavation taking place dangerously close to the existing foundations.

New foundations should not be designed to be deeper than the existing ones. There is sound logic behind this. When the new foundation is deeper than the existing one, the excavation goes further down than the level of the existing foundation (Ill. 11). In the process some of the earth which now supports the foundation is removed or disturbed. The remaining earth is not able to support the loads and the foundation will fail.

*Remember that the footings must be below the frost line.

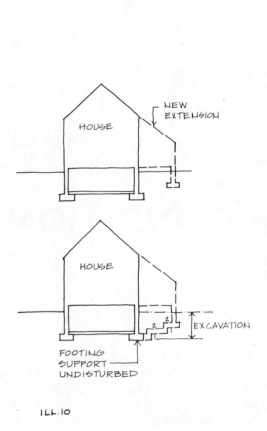

ILL. 10

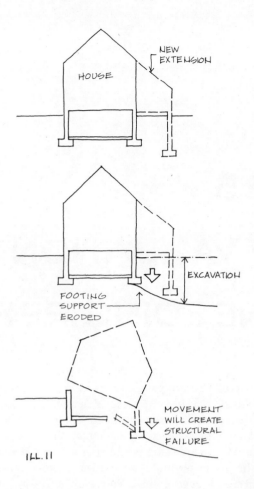

ILL. 11

WATERPROOFING

A few words should be said about waterproofing techniques. If your building sits on piers or piles, you don't need to concern yourself with waterproofing. Houses sitting on crawl spaces are also generally exempted from the headaches of waterproofing, unless they happen to rest on soils of such wetness that the local code or general local practice demands it. When the extension sits over a full basement, however, you have no choice but to deal with waterproofing (particularly if the foundation walls are built of concrete block or fall below the water table).

For average soil conditions, black asphalt, tar, or pitch, or one of a variety of other bituminous compounds (usually referred to by trade names), is applied on the exterior of the foundation walls. Although this does not offer a complete guarantee against leakage, it may help. A much better technique is membrane waterproofing. This type is used in wet soils and consists of alternate layers of hot pitch (tar or asphalt) and felt, which are carefully lapped to the exterior of the foundation wall. Membrane waterproofing offers more protection than any of the rolled-on types but is more expensive.

In addition to either of the above techniques, footing drainage pipes are placed at a slight pitch adjacent to the footing and following the perimeter of the house. A layer of gravel or crushed stone is placed all around the pipe (see Chapter 28, Ill. 22). These pipes may be of porous cylindrical clay (without hubs) or perforated black plastic. Their function is to collect all the excess water accumulated around the footing's perimeter and divert it (generally to a storm sewer, a dry well, or another location on the site), thus preventing water pressure from building up next to the foundations. (See pages 250 and 251 for more details.)

Consult the local code for recommendations or requirements in your particular area. Don't forget, however, that the effectiveness of any waterproofing method is directly proportional to the thoroughness of its application.

Foundation
Design

219

25

EVALUATION OF CONDITIONS NEEDING REPAIR

Many of you are painfully aware of the specific problem areas in your home. You may have lived for years with a basement that periodically floods, archaic plumbing, or an inadequate heating system. We include this checklist as a general guide to help you evaluate those areas of your house that need overhauling. You may not want to tackle all of them at this time, but it is wise to repair critical areas as soon as possible and incorporate the remaining repair jobs in some future master plan.

We have known many renovators who have spent considerable time cosmetically remodeling their homes only to find their work ruined by a leak from an ignored roof. Priorities must be established as to which jobs come first. It's no use concentrating on interior finishes when the electrical work has not been completed. Most important, any renovation effort has to start with making the building structurally and mechanically sound and watertight.

THE EXTERIOR

The Roof

The longevity of the roof will vary with the type of roofing material. Slate and copper last the longest, whereas asphalt shingles and built-up roofing need replacement more often. No matter what roofing material covers your house, check for

breakage, wear, or blistering. Carefully examine the roof around vertical penetrations such as chimneys and vents. Make sure those areas are sealed tight. If the roof is lumpy, uneven, or has lots of patches, check the interior of the building for signs of water leakage below those areas. If you have a pitched roof, look at the ridge. Sags in the ridge can indicate anything from minor settling to major structural problems.

Pay special attention to the condition of the flashing. Flashing prevents water from getting underneath the roofing in critical areas such as chimneys, vents, valleys, and skylights. Rusty, loose, or missing flashing needs to be replaced. Make sure that all gutters are intact and firmly secured to the building. Examine the mortar joints in the chimney. Are they crumbling? Are there cracks in the masonry? When examining your masonry chimney, check to see if the chimney flue is lined with tile. If not, you are living with a fire hazard.

The Walls

Start by checking for structural soundness. Look for bulges and bowing in the exterior walls; they could be a sign of a major structural flaw whose cause should be thoroughly investigated by a structural engineer. Look at the windows and doors. Do they line up squarely in their frames? Doors that do not fit squarely into their frames may be indicative of structural problems. Open and close the doors and windows to make sure they don't jam. Check to see if they are flashed. If properly flashed, you can generally see the edge of the flashing at the top of the windows and doors. The trim should fit tightly to both window and siding. Joints between siding and trim should be caulked. Any decorative woodwork, such as corner boards and eaves trim, should be firmly secured and thoroughly caulked. These are critical points where water can penetrate and cause rot. Joints between dissimilar materials also need to be caulked. Examine the clapboard, shingle, or vertical wood siding. It should not be cracked, split, or show signs of rotting. Missing siding or loose shingles should be replaced and renailed. When removing siding for replacement, check the underlying sheathing.

Masonry buildings should be checked for cracking and mortar condition. Horizontal or hairline cracks are generally not a problem. Vertical cracks through brick or stone could be signs of more serious trouble. Should the mortar be soft or crumbly, it will have to be repointed.

Examine the condition of the paint. Whole areas showing peeling and blistering could point to moisture penetration rather than paint failure. Check for interior leaks and make sure the vapor barrier is intact before repainting. Make sure that the wood siding is never in contact with the earth.

The Foundations

Foundations can be undermined by insects and water problems. There are many insects, including carpenter ants and termites, that can cause serious damage to your building. If you see signs of insect infestation (such as veins of dried mud along foundation walls), have a professional pest-control inspection.

Water has to be kept away from the house. Earth around the building should always slope down, leading water away; otherwise, you are inviting water problems. Where downspouts hit the ground, make sure that the splash block is directing the water away from the house. If the downspout leads to an underground pipe, be sure the outlet empties downhill from the building.

Check for sill damage. Poke a small knife into the sill; if it penetrates without much difficulty, you may have to contend with sill rot. The entire perimeter of the house, including the porches, should be inspected. Call in an engineer for further advice.

THE INTERIOR

The Basement

Look for cracks and signs of bowing in the foundation walls. Hairline cracks usually indicate water-seepage problems. Vertical cracks or bowing are indications of serious structural problems. You should not be able to see daylight between the sill and the foundation wall. If your inspection uncovers any of these conditions, have an engineer check your house. Having checked the sill around the house from the outside, take a look on the inside. Any signs of rot or insect damage?

Is there any evidence of leakage from the plumbing system? Examine the girders and joists supporting the ground floor. They should not sag at midspan. Excessive sagging is sometimes caused by undersized members or by the absence of support posts that either rotted or were removed in previous renovations. Do you see any makeshift props holding up floors? Have any structural members been cut to make room for piping or ductwork?

It is not unusual, particularly in the basement of older houses, to encounter asbestos. Asbestos was quite commonly used in the past in a variety of products: as insulation for boilers, furnaces, heating pipes, ductwork, and electrical materials. Asbestos is also frequently found in siding and roofing materials and in resilient floor tiles. Its use, however, is not limited to the products mentioned above. For this reason, we strongly recommend that before any renovation work begins, you contact a licensed asbestos investigator. He will inspect your entire building and get laboratory tests of any suspect areas.

Living Areas

Start by examining the walls and ceilings. Plaster should be checked for signs of cracking or loosening. Touch the plaster. If it is bulging or soft and spongy, it needs to be replaced. If the walls and partitions are constructed of gypsum board, look for loose nails or screws. Is the joint tape coming loose? Damp plaster (or gypsum board), curling wallpaper, or peeling paint is an indication of a leak from the roof, pipes, or exterior walls. It may also be caused by water from a shower or a wet bathroom floor above. If the leak is extensive or long-standing it may have caused the structure to rot.

Walk across the floor. Is it bouncy? Is there a

pronounced sag? Jump on the floor. Do the windows shake? The floor joists may be undersized or cracked. Look at the window and door trim. Windows and doors that are not plumb and true may be the products of a faulty floor structure. How about the stairs? When you jump, are they very springy or just squeaky? Too much vibration could be a structural problem. Has the original flooring been covered with layers of assorted materials? The bottom layer may bring a pleasant surprise or a bitter disappointment.

Look around the window frames for water leakage. Do the windows move up and down freely or do they stick? Do they fit tightly or can you feel a draft coming through? Cracks in the walls around doors and window frames may indicate weakness in the wall framing.

If you have not used the fireplace yet, open the damper and look up the flue. Can you see light? Darkness may indicate a blocked flue. Smoke damage on the mantel is evidence of a smoky fireplace.

The Attic

The attic should be checked for leaks and for adequate ventilation. Look for water stains under the roof. Chimneys, valleys, dormers, and eaves are particularly vulnerable to leakage. Examine the top plate for rot. Rotted top plates, just like rotted sills, present a very serious problem.

Is the attic ventilated properly? Look around for louvers or fans. The presence of mildew would indicate insufficient ventilation.

Insulation

Look in the attic and the basement to see if they are insulated. Is the insulation properly installed or are some of the sheets hanging loose? Are you planning to insulate the floor joists over the basement? Touch the exterior walls. If they feel cold on a winter day, or damp from condensate, they are probably not insulated.

The Electrical System

Do you have an electrical service panel or a fuse box? If you have a fuse box, you probably have very little incoming power. Anything less than 100 amps of incoming power is inadequate. Most new homes are equipped with 240-volt three-wire service with an entrance capacity of 200 amps. What is the general appearance of the wiring in the cellar? Frayed or tangled wiring is a clear sign of outdated wiring and is a fire hazard. Is the electrical system grounded?

Look at the ceiling fixtures. Do they all have switches or are there some with pull chains?

How about the number of outlets for your needs? The National Electrical Code requires for new houses that outlets be placed a minimum of every 12'. Do all the rooms have a sufficient number of outlets? Do you use many extension cords or multiple plugs? If so, you should consider rewiring. Do the kitchen lights dim when you turn on the toaster? Outlets above the kitchen counter should be part of one or more small-appliance circuits. Anything less is inadequate for today's appliance demand. Do the bathrooms have ground-fault circuit interrupter outlets? This type of outlet is generally installed in rooms with plumbing fixtures for grounding protection. You can distinguish them from regular outlets in that they have two buttons which say "test" and "reset." In addition, any kitchen-counter outlets that are closer to the sink than 6' need a GFI. All receptacles in the house must be grounded (see Chapter 20).

The Plumbing System

Is your water supplied by a well? Have you noticed any problems with the pump? If your water is muddy after running for a long time, you may need a larger storage tank. What is the pipe material? A knife and a magnet will help you to identify the pipe materials. If the magnet sticks, the pipe is either galvanized steel or cast iron. Galvanized steel is gray, whereas cast iron is black. The magnet will not stick to copper, brass, or lead. Scratch the pipe with the knife. Copper pipe will be orange-gold. Brass is a yellowish-gold color. Lead is silvery gray and feels soft when scratched with the knife.

Cast-iron pipes used for the waste lines are durable. Check to see if any of the main waste lines in the basement are cracked. A powdery greenish surface accumulating in the horizontal runs often points to deteriorated piping. Galvanized-steel piping, which is often used for water supply, has a life span of about thirty years. If the house is much older than that, most of the hot- and cold-water supply will need replacement. Galvanized piping corrodes and clogs. Any lead piping will need to be totally replaced (see Chapter 18). Brass can be "red" or "yellow." Yellow brass has a life span of about forty years. Red brass is more durable because it contains more copper. If you have copper pipes, your plumbing system probably needs little, if any repair.

New homes may have plastic piping. Plastic piping in the waste system is acceptable. If the water supply piping is plastic, investigate further as to its specific type and problems related to toxicity (see page 152). Problems with the water pressure generally indicate pipes that are either clogged or of insufficient size. When the sinks are draining, do you hear a gurgling sound from other fixtures? This is a sign of inadequate venting or no venting at all. It could also signify a clogged line or vent. Do you run out of hot water when you are the second in line for the shower? Most likely the hot-water heater is not large enough or it is not operating at full capacity and may need repair. It should provide a minimum of 40 gallons for a family of four.

When was the septic tank last cleaned out?

The utility company should check over the gas lines. If you smell any gas at all, call the gas company immediately. Refer to Chapter 19.

The Heating System

Is the furnace fueled by oil or gas? Has it been converted from coal? Converted furnaces can be wasteful of energy. Was last year's heating bill more than you had anticipated? It could be time to have your house evaluated for energy efficiency.

How old is your furnace? Furnaces generally last an average of thirty years. Many old furnaces are energy-inefficient. Is your furnace operating properly? One way to check is to turn on the thermostat to higher than room temperature. Does it start quickly? Hot-air systems should deliver heat to the registers rather quickly. Hot-water or steam systems may take up to twenty minutes. You should not smell fuel or exhaust in the house. Look at the radiators for signs of leakage. If you have a hot-air system with filtration, change the filters regularly.

26

IN PREPARATION
FOR CONSTRUCTION

With most of the decisions made, you are probably eager to begin demolition. Hang in there for a little bit longer, since there are still a number of technical and administrative chores to put behind us before the wielding of a pickax. We have already determined if the project is legal by checking with all of the required authorities. We will still, however, have to file drawings and papers with the building department, the board of directors, and all other relevant agencies to receive official permission in writing. (Many towns, co-op boards, and managing agents require that an architect or engineer prepare and file drawings for construction or renovation.) In addition, you will have to decide what parts of the work you want to do yourself (assuming you are skilled in these areas). No matter who does the work, you should step up your homeowner's insurance before any construction begins. Speak to your insurance agent, and be sure you tell him exactly what you are doing. Aside from your usual homeowner's policy you may need special coverage to protect you if you do any of the construction or even if you act as your own general contractor during the construction phase. You may have to carry workmen's compensation insurance if you are hiring workers instead of a general contractor. Your local building department may be able to advise you on this matter.

HOW MUCH WILL YOU DO YOURSELF?

If you are thinking of doing any of the construction work by yourself, seriously ask the following questions: Will the law allow me to do this part of the work? Is it practical for me to take on this responsibility given the other demands on my time? Is it economical for me to buy all of the tools and master the skills required to take on a particular construction trade? Is it safe for me to do this part of the work or am I exposing myself and my family to hazardous conditions and toxic materials that I don't know how to handle?

Most important, do you have the requisite skills or experience to tackle this part of the job? Have you successfully completed a construction project similar in complexity and scope to the one being attempted here? It would be foolish to take on the construction of an addition to the house if you made a botch of the back porch you attempted last summer. Being able to put together the components of a barbecue does not mean you can do carpentry, plumbing, or electrical wiring.

This book is not meant to be a beginner's manual. The instructions it contains provide a general outline but are not specific enough to cover all contingencies that may arise as part of your project. It would be unwise of you to use your house as a learning tool and this book as a construction primer.

If you attempt a job you have never done before, there may be some serious consequences. In some cases your lack of experience will simply lead to a sloppy job that may prove expensive to repair. For instance, if you undertake taping and spackling for the first time, it is unlikely that your work will be smooth and seamless. But, bad as the wall may look, sloppy taping won't cause structural failure. On the other hand, sloppy carpentry or electrical wiring can be dangerous to yourself and others. If you want to attempt a task that you have never done before, be sure you read a number of instruction manuals, watch somebody else at work, and, best of all, ask a professional if you can work alongside him as an assistant.

Filing and Other Legal Considerations

Legal requirements are established by the local municipality. Some limited renovation work, such as the replacement of roofing shingles or the substitution of one kitchen cabinet for another, may not have to be filed at all. Most towns require that you file any change in the roofline or the number of rooms, or any modification that may impact on the structure, plumbing, or electrical work. If your building is in a historic landmark area, you may have to file with the proper preservation authority. Local laws often require that a professional prepare and file construction drawings and that the electricians and plumbers be licensed. Some municipalities will allow anyone to file drawings with the building department. Some towns require that the panel box be installed by a licensed electrician, but the rest of the wiring can be done by someone without a license with some professional supervision. It makes little sense for us to anticipate all of the variations since there are so many local rulings. You will have to read the building code that governs your area and consult with an official in the building department (co-op board, managing office, etc.) to be sure you know what your legal responsibilities are.

Practical Considerations

Whether it is practical for you to do all of the work is another question. There are so many different skills required to complete this mammoth job. It may not make a whole lot of sense to take the time out from your regular life to become proficient in all of the skills required. First you have to be a good designer and space planner. Next you have to know how to translate your great ideas into floor plans and elevations. In addition, you should know how things go together

so that they stand up and don't leak. Other skills provided by a design professional include managerial skills. Do you know where to buy all of the materials, how to order them, which trade must be called in and in what order? Even if you have extensive experience in do-it-yourself construction, it may be impractical for you to do all of the construction and mechanical work yourself. Do you have plumbing skills? Can you tape and spackle gypsum-board joints so that they are as smooth as glass? Do you have a permit to drive the heavy equipment that makes the task of excavation less backbreaking?

Go over all of the tasks and skills that are required to complete the renovation and decide which ones make sense for you to do. If you hire professionals to do all of the work, there are many ways you can keep your hand in. For example, let us say you have some very good ideas about how you want to redesign a part of your house or apartment. Measure the existing premises and draw up (in scale) your design ideas. It may be possible to hire a designer (an architect or qualified interior designer) on an hourly consultation basis to review your schematic plans and to provide structural and mechanical details. Perhaps the designer has some ideas of his or her own that will improve the layout or aesthetics. If the job is primarily cosmetic and you are not required to file plans with any authority, that may be the limit of your contact with a design professional. If you want the designer to be more involved, you may discuss his taking on other aspects of the project, such as inspection or supervision. (You may find, however, that many architects will be reluctant to involve themselves in your project in this piecemeal fashion, since—among other reasons—as "architect of record" they could at some future date be held liable for your mistakes. Interior designers may be equally reluctant for these and other reasons.)

Economic Considerations

We have never actually questioned your motives in undertaking the project on your own. Some people want to do the work themselves for the personal gratification of honing their skills and providing their own shelter. Others undertake the work simply to save money. Both of these reasons are valid and well worth the time and effort the project will take. If you are in the first category, we suggest you take off an adequate amount of time from your regular job or resign yourself to a long period of living with construction. If you are

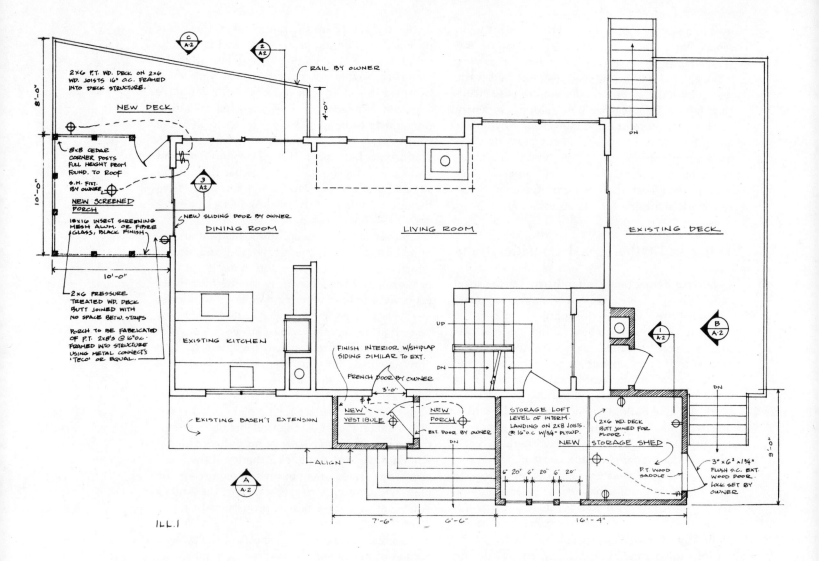

2x6 P.T. WD. DECK ON 2x6
WD. JOISTS 16" O.C. FRAMED
INTO DECK STRUCTURE.

NEW DECK

RAIL BY OWNER

8x8 CEDAR
CORNER POSTS
FULL HEIGHT FROM
FOUND. TO ROOF

S.M. FIXT.
BY OWNER

NEW SCREENED
PORCH

10x16 INSECT SCREENING
MESH ALUM. OR FIBRE
GLASS, BLACK FINISH

NEW SLIDING DOOR BY OWNER

DINING ROOM

LIVING ROOM

EXISTING DECK

2x6 PRESSURE
TREATED WD. DECK
BUTT JOINED WITH
NO SPACE BETW. STRIPS

PORCH TO BE FABRICATED
OF P.T. 2x8's @ 16" O.C.
FRAMED INTO STRUCTURE
USING METAL CONNECT'S
'TECO' OR EQUAL.

EXISTING KITCHEN

FINISH INTERIOR W/SHIPLAP
SIDING SIMILAR TO EXT.

FRENCH DOOR BY OWNER

UP

DN

EXISTING BASEM'T EXTENSION

NEW
VESTIBULE

EXT. DOOR BY OWNER

NEW
PORCH

DN

STORAGE LOFT
LEVEL OF INTERM.
LANDING ON 2x8 JOISTS.
@ 16" O.C W/3/4" PLYWD.

NEW STORAGE SHED

2x6 WD. DECK
BUTT JOINED FOR
FLOOR.

P.T. WOOD
SADDLE

3" x 6² x 1¾"
FLUSH S.C. EXT.
WOOD DOOR.
LOCK SET BY
OWNER

ALIGN

A
A·2

6" 20" 6" 20" 6" 20"

7'-6"   6'-6"   16'-4"

ILL.I

---

in the second category, keep in mind that "time is money." Most construction tasks require a great deal of skill and experience to do the job right. One specialist we have come to admire is the tape-and-spackler. It takes an awful lot of time to learn how to tape and spackle gypsumboard joints so that you can't see where the wall boards meet. It may take you weeks or months of practice to master what this skilled worker can complete in a few days. Another potentially expensive aspect of construction is the cost of tools and equipment. You probably have the tools to do most of the tasks required, such as erecting the framework for partitions and installing gypsum board. On the other hand, some parts of the project may cost more to do yourself than it would to hire a specialist, once you take into account the cost of the tools and supplies. For example, if you have a small amount of plumbing to do, it may be more economical to hire a plumber for the day

rather than purchase the tools you will need to do the work. Last, keep in mind how much it will cost to hire someone to demolish and reconstruct work that you have done yourself but may be of inferior quality.

PREPARING CONSTRUCTION DRAWINGS

The drawings that contain all of the necessary dimensions and details to construct the project are called the "working" or "construction" drawings. The discussion below will help you read working drawings and, to a limited extent, produce a set of drawings usable for construction. Most architects study for five years and then work as apprentices to a professional architect before they

Technical
Decisions
226

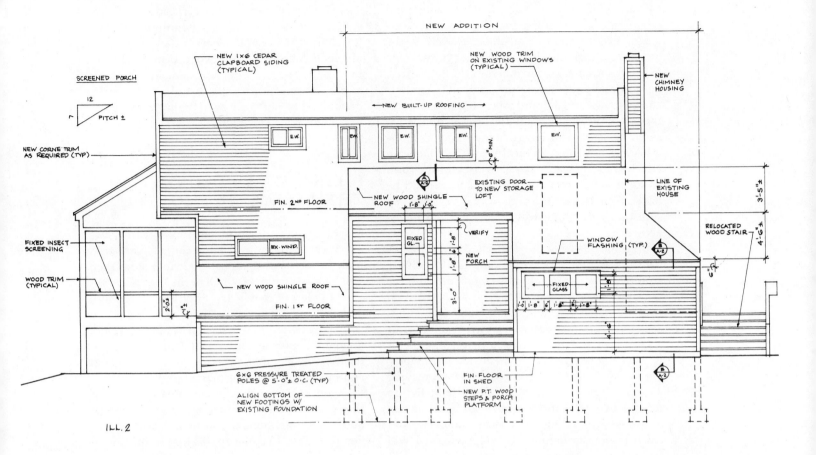

Labels in illustration:
NEW ADDITION
NEW 1x6 CEDAR CLAPBOARD SIDING (TYPICAL)
NEW WOOD TRIM ON EXISTING WINDOWS (TYPICAL)
NEW CHIMNEY HOUSING
SCREENED PORCH
12 PITCH ±
NEW BUILT-UP ROOFING
NEW CORNER TRIM AS REQUIRED (TYP)
E.W.
FIN. 2ND FLOOR
NEW WOOD SHINGLE ROOF
EXISTING DOOR TO NEW STORAGE LOFT
LINE OF EXISTING HOUSE
6" MIN.
FIXED INSECT SCREENING
EX. WIND.
FIXED GL.
VERIFY
NEW PORCH
WINDOW FLASHING (TYP.)
RELOCATED WOOD STAIR
WOOD TRIM (TYPICAL)
NEW WOOD SHINGLE ROOF
FIN. 1ST FLOOR
FIXED GLASS
6x6 PRESSURE TREATED POLES @ 5'-0"± O.C. (TYP)
FIN. FLOOR IN SHED
ALIGN BOTTOM OF NEW FOOTINGS W/ EXISTING FOUNDATION
NEW P.T. WOOD STEPS & PORCH PLATFORM
ILL. 2

can produce a good set of drawings. If you are not a professional, it is likely that your drawings will be rudimentary, but with the help of someone in the field, you may be able to produce a basic, usable set.

Floor plans, the basis of the working drawings, are usually drawn at the scale of ¼" = 1'-0" or ½" = 1'-0". A plan is a horizontal slice through the house or apartment taken at shoulder height (Ill. 1). The plan depicts everything lower than shoulder height in lines and anything over shoulder height (such as an overhead balcony or lighting fixtures) in dashed lines. Any wall that is cut through is shown using thick black lines. Low walls and partitions (less than shoulder height) are drawn using lighter lines. In a renovation project new construction is shown as hatched parallel lines. Windows are shown as thinly spaced parallel lines. All dimensions are indicated using light lines with arrows at the ends. Arrows with circles in the middle are used to show the views of the elevations. An arrow with a tail shows the exact place you are cutting through for a construction section.

Elevations are often drawn at the same scale as the plan but may be enlarged if a great deal of detail has to be shown (Ill. 2). An elevation is a vertical projection that shows only the heights and widths of items such as refrigerators and kitchen cabinets (but not their depths). You can think of the elevation as a vertical section through the building showing everything as if flattened by a rolling pin (Chapter 5, Ill. 17).

A construction section can be either a horizontal or a vertical slice through a specific item (such as a cabinet or lighting cove) that requires greater explanation if you want someone to build it exactly as you have conceived it. Construction sections are usually drawn at a much larger scale than either plans or elevations since they show very fine details.

A good set of construction drawings (which also includes specifications and door and hardware schedules) has all of the information needed to build the project. If you have a good set of construction documents, you should be able to hand them to a contractor and (once he has looked at the job site) expect him to build the

In Preparation for Construction
227

project without any further input from you. The working drawings include all dimensions, and specify the size, location, brand name, and number of every window and door, as well as the finishes for each interior and exterior surface, the location and catalogue numbers of the appliances, lighting and plumbing fixtures, and all the outlets and switches. In addition, there are some areas of the house that may require further detailing, such as how various finishing materials abut one another and how built-in furniture and cabinets are attached to the wall. These are often in the form of construction sections. All decisions should be made prior to construction so that you may be sure that everything will fit and work well together.

Be sure to review the working drawings carefully (even if they have been prepared for you by a professional). It is not unusual for some important item to be left out of the drawings that you may ultimately have to live without. Some things are obvious omissions, such as the front door or a light switch, and either you or the contractor will catch it later. Other items are not so obvious. For instance, what if the drawings do not include an outlet for your computer and a light fixture directly over the bathroom medicine chest? If you are looking over the electrician's shoulder and catch the errors before they are made, you will have to pay extra for the items that were not included in the drawings on which his bid was based. On the other hand, if you are not around to look over his shoulder, it is likely that the renovation will be completed without the outlet or the lighting fixture.

If the drawings are insufficiently detailed, the contractor will provide his own interpretation of what he reads in the sketchy drawings. You, however, may not like the way the contractor chooses to interpret your plans. Very often you make the assumption that the contractor will build an item in a certain way and are astonished to discover that the contractor has a different conception of how it is supposed to look. Even architects and designers have fallen into this trap. For instance, our conception of a tile backsplash behind a kitchen counter is a wall of ceramic tile that extends from the counter itself all the way up to the underside of the overhead cabinet. Not all contractors have the same conception. If you submit a plan to a contractor calling for a "tile backsplash" (and you don't provide an elevation or a construction section), it is likely that the contractor will provide a 6"-high tile backsplash that does not go all the way up to the bottom of the cabinet. Likewise, if you call for a closet with a clothing rod, you may or may not get overhead shelves. Even if you call for overhead shelves, you should include the sizes and mounting heights of the shelves and denote whether they are made of plywood edged with hardwood trim or left with raw edges, covered in plastic laminate or sanded as preparation for painting. A full set of working drawings has notes all over the drawings and a vast number of elevations.

FILING DRAWINGS WITH THE LOCAL AUTHORITIES

Most local governments, even in very rural areas, exert some control over what can and cannot be built in their jurisdictions. Your first stop, then, will be the town or city hall to find out what you need to file and to which authorities. (Hopefully, you have taken our initial advice and have visited them long before.) They should be able to provide you with the forms for filing and all of the zoning regulations, floodplain restrictions, and energy and building codes that may apply.

If you live in a more urban area, chances are that you will have to meet all of the above requirements and more. If you are in a historic area, you may have to make application to the preservation office. You may have to make separate applications to sewer, water, electric, and waste disposal departments. The health department may want to look at your drawings as well. Some areas will insist that you make your home accessible to the disabled.

If you live in a condominium or a cooperative house, you will have to submit your plans to the board of the development. They may have rules and regulations above and beyond what is required by the building department.

If your community requires you to file drawings to obtain a building permit, you may submit the working drawings rather than produce a separate set of drawings for filing. (Even though some building departments do not require as much detail as is provided on a working drawing, it doesn't make much sense to produce two sets of drawings for the same project.) Before filing drawings make sure you know specifically what the building department inspectors expect to find on the drawings. Some departments insist on a site plan (a plan of the property and roof) even if you are renovating only the inside of the house. If you are putting on an addition that will change the roofline of the building, be sure to include the site plan showing the distances from the house to the property lines on all sides. If you are adding another floor, include an elevation showing the total height of the remodeled house. The building department will want to make sure that you are conforming to the zoning restrictions on front, side-yard, and rear-yard setbacks. If the front set-back line in your neighborhood is 30', you are required to construct your house at least 30' back from the front property line. No living space may protrude into this setback, with the possible exception of an exterior stair or an open porch. The building department will check the site plan to make sure that you do not violate any rights-of-way or utility easements.

If you are adding to your house, in addition to all of the above the building department may require calculations proving that you are not exceeding your allowed floor-area ratio (FAR), the ratio of the total number of square feet of the building (calculate the square feet of every floor and add them all up) to the area of the property. If your house is built to its maximum FAR, you may not be allowed to add on to it even if you are in conformance with the height and setback regulations. Also, you must conform to the site coverage requirements. Many areas will allow you to cover only a certain percentage of the lot with building.

If you are renovating all or part of an apartment, the building department may want a site plan of the entire apartment house showing the nearest cross streets, as well as a plan of the floor you live on showing the public halls, the location of your apartment, the staircases, and the elevators. New York City requires that your drawings contain the sizes of all the windows in the apartment and a set of notes outlining how the other tenants in the building will be protected from the noise and dust of your construction.

The building department is concerned with the welfare of the occupants of any building in their jurisdiction and may legislate on a number of pertinent safety issues. Some urban authorities insist that the building be constructed with only incombustible materials and will not allow you to use wood studs and joists. Some municipalities require that your ground-floor windows be large enough to allow you to escape through in case of fire. Buildings that house two or more families may be required to have two means of egress in case of fire, either a second (enclosed) stair or a fire escape, or in lieu of these, a sprinkler system. New York City will not even look at your plans until a report is filed by a certified asbestos inspector. If you have some asbestos anywhere in the building, the authorities may demand that a licensed asbestos technician remove it or contain it before you are permitted to proceed with your renovation.

All states are governed by energy conservation codes. The code in your area may require that you show the sizes of the windows on your construction drawings and indicate the type of glazing. Many energy codes have ratios of allowable glazed area to total wall area. You may have to eliminate some of your windows if you have too many square feet of glass, depending, of course, on the type of glazing you use. Some areas do not permit fireplaces since they allow too much of your mechanically generated heat to escape up the flue. Some municipalities will allow you to use heat-circulating fireplaces or wood stoves or special fireplaces that draw air from the outside.

In addition to supplying drawings you will have to fill out and submit a number of forms. Try to be as knowledgeable as possible before making your submission to the plan examiner. Go down to the town hall and ask someone at the desk what is required to be included in the drawings. Although we have found examiners and inspectors in suburban and rural areas to be very patient and forthcoming with information, it is best not to pester these people too much.

The above listing is in no way complete. You will have to check with the authorities in your area to determine which apply to you. In fact, filing drawings for a building permit is sometimes so complex that the expediting of building department applications is a subspecialty in itself. Most city architects hire such a specialist to advise them on their submissions and to move the papers through the building department. You may find it expedient to hire a code consultant to help you through the filing process. (The code consultant is not usually a licensed professional and, therefore, may not be able to stamp or seal your submission. If your community requires that a licensed engineer or architect take responsibility for the work, you will have to hire one.)

ESTIMATING THE COST OF THE JOB

Sending the Drawings Out to Bid

If you are planning to hire a general contractor or individual tradespeople to construct all or parts of the job, your working drawings will provide the basis for their cost estimates. In professional parlance, the working drawings (together with a list of written specifications and a blank contract form) are called the bid documents.

If you are seeking competitive bids, send your working drawings to a few established and recommended general contractors in the area. If all of the items are specified (the name and model of each light fixture, the name and number of the heating unit, the size and style of the baseboard, the size and quality of the doors), you should be able to get some fairly dependable prices. If you have a thorough set of working drawings, and the underlying structure and plumbing of the building is in good shape, the cost of the extras should be within 10 to 15 percent of the contractor's original bid price.

It may take the contractors a couple of weeks to come back with their prices. Since this is a private job, you are in no way obligated to take the lowest bid. In fact, you may decide to select the contractor with the highest bid if he has the best reputation, or if he can start immediately, or if the bids are very close. Don't make your decision on price alone. All contractors are not equal and there can be a vast difference in the quality of work delivered. You are always best off looking at a number of jobs constructed by the contractor being considered and speaking to his clients as references.

Do-It-Yourself Estimating

The most accurate estimate is obtained by getting bids by competent contractors who are working with a thorough set of construction documents. Nothing else is quite as reliable. The next-best thing is doing a materials takeoff. To do a takeoff you must patiently sit down with a pencil, a scale, and a calculator and translate your plans and elevations into a list of materials to be purchased.

In a takeoff the quantity of each item (with a contingency of 5 to 10 percent added for waste) is multiplied by the price per unit. To estimate the quantity of tile needed for the kitchen floor, measure the floor's area and add a contingency of about 10 percent for cut tiles and waste. Tile is often sold by the square foot and it will be easy to estimate the cost of this material. Remember that you will also have to buy adhesive and grout, a tile cutter, if you don't have one, and perhaps plywood to reinforce the subfloor. It will be more difficult to estimate the cost of labor if a tile installer is to be hired.

Your materials supplier may be of great help while you are doing your takeoff. Suppliers have many rules of thumb that can come in handy. As a matter of fact, it is not unusual for a supplier to do the takeoff. The idea behind it is, of course, that you will give him your business. Unfortunately, you probably will be paying higher prices than a contractor would for the materials. Contractors, unlike the one-time renovator, buy in bulk. They can purchase at lower prices and already own all of the tools and equipment. This may offset the cost of labor. For this reason it may be cheaper for you to hire a contractor to do the job than to do it yourself. It may be helpful to have a subcontractor, such as an electrician or plumber, bid on that aspect of the work so that you can compare the cost of materials only (derived from your takeoff) with his price for the whole job. You can then decide whether the difference between the two prices justifies your doing the work yourself.

You usually compile a materials takeoff by trade (all of the lumber and nails and then all of the gypsum board and spackling supplies) so that the estimate can proceed in some orderly fashion.

PART FOUR: THE CONSTRUCTION PROCESS

AN INTRODUCTION TO DEMOLITION AND CONSTRUCTION

You are finally ready to gather your forces for the demolition and construction ahead. This phase of the work can be both exhilarating and frustrating. Exhilarating because you can see your design slowly taking shape right before your eyes. Potentially frustrating because construction might not move as fast as you would like.

If you are working with a professional designer and a general contractor, this phase should be relatively relaxing (unless you are forced to live in the building while the renovation is going on). We don't advise you, however, to fly off to a South Seas island for the next few months. This is a renovation, rather than new construction, and there may be exigencies that could not be foreseen in advance. Your input may be required to resolve a problem (especially if the resolution generates a costly extra). Even if there are no major complications, it is a good idea for you to visit the site a few times a week, not only to see how the job is progressing but to check that every detail has been included. The designer may fail to notice that an electric outlet has not been installed in precisely the spot indicated on the drawings. Since you know exactly where you want to locate your computer, you are more likely to spot the omission than is the designer.

If you are your own general contractor (or if you have prepared the construction drawings yourself and hired a general contractor), you will have to visit the site daily to resolve problems and answer questions. You will have to check the progress of the work, make sure that it is being constructed as drawn, that the workmanship is of good quality, and that the contractor is using specified materials. If you are scheduling the work, you will have a substantial amount of homework as well. Materials will have to be ordered, received, and paid for. Subcontractors will have to be called in when needed.

The rest of this introduction is for those who will be constructing or supervising part of the work. Be advised that the directions outlined in the chapters that follow cannot be relied upon as your sole means of instruction in any single trade or for any particular procedure. There are a number of excellent comprehensive books available covering carpentry, plumbing, and electric wiring (as well as the other trades) that must be used to supplement this book. Be sure to read extensively before you attempt a job. Book learning, however, does not make up for experience. Think twice before attempting something that you have never actually done before.

In addition, read and memorize the list of suggestions and precautions below before plunging in.

In General

1. The evening before a day's work, pore over the construction plans of the job ahead of you. Familiarize yourself with the details and be sure that you understand what is required in each step of the procedure. If you have any questions, call someone with experience, build a model of the questionable area, or consult your reference books for a solution.

Don't expect the problem to resolve itself the next day. It won't. At best you will be wasting valuable daylight hours pondering; at worst you may have to rip out half a day's work to remedy a mistake. Whenever possible, work with someone to prevent straining yourself. If you have a partner, you can discuss a procedure in advance. Two opinions on the subject may help you avoid doing something foolish.

2. Make sure you have all the materials and tools you will need for the day's work. It is frustrating to have to stop work to search for a missing item. At such a time the temptation is great to substitute an inferior or ill-suited item for the one you are missing—a bad construction practice.

3. Be sure you have read and provided for all the safety admonitions in this book, other books, and the instruction booklets of all power tools and for all materials. Remind yourself that people lose fingers by removing safety guards, and their lives by ignoring grounding rules.

4. Never drink alcoholic beverages or take drugs before or during work. With normal judgment impaired, you may feel like a superman or superwoman—may think that you can work longer, harder, and faster than you ever worked before. This is the best way we know to hurt yourself. Besides, you will probably judge the work to be sloppy the next morning.

5. Don't work where or when it is too dark to see, or when it is very cold or hot. Don't work outdoors if it is raining or if surfaces are slippery.

6. Don't work when you are exhausted or dizzy from the heat.

7. Keep work areas clean. It is very easy to slip on accumulated debris and sawdust. Often the wind sweeps unattached materials and debris onto the heads of workers and passersby.

8. Don't use power equipment in wet or damp areas. Keep tools stored in dry, safe places when not in use. Make sure that all outside electrical outlets are covered by ground-fault interrupters.

9. Make sure you are dressed properly for this kind of work. You will need heavy shoes with thick soles and firm toes, a hard hat, work gloves, and a respirator (or masks rated for the type of work being performed). Use safety glasses when using power saws and other power tools. Do not wear loose clothing, necklaces, or long hair that might get caught in the machinery. Keep a first-aid kit on hand.

10. Be careful when handling, storing, or using flammable materials or chemicals. Avoid using materials with poisonous or noxious fumes. Follow all printed instructions. Use and store these materials in well-ventilated areas. Keep all tools and chemicals away from children.

11. Wear a suitable protective mask when installing fiberglass insulation or applying and sanding spackling compound or whenever a manufacturer suggests it.

12. Make sure that you, your house, any workers you may hire, or any subcontractors are covered by liability and accident insurance. Some co-op buildings require extensive liability and workmen's compensation insurance.

For Demolition

Few items on the construction agenda are more dangerous than demolition. Don't just jump in there and wreck the wall. It may be load-bearing, or alive with electric and gas lines, or full of asbestos.

Since it may be more dangerous to demolish a structure than it is to build one, we urge you to consult an engineer or architect before cutting into or dismantling the structure of your house. Many old houses have complex structural arrangements that may confuse an expert, or may have been built using harmful materials such as asbestos (in pipe coverings, exterior shingles, floor and ceiling tiles, etc.). Even if you are relatively certain that you understand the structure and know what you are doing, get a second opinion.

Before you demolish anything, prepare yourself as follows:

13. Have all your demolition equipment ready. A list of materials and equipment can be found in Inset I.

14. Clear away all items in the room, or else seal them with drop cloths and tape. Even minor demolition generates an enormous amount of airborne dust. It may take four minutes to demolish a partition, but another two months to vacuum and dust the dishes, furniture, and books in the surrounding rooms. After removing everything you can from the room, close the doors and tape around the door seams. Tape around closet doors as well, or tape drop cloths over the doors. (The insidious dust seems to find its way through tiny cracks and around corners.) Open all of the windows and install an exhaust fan.

15. Protect the floors, if they are to be salvaged, by laying down old sheets of plywood (or Masonite) or, at the very least, taping heavy-duty kraft paper to the floors.

16. If possible, move out. Move to a hotel or a friend's house or, if these are not options, set up temporary cooking and sleeping areas (away from the demolition dust) so that you can do without the rooms

- Masks and respirators as required for the procedure
- Straight wrecking bar
- Crowbar
- Sledgehammer (not so heavy that you can't lift it comfortably)
- Reciprocating saw (for cutting wood joist, lathing strips, and gypsum board)
- Impact hammer with a carbide masonry bit (if you are cutting through heavy masonry)
- Ladders and scaffolding
- Temporary lighting
- Wheelbarrows, barrels, shovels, and brooms for the debris
- Shoring (if you have to prop up ceilings, beams, or walls temporarily)
- Plastic sheeting and duct tape
- Old plywood sheets or heavy kraft paper to protect the floor

being worked on for a few days. If you are demolishing part of your kitchen, it is unlikely that you will be cooking dinner there for a while.

17. Shut off the electricity in that part of the building. (You will have to use long, heavy-duty extension cords for any lighting or electrical equipment.) Shut off every circuit (even if it does not service the immediate area) that you can, and, if possible, shut down the whole house and get your electrical power from a neighbor. (To identify which circuits control what outlets, plug in a number of lamps to the outlets and turn off the circuit breakers at the panel box, one by one, until the lights go out.) If you are having work done on your apartment, make sure that, at the very least, your circuits are shut off. It may be impossible to shut down the electricity in the apartments above or next to you. Since there may be live lines in the partitions, the work will have to proceed with extreme caution.

18. If you have any suspicion that the gas line is in the partition you are dismantling, have a plumber or the gas company shut off service temporarily. If your house is relatively new, it will be easy to determine if there are gas lines passing through. Trace the line from the stove and clothes dryer to the gas meter and then to the place where the gas line enters the house. If you are demolishing anything near that route, shut off the gas. In an older house or apartment building you may have more difficulty. Often there are live and dead gas lines that were originally designed to service gas-lit wall sconces and gas fireplaces. Also, an old apartment building may have seen a number of radical renovations. What is now the bedroom may have once been the kitchen. The gas line in the wall may still be active. Proceed with caution and if you hit a gas line call the emergency number for the gas company at once.

19. Shut off any water lines that might be running through the wall or ceiling about to be demolished.

20. Have the place inspected for asbestos. There could be asbestos in floors, pipes, valves, ducts, insulation, radiators, floor underlayments, etc. If the inspector finds evidence of asbestos, you should not do the demolition yourself, but should hire a licensed asbestos-removal company. Should you attempt the demolition yourself, or hire inexperienced labor, you could be endangering yourself, the workers, and your family.

21. Rig up temporary lighting. Since you are shutting off electricity in the area, you will need construction lights on long extension cords.

22. Make sure you know how you are going to get rid of the debris. This might be the most costly and troublesome part of the demolition. If you are going to truck it away yourself, find out where you can legally dump the debris. If you have no way of hauling it off yourself, find a carter who will dispose of the debris legally.

23. Don't pile debris in the middle of rooms. House and apartment floors are designed to support light residential loads only. They are likely to collapse under the weight of the accumulated debris.

Some Demolition Guidelines

24. Try not to demolish more than you absolutely have to. If possible, plan to repair a surface rather than demolish and reconstruct it.

25. Remove everything that is salvageable before the demolition. Unpin door hinges and set the doors and the hardware aside. Doors (especially old, paneled doors or French doors) are very expensive and can be either reused or sold. If the doors have too many layers of chipped paint, they can be stripped and either repainted or stained and varnished. This is easily done by sending them out to a company for chemical stripping.

26. If the wood trim is intricate, you should try to save it for reuse. Gently pry it off using a small bar at the nail points. Wainscoting too should be salvaged if you can retrieve it in one piece and if it is not too dried out. Mantels, of course, should be protected if they are to remain in place or carefully removed and saved for relocation.

27. Demolition* should begin at the top and proceed downward, from the ceiling to the top of the walls,

*After temporary shoring is in place, if required.

down the walls to the floor. Remove all of the plaster (or gypsum board) first (so that pipes, wires, etc., are exposed), the lath next, and the ceiling joists and wall studs last.

28. Be prepared to remove nails immediately from the lumber you will be removing. We suggest this for practical as well as safety reasons. First, you may want to reuse the lumber. Second, nails left in lumber cause nasty puncture wounds to the unsuspecting. Even if you are going to dispose of the wood, hammer the nails down, out of harm's way.

27

PREPARING THE SITE FOR AN EXTENSION

THE LAYOUT

The first and most important step in the construction process is the laying out of the extension on the property. We cannot overemphasize this, since any error made at this point will interfere with every succeeding job. Inaccuracies in the measurement of the building walls or the angles at corners will manifest themselves in the remainder of the construction work. In addition, mistakes relating to the location of the extension on the property, such as being too close to a property line or violating code restrictions, will eventually cost you time and money to rectify.

There are various methods of laying out. We have chosen the layout square method. It provides the degree of accuracy necessary for a small extension and it is very simple.

Materials

The materials and tools required for laying out are not particularly difficult to come by or to operate. Many of them you can easily construct.

You will need the following materials:

- 2″ × 2″ stakes approximately 2′ to 4′ long
- 2″ × 4″ stakes approximately 3′ to 4′ long
- 1″ × 6″ boards approximately 4′ to 10′ long
- Eightpenny nails (8d)
- Mason line
- Weights (bricks will do)

(Some of these materials will be employed in the construction of tools such as the layout square.)

Tools

Two types of tools are needed: tools necessary for laying out and those used for excavation.

The following is a list of layout tools:

- Layout square (see Inset I)
- Plumb line with plumb bob
- Carpenter's, or spirit, level
- Line level
- Claw hammer
- Hatchet
- Crosscut saw
- 6′ and 100′ metallic tape measures
- Folding rule
- Water level

For excavation you will need:

- Licensed backhoe and bulldozer operator
- Shovel
- Pick

Excavation is an exhausting, time-consuming, and tedious project. In addition, excavation close to an existing building requires a great amount of skill and care. This job is best left to a licensed and experienced backhoe and bulldozer operator.* (See section on excavation.)

*A backhoe is used for small excavations. It has two attach-

A layout square is essentially a large 90° wooden triangle. To build it, you need three perfectly straight wood boards approximately 1" × 4" or 1" × 6" and 10' to 12' in length. Take two boards and carefully square off the ends. Make a lap joint at one end. This is done by making identical notches at the end of each board to half the depth of the wood. The pieces are then fitted together and nailed, screwed, or glued to each other. Then proceed as follows (Ill. I-1):

· Take board 1, measure 6' along it, and mark it.
· Take board 2, measure 8', and mark it.
· Take board 3, measure 10', and mark it.
· Place board 1 on the ground.
· Place board 2 on top of board 1, joining the lapped ends.
· Place board 3 on top of boards 1 and 2, joining the 6' and 8' markings.
· Fasten with nails.

· Notch at point P to allow for the dimension of the corner stake.

To use the layout square, place one of its legs directly under the stretched mason's line. The notched end fits around the stake. Check for perfect alignment by means of a plumb bob. The adjacent leg will indicate where the next line should be located to obtain a right-angled corner (Ill. I-2).

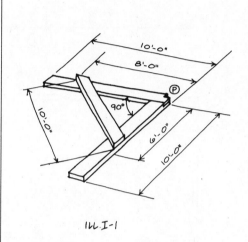

ILL. I-1

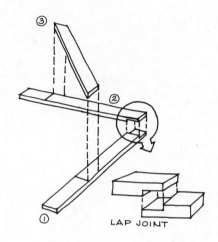

LAP JOINT

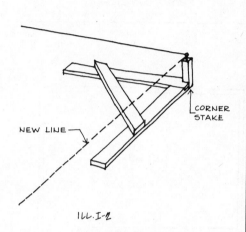

NEW LINE

CORNER STAKE

ILL. I-2

Locating the Extension Corners* and Clearing the Site

We remind you that although laying out the extension is not a difficult process, it does require accuracy. If you are not capable of precise work, we suggest that you subcontract this part to a licensed surveyor or civil engineer. For those of you with tight sites, we also recommend that you hire a surveyor or civil engineer,† both to stake out your property and to site the new extension. There is a simple reason for this advice. We have seen many distressed homeowners requesting zoning variances from town zoning boards, the source of their problem stemming from discrep-

ancies in siting between code requirements and actual dimensions. Those of you with large properties should look at the existing survey. Check to see if the distances between the proposed extension and the property boundaries are greater than the requirements specified by code. Bear in mind, however, that there may be zoning regulations governing the maximum building area or site coverage. (See Chapter 4.)

Before you start clearing the site, post a grading or building permit or any other license needed to start work on your property. Clean the site of any roots, stumps, and tree limbs and remove any debris such as rocks or blocks of wood. Be sure to remove any underground wood that may eventually cause termite problems. If the topsoil is of good quality, remove it with a bulldozer for later use in landscaping.

Be extremely careful about clearing this area. Look in the cellar to see where plumbing and electrical services penetrate the foundation. This will give you a clue as to the possible paths to a power pole, well, septic system, sewer, water main, telephone wires, etc. It is also advisable to

ments: a clawlike one for digging and a scooplike one for removing earth. Bulldozers have a plowlike element for pushing earth. They are used for leveling and large excavation jobs.
*This procedure works for a flat or gently sloping site. For more difficult sites, we advise you to consult a professional surveyor.
†Both licensed surveyors and civil engineers measure land parcels, set boundaries, and draw up site maps.

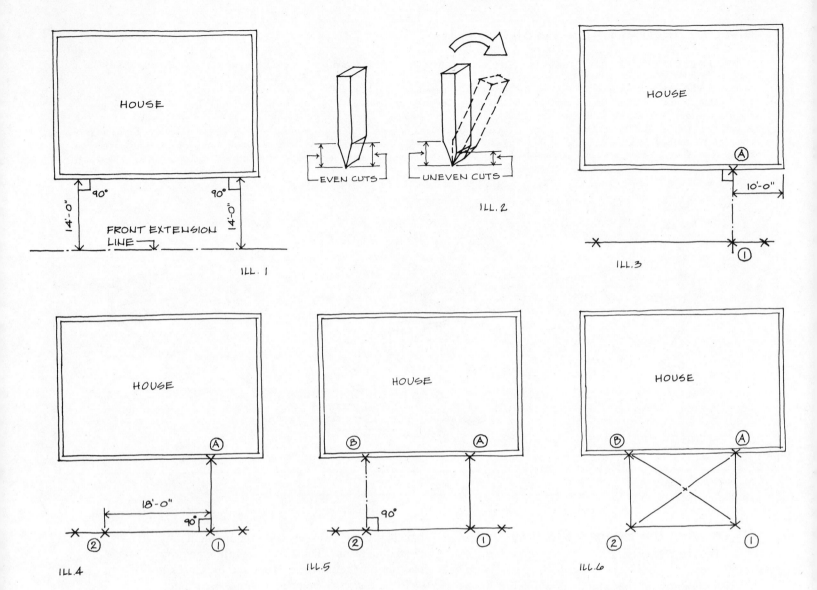

ILL. 1

ILL. 2

ILL. 3

ILL. 4

ILL. 5

ILL. 6

check with the local building authorities for any old plumbing, gas, or sewer lines that were once part of a now demolished structure and might still be underground. These pipes should be properly capped with the required devices. There may be underground plumbing, gas, or sewer lines going through your property which service a nearby structure. The local authorities can also provide you with locations of municipal storm sewers. The power company can assist you in locating any underground electric wire or conduit from either a present or a previous electrical installation. In addition, the company can make sure that any installation is dead.

Let's assume an extension that measures 14' in width by 18' in length. When the site is gently sloping, you need not worry about creating a level platform where the extension is to be built. Using the house as a guide, measure the length that the extension projects into the yard. With the use of a layout square (see Inset I) take measurements 14' away from the house and at right angles to it (assuming the extension is at right angles to the house). These measurements are taken at two points along the house and a stake is driven at each (Ill. 1). Make sure that the stakes are carefully pointed—that is, all cuts are at even lengths; otherwise, the stakes will twist (Ill. 2). Stretch a mason's line between these stakes.

The next step is to establish the intersection between the house and the extension. Measure along the house the appropriate distance from one of its corners to the beginning of the extension. Let's assume 10'. Intersection A has now been located. Drive a nail into the building's wall at this point (Ill. 3). Starting at point A and with the aid of the layout square, find corner 1 by placing one leg of the square parallel to the side of the house. The adjacent leg will indicate the perpendicular. Where this line intersects the 14' line, drive in stake 1 (Ill. 3). Stretch a mason's line between points A and 1. Starting at point 1, measure along the line of the extension 18' to locate corner 2 (Ill. 4). Place one leg of the layout square directly underneath line 1–2; the adjacent leg will locate point B (Ill. 5). Drive a nail at point B. Measure the distances between points A–B and 1–2 and between A–1 and B–2 to make sure that they are 18' and 14', respectively. To double-check the accuracy of the corners, measure the lengths of diagonals A–2 and B–1 (Ill. 6). The diagonals of a perfect rectangle are always equal; should there be any discrepancy, readjust the lines accordingly by repeating the above procedure.

Check to make sure that all yard measurements conform to code requirements. You should also check the lengths of the front and side walls of the extension. Keep in mind that all other construction is based on these first steps!

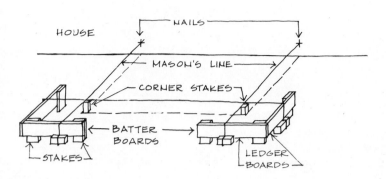

ILL. 7

Erecting the Batter Boards

We now have stakes located at the extension corners and intersections with the main house. In our excavations for footings and foundations these stakes will inevitably be in the way and most likely will be lost. Remember that footings protrude a minimum of 4" outward from the walls of the extension (albeit underground) and that in addition to allowing for the footing projection, we need to allow room in which to construct the footing forms. The excavation should be at least 2' greater than the perimeter of the house. So that we can remove the corner stakes prior to construction and still provide for easy location of the corner points, we erect batter boards. These boards frame the corners of the extension but stand 4' to 8' back from them, depending on the depth of the excavation (Ill. 7).

Erecting batter boards is a very simple procedure. The verbal explanation, however, tends to be somewhat confusing. We suggest that you refer closely to Illustration 8. Let's assume that we are locating the batter boards 6' outside the building lines. The first batter-board stake is located directly in line with the building-line diagonal. The distance away from the extension corner stake should be 10'. The second and third stakes are driven at right angles to the first, making sure that they are parallel to the building line. They should be located past the building corner, as shown in Illustration 8. We are now almost ready

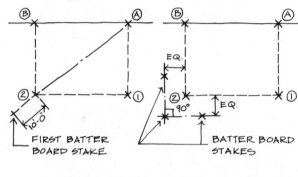

ILL. 8

to nail the ledger boards to the stakes. Before doing this, the elevation of the top of the foundation wall must be determined.

Determining the Floor Level

There are several ways to determine the elevation of the existing floor. The most foolproof method, however, is to open a hole in the exterior wall and expose the house's rough floor framing. A further advantage of this method is that in the event that you don't have a completely level floor, you may adjust the extension's floor wherever the openings between the spaces occur. If you are planning to have only a door between the extension and the house, open the wall in the location of the future door. With the opening in place, calculate the thickness of the new floor by adding up the various layers: framing, subflooring, flooring, and sill. Measure the distance representing the total depth of the new floor down from the existing floor level to determine the height of the new foundation.

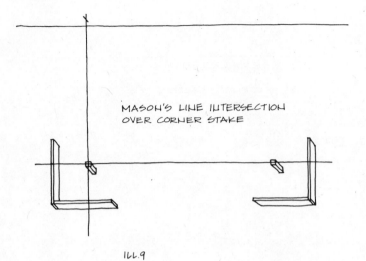

MASON'S LINE INTERSECTION
OVER CORNER STAKE

ILL.9

The next step is to transfer this height to the batter boards. This can be done with the aid of a transit. An easier method is to use a water level. A water level is a tube filled with colored water; it can be purchased at building supply houses. When you extend the tube and the water is level, it gives you a straight line. (The water level was used for the installation of acoustical ceiling tiles before the use of lasers became popular.) Hold up the tube against the building at the appropriate height. Stretch the tube out. When the water is level, transfer the height to the batter boards. If the extension is very small (about 10' wide or less), you can site the elevation by using a straight piece of lumber and a 4' carpenter's level.

Locating the Building Lines on the Batter Boards

Locating the building lines on the batter boards is done by stretching a mason's line between batter boards at right angles to each other (Ill. 9). The mason's lines are kept in place by attaching them to bricks. The lines are adjusted with a plumb bob until they intersect directly over the tack on the corner stake (Ill. 10). Mark the location of the mason's line along the batter board and cut a notch on it. Place the line on the notch, wrap it around the ledger board a few times, and tie it to a nail (Ill. 11). Check the line for levelness by using a line level. The corner building stakes can now be removed.

The nails indicating where the extension meets

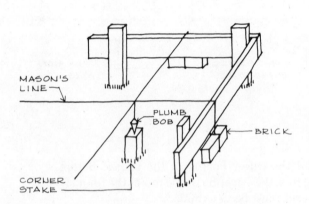

MASON'S
LINE

PLUMB
BOB

BRICK

CORNER
STAKE

ILL.10

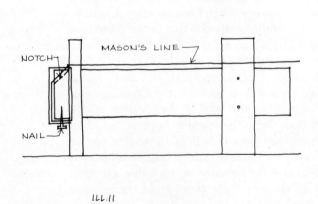

NOTCH

MASON'S LINE

NAIL

ILL.11

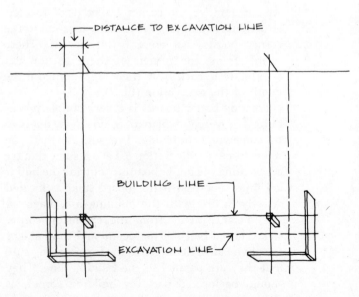

DISTANCE TO EXCAVATION LINE

BUILDING LINE

EXCAVATION LINE

ILL.12

the house are located high enough on the existing foundation to remain undisturbed during the excavation.

Once the building lines have been located, you can mark off the distance along the batter boards to the excavation lines. You should excavate at least 3' out from the actual building lines to allow yourself room to work on the foundations (Ill. 12). (See discussion on excavation. We cannot overemphasize the danger of excavating too close to the foundations of the existing house and the danger of inundation and collapse.) Cut notches at the point where the excavation line will occur and transfer the mason's line from the building line to the excavation-line notch. Using a plumb bob, drive a stake directly under the intersection of the stretched excavation lines. This locates the extension corners. Remove all lines from the batter boards. You are ready to begin excavation.

EXCAVATION

You can now instruct the backhoe operator to start excavating. Make sure that this person is experienced with excavation close to an existing structure. As we already explained in the chapter on foundations, it is very important that the existing building foundations and footings not be disturbed in any way. Undermining the building's foundations by inundating the footings or pushing into foundation walls can prove disastrous. One safety measure which might help is to do the excavation close to the existing foundation (within 3' to 4') by hand rather than with a backhoe.

We recommend (as we already stated in the foundation design chapter) that you have a crawl space for the extension rather than a full basement wall. The reason for this advice is that it will keep the excavation depth shallower than the depth of the existing foundation wall (assuming you have a full basement under your existing house). As we discussed in the foundations chapter, the new foundations will need to step down to the existing ones (see Chapter 24). The crucial point to remember is that you want to keep the excavation line *above* the line of the existing footings (see Chapter 24, Ills. 10 and 11).

In cold areas, you must take into account the depth of the frost line (see page 216, Inset I). The ground expands when it freezes, causing foundations that are not secured by footings placed below the frost line to move, thus damaging the house. Local codes of building authorities can tell you the depth of the frost line in your area.

More on safety: When trimming trenches by hand or doing any work involving digging, a few things should be kept in mind. Sandy soil requires a larger excavation, as it does not hold together. Soil with a high clay content will be more likely to hold up in a straight line. Earth is often unpredictable. Sometimes a bank that looks safe will cave in on you. A few warning signs to look for are cracks along the surface of the earth on top of the trenches or earth trickling down a bank. A good bet is to brace the excavation with boards placed vertically along the banks of the trench. In addition, store any excavated material way back. It should not be piled close to the trenches. If you decide not to use bracing, at least slope the banks as much as possible, particularly in loose soil. Finally, it's not a good idea to let the excavation stand idle for days. Storms, rain, and wind make the excavation unstable and can set off a slide.

28

CONSTRUCTING FOUNDA-TIONS FOR AN EXTENSION

In this chapter we work our way out of the ground and into areas where the progress of construction can begin to be appreciated. It is most important that foundations are built accurately and carefully.

Materials

The materials will vary according to the type of foundation that is to be built. We will limit our discussion to poured footings and concrete-block walls, since we are recommending a crawl space for your extension rather than a full basement wall. The list of materials follows.

For footings:

- 2″ × 8″, 2″ × 10″, or 2″ × 12″ boards to be used for the footing forms, depending on the footing size; length to suit
- 2″ × 2″ or 2″ × 4″ stakes; length to suit
- Ready-mixed concrete
- Nails
- ½″- or ¾″-diameter (nonsmooth) reinforcing steel bars (or as required by code)

For concrete-block walls:

- Concrete blocks (stretchers, corners, and a few sash blocks)
- Mortar (see Inset I)
- Anchor bolts, nuts, and washers (½″ thick and 12″ to 18″ long)
- Horizontal joint steel reinforcement

Tools

The tools required for foundation work are quite varied. Many of them have already been used for site preparation. In addition, masonry and carpentry tools will be required.

- Plumb bob
- Carpenter's level
- Mason's line
- Sledgehammer (choose the size you can best handle) to drive stakes
- Claw hammer
- Windable chalk line
- Wooden rule
- 50′ retractable metal tape
- Hand or electric saw
- Long-handled shovel (for small excavations)
- Pointed trowel
- Hoe or garden rake (for spreading concrete inside footing forms)
- Framing square (preferably steel, 16″ × 24″)
- Screed board
- Mortar board
- Metal tub (to mix mortar)
- Story or course pole (to be built on the job)
- Straightedge or long spirit level
- Brick hammer
- Brick set
- Mason's corner (also called clip or cut nail)
- Joining tool

In order to keep the following discussion relatively simple, we are not including an explanation on the construction of stepped foundations. The following discussion applies to houses with a crawl space or slab on grade where the new foundations will naturally align with the old ones. All foundation work must be coordinated with the floor framing plan. Be sure you know exactly the heights of each wall and pier.

Foundation work starts by reestablishing the building lines on the batter boards. This is done by placing the mason's line in the grooves cut in the batter boards and on the nails on the existing building. A plumb bob is dropped at the intersection of the batter boards to locate the building corner (which is also the foundation-wall corner), and a stake is driven at that exact location as a marker (Ill. 1). When all corners are located, the extension dimensions are checked against the distances between the stakes to make sure everything is still as accurate as when originally measured prior to excavation. The next step is to locate and build the footing formwork.

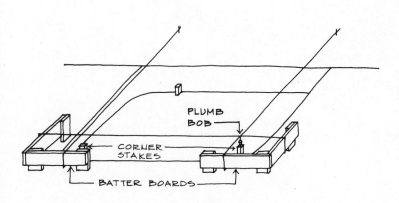

ILL. 1

FOOTINGS

Building the Footing Forms—Outside Perimeter

Footing forms can be trenches dug in the soil or built-up wood forms (Ill. 2). Pouring footings in a trench is possible if the soil is firm and capable of holding a sharp cut. In loose soils, such as sand, gravel, etc., this method cannot be used. Footings

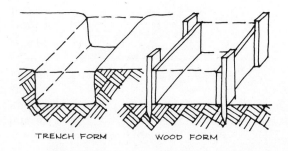

ILL. 2

INSET I / MIXING MORTAR

Mortar is a mixture of cement, lime, sand, and water. There are various types of mortar with different material contents, such as straight-lime mortar or straight-cement mortar. A very popular type is known as masonry cement mortar. This is a mixture of masonry cement which is manufactured for mixing only with sand and water, thus minimizing the variables in the mixing process.

The recommended proportions for mixtures vary with the function of the masonry; for example, mortar mixtures to be used for foundation walls vary from those for non-load-bearing partition walls. For this reason, you should always consult the recommendations made by organizations such as the Portland Cement Association or by the local building code (which often specifies the mortar proportions for the various localities). The most widely used proportions are one part masonry cement to three parts of sand (1:3). When using Portland cement, the proportions are generally one part Portland cement to one-fourth part hydrated lime to three parts sand (1:1/4:3).

The water recommendation is trickier since water increases the workability of the mixture but decreases its strength. The water content should not be such that the mortar slides off the trowel when picked up or falls off the ends of the brick when laid up. The consistency of the final mixture should not be too soft or too stiff.

Mortar can be mixed by hand or with a mixer. The power mixer saves time and effort. When using a power mixer, the procedure starts by adding a little water to the drum. Next, about a third of the sand is added, and finally all the cement (and lime if required). While the machine turns, the remainder of the sand and the water is added until the right consistency is obtained. With all the ingredients in, the mixture continues to be mixed for a few more minutes.

To mix mortar by hand, about half of the sand is placed in a metal mortar box. The cement is laid over the sand (and the lime if required). The rest of the sand is then added and the dry ingredients are thoroughly mixed together until the mass is even in color. Water is added by making an indentation in the center of the pile of dry ingredients, pouring water into it, and mixing until the desired plasticity is obtained.

Mortar must be constantly mixed fresh. If it is more than two or three hours old (depending on the weather), it becomes hard to handle and must be discarded.

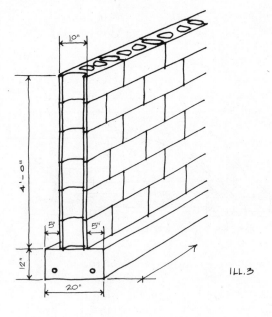

ILL.3

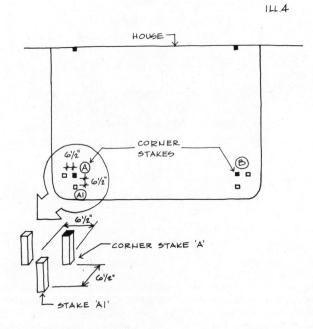

ILL.4

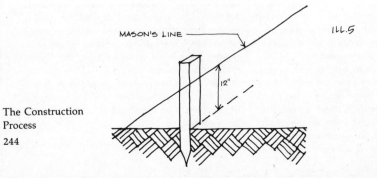

ILL.5

must be poured on undisturbed earth. If the ground has been overexcavated, the footing should be made thicker. Watch for any loose fill at locations that may have previously been backfilled, such as near the existing foundations.

A labor-saving approach is to make the foundation-wall height a multiple of concrete-block courses (including the joints). The depth of the footing can be increased as necessary so that the wall will be made up of the desired number of blocks. For example, for the top of the foundation wall to be level with the first floor, it needs to be 4'-2" high. Concrete blocks are 8" high (including the thickness of the mortar joint). Six courses of concrete block will result in a 4' wall, leaving 2" to be built up. By increasing the depth of the footing by 2", you will have an even concrete-block module to work with. Instead of making the footing 10" deep, increase its depth to 12" (Ill. 3).

The stakes just driven represent the corners of the foundation walls. Footings, however, project a distance outside these walls, and their location has to be established. The extension-corner stakes are used as reference points. Let us assume that the extension has foundation walls that are 10" thick and 4'-0" high resting on footings 12" high (using the above example) and 20" wide (Ill. 4). From one corner stake (we'll call it stake A) measure the distance the footing projects outward from the foundation walls—that is, 5"—and add to this dimension the thickness of the form board you are using—that is, 1½" (a 2" board is actually 1½" thick). Be sure to make this measurement (6½") in both outward directions at each corner and drive a stake at each (Ill. 4). Repeat this procedure at all corners.

Follow this step by marking the height of the footing on one of the outside stakes—that is, 12"—and securing one end of the line to that level (Ill. 5). Repeat this at a second stake (stake B) and stretch the line tightly between them, making sure to check for levelness with a line level. Continue this process until all stakes are joined, delineating the perimeter of the footings (Ill. 6). Intermediate stakes are then driven a fraction of an inch away from the stretched line (Ill. 7). These stakes should be spaced no more than 2½' to 3½' apart. (Concrete is heavy. It is better to have an overstructured form than one that collapses during the pour.) When all stakes are driven, the mason's line can be removed.

It is time to nail the form boards to the stakes. (Make sure that the top of the board is in line with the previously marked height.) Nail one form board to the inside of the end stake and fasten the other end to an intermediate stake.

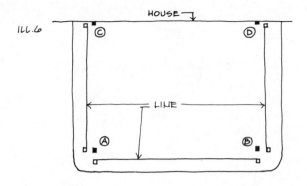

ILL.6

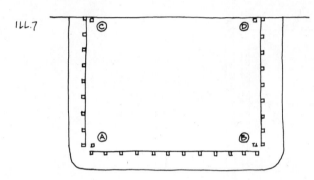

ILL.7

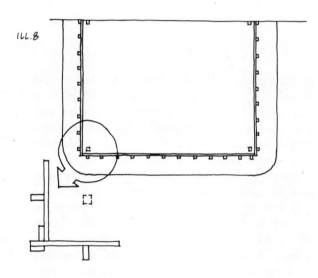

ILL.8

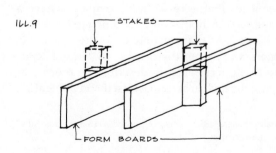

ILL.9

Check the top of the form board for levelness with the carpenter's level. Butt a second board against the first and repeat the same procedure. All the remaining boards are attached in this fashion until the outside perimeter is completed (Ill. 8). Again check for levelness. Once all the boards are nailed, cut the stake tops flush with the top of the forms. This is done to facilitate the leveling of the top of the footing when the concrete is poured (Ill. 9).

Building the Footing Forms—Inside Perimeter

To find the exact location of the inside footing form, measure the width of the footing—that is, 20"—and add to this dimension the thickness of the form material—that is, 1½". Measure 21½" in from the outside perimeter forms and drive a stake where the side and end measurements intersect (Ill. 10). The steps that follow are similar to those described for exterior-perimeter formwork. Measure and mark the footing height at an end stake, stretch a line between two corner stakes, locate intermediate stakes, and nail the boards. Using a carpenter's level, make sure that the inner and outer perimeter forms are level with one another (Ill. 11). The final product should look like a U (Ill. 12).

Preparing to Pour

There are two remaining tasks before pouring the concrete: first, preparing the ground surface to receive the concrete, and second, placing steel reinforcement bars in the formwork or trench. (These procedures must be done in that order. Once the steel bars are in place it is impossible to successfully prepare the ground.) Steel reinforcement bars are not always used for house footings. Unless specifically required by the local building code, footing reinforcement is optional. We recommend its use, however, as reinforcement provides insurance against settling problems.

Immediately before pouring the concrete, wet the base of the footing forms with a garden hose. Be sure not to overwater the forms and see to it that there are no remaining puddles when the concrete is poured. Wet down the soil bed (or, for that matter, any surfaces that come in contact with wet concrete or cement) to prevent the dry soil from absorbing the moisture in the concrete, which would cause it to lose strength. Tamp

Constructing
Foundations for
an Extension
245

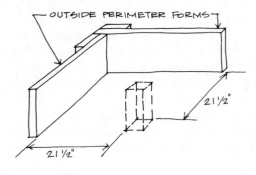

ILL. 10

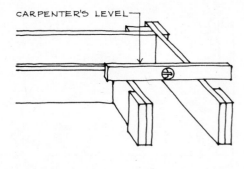

ILL. 11

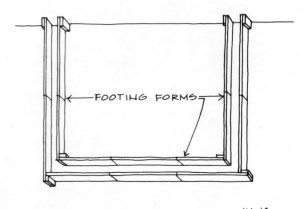

ILL. 12

(press) the earth down firmly with a square shovel and wet again.

Reinforcing bars are usually placed in the lower half of the footing. They must be held up in some way at their final positions (2″ from the bottom of the trench) until the concrete is poured. This temporary support may take a variety of forms. The most professional support is a small metal device called a chair (Ill. 13). A more primitive way of accomplishing the same end is to support the bars on small, thin pieces of masonry such as concrete block or brick. The recommended diameter of reinforcing bars is ½″, unless otherwise specified by local codes. When you have to join two lengths of reinforcement, the bars should overlap about 20″ (40 times the diameter of the bar). It is crucial that the bars are solidly joined where they overlap. Tie them securely together with wire (Ill. 14).

You are now ready to pour. Find out whether the work must be inspected by a building official before pouring; if so, schedule a date with an inspector. When planning the date of the pour, keep two things in mind. First, you will not be able to continue with the foundation work for a couple of days after the footing is poured. The

mixture needs sufficient time to set before the foundation walls can be started. Second, plan to pour in weather that is neither too hot nor too cold, since extreme temperatures can alter the setting process of concrete. Once these two factors have been taken into account, you can call the ready-mix company and have them deliver the quantity and quality of concrete needed.

A few tips on concrete pouring: Concrete is difficult to work with because it sets so fast. Have all the formwork ready before the truck arrives. Should the forms be located in such a way that the truck cannot reach them all, have one or two wheelbarrows, planks, and extra people available. The concrete can be poured from the wheelbarrow into the forms before it sets. The concrete is "worked" while the wheelbarrow goes to get another load. (Some ready-mix companies have a pumper which hooks on to a concrete truck and has a long hose that can deliver concrete up to 50′ or more away from the truck.)* "Working" concrete is the term used to describe the process of helping the mixture compact itself and preventing

*Be sure that the concrete is not poured so that it "free-falls" more than 3′ or 4′.

pockets or voids from forming. With the aid of a flat hoe or a spade, move the mixture at the center of the forms (the sides can be handled by lightly tapping the forms with a hammer). Be careful not to work the concrete excessively since this will tend to separate the materials within the mixture. Never add water to concrete to make it more workable after the initial mix. The water will seriously affect the strength of the concrete.

It is important that the concrete be evenly distributed within the forms. This is done by pouring the mixture at several points and spreading it to where it is needed with a garden rake or a hoe. Work the concrete into the forms by using a pointed trowel, moving it around to fill any depressions and get rid of any excess. To help the mixture flow into gaps and compact itself, tap the sides of the forms lightly with a hammer. The concrete at the top of the footing is leveled with a screed board (this can be any straight piece of wood that is longer than the footing is wide). With a person positioned on either side of the footing, move the board along the top of the form (Ill. 15).

To create a tie between the footing and the concrete-block wall, vertical reinforcing bars are used in the footings. These bars are placed at regular intervals (usually 2', but they vary according to code). The steel is inserted in the footing forms while the concrete is still plastic.

FOUNDATIONS

Erecting Concrete-Block Foundation Walls

Construction begins by reestablishing the building corners and snapping a chalk line between them on the footing as a guide to locate the first block course. In order to visualize any shifting or cutting that might be needed, set one row of blocks without mortar all around the footings. As you are doing this, keep in mind that the joint thickness is approximately ⅜". Most likely, you will find that some blocks need to be cut. Reposition the blocks until they successfully fit the wall length and mark the joint location on the footing with chalk. Then remove the blocks, leaving only the chalk mark behind.

The most important step is to carefully place the corner blocks. It's essential that these blocks be positioned correctly since they will act as a guide for the remaining wall construction. Lay a

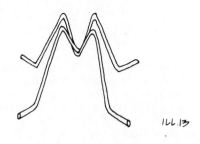

ILL.13

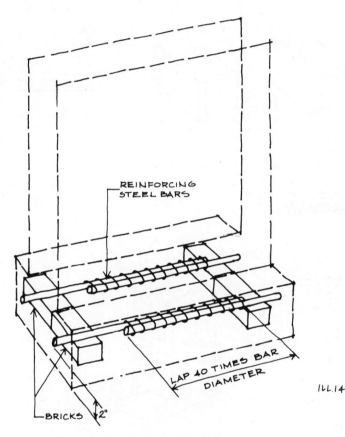

REINFORCING STEEL BARS

LAP 40 TIMES BAR DIAMETER

BRICKS 2"

ILL.14

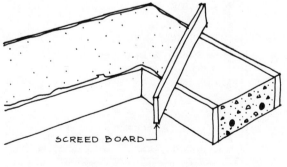

SCREED BOARD

ILL.15

Constructing Foundations for an Extension

247

The first course of block will be set directly over the footing and should rest on a full bed of mortar to ensure complete bonding. The second course will be set over block, and instead of being laid in a full bed, it is laid in a face shell bedding. This means that mortar is applied only to both edges of the block, leaving the core voids and webs undisturbed (below). Blocks must be bonded to each other not only by horizontal but also by vertical mortar joints. Applying mortar to the vertical

edges is referred to as buttering. The buttered block is placed in position (with the thick-webbed side facing up) by pushing downward and forward into the mortar bed (below).

The top block should be level with the mason's line. Should the block be much too high over the line, either there is too much mortar or the mixture is too stiff. On the other hand, if the mixture gives too quickly and the block sinks in, the cause is probably too much water. After a few blocks have

been placed, the correct alignment is checked with a level or straightedge. The excess mortar squeezed out of the side should be cut off (upward motion).

The last step in laying block is the tooling of the joints. This means compressing the mortar squeezed out of the joints tightly back into the joints and taking off the excess. Since tooling is not only for appearance but also for weathertightness, a concave joint is generally used.

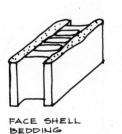

FACE SHELL
BEDDING

FULL
BEDDING

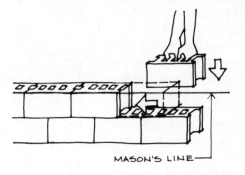

MASON'S LINE

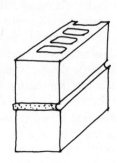

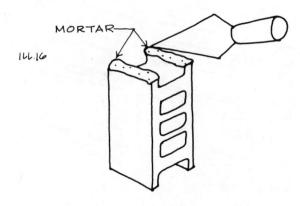

MORTAR

ILL. 16

full mortar bed at the footing corners (Inset II). Take one concrete block, stand it on end, and apply mortar to the end surface (Ill. 16). Picking it up by the webs, set it on the mortar bed. To ensure levelness, place a carpenter's level over the block and tap the block lightly with the trowel handle until the level's bubble is centered. Also see to it that the block is plumb and that it is directly at the building corner. Lay the remaining corner blocks in the same manner. To check for squareness, measure the diagonal distances between corner blocks. They should be equal. If they are not, adjust the corners accordingly. Most likely, relocating a corner block that might not be directly under the string intersection will be the solution (Ill. 17).

The second stage of construction is to build up the corners of the wall by laying three or four courses of block in half lap (Inset III). With the aid of a carpenter's level, make sure that the corners are plumb, level, and aligned. A story or course pole* might come in handy for checking whether the tops of the masonry courses are at the planned height. If they don't line up, the joints might have become excessively thick or thin. Every built-up corner must be the same height. Once all corners

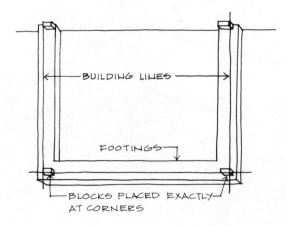

BUILDING LINES

FOOTINGS

BLOCKS PLACED EXACTLY
AT CORNERS

ILL. 17

The Construction
Process

248

*A story pole is a straight piece of wood used to check or transfer key dimensions easily.

are ready, the side walls are constructed with the aid of both a mason's line and the chalk line already drawn on the footing. Secure the mason's line to one built-up corner with a clip attached to the block (be careful that it is not attached to the mortar joint) and stretch it tightly between two of them (Ill. 18). This line serves as a guide to leveling the top edge of the block. (If the line is left overnight, watch out for sagging due to moisture.) The placement of the block on the line is gradually worked out by each individual. A good start, however, is to tip the block toward you so that you can see the edge of the block below. This way you can line it up with the new block by eye. Don't forget that every other course should be provided with horizontal joint reinforcement.

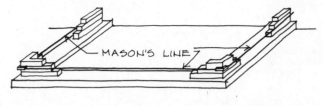

ILL. 18

The last course is made up of regular block with the cavities filled with concrete. To prevent the concrete being poured in the cores from falling all the way to the footing, a piece of metal lath is placed two courses before the last. Anchor bolts which go through two courses (tying the foundation wall to the extension's structure aboveground) are inserted in the filled block cores at approximately every 4' while the concrete is still plastic. They extend down into the foundation wall about the depth of two courses of block and sufficiently above the top course to go completely through the sill (about 3") (Ill. 19). Do not install anchor bolts where the plan calls for doors, sliding doors, posts, etc. Try to place them at the sides of openings.

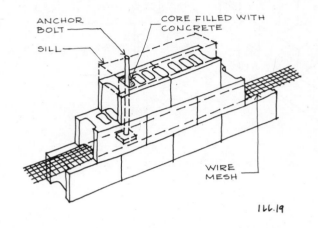

ILL. 19

Any openings for access into the crawl space, vents, pipes, sewer, girders, etc., should be planned out before construction begins by means of a scaled drawing. This advance planning will save you block cutting (which is not easy). Both the heights and the widths of all openings should occur in places that are multiples of 8" (assuming you are using 8" × 8" × 16" concrete block). The vents themselves should be multiples of 8" to fit these openings. (Ill. 20). Girder pockets can easily

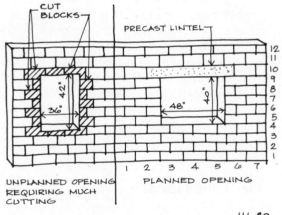

ILL. 20

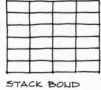
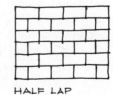

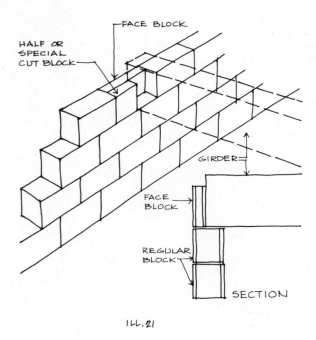

ILL. 21

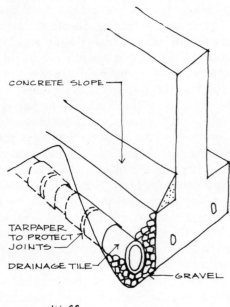

ILL. 22

be provided by using a face block (which is only 4" wide) and a half or special-cut block to fit around the girder and make the wall solid (Ill. 21). Since the girder transfers heavy loads to the wall at that particular point, it is important that the cores of all the blocks under the girder be filled with concrete.

The easiest way to bridge the gap left above vent openings is to use precast reinforced-concrete lintels. These lintels are available where you buy the blocks. Steel angles can also be used. They require periodic painting; otherwise, they will rust and fail.

Pier Foundations

You may need to use intermediary piers if the extension width is more than 16', or you may have chosen to build the extension entirely on piers. The two simplest methods of construction are with concrete blocks and with cardboard tubes.

CONCRETE BLOCK: If you choose this approach, footing pads are located and poured as described earlier. While the concrete is still plastic, four reinforcing bars are set in. Once the concrete sets, a double row of blocks is constructed over the footing (the reinforcing bars go through the cores in the block). The blocks are set in a full bed of mortar (the sides with the small openings

facing up). After laying a row, check for levelness before proceeding to the next course. Make sure all piers are the required height. Place the anchor bolts and fill all the cores with concrete.

CARDBOARD TUBES: In this method, the footings are poured and the vertical steel reinforcing bars placed in the footing while the concrete is still plastic. In order to hold these reinforcing bars in place, metal ties are wrapped around them. The pier reinforcement is then fabricated and tied to that projecting from the footing. Cardboard tubes (which act as the formwork) are then placed over the footing and the reinforcement. Stakes are driven into the ground and diagonal wood bracing is installed around the tube to hold it in place during the pour. A wood collar is placed on top of the tube to make it rigid. Concrete is then poured, vibrated, and the anchor bolts are set in place while the concrete is still plastic. When the concrete is fully set, the cardboard tubing can be peeled away. Steel brackets which act as the connection between the pier and the girders are attached to the anchor bolts.

BACKFILLING

The next step to complete the foundation work is backfilling. Before backfilling the excavation, however, the drainage tile should be installed. It lies directly adjacent to the bottom of the footing and follows the perimeter of the extension until it eventually connects to either the existing drainage tile or a separate dry well, storm sewer, or other means of water disposal. The tile should slope approximately ¼" or ½" per 10' of distance. Tiles are placed end to end, leaving only a small gap between them to allow the water to seep in. The gap is covered with tarpaper to avoid clogging by small stones and silt. Gravel or crushed stone is placed all around the tile. Perforated black plastic pipe may be used in place of drainage tile (Ill. 22).

You are now ready to backfill the excavation and level the inside of the crawl space. Here are a couple of pointers. Be careful of increased earth pressure against a tall unbraced wall. The pressure could knock down the wall. Since you are dealing with a crawl space, the lower wall should not create as much of a problem. You should still be careful. Another piece of advice: don't make the mistake of backfilling the excavation with an expansive soil such as clay or with topsoil. It hurts the drainage.

If you are building the extension in termite country, call in an exterminating company once the foundation work and backfilling have been completed (see Chapter 29, Inset I).

29

CONSTRUCTING AND MODIFYING THE FLOORS

Read this entire chapter on the construction of a new floor system whether you are building an extension or cutting into an existing floor. Even if you have had a good deal of carpentry experience, the more you know about how a house is framed, the less likely you will be to make a dangerous and costly error.

Tools

· Claw hammer
· Crosscut saw
· Power circular saw, stationary or portable
· Framing square or combination square
· Tape measure
· Scratch awl
· Drills (electric and hand)
· Wrench
· Carpenter's level
· Hacksaw
· Chalk-line reel
· Demolition equipment (see Inset I, page 234)
· Nailing gun
· Lath knife

Materials

If you are doing any new construction, and even if you are only framing an opening for a stair or a chimney, it is likely you will need some of the following:

FOR MOST CONSTRUCTION

· Nails: 6d (sixpenny), 10d, 12d, and 16d
· Joist stock, to be used for joists, headers, and trimmers. Specific dimensions and quantity are determined by examining the framing plan. Buy about 10 percent more to compensate for damaged or warped lumber
· Plywood or plyscore for the subflooring
· Timber connectors and joist hangers

FOR CONSTRUCTION OF AN EXTENSION

· All of the above and
· 2 × 6 lumber, pressure-treated for the sills. Order enough lumber to go around the extension's periphery twice. The lumber will inevitably have a considerable number of defects and some of it will have to be discarded
· Sill sealer
· Bolt nuts (to fit over the anchor bolts)
· 1¼ × 4 rough-sawn lumber for the cross bridging or additional joist stock for solid bridging

FOR DEMOLITION AND
RECONSTRUCTION

· Most of the above and
· 2 × 4, 2 × 6, and 4 × 4 lumber (can be used) for shoring

CONSTRUCTING THE FLOOR SYSTEM FOR AN EXTENSION

Examine your framing plan to determine the direction of the joist span and whether you will require a girder. If you are framing between new perimeter walls, you need not disturb the existing house until most of the floor is completed. Follow the instructions below.

If you are framing between the existing house and a new foundation wall, you will have to prepare the existing wall for the extension. Carefully mark off the length of the extension onto the existing siding and plan to remove the strip of siding and sheathing that is covering the existing header or trimmer (Ill. 1). If you are not sure of the depth of the existing header or trimmer, demarcate a strip about 10" high. Cut into the siding with a circular saw that is extended only to cut through the siding (you want to make sure you don't cut through into the header). If your existing siding is clapboard, make sure you have a smooth, flat guide for the saw. Use a worn carbide blade and watch out for nails. Pry off the siding using a utility bar. Repeat the step for the sheathing. You will frame the joists into the now exposed header (or trimmer) using joist hangers. Check the condition of the existing header and sill. If they are rotted, you will have to replace them. If the header consists of short pieces of lumber, you will have to remove and replace it. If the header is not properly secured to the sill and the existing joists, make those connections. The new joists of the extension will frame into the existing header with joist hangers (Ill. 2).

The Girders

A built-up girder is constructed out of three or more pieces of 2" joist material of appropriate depth. Remember that the joints between the segments of lumber must be staggered and should always be over a support (Ill. 3). Line up the first three pieces of wood, sandwiching the shorter piece in between the longer ones. Nail the individual sections of the built-up girder together using 10d nails. Continue nailing on one side and, when complete, turn the sandwich over and nail the other side. It is important to nail the section together so that the girder acts structurally as one unit (Ill. 4).

The built-up girder (or solid section, depending on what is specified in your framing plan) must be set into the pocket framed in the foundations.

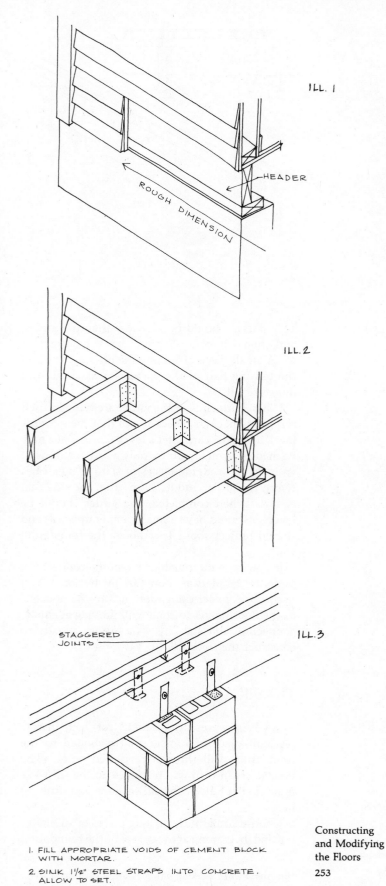

ILL. 1

ROUGH DIMENSION

HEADER

ILL. 2

ILL. 3

STAGGERED JOINTS

1. FILL APPROPRIATE VOIDS OF CEMENT BLOCK WITH MORTAR.
2. SINK 1½" STEEL STRAPS INTO CONCRETE. ALLOW TO SET.
3. CONSTRUCT AND POSITION GIRDER.
4. DRILL HOLES THROUGH STRAP, GIRDER AND LAG BOLT.

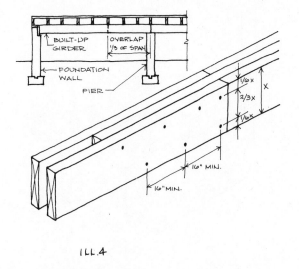

ILL.4

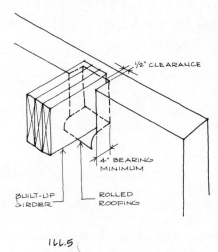

ILL.5

This pocket should be 1" wider than the girder, and should have a minimum bearing surface of 4". A small piece of roofing membrane is put on the bearing part of the pocket for absorption of moisture (Ill. 5).

When both ends of the girder are lying in their respective pockets, check to see that the girder is level, using the carpenter's level. Corrections may be made (if you are off by only a few fractions of an inch) by wedging pieces of slate or metal between the girder and its support on the side that is low. When completed, the girder should be level (or should have a small camber upward) and should project about 1½" above the foundation wall.

If you have intermediate supports, connect the girder to the piers as shown in Illustration 3. You need not connect the girder ends to the pockets, as the flooring yet to come will provide adequate connection and stability. You are now ready to construct the floor (Ill. 6).

The Sill

The sill is a pressure-treated,* rot- and insect-resistant piece of lumber that is bolted to the foundation wall through predrilled holes. (The floor joists in turn will be nailed to the sill.) We must first cut all of the sill sections and drill the holes.

Choose straight, clean, long pieces of sill material and, beginning at the corner of the foundation

*Be careful when working with pressure-treated wood. Wear gloves and consult your health department regarding the proper inhalation protection.

wall, lay the sill alongside the anchor bolts (Ill. 7). Place the combination square's handle on the side of the wood away from the bolts and transfer the marks as shown in Illustration 8. The anchor bolts will not be in perfect alignment with one another. Be sure to measure the distance from the outside of the foundation wall to each bolt and measure that same distance onto the lumber being used for the sill (Ill. 8). Be sure that all of the sill sections butt each other squarely. Mark the sill sections and the foundation wall so that you will know where each section fits and remove the sill sections. Drill ¾"-diameter holes at the points marked. (Although the bolts are only ½" in diameter, drill a slightly larger hole to compensate for small miscalculations.) Notch the sill around the projection of the girder (Ill. 9).

When all of the sill sections are marked and drilled, replace the sections and make sure they fit. Once again remove the sill sections and position the termite shields, if you are going to use them (Inset I). Apply the roll of sill sealer to the top of the foundation wall, snipping or puncturing the holes for the bolts. This material, normally 1" thick, will compress to approximately ⅛" or less when the joists are installed. The sill sealer will protect against insects, air infiltration, and dust.

Reposition the precut, predrilled sill sections and check to see if they are level. If there are gaps, fill them with grout. Grout can be used to some extent to level the top of the foundation wall. When the grout is dry, apply the nuts and washers to the bolts and tighten. Check again for levelness. (Accommodations can be made to raise portions of the sill slightly by loosening the bolts and wedging slate scraps under the sill.)

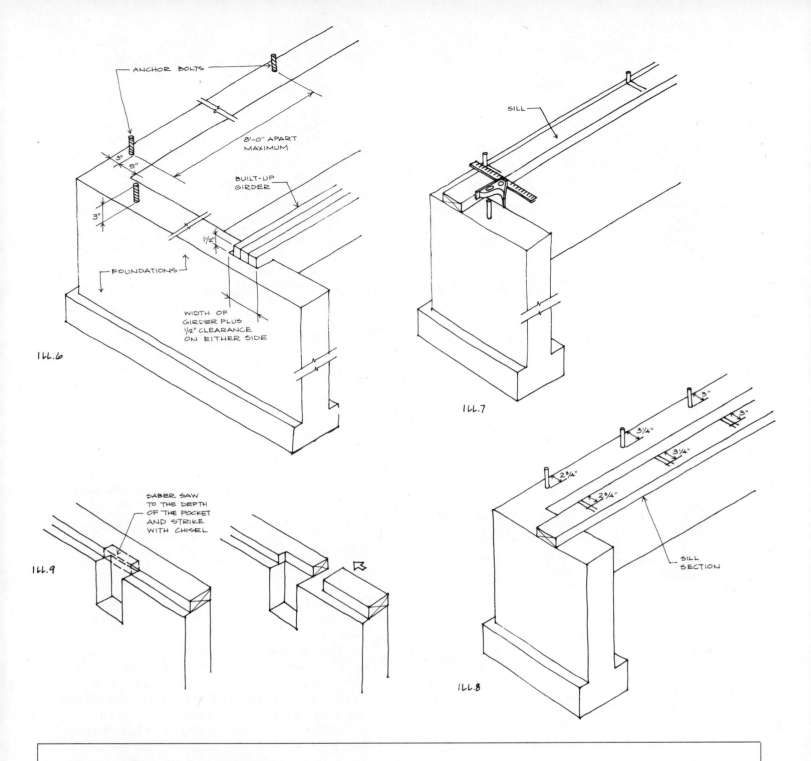

ILL.6

ANCHOR BOLTS

8'-0" APART MAXIMUM

BUILT-UP GIRDER

3"

5"

3"

1/2"

FOUNDATIONS

WIDTH OF GIRDER PLUS 1/2" CLEARANCE ON EITHER SIDE

SILL

ILL.7

ILL.9

SABER SAW TO THE DEPTH OF THE POCKET AND STRIKE WITH CHISEL

3"

3"

3 1/4"

3 1/4"

2 3/4"

2 3/4"

SILL SECTION

ILL.8

INSET 1/TERMITE PROTECTION

Most areas in the United States are subject to termite infestation. To prevent the invasion of these wood-eating insects:

1. Use pressure-treated sills, which resist insect damage and also protect against wet- and dry-rot damage. (Alternatively, use redwood heartwood or cedar heartwood.)

2. In the past termite shields were used extensively, but since the shield is one of the first elements to be installed after the foundation, it is subject to damage that tends to reduce its effectiveness. In theory, a termite or other insect would not be able to negotiate an undamaged termite shield. A series of dents or irregularities in the shield, however, would serve as a pathway for these wood chewers. Therefore, be very careful that you do not damage the shields when you backfill. Chemical treatment of the soil is the alternative to termite shields. Check with local building de-partment and environmental authorities to find out which chemicals, if any, are considered safe and are permissible in your community. In addition, have a reliable exterminator install the chemicals.

3. In areas where termites are not a major problem the careful installation of a termite shield may be considered a form of insect insurance.

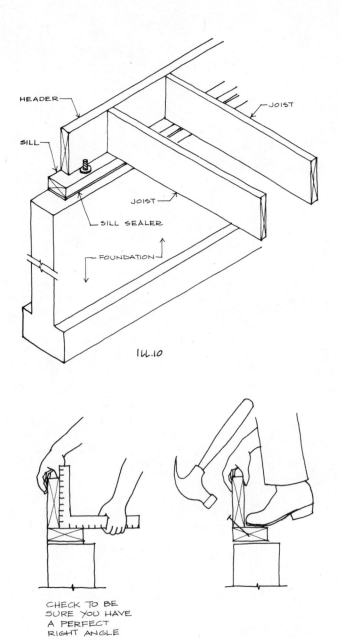

HEADER

JOIST

SILL

JOIST

SILL SEALER

FOUNDATION

ILL.10

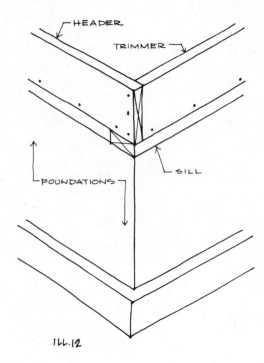

HEADER

TRIMMER

SILL

FOUNDATIONS

ILL.12

CHECK TO BE
SURE YOU HAVE
A PERFECT
RIGHT ANGLE

ILL.11

Headers and Trimmers

A section of joist called the header, which the rest of the joists will abut, is set on the sill (Ill. 10). The last joist on either side of a run of joists is called the trimmer. Together and in conjunction with the sill they enclose the platform floor.

Working flush with the exterior edge of the sill, toe-nail the header to the sill every 16″ using 12d nails (Ill. 11). Make sure that the sill and the headers are at right angles before nailing. Check the framing plan for special details, such as a cantilever, which may eliminate the need for a header in that location, before completing the work.

When the sill turns a corner, be sure to nail the header to the trimmer as shown in Illustration 12.

Marking Off the Joists onto the Headers

The perimeter is complete and now we have to mark the location of the joists onto the headers. Study the floor-framing plan carefully. We will use the lap-joint detail for joining the joists over the girder (see Chapter 21, Ill. 9) and we will hang the joists onto the existing house's header at the other end of the span. The simplest way to mark the joists on the sill is to create a template (also called a story pole). To make a story pole, first find a very straight, long (about 8′) piece of lumber, then measure and mark off the exact demarcations with a tape measure and pencil. Using a combination square (or a framing square), draw lines across the width of the template perpendicular to the edge (Ill. 13). The template will have evenly spaced markings 16″ (or 12″ or 24″) apart on it. It will be used when you have a clear run of joists without interruption. If you have special conditions, such as the doubling of the joist for a partition or to frame an opening, you can mark these special conditions with an X or a different-colored pencil (Ill. 14).

The next step is to transfer the markings from

the template to the header. Measure 15¼" along the header from the corner where the header meets the trimmer. Then lay the template on the sill along the header and transfer the 16" demarcations onto the header. The reason that we first measured a 15¼" spacing is in anticipation of the installation of the subfloor. The subfloor material comes in 4' × 8' sheets. We want the end of the sheet to lie on the center line of the joist (Ill. 15). Use the combination square as an aid in transferring the marks. On the side of the mark closest to the header draw an X. This X mark is a convention used by carpenters to indicate on which side of the mark the joist is to be set.

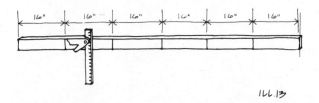

ILL. 13

The template may be used along the rest of the header, marking off the 16" demarcations. Most likely there will be some framing details, such as openings for stairs and the doubling of joists under partitions and bathtubs, that will interfere with this even line of joists. Check the framing plan. Mark the exact location of any additional joists onto the header. Transfer the mark onto the template using a contrasting-colored pencil. Be sure to draw an X indicating on which side of the line the joist is to be placed. Be sure to write the word "start" on the end of the template nearest to the trimmer, so that you will not be confused as to which end of the template is the beginning and which is the end when you start to mark the girder.

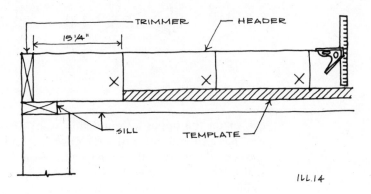

ILL. 14

To mark the girder, transfer the marks from the template onto the girder. When marking the adjacent row of joists (that go from the girder to the other foundation wall), remember that we are using a lap joint over the girder. The joists will not lie in exactly the same places as on the first foundation wall (Ill. 16).

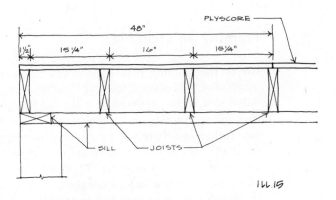

ILL. 15

Installing the Joists

If you are using joist hangers, nail them to the header so that the top of the joists will be level with the top of the header (Ill. 17).

Select the joist lumber. If the joist is to lap over the girder, the exact length isn't important as long as the end sits completely over the girder. The squareness of the cut is not crucial either; that is the advantage of this joint. (If you are using a butt joint, rather than lapping over the girder, or if you are spanning between headers, it is necessary to measure and cut the joists precisely.) When cutting the joists or any other members that must be cut in multiples, be sure to cut only one or two pieces first to make sure that they fit. Set the joist on the sill and on the girder (or in the joist hang-

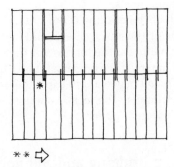

*NOTE: IF THE FRAMING PLAN SPECIFIES JOISTS SPACED 16" O.C., KEEP IN MIND THAT THIS IS A MINIMUM SPACING. YOU COULD ALWAYS MAKE THE SPACING SMALLER THAN 16" O.C., IN ONE OR TWO CASES WHERE IT IS CONVENIENT. WHEN IN DOUBT, THROW IN AN EXTRA JOIST FOR INSURANCE, YOU'LL SLEEP BETTER AT NIGHT. (DOUBLE UP JOISTS UNDER TUBS.)

** ⇨ JOIST LOCATION SHIFTS THE WIDTH OF THE JOISTS.

ILL. 16

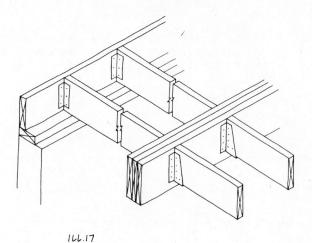

ILL.17

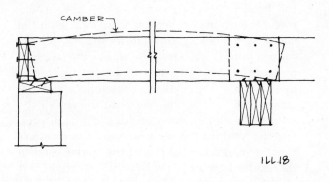

CAMBER

ILL.18

ers, or on the opposite foundation wall). If the joist has a slight camber (desirable) set it with the convex side up (Ill. 18), as the weight of the floor will rectify the camber. Be sure that the joist is right on the line that was so painstakingly marked with the combination square to ensure its being perpendicular to the sill. Nail the joist to the header with three 20d nails.

Framing an Opening

Check the framing plan for the exact size and location of the opening. Install the run of joists on either side of the opening, leaving out the joists that will span the opening and the joists on either side (otherwise there will be no room to swing a hammer). Install the inside trimmers first just as you would ordinary joists (Ill. 19). Mark the location of the four header joists on the trimmers. Cut the header joists to size and install the outside headers. Finally, install the outside trimmers, the crippled joists, and the inside headers, in that order. The stability of the entire system depends on the accuracy of your measurements and on the squareness of the joists.

If the length of the opening is not running parallel to the line of the joists, care should be taken to beef up the nailing at the junction of the headers and the trimmers. If the opening is particularly long (over 10′), you may want to triple the header and triple the trimmer. The section should be calculated as if it were a girder.

Installing the Bridging and Subfloor

Although wood cross bridging is more economical of material than solid bridging, it is much less

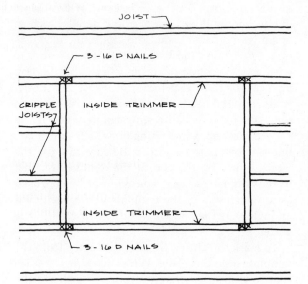

JOIST

3 - 16 D NAILS

CRIPPLE JOISTS

INSIDE TRIMMER

INSIDE TRIMMER

3 - 16 D NAILS

STEP 1

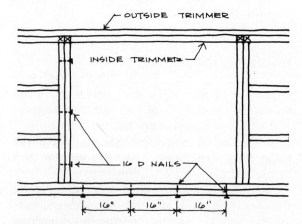

OUTSIDE TRIMMER

INSIDE TRIMMER

16 D NAILS

16″ 16″ 16″

STEP 2

NOTE: LEAVE OUT THE JOISTS ADJACENT TO THE OPENING, UNTIL THE OPENING HAS BEEN FRAMED. OTHERWISE THERE WILL BE NO ROOM TO SWING A HAMMER.

ILL.19

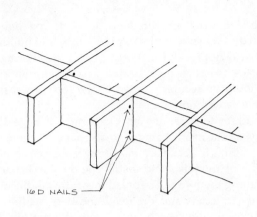

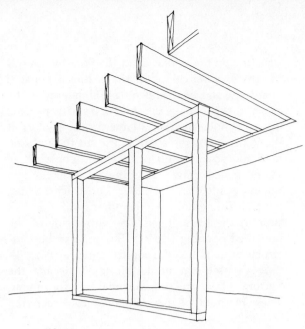

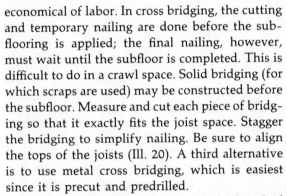

ILL. 20

ILL. 21

economical of labor. In cross bridging, the cutting and temporary nailing are done before the sub-flooring is applied; the final nailing, however, must wait until the subfloor is completed. This is difficult to do in a crawl space. Solid bridging (for which scraps are used) may be constructed before the subfloor. Measure and cut each piece of bridging so that it exactly fits the joist space. Stagger the bridging to simplify nailing. Be sure to align the tops of the joists (Ill. 20). A third alternative is to use metal cross bridging, which is easiest since it is precut and predrilled.

Plywood subflooring ⅝" or ¾" thick is laid with the grain of the outer plies at right angles to the joists. Subflooring is nailed with 10d nails (a better choice may be barbed, screw-type, or resin-coated nails) to each joist every 6" along the edges of the panel and every 10" for the intermediate joists.

Constructing the Second Floor

The second floor or any subsequent floor or balcony is constructed in much the same way as outlined above. The difference is that the header and joists are nailed to the top plate of the wall rather than to the sill.

MODIFYING THE FLOOR OF AN EXISTING HOUSE

It is likely that you will want to cut into the existing floor for a stair or chimney. If you have a choice, make the opening so that its length is parallel to the run of the joists.

For a stair or similar opening, first expose the

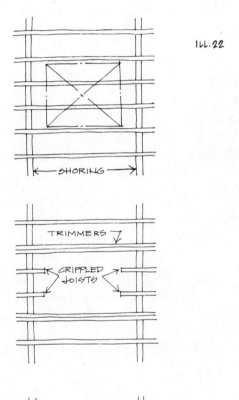

ILL. 22

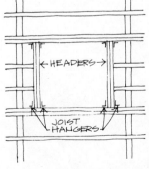

Constructing
and Modifying
the Floors

259

structure on the underside of the floor by removing the existing ceiling. If the ceiling is gypsum board, the size of the opening will determine the tool you use to make the cut. For a small opening, use a keyhole saw. For a larger opening, start at the joint and, using a lath knife, cut through the tape and spackle and remove the whole piece. With a pencil, draw the outline of the opening on the underside of the subfloor. Construct shoring, which is (more or less) a temporary wall that will support the lines of joists on either side of the projected opening (Ill. 21). Shoring can be constructed out of 4 × 4's spaced about 2' apart, with 2 × 4's used for the double top plate and the bottom plate and as diagonal reinforcement. These temporary supports may be constructed in sections that are tilted up, leveled, and tightly wedged or shimmed into place. (In an old building that is not level, it is best to build the shoring in place, so that it is properly secured.) Shoring should be securely nailed to the joists to ensure that it will not slip out.

Refer to "Framing an Opening" on page 258. Install the inside trimmer joists that will frame the opening (Ill. 22). Cut and remove the center portion of the joists and install the outside headers, nailing them to the crippled joists. Install the outside trimmers and the inside headers, nailing all securely. Slip joist hangers from the bottom. Finally, cut through the subfloor and the finished floor.

30

CONSTRUCTING AND MODIFYING THE WALLS AND PARTITIONS

This chapter covers the construction of new walls and partitions for the extension or the existing house and the cutting of openings into existing ones. The preliminary design of load-bearing and non-load-bearing walls and partitions is covered in Chapter 22. Most interior partitions are constructed of 2 × 4 studs. The extension's exterior walls, however, should be constructed of 2 × 6's to allow for at least 5½" of insulation.

Tools

For demolition and carpentry tools, see Chapter 29 and the Introduction to Demolition and Construction.

Materials

· 2 × 4's and/or 2 × 6's for the studs and plates. Wall sections are constructed primarily of 2 × 4 and 2 × 6 stud stock. Most lumberyards stock lumber that is stamped "stud" at the end. Usually this lumber is of slightly poorer quality than the joist or beam material, but it is adequate for the job since most of the loads we will be supporting will be compressive. Try to purchase the studs at exactly the length you will need or a little bit longer. For the posts hidden in walls we will need thicker sections, either 4 × 4's or two 2 × 6's of better quality, or composite sections built up of 2 × 4's or 2 × 6's
· 4' × 8' plywood sheathing for the outside walls
· Window and door headers, if required
· Nails: 6d, 8d, 10d, 16d

CONSTRUCTING NEW WALLS AND PARTITIONS

LAYING OUT THE EXTENSION'S EXTERIOR WALLS: Take a long tape and a spool of chalk line to one side of the platform floor and measure inward 5½" (or 3½" if you are constructing 2 × 4 exterior stud walls) for the width of the sole plate. Snap a chalk line along the exterior wall at the 5½" (or 3½") line (line A on Ill. 1). Do the same for the adjacent exterior wall.

LOCATING THE PARTITIONS: Locate the first partition by measuring the actual dimension of the room (let us say 11') and add ½" or ⅝" each for the gypsum board of both exterior wall and interior partition. (If you are locating a partition in the existing house, you need only add for the new partition.) This is the real dimension between the sole plates. Draw an X on the far side of the chalk line to remind you which side gets the plate. Be careful in laying out the sole-plate locations. There may be some partitions that need to be wider than the usual 2 × 4 stud width to accommodate pipes in the wall or built-in shelves.

LAYING OUT THE TILT-UP SECTIONS: It is easiest to construct short sections of the wall (about 6' to 8' in length) and then tilt them up into place. Longer sections of wall are practical if you have the labor to lift them in place. If you build the walls in sections, determine where the breaks will be. Organize the breaks so that they do not

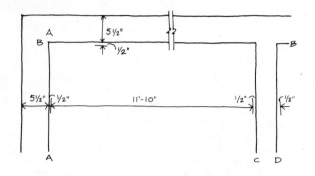

ILL. 1

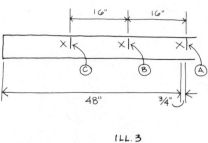

ILL. 3

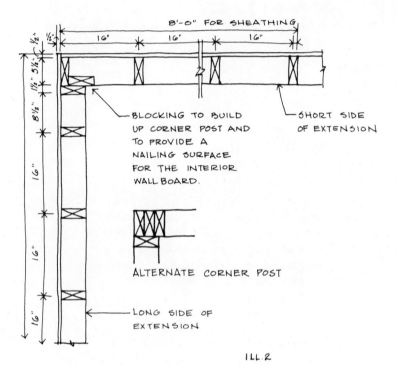

BLOCKING TO BUILD UP CORNER POST AND TO PROVIDE A NAILING SURFACE FOR THE INTERIOR WALL BOARD.

SHORT SIDE OF EXTENSION

ALTERNATE CORNER POST

LONG SIDE OF EXTENSION

ILL. 2

fall in the middle of a door or window, but between these openings.

For the extension's exterior walls, cut the sole plate and lay it around the perimeter edges of the platform, even under doors and sliding glass doors. Tack the plates down at each edge so that they will not shift off position. (Tacking is temporary nailing—you do not hammer the nails all the way down to the wood.) Next construct the corner posts. Corner posts can be arranged in a number of ways as shown in Illustration 2. For the extension, we suggest that you assemble the wall sections first, raise them into position, and then build up the corner posts by joining the sections and adding blocking as shown in Illustration 2. Keep in mind that there we will eventually apply sheathing to these sections which will cover the corner post and add rigidity to the structure.

(Some carpenters build the corner posts as part of one of the tilt-up sections. The topmost plate is later lapped over the lower top plate.)

To lay out the studs on the exterior wall of the extension, start at the corner of a long wall and measure 48" (the width of a sheet of plywood). Add ¾" to the 48" so that the sheathing will be centered on the 1½"-wide stud (Ill. 3). Mark the plate (point A). From that mark measure back 16" and then another 16" and place X's on the side of the marks closest to the corner. From point A outward mark the plate every 16" and add your X's, regardless of where the openings fall. (The plates under the doors will be cut away.)

Having completed the stud markings on the first long side of the extension, cross over to the parallel exterior wall and mark the studs on that side. For the perpendicular wall follow a similar procedure. Mark 8' from the corner of the house plus ¾" and then mark back 16" and then another 16". The distance between the first and second studs in from the corner will be short (only 8½", see Ill. 2), but the sheathing will eventually cover and join the entire corner. When you get to the ends of the walls, be sure that there is a stud 8' from the corner to nail the sheathing to. Since sheathing is so important to the stability of the structure, we want a full-sized piece of sheathing at the corner. It is likely that you will have to make adjustments in the stud spacing and will be required to cut at least one sheet of sheathing down.

New partitions are laid out in a similar manner. Where walls intersect partitions, remember to provide a nailing surface for the gypsum board (Ill. 4).

LAYING OUT THE WALL AND PARTITION OPENINGS: Using a red pencil (so that these markings will stand out from the others), measure and locate both sides of the door and window rough openings and mark them. The rough opening is a bit different from the size of the window, so check the manufacturer's literature to verify. Indicate the location of the inside trimmers, the studs that will support the header, by writing "IT" on the outside of these red marks. Then 1½" beyond write "OT" to indicate the location of the outside trimmers. Add a red "C" to the X's marking the stud locations within the opening, to indicate that they will be cut (or "crippled") (Ills. 5 and 6).

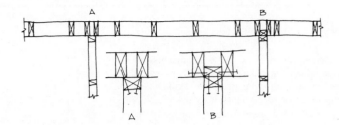

ILL.4

LAYING OUT THE INTERSECTIONS OF PARTITIONS, AND PARTITIONS AND WALLS: Special provisions should be made where the partitions abut the walls. The sturdiest accommodation is made by adding two or more studs as shown in Illustration 4B. It is essential that the partitions have sturdy nailing surfaces.

If you are abutting a new partition to an existing one, make sure there is a stud in the existing wall or partition at the point of juncture. If there is no stud to nail your new load-bearing construction to, you will have to remove the gypsum board and install a few studs at that point. If the partition is non-load-bearing and in a noncritical area, you may be able to nail your new stud into the sole and top plates of the abutting partition.

ASSEMBLING THE TILT-UP SECTIONS: For the top plates cut pieces of 2 × 6 (or 2 × 4) to the lengths of the sole plates. Transfer all of the markings from the sole plates to the top plates by laying the loose pieces of lumber side by side with the sections that are tacked down and transferring marks with a carpenter's square. Remove the tacks from the sole plates and move the matching pairs to a level spot.

Determine the length of the studs and cut them down to size. Be sure to cut the ends at perfect right angles. Once you cut one stud you can use it as a template to measure the other full-length studs. Position the full-length studs as indicated by the X's on the sole plate and nail top and bottom to the plates using two 16d nails. Make sure the assembly is square. Tack diagonal bracing to the frame and completely nail the studs to the plates.

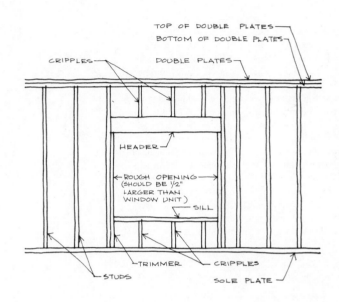

ILL.5

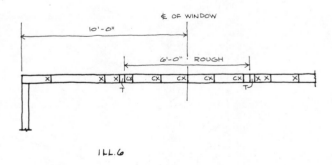

ILL.6

CONSTRUCTING TILT-UP SECTIONS WITH ROUGH OPENINGS: For each window, position the studs that will be used as the outside trimmers and nail them to the OT marks on the plates. Measure and cut the inside trimmers to the height of the rough opening (Ill. 5); cut and nail them to the red IT's on the plates. Measure the distance between the trimmers and cut the sill. On the inside trimmers, measure to the bottom of the rough opening and install the sill. Measure the header lumber and assemble the header (Inset I). Position the header on top of the inside trimmers and nail to both the outside and inside trimmers. Measure and cut the crippled studs for the top and bottom of the rough opening and nail into place. Check for squareness. Tack 1 × 4 tempo-

INSET I/HEADERS

There are many openings in the wall of a house—for windows, doors, pass-throughs, and so on. Since many walls and partitions are load-bearing, some provision has to be made for the transfer of loads over and around these openings. The header, which is framed over the window opening, acts as a beam to transfer the loads to the trimmer studs. The header can be made up of beam material (4 × 6's or 4 × 8's), but it is more economical to build up this piece out of two or three pieces of 2" material (two 2 × 8's or two 2 × 10's). For 3½" walls place two pieces of joist material on edge. Since each piece is 1½" thick, a continuous ½" piece of plywood is nailed in between as blocking to bring the composite width up to the width of the 3½" studs and trimmer. For a 5½" stud you can use three pieces of joist stock. Nail two of them together and fill the space between them and the third piece with blocking. Very often the distance between the header and the double plates is too short to justify the placement of crippled studs. In such cases an oversized header is often used that fills in the space from the top of the window to the plates. The length of the header is equal to the rough opening plus the width of the trimmers (1½" × 2" pieces of trimmers). If the header is longer than 6' you might consider tripling the trimmer so that the header rests on two trimmers on either side.

Recommended Header Sizes

Rough Opening	Header Depth (use two or three pieces)
up to 3'-0"	2 × 6's
3'-6" to 5'-6"	2 × 8's
5'-6" to 7'-6"	2 × 10's
7'-6" to 8'-6"	2 × 12's

PLYWOOD

JOIST STOCK

SPACER BLOCKS

NOTE: IT IS A GOOD IDEA TO USE OVERSIZED HEADERS THAT GO FROM THE TOP OF THE WINDOW TO THE PLATES. THIS AVOIDS THE CONSTRUCTION OF CRIPPLES ABOVE THE HEADER.

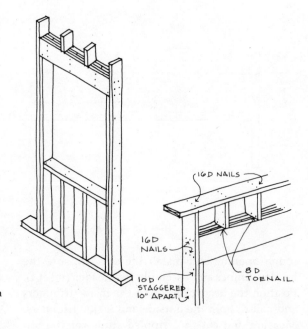

16D NAILS

16D NAILS

10D STAGGERED 10" APART

8D TOENAIL

ILL. 7

rary diagonal bracing to the studs. Make sure that all parts of the assembly are securely nailed, using the nailing details in Illustration 7.

RAISING THE TILT-UP SECTIONS: You may need a few friends to help raise the tilt-up sections. Be sure the sole plates are resting on the correct side of the chalk lines. With a few temporary nails, tack the sole plate to the platform floor, and brace it with 2 × 4's as shown in Illustration 8. Before the wall sections are secured permanently, they will have to be plumbed. This is best accomplished after all of the wall sections are completed.

ASSEMBLING THE CORNERS: When all of the sections are completed and temporarily braced, the corners are plumbed and permanently nailed. For the corners of the extension (Ill. 9), one piece of wall section should come flush with the outside of the platform. The other, intersecting section should butt up against it. A third stud length should be cut and positioned between the two, as shown. This stud not only stabilizes the corner

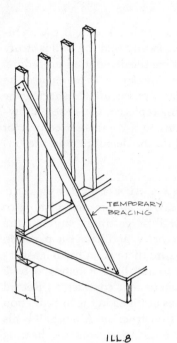

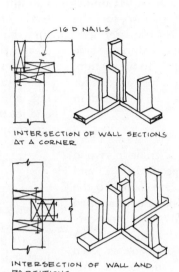

16 D NAILS

INTERSECTION OF WALL SECTIONS AT A CORNER

INTERSECTION OF WALL AND PARTITIONS

TEMPORARY BRACING

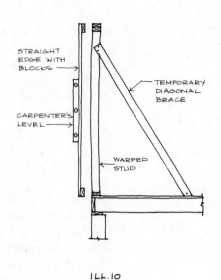

STRAIGHT EDGE WITH BLOCKS

CARPENTER'S LEVEL

TEMPORARY DIAGONAL BRACE

WARPED STUD

ILL. 10

ILL. 8

ILL. 9

but also provides a nailing surface for the interior gypsum board.

SECURING THE TILT-UP SECTIONS: The walls can be plumbed with a plumb bob or with a carpenter's level. The short carpenter's level should be used in conjunction with a long straightedge so that the full height of the wall can be checked. Often there is a slight warp in the stud and the straightedge does not lie flat on the surface of the wall. To rectify this problem, attach blocks to the ends of the straightedge so that the middle section of the straightedge can stand an inch or more off the wall (Ill. 10). Adjust the braces until the sections are plumb.

When all are plumb, and the corners nailed firmly together, nail the top plate of the double plates (Ill. 11) onto the assembled-in-place walls and partitions. Be sure to use the top of the two plates to span the breaks between sections and to connect the partitions to the walls.

Once the walls are leveled and joined by the top plate, the sole plate should be nailed securely to the platform. Be sure to nail the plate into the joists beneath the subfloor. The line of the joists can be found by looking for the nail pattern on the floor. It is important to nail the sole plate to the joists and not merely to the subfloor. Make sure there are at least two nails from the plate to each joist. If you feel that the wall is moving as you nail, you know that the braces are not secure enough.

The interior partitions that are to receive gyp-

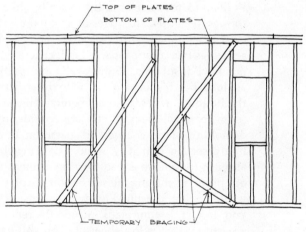

TOP OF PLATES
BOTTOM OF PLATES

TEMPORARY BRACING

NOTE: POSTPONE THE PLACING OF THE TOP OF THE TWO UPPER PLATES UNTIL THE PARTITIONS ARE COMPLETE. THIS WAY THE TOP PLATE CAN OVERLAP THE PARTITION AND THE WALL.

DOUBLE PLATE OVER CORNER

ILL. 11

sum board or wood paneling will be left unfinished for the time being to allow for the placement of mechanical and electrical services. Some carpenters apply gypsum board to one side of the partition to provide stability to the section, while leaving the other side open. Instructions for the finishing of the partitions can be found in Chapter 32.

APPLYING THE SHEATHING TO THE EXTENSION'S WALLS: The exterior-grade plywood used for sheathing is usually specified at ½" and ⅝" thick. The 4' × 8' sheets are nailed to the studs using 6d nails. The sheathing can be applied either lengthwise or horizontally, with most carpenters finding the horizontal application the easiest. Remember that the plywood is used structurally to stabilize the construction. Although there are other products on the market that are called sheathing, we recommend plywood because of its intrinsic strength.

DEMOLISHING AND RECONSTRUCTING WALLS AND PARTITIONS

Walls and partitions are intrinsically alike. The former separates the exterior from the interior (and is equipped with insulation) and the latter separates two interior spaces (and, generally, does not have insulation). Some walls and partitions are load-bearing and are critical to the structure of the building, whereas some merely delineate one room from the next. If you are considering the demolition of either a wall or a partition, be absolutely certain that it is *not* load-bearing. If you attempt to remove a load-bearing element without properly shoring the surrounding structure, it is likely that the building will collapse around you. In fact, if your plans include the removal of a partition that is load-bearing, you will have to see to it that a girder and posts or columns are substituted for the structural partition to be removed. Even if your plans include the cutting of relatively small openings for doors or windows into existing load-bearing walls or partitions, you will have to make sure that special provisions are made to carry the loads around the openings. (See Chapters 16 and 22 for information on structural walls and partitions.)

The removal of a load-bearing wall is so potentially dangerous we strongly suggest that you hire a licensed professional to determine the structural or nonstructural nature of any partition or wall

you intend to remove or break into. If the architect or engineer advises you that the wall is structural, have him outline the demolition procedure, design the beam or lintel that is to replace the partition, and devise a procedure for shoring the wall while it is being replaced. Give these drawings and instructions to a competent contractor and let the experts do the demolition and reconstruction.

DEMOLISHING A NON-LOAD-BEARING WALL OR PARTITION: Before demolishing or cutting into any wall or partition, shut off the water, gas, and electricity, and have the partition inspected to make sure there is no hidden asbestos. (If asbestos is found, have it removed by a licensed asbestos-abatement contractor.) Reread all of the precautions outlined in the Introduction to Demolition and Construction. Almost all walls and partitions have electrical conduit, heating ducts, or pipes running in them. Provisions must be made to cap and/or relocate all of these services. Consult Chapters 33, 34, and 35 (plumbing, heating, and electrical) for instructions.

Since every demolition situation is different, we can only outline the procedure generally. It is best to first remove the plaster, mesh, and lath or the gypsum board from the studs or masonry so that you can get at the wires and pipes in the wall. The gypsum board is removed by cutting the taped joint with a lath knife and prying the sheet from the studs. Plaster on wood or gypsum lath is removed by using a sledgehammer and a crowbar. (Plaster mounted on wire lath is demolished in two steps. First, the plaster is stripped off the lath. Next, the lath is pried or cut off the studs or blocks.) Cap, remove, or relocate all of the services in the wall.

If you have stud walls, carefully remove the existing structure by cutting the studs at one or two points and twisting the ends out. For a non-load-bearing partition made of gypsum block (often found in old apartment buildings) or lightweight cement block, you will need a sledgehammer. Remember to begin demolition at the top to prevent the wall from falling on you, and don't store the heavy rubble in one place on the floor, unless you are sure the area can take the load.

CREATING AN OPENING IN AN EXISTING STUD WALL OR PARTITION: If you are creating an opening in a load-bearing wall* (or partition) for an arch (or window), the procedure

---

*If your opening is wider than 6' have a licensed professional outline the procedure for demolition and reconstruction.

differs from the one outlined above. In this case you must be sure that the header, lintel, or beam that will span the new opening is strong enough to take on the wall and joist loads now supported by the partition to be removed. Also, you may have to reinforce the floor or wall *below* the opening's end supports to receive the increased load. If the new opening's end supports are not directly supported by a joist or stud under the subfloor, use solid blocking to span the gap between adjacent joists or studs.

Since you will be temporarily weakening the wall supporting the floor (or roof) system *above* your head, you will have to provide temporary shoring to support the joists framing into that wall. In the case of a partition between two rooms, you will have to provide shoring on *both* sides to pick up the joist loads (Ill. 12). Shoring is a temporary frame wall consisting of 4 × 4's (or double 2 × 4's)* built about 2' from the bearing wall or partition.

First remove the plaster or gypsum board covering the wall and the adjacent ceilings in the location of the shoring. Remove and relocate the partition's electric or plumbing services. For the shoring, nail a plate to the floor and a 4 × 4 to the underside of the joists. Measure and cut the shoring studs to fit snugly between the top and the bottom plates, then nail them to the plates. To make sure that each individual joist is supported, force hardwood shims in any gaps between the joists and the top plate. It is good practice to construct the shoring at least 3' wider than the opening (Ill. 13).

If you are cutting into an exterior wall, the next step is to remove the siding and the sheathing to the width and the height required for the installation of the header and the jack studs. (Make sure you have a heavy plastic sheet to seal the opening from the weather.)

To demolish the wall, cut the wall studs at the point where they will support the header. (Cut them at the top and bottom and twist them out.) Construct and raise the header (Inset I), wedging it into place, and shore it temporarily. Install the jack studs, the sill, and other framing members and nail the assembly together (Ills. 7 and 13). Remove all of the shoring.

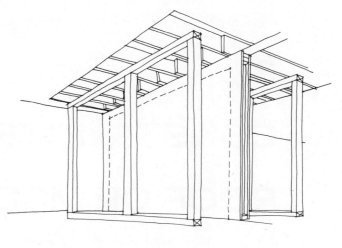

ILL. 12

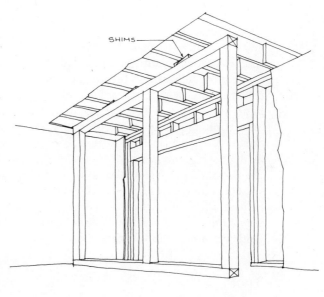

SHIMS

ILL. 13

Constructing
and Modifying
the Walls
and Partitions
267

*Place the vertical supports at 2' o.c.

31

CONSTRUCTING A NEW ROOF OR MODIFYING AN EXISTING ONE

This chapter is important for anyone who is doing any construction that involves the roof. Of course, if you are anticipating an addition to the house, you will want to read this chapter on roof construction. Even if you are only adding a skylight, you should be very familiar with the structural configuration of the roof so that you don't accidentally dismantle it. In this chapter we will be discussing only pitched roofs; the structure of the flat roof is very similar to that of the floor system, and a rereading of Chapter 29 will be helpful. Please note that roof construction can be very dangerous; if you have not done this kind of work before, call in a contractor.

Tools

· Carpentry and demolition tools (see pages 234 and 252)

Materials

· Ceiling joists: If your design requires them, quantity and dimensions can be taken from the framing plan.
· Rafter stock: To determine the length of the rafter stock, you can make a large-scale drawing of the rafter and its supports. Or you can use the formula provided in the section "Preparing the Rafter Stock for Cutting" or Illustration 3. Add to this figure the length of the overhang and about another 9" for cutting.

For the number of rafters required, multiply the length of the roof (the ridge length) × ¾ (for 16"

spacing; for 24" spacing use ½) and add 1 for the end rafter. This gives you the number of rafters for one side of the roof; for the total number of rafters, double the figure. Always add 10 or 15 percent for waste.
· Plywood sheathing: Thicknesses varying from ½" (for 12" or 16" spacing) to ¾" (for 24" spacing). For the number of panels required, multiply 2 × (the length of the rafter + overhang) × the length of the ridge. In the case of plywood roof sheathing, you need order only about 5 percent over the calculated amount required, since there is little waste.
· Ridge stock: 2" thick. For the depth of the ridge, add 2" to the depth of the rafters as determined by the design. The length of the ridge is equal to the length of the building + the gable overhang.
· Nails: 3d, 4d, 8d, 10d
· Roofing underlayment paper
· Asphalt strip shingles: 3 bundles per 100 square feet
· Metal roof flashing, as required
· Flexible roof flashing and cement, if required

FRAMING THE NEW ROOF

The pitched roof and the shed roof can be constructed using light-frame or plank-and-beam construction. Generally pitched roofs have two sloping sides and require tie beams to hold the roof together (unless a ridge beam is used), whereas the shed roof may not need ties. The plank-and-beam roof is composed of heavier sections (spaced farther apart) and may require a crane for construction. Another major difference between light-frame and plank-and-beam con-

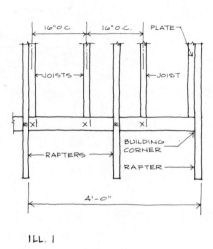

ILL. 1

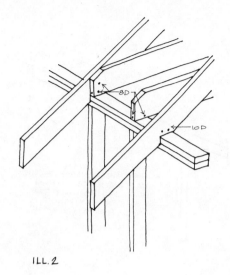

ILL. 2

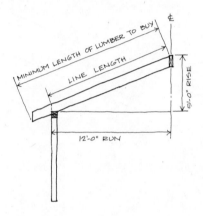

ILL. 3

RISE:
TOP OF PLATES TO TOP
OF RAFTER-RIDGE
INTERSECTION

RUN:
FROM OUTSIDE
SUPPORT TO CENTER
LINE OF RIDGE

LINE LENGTH:
THE HYPOTENUSE OF
THE TRIANGLE MADE
BY THE RISE AND
RUN, MINUS ONE
HALF THE WIDTH OF
THE RIDGE

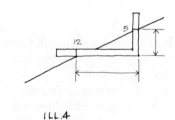

ILL. 4

struction is that the latter uses metal connectors rather than nails.

Laying Out the Rafters and Ceiling Joists

Mark the top plates of the walls to receive the rafters using the method outlined in Chapter 29 on constructing the floors. If your design calls for attic ceiling joists, mark the plates for both the joists and the rafters (Ill. 1). When laying out the rafters and joists, make sure that you have exactly the same markings on the opposite walls unless there is an intermediary support (such as a partition) between the two exterior walls. In that case, plan to use overlapping or butt joints for the ceiling joists as shown in Chapter 21, Illustration 9, and mark the plates accordingly. Position the ceiling joists (if you have them as part of your layout) and toe-nail them to the plates using 10d nails (Ill. 2).

Preparing the Rafter Stock for Cutting

To lay out the rafters you will have to know the slope of the roof (that is, the unit rise to the run) expressed as a ratio (for example, 5:12, 8:12) and the line length of the rafter expressed in feet and inches.

The ratio of the slope of the roof can be calculated by the method outlined in Chapter 23, page 206. The line length of the rafter can be determined by making a large-scale drawing of the assembly and measuring off the drawing, or applying the formula below (and see Ill. 3):

$$\text{line length} = \left\{ \frac{\sqrt{12^2 + \text{the pitch per foot}^2}}{12} \times \text{RUN} \right\} - \tfrac{3}{4}"$$

It is a good practice to cut a few pieces of rafter, test them on the roof, adjust them if needed, and then cut all the remaining rafters, using the first as a pattern. On a framing square, measure (and mark with tape) the rise of the roof on the tongue (short end) and the run on the blade (long end) (Ill. 4). The line length of the rafter is the distance

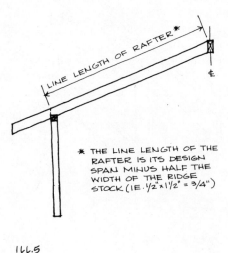

LINE LENGTH OF RAFTER*

℄

* THE LINE LENGTH OF THE
RAFTER IS ITS DESIGN
SPAN MINUS HALF THE
WIDTH OF THE RIDGE
STOCK (IE. ½"×1½" = 3/4")

ILL.5

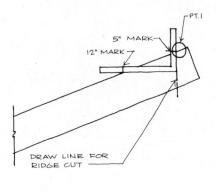

PT. 1
5" MARK
12" MARK

DRAW LINE FOR
RIDGE CUT

ILL.6

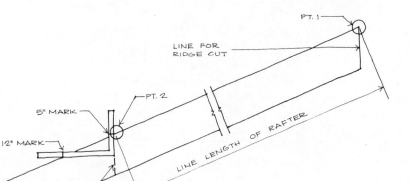

PT. 1
LINE FOR
RIDGE CUT

PT. 2
5" MARK
12" MARK

LINE LENGTH OF RAFTER

DRAW LINE FOR VERTICAL
CUT OF BIRD'S MOUTH

ILL.7

PT. 2
BIRD'S
MOUTH
CUT
3½"

ILL.8

between the bird's-mouth cut (which is the notch that "sits" the rafter onto the plates) and the cut for the ridge (Ill. 5).

Choose a very straight and clean piece of rafter stock. Try to find a piece that does not have a camber, but if it does, position it so that the crown of the camber will be the top of the rafter. Position the framing square (as directed in Ill. 6) on point 1 and draw the ridge cut line. From point 1, along the top of the ridge, measure the line length of the rafter (Ill. 7); this gives you point 2. Position the tongue mark (in this case 5) on point 2, and move the square until the 12 mark on the blade rests on the top of the rafter stock in the position shown in Illustration 7. Draw a line down along the outside of the tongue, from point 2; this will be the vertical cut line for the bird's mouth. Invert the square. Lay it as shown in Illustration 8 and measure off 5½" for 2 × 6 exterior

stud walls (or 3½" for 2 × 4 walls). This is the final cut of the bird's mouth, representing the width (5½" or 3½") of the plates. Measure off the overhang as designed and draw the line for the overhang cut. Prepare five rafters, using the first as a pattern.

Preparing the Ridge

The ridge, as we have learned, serves little structural purpose, yet it is important that the pieces selected for the ridge be as straight as possible. The rafters that will butt against it are cut exactly to fit, and too much of a warp or camber in the ridge will throw off the assembly.

Set the ridge sections alongside the plates and lay out the rafter spacing on the ridge by transferring the marking directly from the plates. If you

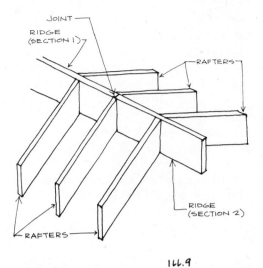

ILL.9

height, and all else looks squarely cut and neat, you can proceed further.

Permanently nail the section already constructed and cut the rest of the rafters using the fifth rafter as a pattern for the rest. Nail the intervening rafters in place following the above procedure of first toe-nailing the rafter to the plate and then to the ridge section. Alternate the installation of the rafters so that only two or three rafters are nailed into place on one side of the ridge before you move to the other side and install the

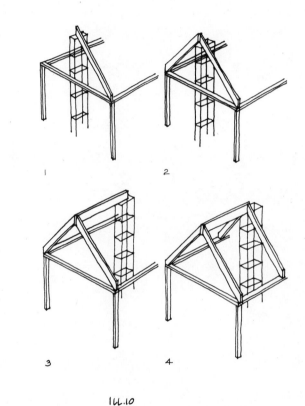

ILL.10

cannot find a single length for the ridge, lay out the ridge pieces so that they will be joined to each other at the point of intersection with two rafters (Ill. 9). Next, move the ridge section to the center of the building and rest it across the ceiling joists (or on a temporary platform supported by scaffolding) directly below where it will be when in its final position.

Raising the Rafters and Ridge

Cut five pieces of rafter stock (and not more until these have been tested for accuracy). The first four pieces will serve as testers and will be nailed temporarily in place to the ridge section. Although it is possible to raise the roof by yourself using bracing and scaffolding, we don't recommend it. It is much better practice to work with one or two helpers. Beginning at one gable end, temporarily nail a rafter to the plate while an assistant holds up the other end at the approximate future height of the ridge. Nail the second rafter to the opposite plate while the assistant holds the two rafters in place. Lift one end of the ridge section, and while a second helper supports the other end of the ridge piece, temporarily nail the rafters to it. Move some scaffolding to support the free end of the ridge temporarily. Move down about six rafter spacings and nail the two remaining rafters temporarily in place. The assembly should now be plumbed and braced, making sure that the ridge is perfectly level (Ill. 10). To check the assembly for accuracy, measure the distance from the top of the ridge section to the top of the ceiling joists. If this conforms to the design

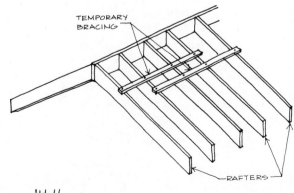

ILL.11

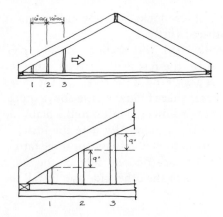

ILL. 12

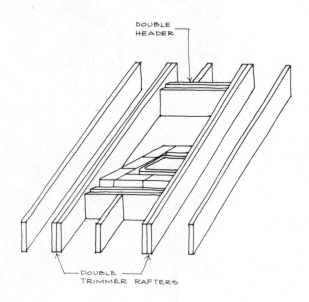

DOUBLE
HEADER

DOUBLE
TRIMMER RAFTERS

ILL. 13

ILL. 14

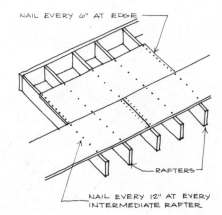

NAIL EVERY 6" AT EDGE

RAFTERS

NAIL EVERY 12" AT EVERY
INTERMEDIATE RAFTER

other half of the rafter pairs. Brace the assembly together by nailing a 2 × 4 as bracing to the top of the rafters (Ill. 11). Since you will be climbing over the roof, bracing the framing is not meaningless work. Nail the rafters securely to their adjoining ceiling joists (Ill. 2). When the roof is complete, drop a plumb line at either gable end to make sure that the end gables are straight.

Use a straightedge to make sure that all of the rafters lie on an even plane. Use a taut line to check that the rafter ends (at the exterior walls) are in a straight line. If there is to be a fascia piece at the end of the rafters, plan for it.

Completing the Gable Wall Section

Lay out the stud spacing at the gable ends at 16" o.c. If there is to be a window or vent opening, lay out the trimmers as well, following the directions outlined in Chapter 30. Hold a piece of stud stock at the first stud space (Ill. 12) and mark the angle at which it intersects the end rafter. Repeat at each stud spacing. Cut the studs and nail them in place. (Care should be taken not to force the gable-end studs into place. The pressure might distort the end rafter.) Not all of the sections need to be custom-fitted as described. The distance between the first and second studs will be standard. If the second stud is 9" longer than the first, then the third stud will be 9" longer than the second, and so forth. The studs can then be laid out on the ground and cut in pairs. The window or vent opening is framed similarly to a conventional opening, as described in Chapter 30, page 263.

Framing Openings in a New Roof

Roof openings (Ill. 13) may be framed by measuring and cutting the rafters before installation in a way similar to the framing of openings in a floor (see page 258). Before framing any openings, be sure that you drop a plumb line down to the house below to make sure that the hole you are framing is directly above the item (for example, the chimney) you are framing.

Erecting the Roof Sheathing

The plywood sheathing, which is installed with its long side perpendicular to the run of the rafters, provides a nailing surface for the roofing. Start applying the plywood sheathing on the lower part of the roof and work your way up to the ridge, cutting the boards where needed. The panels should be applied in an alternating pattern as shown in Illustration 14. As a safety precaution, scaffolding should be erected at the periphery of the house to facilitate the nailing of the lower row of sheathing.

RENOVATING AN EXISTING ROOF

Demolishing All or Part of the Roof

Roof demolition, like the demolition of a load-bearing wall, is potentially very dangerous. First, if you don't do it correctly, the structure may collapse around you. In general, if you are going to remove any part of a pitched roof, read Chapter 23, on roof structure, first. Remember that most rafters are leaning against one another. If you cripple the rafters on half of a pitched roof without providing for support, it is likely that the whole roof will cave in. If you are planning to cut into your roof, have an expert design the opening, plan the temporary shoring, and outline a quick demolition and reconstruction procedure.

Second, unless you have a very large crew of experienced demolishers (unlikely), the work will proceed very slowly. A flash rainstorm can cause a great deal of damage to your unprotected house. For these reasons we strongly advise you to hire a contractor to do the necessary work. If you are making a relatively small opening in the roof, however, you may be able to handle it yourself providing you know (in advance) what you are going to do, you work quickly, and you wrap the work in plastic sheets between workdays.

Cutting into a Sloped Roof for a Skylight or Chimney Opening

Many skylights come with installation instructions. Purchase a unit that has its own curb and has self-flashing. Be sure to have the unit on hand before disturbing the roof. Plan to position the skylight so that the fewest possible rafters will be cut. Buy long, narrow skylights and install the long side parallel to the rafters. If the skylight or chimney is less than 30" wide, you will have to cut into only one rafter (Ill. 13).

First expose the structure on the underside of the roof. Strip off all of the roofing, flashing, insu-

lation, and interior finish but do not yet remove anything structural. If there are electrical wires, drainage pipes, or any other services in the roof, remove or relocate them.

Double the rafters on either side of the future opening and temporarily shore up the rafter that will be cut both above and below the cut marks (Ill. 15). Draw the outline of the exact size of the rough opening required on the underside of the sheathing and drill some critical holes through the roof to locate the opening on the upper side. Remove roofing material along the cut lines of the opening to a width of about a foot outside of the

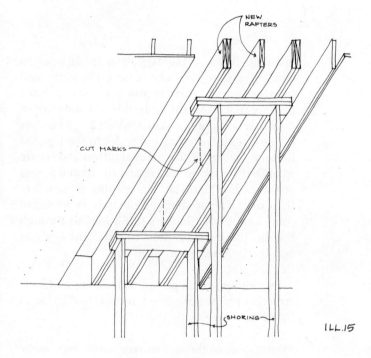

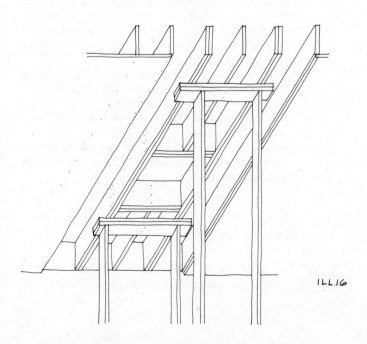

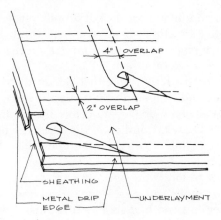

4" OVERLAP

2" OVERLAP

SHEATHING

METAL DRIP EDGE

UNDERLAYMENT

ILL.17

opening. If you have asphalt strip shingles in good condition, carefully remove the strips and save for reuse, so that the patching will match the existing roof. From the underside, cut and remove the rafter section(s). Install doubled 2 × 8 headers (if the opening is up to 48" wide) to the top and bottom sections of the crippled rafters and secure to both the crippled rafters and the doubled ones at the ends (Ill. 16). If the opening is narrower than the rafter spacing, you may have to install some additional trimmers to fill in. Cut through the sheathing and continue to install the skylight and its flashing.

In addition to the general demolition and construction precautions listed in the introduction to Part Four, we include these:

· Don't work on the roof on very windy days, as the materials and equipment have a tendency to blow off.
· Don't store anything, even temporarily, on the roof. We know of an electrician who stepped on an unsecured piece of plywood. He and the plywood fell from the roof together.
· Don't work on the roof on extremely hot or cold days, as you may end up destroying the existing roof, which may be either soft or brittle.
· Use a very secure ladder, wear skid-resistant shoes, and be very careful.
· Since no two roofs are the same, you should consult with an engineer or architect before cutting into any structural members.

ROOFING

The plywood sheathing is by no means watertight, and if you are not adding your roofing ma-

terial immediately, you should protect the roof until it can be finished.

Installing the Waterproofing Underlayment*

There are a variety of underlayments sold to cover the sheathing before the installation of the strip shingles. These products provide an added layer of moisture protection against wind-driven rain. The most commonly available is an asphalt-saturated felt. Use a material that will allow vapor to pass through to prevent the accumulation of condensate between sheathing and underlayment. Fifteen-pound saturated felt paper is considered a good choice in buildings with well-ventilated attics. Plastic sheeting is a bad choice.

Prepare the sheathing to receive underlayment by making sure that there are no nailheads or splinters projecting, the sheathing is dry, clean, and free of dirt, and any knotholes are repaired by nailing metal flashing material over them. Underlayment material consists of asphalt-saturated felt or a similar material, which comes in rolls 36" wide and 72" or 144" long. The paper is laid in long horizontal rows beginning with one layer parallel to the edge of the roof and working the layers up to the ridge. The horizontal joints should overlap about 2" (Ill. 17). Two people are usually required for the job. The underlayment is stapled to the sheathing every 12" and along the edges of the roof. Lap the felt over the ridge. A drip edge (purchased prefabricated) should be installed under the felt at the bottom edge of the roof and over the felt at the side edge (Ill. 17). Install all flashing as directed in Inset I.

Installing Asphalt Strip Shingles

Asphalt strip shingles are very easy and quick to install. The most common shingle is the square-

---

*Steep roofs finished with wood shingles often do not require felt at all because of the tendency of the shingles to quickly shed water. In climates with regular snowfalls the lower 5' of roof should, however, receive the protection of some waterproof underlayment to prevent what is called the ice dam effect. The ice dam is created by an accumulation of melting snow at the periphery of the roof a few days after a snowfall. The snow slides to the edge of the roof and melts. The temperatures fall and the melting snow turns to ice. If more snow should fall, this ice dam will prevent the new accumulation from sliding off the roof. When this second layer begins to melt, the water will be backed up behind the dam and may make its way through the shingles to the sheathing.

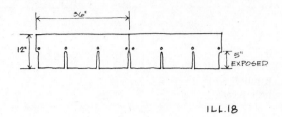

ILL.18

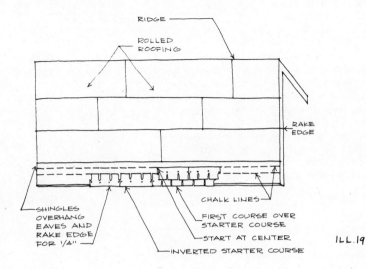

ILL.19

butt strip that is 36" long and 12" wide and has three "tabs" (phony shingles) with two cutouts between the tabs (Ill. 18). The strips are laid up so that 5" is left exposed "to the weather." The strips are sold twenty-seven to a bundle. Three bundles will cover 100 square feet of roof.

Asphalt shingles require a full underlayment of saturated felt. Drip edges of 26-gauge galvanized steel are applied at the eaves and at the rake. Install the flashing that can be applied before the roofing. Some flashing details require the alternate application of roofing and flashing (Inset I). The strips are applied in long horizontal lines. Chalk lines are snapped to keep the rows straight and parallel. (Begin the work by snapping one line for each course. As you get more proficient you will need only one line for every three courses.) Use 1¼" galvanized nails with barbed shanks and large heads. The shingle manufacturer will most likely recommend the type of nails that will best do the job. Nail according to the nailing pattern in Illustration 18 or the manufacturer's instructions, if available. Cut strips with a linoleum knife.

To begin, start at the eaves somewhere in the center between the gable ends and work outward in horizontal lines. Lay a starter strip, which is a layer of strip shingles applied upside down, or a special strip sold for this purpose. The starter strip in effect closes the gaps made by the cutouts at the eaves. Lay this starter strip so that it barely covers the drip edge (Ill. 19). Follow one of the patterns in Illustration 20. Check often to make sure that your rows are straight and even. At the ridge use individual 10"-wide shingles, folded over the ridge and laid one over the other so that the nailing is covered (Ill. 21).

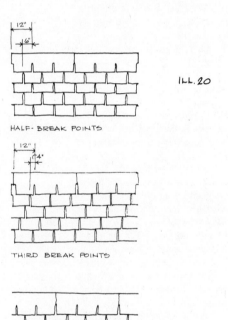

ILL.20

HALF-BREAK POINTS

THIRD BREAK POINTS

RANDOM SPACING

GUTTERS AND DOWNSPOUTS

The system that leads water from the roof to the ground is composed of gutters and downspouts. The gutters are troughlike canals that are attached

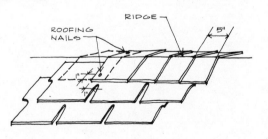

ILL.21

Constructing a New Roof or Modifying an Existing One

275

INSET I/FLASHING

Since flashing material is applied to a building at different points in the construction process, we must discuss it as a separate issue. Flashing is an extremely important aspect of the roofing. Flashing material, which can be metal (such as copper or aluminum) or a flexible fabric, is placed between the intersection of two different materials, at the juxtaposition of two planes, or at any crucial area where moisture penetration may occur.

FLASHING AT THE RIDGE: Flashing at the ridge can be exposed or concealed. We recommend that you use the concealed flashing for aesthetic reasons. Use 16-ounce copper, .019" aluminum, 26-gauge stainless-steel, or 24-gauge galvanized-steel material. Use 10" lengths of flashing material and lap 4". Shingles are applied up to the point where they reach the ridge. The flashing is applied and nailed over the shingles into the sheathing. Special ridge shingles are installed in an alternating pattern (Ill. I-1).

FLASHING THE EDGE OF THE ROOF: The edge of the roof, over the cornice, must be protected from a driving rain. The material to be used is the same as that used for ridge flashing. Details are shown in Illustration I-2. If a gutter is to be installed, see details in Illustration I-3.

FLASHING AROUND THE CHIMNEY: Chimney flashing is particularly difficult because the chimney and the house frame are structured to be discontinuous. There is likely to be some settling of the structural frame of the house, which will create gaps between the chimney and the roof. Therefore, two overlapping layers of flashing are used to prevent the penetration of water while allowing for the independence of chimney from roof. One is attached to the roof itself, and the other is integrated into the construction of the chimney. The overlapping of the layers allows for some movement.

Before any flashing material is applied, the shingles are laid up the roof until they reach the bottom of the chimney opening (Ill. I-4). The base flashing, which is 90-pound mineral-surfaced roofing paper, is cut for the bottom section as

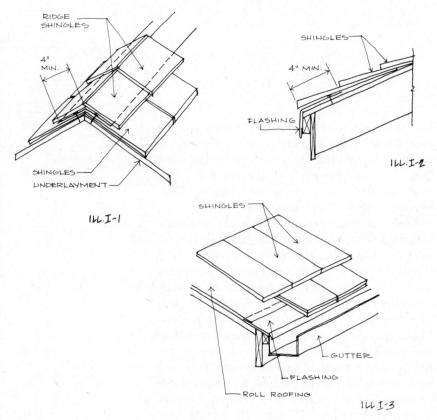

ILL. I-1

ILL. I-2

ILL. I-3

shown in Illustration I-5. The flashing should extend about 10" up the chimney and 10" along the roof. Cut the four pieces of roofing and cement securely to the roof as well as to each other. The flashing must be applied in the following order so that no rain can penetrate as water travels down the roof: bottom, sides, then top.

The flashing that is attached to the chimney is cap flashing, made up of metal flashing material that is set into the joints between the masonry when the bricks are being laid. The first of the pieces applied is the lower section. It is cut the width of the chimney plus enough more to wrap around the corners. The material is set ½" into the mortar joint and overlaps the base flashing (Ill.

I-6). The side pieces must be stepped up the chimney in shorter pieces to conform to the slope of the roof (Ill. I-7). The back of the chimney presents a special problem because it provides a pocket for water and snow accumulation. For this reason, a small cricket or gable is built to keep snow and water from collecting. It is covered with flashing and carried under the shingles and cap flashing (Ill. I-8).

FLASHING AROUND A VENT: Use one piece of sleeve flashing to cover the vent pipe. The sleeve should lap 2" over the vent and flare a minimum of 6" at the base. Use cleats to hold the flashing sleeve in place (Ill. I-9).

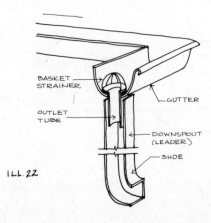

ILL. 22

to the eaves of the roof to channel the rainwater to downspouts, which take the water to the ground. The excess water might be deposited directly onto the grass or some paved area or might be taken down into a dry well.

Gutters are made of either wood (which should be lined), galvanized metal, copper, plastic, or aluminum and come prefabricated and shaped. Wood gutters are installed after the roof sheathing is applied and before the roof is shingled. The

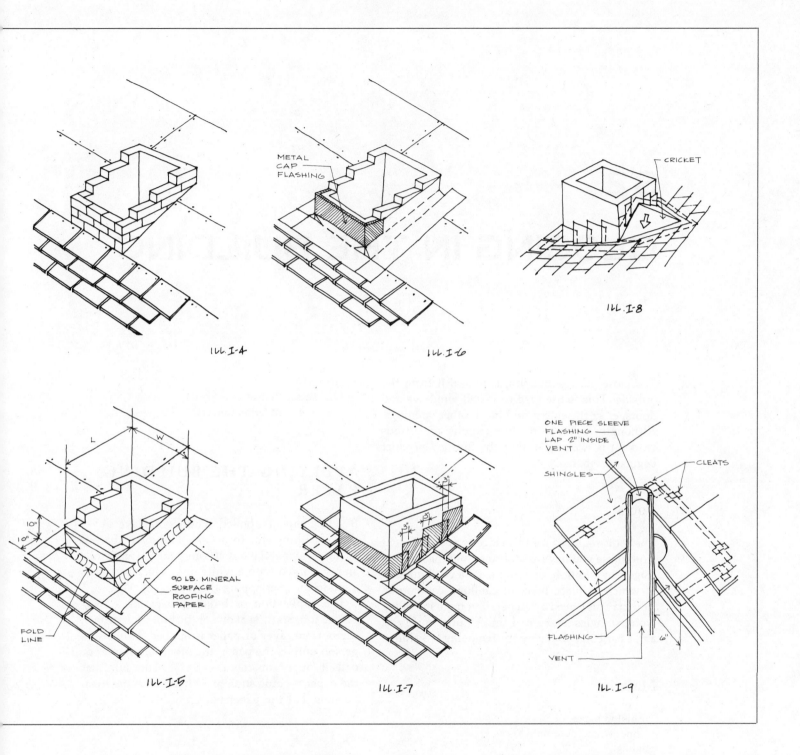

ILL. I-4

ILL. I-6

ILL. I-8 — CRICKET

ILL. I-5

90 LB. MINERAL SURFACE ROOFING PAPER

FOLD LINE

ILL. I-7

ILL. I-9

METAL CAP FLASHING

ONE PIECE SLEEVE FLASHING LAP 2" INSIDE VENT

SHINGLES

CLEATS

FLASHING

VENT

gutter is nailed directly to the fascia using galvanized nails. Be sure that the wood gutter is primed before it is erected. Roof gutters are set so that there is an incline toward the downspouts. The downspouts, usually made of metal, are connected to the gutters at some point where they will be least obvious. A hole is made in the gutter at the point of intersection and the sheet-metal sleeve (for the downspout) is fitted inside (Ill. 22). Galvanized-iron and aluminum gutters and downspouts are designed so that the component parts fit easily together.

Constructing
a New Roof or
Modifying an
Existing One

32

CLOSING IN THE BUILDING

To "close in" the building is to seal it from the outside. This is the time to install windows and doors, erect the siding, and block other openings. Although closing in involves tedious, repetitious work, it is exciting in that the finished product begins to emerge.*

Tools

The tools required for this stage are not different from those you have used throughout the framing stages. In addition, you will need a caulking gun in which to place tubes of caulking compound. You may also need a hatchet, if you are installing wood shingles, and a nail set. A putty knife and a flat bar come in handy for removing old siding.

Materials

- Building paper
- Window and door units
- Siding
- Nails
- Locksets
- Flashing

To finish the overhangs (if you have any) you'll need wood boards for:

- A fascia
- Ledger boards

*Roofing is discussed in Chapter 31.

- Lookouts
- Plywood for the soffit
- Screens or ventilation louvers

APPLYING THE BUILDING PAPER

Building paper is applied in horizontal layers over the sheathing to form an additional barrier against water and wind. It comes in 48"-wide rolls and is marked with a white line, which serves as a guide for overlapping the layers (Ill. 1).

The application of building paper is a two-person job. Starting at one of the building corners, the bottom layer of paper is applied. While one person unrolls the paper, the other one staples or nails it (approximately every 8"). Make sure that the paper is going straight. When you come to an opening, cut the paper with a utility knife.

INSTALLING WINDOWS AND DOORS

Door and window installation is made easier by planning ahead. Be sure as you are framing in the rough openings that they are plumb, level, and square. Although this advice may seem redundant, it is not unusual to find yourself with rough openings that are not plumb. Such an opening will, in turn, throw the windows and doors out of

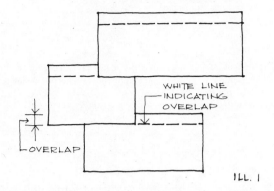

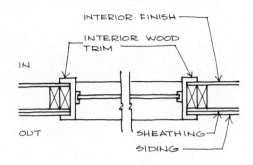

WHITE LINE
INDICATING
OVERLAP

OVERLAP

ILL. 1

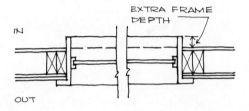

INTERIOR FINISH

INTERIOR WOOD
TRIM

IN

OUT

SHEATHING

SIDING

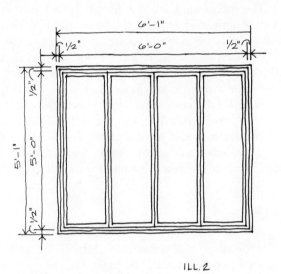

6'-1"

1/2"   6'-0"   1/2"

1/2"

5'-1"   5'-0"

1/2"

ILL. 2

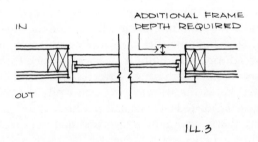

EXTRA FRAME
DEPTH

IN

OUT

ADDITIONAL FRAME
DEPTH REQUIRED

IN

OUT

ILL. 3

level, making their installation trickier. Windows and doors are heavy; the less you have to fuss with them, the better off you are.

Yet another factor to keep in mind while framing in the openings is to allow for sufficient clearance so that window and door units can fit easily. A space approximately ½" all around is usually enough to give you installation leeway. For example, if a window is 5' × 6', the rough openings may be 5'-1" × 6'-1" (Ill. 2). Consult the manufacturer's catalogue for recommended clearances before framing.

Be aware while doing the installation that walls have depth and so do the frames of windows and doors. Consider the depth of the siding and the interior finish and place the units accordingly (Ill. 3). If the frames are too deep and project far into the room, you may find yourself having to cut them down to fit. On the other hand, if they are too shallow, you are also in trouble (Ill. 3). Most manufactured windows come equipped with self-flashing which is nailed to the sheathing. It auto-

matically sets the window in place. Generally these window jambs come designed for 4½" stud walls. If you have 5½" walls, you will need an extension, which can generally be provided by most window manufacturers.

When preparing to install the windows and doors, make sure that you have a helper. Two people are needed to lift the window into place. Once it is in place, one person holds the unit in the rough opening while the other one levels and nails it through predrilled holes according to the manufacturer's recommendations. (Use aluminum or galvanized casing nails spaced every 16" on center.)

Windows

Window units come complete with frame, outside trim, and hardware. There are units that come self-flashed with either top or full perimeter flashing. (Check to see that they come with a drip

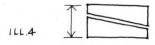

ILL.4

cap; if not, you have to install one after the window is in place.) Start by double-checking the size of the unit against that of the rough opening and make sure they correspond. Most windows require a ½" space on each side and ¾" above the head for plumbing and leveling. From the outside of the building, lift the window unit onto the rough opening. Since it's easier to work from a secure floor than hanging from a ladder, one person holds the window in place while the other goes inside to level and nail it. Check at the sill to see that the window is level and that the space at the top between the frame and the rough opening is not too great. If everything checks, tack the unit in place. (By tacking we mean leaving the nail out about ¼" or so.) Tack the unit at the top, sill, and both sides. Once the window is tacked, open and close it to make sure it's working properly. Again check the sill for levelness. If all is well, drive the nails in (Inset I). To prevent heat loss and drafts, any space left between the window unit and the rough opening is stuffed with fiberglass insulation.

If the window unit isn't level, a little moving around is in order. Shims are used to level the window. (They are any kind of scrap wood that is wedged under the sill until the window is level.) Wood-shingle scraps are particularly good for use as shims because they slope. Using two shingles with slopes in opposite directions, you can arrive at various thicknesses (Ill. 4). With the window level, tack and nail it as previously described.

Doors

Doors can be purchased prehung. This is a great advantage over the old process of constructing the frame, hinging the door, weather-stripping, and so on, particularly for the amateur builder. It saves you time and meticulous work.

The procedure to follow for the installation of a door unit is essentially the same as for a window. Lift the door in place and check it for plumbness on the hinge side. Keep in mind that the sill should be flush with the finish floor. When the door is plumb, tack it in place. Check that it closes well. Be sure to nail the door to the rough opening through shims placed behind hinges and at regular intervals through both jambs. Do not nail through the doorstop. Install the lockset (if it did not come already installed) (Inset II).

Flashing

The top edge of all windows and doors should be flashed to prevent water leakage. Always keep in mind while installing flashing that it should be bent in such a way that it promotes drainage. Once the windows and doors are in place, the upper half of the flashing is nailed directly to the plywood sheathing. It should extend about 4" into the wall's surface. The flashing is then bent into shape to fit over the head (or top) trim. To allow water to drip free from the window or door trim, the flashing should overhang about ¼". There are many doors and windows that come with built-in flashing (Ill. 5).

INSTALLING SIDING

Bevel Siding

REMOVAL OF OLD SIDING: Most renovation work will involve some form of removal and replacement of the existing siding. You must keep in mind that this siding, after years of exposure, is rather delicate. If you want to keep new siding to a minimum (to keep the same weathered look

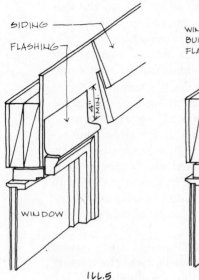

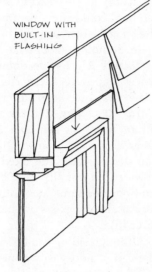

SIDING

FLASHING

WINDOW

WINDOW WITH BUILT-IN FLASHING

ILL.5

boards.) Once the siding is slightly loose, use a flat steel bar or chisel to pry the board loose. Work slowly along the entire length of the board. Once pried, push the board back. This will loosen up the nails. Press the board back down to elevate the nailheads. If the nails are not ribbed or rosin-coated, they will pull out when the board is pushed back. You can now pull out the nails. If the nails don't pop out, you will have to pull everything out (the heads will pull through the wood) and then remove the nails separately. Keep in mind that nails may go through two layers of siding. Make sure you get rid of any remaining nail shanks before replacing the siding. If you are unable to remove the board, break the old siding in pieces and trace the shape onto the new siding stock. The new piece could be driven into place with the aid of a block.

in the wood), you must exercise a lot of care when removing existing siding. The method used to remove bevel siding depends on the condition of the wood, the type of finish (stained or painted), and the type of nails originally used. Expect to do some experimentation.

Take a wide putty knife, insert it under the siding, and gently pull the board up. (Putty knives are thin and can easily be inserted between

INSTALLING NEW SIDING: An important aspect of the application of siding is to use the right nails. Corrosion-resistant, galvanized, stainless-steel, or other nails made of similar metals will not bleed and spot the siding's surface. These nails will cost more but they are worth it. In terms of shape, the nails used for siding are usually thin and have a flat head (box nails). Thin nails are used in order to reduce the risk of splitting the wood. You must be careful, however, to drive

---

INSET II/INSTALLING A LOCKSET

Lockset manufacturers provide instruction sheets and a template to guide you in the installation. Some doors come with predrilled holes to accommodate the locksets, making your job easier. Although the installation of a lockset may vary somewhat with the lockset type, the steps usually required are as follows:

1. Install the latch by inserting it into the bored hole. With a pencil, mark its outline and remove it. In order for the latch to be flush with

the door, chisel out the area where the latch is to be installed. Insert the latch in place and tighten the screws (Ill. II-1).

2. The strike plate is installed next. The template will give you directions on how to find the location of the strike plate's screws. With a pencil, mark this spot on the doorjamb. Drill the latch bolt hole. Place the strike plate on its proper location by matching the center line of the screw holes with the one you've

drawn on the jamb. Draw the strike plate's outline, remove it, and chisel out the outlined area so that the strike plate will be flush with the doorjamb. Install the strike plate by fastening the screws (Ill. II-2).

3. Finally, insert the knob that has a spindle into the latch and push it against the door. The other knob is installed by placing it on the spindle of the first. This knob, too, is pushed against the door and firmly tightened with screws (Ill. II-3).

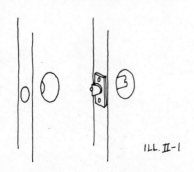

ILL. II-1

ILL. II-2

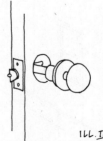

ILL. II-3

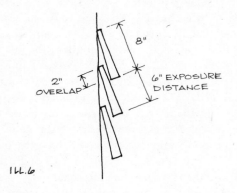

ILL. 6

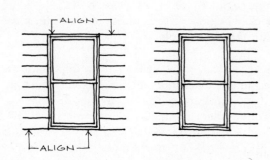

ILL. 7

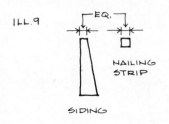

ILL. 9

NAILING STRIP

SIDING

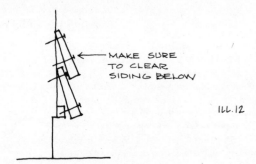

MAKE SURE TO CLEAR SIDING BELOW

ILL. 12

them only to the wood's surface. Driving the nails too hard could show hammer blows and increase the chances of crushing the wood.

Bevel siding should lap no less than 1" and preferably 2". The recommended exposure distances (exposure distance is the amount of siding left exposed to the weather) are 4" for 6" siding, 8" for 10" siding, 10" for 12" siding, and so on (Ill. 6). From the standpoint of both weather resistance and appearance, the exposure distance is adjusted to meet the fixed dimensions of windows and doors (Ill. 7). Obviously, you need to continue the same amount of overlap and exposure as already exists on the rest of the house (see Inset III).

Although siding can be installed by one person alone, it is more easily done by two. The erection of siding starts by securing a nailing strip to the bottom edge of the sheathing (Ill. 8). This strip should be equal in thickness to the "top" thickness of the siding (Ill. 9). Make sure that the nailing strip is level. At either end of the wall, measure up from (the bottom of) the nailing strip the dimension of the siding board and snap a chalk line (Ills. 10 and 11). Using the chalk line as a guide, position the board and nail it on the studs at approximately every 16" on center. When you are through with the first board, simply butt up the next board against the one you've just nailed.

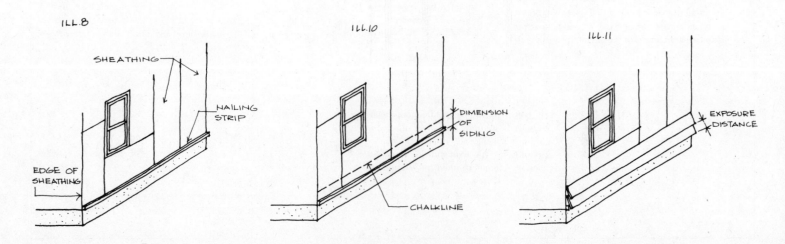

ILL. 8

SHEATHING
NAILING STRIP
EDGE OF SHEATHING

ILL. 10

DIMENSION OF SIDING
CHALKLINE

ILL. 11

EXPOSURE DISTANCE

The procedure used to determine how much the recommended exposure distance has to be adjusted so that the siding aligns with a window is not difficult. Let's say that you are using 8″ siding and the window height is 55″. The number of courses needed between the top and the bottom of the window is found by dividing 6″—the recommended exposure distance for 8″ siding—into 55″—the height of the window (Ill. III-1). You need 55 ÷ 6 = 9⅙, or nine courses. To find out

precisely the exposure the siding must have to get nine courses, divide 55″ (the window height) by 9 (the number of courses). You need 55 ÷ 9 = approximately 6⅛″ exposure for each course of siding to meet the window flush at either end.

The exposure for siding located between the windowsill and the foundation wall should also be adjusted. You may, otherwise, find yourself with two noticeably different siding exposures or a very narrow end course within the same wall (Ill. III-2).

For example, if the distance between the bottom of the windowsill and the top of the foundation wall is 31″, you need 31 ÷ 6 = 5⅙ courses between the two. To arrive at the necessary exposure for the right number of courses, divide 31″ by 5 and you get 6.2″, or approximately 6³⁄₁₆″, which is only slightly over what the exposure will be for siding above the sill. Therefore the difference will hardly be noticeable.

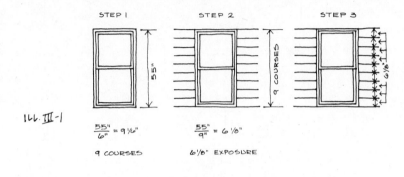

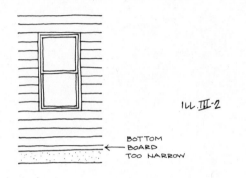

Once the first row of siding is complete, measure up from the top of the first row the exposure distance for the second row (Ill. 11). Snap a chalk line and locate the board. Nail the second row in the same manner as the first. This time, however, make sure that you're nailing up far enough along the siding to clear the lower course (Ill. 12). The remaining courses are installed in the same manner.

To fit around windows and doors, butt the siding up against the frames. Caulk the joints between the siding and the frames, in order to seal them against water penetration.

Here are a few general points to remember while installing siding: Try to minimize joints. Joints are the point of least resistance to weather. The fewer the joints, the more weathertight the wall will be. To minimize joints, use longer sections of siding under windows, over doors, and whenever there is a long uninterrupted stretch of wall. Save the smaller pieces for areas in between openings. Keep in mind that these joints should occur over the studs and should be staggered between courses. For further protection against moisture penetration, dip or brush the ends of the siding in a water-repellent preservative before nailing in place. In addition, check that all the ends are perfectly square. Joints must be good and tight; otherwise, water may find its way in.

Whenever cutting the board is necessary, cut it with a table saw, a radial-arm saw, or a miter box to ensure a square end.

CORNERS: There are two corner conditions you have to worry about: inside and outside corners. Outside corners are easier and can be handled in a number of ways. The two most popular ones are mitering and butting against a wood strip called a corner board.

Mitered corners involve cutting both boards at an angle that will form a 90° corner when butted against each other (Ill. 13). Miters have a tendency to come apart, so add extra nails around the miter joint from both sides.

Another way to handle outside corners is by using a corner board. This type of joint involves nailing two vertical wood strips at the corner of the building; this will serve as a surface against which both pieces of siding can butt (Ill. 14).

Interior corners are trickier. Mitering doesn't work in this type of corner. One solution is to place a corner board in the corner and butt up both surfaces of siding against it (Ill. 15). Another, more difficult joint involves taking one piece of siding and butting it right up to the sheathing (Ill. 16). The other side is coped to fit the first. This is done by holding the siding in place against the one you've just nailed and scribing it at the proper

Closing in
the Building
283

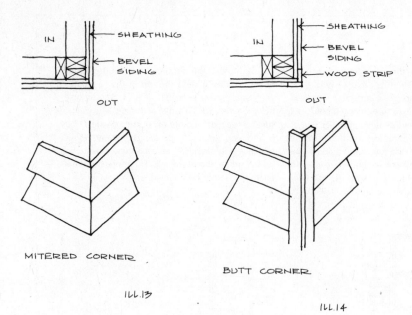

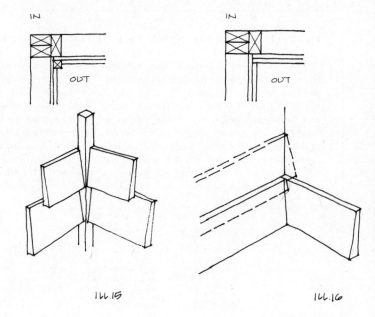

MITERED CORNER

ILL. 13

BUTT CORNER

ILL. 14

ILL. 15

ILL. 16

angle. Cut the siding at this angle and nail in place (Ill. 16).

Shingles

REMOVAL: See discussion under "Bevel Siding."

INSTALLING NEW SHINGLES: The installation of shingles is more time-consuming and difficult than that of bevel siding because they are smaller, are irregular in shape, and have to be applied one by one. There are several things you should be aware of before installing shingles. Shingles come in varying widths. Spread the widths out evenly so that you don't get a concentration of narrow shingles at one end and wide ones at the other (Ill. 17). The maximum recommended exposure for shingles is ½" less than one-half its length. For example, a 16" shingle has an exposure of 7½", an 18" shingle an exposure of 8½", etc. Both the shingle exposure and the pattern should be kept as close as possible to that of the rest of the house. As with siding, shingle joints are the areas of least resistance to weather. For this reason, the joints should be staggered so that no two courses have joints overlapping any closer than 1½" (Ill. 18).

The installation of shingles starts by snapping a chalk line ½" below the bottom of the sheathing on the foundation wall. The shingle overhangs the foundation wall to provide a drip cap (Ill. 19). The chalk line together with a wood board (a straight piece of 1 × 3 or 2 × 4) serves

ILL. 17

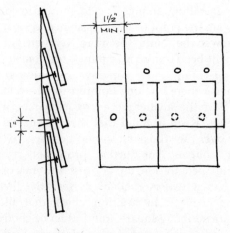

ILL. 18

as a guide to align the shingles. Because the wood board cannot be nailed to the concrete foundation wall for the first course, shingles are nailed to either end of the board to serve as nailers for the sheathing above (Ill. 20).

Nail the board in place aligned with the chalk line. The first row of shingles is located using the wood board as a guide (Ill. 21). The reason for using the bottom of the shingle as a measuring point rather than the top is that shingles may vary slightly in length. Since the bottom is the part that remains visible, that's the part that should be carefully aligned. Use two nails for shingles 8" wide or less and three nails for wider shingles (Ill. 22). Once the shingles are nailed, remove the board and reset it until the first course is complete.

A second layer of shingles is applied directly over the first course. With the double course finished, start the second course by measuring up from the bottom of the shingle the distance it is to be left exposed—that is, 7½" for 16" shingles. Snap a chalk line. Again align the wood board with the chalk line and nail it directly to the sheathing. Rest each shingle on the top of the board and nail it in place. Make sure when you drive in the nails that you do so about 1" clear of the course below (Ill. 18). The following courses are laid in the same manner.

The space that should be left between shingles varies with the amount of moisture present in the wood. If the wood is new and damp, you can butt them against each other. If it's old, leave a space of approximately ⅛" to allow for expansion under moist conditions. Generally, the cheaper the grade of shingle, the drier it is and the more it will expand. When shingles meet windows and doors, merely butt the ends to meet the frame, leaving enough expansion clearance depending on the moisture content of the shingle.

CORNERS: Both exterior and interior corners are handled in essentially the same manner. For an exterior corner, nail one shingle flush with the corner edge of the sheathing. The shingle meeting it from the other side will overlap this one. Nail the overlapping shingle. The excess wood is cut off with a hatchet (Ill. 23). Laps should be alternated in each course.

Interior corners are handled in a similar manner. The only difference is that instead of nailing the second shingle and cutting it in place, it is held in place and scribed. It is then cut and nailed in place.

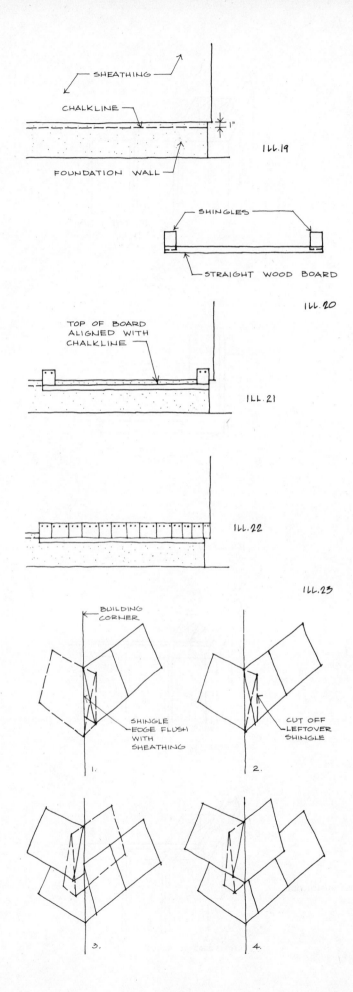

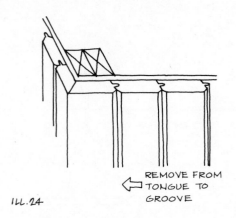

ILL. 24

REMOVE FROM TONGUE TO GROOVE

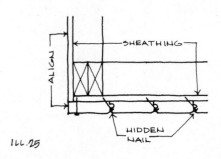

ALIGN

SHEATHING

HIDDEN NAIL

ILL. 25

ILL. 26

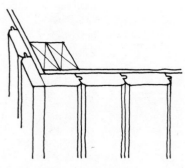

LAPPED CORNER

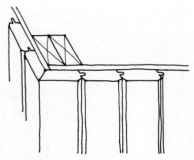

MITERED CORNER

Vertical Tongue-and-Groove Siding

REMOVAL: The first step in removing tongue-and-groove siding is to find out in which direction the tongues are going. (An easy way to do this is to take a look under the siding where the foundation wall and the siding meet.) The boards should be removed from the direction of the tongue side to the groove side (Ill. 24). With a lath knife, cut into the tongue at the center of the groove. Be careful while doing this. Keep in mind that you may hit a nail, which could break the blade. Once the tongue is cut, begin to pry up the adjacent board from the bottom up. (Do this with a pry bar and a piece of wood to protect the adjacent board.) Remove the first board. Start working on the next board by taking a nail set and driving the nails through the tongue. This board can now be pried loose. Keep repeating this procedure for the remaining boards.

INSTALLATION: In order to provide a good nailing surface for the boards, the plywood sheathing underneath vertical siding should be thicker than that used for horizontal applications (approximately ⅝″ to ¾″). In horizontally applied siding, the boards are nailed to the studs every 16″ on center. This is not the case with vertical siding; hence the thicker plywood.

Start the siding application at one of the building corners. Position the board plumb against and aligned with the sheathing. The bottom of the board should overlap the foundation wall approximately ½″ to provide a drip cap. Check to be sure that the board is perfectly vertical. Start nailing from the top of the board. The nails should be located as close to the groove as possible (Ill. 25). Another row of nails is then driven at the tongue side, which will be hidden from view (Ill. 25). Insert the second board into the first and nail it, this time, however, only at the tongue; the other edge is held secure by the groove (Ill. 25).

To fit over an opening, allow a small gap (approximately ⅛″) between the board and the door or window frame. There should also be a small gap left at the sides. Fill them with caulking.

CORNERS: The corner conditions, both exterior and interior, are most easily handled by lapping boards. You will have to cut the board lengthwise. Exterior corners may also be mitered (Ill. 26).

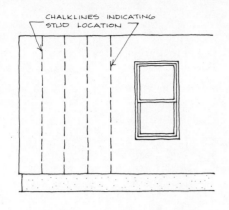

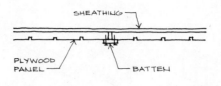

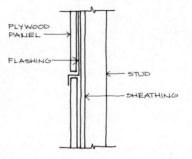

ILL. 28

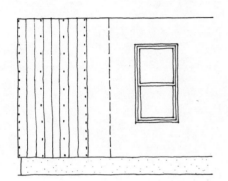

ILL. 27

ILL. 29

Plywood Panel Siding

REMOVAL: Unlike bevel and tongue-and-groove siding, with plywood siding you will most likely not be able to reuse any of the pieces you remove. There's not much finesse to removing plywood siding. Pry along one joint with a pry bar until the panel comes loose. Nails sometimes come out with the wood, but are likely to stay in the wood. If the nails come out with the panel, make sure to either bend them over or remove them. (You may otherwise puncture yourself while throwing away the panels.)

INSTALLATION: Plywood siding is very popular because it is easier and faster to apply than any other type of siding. Because the panels come in 4' widths, their application is not vastly different from that of sheathing. These panels may be applied directly over studs (which is not recommended, for structural stability, water penetration, and energy conservation reasons) or over sheathing.

Panel application over sheathing begins by snapping vertical chalk lines at the location of the studs. These lines will serve as a guide for nailing the paneling over the studs. Pick up the first panel and position it at one corner of the building. Make sure it is plumb against the sheathing. Nail it in place approximately 4" to 6" on center at the perimeter and 8" to 12" at intermediate studs (Ill.

27). The next panel is either butted against or inserted into the edge of the first, depending on whether the edges are square, shiplap, or tongue and groove. Butt joints are protected with a batten strip (Ill. 28). Nail the panel in place in the same fashion as the first.

If a horizontal joint is necessary, flash it well to protect against moisture penetration (Ill. 29). Some panel manufacturers have joining devices specifically designed to protect horizontal joints in their panels. For extra protection against moisture penetration, you can treat the edges with water-repellent preservative.

A space of approximately 1/16" should be left between the panel and door and window frames. This opening is later caulked.

FINISHING THE OVERHANGS

There are two basic types of overhang conditions: the flush or simple overhang and the rafter overhang, which can be opened or closed (Ill. 30).

Flush and Open Overhang

Both the sheathing and the building paper should have been notched to fit around the rafters. The

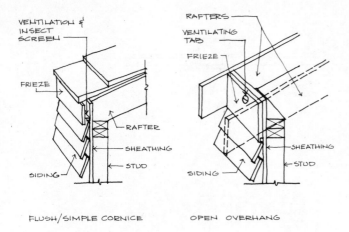

FLUSH/SIMPLE CORNICE   OPEN OVERHANG

ILL.30

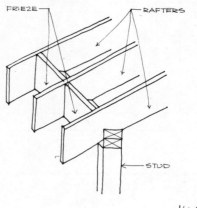

ILL.31

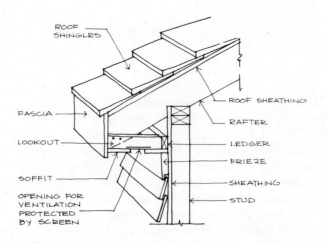

BOX/CLOSED CORNICE

ILL.32

ILL.33

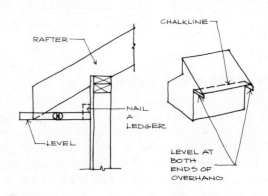

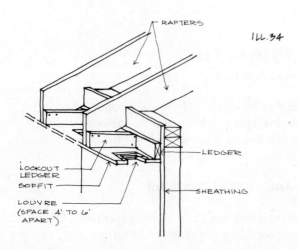

ILL.34

rest of the installation consists of laying out, beveling, notching, and nailing on the frieze (Ill. 30). In the case of open overhangs, cut the frieze to fit between rafters (Ill. 31). For flush cornices, cut the frieze to span between the building's corners. Level the pieces, tack them in place, and nail them. The joints should be smooth and square for a tight fit.

Boxed-In Overhang

A boxed-in or closed overhang requires more work. This type completely hides the rafters with a fascia and soffit (Ill. 32).

Start by leveling across between the rafter overhang to the wall (Ill. 33). Do this at both ends of the overhang and snap a chalk line (Ill. 33). Nail, aligned with this line, a ledger, or nailing strip (Ill. 34). Lay out and cut the lookouts. Set them in place, level, and nail them. (First nail to the rafter and then toe-nail to the ledger.) The lookouts can also be installed in the framing stage and nailed directly to the rafters and studs.

The next step is to cut out the plywood soffit. Openings should be provided in the soffit for ventilation. These openings are protected with a screen to prevent insects from flying into the building. Ventilation louvers are also available, which only require installation into the openings. With the soffit cut out and ready, nail it to the bottom of the lookouts, making sure it's level.

The fascia is installed next. It is nailed directly to the ends of the rafters and lookout (Ill. 32). The fascia should extend about 1″ below the soffit to provide a drip edge. The top is beveled to meet the roof slope. A frieze is later installed under the soffit (Ill. 32).

33

RENOVATING THE PLUMBING

Unlike other aspects of building, the plumbing installation does not follow a rigid pattern. The most important aspect of the system is its proper design (and, of course, a very thorough understanding of what you are doing). You must become proficient in the basic techniques involved in measuring, cutting, and joining the pipes, and also become familiar with the various fittings available (Inset I). You should also be aware of how the pipes are integrated into the building's structure without weakening it in any way (Inset II). In this chapter we will describe plumbing procedures and advise on how to disconnect the existing plumbing and where to start the installation. We will also explain how to extend the existing plumbing and how to organize the pipe assembly. The specific steps to be taken after these basic ones are a function of your particular design.

As discussed in Chapter 18, on plumbing design, most codes require that a licensed plumber do the work. This chapter deals with one-family houses. Some local codes permit the owner of a one-family (and sometimes two-family) residence to do his own plumbing work with the proviso that it be inspected and approved by the "local inspecting authority." For multiple dwellings, codes prohibit do-it-yourself plumbing. A licensed plumber is a must.

Materials

The materials necessary to install the plumbing system depend on the plumbing design. What follows is a basic outline of the materials you may need.

Drainage materials:

· Piping for drainage and venting (plastic, copper, cast iron, or galvanized steel)
· Pipe adapter (if required) to change lines from one material to another—for example, from plastic to metal
· Fittings: couplings, elbows, sanitary tees, Y branches, etc.
· Reducing tees
· Cleanout plugs
· Floor drains (if required)
· Prefabricated flashing curb

Water supply system materials:

· Copper piping: Type K flexible copper tubing for underground installation and Type L flexible copper tubing for aboveground installation
· Pressure and temperature relief valve at your hot-water heater outlet
· Outside water faucets (freeze-proof if you live in a cold climate)
· Valves and fittings, as needed: shutoff valves, unions, tees, etc.

Materials required to aid in the installation of the system:

· Pipe hangers
· Roofing nails
· Steel wool or emery cloth
· Rags

- Pipe-joint "dope" or tape for galvanized-steel screw pipe
- Pipe insulation (where needed)
- Solder compound (for copper piping)
- Solvent (for joining plastic pipe)

Tools

The tools needed for plumbing installation vary with the pipe material you are using. Regardless of materials, however, you will need the following carpentry tools for cutting the woodwork:

- Reciprocating saw
- Wood chisel
- Carpenter's level
- Plumb bob
- Tape
- Folding ruler

In addition to these tools, you should have an adjustable wrench or a wrench set for tightening nuts when installing the fixtures. A ladder is also handy, since a lot of the plumbing work takes place in the ceiling and hard-to-reach places. If you want to avoid a lot of bending, use a workbench instead of the floor to assemble the pipes.

The tools required for the assembly of copper piping are:

- Propane gas torch
- Hacksaw or tubing cutter
- Conduit bender
- Round file
- Wire brush
- Vise
- Jig

Cast-iron piping requires the following tools:

- Hacksaw
- Cold chisel
- Sledgehammer
- Screwdriver or hexagonal wrench

Following is a list of tools needed for the installation of plastic piping:

- Hacksaw and jig
- Round file
- Bristle brush (make sure it is a natural-bristle brush; otherwise, the chemicals in the compound might affect the piping)

The plumbing installation takes place in two stages: the rough stage, when all the normally concealed pipes and fittings are located and assembled, and the finish stage, when fixtures are installed. Before either one of these stages can take place, however, you must disconnect the old fixtures.

DISCONNECTING OLD FIXTURES

The very first step is to find the shutoff valve for every line where a fixture is being removed. These valves are generally located at the base of the pipe serving the fixture. Older houses may have one valve that controls more than one fixture. These are often located in the basement. Occasionally you may find shutoff valves hiding in nearby closets, or concealed inside walls or chases, with handles protruding.

Once the valves are shut, open up the faucets and drain all water. The supply pipes in lavatories and sinks are disconnected by removing the unions with pipe wrenches. There are instances where the supply piping may be attached to threaded faucet stems underneath the basin. Loosen up the nuts with a basin wrench. With the aid of two pipe wrenches, detach the drainage pipe by loosening up the trap's slip coupling. The sink can now be taken off and set aside. Stuff a rag in the drainage pipe to prevent sewer gases from entering the space.

To remove toilets, start by closing the shutoff valve located near the base of the water flush tank. Flush the toilet and make sure there is no water left. If you have a two-piece toilet (with a separate tank and bowl), disconnect the tank from the bowl by loosening the bolts that hold the sections together. The toilet base is then detached by unscrewing the nuts capping the bolts on either side of the base. The last step is to break the wax seal between the toilet base and the floor by gently rocking the toilet base. The base can then be lifted and set aside. Don't forget to block the drainage pipe with a rag.

Tubs are trickier. The connections are often inside the wall at the head of the tub or under the floor. In such cases be prepared to restore tiles, wallboard, plaster, and paint finishes. You will need to remove portions of these finishes to get to the pipes. Again, with the aid of a pipe wrench, the drain-overflow assembly is set apart by loosening up the slip couplings. Disconnect the unions or simply cut through the supply risers. At this point, you should cap all disconnected pipes. This will allow you to turn on the water service

HOW TO MEASURE PIPING

Measure the face-to-face distance the pipe must travel between fittings. To this distance add the depth that the pipe must travel into each fitting. (Make sure to add this quantity to both ends.) Let's say that the distance between fittings is 11" and the distance the pipe will go into each fitting is ½". The total required length of pipe will be 12" (Ill. I-1).

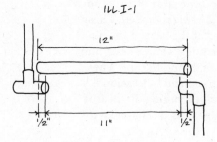

ILL. I-1

HOW TO CUT AND JOIN PIPE

The method of cutting and joining pipes varies with each material. Regardless of material, however, make a few practice cuts and joints before going ahead to the actual installation to get the hang of the material.

Cast-iron pipe: Joining cast-iron pipe may vary with the local code requirements. Most codes no longer require leaded joints, which are cumbersome and difficult to do.

Cast-iron pipe is available in the hub-and-spigot type. It consists of a section of pipe with one end having a larger diameter than the other. The larger-diameter end is called the hub. The opposite end has a slight ridge and is called the spigot. These ends are designed to fit inside each other. The hub is always located at the end facing up (receiving the flow of the drainage). The spigot end fits inside the hub of the section underneath. Cast-iron pipe is also available in a no-hub type (Ill. I-2).

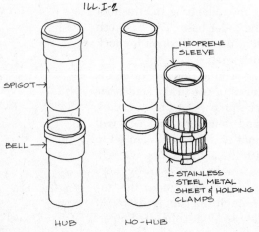

ILL. I-2

SPIGOT →

BELL →

NEOPRENE SLEEVE

STAINLESS STEEL METAL SHEET & HOLDING CLAMPS

HUB   NO-HUB

Cuts in cast-iron pipe are made by means of a cold chisel or a hacksaw, depending on the thickness of the pipe. (There are two thicknesses of cast-iron pipe, a heavy one for exterior use and a lighter one for interior use.) Chalk-mark the length to which the pipe must be cut. Place a piece of wood on the floor and lay the pipe over it. If the pipe is lightweight, use a hacksaw to make a shallow cut all around the pipe. Tap the pipe with a hammer until it breaks. A hacksaw won't work when using heavy pipe. Instead, score the pipe at the chalk line with a cold chisel. The first cut should be a light one all around. Then continue chiseling progressively harder until the pipe breaks (Ill. I-3).

To join no-hub pipe, slip the neoprene gasket over the end of one pipe and the metal band over the end of the other pipe (or fitting) (Ill. I-4). Bring the two ends together and slip the gasket over the joint. The next step is to slip the metal band over the gasket (Ill. I-4). The connection is completed by tightening the clamps in the metal band with a screwdriver (Ill. 1-4). These clamps hold the joint together. An added advantage to the no-hub fittings is that they can be easily taken apart without damage.

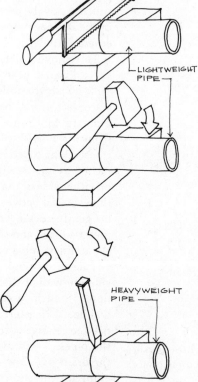

ILL. I-3

LIGHTWEIGHT PIPE

HEAVYWEIGHT PIPE

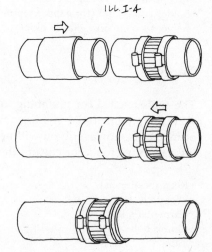

ILL. I-4

Copper tubing: Copper is considerably easier to cut and join than cast iron. To cut copper tubing, chalk-mark the desired length. Copper can be cut with a hacksaw and a jig or with a pipe cutter. Regardless of the method, the important thing is to get a square cut. If you are using a pipe cutter, place the pipe on a vise and the cutting blade of the cutter on the chalk mark. Rotate the cutter around the pipe at the same time that you are tightening the cutter's handle (Ill. I-5). The cut pipe is likely to have burrs, which must be removed with a file.

Before the pipe can be soldered, its ends as well as the inside of the fitting must be cleaned with steel wool. It is wise at this point to check for any dents in the pipe. Remember that the pipe must be perfectly round if the joint is to be successful. With a brush, apply a coat of flux to the inside of the fitting and the outside of the pipe you have just cleaned. The fitting is then slipped on and turned a few times in order to spread the flux evenly all around. Any excess flux should be removed.

The soldering process starts by heating the fitting with a torch. When hot, solder is applied to the edge of the fitting all around the joint, sealing it. (Capillary action allows the melted solder to penetrate into the space between the pipe and the fitting.) Remove the heat after the connection has been filled. Wipe away any surplus solder. (Be careful not to burn yourself.) While the solder joint

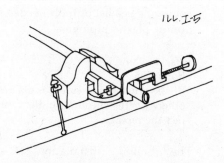

ILL. I-5

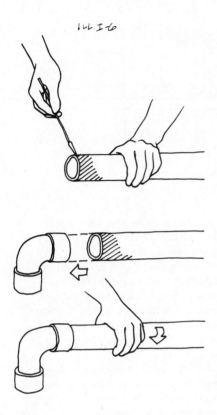

ILL. I-6

is cooling, prevent the solder seal from being broken by making sure that the pipe and fitting are not moved.

Plastic piping: Plastic is by far the easiest material to cut and join. Cutting plastic pipe can be done with a hacksaw, a handsaw, a power saw, and sometimes even a pocketknife. (Make sure that the saw is fine-toothed.) Here again, a square cut is important. This can be easily done by using a jig. Once the pipe is cut, any burrs should be removed with a file.

Plastic pipe is joined by means of solvent. Before it can be applied, however, the inside of the fitting and the outside of the pipe should be cleaned with emery cloth. The solvent is then applied on both the outside of the pipe and the inside of the fitting with a bristle brush, covering the entire area which makes up the joint. It is important to get the correct solvent for the type of plastic pipe you are using. The easiest way to avoid confusion is to purchase the solvent at the time you purchase the pipe. Slip the fitting onto the pipe as far as it should go. Press it against the pipe, and turn it (about a quarter of a turn) to ensure the even distribution of the solvent (Ill. I-6). Hold the joint together for a few seconds and then remove any excess solvent. Do not move the joint until it has had sufficient time to set.

Compare this procedure with that for copper or cast-iron piping and the reason why plastic pipe is gaining in popularity becomes obvious.

to other areas of the house which are still in use. Now go back and check for leaks at these caps.

EXTENDING PLUMBING TO A FIXTURE

If you only need to add a few fixtures, try to use the existing pipes wherever possible. Start by locating the new fixtures with chalk or a crayon. Take a look around that area to assess where the closest drainage and supply pipes are. Cut away the finish wall surfaces to the edges of the nearest studs. Avoid cutting the studs or floor beams. Where new plumbing needs to be run under floors you will have to drop ceilings to allow for the pipe runs (Inset II). Allow yourself enough room to work.

Try to visualize the new piping and new fixtures in place. The next step is to locate the traps. In the case of lavatories or sinks, you need to locate the trap height on the wall (Ill. 1). From the top of the trap run an imaginary line to the soil stack, making sure the pipe pitches downward (Ill. 1). Where this line hits the trap, mark an X. (The bottom of the trap should not be lower than the connection to the stack. Otherwise, water will be siphoned from the trap.) Position the T connection to the soil stack at the X location. Mark the top and bottom of the fitting on the soil stack. To prevent damage to the piping, secure both sides of the pipes next to the cuts (Ill. 2). The next step is to join to the existing pipes by cutting into them (make sure that you have drained the pipes first). Using a pipe cutter, cut out the section of the stack (Inset I). Join the new fitting with hubless connectors. Toilets have built-in integral

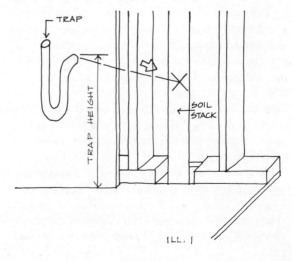

TRAP

TRAP HEIGHT

SOIL STACK

ILL. 1

Renovating the Plumbing

293

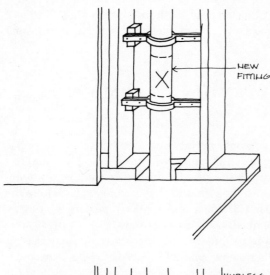

NEW FITTING

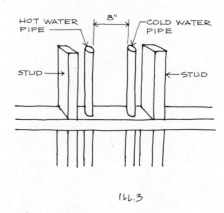

HOT WATER PIPE   8"   COLD WATER PIPE

STUD   STUD

ILL.3

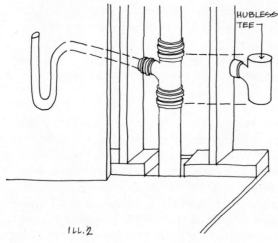

HUBLESS TEE

ILL.2

traps; showers and tubs have the traps at or in the floor below. Toilet traps should connect directly into the soil stack as described earlier. To hook up shower and tub traps, follow the basic procedure described for lavatories.

Positioning the fittings for the supply pipe is not as critical as for drainage pipes. It's a good idea, however, to pitch the pipes slightly downward back toward the supply risers just in case you need to drain the system. The procedure for cutting and fitting new supply and vent pipes is not altogether different from the procedure for drainage pipes. You will need to cut a section of pipe and install a tee to branch into the new line (Ill. 2). If the original supply pipe is galvanized or other material, you need to use adapters to extend pipe with copper.

Here are a few things to keep in mind while installing the hot- and cold-water supply pipes:

· Hot- and cold-water pipes run side by side approximately 8" apart. Where the pipes must cross, be cer-

tain that they are still an adequate distance apart (Ill. 3). Where possible, insulate all such branch supply piping with fiberglass pipe insulation.
· Always provide a shutoff valve at each fixture supply line to facilitate repairs. It is also a good idea to provide each branch pipe leading to a kitchen, bathroom, or laundry room with a shutoff valve. This can prove helpful in the event that the water has to be cut off from an entire area at one time; it eliminates the need to close each individual fixture valve.
· Don't forget to pitch all horizontal branch pipes down toward the stop and waste valve you have already installed at the lowest point in the system. Drainage of the system may otherwise be impossible.
· Hot-water supply pipes are usually located to the left of the fixtures (looking at the fixtures head-on).
· Air chambers must be installed (usually in the wall behind the fixture) above each supply pipe. This is easily done by putting a tee at the top of the vertical supply pipe. A capped length of pipe approximately 12" in length is inserted in the top of the tee and becomes the air chamber (Ill. 4).

When the drainage and venting systems have been installed and until such time as the fixtures are hooked up, debris must be prevented from entering the pipes. This can be done by plugging

ILL.4

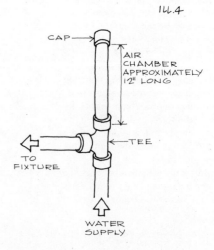

CAP

AIR CHAMBER APPROXIMATELY 12" LONG

TEE

TO FIXTURE

WATER SUPPLY

up all the pipe outlets temporarily with rags. This also prevents poisonous gases from the house sewer from backing up into the house. In addition, check for any unused openings in the tees or other connections. If there are any, plug them up with a cap and nipple.

ADDING A NEW WASTE STACK AND DRAINAGE SYSTEM

Your renovation may include an extension with plumbing for a kitchen or bath. More often than not, the existing soil stack will be too far from the new plumbing. The best solution is to install a new waste stack (secondary soil stack) which in turn is connected to the house drain. The house drain can be extended by tapping into it at the existing cleanout. Remove and replace the existing cleanout with a new length of pipe as required. A new cleanout is then installed at the end (Ill. 5).

With the aid of your plans and templates or dimensions supplied with the fixtures, measure and mark with chalk on the extension floor the location of the new fixtures, their drains, and hot- and cold-water lines and where the waste stack punctures the floor and walls.* Cut a small hole (as marked in chalk) where the waste stack penetrates the floor (or if you have a multistoried extension, the highest floor where the extension has plumbing). Once the hole is open, take a look to see if there are any structural members in your way. Should you encounter joists or beams, you will have to reposition the stack accordingly. If there is no structural interference, drop a plumb bob to the floor below and mark the exact location where the waste stack will fall (Ill. 6). Repeat this procedure for as many floors as necessary to establish the stack run. To determine where the waste stack will pass through the roof, plumb up to the roof from the cutout on the highest floor. Drill a small hole to see if any rafters are in the way. If there are no rafters in the way, you have just established the complete stack run. You can now go back and enlarge the holes (make them slightly larger than the diameter of the stack pipe).

If the extension has a toilet, drill a small hole in the floor where the drain will be located to deter-

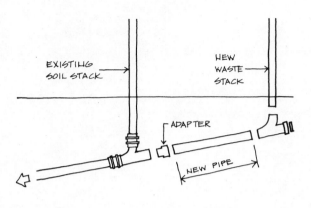

ILL. 5

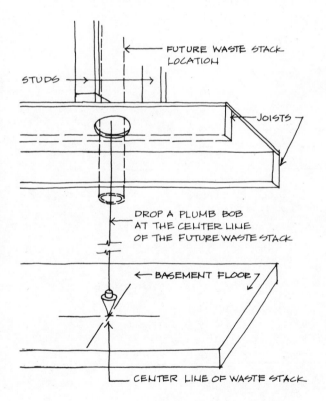

ILL. 6

*If you build an extension that has plumbing, remember to provide access to the crawl space through either the foundation wall or a trapdoor.

Renovating
the Plumbing

295

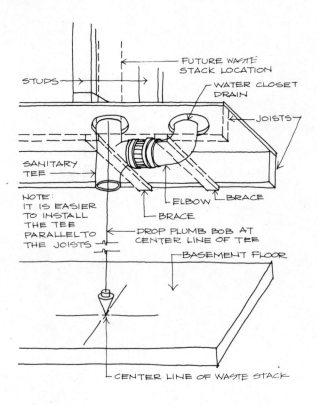

FUTURE WASTE STACK LOCATION

STUDS

WATER CLOSET DRAIN

JOISTS

SANITARY TEE

ELBOW — BRACE

BRACE

NOTE:
IT IS EASIER
TO INSTALL
THE TEE
PARALLEL TO
THE JOISTS

DROP PLUMB BOB AT CENTER LINE OF TEE

BASEMENT FLOOR

CENTER LINE OF WASTE STACK

ILL. 7

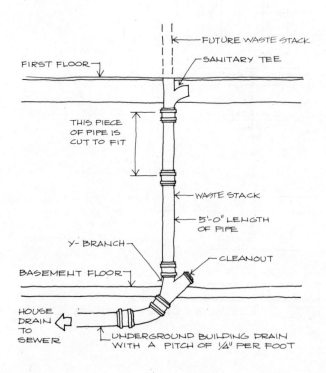

FUTURE WASTE STACK

FIRST FLOOR

SANITARY TEE

THIS PIECE OF PIPE IS CUT TO FIT

WASTE STACK

5'-0" LENGTH OF PIPE

Y-BRANCH

CLEANOUT

BASEMENT FLOOR

HOUSE DRAIN TO SEWER

UNDERGROUND BUILDING DRAIN WITH A PITCH OF ¼" PER FOOT

ILL. 8

mine if there is any structure in the way. (Water closets should drain directly into the waste stack.) If there is no problem, enlarge the hole and position a sanitary tee and elbow together. Hold them temporarily in place with braces directly beneath the two openings provided as shown in Illustration 7.

The waste stack will go down through the basement or crawl space to join the upper end of the building drain. Don't forget that the building drain should have a minimum rise of ¼" per 1' (or as required by code). Install a cleanout (a sanitary Y branch with a cleanout plug) where the soil stack and the building drain come together. Check to make sure that the sanitary Y is plumb and directly underneath the location of the waste stack. You can now start assembling the waste stack from the bottom up. The first run of vertical pipe is connected to the sanitary Y (cleanout). If the material of the house drain is different from that of the waste stack, you will have to use an adapter. Otherwise, continue upward with the stack until it reaches the point where it connects to the first-floor sanitary tee; some pipe cutting will be required (Ill. 8). The tee can have one or more side outlets, depending on the number of branch lines it must receive (Ill. 8). The sanitary-tee connection between the toilet and the waste stack, which had previously been temporarily held in place, can now be joined to the waste stack.

The waste stack continues its run to the roof by joining successive lengths of pipe. Once it reaches the roof, it should extend through the roof and be carefully flashed (see Chapter 31). On its way to the roof, branch pipes connect into the stack as required by the design of the drainage system (Ill. 9). Whenever the waste stack is brought up to a level where branch waste lines occur, they should be connected to the stack before it is built up any further (Ill. 10). The branch lines are located by measuring, cutting, and joining pipes until they follow the path required between the fixture drains (as indicated by the chalk mark) and the waste stack. These runs will sometimes occur inside a wall (as in the case of sinks) and other times under the floor (as in the case of bathtubs and water closets). To allow for free passage of waste, avoid sharp bends. Never use a right-angle pipe fitting in bends or in runs of drainage pipe. Make sure that every fixture is supplied with a trap. Double-check all horizontal drainage lines to be certain that they are pitching at a minimum of ¼" per 1' (or as required by code).

CONNECTING VENTS

The venting network is an integral part of the drainage system and it is installed at the same time. (When installing waste lines, make sure to leave Y's to allow the connection of vent lines later on.) Because they function by gravity, drainage lines pitch down toward the waste stack. Instead of letting these lines terminate at the level of the fixture trap, they are extended upward above the trap and are hooked to a vent riser. When continuation of the fixture drainage pipe upward is impossible, a vent line is connected to a branch line as close to the fixture as possible (Ill. 9). The connection between the drainage line and the vent is done with a Y or T-Y to facilitate waste going in one direction. These connections generally occur inside the walls. A horizontal vent branch is then installed to join the various fixture vents. Horizontal vents should always pitch up toward the vent stack to prevent waste in the drainage lines from entering the vents (Ill. 9).

The vent branch is then connected to a vent riser. Its path through the house is parallel to that of the waste stack, until it is either connected to the waste stack (above the level of the highest fixture) or continues its run directly to and through the roof (Ill. 9). The procedure for locating the vent stacks is similar to that for the waste stack. You may need to jog pipes around to work around the structure of the building. The vent lines for a particular area should be installed at the same time as the drainage lines.

EXTENDING A WATER SUPPLY SYSTEM

The techniques involved in installing the water supply system are essentially those employed in installing the drainage system. The primary difference between the two involves size. Waste and vent pipes are large and often cannot be drilled through studs. They can never be drilled through

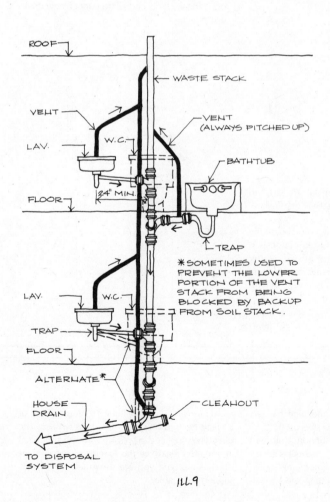

ROOF

VENT

LAV.

FLOOR

LAV.

TRAP

FLOOR

ALTERNATE*

HOUSE DRAIN

TO DISPOSAL SYSTEM

WASTE STACK

VENT (ALWAYS PITCHED UP)

W.C.

BATHTUB

24" MIN.

TRAP

* SOMETIMES USED TO PREVENT THE LOWER PORTION OF THE VENT STACK FROM BEING BLOCKED BY BACKUP FROM SOIL STACK.

W.C.

CLEANOUT

ILL. 9

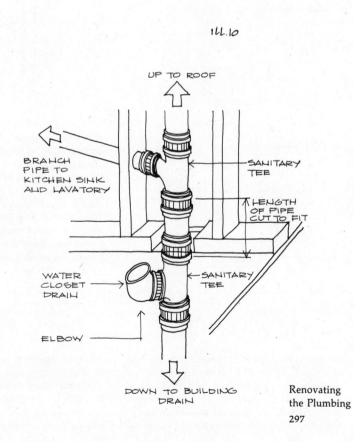

ILL. 10

UP TO ROOF

BRANCH PIPE TO KITCHEN SINK AND LAVATORY

SANITARY TEE

LENGTH OF PIPE CUT TO FIT

WATER CLOSET DRAIN

SANITARY TEE

ELBOW

DOWN TO BUILDING DRAIN

Renovating the Plumbing

INSET II/THE PIPES AND THE STRUCTURAL FRAME

The piping network weaves its way through the structure of the house and is supported by it. It is essential that the structural strength of the frame not be diminished by the holes cut in its members. Cutting away at the house frame to make room for the pipes must not alter the load-carrying capacity of the frame. Nobody wants a sagging floor or, worse yet, a collapsed one.

Here are a few pointers to keep in mind:

· When drilling holes or cutting notches through the studs or joists, the cut should never exceed one-quarter of the total depth of the member (Ill. II-1).

ILL. II-1

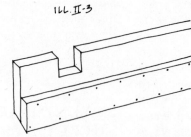

· Holes drilled through joists should be centered between the top and the bottom face of the joists or studs (Ill. II-2).

ILL. II-2

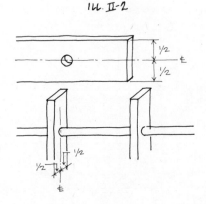

· If a large notch is absolutely necessary in a joist, beef up the joist with additional wood or steel plate or nail in and attach a second joist (Ill. II-3).

ILL. II-3

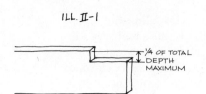

· A steel plate can be added to the side of a notched stud to add to its strength (Ill. II-4).

ILL. II-4

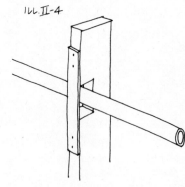

· Wet walls are usually framed out 2″ × 6″ to accommodate pipe thicknesses (particularly waste pipes).
· When studs are too small to accommodate the pipes, the walls need to be furred out. This is done by attaching another layer of studs (either 1″ × 2″ or 2″ × 4″) to those already in place. Keep in mind that notched studs should be reinforced with a steel plate (Ill. II-5).
· Sometimes pipes (particularly drainage pipes) have to be run under the floor to avoid inter-

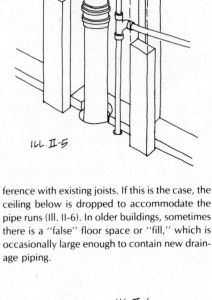

ILL. II-5

ference with existing joists. If this is the case, the ceiling below is dropped to accommodate the pipe runs (Ill. II-6). In older buildings, sometimes there is a "false" floor space or "fill," which is occasionally large enough to contain new drainage piping.

ILL. II-6

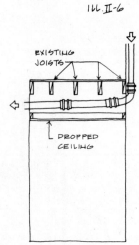

EXISTING JOISTS

DROPPED CEILING

INSET III/PIPE SUPPORTS

Pipes are heavy slender elements that have to span large distances. To prevent their buckling and sagging, supports are provided. When a pipe is traveling horizontally through a wall, the support is provided by studs. At other times the run does not occur within the structure (as may be the case in the basement ceiling) and pipe hangers and other clamping devices must be used.

Horizontal pipes should be supported at least every 6′ to 8′. Larger piping such as steel is generally supported every 10′. Cast-iron piping should be supported at or near every fitting and a maxi-

mum of every 5′ on straight runs. Vertical runs of 1″ pipe need to be supported at every floor. The plumbing supplier can provide you with additional information regarding the spacing of supports for the specific type you are using and the various supports available.

joists. Instead, dropped ceilings or soffits are generally built around them. Supply pipes, on the other hand, are often installed in studs by drilling holes. Drainage pipes can serve as guides for the location of the hot- and cold-water supply lines. The steps required for aligning and erecting the supply pipe assembly are similar to those for the drainage pipes (of course, the actual connection work will vary with the pipe material).

To plot out the route the pipes must take, start by locating the existing hot- and cold-water mains. Take a look at the proposed location of the fixtures. The next step is to figure out the easiest path for the branch pipes to take in order to connect to the fixtures (try to minimize bends and cutting). Areas are cut out for each pipe according to its installation priority. That is, main stacks and supply mains will be installed before branch pipes. Do only enough drilling through woodwork to deal with the specific pipe run you are installing. If you cut the woodwork for all the plumbing at once, inaccuracies between the original layout and the actual pipe assembly might get you in trouble. Be aware that there is a limit to how much wood framing you can cut without causing structural damage (Inset II). For basic guidelines on supply pipe installation, see the section "Extending Plumbing to a Fixture." Remember that pipes have to be properly secured within the structure of the building (Inset III).

FINISHING THE INSTALLATION

The finish installation takes place once all wall, floor, and ceiling finishes are up. It consists of hooking up the fixtures (water closets, tubs, lavatories, sinks, etc.) to the plumbing system. The installation of the fixture varies with both the fixture and its manufacturer. As a general rule, manufacturers supply detailed instructions and recommendations for the installation of their products. Get all the literature and help that you can from them. They're probably the best available source.

Here are a few items to keep in mind while doing the finish installation:

WATER CLOSETS: To make a watertight seal between the bowl and the floor, turn the bowl upside down and apply putty to the outside rim. Then place a ring (rubber, putty, or wax designed for this purpose) around the drainage opening. Turn the bowl right side up and move it slightly until you position it over the floor flange.* Ease the toilet over the flange bolts. Press down on the bowl to make the putty spread evenly. Make sure the top of the bowl is level and that there is no

*The floor flange fits over the top of the water closet drain. It acts as an adapter between the bend and the toilet base.

INSET IV/HOT-WATER HEATERS

Place the hot-water heater in its intended location. Shut off the valve at the water supply main. With the aid of a tee, split the water supply main in two. One branch is connected to the water heater (by means of a union) and becomes the hot-water supply main. The other branch bypasses the water heater and becomes the cold-water main. Install a shutoff valve on both inlet and outlet pipes (Ill. IV-1). Otherwise, you will not be able to stop the water flow into the heater in the event of a breakdown or a necessary repair. The next, very important step is to provide the water heater with a temperature and relief valve (unless the heater comes already equipped with one). The relief valve is a safety measure against an explosion of the water heater (or boiler) due to a buildup of pressure. In addition to being connected to the heater, this valve is joined to a ½" relief or blow-off pipe directed toward the floor (Ill. IV-2). The purpose of the pipe is to permit the release of any

excess water and steam in the event the relief valve "pops" or "blows." It must be directed down toward the floor to prevent anyone's getting hit by a discharge of high-pressure hot water.

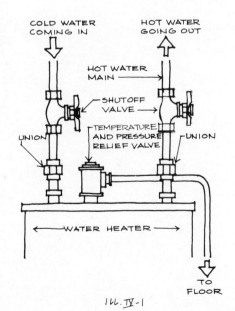

ILL. IV-1

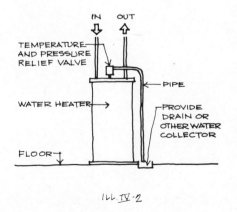

ILL. IV-2

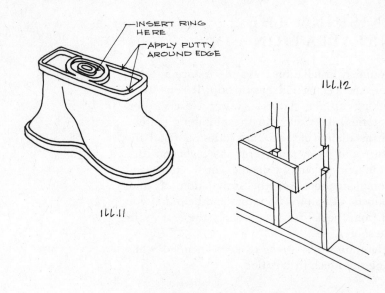

INSERT RING HERE

APPLY PUTTY AROUND EDGE

ILL.11

ILL.12

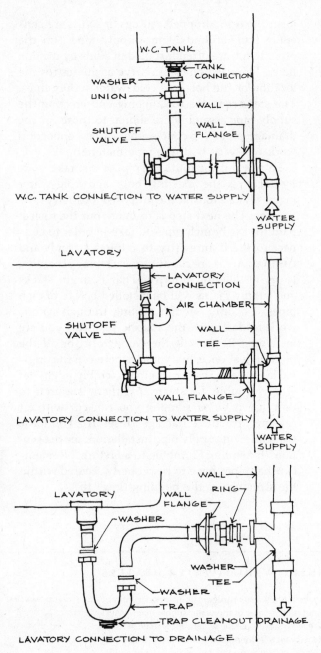

W.C. TANK

TANK CONNECTION

WASHER

UNION

WALL

SHUTOFF VALVE

WALL FLANGE

W.C. TANK CONNECTION TO WATER SUPPLY

WATER SUPPLY

LAVATORY

LAVATORY CONNECTION

AIR CHAMBER

SHUTOFF VALVE

WALL

TEE

WALL FLANGE

LAVATORY CONNECTION TO WATER SUPPLY

WATER SUPPLY

WALL

LAVATORY

RING

WALL FLANGE

WASHER

WASHER

TEE

WASHER

TRAP

TRAP CLEANOUT DRAINAGE

DRAINAGE

LAVATORY CONNECTION TO DRAINAGE

ILL.13

rocking before you tighten the nuts. Do this carefully, without overtightening, to avoid cracking the bowl. You can now install the tank over the bowl as per the manufacturer's instructions (Ill. 11).

SINKS AND LAVATORIES: Unless it rests on a cabinet or pedestal, the sink or lavatory is hung from the wall. In order to do this, a 1" × 6" piece of wood approximately the length of the sink is nailed to the studs. A metal hanger is then bolted or screwed to this board. Before the wall finish is applied, notch the studs to accommodate the thickness of the wood (Ill. 12).

TUBS: If you have a custom tub, keep in mind that the floor of the tub should slope toward the drain. Manufactured tubs come built this way.

CONNECTIONS: For typical hookups of fixtures to water supply and drainage systems, refer to Illustration 13.

34

MODIFYING THE HEATING EQUIPMENT

If you are renovating a house in any way, you will have decided by now if you are going to keep your existing heating system as is, modify or expand the existing service, or completely replace everything. We will attempt to cover all exigencies in this chapter. However, the scope of this book requires us to stick to the basics only, without describing sophisticated equipment.

The installation of most room heating units is easy. Electric radiation units are installed by either plugging in the unit to a grounded outlet or hard-wiring it to a grounded, dedicated circuit. See the manufacturer's instructions and Chapters 20 and 35 for specifying and installing circuiting and wiring. Through-the-window and through-the-wall heat pumps are installed like air conditioners and must have grounded, dedicated circuits. Make sure that you have the requisite circuitry and amperage for these units.

INSTALLING A NEW FORCED-AIR SYSTEM OR MODIFYING AN EXISTING ONE

With the help of Chapter 19 and a heating expert you should have a plan outlining the ductwork and the various duct sections required. If you are completely replacing your system, you should have selected the location of the new furnace, which should be installed by a heating contractor.

As a matter of fact, you may want to have all or most of the system installed by a professional. In any event, if you are going to cut into the ducts, have them checked for the presence of asbestos.

Tools

- Screwdrivers
- Hammer
- Tin snips
- Hand or electric drill
- Hand brace and auger bits
- Keyhole saw
- Ruler
- Tape
- Wood chisels
- Carpenter's square
- Hacksaw
- Level
- Flashlight

Materials

The materials required for the ductwork* depend on your plan. Illustration 1 shows all of the po-

*We have included instructions for the installation of metal ductwork only. You may use fiberglass ductwork for your job if it is permitted in your area. Even if fiberglass ducts are permitted, the code may require that certain parts of the system be metal, so check the code carefully. Fiberglass ducts are easy to install since they are joined primarily with tape and require no additional insulation. Use the proper mask when working with fiberglass.

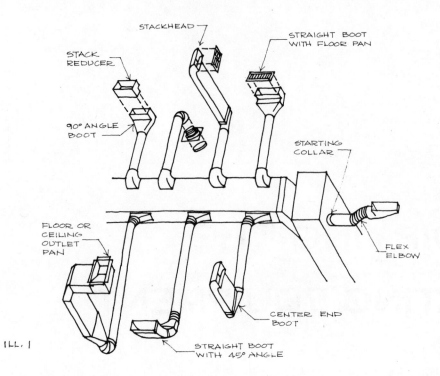

STACKHEAD

STACK
REDUCER

STRAIGHT BOOT
WITH FLOOR PAN

90° ANGLE
BOOT

STARTING
COLLAR

FLOOR OR
CEILING
OUTLET
PAN

FLEX
ELBOW

ILL. 1

CENTER END
BOOT

STRAIGHT BOOT
WITH 45° ANGLE

tential parts of the system. You will most likely have to have your ducts fabricated in a sheet-metal shop. Bring your drawing to the shop and they will custom-make the ductwork to the sizes and shapes specified by the HVAC (heating, ventilating, and air conditioning) designer. There is a small likelihood that you will be able to purchase simple ducts (such as round sections) "off the shelf."

The Installation Procedure for a New System

Generally, the furnace is installed first and the pipes and ducts are then assembled. The return-air runs are installed before the supply ducts. Finally the smoke pipe is installed, the fuel supply connected, and, last, the supply-air and return-air registers are put in place.

Installing Ducts in an Existing House

If you are modifying an existing system that is somewhat oversized, it is likely that you can tap into existing ducts and plenums and extend the system a few feet, adding one or two registers. If the new registers are remote from the furnace,

you may have to play with all of the dampers in the house to balance the system so that heat is forced into these remote runs.

You will probably be taking off smaller ducts from larger, oversized ones. Follow the instructions outlined below for the cutting into and joining of ducts. The most difficult proposition in adding ducts is to make sure that you have an unobstructed run from existing duct (or plenum) to the new register. If you are installing in a ceilingless basement, you may have to run the duct under joists, beams, and plumbing lines. Remember that the efficiency of the system is reduced (and the noise factor increased) with each additional change of direction. Vertical ducts can be installed in closets or along existing partitions and then furred out.

Installing the Furnace

Advanced technology is allowing the furnaces to be smaller and smaller, and if space is at a premium, shop for an efficient, reliable, and safe unit that takes the least amount of space. Some fit in the attic space horizontally. You may even be able to fit one in the upper part of a closet. Make sure that you meet code requirements, that the furnace is surrounded by incombustible materials, and that the furnace has access to the air required for combustion. If the furnace is fueled with oil or gas, the unit will have to be located where it can have a flue or vent. If you are using a heat pump, you will have to find locations for both the interior and the exterior parts of the system, which are connected to each other with a small tube. Hire a heating expert to install the unit and all of its controls.

Assembling the Pipes and Ducts

There is no precise sequence of steps to follow in installing the ducts. It is, however, a good idea to review your plans to determine if a supply line is to cross the return line or another supply line. If so, it makes good sense to install the upper one (the one closer to the ceiling) first.

ROUND PIPE: You can purchase round pipe ready to be installed.* Round ductwork comes with one end flat and the other end crimped. To join sections of the pipe together, fit the crimped end of one pipe section into the flat end of another (Ill. 3). The crimped end should always face away from the furnace. Push the ends together for a tight fit. Seal the joints with a liquid sealer (provided for this purpose) or duct tape. An alternative is to use sheet-metal screws to secure the joints. Drill two holes through the joint and tighten the screws (Ill. 4). Round pipe should be supported every 5' or 6'.

To shorten pipe sections, measure the exact length of the required section onto a section that has not yet been rounded. (It is easier to cut the pipe when it is still open.) Always cut off the plain end, not the crimped end. Open pipe can be cut with tin snips. (If the edge seam gets compressed in the process, pry it open with a screwdriver.)

RECTANGULAR DUCT: Large sections of rectangular duct are used as main trunk lines or plenums. (A plenum is a space, generally above the ceiling, that is used to conduct the flow of air. It is more often used as the return for spent air, but is also used at the beginning of the supply-air system.) Rectangular or round duct can be con-

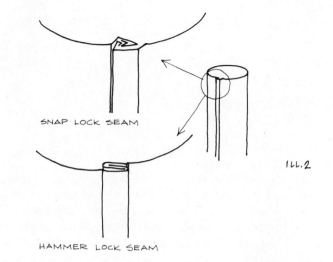

ILL. 2

SNAP LOCK SEAM

HAMMER LOCK SEAM

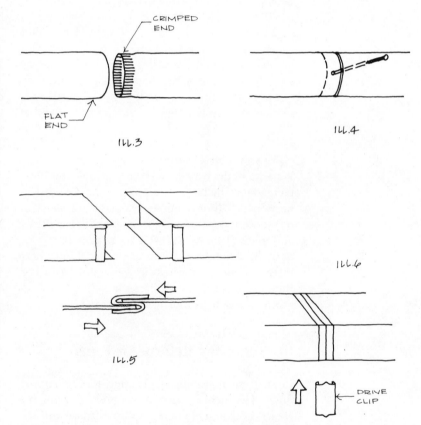

CRIMPED END

FLAT END

ILL. 3

ILL. 4

ILL. 6

ILL. 5

DRIVE CLIP

*Some ductwork is shipped flat and will have to be assembled. The pipe will have either a snap lock or a hammer-lock seam. The snap lock is joined by pressing the tongue on one edge into the slot on the other. The seam will snap closed. The hammer-lock seam will require hammering to get the seam to close. Place the pipe around a piece of 2 × 4 and gently hammer the seam closed (Ill. 2).

nected to the central plenum. Most rectangular ducts come with S-shaped connectors on the long sides. The two short sides are bent back. Push the section together, joining the S seams on the long sides (Ill. 5). Slip drive clips over the two shorter ends. To install the clips, bend one end tab inward. Start the clip upward and, if required, tap it upward with a hammer. When in position, bend the top tab down (Ill. 6). Ducts should be supported with hangers every 5'.

To shorten rectangular duct, measure and cut

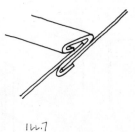

Ill. 7

the section before the long seams have been joined. First assemble all of the regulation-length ductwork, and then measure and cut the last piece. Cut the plain end, not the end with the S clip. It will be necessary to reshape the short sides so that they will join with the regular sections. Cut 1" into the sides and bend the short end backward to receive the drive clip.

SMALL RECTANGULAR DUCTWORK: This type of ductwork is most often used as wall stack because it is designed to fit neatly in between the studs. It is joined with snap locks.* Fit the snap end of one section into the shaped end of the next section and push gently but firmly together (Ill. 7).

CUTTING OPENINGS IN THE SHEET METAL: When one duct meets another, an opening must be made in the larger one to accommodate a connection. Make a template by placing a sheet of paper on the opening of the smaller duct or fitting and tracing its size. Transfer the required opening onto the sheet metal of the larger duct. Drill a hole in the center of the required opening. You can then use metal cutting pliers, tin snips, or a fine-toothed saw to complete the opening.

Installing the Return-Air Runs

Return runs are installed prior to the supply ducts. There are a variety of ways of installing the return-air run, depending on the furnace and the distribution system. Some systems do not have return-air ducts but draw the air from the surrounding area. This is especially true for installations where the furnace is in a utility room on the main floor of the house.

For those systems with return-air ducts an opening must be cut in the plenum chamber of the furnace. Having first determined the exact lo-

cation of this opening, position an offset takeoff collar at that location (Ill. 8). (Clear the floor joists or any other combustible material by at least an inch or two.) Trace the size of the collar onto the plenum chamber. Some systems may require more than one collar. Trace all collars before making cuts. To facilitate the cutting you might consider removing the plenum from the furnace. Cut the holes and position the collars in the openings. The collars are secured to the plenum by bending back the tabs. It is unwise to secure a grill directly to the plenum chamber of the furnace. First place a takeoff collar on the plenum and then attach the grill to the collar.

Return-air plenums can be constructed by lining with sheet metal the already existing stud and joist spaces. These long, vertical and horizontal spaces make ideal ducts. Holes must be cut in the floors and walls to connect the stud spaces to each other. Be sure to block up that portion of the stud spaces above or below the part used as a plenum (Ill. 9).

For the horizontal return ducts, the space between the joists can be used if the bottom section is enclosed with sheet metal (Ill. 10).* This situation is viable only if the duct runs parallel to the line of the joists. If it does not, a regular sheet-metal duct must be used below the joists as the return-air plenum. Holes in the floor must be cut carefully and fully blocked. Cut holes at least as large as the required return-duct size. Larger return-air ducts will not hurt the system, but ones smaller than required might cause vibrations and inefficient distribution. The sheet metal can be nailed directly to the structural wood.

Installing the Supply-Air Runs

Vertical supply ducts in the walls must consist of sheet metal. You want these ducts to be relatively airtight so that the heated air is not lost through cracks. Build up the sheet-metal ductwork as per plan starting from the furnace and working outward to the registers. Remember that the snap end of the small ductwork points to the furnace. Holes cut to accommodate the ductwork should be larger than the ducts. The supply-air plenum at the furnace must be assembled and installed according to the directions supplied with the unit itself. Make all the openings and install the take-off collars before permanently installing the plenum to the furnace.

*Ducts may be joined together by different mechanical locking devices. Some installers further seal the snap-locked joints with adhesives or tape.

*Although it is permissible in some areas to run the return air in unlined stud spaces, we do not advise it.

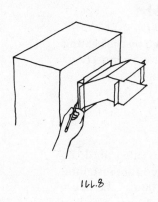

ILL.8

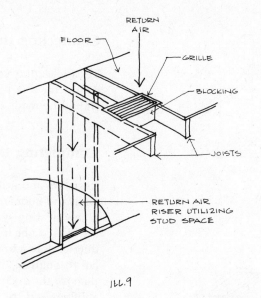

FLOOR

RETURN
AIR

GRILLE

BLOCKING

JOISTS

RETURN AIR
RISER UTILIZING
STUD SPACE

ILL.9

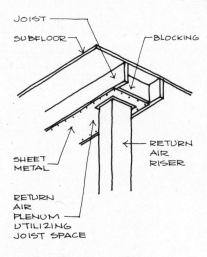

JOIST

SUBFLOOR

BLOCKING

SHEET
METAL

RETURN
AIR
RISER

RETURN
AIR
PLENUM
UTILIZING
JOIST SPACE

ILL.10

Install a volume damper in each run of duct (Ill. 11) so you can control the flow of air. Place it where it will be accessible. Supply runs that pass through unheated spaces should be insulated. Blanket insulation material with a vapor barrier (which is essential for ducts that are also used for cooling), sold in 1"- or 2"-thick rolls for this purpose, is easy to install and may be purchased at the building supply store.

Installing the Smoke Pipe

We suggest that this item be installed by the contractor who is installing the furnace. The smoke pipe leading from the furnace to the outside must be airtight to ensure that there are no leaks of toxic or unpleasant fumes into the house. In addition, the pipe should rise slightly in its horizontal run. The pipe, although light in weight, must be supported properly.

The pieces of the smoke pipe should be laid out on the floor in the order in which they will be needed (Ill. 12). The crimped end of the smoke pipe faces the chimney (if one is required). Properly adjusted elbow sections will be needed to make the required turns. If the smoke pipe is to be installed into a chimney flue, the last piece of

the run is installed in the chimney thimble, with the crimped end forced all the way in. The runs should be assembled starting from the furnace. If a section must be shortened, it should be the last section and a drawband (a thin strip of sheet metal used to tighten and cover the joint) should be used to make the final connection. Wire is used to support the smoke pipe at every turn and at every other pipe section.

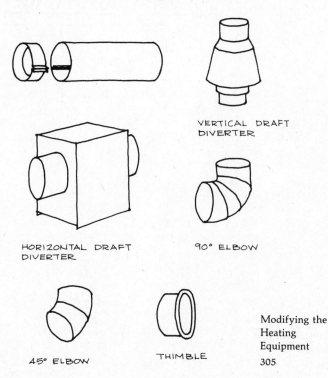

VERTICAL DRAFT
DIVERTER

HORIZONTAL DRAFT
DIVERTER

90° ELBOW

45° ELBOW

THIMBLE

Modifying the
Heating
Equipment
305

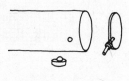

ILL.11

ILL.12

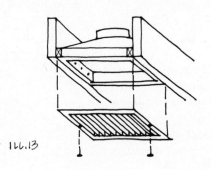

ILL.13

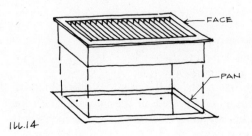

FACE

PAN

ILL.14

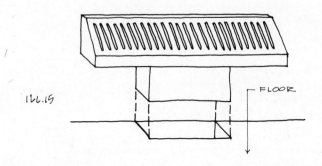

FLOOR

ILL.15

Connecting the Fuel Supply

The fuel supply should be installed by the heating contractor or a plumber. All electric connections should be made by an electrician.

Completing the System

Registers and grills cannot be installed until the walls and floor are completed. If you are installing a new heating system in an old house, the floors are likely to be in place. Even if you are installing ductwork in a brand-new residence, it is easier to cut through an already installed floor than it is to plan for the ductwork while you are installing the subfloor and the finished flooring.

There are a number of different kinds of supply registers, and each variety requires a different kind of opening. The rectangular ceiling register (Ill. 13) requires a rectangular hole between the joists. The round ceiling register requires a round hole cut in the ceiling. The floor register (Ill. 14) requires a rectangular hole through the subfloor and finished floor large enough to fit the pan snugly. The perimeter baseboard register (Ill. 15) requires a floor opening cut flush against the wall. The return-air grills are installed in rectangular cuts in the floor. The opening for the grill is the same size as the shoulders on the underside of the grill.

To cut the opening in the floor, drill four holes (1" in diameter), one in each corner of the opening, and use a saber saw to complete the opening (Ill. 16).

If the register is to be located in the wall it must be positioned between the studs (Ill. 17). This opening must also be lined up with the joists in the floor below (or above if your plan calls for an

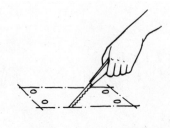

ILL.16

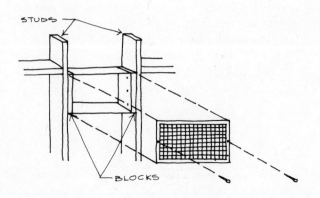

STUDS

BLOCKS

ILL.17

overhead supply) to allow for the supply duct from the basement. (If the walls of the house are already enclosed, cut the hole for the register as required. For cutting gypsum board, use a fine-toothed saw and cut continuously around the outline.)

Installing the Air Supply Registers

Floor registers consist of two parts, a face and a pan. Slip the pan in the hole cut for it and screw through its sides into the opening edges. Slip the register face into the pan (Ill. 14).

Perimeter baseboard registers have a register extension, which fits into a hole cut for it. The back plate is nailed to the wall behind it. The register face is then attached (Ill. 15).

Rectangular ceiling registers have a face and a boot. The boot is designed to fit snugly into the cut hole. Wood blocks are nailed to the joists on each side, and the boot is nailed to the blocks. The face is slipped into the boot and is secured with screws (Ill. 13).

Wall registers attach to boxes called stackheads. The wall opening must have the same dimensions as the stackhead. Wood blocks cut to the required width are nailed to the adjoining studs and the stackhead is secured to them. The register face is positioned on the stackhead and screwed to it (Ill. 17).

Return-air grills fit directly into the openings cut for them. When the grill is in place on the floor, the flanges rest on the periphery of the opening (Ill. 18).

Wall grills fit between the stud spaces. The grill is supported by wood blocks nailed to the studs. The grill is attached to the blocks with screws.

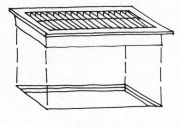

ILL. 18

INSTALLING A NEW HYDRONIC HEATING SYSTEM OR MODIFYING AN EXISTING ONE

If you are adding one or two more convectors to an existing system (check Chapter 19 first to see if the system can handle the additional heat loss), you can tap into existing hot-water pipes.

If you are installing a brand-new hot-water system, five procedures are involved. First, the boiler and its paraphernalia are installed. Second, the connection to the fuel supply is made. Third, the baseboards are assembled and temporarily placed in their final locations so that holes can be drilled through the subfloor. Fourth, the hot-water pipes are run from the boiler to the baseboards and connections are made between boiler and household plumbing. Last, the baseboards are permanently installed after finished walls and floors are completed.

We recommend that you hire a heating contractor to do this work. At the very least (and it is usually required by law), have the contractor install the burner and boiler, connect the fuel supply and smoke pipe, and make the electric and thermostatic adjustments.

Tools

Most of the tools required for joining and cutting pipe are outlined in Chapter 33.

Materials

· Copper tubing: the sizes outlined in the design drawings. Always order about 5 percent more than the lengths measured off the drawings, which are never completely accurate. Extra pipe length will be required where fittings have to be made
· Elbows, air vents, etc., as required
· Flexible connectors used as expansion joints
· Baseboard units, as designed
· All equipment required for the installation of the boiler and burner
· Smoke pipe

Installing the Boiler and the Smoke Pipe

All boiler manufacturers make their products differently. Some are shipped preassembled; others are shipped in parts. Have a heating specialist install the burner and the boiler to ensure that all of the safety equipment is in place. Instructions for installing the smoke pipe can be found in the section on forced-air heating above.

Locating the Baseboard Units

Before installing the hot-water tubing, it is a good idea to determine the exact location of the baseboards even though these units will not be installed until later.

Place the units in their anticipated locations (most likely under the windows). If the gypsumboard walls are not yet installed, allow for their thickness and, if the finished floor is not in place, the thickness of the flooring. Slip on all fittings and connections and temporarily assemble all end panels and accessories.

To determine the location of the supply and return risers drill exploratory holes to make sure you are clear of the joists and any other obstructions. If the assembly coincides with the joists, the baseboard units on the floors above can be shifted a few inches to clear the structure. In the case of a corner baseboard installation, the baseboard can be cut slightly or a flexible connection can be arranged. The exploratory hole is drilled with a ¼″ bit from above in the center of the projected pipe. The hole is inspected by going down to the floor below.

If the exploratory hole should prove to miss the framing and provides a clear path, enlarge it to accommodate the size of the actual riser. Metal expands as it is heated, and the entire system is expected to move somewhat depending on the temperature of the water circulating in the pipes. To accommodate this movement, oval holes—larger than the risers themselves, with the long side of the oval parallel to the long run of pipe in the basement—are cut through the floor. Drill two holes and cut in between them. For up to 25′ of baseboard the long end of the oval should be 1½″. If the length of baseboard assembled in the room exceeds 25′, add another ⅛″ to the hole for each additional 10′ of baseboard length.

Installing the Hot-Water Pipe

The directions for installing the hot-water pipe are the same as those for the installation of the domestic water supply system. Since all of the connections are to be made from rigid copper tubing, directions for cutting the pipe, connecting it,

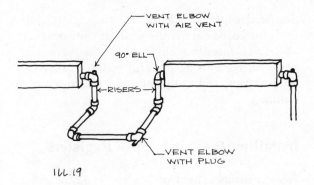

ILL. 19

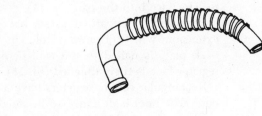

ILL. 20

and running it through the walls and across the floors can be found in Chapter 33.

Install the pipe system, making all connections permanent except those to the baseboards. If there is more than one loop to the system, one entire loop should be completed before another loop is started. Begin at the supply end and assemble the pipe lengths according to plan. Assemble each connection and be sure it is watertight before going on to the next connection. Support the pipe every 10′ or 12′ as you progress.

Hot-water pipe will expand and contract. (Copper tubing can expand as much as 1½″ per 100′ of run.) To accommodate this expansion without placing stress on the pipe you can construct expansion joints from elbows as shown in Illustration 19. It is much simpler, however, to use flexible connectors, which not only take care of expansion but reduce vibrations, eliminate soldering connections, and compensate for errors in measurement. The flexible pipe is made up of ringlike corrugations of copper, allowing the pipe to bend (Ill. 20).

Installing the Baseboard Units

Install the baseboards after the finished walls and flooring are in place. The baseboard units are designed to be screwed to wall framing and rest on the finished floor. Remove the innards from the units—that is, the heating element (the fins) and the front panels—and nail the rear panels to the wall. Use a punch to start the holes, and always nail the panels to the studs. (These can be located by tapping the walls with a small hammer and listening for a solid thunk.) Replace the heating elements and reassemble the units.

Install the air-vent elbows at the return end of the baseboard. (You will not need to install valves for baseboards in a series loop.) The assembly now can be permanently joined. Solder the various components together, removing them, if possible, from the floor to an elevated working area. Soldering instructions for rigid copper conduit can be found in Inset I, page 292.

35

MODIFYING THE

ELECTRICAL WIRING

Electrical installation work demands great care. All connection work must be done meticulously and accurately to avoid short circuits and malfunctions. Code requirements and recommendations need to be followed strictly. It is for this reason that most municipalities do not allow electrical work to be done by anyone other than a licensed electrician. In cities, by code, a licensed electrician is a must. Those of you who live in multifamily dwellings will also find that the codes prohibit do-it-yourself electrical work. There is sound logic behind this requirement. The electrical systems of these buildings are far too complicated for the novice. Occasionally you will find a code that allows the owner of a single-family home to do his own electrical work. Even in this instance, we strongly recommend that you hire a licensed electrician to do your renovation. The following discussion is geared to those renovators in one-family houses who may be assisting a licensed electrician.

A few tips on safety: Whenever you are working on the system, caution must be taken that the wires are dead. Make sure you disconnect all power to the area where you are working. Disconnect the circuits by flipping off the breaker or completely removing the fuse from the box. Use a voltage tester to make sure the circuit is dead. Let everyone know that electrical work is in progress by leaving a note on the service panel. "Hands off panel: electrical work in progress" will prevent any confusion. The last thing you want is for someone to go into the basement and flip the circuit breakers back on while there is work tak-

ing place. Always use tools with insulated handles. Rubber gloves and rubber-soled shoes are also good insulators. Never stand on a damp or wet surface while doing electrical work. Remember, electricity can be hazardous.

Materials

You'll need the following materials:

- Cable: two- and three-wire
- Standard duplex outlets
- High-voltage outlets (both 115 V and 230 V)*
- Weatherproof receptacles
- Lighting outlets
- Switches: two-, three-, and four-way, as needed
- Ground-fault circuit interrupters (GFI's)
- Service panel, as needed
- Boxes: switch, outlet, and junction boxes
- Solderless connectors ("wire nuts")
- Box hangers
- Cable connectors
- Straps
- Finish plates

Tools

Here are some of the most widely used electrical tools:

*The configuration of 115-volt and 230-volt outlets and plugs is different.

- Long-nosed pliers
- Electrician's pliers
- Electrician's multipurpose wiring tool
- Electrician's screwdriver
- Standard ¼" screwdriver
- Pocketknife
- Hacksaw
- Drill or brace and bit
- Metallic tape measure
- Yankee push drill
- Voltage tester
- Continuity tester
- Soldering iron
- Cable ripper
- Compass saw
- Adjustable wrenches
- Fish tape
- Electrical tape

We have divided the roughing-in stage of electrical installation into two sections: new work and old work. New work would apply to those of you doing a "gut" renovation and those building a new extension. Old work applies to renovators who are extending or adding to the existing system. Whether you are doing new or old work, we suggest you read the entire chapter, since most of the techniques discussed are common to both types of projects.

Like plumbing, electrical work takes place during both rough and finish stages of construction. Roughing in refers to concealed wiring; it usually takes place when the house frame is exposed. The finish work occurs after all wall and floor finishes are in place. The steps involved in an electrical installation are:

Roughing In

- Installing the service panel
- Locating and installing the boxes
- Stringing the cable to the various boxes
- Connecting to the box
- Grounding the cable to the box
- Stripping 1" of insulation off the wires
- Testing the circuits
- Inspection

Finish Work

- Wiring the various devices
- Installing the finish plates
- Final hookup at the service panel
- Permanent hookup to the power line

Following are a few pointers to remember:

- All power should be turned off before any work takes place.
- Electrical cables are color-coded to simplify their installation. Always connect white wires to white wires and black wires to black wires. (Exceptions to this rule are described on page 317.)
- White wires are connected to chrome screws. Black wires are connected to brass screws.
- Switches are connected to black wires, not white ones. (See pages 317–318 for exceptions.)

ROUGHING IN: NEW WORK

The Service Panel

The existing service panel may be inadequate to meet your expanded needs. If so, you may need an auxiliary panel or a new service. The service panel may be installed before, after, or at the same time as the interior wiring. Service panels are installed by licensed electricians—for very good reasons. Not all service panels are similar in design. As designs vary, so do the steps necessary for proper installation.

Aside from this problem, the installation work itself is tricky. Its efficient operation, however, is essential to that of the rest of the system. A mistake in the installation of the service panel could become a hazard for the entire system. As a matter of fact, many electrical contracting companies allow the service panel installation to be performed by only their most experienced electricians.

The Distribution System

The code requires that all connections between the cables and the devices (switches and outlets) and all wire splicing take place inside approved boxes or inside special conduit fittings. This is to reduce the possibility of fire or shock brought about by a defective connection left unprotected inside a wall. A few sparks could ignite paper, wood, other combustible construction materials, or accumulated dirt inside the wall cavity. A greater danger is a subsequent fire resulting from an incorrect installation and long-term heating of the wire or conduit. The roughing-in stage starts by locating and installing all the boxes for switches and outlets as indicated in the plan.*

*Although these boxes have traditionally been made out of metal, the use of plastic boxes is becoming more popular. There are still many building codes that do not allow the use of plastic boxes.

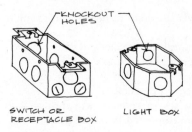

SWITCH OR
RECEPTACLE BOX   LIGHT BOX

ILL. 1

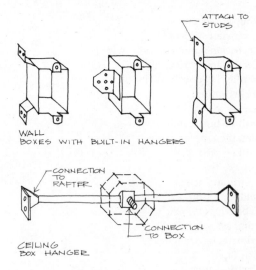

WALL
BOXES WITH BUILT-IN HANGERS

CEILING
BOX HANGER

ILL. 2

There are many boxes available to satisfy a number of different conditions (Ill. 1). The most common ones are rectangular and octagonal. Octagonal boxes are generally used for lighting, and multiples of rectangular boxes are used for receptacles and switches. Square boxes are often used for junctions. (Junctions occur when electrical wires are spliced with no outlet or switch provision.)

The size of the box is determined by the number of outlets or the number of connections and by the quantity of wiring to be contained. There should be enough room in the box to work on the connection, to comfortably house the device, and to store all loose wiring. Avoid working with small boxes. They not only will make the installation work more difficult but will hardly leave sufficient room to house the wiring and the device. (See square-inch requirements in the code.)

Cables enter the boxes through knockout holes (Ill. 1). Knockouts are circular sections of metal or plastic that have been prepunched and can be opened by tapping with a screwdriver and a hammer. The piece of metal is then twisted loose with a pair of pliers. Each box is equipped with more knockouts than required to accommodate various installation conditions. It is important to remove only those knockouts necessary for the connection work. Don't leave an unused knockout open. If you pull one open by mistake, close it with a closure washer.

Switch, receptacle, and junction boxes are attached to the woodwork with mounting brackets (Ill. 2). These brackets are generally built in as part of the box. Ceiling boxes are attached to the frame with hanging bars. Both the bars and the built-in mounting brackets automatically adjust the boxes to be flush with the outside edge of the finish wall surface.

It is helpful to know the heights commonly used for installation of boxes. Those used to house floor outlets are usually 12″ to 14″ above the floor. Over-the-counter outlets are generally placed at approximately 40″ (to the bottom of the outlet) or 42″ (to the center of the outlet) above the floor. Switches are installed at 48″ above the floor (to the center of the outlet). Outlets and switches to satisfy special conditions should be placed accordingly.

With all the boxes in place, the next step is to string the cable to the various boxes according to the circuitry design. (The 115-volt circuit is customarily strung before the 230-volt circuit.) Electrical cables, like plumbing pipes, snake through and around the house structure. (It is a good idea to keep the paths of the electrical cables and the plumbing pipes separate from each other to avoid problems should leaks develop in the pipes.) To minimize interference with the building's structural capacity, keep in mind the tips for drilling outlined in Chapter 33, Inset II. In addition, placing electrical cables in the center of studs or joists helps to prevent finish nails or screws from puncturing the cables during the installation of finishes.

To prevent the cables from sagging and causing possible damage, they are secured to the woodwork by means of special staples. These staples are specifically designed for use with nonmetallic sheathed cable or armored cable, making the installation work considerably easier. (Care should be taken to use the right type of staples for the type of cable you are using; you may otherwise damage the cable.) Check your code for the required spacing of the cable supports. Illustration 3 (page 314) shows ways in which to run the cables in relation to the house structure. Avoid sharp bends.

A few tips on stringing cable: Cable comes

INSET I/BASIC SKILLS

CUTTING CABLE

The procedure varies with the type of cable. We will discuss nonmetallic sheathed cable and armored cable.

Nonmetallic sheathed cable: This type of cable can be stripped with a knife. Slit the outer covering, being careful not to damage the insulation of the wires inside. Once a slit is started on the outer cover, you can pull it off as far as you want with a pair of pliers. A cable ripper can be used instead when type NM cable is used. It will save you some time. For type NMC cable, only a knife is needed (Ill. I-1).

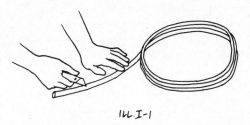

ILL. I-1

Armored cable: Armored cable is more difficult to cut than nonmetallic sheathed cable. With a fine-toothed saw, start a diagonal cut on the cable where the armor is to be removed (Ill. I-2). Be careful as you are sawing the armor not to damage the wire insulation or the bare grounding strip inside. Grab the cable with one hand at either side of the cut and twist the cable against the spiral until the armor breaks off (Ill. I-2).

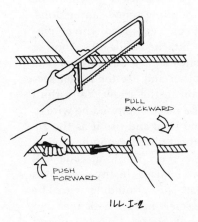

PULL BACKWARD

PUSH FORWARD

ILL. I-2

To prevent the sharp edge of the cut armor from damaging the insulation of the wires, you must install a bushing. A bushing is a small cylinder with one side having rounded edges. It is made out of a tough fiber with a high insulating value (Ill. I-3).

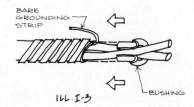

BARE GROUNDING STRIP

BUSHING

ILL. I-3

The bushing is slipped between the armor and the wires. Make sure that the grounding wire is bent back over the outside of the armor (Ill. I-3).

It is very important that a bushing be provided; otherwise, the danger of damaging the wires and a consequent short circuit or ground is increased. No inspector will approve an installation without bushings.

SPLICING THE WIRE

To splice is to join together two or three wires in such a manner that the resulting wire remains as strong mechanically, as good a conductor electrically, and as well insulated as a continuous piece of wire. The first step in making a splice is to remove the insulation from the wire. You can do this with a pocketknife (being careful not to damage the conductor) in the same manner in which you sharpen a pencil. The insulation should decrease smoothly toward the conductor. It should not be a right-angle cut (Ill. I-4). Make sure that there are no traces of insulation left on the wire.

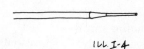

ILL. I-4

The splice can be soldered or solderless. Soldered splices start by mechanically joining the wires. This can be done in a couple of different ways. The most common one is the pigtail splice, which joins two wires (Ill. I-5).

PIGTAIL SPLICE

ILL. I-5

There are instances in which three wires are joined together, and a slightly more complex version of the pigtail called the bunch splice is used (Ill. I-6).

When the wires have been joined mechanically, flux is applied over the splice. Be careful to apply the type of flux used for electrical purposes. Check with your supplier. Hold the wire splice with a pair of pliers and heat it with a soldering iron until the solder melts on contact. Push the solder inward to provide enough solder for a good bond. Make sure that the splice is well soldered on all sides.

After the solder has hardened and cooled, tape the entire splice over with rubber tape (then plastic tape).* Wrap the tape spirally to completely cover the splice and overlap the wire insulation. The proper application of tape is very important since it provides the insulating jacket for the splice.

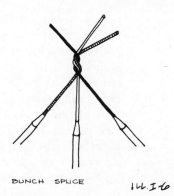

BUNCH SPLICE

ILL. I-6

Solderless splices are easier to do than soldered ones. "Wire nuts" are the most common, although "pressure" connections are sometimes used as an alternative. Both save considerable time. Check the code to see if it allows their use.

A wire nut is a small insulated cap that is screwed onto the ends of wires. Only enough wire is stripped to fit into the connector. The wires are placed side by side and screwed onto the cap (Ill. I-7). Be careful not to leave any bare wire exposed. A "pressure" connection is made with an insulated copper thimble and a special pressure hand tool.

*Plastic, vinyl, and friction tape have no acceptable insulating qualities.

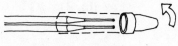

SOLDERLESS CONNECTOR

ILL. I-7

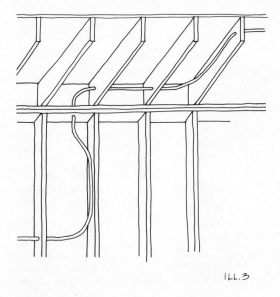

ILL.3

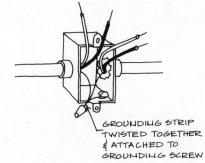

GROUNDING STRIP
TWISTED TOGETHER
& ATTACHED TO
GROUNDING SCREW

ILL.4

BOX WITH PIGTAIL

ILL.5

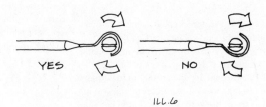

YES   NO

ILL.6

wound in big rolls. Unwind only as much cable from the roll as you will need to make a run between two boxes. When too much cable is unwound at a time, it tends to twist, making the stringing job more difficult. To further avoid twists and bends, unwind the cable by turning the spool. Begin by stringing the cable from the service panel (or projected location of the service panel) to each outlet box along a particular circuit. To avoid a mix-up later on, tag all circuits at the service panel end. Leave 4' to 6' of cable behind for later installation to the panel. Once you get to the box, cut the cable (Inset I), allowing about 1½' extra length for both the incoming and the outgoing cable. (Extra cable comes in handy in case an outlet must be moved to accommodate a molding, cabinet, or other unforeseen construction.) Strip 8" of cover from the cable, leaving the wire exposed. Remove two knockout plates from the box and carefully connect the cable to the box (Inset II).

To provide a continuous ground, the cable is grounded at each box. The grounding procedure varies with the code.* Generally, however, if you are using nonmetallic sheathed cable, the grounding wires in the incoming and outgoing cables are secured or connected together with a wire nut and fastened with a screw to an unused hole in the box (Ill. 4).† (Grounding wire may be bare or

insulated.) There are several ways in which the connection to the grounding screw can be done. There are boxes that come equipped with a "pigtail" wire already attached (Ill. 5). Another method is to allow one of the grounding wires to be longer than the other and use the longer section as the connection to the screw. Yet a third method is to snip off a piece of grounding wire or buy precut grounding wire and use it as the attachment between the twisted grounding wires and the screw. Most likely the local code will specify the method to be used. In any event, it is very important that the grounding wire be wrapped around the screw in such a manner that as the screw is tightened, the wire is being wound and "lays" in the same direction on the binding screw (Ill. 6). This screw should be used only for grounding. The other end of the grounding wire will later on be connected to the neutral bar in the service panel. If you are using armored cable, the grounding will be accomplished together with the connection of the cable to the box (Inset II).

*Keep in mind that the grounding wire, or the ground system, is not the same as the neutral. See Chapter 20.
†When using plastic boxes, care must be taken to follow the grounding procedures as directed by local codes. Since plastic is not a conductor like metal, the grounding techniques for plastic versus metal boxes differ significantly.

INSET II/CABLE CONNECTORS

Cable connectors are used to fasten the cable to the outlet boxes (Ill. II-1). The type of connector varies to accommodate different conditions—for example, straight-run and right-angled connections (Ill. II-1). They are installed by slipping the connector over the end of the cable. The screws (on the connector) are tightened. Before inserting the connector through the knockout in the box, remove the locknut. Once it is in the box, fasten the locknut and connector tightly to each other—and therefore the box (Ill. II-2). Some boxes come with built-in clamps, eliminating the need for connectors (Ill. II-3).

When installing connectors to armored cable, be sure to push the cable into the connector as far as it will go to prevent the bushing from falling out of place. The bare grounding strip should be *in* the connector. This way, when you tighten the screws on the connector to anchor it to the cable, the grounding wire will be squeezed. It should not lie loose. This is very important in order to obtain a good continuous ground.

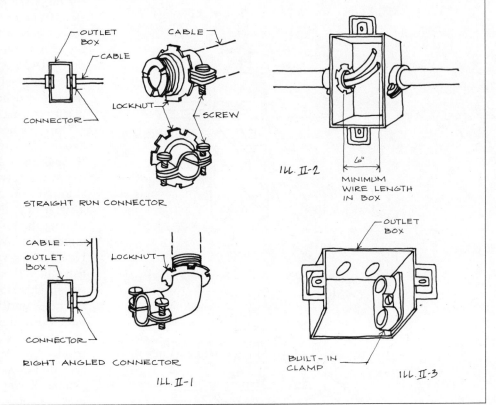

STRAIGHT RUN CONNECTOR

ILL. II-2

MINIMUM WIRE LENGTH IN BOX

RIGHT ANGLED CONNECTOR

ILL. II-1

BUILT-IN CLAMP

ILL. II-3

The last step in the roughing-in process is to strip about 1″ of insulation at the end of the wires (Inset I). These ends will be connected to the devices during the finishing stage. Before moving on to the next box, bend the wires back into the box to keep them out of the way. Repeat the same procedure at every box in the circuit.

With all the circuits in place, the electrician will install the service panel (if he has not done so already). He will also conduct a few tests to check for short circuits, proper current flow, and good circuit ground. Before any of these tests are done, make sure that the power has not been connected at the service panel. The electrical inspector is now called in to check and approve the wiring.

ROUGHING IN: OLD WORK

The basic principles involved in roughing in are common to new work and old work. The primary difference lies in the need for breaking through finish surfaces and routing the electrical wire within the existing walls and floors (with a minimum of disruption in rewiring existing installations). Most commonly, the cable runs in the spaces between studs and joists. There are other possibilities, such as the corners of stairwells. Routing wires behind baseboards, door trim, or other moldings is yet another option. (Wiring should never be run through ducts.)

"Fishing wire" is not easy. The steps involved are more difficult than they sound. This is a two-person job: one person feeds a length of metal or "fish" tape into an opening in the wall, while a second person (with another fish tape) tries to catch the first tape. Once both tapes are connected, a length of electrical cable is attached to one fish tape and pulled through the opening.

Cutting out a series of small openings in the finish surfaces at various locations along the wiring run is usually necessary to snake the wires through. To minimize disruption, find out where the studs and joists are. The openings can then be cut in the spaces between these members. Start by getting access into the wall by means of a new or existing outlet. If you are using an existing outlet, cut all power to the outlet and remove the receptacle.* To open up a hole for a new outlet, trace

*It is important to point out that there are codes which do not allow extending circuits from existing boxes. If the code allows you to do so, do not exceed the ampacity (amperage

Modifying the Electrical Wiring

315

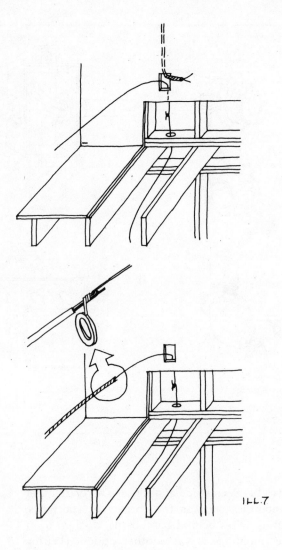

ILL.7

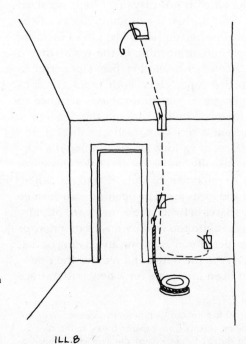

ILL.8

the box itself onto the wall (including all protrusions from the box). The next step is to cut out the space for the box. Where the wall is gypsum board, you can use a keyhole saw to cut out the hole. Plaster walls are trickier. Drill holes at the corners of the box. Cut into the holes very gently (plaster is delicate and can easily crack) with a plaster cutting blade.

Once the holes are in place, insert the fish tape above. The next step is to drill a hole either through the sole plate (if you are trying to get to the space between the joists) or through other studs (if you are working along the wall). As a general rule, the most difficult part of wiring is drilling the holes through plates, studs, or other structures. A ¾" drill bit at the shallowest possible angle is generally used for this task. A second fish tape is then inserted from below (or from the sides). This tape has to make its way through all the holes until it hooks up with the original fish tape. When the two engage, pull the tape into the living space. Using electrical tape, wrap the electrical cable securely to the end of the fish tape (you don't want it to come apart and have to start fishing all over again!). The other person can now pull the cable and bring it into the new outlet location (Ill. 7).

The easiest route for wiring the ceiling is to cut an opening directly from above. This is relatively easy for those who have an unfinished attic directly above the area being rewired. Where there is no attic space, you will need to cut into the finish surfaces where the wall meets the ceiling (Ill. 8).

The space behind baseboards is a convenient place to run cable, since cuts will later be covered during the installation of the trim. Wires can sometimes be easily snaked by removing moldings, installing the wires, and later covering the damage with the reinstalled molding. Care must be taken, however, that finish nails do not accidentally puncture the cable. One way to help prevent this is to chisel out the bottom of the studs (check the local code for allowable depth of cut) and then cover these notches with a steel plate.

capacity) of the individual circuit and make sure that additional outlets do not exceed the ampacity of the wire (see Chapter 20). If extending an existing circuit, be sure to install the new device before returning power to the circuit. If this is not possible, temporarily install wire nuts to the wire ends. Renovators should also keep in mind that all wire splicing must be made in accessible junction boxes.

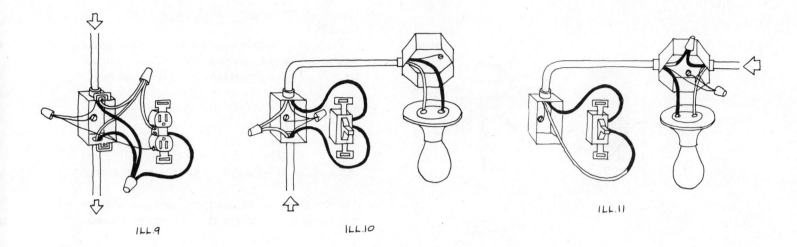

ILL.9   ILL.10   ILL.11

FINISH WORK

With the rough work checked and inspected and the finishes up, you can start to install the devices* (receptacles, fixtures, and switches) to the wires in the boxes.

As a general rule, similar-color wires are connected to each other: black ("hot") is connected to black, white (neutral) to white, red ("hot") to red, and grounding strip to grounding strip. The white or neutral wire runs, without interruption by a switch, circuit breaker, fuse, or other device, up to each point where current is being consumed. This continuity is very important since the white wire is the one connected to the grounding or neutral bar in the service panel (see Chapter 20). There may be instances where a white wire may need to be connected to a black one to respond to a particular wiring condition. You will find, however, that in these instances there is always provision for maintaining the continuity of the white (neutral) wire. Remember: Neutral wires are always continuous, and hot wires are interrupted by switches.

Most devices are connected to the wires by means of two sets of terminal screws, a brass and a chrome set. The black wires are attached to the brass screws and the white wires to the chrome screws. Illustration 9 shows a device wired in parallel. This means that should the wire slip off the terminal screw, the power will continue to flow to the rest of the circuit.

Terminal screws are wired with the aid of small-nosed pliers (wrap the jaws with tape to

*The National Electrical Code defines a device as a unit of an electrical system which is intended to carry but not utilize electrical energy.

avoid damaging the wire). Make a loop in the end of the wire and place it around the screw. The open end of the loop should be in a clockwise direction so that when you tighten the screw, you wind the wire, not the opposite (Ill. 6). Make sure that all bare wire is wound in the screw. Any bare wire left exposed could cause short circuits. Should you have more bare wire than you need to go around the screw, trim it off.

To install wire nuts, hold the wires together with a pair of pliers and twist the exposed ends in a clockwise direction. Snip the twisted ends slightly so that the wires end evenly. (There should be about ½" of bare wire.) Put the wire nut in place and twist it until snug. (Wire nuts come in a variety of sizes and are usually color-coded to indicate the number of wires they are designed to hold.) The wire nut should cover all exposed wire. Make sure that the wire nut is "socked up" solidly; otherwise, it can come loose.

Switches have brass screws as a reminder that only black wires are connected to each other (Ill. 10). (Keep in mind that switches do not consume current.) An exception to this occurs when a switch is located at the end of a circuit. Whenever you have this condition, you will find yourself with only one black wire with which to effect the connection instead of the two you need. To solve this problem, the National Electrical Code allows you in this particular case to connect a black and a white wire to the switch, providing you with the two wires needed. You will note, however, that since the switch is at the end of the circuit, the continuity of the white wire up to the point where the current is being consumed is not broken (Ill. 11). If you have such a condition, paint the ends of the white wire black as a reminder

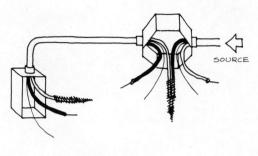

ILL. 12

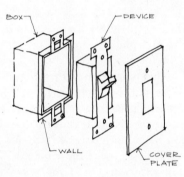

ILL. 14

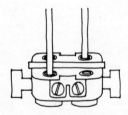

ILL. 15

that it is no longer serving as a neutral wire (Ill. 12).

Three-way switches have a pair of brass terminals and a single darker one called the common terminal. The common terminal is attached inside to a switch arm that can connect internally to either one of the two terminals, depending on which way the outside switch lever is pushed. You will need three-wire cable to make these connections. Three-wire cable comes with a red and a black wire (both hot) and a white (neutral) wire.

Some of the most common wiring conditions are shown in the schematic drawings of Illustration 13.

Following are a couple of tips on device installation:

There are instances when too many wires in a box may cause the screw terminals in the receptacle to be pushed against the side of the box. This can result in a short circuit. A good way to help prevent this problem is to wrap electrician's tape around all the sides of the device.

To avoid working in cramped quarters, pull the wires out of the box. Once the device has been installed, gently curl the wires back into the box, being careful to move them out of the way of devices to be pushed in. Push the device back into the box, making sure that no strains are being induced on the connections. The finish work is completed with the installation of the cover plate (Ill. 14).

A number of devices are available to simplify the finish wiring. Generally, they are more expensive than the ones we've already described and they are often not allowed by code. The most common one is the back-wired type. In back-wired devices, the bare wires are inserted in the back of the device. Once inside, the wire is sandwiched between two plates, which when pushed together grip the wire to make contact. This is done by tightening two screws located at the side of the receptacle (Ill. 15). This device also has a stripping guide to measure the amount of wire that needs to be bared.

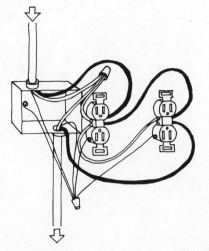

DOUBLE RECEPTACLES AT MIDDLE OF CIRCUIT

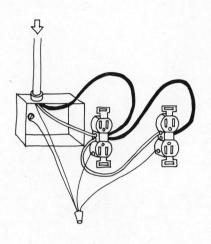

DOUBLE RECEPTACLE AT END OF CIRCUIT

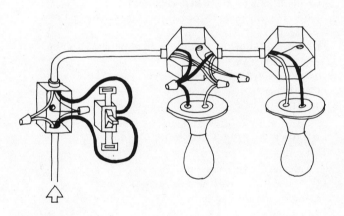

FIXTURES AT END OF CIRCUIT CONTROLLED BY ONE SWITCH

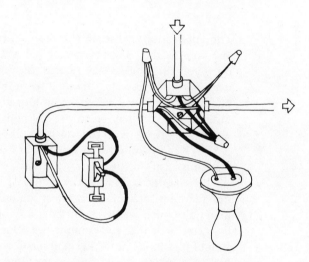

FIXTURE AT MIDDLE OF CIRCUIT CONTROLLED BY A SWITCH

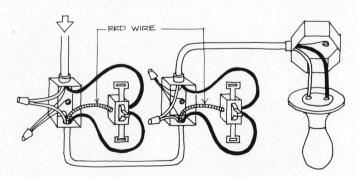

RED WIRE

THREE-WAY SWITCHING: FIXTURE AT THE END OF CIRCUIT

Modifying the
Electrical Wiring
319

ILL. 13

36

APPLYING

INTERIOR FINISHES

The application of the finishes is practically the last step in the long process of renovation. By now you may be so happy that the project is nearing completion that the time spent in the application of the finishes may go unnoticed. On the other hand, you may be so tired of construction work that fussing with the finishes will become a hassle. Keep in mind that finishes are the most visible part of all the work.

This chapter includes a discussion of installation methods for some of the most common finish materials, such as gypsum board, wood-strip floor, resilient tile, and ceramic tile. Our discussion of plaster is limited to small repair work. We feel that major plaster and restoration work is best left to the professional plasterer. In addition, we've incorporated a section on the installation of insulation and vapor barriers.

Materials

The materials necessary for the various finishing jobs include:

FOR THE APPLICATION OF BLANKET INSU-
LATION AND VAPOR BARRIER

· Blanket insulation
· Polyurethane sheets (where needed)

FOR THE APPLICATION OF GYPSUM BOARD

· Gypsum-board panels

· Cementitious board (where required)
· Joint tape (calculate 75' of tape per 200 square feet of surface)
· Ready-mix joint compound (approximately 1 gallon per 200 sq. ft.)
· 1⅝" power-driven drywall screws
· Corner beads
· J moldings

FOR THE APPLICATION OF PLASTER

· Ready-mix joint compound
· Gauging plaster with perlite aggregate
· Gauging plaster and lime
· Metal lath

FOR THE APPLICATION OF WOOD-STRIP
FLOORS

· Tongue-and-groove wood strips
· Flooring nails
· Building paper
· Baseboard and molding

FOR THE APPLICATION OF RESILIENT TILE

· Adhesive (unless tile is self-adhesive)
· Baseboard
· Tile

FOR THE INSTALLATION OF CERAMIC TILE

· Cementitious board (for walls)
· Tile
· Adhesive
· Grout

Tools

Here is a list of tools you'll need to install the various finishes:

BLANKET INSULATION AND VAPOR BARRIER

· Stapler
· Knife
· Gloves
· Approved respirator or mask

GYPSUM BOARD

· Chalk line
· Screw gun
· Pocketknife or utility knife
· Rule or steel tape
· Keyhole saw
· Crimper
· Rubber mallet
· Spackle knives (in 4", 6", and 10" widths) for applying compound
· Sandpaper
· Ladder
· Approved respirator or mask
· Pencil

PLASTER

· Spackle knives (in 4", 6", and 10" widths) for applying compound
· Hawk
· Wood straightedge

WOOD-STRIP FLOORING

· Saw
· Nailer or hammer (for small jobs)
· Chalk
· Nail set (if using hammer)

RESILIENT TILE

· Utility knife
· Notched trowel

CERAMIC TILE

· Notched trowel
· Squeegee or sponge
· Carpenter's level
· Tile or glass cutter
· Nippers
· File

INSTALLING THE BLANKET INSULATION AND VAPOR BARRIER

Blanket insulation is made up of glass fibers. During the installation you should make every attempt to protect your skin and lungs from coming into contact with these fibers; wear long sleeves, gloves, and an approved respirator. The application of blanket insulation is simple. Starting at one corner of the walls, measure and cut the blanket insulation to the proper length. Tack-staple one side of the insulation to the stud at large intervals. Once you are sure it fits, go back and staple it at 6" intervals. If there is a vapor barrier attached to the insulation, make sure that it is facing the predominantly warm side (normally the interior). Once the full length is in place, grab the opposite edge and stretch it well. This side can now be stapled to the stud. With both edges stapled, the top and bottom edges are secured to the floor and ceiling members. It is very important that the insulation be continuous. Don't skimp on joints or edges. It's preferable to overlap or have extra insulation at the ends than to leave gaps.

Whenever openings have to be provided to accommodate outlet boxes or other fixtures, cut a hole of the appropriate size in the backing.

If the insulation you're using doesn't come with a vapor barrier, you must install a polyurethane sheet over the entire area being insulated. This has become a very popular method of condensation control, its main advantage being fewer joints and therefore fewer areas of possible moisture penetration.

To prevent air leakage through cracks in the framing, stuff bulk insulation in the spaces left between door and window frames and the studs. In addition, stuff bulk insulation against any space left between the header and sill plate and the subflooring in all perimeter walls. Be careful not to pack these spaces too tightly, since the effectiveness of the insulation depends on dead air spaces.

Basement ceilings, crawl spaces, and attics are similarly insulated, the difference being that the insulation strips are stapled to the bottom of the ceiling joists rather than the studs and that ceilings and floors over non-air-conditioned areas get thicker insulation, usually 7½" or 9½".

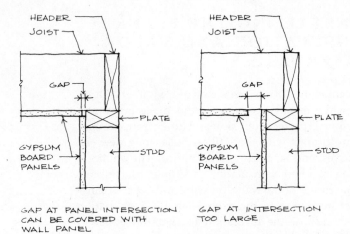

GAP AT PANEL INTERSECTION
CAN BE COVERED WITH
WALL PANEL

GAP AT INTERSECTION
TOO LARGE

ILL. 1

INSTALLING GYPSUM-BOARD PANELS

The installation of gypsum board, although not difficult, requires lots of muscle and tender care. The muscle is needed because gypsum-board panels are heavy (a ½" panel weighs about 2 pounds per square foot; thus a 4' × 8' panel weighs 64 pounds). The care is needed because the seams must be "invisible" at the end of the job, requiring great skill in installing tape and joint compound. For both these reasons be sure to have at least one or two other people on hand while installing the drywall, as well as ample time to spend on your jointwork.

The erection of the gypsum board starts with the ceiling panels both because it's harder to install the ceiling than the walls and because the joints between the ceiling panels and the wall framing can be hidden while installing the wall panels. Of course, this requires leaving a gap of ½" or less between the ceiling panels and the wall (Ill. 1).

Start by checking to see that the corner of the ceiling where you plan to begin is square. If it's out of square, take measurements between the center of the joist where you are planning to screw the panel and the top plate along the wall. This will give you the angle at which the panel should be cut. Transfer these dimensions to the panel and cut it to fit the corner.* With the panel

cut, you're ready to lift it in place. Butt the panel against the wall. As one person holds one side, screw the other one to the underside of the joists at approximately every 6".* Remember that all joints must be centered over wood. Inset the screws a little below the surface of the panel without tearing through the paper. The idea is to be able to cover the indentation with spackle in order to obtain a smooth finish at the end (Ill. 2). The remainder of the ceiling panels are installed similarly, making sure the edges butt against each other.†

Once the ceiling is complete, the wall panels are erected. Any small inaccuracies that have been left at the edges of the ceiling panels can now be covered. Begin the installation at one corner. The first step is to check whether the corner is plumb. Cut the panel to match the corner where necessary.

Gypsum board may be installed either vertically or horizontally. Because the jointwork is difficult, it is wise to apply the panels in whichever manner will result in fewer or no butt joints. In rooms with 8' or less ceiling height, it is better to install the boards vertically. When rooms are taller than 8' (or than the longest available gypsum-board panel) horizontal applications may result in fewer butt joints. Try to avoid vertical joints at the top of doors and the top or bottom of windows by staggering the panel pieces.

For horizontal applications, start by installing the top panels.‡ (There's no way you can do this without the aid of another person.) Butt the panel up against the ceiling and tack-screw it in place. Go back and screw it every 6" around the perimeter and every 12" in the middle (Ill. 3). The lower board is then cut to fit the floor. Any gaps or inaccuracies left between the panels and the subfloor are covered by the baseboard.

For vertical installations, check the corner for plumbness and cut the panel as needed. Butt the panel well against the corner and screw it in place (Ill. 3).

Openings must be provided in the panels to

*To cut gypsum board, mark the panel where it must be cut and place a straightedge on the mark. Score the surface of the paper with a sharp knife, trying to press hard enough to cut into the gypsum core. Cut slowly; a quick cut could get out of control and you can slice your hand instead of the panel.

Bend the board backward until you break the core. Slice the back of the paper with a knife and smooth the edges.
*Some builders put a nailing strip on the ceiling perpendicular to the ceiling joists. This furring can be adjusted in the event that a joist has more crown than the ones next to it.
†Butt joints at the ceiling are difficult to finish. Stagger the panels or try to use (when possible) sheets of gypsum board that are as long as the room is wide. You will, of course, have to enlist some extra help to handle such large sheets.
‡Be sure to purchase an asbestos-free spackle compound and wear a respirator or approved mask.

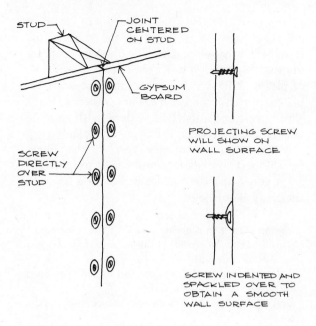

PROJECTING SCREW WILL SHOW ON WALL SURFACE

SCREW INDENTED AND SPACKLED OVER TO OBTAIN A SMOOTH WALL SURFACE

ILL. 2

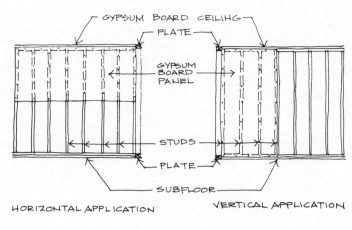

HORIZONTAL APPLICATION   VERTICAL APPLICATION

ILL. 3

allow for outlets, switches, etc. Determine the exact location of the opening and mark it on the face of the panel. Poke holes at the corners of the projected opening with the tip of a keyhole saw, then cut out the remainder.

Tape and Spackle

Taping and spackling involve skill and meticulous work. One of our friends, an experienced carpenter and all-around builder, just completed an extension to his house. Whereas pouring the foundation and the carpentry, roofing, heating, and electrical work did not bother him, he complained at the prospect of having to fuss with taping and spackling. He screwed the gypsum panels in place but brought in a pro to do the jointwork.

While we don't think that taping and spackling are impossible for the amateur to handle, we must make you aware that it is the type of job that requires good, neat workmanship and lots of patience.

You'll be wise to minimize the sanding of the joints by applying the tape and joint compound carefully. Although mistakes can be partially fixed by sanding, they cannot be totally corrected. An alternative to sanding the joints is to even them out with a sponge before they dry.*

*There are contractors who prefer to start the application from the bottom.

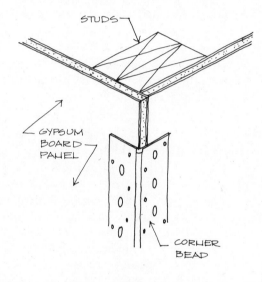

ILL. 4

Before beginning the taping and spackling, install the corner beads at all outside corners (Ill. 4). Cut them out to the required lengths. Hold them in position and secure in place with a crimper and mallet. Install J-molding where gypsum board requires a finished edge or where it abuts a dissimilar surface.

The jointwork requires several precise steps. Once the joint compound dries, it becomes tough to work with. First, with a scraper, apply a small amount of compound over the joint. Start at one end and move all the way to the other. Try to do this in as long and even a stroke as you can. Short strokes give you a rough surface which is hard to smooth out later on.

Applying
Interior Finishes

323

Once the first layer of compound is applied, take the roll of tape and center it over the joint. Hold the tape with one hand while with the other hand you press the tape into the compound with the scraper. The tape shouldn't wrinkle. Where wrinkles appear, lift the tape to a spot before the wrinkles begin and apply the tape over again. Sometimes the tape starts to slant away from the joint. Cut it out and start a new strip. It should be directly over the joint. Scrape over the entire length of tape, removing any excess joint compound.

The second step is to cover the tape with another layer of compound. It should be a thin, smooth layer wider (about 6") than the tape. Be sure to cover all exposed nailheads and exposed corner beads with compound. Leave the compound until it has thoroughly dried (approximately twenty-four hours).

With a wider scraper (about 10"), apply another layer of compound. This layer should be thin and very evenly applied. Once again, give it time to dry. Small irregularities may be wet-sanded (although we prefer feathering and smoothing to wet-sanding). The wall is now ready to receive the primer.

MAKING MINOR PLASTER REPAIRS

The main problem in working with plaster is that it dries very quickly, making it difficult to correct mistakes. For this reason, most amateur renovators prefer to use joint compound for minor plaster repairs. Since it sets slowly, mistakes are easy to correct. The main disadvantage of compound is that it shrinks considerably as it dries.

There are essentially three types of minor plaster repairs: cracks, holes, and failing plaster.

Cracks

Open up the crack by chipping it out with a small chisel, a pointed trowel, or a pointed can opener. With a trowel apply plaster or joint compound over the opened crack. Unless you are quite skilled, you will most likely have to apply more than one coat.

Holes

You will need to patch holes that were created by chopping for electrical wire or plumbing or sim-

ply by failed plaster. The application of plaster is done in three layers or coats: the scratch, the brown, and the white coat. The first two coats are done with gauging plaster with perlite. This type of plaster is lighter and takes longer to dry than plaster of paris (making it easier for the amateur). The "white" or finish coat is done with gauging plaster and lime since it has good workability.

Mixing plaster is not easy. You will most likely get the best advice on mixtures and proportions from your supplier. We are including a few tips that may be of help:

· Mixing plaster in a plastic pan simplifies cleanup.
· Use as much water (cold) as the volume of plaster you want to end up with.
· Sift the plaster through your fingers into the pan until all water has been absorbed.
· Don't stir the plaster and the water since it speeds the setup.
· When mixing lime and plaster, wet the lime a couple of days in advance.
· Amateur plasterers generally use 5 parts of lime to 1 part of plaster.

If the lath is in place, start by cutting back any loose plaster and thoroughly wetting both the lath and the surrounding plaster. You can then apply the scratch coat to the existing lath (as the plaster oozes into the lath it forms a "key"). While the plaster dries, take the tip of the trowel and make diagonal scratch marks. This rough surface provides a bond for the brown coat. Allow the plaster to dry thoroughly between coats. Trowel in the brown coat. To even out bumps and valleys, run a straight board over the patch (long enough to span it). The brown coat should be recessed about ⅛" from the adjacent plaster surfaces. Once it sets, apply the finish coat of plaster. This coat should be built out flush with the adjacent surfaces. The last step is to polish the surface out with water and a trowel.

In those cases where the lath has failed, start by making the hole large enough so that you can securely fasten the new wire lath to existing wood lath or framing. Cut a piece of wire lath the shape of the hole. The wire lath can be attached to the existing wood lath or framing by screwing either to the studs or the wood lath. You must be careful not to loosen the surrounding plaster. For very small holes requiring small pieces of lath, a short-cut approach can be used, in which you mix some plaster and attach the wire lath to the wood lath with the plaster. If you already have metal lath in the walls, you can attach the wire lath with wire. Orient the blades of the wire lath so that they are diagonally facing up and away from the wall.

This provides a good hold for the plaster. With the lath in place, proceed with the application of plaster as described above.

Failing Plaster

When plaster is relatively intact (the three coats and the "keys" are together) but the lath is pulling loose from the beams and causing sagging, you can often use plaster anchors (washers) to fasten it back to the structure. The plaster is pressed back into position, a hole is driven through the plaster and into the supports, and then the anchor is screwed in place. For ceiling applications, make a T brace support out of 2 × 4's and push the ceiling into position. The screws hold best when you can screw into the framing. If you have to screw into wood lath, drive the screws very slowly to prevent them from stripping through the wood. Once the washers are in place, skim over them with a layer or two of joint compound.

INSTALLING FLOORING

The floor is installed last to prevent its being damaged during the application of other finishes. Before putting in the new finish floor you must first remove the existing floor and then make sure that the subfloor is well nailed, level, and clean.

Removing Existing Flooring

Be it linoleum, carpet, tile, or wood, the existing floor surface has to be removed before the installation of the new floor can begin. There's not much advice to be given for carpet, linoleum, or vinyl tile removal.* Removal of tongue-and-groove wood flooring and ceramic tile is more difficult. For the removal of tongue-and-groove wood floors (this includes parquet flooring), use the procedure described for removal of tongue-and-groove siding in Chapter 32, page 286.

Removing ceramic tile requires a good amount of physical strength. Most likely you will be dealing with tile that was installed in cement. In the

*We must point out that asbestos fiber may have been used in linoleum backing, vinyl tiles, and even wood backing. Have an asbestos inspection and analysis of the material before proceeding with the demolition. If the flooring contains asbestos, have a licensed asbestos-removal company do the job.

past, wall tile was installed by applying a gob of cement to the back of the tile. The tile was then stuck onto a wall which had been coated with cement. As a result, this covering must be removed practically tile by tile. With a cold chisel and a sledgehammer, smash the tiles (or take an end tile and put the chisel behind it). Chisel them off one at a time. Floor tiles are removed by hitting them with a hammer, breaking them into pieces, and chiseling them off.

Installing Wood-Strip Flooring

A layer of building paper is customarily laid over the subfloor as the first step in the installation of strip flooring. The building paper prevents dust from passing through to the joists and reduces the risk of squeaking caused by flooring moving against subflooring. It's a good idea to snap chalk lines over the building paper to indicate the location of the joists below.

Strip flooring is installed at right angles to the floor joists (Ill. 5). Older houses may have wood planks as the subfloor instead of plywood. If this is the case, the wood strips are installed at right angles to the subflooring (which will make them parallel to the joists). An alternative is to install the wood-strip flooring on the diagonal. Diagonal installation, though, entails more waste and difficulty in cutting. The strips are matched and grooved on both sides and at either end to provide an easy fit. Keep in mind that wood expands and contracts with the amount of moisture present in the air. Enough room (approximately ¼") should be left between the strips and the wall for this movement to take place. The strips will otherwise buckle, damaging the floor.

Lay out parts of the floor before beginning the installation. Mix long and short wood lengths. Long lengths can be used at the center of the

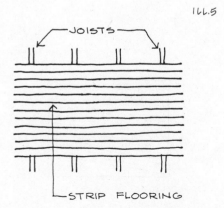

ILL.5

JOISTS

STRIP FLOORING

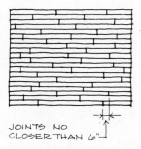

JOINTS NO
CLOSER THAN 6"

ILL. 6

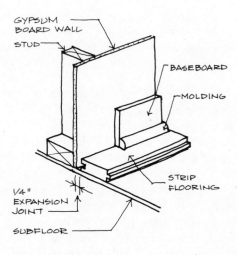

GYPSUM
BOARD WALL

STUD

BASEBOARD

MOLDING

STRIP
FLOORING

1/4"
EXPANSION
JOINT

SUBFLOOR

ILL. 7

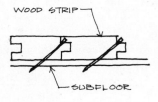

WOOD STRIP

SUBFLOOR

ILL. 8

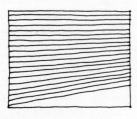

ILL. 9

rooms with short ones left for areas close to the walls. Avoid using all the long strips in one area and all the short strips in another. The floor should look homogeneous. Remember to stagger the joints (Ill. 6).

Lay the first strip about ¼" from the edge of the wall, placing the groove side toward the wall (Ill. 7). With the aid of a nailer and mallet, nail through the top of the tongue into the subfloor and the joist below (Ill. 8). Hook the groove side of the second strip to the tongue of the first. These strips should be driven tightly against each other. You can do this by using a piece of scrap flooring as a driving board.

The remaining strips are installed in the same manner. You may have to cut the last strip lengthwise to fit the room. Here again a gap of approximately ¼" should be left to allow for expansion. Joints between the butt ends of the strip and the wall are not that critical, since most of the expansion and contraction occurs along the width rather than the length. Keep a few things in mind. Butt joints should be staggered, with joints no closer than 6" from each other (Ill. 5). In addition, be particularly careful to keep the boards straight. If they are not aligned, you'll have a problem when you reach the other wall (Ill. 9).

Thresholds and saddles are nailed in place once the floor is completely laid. The baseboard is the last of the trimming to be installed. It is usually made up of a precut molding or a 1" × 4" or 1" × 6" piece of wood and a decorative cap. A quarter-round molding is then added at the floor. The molding is nailed to the floor, not the baseboard. Its purpose is to cover any cracks between the baseboard and the floor due to unevenness (Ill. 7).

Installing Resilient Tile

Resilient tile, unlike wood-strip flooring, does not add to the strength of the floor. For this reason, the use of resilient tile requires a minimum of ¾" of plywood to avoid springy floors.*

Install the underlayment using ring-shanked nails every 6" o.c. at the edges of the panels and approximately 12" o.c. at the intermediate joists. Any indentations in the underlayment should be filled with a floor-leveling compound. Check with your supplier. Joints between underlayment sections should also be filled. The reason for doing this is that the type of tile used for residen-

*Most resilient-tile adhesives are not compatible with particle board.

tial installation is thin. Defects in the underlayment could show through and eventually damage the tile itself.

One way of applying tile is to start at one corner of the room and work your way into the other. A better way is to find the center line of the room and determine how many tiles need to be installed on either side. For example, a room that is 17'-4" wide will require eight full (1' × 1') tiles to both the right and the left of the center line. The edge tile at both ends of the room will be 8" (Ill. 10). The same system is used for the length. The center line can be adjusted slightly to accommodate various conditions. For instance, if the room was 16'-4", the edge tile would be a skimpy 2". By moving the center line to 7'-8" and 8'-8" the edge tile can become 8" (Ill. 11).

If the type of tile you are using is self-adhesive, be careful. Once it's laid down it is quite difficult to lift. When the adhesive is separate, follow the instructions on the can. Adhesive application should be done with a notched trowel.

Start laying the tile by applying adhesive up to one of the center lines. Allow the adhesive to set to the proper dryness. Line up the tile with the pencil line and press it firmly against the adhesive. The following tile is butted tightly against the first. The remaining tiles are similarly installed. Don't try to push tiles into place once you've laid them. Lift and relocate them instead. To cut and fit tiles to walls and other features, place a tile on top of the nearest full installed tile. With the aid of another tile scribe up against the wall and transfer the dimensions to the top tile. This tile is then removed, cut with a lath knife and straightedge, and installed in the same manner as full tiles. When all the tiles are laid, the baseboard is installed.

Installing Ceramic Tile

There are two ways in which ceramic tile can be installed: with mortar or adhesive. We generally recommend mortar over adhesive since it offers a more durable installation. Mortar installation can be the traditional "mud" job or thin-set. Traditional Portland cement or "mud" jobs involve a thick bed of mortar, about ¾" to 1¼" thick (depending on whether it is for floors or walls). There are tiles that because of their irregularity can only be installed in cement. These generally include handmade tiles such as Mexican tiles. This type of installation involves quite a bit of time and skill. Should your tiles require a cement or "mud" installation, hire a good tile person.

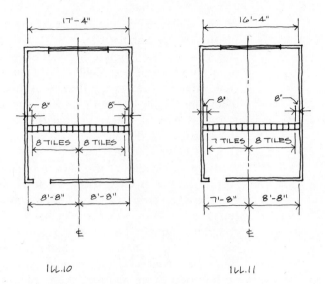

ILL.10   ILL.11

We recommend that you limit your tilework to thin-set installation.* "Thin-set" is a term used to describe various types of mortar compound which offer you the durability of Portland cement and the flexibility of adhesives. These installations can be as thin as ³⁄₃₂" to ⅛". All that is required is to spread the compound over the surface (with a large square-toothed trowel) and set the tiles in place. The best recommendation on the type of thin-set compound to use will come from your supplier. Directions for use are on the bag or container. While applying the tile, keep in mind the compound's drying time. If you apply too much at once, it may be too dry by the time you're ready to set the tile.

The procedures for walls and floors are not vastly different. The walls, however, should be done first. (Walls located in moist areas such as showers or tubs should be backed by cementitious board. Moisture-resistant gypsum panels can be used on other bath walls.) Ceramic tile, like resilient tile, should be centered on the wall or floor. You may otherwise wind up with very narrow edge tiles, which, aside from looking awkward, are quite difficult to cut.† To center the tile

*Thin-set installation requires that the floor base be level and smooth.
†Ceramic tile may be cut with tile cutters or with water saws. These tools can generally be rented where you buy the tile and instructions obtained from the dealer. For other than straight cuts (such as when you need to fit tile around a pipe), you will need to use nippers. Nippers are essentially "tile scissors." Hold the glazed side up and, starting at one edge, make very small cuts until you get the desired shape. Smooth the edges with a file. When a hole is located at the center of a tile, your best bet is to cut the tile in half and, using the nippers, cut out the hole in each half.

on the wall or floor, use the procedure outlined previously for resilient tile.

Begin the installation of the wall tile by setting up a plumb vertical guideline. (You can use the center line you've already drawn on the floor to determine the tile location.) A wood strip is nailed at the edge of the line. (Without the wood strip the line would disappear when you apply the thin-set.) Check to see that the floor is level and start the application of the bottom or cove tile.* Apply the tile in rows, using the level cove tile and the wood strip as guides. Start on one side of the wood strip and work in one direction. When complete, remove the wood strip and repeat the process in the other direction. Some wall tiles are made with concealed tabs which space the tiles with respect to one another. These tabs should be laid in contact with one another. If the tile does not have these features, you will have to insert spacers between horizontal rows of tile in order to prevent them from settling. These are available at tile stores or may be fabricated out of wood. The rows of tile should be checked frequently with a carpenter's level.

Plot out the installation of the floor tile by placing the guideline and wood strip at the opposite end of the room from the door. The reason for this

*For those who are not using a cove tile, we suggest you start the installation with the floor and then proceed to the walls.

is that once you install the tile, you cannot step on it until it sets. Install the tile in the same manner as described above. (Spacers are not required for floor installation.) With the aid of a straight-edge and ruler, check the lines periodically for correct alignment. Once the tile sets, come back to complete the installation of the far edge.

Tiles are set by pressing them firmly against the thin-set. (A slight twisting motion helps to adhere them to the surface.) Every so often, go back over a few rows and tap them down with a wood board to make sure they're all on the same plane. Allow tiles to set as recommended by the thin-set manufacturer.

Now is the time to grout the joints. Grout is the material used to fill the joints between the tiles. It comes in a couple of types, the most popular being a powder, which when mixed with water forms a thick paste. Before applying the grout, make sure that all the joints are free of thin-set. With the aid of a squeegee (some people prefer a trowel), pack the grout well into all the joints, going over them a few times. Wipe off excessive grout. Let the grout set for ten or twenty minutes or as directed by the manufacturer. Wipe clean the film of dry grout with a damp (not wet) sponge. Don't let the grout dry completely before removing the excess. Once it dries, it is quite tough to remove. Most likely, you'll have to wipe off the tile several times before it's completely removed. Polish the clean tiles with a dry cloth.

37

INSTALLING CABINETS

We have limited our discussion of cabinetry to the installation of stock cabinetry. There are good reasons for this. First, we feel that the skills required to do custom cabinetwork are too advanced for the amateur renovator. Second, for those of you willing to attempt cabinetmaking, there are many fine, detailed books readily available to guide you. Fortunately, there is a wealth of stock cabinetry on the market today. You can find cabinets ranging from the very crude to the extremely sophisticated (both in construction and in price). Bear in mind, however, that cabinetry installation, although not terribly difficult, requires a certain degree of care and finesse.

Tools

- Screw gun
- Carpenter's level
- Screwdrivers (both Phillips head and regular)
- Handsaw
- Reciprocating or saber saw
- Electric drill and drill bits
- Hammer
- Table saw
- Router or edge trimmer
- Wood rasp
- Paint roller tray
- Clamps
- Laminate roller
- File
- Metal shears

Materials

- Nails
- Power-driven screws
- Plastic or lead shields
- Grommets
- Plastic laminate
- Glue
- Commercial carpet scraps
- Wood blocking
- Plywood or particle board
- Silicone

Stock cabinetry is delivered boxed or wrapped in protective coverings. Inspect the cabinetry for any damage caused during shipping. If there is damage, don't try to fix it. Instead, bring it to the immediate attention of the delivery company and the dealership. You should also keep in mind that once the original finish of the cabinets is damaged, it is rather difficult to repair. To prevent scratches and dents, keep the cabinets well protected until ready for installation.

BASE CABINETS

If you have wood-frame walls, the cabinets are screwed directly onto the studs. For this reason, the installation begins by establishing the location of the studs on the wall. With a hammer, gently tap along the wall until you hear a thump rather than a hollow sound. A thump indicates

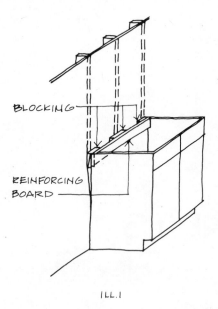

BLOCKING

REINFORCING
BOARD

ILL. 1

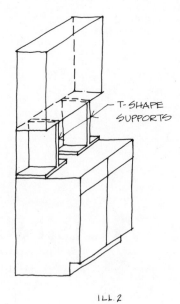

T-SHAPE
SUPPORTS

ILL. 2

the location of the stud. Drive a finish nail into the stud to find the center line. (Studs are generally spaced every 16" o.c., although in older homes the space could be irregular.) Take a level and a pencil and draw the center line of the stud on the wall from floor to ceiling.

There are instances where the existing walls are not wood-frame (gypsum block) or where the walls are so poorly constructed that they cannot support the cabinetry screws. In such cases, the easiest approach is to fur out the wall. This involves constructing a new wood stud wall in front of the old one. The wall can be made out of 2 × 4's on edge to minimize the space loss (1½" stud plus ½" or ⅝" gypsum board gives you a total space loss of 2" to 2⅛"). Secure the furred-out wall to the existing building by nailing the bottom and top plates to the floor and ceiling structure. If your building has concrete floors, you will have to secure it with drilled holes, screws, and shields, or wire-cut nails. A further advantage of this approach is that the new wall will be plumb. Furring out the wall also proves helpful where you encounter solid-brick walls. Not only is it easier to attach to wood than to brick, but the space between the studs can accommodate plumbing pipes and electrical wiring.

The next step is to locate and level the base cabinets. Start by finding the highest point on the floor. This gives you an idea of how much leveling the cabinets will require. Screw together two or three cabinet sections to form a unit not to exceed 5' to 7' in length. Make sure that they are aligned in relation to each other. The cabinets are attached to each other through the side walls with

screws and little rings called grommets. (Grommets are used to prevent the screws from pulling through the cabinetry walls and to give a more finished look.) While screwing the cabinets together make sure that screws do not project through the cabinet walls into places where they interfere with drawer operation or shelf location. This base cabinet section is then set in position, ready to be leveled and plumbed. Place a level on top of the unit. With the aid of wood pieces shim the cabinet base until level. Keep in mind that to get a level and plumb cabinet, you need to level it from front to back and from side to side. Repeat this procedure for each base unit until all of them are level. Replace the temporary shims with solid-wood blocking cut in thicknesses as required.

Most likely the wall behind the base cabinets is not plumb. Take a look to see how much space is left between the cabinet and the wall at the stud location. These gaps need to be closed up with wood blocking at the points of connection before the cabinet can be secured to the wall (Ill. 1). Slip wood blocking in place. Once the gaps have been closed, fasten the cabinetry to the wall by driving screws (with grommets) through the reinforcing board on the back of the cabinet and into the studs in the wall (Ill. 1).

UPPER CABINETS

The installation of the upper cabinets is trickier. Unlike the lower cabinets, upper cabinets hang from the wall. For this reason you need two people to do the installation work—one person to hold the cabinet in place and the other to shim, level, plumb, and screw cabinets together. You should also realize that when full these cabinets can be quite heavy. Because they hang from the wall, it is very important that the connections between the cabinets and the wall be very strong.

With these criteria in mind, you can begin the installation.* The location of the studs has already been drawn on the wall. You can now draw two more lines: one that will indicate the top and one that will indicate the bottom of the cabinet. Check to make sure that these lines are level. The next step is to check the wall for plumbness. There will undoubtedly be some bumps on the wall. Circle any bumps. This way you will know exactly where you will need wood blocking. The installation continues by cutting out and assembling T-shape plywood supports (about 1' deep) which span the distance between the lower and upper cabinets (Ill. 2).† Be sure to compensate for the thickness of the countertop. These supports are used to help hold the cabinets in place. With the aid of your helper and the plywood props, lift the first cabinet into position. In pencil, mark the location of the studs on the inside wall of the cabinet. Since the base cabinets are level and the prop supports are the same length, the cabinet should be level. You should double-check anyway. The front of the cabinet should be checked for plumbness. Slip wood blocking from the top and the bottom of the cabinetry as required to close any gaps.

Wall cabinets should come equipped with hangrails mortised and tenoned, doweled, or screwed to the side panels and under the top member (Ill. 3). These hangrails are designed to reduce the possibility of the back panel pulling away from the case. In addition, they provide a much stronger surface for attaching the cabinet to the wall. Using power-driven screws, screw the cabinet to the wall (at each stud). Try to install a minimum of two screws through each hangrail at the top of the cabinet. You should also screw the cabinet to the stud in at least one other location (near the bottom). When in doubt, install more screws. Keep in mind the potential weight of a fully loaded cabinet. Repeat this procedure for all upper cabinets. Once the first cabinet is installed

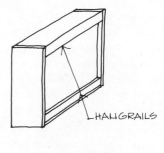

HANGRAILS

ILL. 3

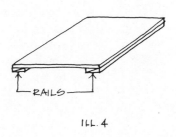

RAILS

ILL. 4

you can clamp the next one to it while plumbing and leveling.

COUNTERTOPS AND BACKSPLASHES

Countertops come in many materials. Those of you who choose stone will find that the company selling you the material will also install it. Once you have the base cabinets in place, give them a call. They will come and take field dimensions. From these measurements (of both counter and backsplash), a plywood template is made which is used to cut out the stone. Other renovators may have decided on composite materials for the countertops and backsplashes. Cabinetmakers usually include installation as part of the job. We do not recommend that you get involved with installation. These materials are expensive and they are not forgiving of mistakes. Should you make an error in cutting or measuring, you will have to discard the piece and purchase another one. The supplier may know of someone who can do the measuring and installing for you.

The following discussion is limited to countertops made of plywood (or particle board) and plastic laminate. The first step is to rough-cut a piece of ¾" plywood, ripping it to a consistent depth (usually 25"). Go to the base cabinets and measure the lengths of countertop that you need. Transfer these measurements to the ripped plywood and cut to the proper length. You can now place the counter in position and scribe to conditions. The front and back edges of the counter are provided with a rail both for rigidity and aesthetics (Ill. 4). Cut two ¾" × 3" wood strips, which will serve as rails and screw them to the underside of the counter (front and back edges).

Place the countertop in its proper location (do not secure it in place). The next step is fitting the backsplash. Backsplashes can range from full

---

*If you have a full backsplash, it should be installed before the upper cabinets. See discussion on backsplash installation.
†Should your base cabinets come without a top surface, cut a piece of plywood and place it over the top of the cabinets as a temporary working surface.

height (from countertop to upper cabinet) to 4"
high (the minimum and most common size). Full
backsplashes are installed before the upper cabinets are in place since they provide some support.
Smaller ones are installed together with the countertop. Start the backsplash by ripping a piece of
plywood to the required height (don't forget to
add ¾" to account for the thickness of the
counter). Going back to the base cabinets, measure along the wall to determine the appropriate
length. Measure and cut it. Place the backsplash
against the wall and mark the location of any
outlet box. Then, using an electric drill (with a
drill bit larger than the blade of the reciprocating
saw), drill two holes at the corners of the box's
diagonals (Ill. 5). With a reciprocating saw, cut
out the diagonal and proceed to cut out the box's
four sides.

You need a tight fit between the backsplash,
the countertop, and the wall. To achieve this, set
the backsplash in position (against the wall and
over the counter) and trace the line from the edge
of the backsplash onto the countertop. Cut the
countertop along that line. Just cut the plywood
layer; do not cut the wood rail underneath. The
wood rail will serve as a small ledge for the backsplash to rest on (Ill. 6). You can now screw the
backsplash to the back side of the countertop. Set

them back in position. It should be a good fit. All
the pieces can now be unscrewed from each other
for the application of plastic laminate.

Applying Plastic Laminate

There are some guidelines for the application of
plastic laminate:

- Spend some time planning out how to cut the sheets.
  This simple procedure will avoid a lot of waste and
  expense (particularly if you are using color-core lami-
  nates).
- Cut plastic laminate with a table saw.
- Install the laminate in a sequence where exposed
  edges occur in the vertical surfaces.
- Plan out the installation to minimize joints.
- To avoid waste and trimming, cut laminate to a size
  about 1" larger than the dimension that you need.
- Make sure that the adhesive you are using is non-
  flammable.
- Keep the area where you are working well ventilated.
- Apply sufficient glue (sometimes up to three coats).
- Make sure the glue is completely dry before applying
  laminate.

Once you have cut the sheet of laminate to the
approximate size, start by applying the adhesive.
We have found commercial carpet scraps and
paint roller trays to be the most effective tools for
the application of adhesive. These scraps are soft
and pliable. In addition, they eliminate the
cleanup time required by brushes. Whenever the
glue hardens, simply cut out the dried-out portion of carpet. Paint roller trays make terrific containers for the adhesive. The contours in these
trays allow you to dip the edge of the carpet in the
glue and also to adjust the amount of glue. We
usually recommend applying the adhesive first to
the plywood and then to the laminate. The reason
for this recommendation is that the number of
coats of glue required depends on the absorbency
of the wood (generally more than one coat). Let
the adhesive dry before proceeding with the application.

Whether the piece you are laminating is large or
small, start by positioning the laminate, making
sure that it is not crooked. If you are dealing with
a small piece, hold the piece from one end and put
it in contact with the wood. Slowly press the
glued laminate to the glued wood. Large pieces
are much trickier to apply and usually require two
people to install. When you are dealing with a
large piece of laminate, start by putting either
wax paper or dowels between the plywood and
the laminate. Place the laminate on top of the

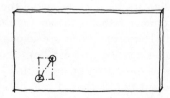

ILL. 5

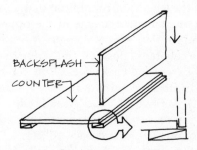

BACKSPLASH
COUNTER

ILL. 6

plywood (with the wax paper or dowels sandwiched in between), making sure that the two are properly aligned. Remove one row of wax paper or dowel and push down the laminate against the wood surface. One person should hold the remainder of the laminate sheet off the wood. Repeat this procedure until the entire sheet of laminate is in place. The plywood and the laminate surfaces have to be pressed firmly together. This is done with the aid of a laminate roller. Start the roller at the center of the piece and work your way slowly toward all the edges. Try to eliminate any air bubbles.

The edges of the laminate are cut to hug the edge of the plywood with the aid of an edge trimmer or router. Carefully set up and test the edge trimmer or router on a bit of scrap wood and laminate. Keep in mind that covered edges of laminate are square-cut and exposed edges slightly bevel-cut. Make sure the cutter is finely and properly adjusted, for misadjustment may cause damage to or destruction of the laminate.

Once the trimmer is properly adjusted, run along the edge to trim off the excess laminate. Corners may need to be trimmed with metal shears and a file or a wood rasp.

Installing the Countertop and the Backsplash

Start by reattaching the backsplash to the countertop using silicone and power-driven screws. (We are using silicone rather than glue because we are attaching wood to a plastic laminate surface, not wood to wood, and we want a watertight joint.) Place the countertop and backsplash in position and secure them to the cabinets. This is done by driving power-driven screws from the underside of the cabinet into the 3" rails at the front and back edges of the countertop. Make sure to use screws shorter than the thickness they are going through ($1\frac{1}{4}$" to $1\frac{1}{2}$" should be fine).

GLOSSARY OF
MAJOR HOUSING STYLES
BIBLIOGRAPHY
INDEX

GLOSSARY OF
MAJOR HOUSING STYLES

SEVENTEENTH AND EIGHTEENTH CENTURIES

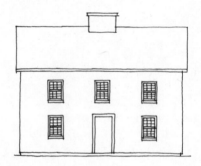

Colonial (1600's to 1770's)

Colonial homes emerged from a functional need for efficiency and energy saving. Every room in the house wrapped around a large central chimney, which gave the house its warmth and provided a place for cooking. Original Colonial homes were one room deep, with additions or "lean-to's" added later on. Houses with these additions came to be known as saltbox houses. Later homes became two rooms deep with a central hallway. A typical Colonial house is two stories high with a gable roof. Houses in the northern states are covered with narrow horizontal wood clapboards, while their southern counterparts are often built out of brick. Window openings are kept small with small windowpanes and simple frames. There are few decorative elements. The classic American farmhouse is a direct descendant of Colonial prototypes. Farmhouses generally have extensions and a front porch, which were added to the basic Colonial framework.

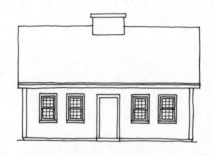

Cape Cod (1700's to 1830's)

The Cape Cod house is derivative of the Colonial house. The primary difference between the two is the height. Cape Cods are one or one and one-half stories high with a deep gable. Like Colonial houses, they are organized around a large central chimney and have small window openings with simple frames. The walls and roof of original Cape Cods were covered with wood shingles. Later homes had horizontal clapboards.

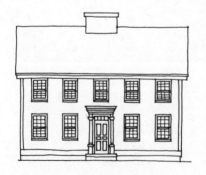

Georgian (1720's to 1780's)

This style grew out of the Italian Renaissance, which emphasized classical details from Roman architecture. In plan, Georgian homes are simple symmetrical boxes with four rooms per floor. These houses are two stories high with a gable roof (although there are some with gambrel and hipped roofs). The plain eaves of Colonial homes are here replaced by cornices. The entrance door is emphasized by framing it with columns or pilasters and a pediment above. Late Georgian models incorporated more classical detailing around windows and doors. Semicircular fanlights commonly appeared above entrance doors and Palladian windows became a popular feature on the second-floor center bay. Northern Georgian homes were covered with clapboards or shingles and had central fireplaces. Those in the middle and southern colonies were built out of brick or stone and had end chimneys.

Federal (1780's to 1820's)

These homes closely resemble Early Georgian models. The heavy use of classical decoration of the Late Georgian period is stripped down, with classical elements used primarily around the front door or small entry porch. The house plan remains a symmetrical box with elaborate projections to the side or the rear.

NINETEENTH CENTURY—FIRST HALF

The beginning of the nineteenth century was much dominated by the Greek Revival style, which took its inspiration from Greek temples. By the middle of the nineteenth century, single architectural styles became less dominant than before. Several different styles became fashionable, with Gothic Revival and Italianate perhaps being the most popular ones.

Greek Revival (1825 to 1860)

This style is often characterized by shifting the main focus of the house from the long side to the gable side. When this occurs a pedimented gable resting on columns gives the building the aura of a Greek temple. The influence of the Greek Revival movement is responsible for many of the gable-front houses throughout the country. The plan is symmetrical with a gabled roof of low pitch. Cornice lines are emphasized with wide bands of undecorated boards. Most Greek Revival houses have porches with square or rounded Doric columns. Front doors are surrounded with narrow, rectangular sidelights.

Gothic Revival (1840 to 1880)

Gothic Revival houses have very steep roofs with cross gables. The plans are almost always asymmetrical, with L-shaped plans being the most common. A one-story entry or full-width porch is yet another traditional feature. Verticality is achieved through the pointed gables with wall surfaces extending into the gable without a break. Windows are tall and slender, sometimes capped by a pointed arch. There is a wealth of decoration throughout the building, primarily around the gables and porch.

Italianate (1840 to 1885)

These houses are two or three stories high with low-pitched roofs. In plan, they vary from a basic box shape to asymmetrical plans. The more formal interpretations have simple hipped roofs with a cupola or tower at the peak. Those inspired by Italian country villas have varying rooflines, including cross-hipped or cross-gabled, front-gabled, and sometimes even with a tower. Italianate buildings have widely overhanging eaves accentuated by a cornice. Windows are tall and narrow and often have arched tops.

NINETEENTH CENTURY—SECOND HALF (VICTORIAN ERA)

Styles that were popular during the last decades of Queen Victoria's reign came to be known as Victorian. Most of these houses have asymmetrical plans and façades. It should be noted that rapid industrialization was taking place in the United States at this time. The development of balloon-frame construction allowed houses to be easily built in more complex shapes than ever before. In addition, the mass production of doors, windows, siding, and decorative detailing made available a wealth of highly ornamented house components at a relatively low cost. The styles usually associated with the Victorian era are the Second Empire, Queen Anne, Stick, and Shingle.

Second Empire (1855 to 1885)

This style, also known as Mansard, is quite easily recognized because of its dual-pitched roof. The roofline is quite functional since it allows for a full floor of usable attic space. Dormer windows interrupt the roof, which is often covered with slate. Because of its functional advantage the mansard roof was often used for the remodeling of older buildings.

Queen Anne (1875 to 1900)

Queen Anne became the dominant style during this time period. It is characterized by unusual massing of forms. These buildings display steep roofs of irregular shapes combined with dormers, turrets, and oriel windows. Front and L-shaped porches are covered with intricate spindlework. Varying textures appear throughout. Wooden houses combine clapboards with shingles, while brick ones introduce terra-cotta decorative elements.

Stick (1875 to 1900)

These houses have steeply pitched gable roofs with decorative trusses in the gables. The entry to the house is most commonly found in the gable end rather than the side. The massing is asymmetrical, with cross gables and overhanging eaves. Stick-style houses are easily recognizable by their richly textured wall panels made up of wood shingles or clapboards interrupted by horizontal, vertical, or diagonal boards. Decorative diagonal or curved support bracing is also found in the porches.

Shingle (1880 to 1900)

The distinguishing characteristic of the Shingle style is that both the walls and the roofs are covered with continuous wood shingles. The plans and massings of Shingle-style houses are quite variable and free. These houses are two or two and one-half stories high with dormer windows and a large porch. Ground floors and foundations are often made out of stone. Shingle-style houses never gained the popularity of the Queen Anne. They remained a high-fashion style that was primarily architect-designed.

fluenced by the English Arts and Crafts movement and by Oriental wooden architecture. Decorative beams or braces are present under the gables. The main roof is extended to cover the porch and is supported by tapered columns.

Tudor (1890 to Present)

These houses are inspired by English half-timbered houses. The façades are dominated by one or more cross gables. Windows are tall and narrow. Tudor houses are most easily recognizable by their decorative half timber and massive chimneys.

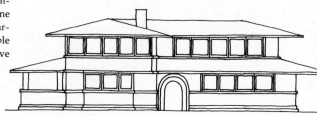

TURN OF THE CENTURY: ECLECTIC REVIVALS

A resurgence of interest in old models occurred at the turn of the century. These eclectic houses drew inspiration from a great number of styles from the past. Colonial Revival and Tudor homes were perhaps the most popular.

Colonial Revival (1880 to Present)

These houses are rarely historically correct. Rather they incorporate details that may have been present in Colonial, Federal, or Georgian buildings. Rooflines vary, but gabled or hipped roofs with dormers are the most common. Façades are symmetrical with double-hung windows. The front door is emphasized with a projecting pediment supported by columns and is further accentuated with fanlights. Classical details may be found throughout the building.

TWENTIETH CENTURY— THE MODERN MOVEMENT

The Modern Movement had two main tendencies: to break with the past and to integrate the rapid growth of industrialization and the machine age into building. Two indigenous American styles emerged at this time, the Craftsman house and the Prairie house. Both of these styles incorporated innovations in planning. Plans became more open and functional, allowing spaces to flow freely into each other. Ornament was not eliminated, but was reinterpreted. Traditional historical ornamentation was replaced by ornamentation that derived from the nature of the materials used in the building. Craftsman and Prairie houses never quite caught on and fell out of favor in the 1920's.

In Europe, the Modern Movement stressed functionalism to the point where anything that was not functional was eliminated. It is for this reason that people often associate modernism with lack of ornamentation. Americans, however, were not as eager as their European counterparts to accept houses without historical precedents. With the exception of architect-designed houses, American homes retained historical elements, even if purely decorative, and combined them with highly functional plans.

Craftsman (1900 to 1930)

This style, which originated in Southern California, was inspired by the work of the Greene brothers. The houses have low-pitched gabled roofs with wide overhangs and exposed rafters. They display a wealth of intricate detailing in-

Prairie (1900 to 1920)

A group of Chicago architects developed this style, with Frank Lloyd Wright as its best-known advocate. This style is characterized by an open plan where spaces flow freely into each other. Prairie-style houses place strong emphasis on the horizontal, attempting to become part of the natural landscape rather than stand separate from it. To accomplish this, the massing of the house combines two-story elements with projecting one-story wings or porches. Roofs are low-pitched and generally hipped. Widely overhanging eaves and horizontal bands of windows are also part of the style's features. Various materials may be found in these houses, ranging from Roman brick and wood to stucco or stone.

Traditional (1935 to 1950's)

Small, one-story gabled or cross-gabled houses emerged during the Depression, particularly in suburban tract developments. These houses have little or no detailing and were built of wood, brick, or stone or a mixture of materials. The garage is usually a separate building close to the house.

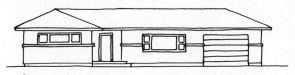

unit intercepted by a one-story unit at mid-level, it places the garage and the family room in the lower level while the mid-level houses the living room, dining room, and kitchen. The top level is reserved for the privacy of the bedrooms.

houses range from boxlike houses with flat roofs to those with many shed roofs or a wealth of geometric shapes.

Ranch (1940's to Present)

Ranch-style houses became popular as suburban areas grew and lots became larger. The houses ramble on the land and integrate the garage into the building. The plan is open, with the kitchen and dining room often sharing the same space. They have low-pitched roofs and big overhanging eaves. The emphasis goes away from the front of the house and into the backyard.

Postmodernist (1970's to Present)

These houses borrow historical details and integrate them with contemporary plans and massings. They do not attempt to copy past styles but allude to them through symbolism. This style emerged from the realization that American houses throughout the centuries have traditionally hung on to historical precedents.

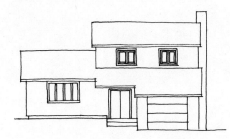

Split-Level (1950's to Present)

A split-level home offers an ingenious solution to functional problems. By having a two-story

Contemporary (1960's to Present)

This is a catchall term for houses with open plans and unusual spaces, such as double-storied rooms with balconies or bridges. These

BIBLIOGRAPHY

Allen, Edward. *Fundamentals of Building Construction: Materials and Methods.* New York: John Wiley & Sons, 1985.

Alves, Ronald. *Living with Energy.* New York: Viking Press, 1978.

Anderson, L. O. *How to Build a Wood Frame House.* New York: Dover, 1973.

————. *Wood Frame House Construction.* Los Angeles: Craftsman Book Company of America, 1971.

Baker, David J. *Respectful Rehabilitation.* (Drawings.) Washington, D.C.: The Preservation Press, 1982.

Bazinski, Stanley, Jr. *Carpentry in Residential Construction.* Englewood Cliffs, N.J.: Prentice-Hall.

Blackburn, Graham. *Illustrated Housebuilding.* Woodstock, N.Y.: The Outlook Press, 1974.

Blankenbaker, Keith. *Modern Plumbing.* South Holland, Ill.: Goodheart-Willcox, 1981.

Browne, Dan. *The House-Building Book.* New York: McGraw-Hill, 1974.

Bryne, Michael. *Setting Ceramic Tile.* Newtown, Conn.: The Taunton Press, 1987.

Buck, Monte. *The Home Cabinetmaker.* New York: Sterling Publishing, 1987.

Butler, Robert Braun. *The Ecological House.* Dobbs Ferry, N.Y.: Morgan & Morgan, 1981.

Callendar, John Hancock. *Time-Savers Standards: A Handbook of Architectural Design.* New York: McGraw-Hill, 1974.

Cary, Jere. *Building Your Own Kitchen Cabinets.* Newtown, Conn.: The Taunton Press, 1983.

Ching, Francis D. K. *Building Construction Illustrated.* New York: Van Nostrand Reinhold, 1975.

Clark, Sam. *The Motion Minded Kitchen.* Boston, Mass.: Houghton Mifflin, 1983.

The Complete Book of Masonry, Cement and Brickwork. New York: Sterling Publishing, 1980.

Daniels, George. *Home Guide to Plumbing, Heating, & Airconditioning.* 2nd ed., New York: Times Mirror/Popular Science Books, 1976.

Debaights, Jacques. *New Interiors for Old Houses.* New York: Van Nostrand Reinhold, 1973.

Demske, Richard. *Plumbing.* New York: Grosset & Dunlap, 1975.

Geary, Don. *Interior and Exterior Painting.* Reston, Va.: Reston Publishing, 1979.

————. *Roofs and Siding.* Reston, Va.: Reston Publishing, 1978.

Harmon, A. J. *The Guide to Home Remodeling.* New York: Grosset & Dunlap, 1972.

Harris, W. Robert. *Drywall: Installation and Applications.* Chicago: American Technical Society, 1979.

Harris, W. S. *Modern Hydronic Heating: Design, Installation, Service.* Columbus, Ohio: North America Heating & Air-Conditioning Wholesalers Association, 1974.

Hedden, Jay. *Best Baths.* Passaic, N.J.: Creative Homeowners Press, 1980.

Irvine, Chippy. *The Farmhouse.* Toronto and New York: Bantam Books, 1987.

Jones, Peter. *Electrical Repair Made Easy.* New York: Butterick Publishing, 1980.

Kicklighter, Clois E. *Modern Masonry.* South Holland, Ill.: Goodheart-Willcox, 1980.

Koel, Leonard. *Carpentry.* Alsip, Ill.: American Technical Publishers.

Lester, Kent, and Una Lamie. *Remodeling Your Home.* White Hall, Va.: Betterway Publications, 1987.

Litchfield, Michael. *Renovation: A Complete Guide.* New York: John Wiley & Sons, 1982.

Mallett, Grant. *New Life for an Old House.* Harrisburg, Pa.: Stackpole Books, 1984.

Mazria, Edward. *The Passive Solar Energy Book.* Emmaus, Pa.: Rodale Press, 1979.

McAlister, Virginia and Lee. *Field Guide to American Houses.* New York: Alfred A. Knopf, 1986.

National Fire Protection Association. *National Electric Code Handbook, 1987.* Quincy, Mass., 1987.

Nisson, J. D. Ned. *The Superinsulated Home Book.* New York: John Wiley & Sons, 1985.

Old House Journal. *Old House Journal Yearbooks.* New York: Old House Journal, 1977–83.

Olivieri, Joseph B. *How to Design Heating-Cooling Comfort Systems.* Birmingham, Mich.: Business News Publishing Co., 1973.

Parker, Harry, Charles M. Gay, and John W. Macguire. *Materials and Methods of Architectural Construction.* New York: John Wiley & Sons, 1958.

Poore, Patricia, and Clem Labine. *The Old House Journal New Compendium.* Garden City, N.Y.: Dolphin, 1983.

Ramsey, Charles G., and Harold R. Sleeper. *Architectural Graphic Standards.* New York: John Wiley & Sons, 1989.

Reed, Mortimer P. *Complete Guide to Residential Remodeling.* Englewood Cliffs, N.J.: Prentice-Hall, 1983.

Ripka, L. V. *Plumbing: Installation and Design.* Alsip, Ill.: American Technical Publishers, 1978.

Rusk, Katherine Knight. *Renovating the Victorian House.* San Francisco: 101 Productions, 1982.

Schuler, Stanley. *The Wall Book.* New York: M. Evans and Co., 1974.

Sears, Roebuck and Co. *How to Install Central Heating & Cooling.* Philadelphia: Sears, Roebuck and Co.

————. *How to Install Hydronic Heating.* Philadelphia: Sears, Roebuck and Co.

Shapiro, Cecile. *Better Kitchens.* Passaic, N.J.: Creative Homeowners Press, 1980.

Snow, Anthony, and Graham Hopewell. *Planning*

Your Bathroom. London: Design Center Book, 1976.

Solar Age Magazine, ed. *The Solar Age Resource Book*. Manchester, N.H.: Solar Age Magazine, 1979.

Stagg, W. D. *Plastering: A Craftsman's Encyclopaedia*. London: Granada, 1976.

State of New York. *State Energy Conservation Construction Code*. New York State Energy Office.

Stein, Benjamin, John S. Reynolds, and William J. McGuinness. *Mechanical and Electrical Equipment for Buildings*. New York: John Wiley & Sons, 1986.

Stillman, Richard J. *Do-It-Yourself Contracting to Build Your Own Home*. Radnor, Pa.: Chilton Book Company, 1974.

Sweet's Catalogue File. *Products for General Building and Renovation*. New York: McGraw-Hill Information Systems, 1989.

Syvanen, Bob. *Carpentry: Some Tricks of the Trade*. Charlotte, N.C.: The East Woods Press, 1982.

Time-Life:
Kitchens and Baths, 1977.
Floors and Stairways, 1978.
Doors and Windows, 1978.
Adding On, 1979.
Weatherproofing, 1977.
Plumbing, 1977.
Advanced Wiring, 1979.
Basic Wiring, 1978.
Roofs and Siding, 1979.
Alexandria, Va.: Time-Life.

Ulrey, Harry F. *Audel Building, Construction & Design*. Indianapolis, Ind.: Theodore Audel & Co., 1970.

——. *Audel Carpenters and Builders Library*, Vol. 3. Indianapolis, Ind.: Theodore Audel & Co., 1970.

U.S. Gypsum. *Gypsum Construction Handbook*. Chicago: U.S. Gypsum.

Wagner, Willis H. *Modern Carpentry*. South Holland, Ill.: Goodheart-Willcox, 1983.

Walker, Les, and Jeff Milstein. *Designing Houses: An Illustrated Guide*. Woodstock, N.Y.: Outlook Press, 1976.

Weismantel, Guy E. *Paint Handbook*. New York: McGraw-Hill, 1981.

Wilson, Douglas J. *Practical House Carpentry: Simplified Methods for Building*. New York: McGraw-Hill, 1973.

Wilson, John, and S. O. Warner. *Simplified Roof Framing*. New York: McGraw-Hill, 1927, 1948.

Wright, Rodney, and the Hawkweed Group. *The Hawkweed Passive Solar House Book*. Chicago: Rand McNally, 1980.

INDEX

Note: Page numbers in *italics* refer to illustrations.

A NOTE ABOUT THE AUTHORS

PHYLLIS SPERLING, a registered architect, is a graduate of Pratt Institute's School of Architecture, holds a master's degree from Columbia University's School of Architecture and Planning, and has worked as a designer and as an architectural representative on construction sites. She is currently a Professor of Architectural Technology at New York City Technical College of the City University of New York and is a principal of Sands and Sperling, Architects, P.C., which has offices in New York City and West Cornwall, Connecticut.

LUPE DiDONNO, a registered architect and NCARB certified, is a graduate of Pratt Institute's School of Architecture. Her professional background includes graduate training at Pratt Institute School of Urban Design, several years' experience in architectural firms, and lecturing at New York City Technical College and Pratt Institute. She is currently a principal of DiDonno Associates, Architects, P.C., and a member of the American Institute of Architects.

A NOTE ON THE TYPE

The text of this book was composed in Palatino, a typeface designed by the noted German typographer Hermann Zapf. Named after Giovanbattista Palatino, a writing master of Renaissance Italy, Palatino was the first of Zapf's typefaces to be introduced in America. The first designs for the face were made in 1948, and the fonts for the complete face were issued between 1950 and 1952. Like all Zapf-designed typefaces, Palatino is beautifully balanced and exceedingly readable.

Composed by The Haddon Craftsmen, Inc., Scranton, Pennsylvania. Printed and bound by The Courier Book Companies, Westford, Massachusetts.